GANGS AND ORGANIZED CRIME

In *Gangs and Organized Crime*, George W. Knox, Gregg W. Etter, and Carter F. Smith offer an informed and carefully investigated examination of gangs and organized crime groups, covering street gangs, prison gangs, outlaw motorcycle gangs, and organized crime groups from every continent. The authors have spent decades investigating gangs as well as researching their history and activities, and this dual professional-academic perspective informs their analysis of gangs and crime groups. They take a multidisciplinary approach that combines criminal justice, public policy and administration, law, organizational behavior, sociology, psychology, and urban planning perspectives to provide insight into the actions and interactions of a variety of groups and their members. This textbook is ideal for criminal justice and sociology courses on gangs as well as related course topics like gang behavior, gang crime and the inner city, organized crime families, and transnational criminal groups. *Gangs and Organized Crime* is also an excellent addition to the professional's reference library or primer for the general reader. More information is available at the supporting website – www.gangsandorganizedcrime.com.

George W. Knox authored the first full textbook on gangs in 1991 (*An Introduction to Gangs*) and the book *National Gang Resource Handbook* (1995). He has co-authored several other gang books: *Hate Crime and Extremist Gangs* (with Gregg Etter, 2008); *Gang Profiles: An Anthology* (with Curtis Robinson, 2004); *The Vice Lords: A Gang Profile Analysis* (with Andrew V. Papachristos, 2002); and *Schools Under Siege* (1992). He has contributed about 10 book chapters and has over 50 journal publications, mostly on gang issues. He is the founder and executive director of the National Gang Crime Research Center and editor-in-chief of the *Journal of Gang Research*. He has done gang research for over 30 years, and has taught gang courses for 22 years.

Gregg W. Etter, Sr. Ed.D., is a Professor of Criminal Justice at the University of Central Missouri. Prior to academic life, he had law enforcement experience with the Sedgwick County Sheriff's Office. He has written extensively and presented classes on gangs, white supremacist groups and police management topics in the United States and Canada. He is a member of the American Society of Criminology, the Academy of Criminal Justice Sciences, and the National Sheriff's Association. He is a multiple recipient of the Frederic Milton Thrasher Award and is an editor of the *Journal of Gang Research*. He is the co-author of *Hate Crime and Extremist Gangs* (Knox and Etter, 2008). He has about 20 journal publications.

Carter F. Smith, J.D., Ph.D., is a retired U.S. Army CID Special Agent and has been with the Department of Criminal Justice Administration at Middle Tennessee State University, Murfreesboro, since 2006. He is the author of *Gangs and the Military: Gangsters, Bikers, and Terrorists with Military Training* (2017), a multiple recipient of the Frederic Milton Thrasher Award and an editor of the *Journal of Gang Research*. He received a law degree from Southern Illinois University–Carbondale and a Doctorate of Philosophy from Northcentral University in Prescott Valley, Arizona.

GANGS AND ORGANIZED CRIME

GEORGE W. KNOX,
GREGG W. ETTER,
AND CARTER F. SMITH

Routledge
Taylor & Francis Group

NEW YORK AND LONDON

First published 2019
by Routledge
711 Third Avenue, New York, NY 10017

and by Routledge
2 Park Square, Milton Park, Abingdon, Oxon, OX14 4RN

Routledge is an imprint of the Taylor & Francis Group, an informa business

Library of Congress Cataloging-in-Publication Data
Names: Knox, George W., 1950– author. | Etter, Gregg W., author. |
    Smith, Carter F., author.
Title: Gangs and organized crime / George W. Knox, Gregg W. Etter, and
    Carter F. Smith.
Description: New York, NY : Routledge, 2018. | Includes bibliographical
    references and index.
Identifiers: LCCN 2018011010 (print) | LCCN 2018012714 (ebook) |
    ISBN 9781315118604 (master) | ISBN 9781482244236 (hardback) |
    ISBN 9781138614772 (pbk.)
Subjects: LCSH: Gangs. | Organized crime.
Classification: LCC HV6437 (ebook) | LCC HV6437 .K66 2018 (print) |
    DDC 364.106—dc23
LC record available at https://lccn.loc.gov/2018011010

ISBN: 978-1-4822-4423-6 (hbk)
ISBN: 978-1-138-61477-2 (pbk)
ISBN: 978-1-315-11860-4 (ebk)

Typeset in Adobe Garamond Pro
by Apex CoVantage, LLC

Visit the eResources: www.routledge.com/9781138614772

This book is dedicated to the professionals who strive to protect
our communities from the gangs and organized crime groups
in the book, the scholars who study them, and the students who
hope to be like either.

CONTENTS

ACKNOWLEDGMENTS

This book would not have been possible without the contributions of countless scholars, researchers, and investigators, past and present. The many contributors to the *Journal of Gang Research* and the attendees at the annual conference hosted in Chicago, Illinois, by the National Gang Crime Research Center ensures our information and interests are relevant, current, and accurate. For all serving in police, courts, corrections, and elsewhere in both the public and private sectors, we hope this endeavor provides you with a compilation of excellent insight to the challenge we face with gangs and organized crime in our communities.

CHAPTER 1 Gang and Organized Crime History and Foundations

CHAPTER OBJECTIVES

After reading this chapter students should be able to do the following:

- Explore the first indicators of gangs in America.
- Identify key historical developments in the evolution of gangs.
- Consider some of the community issues present when gangs are involved.
- Discuss definitions of gangs and organized crime.
- Identify activities that are considered gang related.
- Examine group-focused theoretical approaches to the study of gangs.
- Understand ways that gangs serve as an alternative means of economic success.

Introduction

Gangs have been part of the American experience since the founding of this nation. They have been called street gangs, street corner gangs, inner-city gangs, urban gangs, suburban gangs, rural gangs, male gangs, female gangs, juvenile gangs, youth gangs, delinquent gangs, criminal gangs, outlaw gangs, biker gangs, drug gangs, and prison gangs. In a 1927 study, gang researcher Frederic M. Thrasher (2000) reported that gangs found among Chicago's neighborhoods primarily comprised the following immigrant populations: Bohemians, Croatians, Germans, Greeks, Gypsies, Italians, Irish, Jews, Lithuanians, Mexicans, Poles, and Russians. In the decades since Thrasher's study, we have discovered gangs in all 50 states, in many other countries, and on most continents, with only Antarctica as the exception. Gangs tend to appear in response to a social need.

Needs in that category can be seen as protection against aggressors, providing social services, and generating revenue. Once the presence of the gang addresses the need, the gang may grow beyond the need. That would mean they could begin to become the aggressor, offer protection to others, or compete for revenue opportunities with legitimate organizations. Gangs seem to be drawn from every possible combination of demographic variables.

Organized crime, too, is a part of the culture of many societies. Organized crime groups often form from gangs, sometimes form independently, and are often less visible to police and the community than gangs, as they are often more advanced in their criminal organization and behavior. Organized crime groups, like gangs, tend to appear when the police and the politicians lack control. Organized crime groups are typically focused on profit.

This textbook was written to share information on gangs and organized crime groups in America. Readers of all types and experience levels should find value in the book, as the authors strive to share what they have learned about gangs in their respective professional and academic endeavors. You will see three common threads throughout the book. First, gangs and organized crime groups are made up of many individuals, hence their analysis and treatment should be focused more on the group than the individual. The second theme of the book is that the members of gangs and organized crime groups are typically adults, or led by adults. Finally, while at any given point in history there may be one predominant culture seen as being mostly engaged in gangs or organized crime, members of these organizations have come from many continents, countries, and cultures.

What you will not see is a focus on hate groups, domestic terrorists, or extremist groups. Hate groups advocate and practice hatred, hostility, or violence towards specific members of society. Domestic terrorist or extremist group members commit crimes that endanger human life intending to intimidate or coerce people, influence government policy, or change government conduct within the United States. Those groups are significantly different than the groups we identify here.

There is a lot of detail in some of the sections. We realize that there are many applications for this information, and did not want to limit the contents for one use while limiting the usefulness for another. For students, professors, and professional researchers, each chapter can serve as a stand-alone study topic. We recommend choosing the areas that are most relevant to the reader, either for the whole class or for a significant portion of it. For example, if you want to spend less time on a certain type of organized crime and more on investigation and prosecution of gang violence, simply using the selected chapters for study would serve that purpose. This recommendation would apply to a typical 15-week semester with midterm and final examinations.

For anyone working in one of the criminal justice fields, whether police, courts, corrections, or security, or another practitioner for whom gangs and organized crime groups are an interest, you should find the book useful as reference material, though hopefully as a bit more of an interesting read than other reference material in your professional library. Should you encounter updated information on any of the topics in the book, please don't hesitate to contact us by email – author@gangsandorganizedcrime.com.

The Early Gangs

Gangs were not always seen as criminal organizations. Gang violence was a part (often a condition) of life where the gang members lived (Sante, 1991). Gangs have been in existence in some form in Western society for about four centuries. Pearson found there were organized gangs like the Muns, Dead Boys, Blues, and Nickers in London in the 1600s. They terrorized their communities by breaking windows, assaulting the Watch (the police), and "rolling old ladies in barrels" (Pearson, 1983, p. 188). Like more contemporary gangs, they wore colored ribbons to differentiate themselves and often fought each other for control of turf.

Gangs first emerged in the eastern cities of North America, which had conditions conducive to gang formation and growth, mostly created by the many waves of immigration and urban overcrowding (Sante, 1991). Haskins (1974) and Bonn (1984) reported that the makings of criminal gangs existing in America as early as 1760. Haskins noted that between 1660 and 1776, New York had evolved from a population of 1,000 with both an orphanage and a poorhouse and still had a group of "young, homeless boys" who were a nightly "source of trouble to respectable citizens" (Haskins, 1974, p. 16). Before the Revolutionary War, around 1764, Ebenezer Mackintosh led a gang-like group of men in Boston called the South Enders. Mackintosh was a shoemaker in his late twenties, and his gang looted the homes of several government officials in their protest of the Stamp Act of 1776, leading Mackintosh to become a powerful figure in the community (Haskins, 1974).

As with contemporary society, the problems with deviant youth were identified back then as either a lack of role models or insufficient supervision by authority. The earliest identifiable gangs in the U.S. came to existence shortly after the Revolutionary War (1775–1783; Sante, 1991). Haskins (1974) explained that following the Revolutionary War there was a time of lawlessness. When the British rulers were driven out, the police forces and other institutions were driven out as well. Combining that environment with the presence of idled young men who had left their country villages to seek a better life in the city, it may be easier to see why the resulting violence and mob activity occurred (Haskins, 1974). In New York, many of the gangs formed in the Five Points area, then on the outskirts of town. It was a wilderness surrounding a large lake referred to as the Collect.

Gangs of that period included the Bowery Boys, The Broadway Boys, and the Smith's Vly gang, all of whom were white, and the Fly Boys and Long Bridge Boys, which were

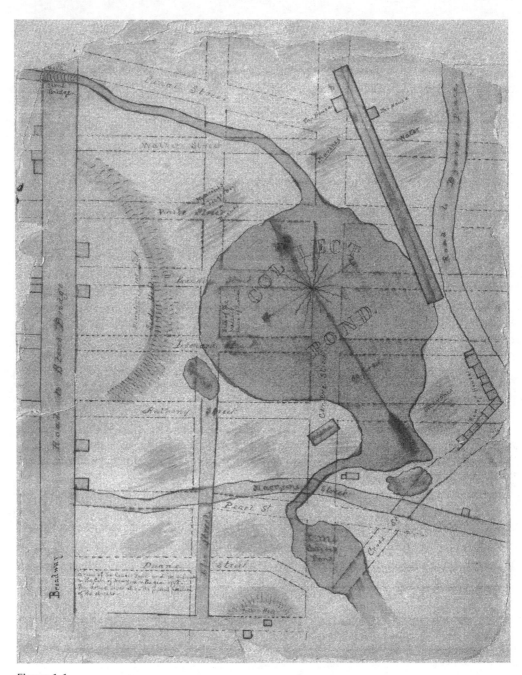

Figure 1.1

Map of the Collect Pond and Five Points, New York City. Public domain.

Geographicus Rare Antique Maps, a specialist dealer in rare maps and other cartography, via Wikimedia Commons as part of a cooperation project

all-black gangs (Sante, 1991). Those gang members were nearly all employed in respectable trades like mechanics, carpenters, and butchers. Most of their gang activity consisted of arguing (and fighting) over the portion of territory each could claim as their own, much as contemporary neighborhood-based gangs do (Sante, 1991).

In the years that followed, America began receiving "scores of poverty-stricken immigrants" (Haskins, 1974, p. 22). A historical review of American gangs would suggest they emerged along both racial and ethnic lines. The early street gangs of New York and Chicago were almost exclusively made up of immigrants. Bonn described gangs as clearly having ethnic homogeneity in terms of their organization. "Irish gangs were the first to emerge," followed by German, Jewish and Italian gangs (Bonn, 1984, pp. 333–334). According to Howell (2012), in both New York and Chicago, the earliest gangs formed in concert with the arrival of predominantly white European immigrants, particularly German, French, British, and Scandinavians, from 1783 to 1860.

The first criminal gang with a definite, acknowledged leadership, the Forty Thieves, formed around 1826 in the Five Points area of New York (Haskins, 1974). The name Five Points denoted the geographic location where five streets intersected, and a park named Paradise Square was situated at the hub. The second recorded gang, the Kerryonians, was named after the county in Ireland from which they came. Similar gangs with equally interesting names also formed in the Five Points area, including the Chichesters, Roach Guards, Plug Uglies (named after their large plug hats), Shirt Tails (distinguished by wearing their shirts outside their trousers), and Dead Rabbits (Haskins, 1974).

Figure 1.2

Early gangs. A fight between the Dead Rabbits and the Bowery Boys in New York City. From the newspaper article "Four Scenes From the Riot in the Sixth Ward" (1857). Public domain.

Illustrated in Frank Leslie's illustrated newspaper, v. 4 (July 18, 1857), p. 108

The second generation youth of immigrant groups were most susceptible to gang involvement. Asbury recorded crimes in Chicago in the late 1850s ranging from burglaries to holdups being committed by bands of men who were recently unemployed (1986). He identified one specific gang that was based out of the Limerick House and committed dozens of robberies. A thief known as John the Baptist led another gang of pickpockets (Asbury, 1986). He was apparently so named because of his attire and behavior, as he often left religious tracts behind.

New York–area gangs of the late 1850s included the Daybreak Boys, Buckaroos, Slaughter Housers, and the Border Gang (Sante, 1991). Many of the New York gangs hung out along the waterfront, so their crimes focused on people who lived and worked in that area. Muggings, murders, and robberies were their crimes of choice, and the area was considered so dangerous that the police avoided it unless there were at least six of them (Sante, 1991). In the late 1860s, German gangs began forming in New York. One gang, the Hell's Kitchen Gang, terrorized the district for which they were named, committing robberies, assaults, and burglaries (Haskins, 1974).

Gangs in post–Civil War New York were snappy dressers, joining together for identity, wearing distinctive clothing (specifically headwear), and seeking publicity (Haskins, 1974). Haskins identified New York gangs of that era with names like the Stable Gang, the Molasses Gang, and the Silver Gang. Many came from poverty, and sought a group with which they could ally. Those gangs differed from previous gangs, as many of them were drug users (Haskins, 1974). When soldiers returned from the war addicted to the morphine they were given to ease the pain of their war wounds, they sought out more of the drug than they could legally obtain (Haskins, 1974). Gangs willingly provided a source for illicit drugs, and some gang members also became users. The most popular drug at the time was cocaine, which added a whole new dimension to gang activities.

The Whyos were the "most powerful downtown (New York) gang between the Civil War and the 1890s" (Sante, 1991, p. 214). The gang was made up of pickpockets, sneak thieves (stealing without detection or violence), and brothel owners. The gang members were very resourceful, offering their services to those in need in the form of a menu, listing the provision of two black eyes for $4, a leg or arm broken for $19, and a stabbing for $25 (Sante, 1991). The "big job" (presumably a murder) cost at least $100.

Perkins (1987) found that white street gangs had been documented in Chicago since the 1860s. Thrasher (1927) reported that most of the Chicago gang activity in the 1860s consisted of breaking fences and stealing cabbages from people's gardens, as there was "not much else to take" (p. 4). Other groups, including Irish, Italians, Jews, and Poles, arrived from 1880 to 1920. Gangs of some type existed in Chicago as early as the 1880s, with groups like the Hickory Street gang spending their time reading, "play[ing] cards, study[ing], and drink[ing] their beer" (Thrasher, 2000, p. 4). Irish gangs like the Dukies and the Shielders influenced activity around the Chicago-area stockyards during that time, robbing men leaving work and terrorizing other immigrants (Howell, 2012).

The gangs fought constantly among themselves, but sometimes joined together to war with the black gangs. Many blacks (African Americans) had arrived from the southern states after the U.S. Civil War, most leaving to escape the oppressive Jim Crow laws and the life of the sharecropper. Cureton (2009) traced the origin of Chicago's black street gangs to the segregated inner-city areas, beginning in the early 1900s. Cureton (2009) argued that the street gang (not the family or the church) was the most important social network organization for urban youth, even though it was the surest way to end up a felon, convict, or dead.

Elsewhere in the nation, criminal gangs that engaged in robbery were plentiful following the Civil War. Jesse and Frank James, for example, were motivated by their hatred of the Union to commit bank and stagecoach robberies. The brothers had fought on the Confederate side of the Civil War and, like many Southerners at the time, opposed the Union Army even after the war.

Early Juvenile Gangs

Historical accounts identify the institution of apprenticeships as a culprit, if not a contributor, to the prevalence of young, unsupervised men in the cities. The practice of apprenticeships matched a young male of 14 and above with an employer, who was presumed to be responsible for teaching the young boy a trade or employable skill. In those times, even young children were expected to contribute to the household income in many families (Pearson, 1983). Sadly, the system that supported the young teenage boys seeking apprenticeships appeared to be ineffective.

The apprentice system had been considered a problem since the early 1700s, as both the supervision of masters and the behavior of apprentices were being questioned. In the 1790s, as the increased supply of slave labor created an unnecessary surplus of apprentices, many an idled youngster was shuffled off to the orphanages. They often escaped and formed up with like-minded young men in "armies of homeless boys wandering about, stealing food, and sleeping in alleyways" (Haskins, 1974, p. 21). The apprentice system was an easy target for complaints regarding the increase in what was becoming known as "juvenile delinquency" (Pearson, 1983, p. 191). Pearson noted that some blamed it for causing the problem in the first place. Many of the young boys who were recruited as apprentices were described as idle and often violent, and were so numerous that they were a subculture of their own.

While previously there was a thriving business of child labor, either through apprenticeships or the early stages of the Industrial Revolution, the dynamics of the labor force changed when a concerted effort to stop child labor was started (Haskins, 1974). By the mid-1870s, over 100,000 children were working in New York factories, and when the reformation began, many of them were idled overnight. While many government efforts were implemented, at least 10,000 of those children became easy recruits for the street gangs of the time (Haskins, 1974). Those children aligned in support gangs such as the Forty Little Thieves, the Little Plug Uglies, and the Little Dead Rabbits, according to Asbury (1927).

Twentieth-Century Gangs and Organized Crime Groups

The gangs that ruled New York from the 1890s onward included gang conglomerates known as the Five Pointers, the Eastmans, the Gophers, and the Hudson Dusters (Sante, 1991). Gangs then appeared to be more like organized crime groups, as they mirrored the practices of the business community, and merged with like-minded organizations to increase their geographic exposure and control. The gangs were increasingly more sophisticated than their predecessors, and in some cases required written reports for contracted work (Sante, 1991). As has been seen in eras since, those adult gangs had a succession plan in place, with a strategy for replacing and supplementing their membership with new recruits from their farm teams. Many of the gangs had female auxiliary support groups as well (Sante, 1991).

As the numbers of Chinese immigrations were added to the population of New York in the latter part of the nineteenth century, their secret societies, known as tongs, started forming. The tongs first formed for mutual aid, but then became powerful and often violent (Haskins, 1974). Some of them ran grocery stores with areas for illicit gambling, while others provided areas for opium consumption. As their activities became more profitable, other gangs started looking for business in the area of New York known as Chinatown, especially the gang known as the Five Pointers, of which Al Capone was a member before he moved to Chicago (Anbinder, 2001).

One of Asbury's (1986) noteworthy findings was a group of Negro women in 1890s Chicago that committed hundreds of holdups before they were arrested and convicted. They were known as footpads, a term used at the time to describe a robber or thief who focused on victims who were walking around town. The women were armed with guns, knives, and baseball bats and often worked in pairs. They cut many a victim across the knuckles if they failed to respond fast enough when confronted (Asbury, 1986). Some were so sophisticated that they had fortified hiding places for when the police came looking for them.

From the 1890s to 1910, Chicago grew in both size and status. It passed the 200 square mile mark in size and recorded over 2 million citizens living within its borders, making it second only to New York in both population and importance in commerce (Asbury, 1986). Chicago's problems included an overwhelming amount of political corruption and an inefficient police department. As immigration was neither checked nor regulated at the time, Chicago quickly became the home to a diverse group of Swedes,

Norwegians, Poles, and Germans, as the "good and bad of Europe" brought their "customs and hatreds, their feuds and vendettas" (Asbury, 1986, p. 204).

Gangs in Chicago around 1900 engaged in human trafficking, too. As with other large American cities, brothels supplied young women for their customers, and that required a system that constantly sought out a "fresh" supply (Asbury, 1986). The average age of prostitutes in those times was 23.5 years, and many of the women were identified and supplied by gangs of white-slavers. Although a nationwide outfit was never identified, the methods the gangs used and the precise and effective coordination between the groups indicated there was more than simply a professional relationship. One such gang in Chicago was affiliated with similar gangs in New York, St. Louis, and Milwaukee. While some of their "products" were apparently willing participants in prostitution, many stories surfaced of young teenagers who were promised legal employment in the big city, only to be forced into prostitution (Asbury, 1986). Even back then, many of these gangs had international connections.

Also, around 1900, the American version of the Mafia started to establish itself in New York (Sante, 1991). Sante (1991) identified the genealogy of one contemporary organized crime group, starting with the Chichesters of Five Points, to the Whyos, to the Gambino family. Regardless of whether that line of succession is accurate, the underlying political and economic framework in each of the eras represented a fertile ground in which criminal groups thrived. Once the Mafia took over, the organization of criminal activity by typical street gangs was limited.

Many of the gangs were encouraged to profit from the institution of Prohibition, a constitutional ban on the production, importation, transportation and sale of alcoholic beverages in the United States from 1920 to 1933. Organized crime group leaders like Al Capone and Johnny Torrio had been running prostitution rings and other vice crimes for some time and saw the opportunity to profit from the demand for alcohol (Asbury, 1986). Torrio persuaded the leaders of many a criminal gang to shift their profit center from burglaries and bank robberies to bootlegging (Asbury, 1986). Breweries were purchased and territories were assigned. This distribution network worked well for a time, and only folded when renegade gangs who were not part of the initial agreement got involved in the industry.

Black gangs in Chicago did not appear until the 1920s, and Perkins (1987) asserted that most Blacks who lived in Chicago before 1930 were the offspring of Blacks who moved there from the Southern U.S. The residences of those blacks were typically confined to underdeveloped, segregated areas. That compounded the overcrowding problem in the substandard housing that was available. Many of the males were chronically unemployed, resulting in many spending countless idle hours in the street (Perkins, 1987).

Between 1910 and 1930, Chicago gained almost 200,000 black residents during the Great Migration of more than a million blacks from the southern states. That gave the city an enormous urban black population, along with New York City, Cleveland,

Detroit, Philadelphia, and other Northeast and Midwest cities (Alonso, 1999). Black gangs in Chicago likely formed to protect their members (and perhaps their neighborhood) from gangs of white youth.

In 1927, Thrasher identified the 1,313 early gangs (with an estimated 25,000 members) that were active in Chicago's neighborhoods at the time, including groups with names such as the Onions, Kenwoods, hard-boiled Crawfords, and Bloody Broomsticks. In Thrasher's study of Chicago gangs, he observed a specific gang in Chicago during the 1920s called the Dirty Dozens. During the Chicago race riots of 1919, Dirty Dozen members chased and threatened several black men in a 30-block stretch of run-down housing on the South Side known as the Black Belt. Moore (1998) found that the dominance of Chicago's white ethnic gangs ended shortly after Thrasher's research was completed. He found that "the gangs of the 1920s were largely a one-generation immigrant ghetto phenomenon" (p. 68).

By the start of the 1930s, gangs had firmly established in Chicago's African American communities. The school system was "ineffective and alienating" for African Americans, and unemployment in the 1930s was said to be eroding traditional family structures (Moore, 1998). Active racial discrimination limited the number of legitimate employment opportunities, while the number of illegal employment opportunities flourished, tied to the notorious political machine that was active in Chicago.

Cureton (2009) found the proliferation of gangs in most major urban areas and even some smaller poverty-stricken areas was significantly related to black migration and overcrowding in socially disorganized areas, a subculture of conflict deviance, crime, and violence, dysfunctional family dynamics, and blocked access to legitimate opportunities, among other factors. As was seen in the Northeast and Midwest, the migration of blacks to historically white southern Los Angeles began with the move of blacks from the South, mostly from Louisiana and Mississippi. Blacks were simply looking for a better life than they had in the South, and the non-black European immigrant communities in the West offered more employment opportunities in factories and an escape from southern oppression. The move turned out to be the trigger for traditional white supremacist ideology, institutional inequality (in housing, education, and employment), and restrictions relative to where blacks could socialize. That led to a civil rights movement of sorts in that region in the late 1940s (Cross, 1973).

Miller (1975), in a report for the Justice Department, found that by 1975 the membership of most U.S. gangs was no longer predominantly white. Prior to the 1970s, most street gangs in America consisted of the sons (and sometimes daughters) of Jewish, Irish, Italian, Polish, German, and other European Americans. Miller's work was documented in the pilot National Youth Gang Survey, which found high levels of gang violence in New York, Chicago, Los Angeles, Detroit, Philadelphia, and San Francisco, among other cities, and a shift in the demographics of the typical gang member. Today we can find gangs that are composed of many different ethnic or racial groups (i.e., they can be heterogeneous).

The basic truth, though, is that today most street and prison gangs and other organized crime groups remain relatively homogeneous with respect to race and ethnicity.

How Many Gangs and Gang Members Are There Today?

Gangs have been reported in all 50 states. According to the National Gang Center (NGC), funded by the Office of Juvenile Justice and Delinquency Prevention (OJJDP), after a decline from the mid-1990s to the early 2000s, the prevalence of gang activity significantly increased between 2001 and 2005, remaining constant thereafter (Egley, Howell, & Harris, 2014, p. 2). In 2010, the numbers started climbing again, and reached an estimated 850,000 gang members nationwide by 2012 (Figure 1.3). At the same time, the OJJDP reported that the estimated number of youth gangs steadily increased from 27,300 to 30,700. While during this same period (2007–2012) the number of problem jurisdictions declined, the number of gang-related homicides increased by 19.6%.

The Federal Bureau of Investigations' National Gang Intelligence Center (NGIC) gathers statistics on several gang variables. NGIC surveys specifically ask respondents to estimate the number of gang members in their jurisdictions. The 2009 and 2011 surveys identified 1 million and 1.4 million gang members, respectively (NGIC, 2009, 2011). The 2013 and 2015 surveys were unable to provide an estimate due to inconclusive reporting and a lack of confidence in estimates, and no attempt was made in 2017.

Most Gang Members Are Adults

Though differences have existed based on region and population size of the jurisdiction, police typically have reported that most gang members were adults (Klein &

Indicator	2007	2008	2009	2010	2011	2012
Gang-Problem Jurisdictions	3,550	3,330	3,500	3,500	3,300	3,100
Gangs	27,300	27,900	28,100	29,400	29,900	30,700
Gang Members	788,000	774,000	731,000	756,000	782,000	850,000
Gang-Related Homicides	1,975	1,659	2,083	2,020	1,824	2,363

Figure 1.3

Gang Magnitude Indicators.

Egley, Howell, and Harris (2014, p. 2), Table 1

Maxson, 2006). In fact, both government and academic gang researchers have found a progressive increase in the proportion of adult gang members for almost every year since 1996. Analysts and researchers who use the phrase "youth gangs" find their results hard to apply to the real world of criminal justice—there are no "youth laws," there are juvenile laws and adult criminal codes. Anyone 17 or older in Illinois, for example, is an adult under law, and their behavior in violating the law is not regarded as "juvenile delinquency," it is "adult criminality." In fact, as was previously addressed, research since then tends to show there are significantly more adult gang members than juveniles. The problem, then, with using the term "youth gang" is that it inaccurately describes the social reality of American gangs. Further, it implies that such gangs have no adult leaders to whom they are accountable.

Sante (1991) showed that adult gangs had a strategy for replacing and supplementing their membership with new recruits from their farm systems. As Asbury (1927) noted, some of the support gangs acknowledged the adult gangs they were supporting, with names such as the Forty Little Thieves, the Little Plug Uglies, and the Little Dead Rabbits. Thrasher (2000) observed that older gang members might have allowed younger boys to hang around, though they may have prohibited them from actual membership in the gang.

Annual surveys of the NGC, formerly the National Youth Gang Center (NYGC), have shown a progressive increase in adult gang members for almost every year since 1996. In 1996, the percentage of gang members was reported to be 50 percent juvenile and 50 percent adult. In 2006, the distribution was 36.5 percent juvenile and 63.5 percent adult. In the 2007 (and previous years) report, the survey results specifically excluded exclusively adult gangs (NYGC, 2009).

Another study found a significant increase in the average age of gang members in a Midwestern city (Etter & Swymeler, 2008). In a comparative study of police-identified active gang members in 1996 and 2006, all four major national street gangs and each of the independent local gangs studied showed increases in the number of older members. The average age of gang members in that study increased from 20.03 to 26.59. Along with the increase, the study revealed that approximately 34.87 percent of the gang members remained active in the gang for 10 years or more (Etter & Swymeler, 2008). Those increased average ages may have indicated not only an aging of the gang population but also an increase in the recruiting of older gang members.

Some communities have had a significant number of adult gang members (Katz & Webb, 2006). In a multisite study covering 1998–1999, Katz and Webb (2006) examined the police response to gangs to identify the factors that led to the creation of a gang unit, alternative responses to community gang problems, and the relevant beliefs held by gang unit officers. Most (79% and up) of the gang members in Albuquerque, New Mexico, Las Vegas, Nevada, and Phoenix, Arizona, were young adults between 18 and 36 years old.

In 2007, the New Jersey State Police (NJSP) Street Gang Bureau collected information about gang activity and analyzed gang trends. In their summary of recent NJSP Gang Surveys, analysts found that most (60%) gang members in 2001 were adults. In 2004, 53% of the reported gang members were adults. Though there was an overall decrease, the number of adult gang members still exceeded the number of juvenile gang members.

The Florida Department of Law Enforcement (FDLE) 2007 Statewide Gang Survey indicated 56.5% of the state gang population was adults. The focus of the research was clearly on youth gangs, and the authors of the report noted an average 38.4% of gang members were between 15 and 17 years of age. The results of the study showed that over half of the gang members were adults (FDLE, 2007). While these estimates may be dated, the limited research conducted to determine the percentages of adults involve in gangs requires us to use that data.

While the NGC and the NGIC have tried to identify the number of gang members in the U.S. by asking police officers about the people in their jurisdictions, gang researchers Pyrooz and Sweeten recently (2015) suggested there were significantly more young people involved with gangs. Using a combination of the National Longitudinal Survey of Youth and the U.S. Census to produce a national estimate of gang membership, they estimated that there were 1,059,000 juvenile gang members, representing 2.0% of persons (about 1 of every 50) between the ages of 5 and 17 in the U.S. population. They also found about 400,000 juveniles leave gangs each year, and about the same number join gangs each year. They also noted most who joined a gang left it long before adulthood.

TABLE 1.1 Summary of Findings by Age

Location	Adult %	Juvenile %
Arizona (Phoenix) (2000)	84.2	15.8
Florida (2007)	56.5	38.4
Nevada (Las Vegas) (1998)	79.0	11.0
New Jersey (2004)	53.0	47.0
New Mexico (Albuquerque) (1999)	88.6	10.5
United States (2006)	63.5	36.5
Average	70.8	26.53

Adapted from "2007 Statewide Gang Survey Results," by the Florida Department of Law Enforcement; "Policing Gangs in America," by Charles M. Katz and Vincent J. Webb, 2006, New York, NY: Cambridge University Press, pp. 98–114; National Youth Gang Survey Analysis, by the NYGC, 2009, and Gangs in New Jersey: Municipal Law Enforcement Response to the 2007 NJSP Gang Survey.

So, if Pyrooz and Sweeten's estimates that there were over 1 million juvenile gang members were accurate, there would be no fewer than an additional 1.1 million adult gang members (if the 53:47 ratio found by the New Jersey State Police is accurate) to as much as 5.6 million (if the higher 85:15 ratio found in one of the studies by Katz and Webb is accurate). That would mean there were actually at least 2.1 million gang members in the United States when the last recorded NGIC tally was conducted in 2011. It could also mean that there were close to 2.6 million in 2013, 2.8 million in 2015, and as many as 3.5 million and 4 million gang members in the United States in 2017 and 2019, respectively, if those numbers continued to climb.

Gangs in the Community

The essential question here is: can anything be done about the gang crime problem in the community? Some may say that it is possible to greatly impact gangs, perhaps even dismantle them. Others may say through social services we can work directly with gangs and gang members, and perhaps show them a better way of life. The most extreme form of this therapeutic intervention would be that we can "de-program" gang members. Still others may say that no one has ever come up with the one-size-fits-all rehabilitation or prevention solution. Therefore, it may be impossible to turn around the gang crime problem.

So how do people come to perceive gangs as a social problem? If a group of gang members hang out on the street corner by the neighborhood grocery and their presence scares off customers, then that is often seen as a private matter for the small business owner. Over time, other area shop owners may talk to a local police officer and mention a similar impact by gang members on their businesses. Former customers may also mention the gang members on the corner to the police officer. To most of us, the gang members on the street corner are perceived as a private problem—a personal matter. But to the police officer, the gang members' presence has become a public matter. The many similar personal matters of individuals become a collective public matter when recognized by a whole community; they become an acknowledged social problem (Mills, 1959).

Gangs became a serious community problem in the late 1990s. Gang-related crime, particularly drugs and shootings, popped up in the suburbs and rural counties. Some researchers argued that the media whipped up a "moral panic" among the people. As such, state legislators passed new laws targeting gangs and gang members. William Recktenwald (1997) made statements in a newspaper article that reflected the standard presentation of gangs in the media: "The sale and use of crack cocaine . . . has spread across the entire state" (p. 1), and "Illinois is experiencing an alarming increase in gang-related violence . . . with gang homicides jumping fourfold to 215 from 1987 to 1995 in Chicago" (p. 2). David E. Neely (1997) suggested gang-associated problems were becoming "an inescapable concern for mainstream America" (p. 37).

Suman K. Sirpal identified perceptions of gangs held by the public and law enforcement, and the portrayal of gangs in the media. He suggested that gang members are portrayed as "mean and cruel, have no respect for their own or others' lives, and commit senseless crimes for personal profit . . . who have no aim in life but the destruction of the society for personal gain" (Sirpal, 1997, p. 13). Researchers Claire Johnson, Barbara Webster, and Edward Connors (1995) suggested that street gangs were a social and political concern due to the crimes that their members committed. Other authors have suggested a relationship between gangs and social problems: "gangs are a community problem" (Virginia Commission on Youth, 1996); "The gang problem is not a 'their problem'; the gang phenomena is an 'our problem'" (Kirk-Duggan, 1997, p. 24); and "Communities are implementing a combination of prevention, intervention, and suppression strategies to address the gang problem" (Burch & Chemers, 1997, p. 1). In their review of findings from a nationwide survey sponsored by the National Institute of Justice, Johnson et al. (1995) found more than 80% of prosecutors acknowledged a gang problem in their jurisdiction.

Gangs are no longer just a problem for the inner city. Gangs are also found in the suburbs and even in rural areas of the country. Recktenwald (1997) cited a report prepared by the Illinois Criminal Justice Information Authority that stated, "While urban areas were hit particularly hard, suburban and rural communities were far from immune from the problem" (p. 1). That assessment was supported by John P. Moore's (1997) assertion that the number of cities, towns, and counties experiencing gang problems was growing. The federal government joined private citizens and researchers in the perception of gangs as a social problem in the 1990s.

More recent analysis showed while 41.6 percent of gangs were in larger cities, an estimated 27.1 percent were in smaller cities (NGC, 2013). Another 25.8 percent of gangs were in suburban counties and 5.5 percent are in rural counties. Comparing the OJJDP (Egley et al., 2014) numbers for total estimated youth gang members in 2012 (850,000) with the U.S. Census Bureau's (2013) estimated total population in 2012 (about 314 million), it appears that perhaps 1 out of every 370 U.S. residents may be a gang member. The numbers would likely be higher if the NGIC had continued their tally since 2011. The statistics stand as seemingly objective and accurate measures of the gang threat in America. However, many gang researchers believe that the overall number of gangs and gang members has been underestimated. Independent estimates of the scope and extent of gang crime in America generally give higher estimates than OJJDP figures. Since many self-reporting studies have indicated that gang membership peaks around age 14 or 15, some scholars have questioned the validity of police reporting (Klein & Maxson, 2006).

The federal government typically has several agencies at work to address the gang problem. However, it is the position of some researchers that the federal government may have ignored the issue of gangs for too long early on, and has now underestimated, and underaccounted for, the real extent of the gang problem. Thus any presentation of gangs may reflect either public perceptions, government goals, or the actuality of the issue. Since gangs and gang-related crime may reach out and touch anyone at any time, gangs are a topic worthy of every person's study, regardless of his or her academic discipline or career field.

Gangs need not have a publicly known label or name for their group, although most American gangs do. Yablonsky recorded the naming process of one gang in New York in the 1960s:

> How did we get our name? Well, when we were in the police station, the cops kept askin' us who we were. Jay was studying history in school—so he said . . . let's call ourselves Balkans. So we told the cops—we're the Balkans—and that was it.
>
> (Yablonsky, 1970, p. 42)

Indeed, in the early stage of gang formation, the name itself emerges as a function of identity and crystallization. Gangs often do not consider themselves "gangs," rather as some type of legitimate community organization. Do gangs necessarily have to have illicit goals, functions, or engage in law violation collectively or as individuals? Or can a gang have prosocial purposes? Gangs have sometimes cloaked themselves in a veneer of possessing conspicuous prosocial functions as a public relations function, and members of motorcycle gangs get involved in collecting toys for needy children.

Gangs like the Gangster Disciples in Chicago, for example, prefer being called a community support or political organization, because they have been able to stage protests with several thousand members marching in unison in front of City Hall and claim the name "Growth and Development." The Gangster Disciples also engaged in political endeavors with their 21st Century Voices of Total Empowerment (21st Century V.O.T.E.), claiming that gang leaders had found solutions for urban problems ranging from drugs to unemployment to homelessness (Papajohn & Kass, 1994). The Gangster Disciples were not the only gang involved in the political scene. The P-Stone Rangers (later known as the El Rukns and the Black P Stones) applied for and received over a million dollars in anti-poverty funds in the 1960s. The Avenues, predecessors to the Crips, were involved with the Black Panther Party in California in the 1960s. Many of the outlaw motorcycle gangs have engaged the community by conducting toy drives for kids and have shown support for various political candidates. The Mafia was also well known for supporting political figures.

To some extent, gangs gain acceptance in the community through the tendency of American culture to romanticize and often idolize gang exploits. This has been particularly seen in Broadway productions, Hollywood movies, television shows, and "true crime" paperback books. Gorn (1987) reported the case of massive public attendance involving thousands of people at a gang leader's funeral back in the 1850s. What all gangs and those in the funeral procession seemed to have in common was their social class. Al Capone as a gang leader has been significantly represented in fiction, myth, and through the Hollywood movie industry. Even the tourist industry in Chicago adapted itself. Bus tours routinely take tourists through the city to show them where Capone conducted business, where mobsters were slain, and so forth.

An "Al Capone" museum was opened as a tourist attraction in Chicago as well. A bar in Peotone, Illinois, locally referred to as "Capone's place," features a large picture of him and a sign reading *Gangster's Hall*. Gang members of today also have their own place, or niche, in some music genres and television shows, and enjoy the notoriety of public affiliation with sports professionals and actors alike. Several well-known entertainers have gang or organized crime member or gang-affiliate roots, either unknown, overlooked, or appreciated by their fans, including Ice-T, Suge Knight, Snoop Dogg, Chris Brown, Elizabeth Hurley, James Caan, Al Pacino, Robert DeNiro, and Mark Wahlberg.

Defining Gangs and Organized Crime

Some of the literature on gangs tends to describe "wannabe" gang members, discounting those "wannabe gangs" and their members as not posing a threat to society. We should be very concerned about wannabe gang members. The reason is this: when one wannabe shoots another wannabe, we do not have a "wannabe homicide"; we have a real gang homicide on our hands. But we should be wary of anyone who discounts their local gang problem as consisting only of wannabe gang members, because in far too many cases the "wannabe" is really a "gonnabe." Eventually, wannabes meet and likely learn from the "real thing" (i.e., hard core OGs—Original Gangstas) when they get processed into the criminal justice system and are sent off to a correctional facility. Additionally, those folks often feel they have something to prove and little in the way of guidance and supervision from someone who has done what they aspire to do. That could make them more dangerous and unpredictable than the typical gang member.

Often, the excuse is made that gang members get a bad label from society. Gang members seek out reputations on the street ("street cred" or a "rep") as a shooter, killer, thug, enforcer, brutal, badass, and a host of other terms that most of us would consider immoral or illegal. They do not seek out a rep as the guy who helps at the local library reading to children or assists the local non-profit by volunteering as a mentor. It is not a gang researcher who puts labels on the gang member—it's other gang members.

The most essential feature of the criminal gang is that its members routinely engage in unlawful violent behavior. This is done individually, in small groups, and often in an organized continuing fashion. The nature of this involvement with crime will be seen to provide the basis for examining gangs from a social organizational perspective. Thus, without crime, we would not have a gang: it would be a deviant group or deviant organization at best. As an example, Thrasher's study of gangs included many Social Athletic Clubs (SACs) that today might be viewed at most as a nuisance, but not gangs (2000).

We also cannot oversimplify the term gang by taking the viewpoint that any organized group containing offenders must necessarily constitute a gang. Were that kind of ambiguous definition used in gang analysis, then correctional officials would have to conclude that any prosocial club or organization behind the walls of correctional institutions constitutes a social gang. Police and corrections officers do not encounter social gangs, those who never come to the attention of the criminal justice system. Rather, they see the hardcore criminal gang members. It is mostly the criminal gang member whom we find in our jails and prisons.

Gangs represent a group, collective behavior, organizational patterns, and other features that have historically been the turf of the sociology discipline. However, other disciplines have much to add to this area of study; those include the perspectives from law, psychology, economics, social service administration/social work, human development, urban studies, anthropology, criminal justice, corrections, and other areas of social sciences. That means the study of gangs should be interdisciplinary. It also means students should seek out, when possible, reliable research about gangs. A student must be vigilant and learn to identify the mistakes that can be made in misinterpreting research findings and drawing conclusions, as well as learn to defend oneself against misinformation and intentional disinformation.

Emile Durkheim (1965) suggested, "The sociologist's first step must therefore be to define the things he treats, so that we may know . . . exactly what his subject matter is" (p. 74). A specific definition is "needed precisely because a researcher or theorist cannot take everyone [or everything] to the phenomenon in question" (Ball & Curry, 1997, p. 4). However, there exists no consensus for a definition of the terms "gang" or "gang-related crime" as they are used within academe, among government agencies, or by the U.S. criminal justice system.

Knox (1994, p. 5) raised the question: "Does calling a group a gang make it a gang?" He suggested that it depends on who is forming the definition. He further stated (1994, p. 5) that "[t]he difference is power." The voice of a community resident differs in definitive power from the voice of a U.S. attorney or a local prosecutor. The difference is the power to establish and assign formal definitions for a society. Accepting the argument that definitive power is a determining factor, it is logical to surmise that a sociological or political definition was most likely used in publications rather than one constructed by a community resident.

Legally, we need to recognize that specific laws addressing gangs have only recently come into being. There is the federal Racketeer Influenced and Corrupt Organizations

Figure 1.4
Emile Durkheim. Public domain.
www.marxists.org

(RICO) statute and its many mini-RICO versions at the state level of criminal law. These define organizations engaged in violation of the law and can be used for both criminal and civil prosecution. Again, however, language is no friend of social science. For example, Illinois, among other states, has a "mob action" criminal statute which covers crimes committed in a group, including civil protest demonstrations. Literally thousands of persons have been arrested under this statute for protests associated with the "right to life" movement and banning abortion. Most people arrested for protesting the operation of an abortion clinic would probably reveal a prosocial motivation of a higher social purpose and an intent to be arrested, not to avoid arrest. Their behavior is a matter of civil disobedience in their minds. Indeed, they may be a very religious persons who knows that mass media attention will come their way due to their protest and arrest, and not because of their "cause."

Groups with internalized higher moral imperatives (e.g., to protect the environment) may engage in civil disobedience knowing they will be arrested for their behavior and willfully continuing such behavior as a moral protest. They cannot be considered "gangs" in any sense. The reasoning here rests with the fact that their intent is not to do harm through violence or to benefit economically through criminal code violation. Furthermore, in such civil disobedience they do not seek to evade arrest.

It is appropriate, therefore, to review some of the definitions in use by social scientists and government agencies. Social scientists are generally considered to be the "experts" or "authorities" based on the extent of their experience and research in specific areas, and the extent of professional acceptance of their academic publications. Gusfield (1980) stated that sociological perspectives are "systematic maps for understanding" and "carry messages . . . that are wise, proper and effective in responding to public issues" (p. 1).

Four recurrent themes exist among a representative sampling of gang definitions offered by social scientists: self-recognition as an identifiable group, perception and labeling by the community as a group, delinquent or criminal acts, and an actual or a willingness to use violence and force to achieve goals (Kirk-Duggan, 1997; Klein, 1971; Miller, 1975; Moore, 1997; Sanders, 1994). More recently gang scholars have defined street gangs as "any durable, street oriented youth group whose own identity includes involvement in illegal activity" (Klein, 2007, p. 18). Contemporary street gangs "have generally been in existence for 20 or more years: they keep regenerating themselves" (Klein & Maxson, 2006, p. 176). All gangs (like other organizations) have an identified hierarchy, with a defined set of leaders and followers (Sheldon, Tracy, & Brown, 2001; Weisberg, 2003).

A group is a gang when it exists for or benefits substantially from the continuing criminal activity of its members. Some element of crime must exist as a definitive feature of the organization for it to be classified as a gang. That need not be income-producing crime, because it could also be violent crime. Conspiracy laws have some application here. To prove a conspiracy it is generally necessary to prove one or more overt acts in furtherance of the conspiracy. The key word is "overt." It must be open and clearly regarded as law violating behavior. That is, they know it is wrong, they know it is against the law, and they do it anyway. Some element of criminal conspiracy to avoid detection for law violation must therefore be present, whether the actual/objective/material skill/knowledge/ability to avoid or limit the probability of arrest exists.

Thus from the perspective of the analysis advanced in this book, a group is not a gang simply because it is labeled as being in some sense deviant. A group is a gang if and only if it meets the higher requirement of having a known involvement with crime. It can therefore include the Crips, Bloods, Gangster Disciples, Vice Lords, Latin Kings, Pagans, Hells Angels, Outlaws, and a host of others whose primary function is income-producing crime or those who benefit substantially from it. Such crime patterns, particularly of more organized gangs who have been able to accumulate economic assets, can also include a mixture of legitimate income (small businesses, hustling, etc.) and criminal pursuits.

Gang definitions used by law enforcement agencies have typically included some variation of these requirements: a group of individuals (often specified as three or more persons) who associate on a continuous basis; self-recognition as an identifiable group using a group name, symbols, structured style of dress, and hand signals; claim a particular geographic territory, neighborhood or turf; and through its membership engages in a course or pattern of recurrent criminal activity directed towards rival gangs and the general population (Illinois State Police, 1997; San Diego County Deputy Sheriffs' Association, 1994; Virginia Commission on Youth, 1996). The National Alliance of Gang Investigator Associations has proposed a standard definition for law enforcement: a gang is a formal or informal group or association of three or more persons with a common identifying sign, symbol, or name who individually or collectively engage in criminal activity that creates an atmosphere of fear and intimidation (NAGIA, 2005).

Research and analyses on differences between gangs and organized crime groups has been relatively well documented (Thrasher, 1927; Howell & Decker, 1999; Klein & Maxson, 2006). Organized crime groups have been said to differ from gangs as they typically reinvest the profits from their crimes to further the group (Decker & Pyrooz, 2011).

Cressey (1969) was one of the first to suggest a standardized definition of organized crime:

> An organized crime is any crime committed by a person occupying, in an established division of labor, a position designed for the commission of crimes providing that such division of labor include at least one position for a corrupter, one position for a corruptee, and one position for an enforcer.
>
> (p. 319)

The United Nations Office on Drugs and Crime (2004) defined organized crime as

> a structured group of three or more persons, existing for a period of time and acting in concert with the aim of committing one or more serious crimes or offenses established . . . in order to obtain, directly or indirectly, a financial or other material benefit.
>
> (p. 5)

Gang-Related Crime

Generally, what the study of gangs implies is much different from loner or individual crime. A single gunman acting alone in a robbery, simply put, differs from a gang member committing a crime based on his or her gang association. The gang has something that the lone criminal offender does not have, that being some sense of organizational capability. The gang also implies a continuing or persisting threat over time that can increase. It is this emphasis on organizational characteristics that is common to the study of gangs, but which is at the same time most underdeveloped in the sense of linking what we know about social organization generally to the more specific problem of the study of gangs. An organizational viewpoint allows for more effective law enforcement, greater choices in managing the problem in the field of corrections, and much more latitude in addressing the gang problem from all levels of prevention—primary, secondary, and tertiary (e.g., aftercare services).

An extensive list of gang-related activities could be readily constructed by drawing from personal observation, a host of gang researchers, newspaper articles, or television documentaries. This list would probably include everything from the beer drinking of minors while playing games of dominoes, to littering and graffiti, to the sale of controlled substances and to murder. One may safely suggest that gang-related activities generally fall under the title of "crime," representing offenses from statutory, civil and criminal codes.

One issue in the problem of defining "gang-related crime" was that of determining when to count a crime as related to, or unrelated to, a gang. Many suggest that the gang or its leader must have prior knowledge of, and give approval for, the commission of a criminal act. In other words, "[a] gang incident is an incident in which there was gang motivation, not mere participation by a gang member" (Spergel, 1991, p. 23). Thus one is faced with having to decide whether a crime must be committed under the auspices of a gang or its leader, and whether it was to their mutual benefit. Many gang-enhancement laws require the demonstration of a benefit of the gang to bring an increase in the penalty.

Why Do Gangs and Organized Crime Groups Exist?

Theories of crime are explanations of causation that apply to all people and all crimes. Theories are not absolute, but they are significant. Theory guides practice. If we know why people join gangs, then it would be possible to devise strategies that prevent that from occurring. Some of the theories may make sense to the reader, and some may not. The theories presented here are by no means all-inclusive. They are presented for consideration by present and future criminal justice professionals to explain the existence of gangs and organized crime groups.

A gang is a group. Organized criminals operate in a group. Therefore, we will examine various theories of group criminality. As a result, many traditional gang theories have been omitted, especially those related distinctly to youth gangs. The absence of those theories in no way serves to dismiss their validity or application in other contexts. Most theorists view the gang as a group or tribe while others view the gang as an illicit alternative economic enterprise. Both schools of thought will be examined.

The Gang as a Group or a Tribe

For over 100 years, theorists have examined the gang from the standpoint of a group or self-affiliated tribe. As such, these criminal groups combine themselves into self-affiliated tribal structures to help them conduct their criminal enterprises and to avoid the police. In these criminal groups, they have adopted a pseudo-warrior culture to facilitate their criminal society. These self-affiliated tribal groups exhibit many of the characteristics of traditional tribes such as a self-declared identity or tribal name for their gang and use totems or symbols to identify with the group. Many have established social interactions and practice ritualism and selective membership in the same manner as fraternities or sororities, although for very different reasons. Reasons for joining such voluntary criminal associations can include a wish to belong to something, protection from other hostile gangs and perceived opportunities for power or economic success (Etter, 1998).

Frederic M. Thrasher (1920s)

Thrasher was one of the first researchers to study gangs as a group. Thrasher's work *The Gang: A Study of 1,313 Gangs in Chicago* is worth discussing not simply because it was an early study of gangs, but because of the enduring influence of Thrasher's approach to gang research. Thrasher's approach can be called the natural history approach, which has been heavily associated with the Chicago School of sociology. But the gangs Thrasher analyzed were youth gangs and were at best periodically delinquent, and certainly did not reach the level of violence associated with modern gangs in the twenty-first century (2000).

An etiological sequence is suggested by Thrasher for gang development that revolves around associations between members. This developmental sequence recognizes five sources of gang input: (1) a spontaneous play group, (2) a casual crowd, (3) the family itself, (4) intimacy groups (adolescent dyads), and (5) the formal group. Thrasher saw eight developmental outputs of the gang: (1) a mob (not implying organized crime), (2) a secret society, (3) public, (4) ring, (5) criminal gang, (6) orgiastic group, (7) political machine, and (8) a psychological crowd (both action type and orgiastic type).

Thrasher's gang etiology sequence recognizes a difference between the pseudo-gang, the gang itself, and separately the criminal gang. The gang itself can develop, incrementally, into three stages: (1) diffuse or amorphous, (2) solidified or well-knit, and (3) conventional or formalized. The gang in its embryonic state can first emerge from a variety of sources such as the spontaneous play group, a casual crowd, the family, a small intimate dyad, or even a formal group. The kind of gangs studied by Thrasher were mostly at the lower end of the organizational sophistication spectrum.

William Foote Whyte (1930s)

Whyte made an ethnographic study of gangs and urban life in Boston's North End. In his book *Street Corner Society* (1943), he explained the study of one Italian community called Cornerville, circa 1937. Like Thrasher, Whyte described the behavior of local street corner groups that drifted into gang and criminal behavior while still engaging in some legitimate behaviors including organized bowling tournaments. Whyte viewed this criminal youth gang association as temporary and observed that most of the gang members married and moved out of the neighborhood, thus ending their involvement in the group. Whyte (1943) observed that new youth gangs formed along the same pattern to replace the existing gang members. The local youth street gangs were also involved in local politics. Whyte saw the street corner gang as arising from "the habitual association of members over a long period of time." When some gang members left the community, a group would disintegrate, and its members merged with another group.

Edwin Sutherland (1940s)

Sutherland's (1940) Differential Association Theory explained how gang and organized crime group members acquire the knowledge and skills to be of use to the criminal organization. Sutherland noted that:

1. Criminal behavior is learned.

2. Criminal behavior is learned in interaction with other persons in a process of communication.

3. The principal part of learning criminal behavior occurs within intimate personal groups.

4. When criminal behavior is learned, the learning includes (a) techniques of committing the crime, which are sometimes very simple; and (b) the specific motives and drives, rationalizations, and attitudes (pp. 6–7).

With the theory of differential association, Sutherland suggested that all behavior, lawful and criminal, was learned in intimate personal groups, whereas learning the techniques of sophisticated criminality required the proper environment (Sutherland, 1940). It was also noteworthy that he observed illegitimate opportunity for success, like legitimate opportunity, was not equally distributed throughout society and access to criminal ladders of success were no more freely available than are non-criminal alternatives.

Albert K. Cohen (1950s)

While Cohen is more remembered for his views on why youth participate in individual criminality (he blamed class frustrations and blocked needs), he made several observations of gangs as well. In Cohen's (1955) *Delinquent Boys: The Culture of the Gang*, Cohen engaged in a theoretical discussion of delinquent subcultures. The general theory of subcultures advanced by Cohen was termed the psychogenic model. Basically, Cohen saw youth gangs emerging as a reaction formation to status frustration among working class youths who are less likely to have been socialized into middle class values.

Cohen (1955) argued that the delinquent subculture rejected the social norms of the dominant larger culture and thus engaged in anti-social activities. For example, Cohen described stealing by gang members as a "diversified occupation." Cohen also observed that another characteristic of youth gangs was "short-run hedonism" and that little interest was shown in long term goals. Cohen also noted the youth gang's desire for "group autonomy or intolerance of restraint" (pp. 28–31). He assumed all behavior including gang behavior is problem-solving behavior (p. 50), and acknowledged that some gang members might be motivated by Merton's (1938) "illicit means theory" (p. 35).

Herbert Bloch and Arthur Niederhoffer (1950s)

Bloch and Niederhoffer (1958) advanced the hypothesis that gangs seemed to provide the adolescent with those things not provided by traditional social institutions, such as rites of passage from youth into perceived adulthood. Therefore, they suggested, the gang becomes a surrogate family and provides other necessary functions as well which may not be satisfied through the existing social structure.

Walter B. Miller (1950s)

Miller (1958) developed the Subculture Theory based on his study of juvenile gangs in Roxbury, Massachusetts. He discovered that youth in gangs had different focal concerns than those of the rest of the population. The cultural things that were important to juvenile gang members included trouble, toughness, smartness, excitement, fate and autonomy.

Lewis Yablonsky (1960s)

In Yablonsky's work *The Violent Gang* (1962) Yablonsky's classification of gangs included three types: (1) delinquent gangs, (2) violent gangs, and (3) social gangs (1962, p. 149). What dominates the gang ethos explains its gang function (delinquency, violence, social, etc.). Thus, what kind of gang it is depends on the type of norms, behavior patterns, and personalities of the gang membership.

It was the violent gang organization that Yablonsky analyzed in detail. The picture that emerges of the violent gang according to Yablonsky (1962) is as follows: the gang emerges spontaneously; it provides a sense of power; joining is easy; initiation rites are pretty much a myth; it is easy to quit the gang, but leaders and core members seldom leave the gang (p. 155); the leaders are self-appointed manipulators who "manifest paranoid delusions of persecution and grandeur" (p. 156); they use the myth of vast alliances with other gang nations and affiliates; and gang warfare is like a group contagion and often has no clear purpose other than trivial things that trigger conflict. The sociopathic members live in slums in urban communities facing negative forces of decay and erosion. Prejudice and discrimination aggravate the gang problem (p. 184).

From Yablonsky came the differentiation between "core" versus "marginal" members, a continuum of organized-unorganized with respect to the gang infrastructure. In this scheme a mob fits the pattern of unorganized, while the violent gang fits the pattern of being a near group, and social/delinquent gangs fit the pattern of being most organized. Basically, the differences in personalities mediate all causal factors and the personality types determine what kind of gang a youth joins.

James F. Short Jr. and Fred L. Strodtbeck (1960s and 1970s)

In *Group Process and Gang Delinquency*, Short and Strodtbeck (1965) extended the Chicago School tradition of gang studies to be the first major study with a large sample size using multivariate statistical analysis. They provided the first comprehensive comparison along racial lines and documented white racist bias crime through qualitative data. Thus, the basic position taken by Short and Strodtbeck (1965; 1974) was that status related to general society (employment aspirations, legitimate career potential, educational attainment, etc.) was important but that status within the small group context is more immediately likely to have impact on outcomes like gang violence (e.g., status threats, and status enhancing functions of the gang). Both the social structure and the group process must be considered.

Malcolm W. Klein (1970s to 1990s)

Defining what he perceived to be a gang, Klein (1971) observed that a gang refers

to any denotable adolescent group of youngsters who (a) are generally perceived as a distinct aggregation by others in the neighborhood, (b) recognize themselves as a denotable group (almost invariably with a group name), and (c) have been involved in a sufficient number of delinquent incidents to call forth a consistent negative response from neighborhood residents and/or law enforcement agencies.

(p. 111)

It was a definition that would be adopted by many gang researchers in the following years.

In his later works, Klein (1990) observed there are different varieties of street gangs and the gangs of Los Angeles did not adhere to a specific hierarchical structure. Klein found that the modal age of the average gang member in the Los Angeles area had increased from 16 to 20 (p. 6). He noted that different ethnic groups had become involved in local gangs and cited Asians as an example (p. 7). Klein also found that the street gangs were engaging in an increased amount of violence and noted that nearly 40% of all Los Angeles County homicides "were gang related" (p. 6).

Klein (1990) stated that gang members do not spend their days enmeshed and engulfed in a full schedule of violence; they also have normal lives (p. 14). Klein created controversy especially with the law enforcement community when he advocated that evidence does not exist that gangs truly control all or even a significant share of drug sales in America (p. 15). Klein also professed that no evidence existed that Los Angeles based gangs like the Crips and Bloods had franchised and exported crack distribution rings to the rest of the United States (p. 15). Most American law enforcement officials disagreed with this view based on what had occurred in their communities.

James D. Vigil (1980s)

Vigil focused on the barrio gangs of East Los Angeles and his ethnographic study saw the gang arising and persisting because of the marginality of gang members in terms of ecological, socioeconomic, cultural and psychological factors. Vigil argued that it is not a simple matter of alienation, but rather gangs arise and persist because of an accentuated estrangement. He discussed the psychodynamic factors of gangs in terms of Erikson's identity and related ego and self-identity formations. Vigil argued that family conditions, when stressful, also are seen as important ingredients in gang affiliation, and why the gang itself becomes a kind of surrogate family.

Irving Spergel (1990s)

In his study of youth gang subcultures for the National Youth Gang Center, Spergel (1993) found the structure of the gang was based on its needs for maintenance or development. The structure requires that certain roles be performed by core members, peripheral or fringe members, and recruits. The core describes the inner clique of leaders and members that is actively engaged in the everyday functioning of the gang. Core members interact frequently and relate easily to each other. They have been described as "those few who need and thrive on the totality of the gang's activity" (p. 36).

William B. Sanders (1990s)

Sanders provided perhaps the best sociologically grounded approach to ethnographic research on gangs. The study dealt with gang violence in San Diego. It explained why some social values like loyalty have different meanings to gangs than they do to others, or rather how in the gang context the value of loyalty is "grounded" in the specific gang culture. That may help to explain how some have regarded gang members as having twisted or upside-down value systems. Sanders showed that gang members are focused on the group and the concerns of the gang.

George W. Knox (1980s and 2000s)

Knox (1981) proposed the use of a synthesis of structural and subcultural models of social and reintegration for ex-offenders in the concept of differential integration. The concept of differential integration was based on the commonality of emphasis on group affiliation in both structural and subcultural approaches (Knox, 1981). Knox observed that ex-offenders had limited legitimate opportunities and were, as a result, less integrated into the traditional, law-abiding community while having ready access to many subgroups in the community more inclined toward deviance. Differential integration states that the explanation for why ex-offenders return to criminal activity (recidivate) involves both the limited opportunities they face and the attraction of the deviant subculture to which they are exposed.

In his extensive study of Chicago based street gangs (2006), Knox found that the gangs exhibited a patriarchal and hierarchical organizational structure. The gangs exhibited a pseudo-warrior culture and claimed defined areas of turf. In keeping with the pseudo-warrior culture, the Chicago based gangs often embraced group identities that reflected a value for mental illness, with words like insane added to the gang's name to make them seem more fierce to their rivals. Unlike Los Angeles based gangs, Knox observed that the Chicago based gangs were involved in local politics. The gangs used political corruption and misuse of social services funds for economic gain. Although the Chicago based gangs began as youth gangs, they have evolved into adult gangs and have lasted for over 60 years spreading with the drug trade all over the United States.

Gangs as an Alternate Economic Means of Success

Some theorists (beginning with Merton in 1938) view the gang as an illicit alternative economic enterprise. Those theorists saw the primary purpose of the gangs was making money. The gangs used the commission of crimes along with the providing of illicit goods and services to achieve these goals. As new opportunities arose, the criminal gang was able to respond to these new opportunities through innovation to exploit the opportunity and benefit the criminal organization.

Robert K. Merton (1938): Social Structure and Anomie

Merton expanded the anomie theories of Durkheim. Merton saw the United States of the 1930s as a culture that placed an overstressing of economic success without providing an equal access to the same opportunities to achieve that economic success. Thus those who could not achieve material success through traditional means such as work, education, or family felt strain by being excluded from the opportunities to achieve success. Merton theorized that individuals engaged in various adaptions because of this strain, including:

- Conformity—some people would simply accept that they would never be a success and would conform to the established social values.

- Ritualism—the effect of being so caught up in the rules or means of achieving success that they have lost sight of the goals.

- Retreatism—A retreatist rejects both the means and the ends of success. Examples are often cited as drug abuse, drunkenness, mental illness, or suicide.

- Rebellion—rejecting both the means and goals that define success, attempting to substitute alternative ones to change the existing order.

- Innovation—accepting the goals but often rejecting the established means of success, perhaps using illegitimate means.

Richard A. Cloward and Lloyd E. Ohlin (1960): Differential Opportunity Theory

Building on the theories of Merton (1938) and Sutherland (1947), Cloward and Ohlin (1960) assumed that in every community there are both legitimate and illegitimate opportunities for success. However, when a youth experiences or perceives closure in the legitimate opportunity and simultaneously has chances to make a living in the illicit or illegal opportunity structure, then delinquency occurs.

Cloward and Ohlin believed that youth who transcended into an adult criminal career often participated in delinquent subcultures. They observed (1960) that these delinquent subcultures "are often integrally linked to adult criminal groups" such as gangs (p. 10). Cloward and Ohlin found that there were three basic delinquent subcultures: criminal, conflict and retreatist. They felt that the criminal subculture developed in slum neighborhoods and embraced criminal acts as an illegitimate means to success. In the conflict subculture, both legitimate and illegitimate means of success were rejected. Violence and defense of turf was used to enhance prestige. Cloward and Ohlin also observed that those who could not achieve some measure of success using either legitimate or illegitimate means often turned to the retreatist subculture where they in effect "dropped out" and sought "kicks" by participating in drug abuse (pp. 161–186).

R. Lincoln Keiser (1969): The Vice Lords: Warriors of the Streets

In this ethnographic study of the Vice Lords, Keiser found that the gang engaged in activities for economic gain. He witnessed the "franchising" of gang branches within the gang organization, including their operation of a restaurant, a recreation center, an employment service, their business office, and their status as a legally incorporated not-for-profit corporation as far back as 1968.

Richard W. Poston (1971): Gangs as Grant Funding Hustlers

Poston's (1971) *The Gang and the Establishment: A Story of Conflict Rising Out of the Federal and Private Financing of Urban Street Gangs*, is a detailed historical chronology of an indigenous social program managed by an ex-gang member originally called the "Real Great Society" (RGS) located in New York City. Its leaders use theatrics, myth, mass media manipulation, and political grandstanding to generate contributions from government, corporate, and private foundation sources. This is a prime example of the type of adaptation and innovation mentioned by Merton (1938). Although this example occurred in New York City, similar social service agency scams were run by both the Folk and People Nation gangs in Chicago during the same period.

Joan W. Moore (1978): Homeboys—Gangs, Drugs, Prisons, Barrios

In Moore's (1978) *Homeboys: Gangs, Drugs, and Prison in the Barrios of Los Angeles*, the essence of the viewpoint presented tends to follow, to some extent, a racial oppression thesis. Gang structure becomes defined as having the following components: territoriality based, age-graded, "with a new klika, or cohort, forming every two years or so," and all Chicano gangs are fighting gangs with high levels of drug use (pp. 35–36). The gang is regarded as a quasi-institution in the barrio and involves the adult world. An illicit economic view of drug trafficking and marketing in the barrio are presented (pp. 78–87). A theme is also developed is that barrio men sent to prison made new connections and became more sophisticated in their criminal operations (p. 87).

John Hagedorn and Perry Macon (1988): Gangs as Part of the Underclass

In their work, *People and Folks: Gangs, Crime and the Underclass in a Rustbelt City*, Hagedorn and Macon (1988) focused on the previously unexplored aspects of racial oppression in explaining predominantly minority group membership in Milwaukee's youth gangs. Rather than a single theory, the authors present their tape recorded oral history data from 47 "top dogs" or gang founders, and then evaluate previous contributions in terms of what fits the Milwaukee context.

As proof of their views, Hagedorn and Macon (1988) cited employment data to show a declining economic opportunity for inner-city minority group members. Gang members were uniformly school dropouts (p. 44). They felt that gang formation occurred in Milwaukee in the context of a race relations crisis, thus racial oppression has some causal significance to gangs (p. 50).

Phillippe Bourgois (1989): Drugs as an Alternative Business

Bourgois's (1989) ethnographic study of the illegal crack trade in New York, *In Search of Horatio Alger: Culture and Ideology in the Crack Economy*, observed that gangs engaged in the drug trade as a business and as an alternative illicit means to success. The study found that the gangs participated in a pseudo-warrior culture and claimed and enforced their territories for their drug trade using violence. He found that the gangs had a clearly defined hierarchy, with bosses who directed workers in the drug trade, maintained records of business transactions (such as collecting receipts), and protected the interests of their drug business through violence (p. 632).

Martin Sanchez-Jankowski (1991): Study of Urban Gangs

In *Islands in the Street: Gangs and American Society*, Sanchez-Jankowski (1991) observed in low income urban areas that gangs were a natural response in the competition for scarce resources and they constituted an alternate social order. Sanchez-Jankowski observed that to function efficiently, gangs establish three particular structures. In the first, leadership categories are labeled and assigned authority. In the second, roles and duties for both leadership and membership are defined. In the third structure, codes are created and enforced to ensure order. Sanchez-Jankowski also found that criminal organizations adapted to their circumstances using five entrepreneurial attitudes that included:

- Competitiveness, both with others and themselves
- The desire and drive to accumulate money and material possessions

- Status seeking
- The ability to implement both simple and complex plans
- The ability to undertake risks in pursuit of their goals.

Felix M. Padilla (1992): The Gang as a Business Enterprise

Padilla examined the economic model of gang organization that provides insight to the motivations of why gangs exist. His study of former members of a Chicago gang focused on an important aspect of gang life: drug selling as "work." It is work that is not very rewarding, but provides a "hand to mouth" subsistence with the real profits going to the higher-up gang leaders. Despite the rhetoric in their gang constitutions, the gangs basically mimic their capitalistic society and seek to exploit the "workforce" of gang members willing to push drugs or commit other crimes of economic profit.

Padilla (1993) observed that some gangs attempted to achieve economic success by the sale of drugs to the point that the sale of drugs had become the gang's primary enterprise and focus (p. 91). A violent pseudo-warrior culture developed among the Los Angeles based street gangs to maintain turf, control drug trade, control competition in the drug trade, control internal personnel, and fight off threats from rival gangs (FBI, 2014a, Bloods and Crips Gangs; Etter, 1998, p. 31; Cureton, 2008, p. 2).

Steven D. Levitt and Sudhir A. Venkatesh (2000): Economic Analysis of a Drug-Selling Gang's Finances

Levitt and Venkatesh (2000) observed that prior to 1980, gangs were largely a local affair that were organized around social peer groups. However, they cited the rise of crack cocaine in the 1980s as creating a change in the mission, organizational structure, and operations of street gangs that they labeled "corporatization." They observed that due to the lucrative monetary incentives that became available in the drug trade, many if not most gangs became involved in the selling of drugs.

In their study of drug dealing by gangs as an alternative to participation in the legitimate labor market, they found:

- Earnings in the gang are somewhat above the legitimate labor market
- The risks of drug selling more than offset that amount
- Compensation is highly skewed, and potential future riches are the primary economic motivation
- The gang engages in repeated gang wars
- The gang sometimes establishes prices below cost.

Their results suggested that economic factors alone were unlikely to adequately explain individual participation in the gang or gang behavior.

Simon Harding (2014): London's Street Casino

Simon Harding's ethnography of the youth gangs in London used what is called Bourdieu's field analysis. This social field analysis of gangs represented a sociological approach to methodology and analysis developed by Pierre Bourdieu, a French sociological game theorist. It assumes that economic capital and social capital are closely related. In this way, Harding describes how gang members are the players on the field in the us-versus-them gangster game in positions to attack or defend a set of rules (which Bourdieu called "doxa"). In the London street gang game, gang members seek to acquire money and street capital (street cred). Like the role of the dice, the likelihood of accumulating a lot of chips (accumulation of wealth) or losing it all (the house holds the advantage always) is a matter of chance and probability. The possibility of prison and violent injury exist in gang life as some of the possible random outcomes of the game.

Summary

There is good reason to be concerned about the gang crime problem in America. Minimally we need to know whether gang-related crimes make up a large or small share of our national crime statistics. Unfortunately, very little raw data are collected, and as a result almost no hard, information exists. We are left relying on after-the-fact, self-reported surveys filled out by employees of law enforcement agencies using their memories and gut feelings.

Additionally, many persons who work at all echelons in the criminal justice system need a comprehensive analysis of gangs in America today as part of their training (i.e., in law enforcement, corrections, probation, parole, judges, private and corporate security, as well as program/service/intervention staff, teachers and many others dealing with the problems of gang crime daily). This book may not answer all their questions, but it attempts to address all the major issues.

The chapter has provided a short overview of some of the major theories in the study of gangs and organized crime groups. We have not provided a simplistic summary of all criminological theories as they might pertain to, or could conceivably be interpreted as apply to, gangs. Theories examining both how the gangs as a group came to be and theories about the gang as an economic enterprise are presented. While gangs existed in the United States long before the 1920s, it was the 1920s before American criminologists like Thrasher (1927) began to look at groups of criminals as a group rather than as individual criminals. It was Merton (1938) that began to look at gangs as an economic enterprise that engaged in criminality as an alternate road to success in American society.

The theories presented in this chapter show that the gangs are groups with a set of common interests that are tribal in nature. Due to the wide geographical differences in the areas that the gangs formed in, there is no set gang leadership structure. Some gangs exhibit a hierarchical leadership structure that is almost stratified (especially Chicago based street gangs, outlaw motorcycle gangs, triads, etc.). Others are almost anarchistic in their lack of an established, well-defined leadership structure (Los Angeles based street gangs). Both types of gang structures are largely paternalistic. Almost all gangs engage in crime to make money as an alternative means to success. The gangs in these self-affiliated urban tribes engage in a pseudo-warrior culture that routinely uses violence or the threat of violence to achieve their desired ends.

What this chapter demonstrates is a diversity of approaches to the understanding of gangs. Along with this comes a range of research approaches that have been used. The analysis of gangs has also represented a theoretical and social policy focus. These contributions must be considered to understand the history and evolution of gangs in society.

DISCUSSION QUESTIONS

1. How accurate do you think attempts to estimate the number of gangs and gang members are? What method would you propose?
2. Why would gangs emerge or organize along ethnic lines?
3. Would the most effective gang be one that is racially/ethnically integrated or one that is homogeneous?
4. How would you define a gang based on your current understanding of the law?
5. How would a gang see itself as a tribal group?
6. Define the economic model of gangs.

CHAPTER 2 Los Angeles Area Street Gangs

CHAPTER OBJECTIVES

After reading this chapter students should be able to do the following:

- Examine the history of Los Angeles area street gangs.
- Identify the major Los Angeles area street gangs.
- Consider how local Los Angeles based street gangs became a nationwide criminal justice problem.
- Explain how street gangs adopted changes in technology to facilitate communication.
- Distinguish the differences between Black and Hispanic gangs.
- Explain how Hispanic gangs became an international criminal justice problem.
- Identify the connections between Native American gangs and Los Angeles area street gangs.

Introduction

As we saw in the previous chapter, street gangs quickly formed in the major cities to further their criminal enterprises. The urban street gang culture and criminality Asbury (1989) documented in New York in the 1820s was still operating almost 200 years later in many traditional gangs in American urban areas (Howell & Moore, 2010). Typically, most street gangs have been a primarily local operation.

Traditional gangs commit their crimes for largely economic reasons—they want to make money. Many of them formed to defend their members from aggression by other groups, and then, as many do, they became hunters instead of prey. But they seldom stray from their claimed territories or turf. They will defend their turf to the death and they are not very mobile (Etter, 1998). However, as any organization grows, it tends to evolve (Etter, 1998). Los Angeles (L.A.) area street gangs were no different. The early

L.A. gangs, like in New York, were aligned by race and often had both adult and juvenile members. The demographic shifts may have affected the racial alignment, while the process of membership likely guided the age distribution.

Los Angeles Pre-gang History

California became part of the United States in the late 1840s, shortly after the Mexican-American War. For many years afterwards, the area was controlled by military governors. While the discovery of gold brought an influx of people to some parts of the state, the growth of Los Angeles did not noticeably begin until the railroad was finished much later in the 1800s.

During the 1890s, the population of African Americans in Los Angeles increased from 1,258 to 2,131, and by 1920 African Americans in the city numbered over 15,000 (Brown, Vigil, & Taylor, 2012). As was seen in the Northeast and Midwest, the migration of African Americans looking for a better life triggered several social and cultural issues in Los Angeles (Cureton, 2009). Cureton observed that the existence of African American street gangs in urban cities evolved from four community transitional stages: defined community (stage 1: 1920 to 1929); community conversion (stage 2: 1930 to 1965); gangster colonization (stage 3: 1966 to 1989); and gangster politicization (stage 4: 1990 to 2000).

In the defined community stage, the mass migration of blacks put the new arrivals in cities near all-white neighborhoods. In response, some whites moved away, while others created community covenants to effectively ban African Americans from establishing residency in certain neighborhoods (Cureton, 2009). Racially restrictive covenants, the nation's first, were established in 1922, and designed to maintain social and racial homogeneity of neighborhoods (Alonso, 1999). They denied non-whites access to property ownership, making much of Los Angeles off-limits to a lot of minorities. That further fueled the racial conflict, as white male youth groups formed and violently resisted attempts at racial integration in their neighborhoods, which led to African American brotherhoods evolving into social protection groups (Alonso, 1999).

During the stage Cureton identified as community conversion, the Great Depression (1930 to early 1940s) and the civil rights movement (1955 to 1965) produced an underclass. The Depression crippled the economic foundation of the African American community, and the civil rights movement was selectively beneficial to better educated, professional, and vocationally skilled African Americans, he observed. Cureton (2009) found that the migration of African Americans to historically white southern Los Angeles began with their move from the South, mostly Louisiana and Mississippi, to non-black European immigrant communities. They were simply looking for a better life than they had in the South, and California offered more employment opportunities in factories and an escape from southern oppression. The move turned out to be the trigger for traditional white supremacist ideology, institutional inequality (in housing, education, and employment), and restrictions relative to where African Americans could socialize. That led to a regional civil rights movement between 1946 and 1950 (Cureton, 2009).

From 1945 to 1948, many black residents challenged the restrictive covenants in court. Those attempts prompted the resurfacing of the racist domestic terror group the Ku Klux Klan, and some white youths formed street clubs to battle integration in both the community and schools of black residents. Alonso (2004) proposed that it was racial intimidation and exclusion, not economic restructuring and poverty, that played significant roles in the formation of African American gangs in Los Angeles. He found that one of the most infamous groups of white youths were the Spook Hunters. The name of the club emphasized their racist attitude towards blacks, as "Spook" was a derogatory term for blacks. The club members' jackets had an animated black face with exaggerated facial features with a noose hanging around the neck (Alonso, 1999). If blacks were seen outside of the black settlement area, they were often attacked.

Perkins (1987) learned it was not until the mid-1950s that African American street gangs turned their outrage and attacks toward the African American community. Prior to that, their activity was limited to conflicts with other groups, drinking, gambling, and committing misdemeanor crimes. Those gangs were typically turf oriented and seldom left their neighborhoods. By the 1960s, some politicians tried to harness the power and unity of the gangs for their own political benefit by encouraging gang members to participate in political rallies, demonstrations, and public discussions (Perkins, 1987).

The freedoms and social gains experienced by those interracial confrontations were short-lived because African Americans still had to contend with structural oppression like community crowding, strained resources, and physical and social deprivation, which led to interracial strife and eventually urban unrest (Alonso, 1999; Cureton, 2009). By 1960, several African American clubs were operating, initially as a defensive reaction to the white violence plaguing the African American community (Alonso, 1999). By 1960, although it was still largely segregated, Los Angeles had the fifth largest African American population in the country (Brightwell, 2012).

Cureton (2009) identified stage 3: gangster colonization (1966 to 1989) as the time when police law and order threatened many of the African Americans in the city. In that stage, street gangs gained a foothold in the underclass. Historically marginalized residents (mostly males) wanted access to the opportunities offered by society, so they traded in drugs, guns, and stolen goods, prostitutes, and gambling to make their living. Respect governed street interaction and affected the chance of survival. Sadly, respect was often earned and maintained by engaging in violence and murder.

Some African Americans responded with the launch of the Black Panther Party for Self-Defense. Many African American youth were attracted to the Panthers' defiant speech, bold display of guns, and military-styled organization. As the Black Panthers' appeal spread, chapters were started across the country (Cureton, 2009). As a result of the FBI's counterintelligence program (COINTELPRO), many Black Panther leaders were arrested and imprisoned. We will see more of a gang connection to the Black Panthers later in the chapter.

L.A. Based Street Gangs

Prior to 1968, street gangs in the Los Angeles area were largely a local affair. Each ethnic group had their own gangs and turf area. Although African American street gangs had existed in the Los Angeles area since the 1920s, after 1969 two particular groups, the Crips and the Bloods, began to dominate the Los Angeles gang scene (Clemons,

Figure 2.1

Crack cocaine. Gangs grew their drug sales in the 1980s with crack cocaine.

By Argv0[CC BY-SA 4.0 (https://creativecommons.org/licenses/by-sa/2.0)], via Wikimedia Commons

Rossi, & Van De Kamp, 1990, p. 1). Quicker and Batani-Khalfani observed that in the early 1970s groups identifying themselves as Crips and Bloods began to appear all over South Los Angeles "like wildflowers after a spring rain storm" (Quicker & Batani-Khalfani, 1998, p. 20). The gangs began to supplant or replace local street gangs in the area. Even with their expansion, the Crips and Bloods still remained a very local affair in the Los Angeles area until the early 1980s.

In the 1980s the fast-growing trade in "rock cocaine" or crack fueled a rapid expansion of both the Crips and the Bloods from their local Los Angeles roots. The Crips and Bloods expanded their drug selling operations eastward to the Mississippi River in the 1980s. By the early 1990s the Crips and Bloods had expanded their gang franchise nationwide with an estimated 40,000 to 50,000 gang members (Clemons et al., 1990, p. 1). These new gangs often operated like hamburger restaurant franchises, selling their product under the national brand name but with a local flair to meet local conditions. To conduct their criminal operations, the Crips and Bloods operated in small groups. Individual groups of Crips and Bloods are known as "sets." The sets often take geographic locators as a part of their set name, such as 22nd Street. Often the geographical locators do not refer to the actual area that the set operated in, but rather a street or location in the Los Angeles area. Typical sets run from around 10 to 40 members each.

During Cureton's (2009) gangster politicization stage 4 (1990 to 2000), neighborhoods became ganglands. They were socially organized around typical male rites of passage (baby gangster to original gangster) and normative expectations (following protocol, dealing with enemies, the value of gang alliances). Cureton found that during this period, the gang became further embedded in the fabric of the underclass black community as each generation of young male gangsters received a street education. Older gangsters passed on knowledge of gangster history, protocol, and politics.

Speaking about Los Angeles based street gangs expanding to other states, Los Angeles County Sheriff Sherman Block (January 1982–October 1998) observed:

> the Crips and Bloods from L.A. went into those areas to try to deal drugs. And there were some conflicts with the local people. So the L.A. gangsters got into the entrepreneurial system and became brokers and jobbers by supplying local dealers and recruiting local kids to go out and sell the dope.
>
> (Bing, 1991)

Unlike their counterparts in the Chicago based gangs, Crips and Bloods are basically apolitical, and generally do not get involved in politics. They are not above trying to bribe a local politician or law enforcement officer to help protect their illegitimate criminal activities, but the social action fronts employed by the Chicago based street gangs are not a factor in the daily operations of a Los Angeles based street gang. L.A. based street gangs are strictly an economic enterprise.

Gang Communication

To facilitate their economic enterprise and maintain internal/external communications and maintain morale or cohesiveness within the gang, L.A. based street gangs became very adept at using various means of communication. The means of communication were both traditional and non-traditional and generally furthered the goals of the gang. Traditional methods of passing gang culture, such as oral history, were used extensively when training or recruiting new gang members. The deeds of founding original gangsters are told and retold until they become legend. Originally the tradition was developed because some of the gang elders were either illiterate or semi-illiterate and did not write down the gang's history, so the history and culture of L.A. based street gangs was passed from generation to generation largely by oral history. Some of the individual

Figure 2.2

Gang graffiti. Gangs use graffiti to mark turf, celebrate exploits, mourn their dead, and disrespect or declare war on rival gangs.

Greg Etter

set's websites now include a section on the history. Another more recent reason to continue the oral tradition was security. Documents can be seized by law enforcement and used as evidence in court (Etter, 1998; Cureton, 2008). Other than attempting to compel testimony, courts have a difficult time "seizing" oral history.

Music is an important part of this oral history tradition. Often the dreams, deeds, and desires of gang members are combined with their complaints and frustrations to form their music (Etter, 1998, p. 30). According to Sgt. Ron Stallworth, former Gang Intelligence Coordinator for the Utah Department of Public Safety, many L.A. based gang members have participated in this type of music: the group N.W.A. (Crips), Ice-T (Hoover Crips), D.J. Quick (Bloods), and so forth (Stallworth, 1994).

Another traditional method of communication for gang members is graffiti. Graffiti consisting of drawing, painting, or otherwise putting pictures, words or symbols on walls and other objects is a time-honored gang tradition. Often called the newspaper of the streets, graffiti is used to mark turf, celebrate gang exploits, mourn dead gang members, show disrespect for rival gangs, or declare war on rival gangs (Etter, 1998; Jackson & McBride, 1986). However, tagging (which is street art) is often mistaken by law enforcement as gang graffiti (Ferrell, 1993).

One of the oldest and simplest traditional ways of gang communications is the use of hand signs by gang members. Hand signs are used by gang members for identification, intimidation, challenges, and general communication. Both L.A. based street gangs and Chicago based street gangs use hand signs. However, they call them different things. A member of an L.A. based street gang may say they are throwing a sign, while a Chicago based gang member would refer to the activity as representing. Hand signs provide a definite statement as to the identity and often to the intentions of gang members (Etter, 1998; Jackson & McBride, 1986). The use of hand signs by gang members for communication is nothing new. The Chinese triads used hand signs for identification and communication as early as 1662 (Booth, 1990, p. 8).

Gangs and Technology

Gangs have adapted to new technology often faster than law enforcement. In the 1980s gang members used pagers to communicate with sending codes, alerts, and notices to call via pay phone to avoid wiretaps. Prospective drug customers would call in orders to a pay phone on the gang's corner, or in another variation the drug customer would arrange to buy drugs from one gang member at one location and the pickup would be at another gang arranged location after a confirming phone call was placed on the pay phone. Assaults and even killings occurred when a non-gang member attempted to use the "drug phone." The police countered by coordinating with the phone companies and severely limiting the ability of pay phones to receive calls.

Car phones were a luxury in the late 1980s, but by the early 1990s many people had them. They were easy to tap as they were simple radio-telephone signals, and no warrant was required. Car phones were hard to locate by triangulation, as the car was moving. Despite the police issues, gang members loved them and, like pagers before them, car phones became a status symbol. They also were an easy way to conduct the drug trade while on the move.

The invention of the cell phone in the 1990s limited the use of the car phone and relegated the pager to service as a backup or warning device. Texting and the usage of codes became popular among gang bangers. Cell phones were a little harder to tap by law enforcement, but it could be done (a search warrant was usually required). Most cell phones also had a global positioning system (GPS) function that proved useful to law enforcement.

Gang members quickly figured out that a cell phone and its contents could become evidence against them and the gang, and started using disposable phones (known as burners). Sold as a way to protect privacy, a burner phone is a type of cell phone that can be purchased at a truck stop, Walmart, or convenience store without a contract. As a result, identification of the purchaser is rarely accurate. The phone comes with a predetermined number of minutes. To obtain more minutes a separate, unrelated purchase is made. Gang members buy the phones, use them once or twice, and throw them away. They are a cheap ($29.95 or less) and secure means of communication. Any area code may be obtained by the consumer at the time of purchase (Sarconi, 2017).

Since about 2002, an increasing number of cell phones have been able to access the internet. Many internet-based communications are now available for use on the phones, independent of the phone number attached to the device. Satellite phones (such as those sold in Europe and Mexico) are favored by many transnational gangs not only for their ability to contact overseas partners but also for their secure mode of transmission. Regular U.S. cell providers cannot access or tap satellite signals, thus law enforcement is often unable to monitor the calls (even with a warrant).

The gangs quickly adapted to the growth of the internet by following the example of leaderless resistance by domestic terrorist (white nationalist) Louis Beam in the late 1980s. The websites of many criminal groups were initially open, broadcasting their propaganda to an anonymous audience. After law enforcement started targeting many of the groups, their strategy changed. Led by the example of many outlaw motorcycle gangs, the street gangs began to take security countermeasures, hosting secure members-only sections, communicating in code, and using less oblivious website names.

Street gang websites have numerous uses for the gang. Gang websites are used to socialize with other gang sets. Gang websites are used to recruit and communicate. Like graffiti, they are the newspaper of the virtual street. Gang websites often show pictures of gang members and activities, therefore they are good for law enforcement intelligence purposes. Some outlaw motorcycle gangs (OMGs) learned to prevent the copying of their pictures by website visitors, and many street gangs followed that practice. Other ways to retain photos exist.

Gangs took to social media quickly, and have used it for many purposes. Myspace.com began in 2003 and allowed users to fashion a personal homepage. Some gangs began an official presence on Myspace. With the advent of Facebook in 2004, Myspace began to lose popularity, however, some gang-related hip-hop groups are still on Myspace. Those sites are good for roll call shots, photos, and other intelligence collection purposes by law enforcement. While Facebook was initially restricted to users with college and university (.edu) email accounts, it was opened for general use not long afterward. Many gang members quickly obtained accounts for their personal usage (along with millions of non-gang users) and began to talk about their gang activities. Some street gangs created Facebook pages for their groups. Facebook site postings can be restricted to limit what non-friends can view.

In 2005, YouTube began allowing people to post short videos for all to see. Gang members quickly took advantage of this new technology. Many posted music videos of their band. Those posts were good for intelligence purposes by law enforcement as they showed association with a group of people. Sometimes gang members even posted crime trophy photos or photos of gang initiations. Those posts were good for intelligence, evidence, and developing probable cause.

Computers provide a whole world of new communications possibilities. Additionally, most youth like to play action video games. Gang members are no exception. However, when they use messaging services on gaming systems like PlayStation and Xbox, gang members can directly communicate with each other in a secure and non-recordable fashion.

Email documenting is a new form of secure communication that has been used by some gangs. Picture two gang members ("bangers"), each with the access to the *same* email account and using the exact same password. Banger #1 composes a message or document and saves it in the drafts folder, *not* sending it. Banger #2 opens Banger #1's email account and retrieves the message or document, opening it and placing his answer on the original document. He then *saves* the document or message as a draft *without* sending it. Because it is a draft, it is not actually sent and therefore cannot be intercepted.

Gang members have made good usage of modern communication opportunities provided by such devices as cell phones and computers. Hard drives need to be seized during search warrants for cyber forensic analysis. Emails for accounts not based on a website are generally not erased from hard drives unless specifically purged. Every time law enforcement figures out what the street gang members are doing and uses that knowledge to get a warrant and make a case, the steps law enforcement uses are discovered in the resulting trial. Thus, gang members change their operation to something new. It is a never-ending cycle.

Crips

Clemons, Rossi and Van De Kamp found that the Crips formed at Washington High School in South-Central Los Angeles in 1969. Crips gangs grew within a short time and quickly earned reputations as violent and dangerous street gangs. The color blue was selected for their clothing to set them apart from other gangs. Some people believe that blue was selected because it was one of Washington High School colors (Clemons et al., 1990).

Sundiata Acoli (n.d.), a former Black Liberation Army member who was sentenced in 1974 for murdering a New Jersey State trooper, claimed that Alprentice "Bunchy" Carter and Raymond Washington were very much attracted to the Black Panthers. Carter was a gang member in the Slauson Renegades, a street organization that predated the Crips and Bloods. The Slausons started in 1952 and were defunct by 1965, according to Alonso (2004). Cureton (2009) found that Carter was killed in 1969 and there is no law enforcement documentation that he was ever a Crip. Washington organized the Crips in 1969.

Former Orange County District Attorney Investigator Al Valdez observed that two of the Crips founding members were Raymond Washington and Michael Conception. Raymond Washington was originally a member of another gang called the Avenue Boys when he began attending Washington High School in Los Angeles (Valdez, 2001). Valdez cited two possible originations of the name Crips for the group. First, some accounts have a member of the group having a limp and thus being mocked by early Bloods members. A second account says that the name comes from a comic book that was popular at the time called *Tales of the Crypt* (Valdez, 2001; OSS, 1992).

Washington's Baby Avenues renamed themselves the Eastside Crips and soon joined forces with the Westside Crips led by Stanley "Tookie" Williams, who had been kicked out of the Gladiators street gang, and "Big Jamel" Barnes from the Avalon Gardens Crips. The Eastside and Westside Crips were soon joined by other gangs who became Compton Crips.

According to Walker (2014), while Stanley "Tookie" Williams was an early member of the Crips, he was not a founding member of the gang. Williams (2007) himself acknowledged that and wrote in his book *Blue Rage, Black Redemption* that he had been recruited into the Crips in the spring of 1971 by Raymond Washington while they were both students at Washington High School.

Walker went on to observe that:

The original Crip Gang members had some common bonds. They either had an association through their high schools (Fremont, Locke or Washington), Fred Shaw Home for Boys, Bob Simmon's Homes for Boys, or detention camps. In

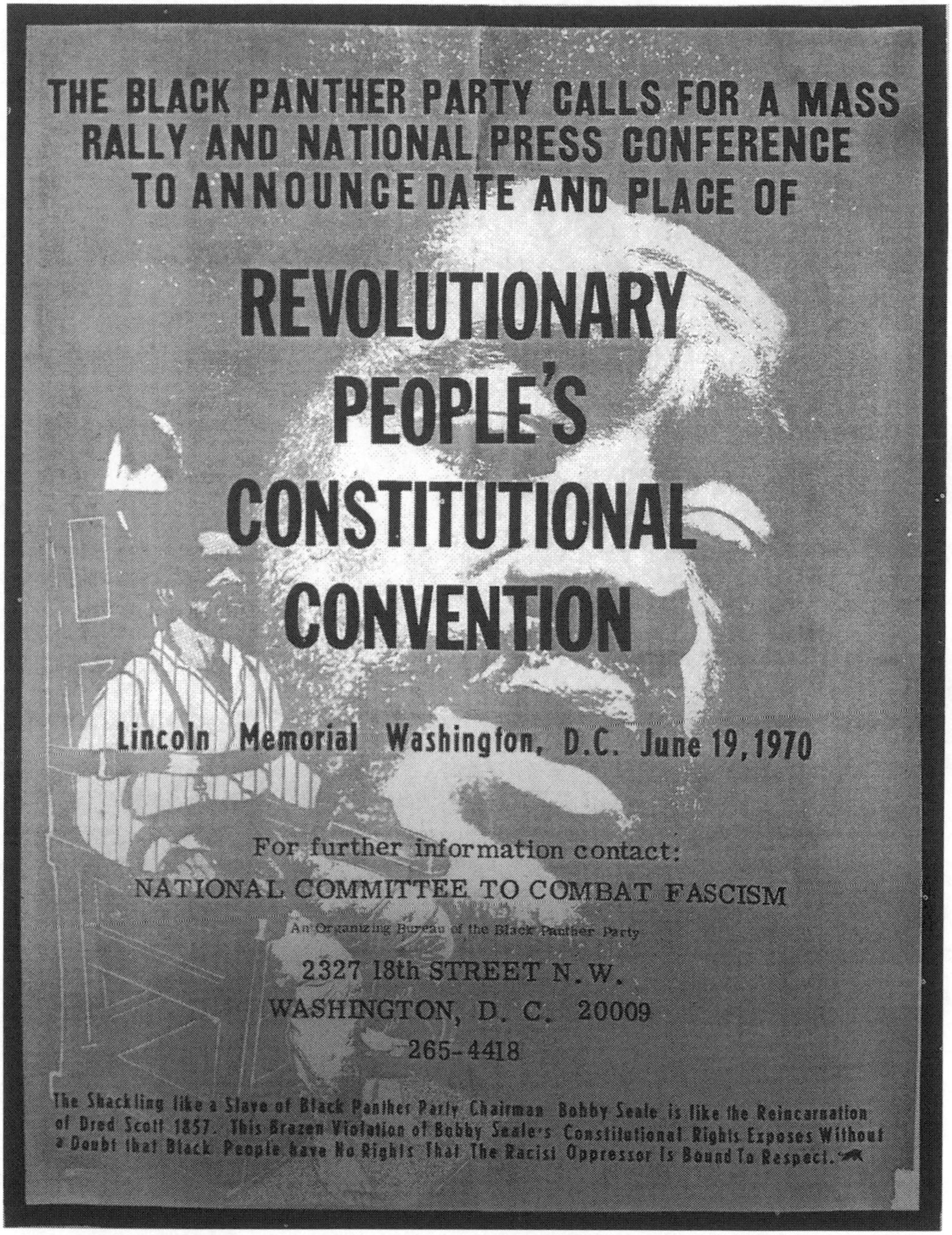

Figure 2.3

Black Panthers. Black Panther DC Rally Revolutionary People's Constitutional Convention 1970. Public domain.

Gelman Library, George Washington University. Special Collections Research Center, Radical Left-Wing Publications Collection

some cases all four. Most of the OG's were troubled youths who craved personal recognition.

(Walker, 2014, p. 85)

Raymond Washington was killed in a drive-by shooting in Los Angeles on August 9, 1979. The murder was never solved.

According to Acoli (n.d.), the Crips members were originally identified as Community Relations for an Independent People or Community Revolution In Progress (CRIP), a community helping association. Many gang researchers and practitioners disagree with the claims that the CRIP was started as a benevolence organization. With changes in leadership, following and resources, the Crips shifted to more self-centered activities such as drug distribution and weapon trafficking (Cureton, 2009).

Crips Organizational Structure

While the Crips have expanded from a neighborhood based local gang in L.A. to a nationwide drug selling operation, they have no central organization. They are a series of independent operations sometimes cooperating with each other, other times not. Walker (2014) observed that

The Crips is a loose association of some 200 gangs, many of which are at war with one another, and none of whom recognizes or exerts any kind of authority. Individual groups are equally marginal in their organization. Most are loosely knit coalitions of small, autonomous cliques.

Because of their loose organizational structure combined with their long history, Buccellato (2013) described the Crips as an institutionalized gang.

While the Crip sets do not recognize any central leader, they do recognize a type of seniority within the set. A gang member who was there when the set was founded is known as an "O.G." or original gangster. The Crips prefer a leaderless type of organization, rationalizing that if they elect or appoint a leader, when that leader is killed or captured it will adversely affect the operations of the set. The Crips have a saying as to their organizational structure and plans, "We don't die, we just multiply!" (Shalur, 1993).

Knox (1997a) found that the structure of the Crips assisted in their rapid expansion throughout the United States, saying:

Because Crips have an imitative informal structure, it is a gang that is easily "transplanted." Using the "familial gang transplant phenomenon" as an explanation, a mother might upon discovering her son was a "Crip" decide to "move" to a new geographical area, thinking this move would remove her son from the evil clutches of gang influence, only to find that in the new location her son starts up a new chapter of the same gang.

A Crip gang is easily "imitated" as well and can therefore begin within in any new geographical area simply by means of "emulation." There are few rules, few "prayers," no lengthy written constitution to remember. Unlike other gangs like the Gangster Disciples, there are no detailed typed "memos" from the top leader that are regularly distributed to the "troops" on the front line. The dress colors, the demeanor, the hand signs, the music forms, the cultural argot and linguistic expressions, the "values"—those are all spread through the mass media, and are therefore readily available to the "wannabe" gang member.

(p. 61)

Waldorf (1993) found that in San Francisco when a southern California gang moved into northern California where the gang structure was very different, two basic factors were involved. One, some Crips had migrated to the area for the purposes of conducting the drug trade. In their expansion, their tactics were adaptable: sometimes assimilating local gangs, sometimes supplanting them. Two, some local gangs wanted to "ride" on the reputation of the Crips gang and began calling their gangs Crips. Thus by copying the Crips, they eventually became accepted as Crips (pp. 11–16).

The Crips grew to be the larger of the two main factions of Los Angeles based street gangs. However, due to the lack of centralized or organized leadership, each set acted in its own best "business" interests and thus Crip sets often found themselves fighting against other Crips sets over drug trade areas and other criminal pursuits. The Crips maintain a very loose alliance with the Chicago based Folk Nation, but will fight sets from that group if interests in drug trade or turf occur.

Although they were initially primarily an African American gang, as the Crips began to expand they began to acquire some Hispanic and Asian sets. The new sets were generally all one race. Grape Street Crips initially were known as Watts Varrio Grapes and had both black and Hispanic members. However, in the 1970s the Latino members had aligned themselves with the Sureño gang groups (while still remaining Crips as South Side Watts Varrio Grape 13) and the African American members formed a different set called Watts Baby Loc/Grape Street Crips (United Gangs, 2014).

Crips Criminal Activities

The criminality of the Crips was an evolving process. Originally the Crips committed typical gang crimes such as assault, burglary, robberies (armed and strong arm), thefts, and drug dealing (Walker, 2014). However, criminality as practiced by the Crips quickly began to evolve into a full-blown economic criminal enterprise. The primary

Figure 2.4

Crips Tag on Dumpster.

Jason Taellious from Olympia, USA (24th St Crip Uploaded by SaltyBoatr), Creative Commons

source of the Crips' income became the sale of illicit drugs. The Crips transitioned from simple street sales into all phases of the drug selling operations. Crips began to act as mid-level drug wholesalers in the 1980s, and this fueled their rapid expansion across the United States as they had the drugs to sell. To ensure their drug supply in the late 1980s and early 1990s the Crips began to directly deal with the Medellin Cartel to purchase the drug supplies wholesale. In one FBI arrest in 1992, the Crips purchased over 50 tons of cocaine and made an estimated profit of $30 million in the previous decade (Weinstein, 1992). According to the National Gang Intelligence Center (2015), the Crips have maintained direct ties with the following Mexican drug cartels: Los Zetas, Gulf Cartel and La Familia Michoacan (and presumably with their successor group, Los Caballeros Templarios) to purchase drugs.

The Crips also have engaged in other primary crimes to make money such as prostitution, weapons violations, money laundering, extortion/protection rackets, and theft/ fencing. In addition, secondary crimes such as murder, assault, and terroristic threats were often committed in support of the primary crimes. The Crips have been extremely violent in the protection of their drug trade areas or in the defense of the perceived "honor" of their set or gang.

Crips in Jail/Prison

When you commit crimes, you often find yourself incarcerated. When Crips have been arrested, the first stop has been county jail. In county jail, they still retained their local gang loyalties and quickly became a Security Threat Group within the jail to other inmates and rival gang members. This resulted in correctional authorities having to take measures to maintain order and protect inmates within their facilities. The L.A. County Sheriff's Department began to house inmates that were Crips and Bloods in separate cell blocks. This helped to maintain order but actually gave some social status to the gang members (Jackson & McBride, 1986).

Crips that were convicted of felonies have often found themselves in the state or federal prison systems. Prior to 1990, the Crips either joined other prison gangs for protection, paid street tax to other prison gangs for protection, or became easy prey for other prison gangs. Because of the problem that Crips have faced in prison, Prisonoffenders.com (2014) observed:

> In 1990, the leaders of different Crip sets decided to organize a unity structure for all Crip members. Under the organizations rules, all Crip members were required to join forces in prison and assist each other in any conflict involving non-Crip gang members. As a unified prison structure, the Crips became one of the nation's largest prison gangs. In most states, the gang now out numbers most traditional prison gangs such as the Mexican Mafia and Aryan Brotherhood.

As of yet, this "prison unity" has not transferred to Crips sets on the street or in county jails (Jackson & McBride, 1986).

Common Crips Markings

The Crips use blue as their primary color. However, there are variations between sets, for example Neighborhood Crips use light blue, Grape Street Crips use purple, Spooktown Crips use brown and Asian Boyz Crips use fluorescent yellow. Other markings include BK (Blood Killer), the letter B crossed out, tattoos indicating membership, and athletic sportswear in gang colors (Jackson & McBride, 1986, pp. 76–77).

Where the Crips Are

A recent National Gang Intelligence Center, National Gang Threat Assessment reported that Crips were found in 37 states and the District of Columbia (NGIC, 2013, pp. 49–79). Other sources report the presence of Crips in Belize and Canada.

Figure 2.5
Rollin '60s Neighborhood Crips.
Phil Brooks

Bloods

In 1969 a rival gang called the Bloods also formed in Los Angeles. Clemons, Rossi and Van De Kamp found that "The Bloods originally developed to protect themselves from the Crips gang members. The Bloods gangs originated in the Compton area in southern California. The first Bloods gang was a group of youths from Piru Street in Compton who named themselves the Compton Pirus. They adopted the color red because most members attended or lived near Centennial High School in Compton where red is a school color" (Clemons et al., 1990, p. 3).

The Bloods, too, claim that they can trace the lineage of their organization to the Black Panther Party. Sundiata Acoli (n.d.) suggested that the leaders of the gangs that became the Bloods formed a constitution that was patterned on the constitution of the Black Guerrilla Family (BGF). The organization was started by Black Panther members when they were incarcerated at San Quentin State Prison.

The first Blood set actually came out of Compton on Piru Street and was started by Vincent "Pudding" Scott and Sylvester Owens. As the Crips began to rapidly spread throughout the Greater Los Angeles area, often converting existing local gangs to add

Crip to their name, non-Crip gang sets like the Pirus became known as Bloods. Soon, the polarization among L.A. Black youth gangs became so strong that they were given an option: "become Crip or die!" Those who refused, Compton Pirus, and gangs outside of Compton like Brims, Bishops, and Bounty Hunters, joined under the banner of "Bloods."

Valdez observed that Scott and Owens were both students at Centennial High School in Compton (2001). The Bloods began as a local affair and conducted their criminal

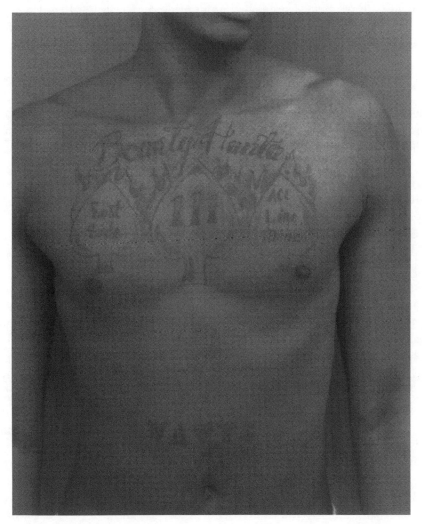

Figure 2.6
Bounty Hunter Bloods.
Eric Qualls

activities locally. With the advent of crack cocaine and the expanding opportunities that drug presented, the Bloods (like their Crip opponents) began to rapidly expand. At first, the Bloods expanded throughout California and later eastward across the United States.

In his book, *War of the Bloods in My Veins*, Dashawn "Jiwe" Morris (2008) related how he joined the Bloods in Phoenix, Arizona, when his family moved there from their home in New Jersey (pp. 18–19). Morris described how he returned back east as a football player and enrolled in Delaware State University (p. 144). Morris continued his involvement with the Bloods and ended up in prison in Delaware after being involved in a stabbing (p. 177). The activities of that young Blood member are typical of how the L.A. based street gangs moved from West to East in the United States during the 1990s.

Bloods Organizational Structure

Prior to 1993, the Bloods sets had a similar organizational structure to their rivals the Crips. That is to say, there was no central organized leadership and original gangsters (OGs) held power within individual sets. The Bloods never had as many sets as the Crips, but they did not usually fight among themselves. Because of their loose organizational structure combined with their long history, Buccellato (2013) described the Bloods as an institutionalized gang.

Beginning in 1993, Bloods incarcerated at Rikers Island in the New York City jail system began to organize among themselves into a prison gang. The result of that activity was the United Blood Nation (UBN). The UBN is a hierarchical gang with a much more formal leadership structure than the traditional Bloods sets. The UBN spread from the jails to the streets and westward back toward California.

Some Bloods sets have embraced the new structure of the UBN and others have chosen to remain with the looser traditional Bloods gang structure. The mixture apparently has caused some inter-set fighting among the Bloods. The Bloods maintain a very loose alliance with the Chicago based People Nation, but will fight sets from that group if interests in drug trade or turf occur.

Bloods Criminal Activities

Moving from common street crimes such as theft, robbery, and burglary, the primary source of the Bloods' income became the sale of illicit drugs. Like the Crips, the Bloods began to evolve from simple street sales into all phases of the drug selling operations. Bloods began to act as mid-level drug wholesalers in the 1980s and this fueled their rapid expansion across the United States as they had the drugs to sell. According to the National Gang Intelligence Center, the Bloods maintain direct ties with the following Mexican drug cartels to purchase drugs: Los Zetas, Gulf Cartel, and Sinaloa Cartel (NGIC, 2015, pp. 22–23).

Figure 2.7

Rikers Island. In 1993, Bloods incarcerated at Rikers Island organized the United Blood Nation (UBN). Public domain.

U.S. Geological Survey

The Bloods also engage in other primary crimes to make money, such as prostitution, weapons violations, money laundering, extortion/protection rackets, and theft/fencing. In addition, secondary crimes such as murder, assault, and terroristic threats were often committed in support of the primary crimes. The Bloods were extremely violent in the protection of their drug trade areas or in the defense of the perceived "honor" of their set or gang.

Bloods in Jail/Prison

The Bloods have gone to jail for their crimes just as anyone else. While in county jail they generally stayed true to their sets and acted as a Security Threat Group inside the jail. The Los Angeles County Sheriff's Office in California placed the Bloods in their own segregated cell block to maintain security and order in the facility. This had the same effect on the Bloods as it did on the Crips. The gang was unintentionally given some social status by this move and made to seem more important to other non-gang members. In 1993, Bloods that were incarcerated became a prison gang as they unified into the United Blood Nation in the New York City jail system at Rikers Island.

Common Bloods Markings

The Bloods use the color red as their primary color. Other markings include CK (Crip Killer), the letter C crossed out, tattoos indicating membership (especially 031, M.O.B. [Member of Bloods], dawg or Mack Truck logos), and athletic sportswear in gang colors (Jackson & McBride, 1986, pp. 76–77).

Where the Bloods Are

The National Gang Intelligence Center's National Gang Threat Assessment reported that Bloods were found in 40 states and the District of Columbia (NGIC, 2013, pp. 49–79). Other sources report the presence of Bloods in Belize and Canada.

Sureños

Hispanic American gangs often unite under the Sureño or Norteño organizations depending on the locations of their hometowns. The dividing line is around Bakersfield, California (Sheldon, Tracy, & Brown, 2001). Sureño means "southerner" in Spanish. Sureños align with the Mexican Mafia in prison. Even though Sureños were established in 1968, the term was not used until the 1970s because of the continued conflict between the Mexican Mafia and Nuestra Familia in California's prison system.

The Mexican Mafia was formed in 1957 by street gang members from different Los Angeles neighborhoods that were incarcerated in the Deuel Vocational Institution, a California Youth Authority facility. The contemporary Mexican Mafia is the controlling organization for almost every Hispanic gang and gang member in southern California. Sureños, including MS-13 and Florencia 13, use the number 13 to show allegiance to the Mexican Mafia. M is the thirteenth letter of the alphabet. Members of almost all related Hispanic gangs are obliged to carry out orders from made (affirmed) Mexican Mafia members. The order is best understood with the assumption that since most gang members are involved in criminal activity, there is a likelihood that they will at some point be incarcerated. The Mexican Mafia has control in many jails and prisons. The Mexican Mafia has an alliance with the Aryan Brotherhood, a white supremacist prison gang.

Sureños Organizational Structure

Although there are hundreds of Hispanic street gangs that claim Sureños, such gangs share no common organizational structure; however, they are all subordinate to the Mexican Mafia (Latino Prison Gangs, 2009b).

Sureños Criminal Activities

According to the Latino Prison Gang: Gang Identification Task Force (2009b):

Although Sureño gangs primarily profit from drug distribution, they will engage in almost any criminal activity that will turn a profit, including major theft and alien smuggling. Sureño gangs have also been associated with drug trafficking organizations (DTOs) and conduct enforcement activities on their behalf. The DTOs prefer to use these soldiers in some instances so that they do not risk the arrest of high level DTO members.

Sureño gangs working with Mexican Drug Trafficking Organizations primarily work with the Gulf Cartel (Valdemar, 2010).

Sureños in Jail/Prison

Many Hispanic gangs in prison align with the Sureños, especially those with southern California roots. Sureños in prison are subordinate to and pay street tax to the Mexican Mafia (Latino Prison Gangs, 2009b).

Common Sureños Markings

Sureño gang members marking include claiming their original Los Angeles Varrio such as "WF," "F-13," "XV3," and "MS-13" (Valdemar, 2010). They might also write "So Cal," "213" or "310" (telephone prefix numbers), and sometimes the words "SUR 13," "South Side" or "Sureños." Other Sureño markings include "Pandilla Sureño" (Sureño Gang), "Sureños Mejicanos," "13," "XIII," "X3," "trece" (Spanish for 13), "3ce," and "kanpol" (Aztec for "southerner"; Valdemar, 2010).

Figure 2.8

Sureños tattoo. Right hand SUR13 left hand has the roman numerals for 13.

Eric Qualls

Where the Sureños Are

Sureños have been reported in 35 states and Mexico (DOJ, 2015a).

Norteños (Norte 14)

Nuestra Familia is the criminal organization of choice for incarcerated Hispanic gang members from northern California. Nuestra Familia was organized in California correctional facilities in 1968. After the Mexican Mafia formed in 1957, Hispanics affiliated with northern California gangs looked for a way to protect themselves and their interests.

Norteños means "northerners" in Spanish. The Norteños align with the Nuestra Familia while in prison. Norteños may refer to northern California as Norte. While members of the Norteños gang are affiliated with Nuestra Familia, being a member of Nuestra Familia does not signify association as a Norteño.

The Nuestra Familia gang influences much of the criminal activity of Norteño gang members in California much like the Mexican Mafia does with their affiliated gangs. Norteños use the number 14 which represents the fourteenth letter of the alphabet. Nuestra Familia has a loose alliance with the Black Guerrilla Family prison gang, a prison gang for African American prisoners.

Norteños Organizational Structure

The Norteños are organized into cliques. They maintain a paramilitary rank structure that includes generals as leaders (Latino Prison Gangs, 2009c).

Norteños Criminal Activities

Criminal activities of the Norteños affiliated gangs include drug trafficking, assault, auto theft, burglary, homicide, and robbery. The Norteños are allied with the Sinaloa drug trafficking organization (DTO).

Norteños in Jail/Prison

Norteños members in prison are subordinate to the Nuestra Familia (NF). According to Prisonoffenders.com (2017):

The Northern Structure is a sub group of the Nuestra Familia and carry out most of the NF's dirty work. Nuestra Familia leaders decided to organize a structure

Figure 2.9
Norteños Hat.
Shawn Williams

division called Nuestra Raza, more commonly known as Northern Structure. The new branch would serve as a prospect base for those interested in joining Nuestra Familia. Northern Structure prospects would have to earn membership into NF by following the gang's orders. Gang hits were always handed down to Northern Structure prospects and gave wanna be's the opportunity of proving themselves to the NF. Before a sponsored prospect can qualify as a member of the NF, the offender must gain knowledge of the gang's constitution officially known as the XIV Bonds. The Northern Structure became the ears of the senior Nuestra Familia and was required to deal drugs for its father hierarchy. Northern Structure sold drugs in the streets and brought in funds for ranking NF members behind bars.

Common Norteños Markings

According to the Latino Prison Gangs: Gang Identification Task Force (2009c), Norteños may

> refer to each other by using the term "Ene," Spanish for the letter "N." Norteños use the number 14 in tattoos and graffiti because "N" is the fourteenth letter of the alphabet. It is sometimes written as "X4," or in Roman numerals as "XIV." Some Norteños will tattoo themselves with four dots. Norteño derogatorily refers to a Sureño as a "Scrap" or "Sur (Sewer) Rat," while a Sureño will likewise refer to a Norteño as a "Buster" or "Chap" (Chapete). Norteños also lay claim to images of the Mexican-American labor movement, such as the sombrero, machete, and "Huelga bird," symbols of the United Farm Workers.

Other Norteño markings include "N," "NORTE," "NORTEÑO," and "ENE." They prefer the colors red and black. According to Morales (2007a):

> Norteño members represent their affiliation with a wide variety of clothing and symbols. In many areas of the west and northwest, gang members wear San Francisco 49ers gear. In the Midwest and on the East Coast, Norteño gang members commonly wear Nebraska jerseys, shirts and hats. In parts of the southwest and other areas, the gang members may wear University of Nevada—Las Vegas (UNLV) gear, which they claim represents the phrase "Us Norteños Love Violence." In Northern California's Bay Area, Norteño gang members often use light blue and North Carolina clothing—representing Norteño Control (NC)—as a means to confuse the police and undermine California's 186.22 PC Street Terrorism Gang Act; a law that could cause them to face enhanced sentences for certain crimes if they were documented as gang members. Another non-verbal identifier for the Norteños in the past has been the Mongolian hairstyle (a top knot or ponytail growing from the top/back portion of the head). This came out of CDC and was adopted on the street.

Where the Norteños Are

Although the majority of Norteños are in northern California, Norteños have been reported by law enforcement in 10 states (DOJ, 2015a).

Mara Salvatrucha (MS-13)

Beginning as a street gang, the Mara Salvatrucha 13 gang was started by Salvadoran refugees in the Rampart section of Los Angeles in the late 1980s (Rather, 2005). MS-13 was established as a defense against established L.A. street gangs. Two teenage friends, Ernesto "Smokey" Miranda and Julio Cesar, started MS-13 when they felt that they were not being accepted by the predominately Mexican street gangs in their neighborhood (Corbiscello, 2008). The name Salvatrucha comes from La Mara Street in San Salvador and the Salvatrucha guerrillas (Farabundo Marti National Liberacion) who fought in the civil war in El Salvador from 1981–1992. According to some, the gang was originally called the Mara Salvatrucha Stoners, but they dropped the "Stoners" and adopted 13 to show solidarity

Figure 2.10

Mara Salvatrucha (MS-13). Public domain.

FBI 2011 National Gang Intelligence Center Report

with other Mexican Mafia affiliates in southern California. They adopted the *cholo* attire (stereotypically baggy khaki style pants, white sleeveless t-shirts, knee-length white socks, and flannel shirts buttoned all the way to the top; Etter, 2010; Anonymous, 2006).

The civil war in El Salvador was brutal and killed at least 62,000 people and wounded thousands more. Many of those killed were civilians, and both sides used "death squads" as well as conventional or guerrilla forces. During the Salvadoran Civil War, many children as young as 14 were inducted into either the guerrilla or government forces. This gave many of the original MS-13 members paramilitary training. The civil war also led to masses of refugees fleeing the war looking for work and safety. The war displaced an estimated 1 million Salvadorans, many of whom came to the United States either legally or illegally (Franco, 2008; Grascia, 2004).

The MS-13 admits members from the Hispanic community, and ethnicity is more important than race. The ages of MS-13 member vary widely from 11 to over 40. The initiation rites are often violent. Membership in MS-13 is for life. The rules, such as a code of silence, are strictly enforced (Domash, 2005, p. 31; Friedan, 2005). Alleged violators of MS-13 rules are often tried internally in a *juzgado* (court) held by senior MS-13 members in the clique (DeCesare, 1998).

An interesting way that some MS-13 cliques (groups) recruit is through the use of youth soccer teams. Soccer is possibly the most popular sport among Hispanic youth. MS-13 has at least two soccer teams in Los Angeles that play regular games against other clubs. There has been information that there is a possible MS-13 soccer team in Galveston, Texas. Most MS-13 soccer teams wear some variation of the Salvadoran National Team jersey with the colors blue and white. Playing organized sports allows the MS-13 to legitimize itself as a community organization with the Hispanic community and also acts as a good place to recruit new members (Etter, 2010, p. 7).

MS-13 Organizational Structure

The MS-13 is organized into cliques. Each clique operates sort of like a hamburger franchise, being independently owned and operated while retaining their affiliation with the national brand of MS-13. Wolf (2012) described the MS-13 clique structure as

> best understood as an informal network of autonomous gangs bound by a shared symbolic and normative affiliation . . . MS-13 has moved past the traditional street gang, yet it remains a social phenomenon . . . increasingly participate in the underground economy, but instead of constituting an efficient and highly disciplined delinquent entity, the gang incorporates both fun seeking adolescents and older, more criminally dedicated members who operate as foot soldiers for organized crime.
>
> (p. 94)

Cliques have business meetings with agendas, goals, reports, and so forth. Members cannot skip meetings. The National Drug Intelligence Center (2004) found that

> Mara Salvatrucha cliques conduct annual meetings that vary from clique to clique. Some cliques also have weekly or monthly meetings. The cliques use the meetings to plan criminal activity, discipline members, resolve dispute, and initiate new members. Most meetings are held at local restaurants, outdoor recreation facilities, parks, pool halls, private homes, and rented hotel rooms. Occasionally the gangs hold a national or regional level meeting, referred to as a Universal, with representatives of cliques from multiple states attending.

The local boss is called the shot caller (*palabrero*). Members of MS-13 cannot act without the boss's consent. "Runners" are messengers who travel between cliques and are treated with great respect. Originally, these cliques operated totally independently of one another, but there have been recent attempts by MS-13s from the West Coast to get things more formally organized through *misas janeras* (conferences). The goal is to be the leading Hispanic gang (Carter, 2007).

Wolf (2012) observed that in addition to the palabrero (shot caller), some cliques had a *solsado* (territorial defender) and *misionero* (assignment executer) as a part of their structure (p. 75). However, according to the FBI (2015b), the MS-13 has no official national leadership structure. MS-13 originated in Los Angeles, but when members migrated eastward, they began forming more independent cliques. Those cliques maintained regular contact with members in other regions to coordinate recruitment/criminal activities and to prevent conflicts.

MS-13 Criminal Activities

Violence is an inherent part of gang life in most street gangs in the United States. This is especially true in MS-13. An interesting thing about violence and MS-13 is that the gang has a set of rules as to when and how a MS-13 member can engage in violent acts and style counts. Permission to kill is called a "green light" and must come from the shot caller (Stockwell, 2005).

Assassinations have strict rules that call for at least one head shot to the victim. There are penalties for the MS-13 assassin who fails to score at least one head shot on the victim. If a victim is shot in the head and somehow survives, it is considered to be OK because the rules were followed. Murder weapons (guns) are often sent to another city to be used in another murder. Notes are often left with the body of the victim either listing the reason that the victim was killed or containing further threats against rival gangs or law enforcement. That has been observed with MS-13 killings in the United States, Mexico, Honduras, and Guatemala (Etter, 2010).

Another favorite weapon for MS-13 members is the machete. Machete attacks on the East Coast and in Central America have decapitated many victims. Fingers are often chopped off the hands of gang rivals, such as in the 2005 attack in Fairfax, Virginia, in which three MS-13 members used a machete to chop three fingers off the left hand of a victim. The victim was a member of the South Side Locos (Jackson, 2005). This attack followed a machete attack on a South Side Locos gang member in May 2004, where the victim lost four fingers to MS-13 machete-wielding members. Local military surplus stores noted a sharp rise in machete sales to groups of individuals who did not look like the camping "types" (Shapira, 2005).

Drug rip-offs and attacking other gang's drug houses have become an MS-13 trademark. Paramilitary tactics are often used including heavily armed assault teams conducting sweeps of the residence to be hit. In describing a raid by MS-13 in Houston, Texas on a rival gang's drug house, *USA Today* reporter Kevin Johnson (2006) quoted a Houston Police Department spokesman's description of the attack:

> The MS-13 suspects swept through the house like a well-trained assault team, using paramilitary tactics including perimeter lookouts, high powered weaponry (an AK-47 rifle was among the weapons recovered later), and a quick, room-by-room sweep of the house that was notable for its precision and sophistication.

When law enforcement authorities challenged the raiders, a shootout broke out that left two MS-13 suspects dead. MS-13 has used hand grenades during attacks in Central America. In 2006, the rapid spread to MS-13 on the East Coast and the violence associated with that spread was the subject of a congressional hearing (Davis, 2006). According to the FBI (2015b): "MS-13 members engage in a wide range of criminal activity, including drug distribution, murder, rape, prostitution, robbery, home invasions, immigration offenses, kidnapping, carjackings/auto thefts, and vandalism." One of the characteristics of the MS-13 is that they are very adaptable and have a short learning curve. They readily adapt to new conditions and are open to all types of new criminal activities. The DOJ (2015a) estimates that there are approximately 8,000–10,000 MS-13 members in the United States and approximately 30,000 to 50,000 MS-13 members and associates worldwide.

MS-13 in Jail/Prison

MS-13 members who find themselves in prison usually operate as their own prison gang. However, MS-13 is often allied with the Sureños and the Mexican Mafia both on the street and while in custody (Etter, 2010).

Common MS-13 Markings

Members of MS-13 use blue and white as their primary colors. These are the same colors found on the Salvadoran flag. MS-13 members use the number 13 to show their origination in southern California. Sometimes they use different numbers such as 76 and 67 which add up to 13. MS-13 gang members will sport tattoos denoting membership in MS-13. Gothic script is preferred for most tattoos using letters (MS-13, MS XII, La Mara, comedy and tragedy masks indicating laugh now/cry later, three dots in a triangle indicating *mi vida loca* ["my crazy life"], dice, crossbones, daggers). Other tattoos, such as teardrops located under the eyes of the gang members can indicate fallen gang members or a person that the MS-13 member assaulted or killed.

Tattoos of bricks sometimes indicate that the MS-13 member has served time in prison. Each brick tattoo represented 1 year of time served. On West Coast members of MS-13, these tattoos may not be visible when the gang member is wearing clothing such as a long-sleeved shirt. MS-13 members from the East Coast and those in Central America follow a more Mayan based cultural tradition in the selection of their tattoos, and often will have their entire body tattooed including their face. This type of facial tattooing is especially popular among MS-13 members who have served prison time in Central America. Tattoos on the inside of lips and on upper eyelids have also been seen (Etter, 2010).

MS-13 gang members are fond of heart-shaped jewelry (making closed M) and multicolored rosaries (usually blue and white). Like most gangs in the United States, MS-13 members also use hand signs for challenge and identification. The usage of graffiti to mark turf, declare war, show mourning, or intimidate rivals is as common in MS-13 as it is in other street gangs across the United States (NDIC, 2004).

Where the MS-13 Are

The MS-13 has been reported in 45 states in the United States. MS-13 has also been reported in Belize, Canada, Costa Rica, El Salvador, Guatemala, and Honduras (Breve, 2007; News 5, 2012).

18th Street Gang (aka La-18, Mara-18, M-18)

According to Franco (2008):

The 18th Street gang (M-18) was originally formed by Mexican migrants in the 1960s in the Rampart neighborhood of Los Angeles who were blocked from joining other native-born Mexican American gangs. The 18th Street gang grew by expanding its membership to other nationalities and races, and it was among the first multiracial, multiethnic gangs in Los Angeles.

(p. 4)

It was the rejection in the 1980s by the 18th Street Gang of Salvadoran immigrants that was partially responsible for the formation of MS-13, and that rejection still contributes to why both gangs are bitter enemies to this day. It is estimated that there are over 200 autonomous 18th Street Gangs currently in operation, making it one of the largest Hispanic gangs in the United States (Valdez, 2009a, p. 137).

18th Street Organizational Structure

18th Street groups are organized into cliques and use a "shot caller" system of leadership, similar to their bitter enemies the MS-13. That lack of a formal organizational structure has made them more difficult for law enforcement to eradicate (Griffith, 2017).

18th Street Criminal Activities

Primary crimes of the 18th Street Gang include drug trafficking, auto theft, carjacking, extortion, identification fraud, robbery, prostitution, weapons trafficking, human trafficking, and money laundering (DOJ, 2015a; Valdez, 2009a, p. 139). While the 18th Street Gang admits primarily Hispanics as members, other ethnic and racial groups have been admitted in various locations. The DOJ (2015a) estimates that there are approximately 30,000–50,000 members of the 18th Street gang.

18th Street in Jail/Prison

18th Street members who find themselves in prison usually operate as their own prison gang. However, 18th Street is often allied with the Sureños and the Mexican Mafia, both on the street and in custody (Latino Prison Gangs, 2009a).

Common 18th Street Markings

Members of 18th Street Gangs use blue and black as their primary colors. Valdez (2009a) discovered that 18th Street gang members often have tattoos indicating membership. Valdez observed:

Most common tattoo is some form of the number 18. Gang tattoos can be located anywhere on the body. Some members will cover their entire body with 18th Street tattoos. Other 18th Street gang members have been known to tattoo the number 18 on their foreheads, or above their eyebrows. Some gang members have used the number 666 to represent 18th Street.

(pp. 140–141)

Where the 18th Street Gangs Are

The 18th Street Gang has been reported in 20 states (DOJ, 2015a). The 18th Street Gang has also been reported in El Salvador, Guatemala, Honduras, and Mexico (Breve, 2007; Franco, 2008).

Native American Gangs

Compared to many racial or ethnic groups in the United States, the Native American population is fairly small. Since most people in any given group are not criminals, the number of individuals engaged in criminal activity within that group is even smaller. Noting the trend to adopt affiliations of existing gangs by Native American youth, Grant (2013) observed:

> it is not unusual for the individuals involved to identify by a unique, localized name (i.e., Odd Squad, The Boyz, Red Nation Klique, etc.). However, the usual trend in most tribal communities involves the gang identifying with, and adopting the names and symbols of, major urban gangs (i.e., Native Gangster Bloods, Native Gangster Crips, Native Gangster Disciples, Native Latin King).

(p. 15)

Thus, most of the gang activity in Indian Country fits the "local hybrid" form of gang behavior. Native American gangs on the reservation often have formed as a result of gang migration and thus take the affiliations of existing gangs. This is due to the movement of Native American populations back and forth between urban areas and the reservation. As was true with other ethnic and racial groups, the relocation of Native American families also moves any family members who might have been involved in gang activities into new territories (Freng, Davis, McCord, & Roussell, 2012; Armstrong et al., 1999; Donnermeyer, Edwards, Chavez, & Beauvais, 2000; Maxson, 1998). That caused many Native American youth gangs to be influenced by urban street gangs or other gangs outside of their immediate environment (Freng et al., 2012; Major et al., 2004; Valdez, 2009a, pp. 256–258). However, while there is evidence of gang migration and assumed existing gang affiliation by Native American youth gangs, the majority of gangs on Native American reservations (SUR 13, Crips, Bloods, Folks, etc.) have been found to be "home grown" smaller groups that were founded by youth in the immediate area (Freng et al., 2012; Grant & Feimer, 2007; Maxson, 1998; Valdez, 2009a, p. 258). According to Morales (2007b):

> Many of the tribes have tried to bring youth back to the reservations as well as provide jobs through the growth of Indian gaming. This has been successful in many respects, but the gang affiliated youth may see a jackpot and use their money for criminal acts. Native American street gang members will visit rural communities to recruit members. There is evidence that some Native gangs are also working with Outlaw Motorcycle Gangs in the U.S. and in Canada.

Grant (2013) also found that Native American gangs tended to either adopt the culture and membership of mainline gangs in the area or be strictly local tribal affairs. Grant stated that the numbers of Native American youth involved in gangs was relatively small (p. 15). Those gangs tend to be L.A. based, though there is no such requirement. Hence they are included in this chapter.

Common Native American Gang Markings

Native American Youth who are members of gangs in trial areas tend to adopt the colors or symbols of the gang identities that they identify with. However, local tribal tattoos or gang names have been observed (Grant, 2013, p. 15).

Native American Gangs Organizational Structure

Grant (2013) observed:

> The majority of Native American street gangs are fragmented, unorganized and leaderless. If leadership in any form exists within such gangs, it usually takes the form of "shot callers" or individuals within the gang that have the ability to influence others; have access to money, alcohol or drugs; or who have a reputation for being prone to criminality or violent, aggressive behavior.
>
> (pp. 19–20)

Grant (2013) also observed that Native American gangs that identified with traditional mainline street gangs in their area tended to adopt the organizational structure of the gang that they identified with.

Native American Gang Criminal Activities

Native American gangs tend to commit crimes in the immediate area in which they live. Crimes include drugs, burglary, robbery, felony assaults, and murder (Grant, 2013, p. 22).

Native American Gangs in Jail/Prison

Prisons that have large numbers of incarcerated Native Americans often have Native American prison gangs. Grant (2013) found:

> Unlike most Native American street gangs Native American prison gangs tend to be more organized and disciplined; and it is not unusual for a Native American prison gang to have rules and regulations, as well as a rank structure and leadership hierarchy.
>
> (p. 23)

Where the Native American Gangs Are

Native American sets of gangs are located in tribal lands and reservations throughout the United States. They are also to be found in urban areas with large Native American populations (Grant, 2013).

Gang Enemies

Because of turf disputes and conflicts of interests in the drug trade, the Crips and Bloods are usually in a state of continuous street warfare. This stems from showing disrespect of the other gang's graffiti to violent reactions when members of the two groups find themselves in the same space. Crip member Colton Simpson (2006) joined the Harlem Crips in Los Angeles at the age of 10. Simpson described the predominant gang member attitude:

> I'm a Crip. You're a Blood. I see you. I'm going to kill you. You see me; you're going to kill me. I'm not ready to die, so I'm going to kill you first. It's all business. There it is. War.
>
> (Simpson & Pearlman, 2006, p. 29)

Gang Alliances

During the late 1970s and early 1980s, African American street gangs began to evolve very rapidly due largely to changes in the cocaine drug market and the newly available product of rock or crack cocaine (NDIC, 1998, p. xii). Two groups developed separately in different cities and in different areas of the country, but came to dominate the drug market and often absorbed local gangs or forced them out through hostile takeovers. The two groups were the Los Angeles based street gangs (Crips and Bloods) and the Chicago based street gangs (Folk and People).

The structures of the two groups were very different. Buccellato (2013) observed that the Chicago based street gangs were based on a hierarchical structure, while Los Angeles based street gangs were described as being institutionalized with a much looser structure. The expansion of Chicago based and Los Angeles based street gangs from their home cities changed the face of gang crime in the United States. Local law enforcement, being unfamiliar with these new groups, had to face some very new challenges and make changes in their own operations to meet this new criminal threat. The gang problem went from being a largely local issue to becoming a nationwide law enforcement problem.

The gangs also evolved as they expanded. Observing this trend in analyzing data from the National Street Gang Survey Report of 1998, the National Drug Intelligence Center observed:

> Gangs have become extremely mobile in order to conduct their illegal activities while avoiding detection by law enforcement. Respondents commonly noted that gangs were traveling from city to city, within the same state or to a neighboring state, to sell drugs or commit other crimes. As gangs engage in crime and move from their original bases, they seem to diversify membership to include persons from varied backgrounds.
>
> (NDIC, 1998, p. xi)

Another change occurred in the demographics of these expanding gangs: their membership aged. The traditional gang age demographic of 12–24 began to change, and gang members began to stay well into adulthood. These were no longer youth gangs being led by other youngsters. The gangs grew their own internal adult leadership (Etter & Swymeler, 2008). As with the original New York gangs, there are more adult gang members than juveniles, and have been for decades.

Summary

Beginning in the 1980s, the illicit trade in crack or rock cocaine fueled the rapid expansion of local street gangs into nationwide drug selling organizations. Two basic types of gangs rapidly expanded their drug dealing operations during this period: L.A. based street gangs (institutional-style gangs) and Chicago based street gangs (hierarchical-style gangs). Many of the early leaders of both types of gangs met a bad end, either ending up imprisoned or dead (murdered, executed, or dead of natural causes at an early age). Literally thousands of gang members were either killed or wounded in the street gang wars that followed the rapid expansion of gangs across the United States. Almost as many (if not more) citizens and more than a few law enforcement officers were also killed or wounded in these drug wars. Those gangs have a multistate following and often absorb local gangs when they arrive in an area. Together the L.A. based street gangs and the Chicago based street gangs changed the way that drugs were dealt in the United States during the 1980s and 1990s. They continue in the operation of their criminal enterprises today. We will examine the Chicago based gangs in the next chapter.

Ethnic gangs are usually formed from members of their own ethnic groups, and like most gangs they provide a variety of illicit goods and services to their clients. Ethnic gangs use language, culture, race, religion, and ethnicity to shield them from law enforcement. Many of the crimes of ethnic gangs are initially committed against members of their own ethnic groups. Some ethnic gangs have grown from their local beginnings and have achieved a multistate or national presence. Others, such as Native American gangs, have a very limited territory. Some ethnic gang such as MS-13 have a very loose organizational structure and franchises operate somewhat independently of each other, but coordinate when it is to their advantage. Other ethnic gangs such as the yakuza have an almost rigid hierarchical organizational structure and have set offices for their leaders. The lack of understanding by law enforcement of the language, culture, religion, and ethnicity hinders the investigation of these groups by law enforcement.

DISCUSSION QUESTIONS

1. Describe how Los Angeles based street gangs originated.
2. Describe the impact of crack cocaine on the expansion of neighborhood gangs into multistate and national organizations.
3. Describe the criminal activities engaged in by Los Angeles based street gangs.
4. Identify the evolution of the Sureños-connected gangs in and out of prison.
5. Examine the Norteño-allied gangs on the streets and in the prisons.
6. Explain the originations of the Mara Salvatrucha (MS-13).
7. Explain the originations of the 18th Street Gang.
8. Identify issues with Native Americans and gangs.

CHAPTER 3 Chicago Area Street Gangs

CHAPTER OBJECTIVES

After reading this chapter students should be able to do the following:

- Examine the history of Chicago based street gangs.
- Identify the major Chicago based street gangs.
- Evaluate the structure and leadership of Chicago based street gangs.
- Explain the differences in between the L.A. based and Chicago based street gangs.
- Explain how Chicago based street gangs became a nationwide criminal justice problem.

Introduction

In Chicago, Illinois, the gangs were not nearly so organized prior to the 1850s. Crimes of violence were commonplace, but the perpetrators were bands of boys and men acting in response to the economic suffering of their families. Asbury (1986) observed that by 1857, large groups of armed criminal thugs in Chicago had formed gangs, engaging in murders, robberies, burglaries, thefts, prostitution, and illegal liquor sales on Sunday. The gangs in Chicago quickly became involved in local politics; however, they largely remained a local affair and focused on their own neighborhoods (Asbury, 1986, p. 103).

In Asbury's research of the city's gang history, there was no record of criminal activity in Chicago until 1833. According to Perkins (1987), white street gangs had been documented in Chicago since the 1860s. Lindberg (2016) found that gangs in early Chicago made use of the first military-style home invasions following the Civil War, although none of the members apparently served in the military. After surveilling a home, they camouflaged their faces with boot polish and entered homes at night. Many a social gathering and house party was interrupted by those gang members. The first gangs in Chicago were almost exclusively immigrants, including Irish, Italians, Jews, and Poles. Groups of immigrants often formed community support groups that evolved into gangs from 1880 to 1920.

Chicago saw an influx of African American gangs following the Civil War, as many sought to escape the punishing and limiting laws in the South. Howell (2015) found that a lot of African Americans were marginalized by the racially restrictive covenants on real estate. They were also affected by the racist attitudes and actions of the established white gangs in the area.

By the late 1920s, the street gang problem in Chicago had grown exponentially with the population of the city. A 1927 study by Frederic M. Thrasher found that there were 1,313 youth gangs in Chicago, and that did not even count the more traditional adult gangs like Al Capone's gang and other mobsters who were in the middle of a bloody gang war at the time (Thrasher, 2000, p. 1). While the adult gangs were involved in local politics, Chicago's gangs were still a largely local operation. The gangs stayed within their well-defined territories. To stray outside of those territories meant war with the neighboring gang and their allies (Lindberg, 2016, p. 41; Howell & Moore, 2010, p. 5).

However, in the late 1950s and early 1960s Chicago street gangs began to evolve. Beginning in the jails and juvenile correctional facilities of Cook County, new players began to form gangs. Those gangs were strictly local affairs at first and did not have very many members. The drug trade in the 1960s and 1970s changed all of that. Chicago based street gangs became very organized with visible leadership structures. The gangs divided into two basic groups—the Folk and the People—and began to grow. The Folk and the People gradually evolved into 28 distinct gangs in each alliance. The Chicago based street gangs developed a hierarchical leadership structure, often with a business or paramilitary model. Some gangs even gave their members business cards that listed the members of their particular set. Some of the original gangs wore "War Sweaters" that looked like a high school letterman's sweater with gang insignia or patches to identify gang membership. They also began to use two and sometimes three colors to identify their gang. Because more than one gang might use the same colors, the way that the colors were arranged indicated which gang was being represented.

The Folk would generally wear their clothing or accessories favoring the right side and the People would generally wear their clothing to the left (Knox, 2006). As the Chicago based street gangs expanded their membership, they also began to expand their areas of operation into the surrounding cities and even into surrounding states, following the drug markets and the movements of their members. Some gang expansion was based on drug supply and some on the movements of gang members into other areas. Laskey (1996) observed that well-meaning family members who tried to remove their gang-involved children from the gang environment would often relocate them to another city or state. That did not end the child's gang membership, however. The gang member simply started a new branch of their gang in the new area. Laskey called this "The Familial Gang Transplant Phenomenon" (1996, pp. 1–15). In Milwaukee, Wisconsin, Hagedorn (1998) observed that in the 1980s many local Milwaukee gangs began to identify with Chicago based street gangs either because of contact with Chicago gang members or to protect themselves from other local gang rivals (pp. 67–77). The result of this gang expansion and the competition for turf area in the drug trade was a series of street gang wars that dramatically increased the levels of violent crime in Chicago (Block & Block, 1993, p. 2). By 2004, the Chicago Police Department said that there were over 100 open-air drug markets that were in operation 24 hours a day, and they estimated that as many as one-third of their customers came from the surrounding suburbs (CPD, 2005).

The gangs of Chicago have continued to evolve. They were typically aligned with either the Folk or People Nation. However, as time has passed some individual gangs in each alliance have disbanded either through death, imprisonment or disinterest. Some have even switched sides from Folk to People or People to Folk. New neighborhood gangs have stepped up to take their place in the alliances. Although the Chicago based street gangs did not spread as fast or as far as their Los Angeles based counterparts, they did expand and are continuing to do so. Some of the gangs in both the Folk and the People now have expanded over several states to be nationwide. Some of the gangs in the Folk and the People are still only operating in the neighborhood that they started in or nearby areas. However, those neighborhood gangs have been in continuous operation for over 50 years (Knox, 2006).

Folk Nation

The Folk Nation began as a loose alliance of 28 gangs that originated in the Chicago area jails and juvenile facilities in the early 1960s. In the 1980s and 1990s, the Folk expanded to operate from east of the Rocky Mountains to the East Coast of the United States. By 2014, the Folk had a truly national presence, although there are not that many sets on the West Coast of the United States. The gangs in the Folk Nation are hierarchical and have a paramilitary structure and organization (Buccellato, 2013). Many Folk Nation gangs have formal constitutions and celebrate set gang holidays. Folk Nation gangs are very territorial and engage in turf wars. Folk Nation gangs are sometimes involved in political movements or political action groups as well as criminal acts. Folk Nation gangs have set up social service groups that acted as a front for criminal activities and facilitated fraud from U.S. government grants.

As a group, the Folk generally aligns to the right in dress and symbols. Folk members vary racially by gang and set. The Folk Nation maintains a very loose alliance with the Los Angeles based Crips, but will fight sets from that group if interests in drug trade or turf occur. Gangs sometimes grow and expand. They also shrink and disappear because of imprisonment, death, or disinterest. The following are some Folk Nation gangs that are no longer active: 2–1 Boys, Braizers, Campbell Boys and Ridgeway Lords (Chicago Gang History, 2017).

BOX 3.1 The Three Kings of the Folk Nation

Whenever a Folk Nation member speaks about the "Three Kings," who are they talking about? The "Three Kings" were all founding members of the Folk Nation.

1. David Barksdale (aka "David Jones" or "King David") was born as Doinse David Barksdale in Sallis, Mississippi, on May 24, 1947. King David moved with his family to Chicago in 1957 at the age of 10. In 1960, Barksdale and Don Derky began a gang in Chicago called the Devil's Disciples. The gang was made up of African American youth from the neighborhood. As the gang grew it began absorbing other gangs; by 1966 the gang had become known as the Black Disciple Nation. Conflicts with the Blackstone Rangers leader Eugene Harrison resulted in Barksdale being shot six times in 1968 in a failed assassination attempt. In 1969, Barksdale allied with Larry Hoover of the Gangster Nation, and the Black Gangster Disciples Nation (BGDN) was formed with Barksdale as the president and Hoover as the chairman or vice president. In 1969, Barksdale again survived being shot by another gang member, however the gunshot wounds suffered during this shooting would eventually lead to Barksdale's death in 1974 of kidney failure. His wife, Yvonne Barksdale, was murdered in 1977. The Disciples and most Folk factions use a six-pointed star as an emblem in honor of "King David." The Folk also celebrate David Barksdale's birthday as a holiday (Knox, 2006, p. 780).
2. Jerome "Shorty" Freeman or "King Shorty" was born in 1951. Freeman was barely five feet tall, and as a result acquired the nickname Shorty. Freeman was a close associate of David Barksdale. After Barksdale's death in 1974, Freeman broke away from the BGDN and formed the Black Disciples. Freeman led the group into the Folk Nation in 1978. Freeman spent much of his life in prison and ran the gang from there. In 1992, Freeman's seven-year-old nephew was murdered by a sniper who was a rival gang member (Kass & Blau, 1992). By 2001, Freeman had had enough and told authorities that he had retired and given up gang life. Freeman began to publicly speak out about ending gang violence in Chicago. Freeman died of natural causes in 2012 in Chicago (Konkol, 2012). Freeman's funeral generated a major Chicago Police presence to prevent violence by rival gangs (Main, 2012).
3. Larry Hoover or "King Larry" (aka "King of Kings") was born on November 30, 1950, in Jackson, Mississippi. Hoover's family moved to Chicago when Larry was four years old. As a teenager, Hoover became the leader of a gang called the Supreme Gangsters and later the Gangster Nation. In 1969, Hoover joined with David Barksdale to form the BGDN. In 1973, Larry Hoover was sentenced to 150 to 200 years in prison for a murder he committed in Illinois. Hoover assumed command of the BGSN upon Barksdale's death in 1974, although there were breakaway groups like Freeman's Black Disciples. Hoover led the gang from prison

in Stateville Correctional Center (NDIC, 2003, pp. 1–2, Knox & Fuller, 1995, p. 67). In the late 1970s, Hoover helped form the Folk Nation alliance of gangs to oppose Jeff Fort's People Nation alliance. In the 1990s, Hoover directed his gang to try another approach. The Gangster Disciples became involved in social outreach (i.e., Growth and Development Organization) and political organizations (i.e., 21st Century V.O.T.E.) in the Chicago area. The idea was to tap into U.S. government neighborhood development grants and to affect local politics in the Chicago area (NDIC, 2003, p. 2; Martin & Thomas, 1996). In 1997, Hoover was convicted on federal drug and Racketeer Influenced and Corrupt Organizations (RICO) Act violations for his activities running the gang from prison. Hoover is currently incarcerated in ADX Florence supermax prison, serving six life sentences (NDIC, 2003, p. 2; O'Conner, 1996a; O'Conner, 1996b).

2–2 Boys (aka Insane Twenty Second)

The 2–2 Boys began in Chicago's Pilsen neighborhood in the 1960s. The gang was originally known as the Twenty Second Street Boys. The 2–2 Boys joined the Folk Nation in 1978 as one of the first gangs to pledge to the alliance. Primary crimes of the 2–2 Boys include drug trafficking, armed robbery, and auto theft. The 2–2 Boys admit mostly Latino and white members. The Chicago Crime Commission estimates that the 2–2 Boys have at least 150 members (Hubbard, Wyman, & Domma, 2012, pp. 178–179; Chicagogangs.org, 2014, 22 Boys).

Common 2–2 Boys Markings

The 2–2 Boys use black and blue as their primary colors. Secondary colors include brown and beige. Other markings include a four-point crown, four insane lines, shield with 22, two dice showing the number 2, and lions guarding dice (Hubbard et al., 2012, pp. 178–179; Chicagogangs.org, 2014, 22 Boys; Petrone, 1997, pp. 159–163).

Where the 2–2 Boys Are

Members of the 2–2 Boys have been reported in Arizona, California, Florida, Illinois, Kentucky, and Wisconsin (Hubbard et al., 2012, pp. 178–179; Chicagogangs.org, 2014, 22 Boys).

2–6 (aka 2–6 Boys, Gangster Two-Six, GTS, G26 TSN)

The 2–6 gang began in Chicago in 1964. The gang consisted of Hispanics and whites from the neighborhood around 26th street. The 2–6 joined the Folk Nation in 1975.

Primary crimes committed by 2–6 members include drug trafficking, thefts, and robberies. The 2–6 now admits mostly Latino members. The Chicago Crime Commission estimates that the 2–6 has at least 2,370 members (Hubbard et al., 2012, pp. 174–177; Chicagogangs.org, 2014, Two Six; avm.gangs.tripod, 2007).

Common 2–6 Markings

The 2–6 uses beige or tan and black as their primary colors. Other markings include Playboy bunny with right ear bent, wearing fedora and sunglasses; hooded bunny; dice showing 2 and 6; and playing cards saying *Amor de Konejo* (Hubbard et al., 2012, pp. 174–177; Chicagogangs.org, 2014, Two Six; avm.gangs.tripod, 2007; Petrone, 1997, pp. 164–168).

Where the 2–6 Are

Members of the 2–6 have been reported in Illinois, Indiana, Iowa, and Texas (NGIC, 2013, pp. 49–79; Hubbard et al., 2012, pp. 174–177; Chicagogangs.org, 2014, Two Six; avm.gangs.tripod, 2007).

Ambrose (aka Almighty Ambrose)

The Ambrose was formed in 1960 from a previous existing neighborhood gang by Walouie Lemas in the West Side Pilsen area of Chicago. The Ambrose began as a primarily Hispanic gang and remains so. They began to expand into surrounding areas, and the Chicago Crime Commission estimated they have at least 600 members (Hubbard et al., 2012, p. 21; Chicagogangs.org, 2014, Almighty Ambrose).

Common Ambrose Markings

The Ambrose use light blue and black as their primary colors. Other common markings include plumbed helmet with spear with four-point diamond shaped tip, Old English A, Folks Alliance logos, sportswear in gang colors, and Oakland A's athletic wear (Hubbard et al., 2012, p. 21; Chicagogangs.org, 2014, Almighty Ambrose; Petrone, 1997, p. 174).

Where the Ambrose Are

Members of the Ambrose have been reported in Illinois, Indiana, Iowa, and Texas (NGIC, 2013, pp. 49–79; Hubbard et al., 2012, p. 21; Chicagogangs.org, 2014, Almighty Ambrose).

Ashland Vikings (aka Almighty Viking Nation, AVS, Vikings)

The Ashland Vikings began in the early 1960s in Chicago in the East Village area around Ashland and Augusta Boulevards. Originally members of the Insane Family under the Spanish Cobras, the Ashland Vikings were opposed to the Latin Kings. The Ashland Vikings consists mainly of Hispanic members. The Chicago Crime Commission estimated there were at least 240 members of the Ashland Vikings (Hubbard et al., 2012, p. 26; Chicagogangs.org, 2014, Ashland Vikings).

Common Ashland Vikings Markings

The Ashland Vikings use green and black as their primary colors. Other markings include Viking helmet, Viking image, eight-pointed star, the number 8, hatchet, AVN, Minnesota Viking sportswear, and Philadelphia Eagles athletic wear (Hubbard et al., 2012, p. 26; Chicagogangs.org, 2014, Ashland Vikings; Petrone, 1997, p. 178).

Where the Ashland Vikings Are

Members of the Ashland Vikings have been reported in Illinois and Wisconsin (Hubbard et al., 2012, p. 21; Chicagogangs.org, 2014, Ashland Vikings).

Black Disciples (aka 2–4, 3rd World Black Disciple Nation, Sons and Daughters of the Star, Sons and Daughters of the Divine Star, Sons and Daughters of the Divine Universal Star)

The Black Disciples began in Chicago in 1960 and were started by David Barksdale and Don Derky as the Devil's Disciples. The gang was made up of African American youth from the neighborhood. As the gang grew, it began absorbing other gangs, and by 1966 the gang had become known as the Black Disciple Nation. In 1969, Barksdale allied with Larry Hoover of the Gangster Nation, and the Black Gangster Disciples Nation (BGDN) was formed with Barksdale as the president and Hoover as the chairman or vice president. Internal struggles occurred in the BGDN after the death of Barksdale in 1974.

As a result, Jerome "Shorty" Freeman split the Black Disciples away from the BGDN. However, Freeman brought the Black Disciples into the Folk Nation alliance in 1978. The Black Disciples is a hierarchical gang with an organized structure including Minister, Co-minister, Demetrius, etc. (Knox, 2004b). The Black Disciples admits mostly African American members. The Chicago Crime Commission estimates that the Black Disciples has at least 4,200 members. Other estimates go as high as 6,000 members (Hubbard et al., 2012, pp. 57–63; Chicagogangs.org, 2014, BDN; Knox, 2004b).

Common Black Disciples Markings

The Black Disciples use blue and black as their primary colors. Other markings include a six-pointed star with the roman numeral III, the number 78, pitchfork, and sayings including "Treys for Days" (Hubbard et al., 2012, pp. 57–63; Chicagogangs.org, 2014, BDN; Knox, 2004b; Petrone, 1997, pp. 189–194).

Where the Black Disciples Are

Members of the Black Disciples have been reported in Arkansas, Florida, Illinois, Indiana, Iowa, Massachusetts, Michigan, New York, Tennessee, and Wisconsin (NGIC, 2013, pp. 49–79; Hubbard et al., 2012, pp. 57–63; Chicagogangs.org, 2014, BDN).

Black Gangster Disciples

(See Gangster Disciples)

Black Souls (aka 40s, 440, Gangster Black Souls, Mad Black Souls, Mafia Black Souls)

The Black Souls was founded in 1962 by "King Wee" after a split from the Black Gangster Disciples. King Wee ran the Black Souls until he was killed in 1975. The gang has primarily African American members. The Chicago Crime Commission estimates that the Black Souls has at least 1,100 members. The gang deals in drugs and illegal firearms as their primary crimes (Hubbard et al., 2012, p. 26; Chicagogangs.org, 2014, Black Souls). On June 13, 2013, over 40 senior members of the Black Souls had the "distinction" of being the first gang members charged under Illinois's new RICO laws (Wojceichowski, 2013).

Common Black Souls Markings

The Black Souls use black and white as their primary colors. Others markings include a cross with two slashes, the number 440, a heart with wings, and a diamond (Hubbard et al., 2012, pp. 38–39; Chicagogangs.org, 2014, Black Souls; Petrone, 1997, p. 202).

Where the Black Souls Are

Members of the Black Souls have been reported in Illinois, Indiana, Missouri, Ohio, and Wisconsin (Hubbard et al., 2012, p. 26; Chicagogangs.org, 2014, Black Souls).

C-Notes (aka Insane C-Notes)

The C-Notes began as a Chicago neighborhood gang in the 1950s whose members were whites of Italian ancestry. In the 1960s the C-notes were a "greaser" gang and expressed racist "white power" views. Due to changing demographics in their neighborhoods, the C-Notes began admitting Hispanic members in the 1980s. In 1995, the C-Notes joined the Folks Alliance. The C-Notes are a small gang that the Chicago Crime Commission estimates at having at least 60 members. The C-Note's primary crimes are drug sales, armed robbery, auto theft, and racketeering (Hubbard et al., 2012, pp. 40–41; Chicagogangs.org, 2014, Insane C Notes).

Common C-Notes Markings

Initially the C-Notes used the colors of the Italian flag as their primary colors (green, red, and white). However, currently the C-Notes use green and black as their primary colors. Other markings include a dollar sign, dollar sign with pitchfork raised, letter C, and six-point star (Hubbard et al., 2012, pp. 40–41; Chicagogangs.org, 2014, Insane C Notes; Petrone, 1997, p. 209).

Where the C-Notes Are

Members of the C-Notes have only been reported in Illinois (Hubbard et al., 2012, pp. 40–41; Chicagogangs.org, 2014, Insane C Notes).

Cullerton Deuces

The Cullerton Deuces were established as a Chicago neighborhood gang in the 1970s. Originally aligned with the People Nation, the Cullerton Deuces joined the Folk Nation in 1993. The gang consists of largely Hispanic members. The Chicago Crime Commission estimates that the Cullerton Deuces have at least 60 members (Hubbard et al., 2012, pp. 40–41; Chicagogangs.org, 2014, Cullerton Deuces).

Common Cullerton Deuces Markings

The Cullerton Deuces use gray and black as their primary colors. Sometimes the gang members have used white and black instead. Other markings include a spade with a 2 in the center, two dots, spade cards, the roman numeral II, and two dice showing snake eyes. Cullerton Deuces say "*amor de dos*" (Hubbard et al., 2012, pp. 40–41; Chicagogangs.org, 2014, Cullerton Deuces; Petrone, 1997, p. 214).

Where the Cullerton Deuces Are

Members of the Cullerton Deuces have only been reported in Illinois (Hubbard et al., 2012, pp. 40–41; Chicagogangs.org, 2014, Cullerton Deuces).

Gangster Disciples (aka 7–4, BOS, Brothers of the Struggle, Gangsters; BGN, BGDN, GDN)

In 1960, David Barksdale and Don Derky began a gang in Chicago called the Devil's Disciples. As the gang grew, it began absorbing other gangs, and by 1966 the gang had become known as the Black Disciple Nation. In 1969, Barksdale allied with Larry Hoover of the Gangster Nation and the Black Gangster Disciples Nation (BGDN) was

Figure 3.1

Gangster Disciples Graffiti on the Side of a Building.

Uploaded by OgreBot/2015 December 27 21:00 [CC BY-SA 2.0 (https://creativecommons.org/licenses/by-sa/2.0)], via Wikimedia Commons

formed with Barksdale as the president and Hoover as the chairman or vice president. Although he was in prison, Hoover assumed command of the BGSN upon Barksdale's death in 1974. Internal struggles occurred in the BGDN after the death of Barksdale in 1974. As a result, in 1978, Jerome "Shorty" Freeman split the Black Disciples away from the BGDN. The Black Gangster Disciples Nation was one of the initial gangs to join the Folk Nation in the late 1970s when Hoover forged the alliance. In 1991, conflicts within the Folk Nation between the BGD and the BD led the Black Gangster Disciples to drop the B from their name and became the Gangster Disciples (Chicagogangs.org, 2014, BGD).

The Gangster Disciples is a hierarchical gang with a written formal constitution and a stratified formal leadership structure. The Gangster Disciples exerted influence in various public housing units in Chicago and used them to conduct the gang's drug selling operations (Knox & Fuller, 1995, p. 65). Hoover also levied a "street tax" on other drug dealers for the privilege of selling drugs in the gang's territory.

In the 1990s, the Gangster Disciples became involved in social outreach (i.e., Growth and Development Organization) and political organizations (i.e., 21st Century V.O.T.E.) in the Chicago area. The idea of these groups was to tap into U.S. government neighborhood development grants and to affect local politics in the Chicago area (NDIC, 2003, p. 2; Martin & Thomas, 1996). In 1993, Hoover's allies in some of the gang's political operations began a sustained unsuccessful political campaign to secure Hoover's parole from prison (Knox & Fuller, 1995, p. 62). However, Hoover's 1997 federal conviction on drug dealing and RICO violations because of his activities leading the Gangster Disciples from prison not only put an end to the efforts to parole Hoover but removed him from an active leadership role in the gang (NDIC, 2003, p. 2; O'Conner, 1996a; 1996b).

The Gangster Disciples engage in drug trafficking, robbery, extortion, social services fraud, mortgage fraud, money laundering, and kidnapping. The Gangster Disciples admits mostly African American members. The Chicago Crime Commission estimates that the Gangster Disciples has at least 10,000 members, however other estimates run as high as 30,000 (Hubbard et al., 2012, pp. 56–63; Chicagogangs.org, 2014, GDN).

Common Gangster Disciples Markings

The Gangster Disciples use blue and black as their primary colors. Other markings include a six-pointed star; pitchforks; heat with wings, tail and horns; Brother of the Struggle (BOS); 7–4 (for the seventh and fourth letters of the alphabet); and the letters G and D. Sayings include "All is one," "What up, G?," and "GD till the world blow" (Hubbard et al., 2012, pp. 56–63; Chicagogangs.org, 2014, GDN; Petrone, 1997, pp. 192–194, 224–236).

Where the Gangster Disciples Are

The National Gang Intelligence Center reported that Gangster Disciples were found in 34 states (NGIC, 2013, pp. 49–79).

Harrison Gents (aka Almighty Harrison Gents, HG, HGN)

The Harrison Gents began as the Harrison Gentlemen in the late 1950s and early 1960s and was started by Hispanic students at Harrison High School in the Chicago area. The gang still consists of mainly Hispanic members. The Harrison Gents maintain a Facebook page. Their primary crimes include drug trafficking, auto theft, larcenies, armed robberies, arson, and kidnapping. The Chicago Crime Commission estimates that the Harrison Gents have at least 240 members (Hubbard et al., 2012, pp. 68–69; Chicagogangs.org, 2014, Harrison Gents).

Common Harrison Gents Markings

The Harrison Gents use purple and black as their primary colors. Other markings include two crossed canes with a top hat and an H and G on either side, a skull with top hat, a cane with four dots above it, Colorado Rockies athletic wear, and "HG Love" (Hubbard et al., 2012, pp. 68–69; Chicagogangs.org, 2014, Harrison Gents; Petrone, 1997, p. 237).

Where the Harrison Gents Are

Members of the Harrison Gents have only been reported in Illinois (Hubbard et al., 2012, pp. 68–69; Chicagogangs.org, 2014, Harrison Gents).

Imperial Gangsters (aka Almighty Imperial Gangsters, AIG)

The Imperial Gangsters began as the Imperial Bachelors in the 1960s in Chicago. The name of the gang changed to the Imperial Gangsters after a power struggle within the group in the 1970s. Two Imperial Gangster leaders, Casper G and Baby Huey, were sent to prison in 1979. Baby Huey died in prison in 1980. One of the original gang leaders, Falco G, was murdered in gang-related violence in 1988 or 1989. Casper G was killed in 1996 while riding an "L" train in Chicago near Fullerton Street. The Imperial Gangsters has a mixed-race membership of Latinos, African Americans, and Caucasians. The Chicago Crime Commission estimates that there are at least 1,110 members of the group (Hubbard et al., 2012, pp. 70–73; Chicagogangs.org, 2014, IMP_GANGSTERS).

Common Imperial Gangster Markings

The Imperial Gangsters use pink and black as their primary colors. Other markings include a six-point crown with seven dots; a rounded crown, sometimes with a cross on top; the Pink Panther; a shotgun, and the number 197 (Hubbard et al., 2012, pp. 70–73; Chicagogangs.org, 2014, IMP_GANGSTERS; Petrone, 1997, p. 241).

Where the Imperial Gangsters Are

Members of the Imperial Gangsters have been reported in Alabama, Florida, Illinois, Indiana, Iowa, and Wisconsin (NGIC, 2013, pp. 49–79: Hubbard et al., 2012, pp. 70–73; Chicagogangs.org, 2014, IMP_GANGSTERS; FBI, 2014b, Imperial Gangsters).

Insane Deuces (aka I2D, 2's IDN, I2DN, ID)

The Insane Deuces formed in the 1960s from two other existing North Side Chicago Street gangs (Barons and Blackhawks). The Insane Deuces admit Hispanic and Caucasian members. The Chicago Crime Commission estimates that that there are at least 310 members in the gang (Hubbard et al., 2012, pp. 74–75; Chicagogangs.org, 2014, Insane Deuces).

Common Insane Deuces Markings

The Insane Deuces use green and black as their primary colors. Other markings include a playing card (deuce of spades), a spade with two dots, dice showing 2, the number 2, the number 2 with a spear and the letters ID, letter D with 2 in the center, and the roman numeral II (Hubbard et al., 2012, pp. 74–75; Chicagogangs.org, 2014, Insane Deuces; Petrone, 1997, p. 245).

Where the Insane Deuces Are

Members of the Insane Deuces have been reported in California, Illinois, Texas, and Wisconsin (Hubbard et al., 2012, pp. 74–75; Chicagogangs.org, 2014, Insane Deuces).

Insane Dragons (aka IDRS)

The Insane Dragons began in Chicago in 1964 after a group of Puerto Rican members split from the Latin Kings. The Insane Dragons now consists of mostly Latino members. The Chicago Crime Commission estimates that the Insane Dragons have at least 240 members (Hubbard et al., 2012, pp. 76–77; Chicagogangs.org, 2014, Insane Dragons).

Common Insane Dragons Markings

The Insane Dragons use maroon and gray as their primary colors. Other markings include a dragon breathing fire, a six-pointed star, a torch, three dots, a claw with diamonds, Morehouse College Tigers clothing, University of Alabama Crimson Tide clothing, and Washington Redskins athletic clothing. Sayings include "DR's F**k the Rest" and "Insane to the Dragon's Brain" (Hubbard et al., 2012, pp. 76–77; Chicagogangs.org, 2014, Insane Dragons).

Where the Insane Dragon Are

Members of the Insane Dragons have been reported in Illinois and Michigan (Hubbard et al., 2012, pp. 76–77; Chicagogangs.org, 2014, Insane Dragons).

Insane Popes (aka IP, IPN, Royal Popes)

When talking about the Popes, a researcher or police officer needs to know whether they are talking about the North Side of Chicago, where the Popes affiliate with the Folk Nation, or the South Side of Chicago, where the Popes affiliate with the People Nation. What makes it even more confusing is that both groups use different variations of the same colors to identify the group: blue, black, and white. However, "North Side" and "South Side" are clearly printed on their business cards. The Popes on the North Side of Chicago began as a greaser gang in the late 1960s and early 1970s. The Insane Popes membership consisted of white youth from the neighborhood and opposed Hispanic gangs in the area. The very name "Popes" was said to stand for "Protect Our People Eliminate Spics/Scum." One of the early leaders in the 1970s of the Insane Popes on the North Side was Larry "Larkin" Morris. Morris was murdered by members of the Gaylords in 1975. The Popes on the North Side joined the Folk Nation in 1978. Those on the South Side went a different path. The Insane Popes now admits members of different races but is still mostly white. The Chicago Crime Commission estimates that the Insane Popes have as least 150 members (Hubbard et al., 2012, pp. 144–147; Chicagogangs.org, 2014, Insane Popes North; Stonegreasers.com 2014b, Larkin Popes).

Common Insane Popes Markings

The Insane Popes use either black and blue or black and white as their primary colors. Other markings include a pitchfork, a cloaked figure with cross, the grim reaper, and the letter P (Hubbard et al., 2012, pp. 144–147; Chicagogangs.org, 2014, Insane Popes North; Petrone, 1997, pp. 248–250).

Where the Insane Popes Are

Members of the Insane Popes have been reported in Illinois and Iowa (NGIC, 2013, pp. 49–79; Hubbard et al., 2012, pp. 144–147; Chicagogangs.org, 2014, Insane Popes North).

Krazy GetDown Boys (aka KGB)

This gang began as a party crew in Chicago in the 1980s. Many KGB members will tell law enforcement that they are not gang members but party crew members upon contact with law enforcement authorities. However, by the 1990s the level of criminal conduct of the group and associations or alliances with existing street gangs in Chicago left no doubt that the Krazy GetDown Boys were a full-fledged gang in their own right. In 2011, KGB members were involved in the shooting of a Cape Coral, Florida, police officer (Ruane, 2011). The members of KGB are mostly Latino or Caucasian. The Chicago Crime Commission estimates that there are at least 90 members of the KGB. KGB members have been involved in drug trafficking, theft, and armed robbery (Hubbard et al., 2012, pp. 80–81; Chicagogangs.org, 2014, KGB).

Common Krazy GetDown Boys Markings

The Krazy GetDown Boys use black, purple, and white as their primary colors. Other markings include a sword, a shield, six dots (usually around the sword), a sword with ball and six slashes, a six-pointed star, and "Purple City" written in tattoos or graffiti. KGB sayings include "Purple and white stay rite shootings RAZAs left and right" (Hubbard et al., 2012, pp. 80–81; Chicagogangs.org, 2014, KGB).

Where the Krazy GetDown Boys Are

Members of the Krazy GetDown Boys have been reported in Florida, Illinois, Indiana, and Missouri (NGIC, 2013, pp. 49–79; Hubbard et al., 2012, pp. 80–81; Chicagogangs.org, 2014, KGB; Ruane, 2011).

La Raza (aka LRZ)

The name La Raza is kind of confusing when taken in the gang context. First there is the National Council of La Raza (NCLR), which is a legitimate political advocacy group serving the needs of Hispanics nationwide. The NCLR was founded in 1968. The NCLR has its headquarters in Washington, DC, and is not affiliated with the Chicago based street gang La Raza.

The Chicago based street gang called La Raza was founded in Chicago in 1972. La Raza was originally a part of the Party People and splintered away from that group. La Raza generally admits Hispanic members of Mexican ancestry. Although a member of the Folk nation, La Raza has at times warred against other Folk Nation gangs over turf and drug trade issues. According to the National Gang Intelligence Center (2013), La Raza maintains direct ties with the Mexican drug cartel Los Zetas to purchase drugs (NGIC, 2014, pp. 22–23). According to the Chicago Crime Commission, La Raza has at least 830 members (Hubbard et al., 2012, pp. 82–85; Chicagogangs.org, 2014, La Raza).

Common La Raza Markings

La Raza uses red, white, and green as their primary colors. These are the same colors as the Mexican flag. Other markings include the Mexican Flag, a brown eagle's head, a cross, a six-pointed star, and clothing displaying the Mexican flag. Sayings include "*Amor de Bandera*" (Hubbard et al., 2012, pp. 82–85; Chicagogangs.org, 2014, La Raza; Petrone, 1997, pp. 282–283).

Where the La Raza Are

Members of La Raza have been reported in Alaska, Arizona, Florida, Georgia, Illinois, Indiana, Iowa, Michigan, Nebraska, New York, Ohio, Virginia, and Wisconsin (NGIC, 2013, pp. 49–79; Hubbard et al., 2012, pp. 82–85; Chicagogangs.org, 2014, La Raza).

Latin Dragons

The Latin Dragons began in Chicago in the early 1980s and were associated with the Latin Kings. The Latin Dragons also claimed People Nation affiliation. A split with the Latin Kings during the 1990s resulted in the Latin Counts abandoning the People Nation and joining the Folks Nation. That resulted in a war between the Latin Kings and the Latin Counts that continues to this day. The members of the Latin Dragons are mostly Hispanic. The Chicago Crime Commission estimates that the Latin Dragons has at least 330 members (Hubbard et al., 2012, pp. 94–95; Chicagogangs.org, 2014, Latin Dragons).

Common Latin Dragons Markings

The Latin Dragons use white and black as their primary colors. Other markings include a dragon, a five-point diamond, a diamond with six dots, and a black jogging suit with white stripes (Hubbard et al., 2012, pp. 94–95; Chicagogangs.org, 2014, Latin Dragons; Petrone, 1997, pp. 298–299).

Where the Latin Dragons Are

Members of the Latin Dragons have been reported in Illinois and Indiana (Hubbard et al., 2012, pp. 94–95; Chicagogangs.org, 2014, Latin Dragons).

Latin Eagles (aka Almighty Latin Eagles)

The Latin Eagles sprang out of two Latino political movements in Chicago in the 1960s. Among the founders of the Latin Eagles was Thomas "Pops" Jimenez (paroled from Illinois Department of Corrections in 2009 for armed robbery), who has an extensive arrest record. The Latin Eagles consists of mostly Latino members, and their criminal activities include drug trafficking, auto theft, and armed robbery. The Chicago Crime Commission estimates that the Latin Eagles have at least 215 members (Hubbard et al., 2012, pp. 96–97; Chicagogangs.org, 2014, Latin Eagles; National Young Lords, 2014).

Common Latin Eagles Markings

The Latin Eagles use grey and black as their primary colors. Other markings include three dots, an eagle, a cursive letter E, and Philadelphia Eagles sportswear (Hubbard et al., 2012, pp. 96–97; Chicagogangs.org, 2014, Latin Eagles; Petrone, 1997, pp. 305–308).

Where the Latin Eagles Are

Members of the Latin Eagles have been reported in Illinois, Iowa, and Texas (Hubbard et al., 2012, pp. 96–97; Chicagogangs.org, 2014, Latin Eagles).

Latin Jivers (aka Insane Latin Jivers, Insane Latin Jivers Nation, 12–10, LJs)

The Latin Jivers formed in Chicago from a splinter group of the Maniac Latin Disciples in the 1980s. The gang included some members of a disbanded gang known as the Latin Stars. The Latin Jivers admit mostly Latino members, and are involved in drug trafficking, auto theft, and armed robbery. The Chicago Crime Commission estimates the Latin Jivers have at least 150 members (Hubbard et al., 2012, pp. 98–99; Chicago-gangs.org, 2014, Latin Jivers).

Common Latin Jivers Markings

The Latin Jivers use brown and black as their primary colors. Other markings include a skull with top hat and cane, and a hooded figure with pitchfork. Sayings include "Black n brown cracking crowns throwing forks down," "Jivers Crazy," and "Run up and gun up" (Hubbard et al., 2012, pp. 98–99; Chicagogangs.org, 2014, Latin Jivers).

Where the Latin Jivers Are

Members of the Latin Jivers have only been reported in Illinois (Hubbard et al., 2012, pp. 98–99; Chicagogangs.org, 2014, Latin Jivers).

Latin Lovers (aka Insane Latin Lovers, LLN, ILLN)

The Latin Lovers were formed in Chicago in the 1970s as a People Nation gang from former members of the Latin Kings and the Spanish Lords. Internal disputes over drug turf with other People Nation factions led the Latin Lovers to flip and join the Folk Nation around 1990. The Latin Lovers admit mostly Latino members, and the Chicago Crime Commission estimates that the Latin Lovers have at least 120 members (Hubbard et al., 2012, pp. 108–109; Chicagogangs.org, 2014, Latin Lovers).

Common Latin Lovers Markings

The Latin Lovers use red and yellow as their primary colors. Other markings include a heart surrounding an N with a line through it and three dots above, a heart with an N in the middle with or without wings, and a pitchfork with an N on top and three dots above. Sayings include "*Los Pocos Locos*" and "The Few But Crazy" (Hubbard et al., 2012, pp. 108–109; Chicagogangs.org, 2014, Latin Lovers; Petrone, 1997, pp. 320–321).

Where the Latin Lovers Are

Members of the Latin Lovers have been reported in Florida and Illinois (Hubbard et al., 2012, pp. 108–109; Chicagogangs.org, 2014, Latin Lovers).

Latin Souls (aka Insane Latin Souls, Maniac Latin Souls, LSN)

The Latin Souls began in Chicago in 1962 or 1964. One of the founding members was Hector Sanchez (aka "Poncho"). Sanchez died in 1995 of a heart attack. The Latin

Souls admits mostly Latino members, and their primary crimes are drug trafficking, armed robbery, arson, auto theft, and theft. The Chicago Crime Commission estimates that there are at least 105 members, but other estimates range as high as 400 (Hubbard et al., 2012, pp. 110–111; Chicagogangs.org, 2014, Latin Souls; Chicagonations.webs, 2014, Latin Souls).

Common Latin Souls Markings

The Latin Souls use maroon and black as their primary colors. Other markings include a cross with three circles on each point. Sayings include "*Amor de Alma*" and "Soul Love or No Love" (Hubbard et al., 2012, pp. 110–111; Chicagogangs.org, 2014, Latin Souls; Chicagonations.webs, 2014, Latin Souls; Petrone, 1997, pp. 329–331).

Where the Latin Souls Are

Members of the Latin Souls have been reported in Florida, Illinois, Mississippi, Missouri, New Jersey, and Texas (Hubbard et al., 2012, pp. 110–111; Chicagogangs.org, 2014, Latin Souls; Chicagonations.webs, 2014, Latin Souls).

Latin Stylers (aka Insane Latin Stylers, LSN, MLSN)

The Latin Stylers began in Chicago in the 1960s, and consist of mostly Hispanic members. The primary crimes of the Latin Stylers are drug trafficking, armed robbery, and auto theft. The Chicago Crime Commission estimates that the Latin Stylers have at least 110 members (Hubbard et al., 2012, pp. 112–113; Chicagogangs.org, 2014, Latin Stylers).

Common Latin Stylers Markings

The Latin Stylers use maroon and gray as their primary colors. Other markings include a shield with "LS" in the middle. Sayings include "*Amor de Estilo*" (Hubbard et al., 2012, pp. 112–113; Chicagogangs.org, 2014, Latin Stylers).

Where the Latin Stylers Are

Members of the Latin Stylers have only been reported in Illinois (Hubbard et al., 2012, pp. 112–113; Chicagogangs.org, 2014, Latin Stylers).

Maniac Latin Disciples (aka MLD, MLDN, FMLDN)

The Maniac Latin Disciples were founded in Chicago in 1966 by Albert "Hitler" Hernandez, who was known as the "King" of the club. In his honor, they adopted a backwards swastika as their symbol. The gang largely consisted of Hispanics and fought with Caucasian gangs in the neighborhood over turf issues. Hernandez was murdered in 1970 by the Latin Kings. In the mid-1970s the Maniac Latin Disciples had joined United Latino Organization, but by 1978 they had joined the Folk Nation. The MLD is a hierarchical gang with given ranks. Hernandez was the King, and no other member has held that title since his death. Other titles include Prince, Don, Chief of Security, Enforcers, Soldiers, and Shorties; some gang sets make up their own titles. The MLD also operate as a prison gang. Primary crimes of the MLD include drug trafficking, armed robbery, auto theft, kidnapping, and extortion. The MLD still largely consists of Hispanic members but also admits Caucasians and African Americans. The Chicago Crime Commission estimates that the MLD has at least 2,700 members (Hubbard et al., 2012, pp. 114–117; Chicagogangs.org, 2014, MLD; latinprisongangs.blogspot.com, 2009b, Maniac Latin Disciples).

Common Maniac Latin Disciples Markings

The Maniac Latin Disciples use light blue and black as their primary colors. Other markings include a heart with wings, horns and tail; a backwards swastika; a devil's head; a pitchfork; a hooded figure with horns; Georgetown Hoyas sportswear; University of North Carolina Tar Heels sportswear; and Detroit Tigers sportswear (Hubbard et al., 2012, pp. 114–117; Chicagogangs.org, 2014, MLD; latinprisongangs.blogspot.com, 2009b, Maniac Latin Disciples; Petrone, 1997, pp. 294–295).

Where the Maniac Latin Disciples Are

Members of the Maniac Latin Disciples have been reported in Florida, Illinois, Massachusetts, Michigan, Tennessee, Texas, Wisconsin, and Puerto Rico (Hubbard et al., 2012, pp. 114–117; Chicagogangs.org, 2014, MLD; latinprisongangs.blogspot.com, 2009b, Maniac Latin Disciples).

Milwaukee Kings (aka 13–11, MKN, MKz)

The Milwaukee Kings formed as a faction of the Latin Kings in the 1970s. Due to disputes with the Latin Kings in the early 1980s, the Milwaukee Kings split from the Latin Kings and joined the Folk Nation. The Milwaukee Kings' primary crimes include drug trafficking, theft, robbery, and kidnapping. The Milwaukee Kings admit mostly Latino members. The Chicago Crime Commission estimates that the Milwaukee Kings have at least 170 members (Hubbard et al., 2012, pp. 122–123; Chicagogangs. org, 2014, MKN).

Common Milwaukee Kings Markings

The Milwaukee Kings use black and orange as their primary colors. Other markings include a king with a five-point crown and the numbers 13 and 11 (Hubbard et al., 2012, pp. 122–123; Chicagogangs.org, 2014, MKN; Petrone, 1997, pp. 332–334).

Where the Milwaukee Kings Are

Members of the Milwaukee Kings have been reported in Illinois, Wisconsin, and Canada (Hubbard et al., 2012, pp. 122–123; Chicagogangs.org, 2014, MKN).

Morgan Boys

The Morgan Boys are a small Latino gang that began in Chicago in 1989. The founder, known as "Chuckkie," initially aligned his group with the Party People and joined the Folk Nation. The Morgan Boys broke away from the Party People shortly after that and a war with the Party People resulted. Chuckkie was murdered in 1990 allegedly by the Party People. The gang lives on but has never been very large (Hubbard et al., 2012, pp. 124–125; Chicagogangs.org, 2014, Morgan Boys).

Common Morgan Boys Markings

The Morgan Boys use red and blue as their primary colors. Other markings include downward spears, the letters M and B, a six-pointed star, six dots, and a cross with slashes through the center (Hubbard et al., 2012, pp. 124–125; Chicagogangs.org, 2014, Morgan Boys; Petrone, 1997, pp. 335–337).

Where the Morgan Boys Are

Members of the Morgan Boys have been reported in Illinois and Indiana (Hubbard et al., 2012, pp. 124–125; Chicagogangs.org, 2014, Morgan Boys).

New Breeds (aka 2–7, Black Gangsters, Breed, New Breed Disciples, Trey-L's)

The New Breed is an African American street gang that began in Chicago as a split from the Gangster Disciple Nation (GDN). The gang has undergone various name changes over the years beginning as the Black Gangsters. George E. Davis (aka Boonie Black) split the Black Gangsters from the Gangster Disciple Nation after the death of David Barksdale in 1972 and the resulting power struggle within the GDN. Davis was an inmate in the

Illinois Department of Corrections at the time and ran the gang from the prison. Davis was stabbed in prison by a member of the Black Souls gang in 1987 in an attempted hit. One of his lieutenants was killed in the attack (Knox, 1996, p. 67). The Black Gangsters are a hierarchical organization and modeled their organizational structure after the royal family concept of the Mafia. New Breed ranks include Don, King, Prince, General, Field Marshall, Commander, Lieutenant, and Members. Davis became the Don of the gang. Although they were in conflict with the Black Souls and the Gangster Disciple Nation, the Black Gangsters remained as a part of the Folk Nation. The group also was known as the Trey-L's because of their philosophy (Love, Life, and Loyalty). The Black Gangsters gained recruits from other Folk groups that opposed Larry Hoover's harsh "street taxes" on criminal activities and complaints about lack of gang support for incarcerated members. Sometime in the 1990s Davis changed the name of the gang again to the New Breeds. Davis died of cancer in 2009. Thousands attended his funeral (Brown, 2009).

In the early 1980s, the Black Gangsters followed the lead of some other Folk Nation groups and established a short-lived political action group known as the Concerned Youth Association (CYA) in the area of Cook County, Illinois. These groups were designed to give political cover and influence to the group, however CYA did not last very long. The New Breeds criminal activities include drug trafficking, armed robbery, theft, kidnapping, illegal dog-fighting, gambling, illegal firearms trafficking, and money laundering. The Chicago Crime Commission estimates that the New Breed has at least 1,740 members. However, other estimates range as high as 15,000 (Hubbard et al., 2012, pp. 128–131; Chicagogangs.org, 2014, New Breed; Knox, 1996, pp. 64–76).

Common New Breed Markings

The New Breeds use the colors black and blue or black and gray as their primary colors. Other markings include COS in a diamond, the letters LLL, the roman numeral III, the numbers 2 and 7, BGN, and a box with a circle in it (Hubbard et al., 2012, pp. 128–131; Chicagogangs.org, 2014, New Breed; Knox, 1996, pp. 64–76; Petrone, 1997, pp. 195–197).

Where the New Breeds Are

Members of the New Breeds have been reported in Georgia, Illinois, Indiana, Iowa, Louisiana, and Wisconsin (NGIC, 2013, pp. 49–79; Hubbard et al., 2012, pp. 128–131; Chicagogangs.org, 2014, New Breed; Knox, 1996, pp. 64–76).

Orchestra Albany (aka OA, IAO, OAN, Insane Orchestra Albany Nation)

The Orchestra Albany (La Orquesta Albany) began in Chicago as a salsa band. In 1971, one of the members of the band was murdered by a member of the Latin Kings. "Sugar

Bear" founded the gang and used the same colors as the band (black and gold) for their symbols. The gang joined the Folk Nation because of their opposition to the Latin Kings who were with the People Nation. In 1978, Sugar Bear murdered Queen Lefty (a Latin King female) in retaliation for the murder of another Orchestra Albany member named Half Pint by the Latin Kings. Sugar Bear then fled to Puerto Rico to avoid prosecution. After joining the Folks, the OA was heavily allied with the United Latino Organization and the Young Latino Organization. The Orchestra Albany admits mostly Latino members. The Chicago Crime Commission estimates that the Orchestra Albany has at least 230 members (Hubbard et al., 2012, pp. 132–135; Chicagogangs.org, 2014, Orchestra Albany).

Common Orchestra Albany Markings

The Orchestra Albany uses black and gold or yellow as their primary colors. Black and brown are sometimes used by OA members. Other markings include the letters O and A in various configurations, a four-point diamond tipped spear with three dots, and the letter O with an A inside the circle (Hubbard et al., 2012, pp. 132–135; Chicago gangs.org, 2014, Orchestra Albany; Petrone, 1997, pp. 342–345).

Where the Orchestra Albany Are

Members of the Orchestra Albany have only been reported in Illinois (Hubbard et al., 2012, pp. 132–135; Chicagogangs.org, 2014, Orchestra Albany).

Party People (aka PP, PPN, Gangster Party People, GPPN)

The Party People began in Chicago in the 1970s as a party crew in the Pilsen area. The initial leader of the Party Crew, Michael, was stabbed to death. The party crew gradually became a street gang within the Folk Nation. The Party People admits mostly Latino members. The Chicago Crime Commission estimates that the Party People has at least 215 members (Hubbard et al., 2012, pp. 138–141; Chicagogangs.org, 2014, Party People).

Common Party People Markings

The Party People use white and black as their primary colors. Other markings include a Playboy bunny and a cross with three slashes above and a circle on the bottom (Hubbard et al., 2012, pp. 138–141; Chicagogangs.org, 2014, Party People; Petrone, 1997, pp. 350–353)

Where the Party People Are

Members of the Party People have been reported in Illinois and Kentucky (Hubbard et al., 2012, pp. 138–141; Chicagogangs.org, 2014, Party People).

Racine Boys (Insane Racine Boys, RB's, IRB's, RBz)

The Racine Boys are a small, mixed-race gang that began in Chicago prior to 1997. The gang has never been very large, but it has survived as a part of the Folk Nation for many years in Chicago and the surrounding areas (Hubbard et al., 2012, pp. 124–125; Chicagogangs.org, 2014, Racine Boys).

Common Racine Boys Markings

The Racine Boys use navy blue and light blue as their primary colors. Other markings include the letters R and B, a knight's helmet with a spiked plume, and a cross with a curved horizontal line and three dots above it. Sayings include "Racine" (Hubbard et al., 2012, pp. 124–125; Chicagogangs.org, 2014, Racine Boys; Petrone, 1997, pp. 363–365).

Where the Racine Boys Are

Members of the Racine Boys have only been reported in Illinois (Hubbard et al., 2012, pp. 124–125; Chicagogangs.org, 2014, Racine Boys).

Satan Disciples (aka Insane Gangster Satan Disciples, SD's, SDN, IGSD's, IGSDN)

The Satan Disciples began in Chicago in the Pilsen neighborhood in the early 1960s. The Satan Disciples were initially allied with David Barksdale and the Devil's Disciples. In 1978 the Satan Disciples joined the Folk Nation. The Satan Disciples is a hierarchical gang with a business-style command structure, formal constitution and set holidays (Knox, 2008a). Two of the primary Satan Disciples leaders, Danny "Gizmo" Velencia and Agapito "King Aggie" Villalobos, clashed in 1995 over internal differences, and Velencia was murdered. Villalobos and another gang member named Jose "Vicious" Trejo were prosecuted for the murder. Trejo was convicted of the murder of Velencia and Villalobos was acquitted (*Trejo v. Hulick*, 2004). The Satan Disciples is now run by a commission. The primary crimes committed by the Satan Disciples include drug trafficking, armed robbery, theft, ramming, and kidnapping. The Satan Disciples admits mostly Latino members. The Chicago Crime Commission estimates that the Satan Disciples have at least 2,700 members. Other estimates run as high as 9,000 members (Hubbard et al., 2012, pp. 152–155; Chicagogangs.org, 2014, Satan Disciples; Chicagonations.webs, 2014, Insane Gangster Satan Disciples; Knox, 2008a).

Common Satan Disciples Markings

The Satan Disciples use yellow and brown as their primary colors. Other markings include a devil, a pitchfork, a heart with wing horn and devil tail, a. six-pointed star, Grambling University sportswear, and Detroit Tigers sportswear. Sayings include "*Amor de Diablo*" (Hubbard et al., 2012, pp. 152–155; Chicagogangs.org, 2014, Satan Disciples; Petrone, 1997, pp. 368–372).

Where the Satan Disciples Are

Members of the Satan Disciples have been reported in 25 states (Hubbard et al., 2012, pp. 152–155; Chicagogangs.org, 2014, Satan Disciples; Chicagonations.webs, 2014, Insane Gangster Satan Disciples; Knox, 2008a).

Simon City Royals (aka Almighty Simon City Royals, SCR, ASCR, ASCRN, R's)

The Simon City Royals began in Chicago in 1960 after several white greaser street gangs in the Simons Park area combined to oppose the influx of Hispanic gangs coming into their neighborhoods. One of the original founding members, Rasher Zayed (aka "Arab"), was murdered in 1974 along with another Simon City Royals leader known as "Bimbo." The Simon City Royals joined the Folk Nation in 1976. The Simon City Royals are considered a prison gang that is allied with the Gangster Disciples by the Illinois Department of Corrections.

The primary crimes committed by the Simon City Royals include drug trafficking, illegal firearms trafficking, armed robbery, theft, extortion, money laundering, and kidnapping. The Simon City Royals admit mostly white members, and the Chicago Crime Commission estimates that the Simon City Royals have at least 360 members (Hubbard et al., 2012, pp. 156–157; Chicagogangs.org, 2014, Satan Disciples; Chicagonations.webs, 2014, Almighty SCR; stonegreaser.com, 2014c, SCR; whiteprisongangs.blogspot.com, 2014b, Simon City Royals; Ferranti, 2013b).

Common Simon City Royals Markings

The Simon City Royals use blue and black as their primary colors. Other markings include a cross with three slashes above it, a three-pointed crown, a Playboy bunny with ear bent, crossed shotguns, Kansas City Royals sportswear, and Colorado Rockies sportswear. Sayings include "Ain't No Pity in Simon City," "Cross is boss," "Black and Royal Blue burn through ur whole lil crew," and "R world" (Hubbard et al., 2012, pp. 156–157; Chicagogangs.org, 2014, Satan Disciples; Chicagonations.webs, 2014, Almighty SCR; stonegreaser.com, 2014c, SCR; whiteprisongangs.blogspot.com, 2014b, Simon City Royals; Ferranti, 2013b; Petrone, 1997, pp. 373–377).

Where the Simon City Royals Are

Members of the Simon City Royals have been reported in Florida, Illinois, Mississippi, Oklahoma, Tennessee, and Wisconsin (Hubbard et al., 2012, pp. 156–157; Chicagogangs.org, 2014, Satan Disciples; Chicagonations.webs, 2014, Almighty SCR; stonegreaser.com, 2014c, scr; whiteprisongangs.blogspot.com, 2014b, Simon City Royals; Ferranti, 2013b).

Sin City Boys (aka SCB, SCBN, Spanish Gangster SCB)

The Sin City Boys are a very small gang in the Chicago area that claims affiliation with the Folk Nation. Members of the Sin City Boys have been involved in some shootings and burglaries in the Chicago area and suburbs (Ahmed-Ullah & Ruzich, 2009). The members of the Sin City Boys are mostly white and Latino, and the Chicago Crime Commission estimates that the Sin City Boys have at least 25 members (Hubbard et al., 2012, pp. 158–159; Chicagogangs.org, 2014, Sin City Boys).

Common Sin City Boys Markings

The Sin City Boys use black and blue as their primary colors. Other markings include a hooded Playboy bunny with blunt, hearts and clubs symbols, and a sword with two lines and two dots (Hubbard et al., 2012, pp. 158–159; Chicagogangs.org, 2014, Sin City Boys).

Where the Sin City Boys Are

Members of the Sin City Boys have been reported in Illinois and Texas (Hubbard et al., 2012, pp. 158–159; Chicagogangs.org, 2014, Sin City Boys).

Spanish Cobras (aka Insane Spanish Cobras, S/C, ISCN)

The Insane Spanish Cobras began in Chicago in the early 1950s. The founder of the gang was Richard "King Cobra" Medina, who was murdered by rival gang the Insane Unknowns on April 13, 1979. The date is still celebrated as a holiday by the Spanish Cobras. King Cobra's brother, William Medina, helped to spread the Spanish Cobras to Wisconsin. William Medina was convicted of a murder in Wisconsin and sentenced to prison there. While in prison, William Medina led a prison uprising in 1983, and in 1993 he stabbed the warden of the Columbia Correctional Institution in Portage, Wisconsin (Tuerina, 1993).

The Spanish Cobras is considered to be a prison gang by the Illinois Department of Corrections and the Florida Department of Corrections (dc.fl, 2014). The Spanish Cobras' primary crimes include drug trafficking, illegal firearms trafficking, extortion, armed robbery, theft, kidnapping, and arson. The Spanish Cobras were founded by Puerto Rican youth originally and still admit mostly Latino members. The Chicago Crime Commission estimates that the Spanish Cobras have at least 1,570 members (Hubbard et al., 2012, pp. 160–163; Chicagogangs.org, 2014, Spanish Cobras).

Common Spanish Cobras Markings

The Spanish Cobras use green and black as their primary colors. Other markings include a king cobra snake, a four-point diamond with three dots, a diamond on a staff with three dots, and New York Jets sportswear. Sayings include "*Amor de Culebra*" (Hubbard et al., 2012, pp. 160–163; Chicagogangs.org, 2014, Spanish Cobras; Petrone, 1997, pp. 260–267).

Where the Spanish Cobras Are

The National Gang Intelligence reported the Insane Spanish Cobras were found in Illinois, Iowa, and Wisconsin (NGIC, 2013, pp. 49–79). Other sources report that the Spanish Cobras have been found in Connecticut, Florida, Indiana, New York, and Ohio (Hubbard et al., 2012, pp. 160–163; Chicagogangs.org, 2014, Spanish Cobras).

Spanish Gangster Disciples (SGD)

The Spanish Gangster Disciples began in Chicago in 1974 as a faction of the Maniac Latin Disciples. The gang was founded by former MLD member Rudy Rios after his release from prison. Rios was latter killed. The Spanish Cobras admit mostly Latino members, and the Chicago Crime Commission estimates that the Spanish Gangster Disciples have at least 470 members (Hubbard et al., 2012, pp. 166–167; Chicagogangs.org, 2014, SGD).

Common Spanish Gangster Disciples Markings

The Spanish Gangster Disciples use baby blue and black as their primary colors. Other markings include a heart with horns, wings and tail; a six-pointed star; a gangster crown; and Duke University sportswear (Hubbard et al., 2012, pp. 166–167; Chicagogangs.org, 2014, SGD; Petrone, 1997, pp. 378–382).

Where the Spanish Gangster Disciples Are

The Spanish Gangster Disciples have been reported only in Illinois (Hubbard et al., 2012, pp. 166–167; Chicagogangs.org, 2014, SGD).

People Nation

The People Nation began as a loose alliance of 28 gangs that originated in Chicago area jails in the late 1950s and early 1960s. In the 1980s and 1990s, the People expanded to operate from east of the Rocky Mountains to the East Coast of the United States. During this period, the People were one of the first non–New York gangs to thrive in New York City. By 2014, the People had a truly national presence, although there are not that many sets on the West Coast of the United States. The gangs in the People Nation are hierarchical and have a paramilitary structure and organization (Buccellato, 2013). Many People Nation gangs have formal constitutions and celebrate set gang holidays. People Nation gangs are very territorial and engage in turf wars. Like the Folk Nation, People Nation gangs are sometimes involved in political movements or political action groups as well as criminal acts. People Nation gangs have set up social service groups that acted as a front for criminal activities and facilitated fraud from U.S. government grants. People Nation gang members generally aligns to the left in dress and symbols. The People Nation maintains a very loose alliance with the Los Angeles based Bloods, but will fight sets from that group if interests in drug trade or turf occur.

Gangs sometimes grow and expand. They also shrink and disappear because of imprisonment, death, or disinterest. The following are some People Nation gangs that are no longer active: Freaks (aka Insane Freaks, Rebel Freaks, Stone Freaks), Future Stones, Jousters (aka Taylor Street Jousters), Kenmore Boys, Kents (aka Stone Kents), King Cobras, Latin Lovers, Noble Knights, Party Gents, Villa Lobos, and Warlords (Chicago Gang History, 2017).

BOX 3.2 Jeff Fort and the Founding of the People Nation

Jeff Fort was born on February 20, 1947 in Aberdeen, Mississippi. His family moved to the south side of Chicago in 1955 when Fort was eight. Fort dropped out of school after the ninth grade and soon found himself in trouble with the law. As a juvenile, Fort was incarcerated at various times at the Cook County Temporary Juvenile Detention Center (Audy Home) and at the Illinois State Training School for Boys in St. Charles, Illinois. It was at the latter institution that Fort met fellow inmate Eugene "Bull" Hairston, and they and a few friends formed a gang that became known as the Blackstone Rangers in 1959.

The gang expanded and grew becoming the Black P. Stone Nation (BPSN) and was ruled by a council called the "Main 21." The BPSN under the leadership of Fort, Hairston, and Mickey Cogwell expanded beyond street crime and became involved in political organizations in the Chicago area. They also founded social service organizations which they used as a front for gang activities and to defraud the government and private foundations out of grant monies. In 1972, Fort was convicted of defrauding the government and misuse of federal funds (Lindberg, 2016, pp. 306–316).

While he was in prison, Fort converted to Islam. Upon his release from prison in 1976, Fort seized control of BPSN in what has been described as a coup. He changed the name of the gang to El Rukn to reflect his embracing Islam and to aid in shielding the gang's activities from law enforcement. In 1978 Fort helped form the alliance that became the People Nation. Many People Nation gangs use the five-pointed star of Islam as a symbol to reflect and honor Jeff Fort's Islamic beliefs.

12th Street Players (aka TPN, Almighty TPN, Players)

The 12th Street Players formed in Cicero, Illinois, in the 1960s around the corners of 12th Street and Austin. The gang was formed largely of Italian Americans at its founding and latter Slavic Americans. The 12th Street Players are still largely white, although some members are not. The 12th Street Players were run out of Chicago for a while after intergang warfare with the Folks, Latin Kings and Latin Counts in the 1980s up to 1996. However, beginning in 2000 the gang has reemerged and expanded into Chicago and the surrounding suburbs. The Chicago Crime Commission estimates that they have at least 50 members in seven identified sets in the Chicago area (Hubbard et al., 2012, p. 20; Chicagogang.org, 2014, 12th Street Players; Stonegreasers.com, 2014a, 12th Street Players).

Common 12th Street Players Markings

The 12th Street Players use black and white as their colors. The gang also uses the symbols of a cane, top hat, five-pointed star, Playboy bunny, and shield. Sayings include "Almighty Don't Like Nobody!" (Hubbard et al., 2012, pp. 20–21; Chicagogangs.org, 2014, 12th Street Players; Stonegreasers.com, 2014a, 12th Street Players; Petrone, 1997, p. 169).

Where the 12th Street Players Are

Members of the 12th Street Players have only been reported in Illinois (Hubbard et al., 2012, p. 20, Chicagogang.org, 2014, 12th Street Players; Stonegreasers.com, 2014a, 12th Street Players).

Belizean Bloods

The Belizean Bloods are a relatively new gang in the Chicago area. They formed in the late 2000s and operate in a rather narrow area around the Wrigleyville neighborhood and Evanston, mainly in Rastafarian bars. The membership consists of immigrants from Belize. While the Bloods in the country in Belize maintain their affiliation as an L.A. based street gang, the Belizean Bloods in the Chicago area claim a People Nation affiliation. The Belizean Bloods engage in primarily in the drug trade and in passport fraud. This group is estimated to have about 100 members (Hubbard et al., 2012, p. 28; Olivo, 2011).

Common Belizean Bloods Markings

The Belizean Bloods use red and black as their primary colors (Hubbard et al., 2012, p. 29).

Where the Belizean Bloods Are

Members of the Belizean Bloods have been reported in California, Illinois, Indiana, New York, and Ohio (Olivo, 2011).

Bishops (Almighty Bishops)

Beginning as a baseball team in the 1960s, the Bishops gradually around 1970 became a faction of the Latin Counts. Then as a splinter group from the Latin Counts, the Bishops began as a separate gang in the early 1980s in the Chicago area near 18th Street and Bishop Avenue. The Bishops are largely Hispanic, and according to the Chicago Crime Commission they have at least 240 members. The gang engages in the drug trade, theft, and robbery, and is known for its violence (Hubbard et al., 2012, p. 26; Chicagogangs.org, 2014, Bishops).

Common Bishops Markings

The Bishops use copper (sometimes brown) and black as their primary colors. A common Bishops saying is "Black and Copper Always Proper." Other symbols include a bishop's miter (although this has no religious significance), a cross, a bishop figure, the letter B, and a five-pointed star (Hubbard et al., 2012, p. 30; Chicagogangs.org, 2014, Bishops; Petrone, 1997, p. 185).

Where the Bishops Are

Members of the Bishops have been reported in Illinois, Iowa, and New York (NGIC, 2013, pp. 49–79; Hubbard et al., 2012, p. 26; Chicagogangs.org, 2014, Bishops).

Black P. Stone Nation (aka BPSN, Almighty Black P-Stones)

The Black P. Stone Nation began in Chicago as a local street gang in about 1957–1960. They were originally called the Blackstone Rangers. The gang started among inmates at the Illinois Youth Center, St. Charles. One of the original founders of the gang was Jeff Fort (aka "King Bull"), along with his fellow inmate Eugene "Bull" Hairston (aka "King Ball"; Knox, 2006, p. 803). About 1959, the Blackstone Rangers began to combine with other local gangs to form an even larger gang that eventually became the Black P. Stone Nation (Sale, 1971, pp. 63–64). The BPSN is a hierarchical gang with a formal leadership structure. Initially in the 1960s the Blackstones gang was ruled by a ruling council known as the "Main 21," which included various gang faction leaders including Fort, Hairston, and Henry "Mickey" Cogwell.

During this period, many leaders of the Blackstones were advised by the Reverend John Fry of the First Presbyterian Church, who was trying to provide social services and counseling for youth and gang members (Moore & Williams, 2011, pp. 49–53). Hairston and Fort used the opportunity to develop social service organizations that served as fronts for gang activities. They applied for and received over a million dollars in grants from the federal government and private foundations. Rev. Fry disassociated himself from BPSN in 1971.

Hairston went to prison in 1966. Fort became the leader of the Blackstones and in 1968 renamed the gang the Black P. Stone Nation. The gang also became politically active and formed "The Grassroots Independent Voters of Illinois." In 1969, Jeff Fort received an invitation from President Richard Nixon to attend his inaugural ball. Fort declined and sent Mickey Cogwell and another gang member instead. In 1972, Fort was convicted and sent to prison for defrauding the federal government and misuse of federal funds.

El Rukn and the Islamic Faction of BPSN

During Fort's incarceration in the U.S. penitentiary at Leavenworth, he became interested in Islam. By the time he was released from federal prison in 1976, he had converted to Islam and adopted the name Prince Imam Malik. Fort joined the Moorish Science Temple and renamed the Black P. Stone Nation as El Rukn. In 1976, the Main 21 disbanded after disagreements between Fort and Harrison and the rise of BPSN's Islamic faction El Rukn (Moore & Williams, 2011, pp. 34–38). Fort began to hide the gang's activities behind the façade of a religious movement, knowing that law enforcement's investigations into religions were severely limited by the First Amendment of the U.S. Constitution. Original Main 21 member Henry "Mickey" Cogwell was murdered on February 25, 1977. The crime was never solved. However, the Cobra Stones blamed Jeff Fort for the killing because there had been disagreements between the two gang leaders. In 1978, Jeff Fort led the El Rukns to join with several other gangs into the formation of the People Nation (Lindberg, 2016, pp. 306–316).

Fort went to prison again in 1983 for drug charges and was sentenced to 13 years. Fort continued to run the gang from prison at the Federal Correctional Institution at Bastrop, Texas. In 1987, Fort was convicted of conspiring with Libya to commit domestic terrorist acts in the United States and trying to illegally obtain heavy weapons. Fort was sentenced to 80 years and moved to the USP Marion supermax (Lindberg, 2016, pp. 306–316).

Original Blackstone Rangers founder Eugene "Bull" Hairston was murdered in September 1988. Although Fort was in prison at the time of the murder, he was suspected of ordering the hit on Hairston (Thorton & Blau, 1988). In 1988, Fort was again charged and convicted with the 1981 murder of another gang leader, resulting in another 75-year sentence. This time the federal government moved Fort to the newly opened ADX Florence supermax prison in Colorado and banned him from all human contact (Hubbard et al., 2012, p. 33; Chicagogangs.org, 2014, BPSN). By 1991, further convictions of El Rukn leaders and members had severely reduced El Rukn's effectiveness as a street gang, but it still remained a factor in prison (Blau & O'Brien, 1991).

The Reformation of BPSN

Although El Rukn is inactive as a street gang, the BPSN has reorganized on the streets of Chicago and elsewhere. The BPSN admits mainly African American members, and the Chicago Crime Commission estimates that the BPSN could have as many as 20,000 members on the street and another 3,000 currently in prison (Hubbard et al., 2012, pp. 32–37; Chicagogangs.org, 2014, BPSN).

Factions of the BPSN

According to the Chicago Crime Commission, there are currently seven subfactions of the Black P. Stone Nation still operating in the Chicago area: Apache Stones, Black P. Stones, Familia Stones, Gangster Stones, Jet Black Stones, Rubinite Stones and Titanic Stones (Hubbard et al., 2012, pp. 64–65). Some of the factions still claim allegiance to BPSN, while others do not.

Common BPSN Markings

The BPSN use green, red and black as their colors. Other markings include a pyramid with 20 bricks, a rising sun and eye, a crescent moon, the number 7, and a five-pointed star. Sayings include "All is well," "Stone to the Bone," and "High Five-Six Must Die" (Hubbard et al., 2012, pp. 32–37; Chicagogangs.org, 2014, BPSN; Petrone, 1997, pp. 198–210, 217–218).

Where the BPSN Are

The BPSN has been reported by the National Gang Intelligence Center in Florida, Illinois, Indiana, Iowa, Massachusetts, Minnesota, North Carolina, and Wisconsin (NGIC, 2013, pp. 49–79). Other sources report BPSN members in Arkansas, California, Georgia, Kentucky, Michigan, Mississippi, Missouri, New Jersey, New York, Ohio, South Carolina, South Dakota, Tennessee, Texas, and Virginia (Hubbard et al., 2012, pp. 32–37; Chicagogangs.org, 2014, BPSN).

Familia Stones (aka La Familia Stones, Puerto Rican Stones)

The Familia Stones was formed in 1968 as the Puerto Rican Stones by Danny Velez in the Chicago corrections facilities and the area around the Logan Square neighborhood in Chicago. The gang was affiliated with the Blackstone Rangers. However, Velez was not given a seat on the "Main 21" ruling council by Jeff Fort. In 1977, when Fort split off into El Rukn, the Puerto Rican Stones went their own way. In the mid-1990s the "Puerto Rican" designation was dropped from the gang's name to better reflect the current membership. The Familia Stones consist largely of Hispanic members but allows some African American and Caucasian members, and the Chicago Crime Commission estimates that Familia Stones has at least 300 members. The gang is involved in drug sales in the Chicago area (Hubbard et al., 2012, pp. 40–41; Chicagogangs.org, 2014, Familia Stones).

Common Familia Stones Markings

The Familia Stones use orange and black as their primary colors. Other markings include a sword, a pyramid with a 5, a diamond, a crescent moon, and San Francisco Giants sportswear (Hubbard et al., 2012, pp. 40–41; Chicagogangs.org, 2014, Familia Stones; Petrone, 1997, p. 359).

Where the Familia Stones Are

Members of the Familia Stones have been reported in Illinois and Iowa (NGIC, 2013, pp. 49–79; Hubbard et al., 2012, pp. 40–41; Chicagogangs.org, 2014, Familia Stones).

Four Corner Hustlers (aka 4CH)

The Four Corner Hustlers was founded in Chicago by King Walter Wheat (aka "Walt," "Al-Bahdee Hodari"), Freddy Gage Jr. (aka "Freddy Malik," "Al-Malik Hodari"),

Monroe Banks Jr. (aka "Money," "Al-Ghani") and Richard Goodwin (aka "Lefthand," "Al-Mustafa") in an area that covered four corners on six square blocks on the West Side. Freddy Gage died in the late 1980s while he was incarcerated (Gangworld, 2009). Monroe Banks was killed in 1992 during a drug deal. Walter Wheat was murdered in 1994 in an internal gang conflict (Papajohn, 1994). Richard Goodwin was also murdered in 1994 in an internal gang conflict shortly after the murder of Wheat (Hill, 1997).

The apparent winner of the internal gang conflict within the Four Corner Hustlers was Angelo Roberts. He began to expand the gang and undercut the street tax (an amount to be paid to the gang for the privilege of doing business on their corner) that had been set by the Vice Lords, of which at one time they were either a faction or allied with. Roberts hated the Chicago Police Department and was so bold as to actually plot to attack a police precinct headquarters in the 1990s in Area 4. Robert's frozen body was found in a car trunk in January 1995 (Hubbard et al., 2012, pp. 48–51; Chicagogangs. org, 2014, 4CH; Gangworld, 2009).

Today the modern Four Corner Hustlers is estimated to have at least 6,500 members by the Chicago Crime Commission. The gang's membership is largely African American, however there is a subset of about 70 members that identifies as the Spanish Four Corner Hustlers in Chicago and uses black and red as their colors. New members are required to memorize "The Lit," which is the gang's creed and a statement of conduct. The Four Corner Hustlers are still involved in the drug trade and noted for their violence. However, they are also known for their incredible diversity and adaptability in committing crimes such as armed robbery, extortion, prostitution, weapons sales, and money laundering. The gang is even known to operate legitimate businesses (always good for money laundering; Hubbard et al., 2012, pp. 48–51; Chicagogangs.org, 2014, 4CH; Dwyer, 2012).

Common Four Corner Hustler Markings

The Four Corner Hustlers use gold and black as their primary colors. They also sometimes use red and black as their alternate colors. Other markings include a pyramid with a crescent moon, a top hat with cane and gloves, a champagne glass, a Playboy bunny head with straight ears, a crescent moon with a five-pointed star, a dollar sign and globes, the number 4 and the letters CH, and New Orleans Saints or Purdue University sportswear (Hubbard et al., 2012, pp. 48–51; Chicagogangs.org, 2014, 4CH; Petrone, 1997, p. 397).

Where the Four Corner Hustlers Are

Members of the Four Corner Hustlers have been reported in Illinois, Indiana, Iowa, Kansas, Minnesota, New York, Ohio, Tennessee, Texas, Washington, and Wisconsin, as well as Mexico (NGIC, 2013, pp. 49–79; Hubbard et al., 2012, pp. 48–51; Chicago gangs.org, 2014, Four Corner Hustlers).

Fourth Generation Messiahs (aka 4GM, Almighty Fourth Generation Messiahs)

Starting as a tagging crew in the Cicero, Illinois, area in the 1980s, by the 1990s the Fourth Generation Messiahs had evolved into a criminal street gang that claimed alliance with the People Nation. The group began to spread into surrounding areas. The Fourth Generation Messiahs have both Latino and white members, and the Chicago Crime Commission estimates they have as least 20 members in the Chicago area (Hubbard et al., 2012, pp. 54–55; Chicagogangs.org, 2014, 4GM).

Common Fourth Generation Messiahs Markings

The Fourth Generation Messiahs use gold and white as their primary colors. Other markings include a four-point crown with the letter M, and the roman numeral IV. Sayings include "Quad Love" (Hubbard et al., 2012, pp. 54–55; Chicagogangs.org, 2014, 4GM).

Where the Fourth Generation Messiahs Are

Members of the Fourth Generation Messiahs have been reported in California, Illinois, and Wisconsin (Hubbard et al., 2012, pp. 54–55; Chicagogangs.org, 2014, 4GM).

Gaylords (aka GL, Almighty Gaylord Nation)

The Gaylords formed from an Italian youth gang on the North Side of Chicago in the 1950s. Gaylords stands for "Great American Youth Love Our Race Destroy Spics/Scum." The gang initially had white supremacist leanings. In the late 1950s and 1960s, the Gaylords were a white "greaser" gang. By the 1970s, the Gaylords had an estimated membership of over 1,000 (White Prison Gangs, 2014a). During the 1970s and 1980s the Gaylords fought other street gangs for turf in several Chicago area neighborhoods (Scott, 2009, pp. 3–4). However, in the 1980s the Gaylords became affiliated with the People Nation and abandoned (at least publicly) most of their racist attitudes. Although the Gaylord members are still primarily Caucasian, the Chicago Crime Commission estimates that there are at least 210 members of the Gaylords (Hubbard et al., 2012, pp. 66–67; Chicagogangs.org, 2014, Gaylords).

Gaylords in Jails and Prisons

In county jails, Gaylords usually maintain their cohesive gang structure, especially in areas where they are most active. The Illinois Department of Corrections classifies them as a prison gang (White Prison Gangs, 2014a).

Common Gaylord Markings

The Gaylords use light blue and black as their primary colors. Alternate Gaylord colors are light gray and black. Other markings include a Maltese cross with flames at the center, a cross with two slashes, a swastika, the letters G and L, a hooded figure, and the number 3. Gaylord sayings include "God forgives, Gaylords Don't" and "Cross is Boss" (Hubbard et al., 2012, pp. 66–67; Chicagogangs.org, 2014, Gaylords; Petrone, 1997, pp. 230–231).

Where the Gaylords Are

Members of the Gaylords have been reported in Illinois, Iowa, Kentucky, and Missouri (Hubbard et al., 2012, pp. 66–67; Chicagogangs.org, 2014, Gaylords).

Insane Popes [Southside] (aka Almighty Royal Insane Popes, IPN, IIPN, Ips)

When talking about the Popes, a researcher or police officer needs to know whether they are talking about the South Side of Chicago, where the Popes affiliate with the People Nation, or the North Side of Chicago, where the Popes affiliate with the Folk Nation. What makes it even more confusing is that both groups use different variations of the same colors—blue, black, and white—to identify the group. However, "North Side" and "South Side" are clearly printed on their business cards. In 1974 or 1975, the Popes leader Larry "Larkin" Morris started a branch of the Popes that was on the South Side of Chicago.

When Morris was murdered in 1975 by the Gaylords, the North Side Popes joined the Folk Nation and the South Side Popes initially chose to remain independent. In 1978, the South Side Popes joined the People Nation. The Popes from the South Side are a mostly white gang but admit blacks and Hispanics as members. The gang from the South Side has never been as large as their cousins from the North Side (Hubbard et al., 2012, pp. 144–147; Chicagogangs.org, 2014, SSPopes).

Common Insane Popes (Southside) Markings

The Insane Popes use either black and white as their primary colors. Other markings include a cloaked figure with or without two slash marks and/or a halo, a shotgun, the letter P, a four-pointed diamond with/or without three slash marks, white t-shirts, black pants, and black Converse high-tops (Hubbard et al., 2012, pp. 144–147; Chicago-gangs.org, 2014, SSPopes; Petrone, 1997, pp. 251–254).

Where the Insane Popes (Southside) Are

Members of the Insane Popes have been reported in Illinois, Indiana, and Iowa (NGIC, 2013, pp. 49–79; Hubbard et al., 2012, pp. 144–147; Chicagogangs.org, 2014, SSPopes).

Insane Unknowns (aka IUKN, UNKNS)

The Insane Unknowns began in Chicago in 1967 after a merger of the Division Skulls and the Unknown Souls gangs. The two gangs had been factions of the Latin Kings at one time. The Insane Unknowns admit mostly Latino members, and the Chicago Crime Commission estimates that there are at least 120 members in the gang. The Insane Unknowns deal in drugs, firearms, thefts, and armed robberies (Hubbard et al., 2012, pp. 78–79; Chicagogangs.org, 2014, Insane Unknowns).

Common Insane Unknowns Markings

The Insane Unknowns use white and black as their primary colors. Other markings include a hooded figure with a shield and "UK" on the inside of the shield, a white figure holding a rifle, a cross with UKNS, and a shotgun. Sayings include "Black to white, day to night" and "Folk 2 Killer" (Hubbard et al., 2012, pp. 78–79; Chicagogangs.org, 2014, Insane Unknowns; Petrone, 1997, p. 255).

Where the Insane Unknowns Are

Members of the Insane Unknowns have been reported in Illinois, Michigan, Pennsylvania, and Wisconsin (NGIC, 2013, pp. 49–79; Hubbard et al., 2012, pp. 76–77; Chicagogangs.org, 2014, Insane Unknowns).

Latin Angels (aka Almighty Latin Angels, LA)

The Latin Angels began in the Cicero, Illinois, area in the 1980s as a low-rider car club. Around 1993, due to associations with 2–2 Boys and conflicts with Latin Kings, the Latin Angels began to consider affiliating with either the Folk or the People Nation. A conflict between the Latin Angels and the 2–6 gang settled the issue, and the Latin Angels joined the People Nation alliance. The Latin Angels admits Hispanic members, and the Chicago Crime Commission estimates that the Latin Angels has at least 30 members (Hubbard et al., 2012, pp. 86–87; Chicagogangs.org, 2014, Latin Angels).

Common Latin Angels Markings

The Latin Angels use blue and white as their primary colors. Other markings include a halo with five points, a hooded man with wings, and a five-pointed star.

Where the Latin Angels Are

Members of the Latin Angels have only been reported in Illinois (Hubbard et al., 2012, pp. 86–87; Chicagogangs.org, 2014, Latin Angels).

Latin Brothers (aka LBO's, Insane Latin Brothers)

The Latin Brothers formed in 1970 as a splinter group from the Latin Counts. The LBO admits mostly Hispanic members. One of the original leaders named Butler was murdered by another gang in 1970. The Chicago Crime Commission estimates that the LBO has at least 140 members, but other estimates go as high as 300 (Hubbard et al., 2012, pp. 88–89; Chicagogangs.org, 2014, Latin Brothers; Chicagonations.webs, 2014, Insane Latin Brothers).

Common Latin Brothers Markings

The Latin Brothers use purple and black as their primary colors. Alternate colors include black and white. Other markings include a knight's helmet with "LBN," a spear with conical point with or without hand guard, a spear with 5 dots, a shield, and a cross. Sayings include "Ain't no other but a Latin Brother" and "LBN Til da end" (Hubbard et al., 2012, pp. 88–89; Chicagogangs.org, 2014, Latin Brothers; Chicagonations.webs, 2014, Insane Latin Brothers; Petrone, 1997, p. 285).

Where the Latin Brothers Are

Members of the Latin Brothers have been reported in Illinois and Wisconsin (Hubbard et al., 2012, pp. 88–89; Chicagogangs.org, 2014, Latin Brothers; Chicagonations.webs, 2014, Insane Latin Brothers).

Latin Counts (aka Almighty Latin Counts, ALCN, Cz, LCz, Almighty Insane Latin Counts)

The Latin Counts began in Chicago as a gang called "The Sons of Mexico City" in the 1950s. By 1960 the gang had changed its name to the Latin Counts. The original members were of Mexican ancestry. However, because of the neighborhood that the gang was located in (Pilsen), the gang began to recruit some whites as well. Initially new members were known as Junior Counts while original members were known as Senior Counts. The Latin Counts began to expand and even sponsor other gangs such as the Bishops and the Latin Brothers, although they have fought with them over the years. The Latin Counts are still largely made up of mostly Hispanic members. The Chicago Crime Commission estimates that the Latin Counts has at least 590 members, but other estimates range as high as 7,000 members (Hubbard et al., 2012, pp. 90–93; Chicagogangs.org, 2014, Latin Counts).

Common Latin Counts Markings

The Latin Counts use red and black as their primary colors. Other markings include a knight's helmet with plumage, a cross with five slashes, a five-pointed star, a shield with "LC," and Chicago Bulls sportswear. Sayings include *"Amor De Conde"* (Hubbard et al., 2012, pp. 90–93; Chicagogangs.org, 2014, Latin Counts; Petrone, 1997, pp. 288–289).

Where the Latin Counts Are

Members of the Latin Counts have been reported in Florida, Illinois, Indiana, Iowa, Michigan, Missouri, New York, Ohio, and Oklahoma, as well as Mexico (NGIC, 2013, pp. 49–79; Hubbard et al., 2012, pp. 90–93; Chicagogangs.org, 2014, Latin Counts).

Latin Kings (aka Almighty Latin King and Queen Nation, ALKQN, LK, ALKN)

The Latin Kings were founded in Chicago in the 1940s from Puerto Rican youth. Latin Kings founding members included Papa King (aka "Papa Santos"), Jose Rivera (aka "Cadillac Joe"), Eddie Rodriguez (aka "Tiger"), Joe Gunn and Fast Eddie. The founding members were known as the "King of Kings" (Knox, 2010). The Latin Kings are a hierarchical gang with a structured organizational system. They have Kings, Lords, a Crown Prince, Advisors, Crown Councils, Incas, and so forth. The Latin Kings have a formal constitution and celebrate set holidays (Knox, 2010). Papa King was killed in 1988. The new leader of the Latin Kings was Gustavo "Lord Gino" Colon on the North Side of Chicago and Raul "Baby King" Gonzales on the South Side. Lord Gino went to prison in Illinois for a heroin charge but continued to run the gang from prison. In 1998, Colon was convicted on federal charges and is now an inmate at ADX Florence supermax. In 1999, "Baby King" was indicted on drug charges. Gonzalez was convicted and sent to Stateville Correctional Center in Illinois, where he was allegedly involved in the murder of a rival gang member. The Latin Kings have ties to the FALN (Fuerzas Armadas de Liberación Nacional), a Puerto Rican terrorist group. Latin King member Luis Rosa was among those arrested and convicted of aiding the FALN in a plot in 1980 (Marx, 1999; latinoprisongangs.blogspot.com, 2009a, Latin Kings; Knox, 2010; Hubbard et al., 2012, p. 100).

Figure 3.2

Latin Kings Graffiti on the Side of a Building.

Brian Dunnette (Amor de Rey) [CC BY-SA 2.0 (https://creativecommons.org/licenses/by-sa/2.0)], via Wikimedia Commons

Although largely Latino, the Latin Kings admit members from other races and ethnic groups, especially in chapters outside Chicago. The Latin Kings specialize in drug trafficking, identity theft, auto theft, robbery, and extortion. According to the National Gang Intelligence Center (2014), the Latin Kings maintain direct ties with the following Mexican drug cartels: Los Zetas, La Familia Michoacan (and presumably with their successor group Los Caballeros Templarios), Arellano-Felix Cartel, and the Juarez Cartel to purchase drugs (NGIC, 2015, pp. 22–23). The Chicago Crime Commission estimates that the Latin Kings have at least 9,900 members, but other estimates range as high as 35,000 members nationwide (Hubbard et al., 2012, pp. 100–107; Chicagogangs.org, 2014, Latin Kings; Knox, 2010; latinoprisongangs.blogspot.com, 2009a).

Common Latin Kings Markings

The Latin Kings use gold and black as their primary colors. Other markings include a crown with three or five points, a lion's head, a king with crown (known as the master), a five-pointed star, five-pointed castles, Los Angeles Kings Hockey sportswear, and yellow shoes with black laces (Converse or British Knights). Sayings include "*Amor de Ray*" and "Love to the Kings" (Hubbard et al., 2012, pp. 100–107; Chicagogangs.org, 2014, Latin Kings; Knox, 2010; Petrone, 1997, pp. 312–313).

Where the Latin Kings Are

The National Gang Intelligence Center's 2011 Gang National Gang Threat Assessment reported that Latin Kings were found in 35 states, the District of Columbia, and Puerto Rico (NGIC, 2013, pp. 49–79). Other reported Latin Kings locations include Canada, Mexico, and Spain (Hubbard et al., 2012, pp. 100–107; Chicagogangs.org, 2014, Latin Kings; Knox, 2010).

Latin Saints (aka Saints, Almighty Saints, Almighty Renegade Saints, STN, ASTN)

The Saints began in Chicago in the Back of the Yards district in 1959 or 1960. The gang was named after a television show that was popular at the time called *The Saint*. The initial gang was made up of Polish American youth from the neighborhood but now is largely Hispanic (Mills & Brunuel, 1998). Sometime during the late 1980s or early 1990s, the Latin Saints joined the People Nation. The Saints still hold on to their original territory but are not active in many areas outside of it. The Chicago Crime Commission estimated that the Latin Saints has at least 570 members (Hubbard et al., 2012, pp. 148–151; Chicagogangs.org, 2014, Almighty Saints).

Common Latin Saints Markings

The Latin Saints use light blue and black as their primary colors. Other markings include a halo with three slashes, a stick figure with halo/wings and three slashes, and University of North Carolina Tar Heels sportswear. Sayings include "*Amor de Santos*" (Hubbard et al., 2012, pp. 148–151; Chicagogangs.org, 2014, Saints; Petrone, 1997, pp. 325–328).

Where the Latin Saints Are

Members of the Latin Saints have only been reported in Illinois (Hubbard et al., 2012, pp. 148–151; Chicagogangs.org, 2014, Saints).

Mickey Cobras (aka Cobra Stones, Mickey Stones, Rock Boys)

James Cogwell founded a gang in Chicago in 1954 known as the Egyptian Cobras. The initial membership was mostly African American and remains so today. In the 1960s, conflicts with the Vice Lords led the group to move neighborhoods and change their name to the Egyptian King Cobras. James Cogwell was murdered in 1961 and his brother Henry "Mickey" Cogwell assumed command of the gang. In 1966, Mickey Cogwell was offered an alliance by Eugene Hairston of the Blackstone Rangers and the gang became part of the BPSN. Hairston went to prison and Jeff Fort assumed command of BPSN, with Cogwell becoming a chief spokesperson for BPSN and a part of the "Main 21" BPSN ruling group.

In 1969, Cogwell was sent with Herman "Moose" Holmes by Jeff Fort to meet with President Richard Nixon, who had invited Jeff Fort to a social function for his political support. In 1972, Mickey Cogwell and other BPSN leaders were convicted on federal charges of defrauding the federal government of $927,000 in grants from the U.S. Office of Economic Opportunity. Sometime after this, there was a disagreement and falling-out between Cogwell and Jeff Fort over Fort's inclusion of Islamic doctrine into BPSN. The Cobras (who by this time were known as the Cobra Stones) left the BPSN but stayed in the People Nation.

Fort also was rumored to be upset with Cogwell's union organizing activities because he felt that this conflicted with traditional organized crime. Mickey Cogwell was murdered on February 25, 1977. The crime was never solved. However, the Cobra Stones blamed Jeff Fort for the killing and changed the name of the gang to the Mickey Cobras to honor their fallen leader. The Mickey Cobras still celebrate "Mick Day" on July 27 to honor Mickey Cogwell's birthday. As they exist today, the Mickey Cobras are one of the larger of the gangs in the People Nation. Their primary crimes include drug trafficking, armed robbery, auto theft, kidnapping, and theft. The Chicago Crime Commission estimates that the Mickey Cobras have at least 1,300 members (Hubbard et al., 2012, pp. 118–121; Chicagogangs.org, 2014, Mickey Cobras).

Common Mickey Cobras Markings

The Mickey Cobras use red, green, and black as their primary colors. Other markings include a pyramid with 21 bricks, a pyramid with an eye, the number 7, a coiled cobra, and a five-pointed star. Sayings include "MC Love," "All is seen in the eye of the Cobra," and "Snakebite" (Hubbard et al., 2012, pp. 118–121; Chicagogangs.org, 2014, Mickey Cobras; Petrone, 1997, pp. 211–213).

Where the Mickey Cobras Are

Members of the Mickey Cobras have been reported in Illinois, Iowa, Missouri, South Carolina, South Dakota, and Wisconsin as well as Canada (Hubbard et al., 2012, pp. 118–121; Chicagogangs.org, 2014, Mickey Cobras).

Party Players (aka Players, APPN, PP)

The Party Players began as a party crew in Chicago in the late 1970s in the area known as the Back of the Yards. Conflicts with street gangs in the area caused them to become a full-fledged street gang. The Party Players initially joined the Folk Nation. In 1988, the Party Players had formed new alliances with the Latin Kings and flipped to the People Nation. The Party Players admit mostly Latino members, and the Chicago Crime Commission estimates that the Party Players have at least 60 members (Hubbard et al., 2012, pp. 142–143; Chicagogangs.org, 2014, Party Players).

Common Party Players Markings

The Party Players use maroon and white as their primary colors. Other markings include a Playboy bunny with bent right ear, a hatchet, a cross with five dots, and five circles (Hubbard et al., 2012, pp. 142–143; Chicagogangs.org, 2014, Party Players; Petrone, 1997, pp. 354–355).

Where the Party Players Are

Members of the Party Players have been reported in Illinois and Wisconsin (Hubbard et al., 2012, pp. 142–143; Chicagogangs.org, 2014, Party Players).

Pachucos (aka Latin Pachucos, Almighty Latin Pachucos, LPz)

The Pachucos began in Chicago in the early 1980s. The Pachucos used the image of a 1940s Latino "zoot suiter" as a part of the persona. The Pachucos admit mostly Latino members, and the Chicago Crime Commission estimates that the Pachucos have at least 170 members (Hubbard et al., 2012, pp. 136–137; Chicagogangs.org, 2014, Latin Pachucos).

Common Pachucos Markings

The Pachucos use white and black as their primary colors. Other markings include a head with hat, sunglasses, and goatee (sometimes called a *cholo*); a rayed cross with the letter P; a cartoon Panama Jack; the letter P with downward pitchforks; a cross with three rays; and brown fedoras with black bands (Hubbard et al., 2012, pp. 136–137; Chicagogangs.org, 2014, Latin Pachucos; Petrone, 1997, pp. 323–324).

Where the Pachucos Are

Members of the Pachucos have been reported in California, Illinois, Missouri, and New Mexico, as well as Mexico (NGIC, 2013, pp. 49–79; Hubbard et al., 2012, pp. 136–137; Chicagogangs.org, 2014, Latin Pachucos).

Spanish Lords (aka AL, SLN, ASL, ASLN)

The Spanish Lords began in Chicago in the mid-1960s. The Spanish Lords admits mostly Latino members, and the Chicago Crime Commission estimates the Spanish Lords has at least 120 members (Hubbard et al., 2012, pp. 168–169; Chicagogangs.org, 2014, Spanish Lords).

Common Spanish Lords Markings

The Spanish Lords use red and black as their primary colors. Other markings include a Spanish cross with a heart in the middle, a ruby on a staff, a staff with a circle and five dots, a sword, and St. Louis Cardinals sportswear. Sayings include "All is well with the FSL," "FSL make your head swell" and "12-gauge gunning with the FSL" (Hubbard et al., 2012, pp. 168–169; Chicagogangs.org, 2014, Spanish Lords; Petrone, 1997 pp. 383–387).

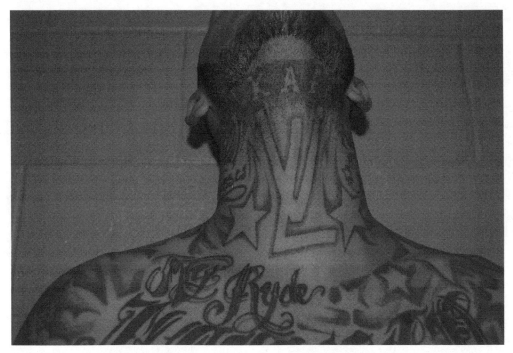

Figure 3.3

Vice Lords tattoo on throat. Latin Kings graffiti on the side of a building.

Eric Qualls

Where the Spanish Lords Are

Members of the Spanish Lords have been reported in Florida and Illinois (NGIC, 2013, pp. 49–79; Hubbard et al., 2012, pp. 168–169; Chicagogangs.org, 2014, Spanish Lords).

Vice Lords (aka Conservative Vice Lords, CVL, ACVL)

The Vice Lords began in Chicago in 1958 when Edward "Pepalo" (also spelled Pepilow or Pep) Perry and others from the Illinois State Training School for Boys in St. Charles, Illinois, formed a gang in the Lawndale neighborhood. The Vice Lords grew as their criminal activities expanded, however the gang was very adaptable. In 1964 the gang changed its name to Conservative Vice Lords in an effort to "soften" its image (Gore, 2014). In the 1960s, the Vice Lords developed social services organizations and portrayed themselves as helping people in the neighborhood with their lives (Dawley, 1992, pp. 122–124). Vice Lords leaders Fred "Bobby" Gore and Alfonso Alfred were able to obtain a $275,000 grant from the Rockefeller Foundation to aid in their alleged social work activities (Williamson, 2013). However, many of these social work activities were fronts to hide the Vice Lords criminal activities.

The gang leaders also became involved in politics, and some leaders even marched with Dr. Martin Luther King Jr. when he visited Chicago in the 1960s. In 1969, the Vice Lord gang leader Kenneth Parks wrote Chicago Mayor Richard J. Daley about how the group was trying to prevent violence on the streets in Chicago and provide social services to the community. The stationery on which the letter to the mayor was written had the gang's name and logo embossed on the top of the page. The letter asked for a personal meeting with the mayor (Dawley, 1992).

But then Fred "Bobby" Gore was arrested in 1969 for murder. He was convicted and sentenced to prison. When Gore was released from prison in 1979, he declined to rejoin the CVL and he spoke out against gang violence. Gore died of natural causes in 2013. Perry resigned as a leader of CVL, and Alfonso Alfred died of natural causes in 1970 (Main, 2013; Dawley, 1992, pp. 172–176).

The Vice Lords are a hierarchical gang that admits mostly African American members. The CVL joined the People Nation alliance in 1978. Estimates of Vice Lords membership range as high as 30,000–40,000 members, including thousands of members in prison (Hubbard et al., 2012, pp. 180–191; Chicagogangs.org, 2014, CVL).

Common Vice Lords Markings

The Vice Lords use gold and black as their primary colors. Secondary colors used include red and black. Other markings include a five-pointed star, a top hat and cane, the letters CVL, a Playboy bunny with straight ears, gloves, University of Nevada sportswear, Chicago Blackhawks sportswear, and Chicago Bulls sportswear. Sayings include "If you ain't conservative u don't deserve to live" and "Fluid for life" (Hubbard et al., 2012, pp. 180–191; Chicagogangs.org, 2014, CVL; Petrone, 1997, pp. 389–397).

Where the Vice Lords Are

The National Gang Intelligence Center's 2011 Gang National Gang Threat Assessment reported that Vice Lords were found in 24 states (NGIC, 2013, pp. 49–79). Other sources have reported Vice Lords in Canada (Hubbard et al., 2012, pp. 180–191; Chicagogangs.org, 2014, CVL).

Summary

Beginning in the late 1950s, Chicago based street gangs developed into a hierarchical-style gang structure in the juvenile facilities and jails of Chicago and expanded throughout Cook County, Illinois. As with Los Angeles based gangs, many of the early leaders of Chicago based gangs met a bad end, either ending up being imprisoned or dead (murdered, executed, or dead of natural causes at an early age). Gang wars killed literally thousands in the rapid expansion of gangs across the United States. Chicago based gangs have a multistate following and often absorb local gangs when they arrive in an area.

DISCUSSION QUESTIONS

1. Describe how Chicago based street gangs differ from Los Angeles based street gangs.
2. When examining the Gangster Disciples of the Folk Nation, who are the "Three Kings" and how did they contribute to the development of the group?
3. Describe the impact of Chicago based street gang involvement in Chicago politics.
4. Identify some differences between L.A. based and Chicago based street gangs.

CHAPTER 4 Outlaw Motorcycle Gangs (OMGs)

CHAPTER OBJECTIVES

After reading this chapter students should be able to do the following:

- Identify the major outlaw motorcycle gangs (OMGs).
- Identify the crimes committed by these groups.
- Compare and contrast the organizational structures of street gangs and OMGs.

Introduction

The International Outlaw Motorcycle Gang Investigators Association (IOMGIA) estimated that there are 375 outlaw motorcycle clubs in the United States. Outlaw motorcycle clubs can range from fewer than 25 members with single chapters to outlaw motorcycle clubs with several thousands of members and hundreds of chapters worldwide. Many of the smaller outlaw motorcycle clubs are allied with larger outlaw motorcycle clubs for protection or drug distribution. These smaller outlaw motorcycle clubs are often known as support clubs, duck clubs, or bunny clubs (Barker, 2007, p. 88).

The National Gang Intelligence Center estimated that in 2011 there were approximately 44,000 members of outlaw motorcycle gangs in the United States (NGIC, 2013, p. 11). The IOMGIA estimated that for every OMG member there were an additional 10 OMG associates who supported the gang in its legal and illegal activities. The IOMGIA also estimated that there were over 100 outlaw motorcycle clubs in Canada, Asia, Africa, and Europe. Most outlaw motorcycle gangs outside the United States have ties to U.S. counterparts with the same name.

There are more than 300 active OMGs in the United States. They range in size from single chapters with five or six members to hundreds of chapters with thousands of members worldwide. OMG members engage in criminal activities such as violent crime, weapons trafficking, and drug trafficking, and some have become a serious national domestic threat, especially with their cross-border drug smuggling.

Most OMGs recruit from groups of motorcycle enthusiasts and the biker community at large (NGIC, 2015). Larger OMGs often have proxy gangs or support clubs, which account for the clear majority of OMG recruits. Some larger OMGs have required smaller motorcycle gangs or sport bike clubs to wear support patches. Those OMGs demand monthly payments from each motorcycle club or sport bike club member in exchange for their use of support patches. Refusal to wear a support patch has resulted in violence.

Traditionally all-white OMGs and predominantly African American OMGs associate with white supremacist groups and black separatist groups, respectively. Some gang members may also adhere to anti-government ideologies, for example claiming sovereign citizen status (a domestic terrorist extremist, or DTE) to escape criminal charges or indictment.

The 2011 NGIC report observed there were 44,000 OMG members in 3,000 gangs. OMGs members represented 2.5 percent of gang members in the United States. In the 2011 NGIC report, 1.4 million gang members were identified, so 2.5 percent of that was 35,000.

The largest OMGs are the Hells Angels Motorcycle Club, Pagans, Vagos, Sons of Silence, Outlaws, Bandidos, and Mongols (NGIC, 2015). All are classified as "one percenter" clubs. The term originated following the "Hollister Incident," which occurred on July 4, 1947, when the president of the American Motorcycle Association (AMA) released a statement saying that 99 percent of the motorcycle riding public was honest, law-abiding citizens and only 1 percent constituted troublemakers. Motorcycle gangs have evolved since the middle of the twentieth century from barroom brawlers to sophisticated criminals. OMGs have spread internationally and today they are a global phenomenon.

BOX 4.1 The Hollister Incident

No single element of biker history is more critical to biker culture than the Hollister Incident. The AMA held a sanctioned Gypsy Tour motorcycle rally on July 3–6, 1947, in Hollister, California. During the rally, some bikers began to cause trouble after they had been drinking heavily. Several members of the Boozefighters and the Pissed Off Bastards of Bloomington began to fight with other motorcycle club members (Hayes & Quattlebaum, 2009). Several arrests were made and there was only minor damage. A photographer took a photograph of a drunken biker sitting on a motorcycle, which ran in *Life* magazine on July 21, 1947 (which some latter claimed was staged). The head of the American Motorcycle Association made a comment to the press to the effect that 99% of motorcycle owner were decent people and only 1% caused the problems. Outlaw motorcycle members seized that thought and proudly wear a 1% patch on their colors to this day (Bovsun, 2013; Barker, 2007, pp. 28–30). Hells Angels leader Ralph "Sonny" Barger claims to have been in on the designing of the 1% patch that many outlaw motorcycle gang members wear. He said it was done to "be a thorn in the side of the AMA" (Barger, 2001, p. 41). The Hollister Incident also established the tradition of the Fourth of July biker run.

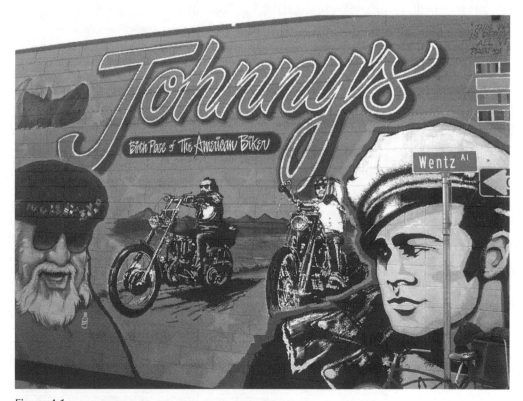

Figure 4.1

Johnny's, the Famous Bar in Hollister, California.

Ashi Fachler from San Diego [CC BY-SA 2.0 (https://creativecommons.org/licenses/by-sa/2.0)], via Wikimedia Commons

Outlaw motorcycle gangs (OMGs) are highly structured criminal organizations whose members engage in criminal activities such as violent crime, weapons trafficking, and drug trafficking. OMGs range in size from single chapters with five or six members to hundreds of chapters with thousands of members worldwide (NGIC, 2013). OMGs differ from street gangs primarily in their demographics and typical mode of transportation, although for criminal enhancements they may be prosecuted under laws designed for street gangs. OMGs are associations or groups of three or more persons with a common interest or activity characterized by the commission of, or involvement in, a pattern of criminal conduct. Members must typically possess and be able to operate a motorcycle to achieve and maintain membership within the group. Most OMG members are older, white, and male. There are OMG members of other races, but they are predominately white. Their preferred mode of transportation is the motorcycle, supplemented by a variety of four- (or more) wheeled vehicles.

OMG members use their motorcycle clubs as conduits for criminal enterprises. The U.S. Department of Justice defines OMGs the same as street gangs, namely:

(1) an association of three or more individuals;

(2) whose members collectively identify themselves by adopting a group identity which they use to create an atmosphere of fear or intimidation frequently by employing one or more of the following: a common name, slogan, identifying sign, symbol, tattoo or other physical marking, style or color of clothing, hairstyle, hand sign or graffiti;

(3) the association's purpose, in part, is to engage in criminal activity and the association uses violence or intimidation to further its criminal objectives;

(4) its members engage in criminal activity, or acts of juvenile delinquency that if committed by an adult would be crimes;

(5) with the intent to enhance or preserve the association's power, reputation, or economic resources;

(6) the association may also possess some of the following characteristics: (a) the members employ rules for joining and operating within the association; (b) the members meet on a recurring basis; (c) the association provides physical protection of its members from other criminals and gangs; (d) the association seeks to exercise control over a particular location or region, or it may simply defend its perceived interests against rivals; or (e) the association has an identifiable structure.

(U.S. DOJ, 2016)

Figure 4.2

Outlaw Motorcycle Patch. The patch colors worn by many motorcycle clubs are typically: one-piece for nonconformist social clubs, two-piece for clubs paying dues, and three-piece for outlaw clubs.

Phil Brooks

OMGs should be contrasted with motorcycle clubs, which are groups of individuals whose primary interest and activities involve motorcycles. Motorcycle clubs vary in their objectives and organizations and are often organized around a brand or make, or around a type of riding (e.g., touring). Some of the more well-known (or oldest) clubs include the Yonkers Motorcycle Club, the Pasadena Motorcycle Club, and the Patriot Guard Riders. Motorcycle clubs are not considered OMGs.

Which of the 1% Gangs Are the Most Dangerous?

Although most 1% outlaw motorcycle gangs are dangerous and engage in some type of criminality, there is no generally accepted agreement about which outlaw motorcycle gangs are the most dangerous. Barker (2007) lists what he calls the Big Five Outlaw

Motorcycle Clubs (MC) as being Hells Angels MC, Banditos MC, Outlaws MC, Pagans MC, and the Sons of Silence MC. Barker (2007, pp. 76–82) went on to note that three major independent outlaw motorcycle clubs existed: Warlocks MC, Mongols MC, and the Iron Horsemen MC (pp. 84–87). The ex-national president of the Mongols, Ruben Cavazos (2008), listed the Mongols MC, Pagans MC, Outlaws MC, Hells Angels MC, Banditos MC, and the Sons of Silence MC as being the most influential 1% outlaw motorcycle gangs (pp. 118–119). In a presentation for the National Gang Crime Research Center in 2008, retired ATF Agent Ron Holmes (2008) stated that there were as many as 40 significant 1% outlaw motorcycle gangs in the United States. However, Holmes noted that many of these groups, while 1% gangs (Avengers, Boozefighters, El Forasteros, Galloping Goose, Invaders, Kingsmen, Phantoms, etc.) were regional gangs with a presence in only a few states.

In 2013, the National Gang Intelligence Center listed rapid expansion in several states by the Mongols MC, Outlaws MC, Pagans MC, Vagos MC, and the Wheels of Soul MC as emerging threats (p. 11). However, the 2013 National Gang Report listed the Hells Angels MC, Pagans MC, Banditos MC, Outlaws MC, and the Iron Horsemen MC "as the most significant OMG threat." The report also chronicled a major federal case that had been brought against members of the Wheels of Soul MC (NGIC, 2015, pp. 19–20).

Outlaw Motorcycle Gang Organizational Structure

Almost all outlaw motorcycle gangs exhibit a hierarchical gang structure. The individual motorcycle clubs are divided into individual chapters. Most chapters have an elected president, vice president, treasurer, sergeant at arms, and enforcers. Many OMGs have national officers. Some have regional officers (RCMP, 2007, pp. 206–212). The exception is the Pagans MC, which has a ruling council. Most outlaw motorcycle gangs maintain a clubhouse as a place to hold their meetings (which they call "church"). Many of these clubhouses have a bar. The clubhouse is not only a place to hold meetings or party; they are often used to store weapons, drugs, or stolen property.

All organizations have rules for their members. Outlaw motorcycle gangs are no exception. Most clubs favor written constitutions. Loyalty is demanded first and foremost from all members. Violation of the rules is punished severely and can result in punishments ranging from fines to having to go through the probation process again, to patch pulling, beatings or even death (Ball, 2011, p. 163; Hayes & Quattlebaum, 2009, pp. 275–276; Barger, 2001, pp. 41–47).

As a group, outlaw motorcycle gangs use various means of internal gang communication. Telephone trees are common. They are very internet savvy, and almost every national level outlaw motorcycle gang that considers itself to be a one-percenter group has its own website. Many individual chapters do as well. Most of these websites have a public side and a members-only site for security purposes (Etter, 1998).

Outlaw Biker Culture

Being a member of an outlaw motorcycle gang is a lifestyle. There exists a definitive biker culture. The biker culture rejects society and commonly accepted social norms. Pranger and Etter (2011) found that

> Normality is not a common thing among outlaw bikers; in fact, they blatantly reject societal norms. Deviancy and hedonism are not abnormal characteristics but expected norms in the outlaw biker sub-culture. This is apparent in the way that outlaw bikers incorporate them into their everyday life by entwining them with almost every single aspect of their life. Nothing is normal about the way these men live, even the way they treat women is mired in deviancy.
>
> (pp. 21–22)

The outlaw motorcycle gangs have developed a pseudo-warrior philosophy and live for conflict. Outlaw motorcycle gangs practice a weapons culture and the possession of a weapon is a symbol of manhood. They view themselves as "road warriors." The average biker wants to ride free of governmental controls. They reject society and have developed a "f**k the world" philosophy that governs many of their actions. Bikers are often racist, but seldom anti-Semitic.

The outlaw motorcycle gang members openly display artifacts of their member-ship in the club. The full members of an outlaw motorcycle gang proudly wear a patch on the back of their vests or jacket that declares to the world their membership. This patch is known as their colors or cuts. There are often other patches or wings that are attached to the front of the vest or jacket that declare the wearer's office, beliefs, drug usage, prison time, or sexual exploits. Many of the insignia displayed often have a Nazi or neo-Nazi affiliation. Hells Angel leader Sonny Barger (2001) explained the infatuation with Nazi insignia began when Barger began wearing a Nazi belt buckle that he was given by another member in the late 1950s. He received the belt simply to hold up his pants, and the other member gave him the belt his father had brought back from World War II as a souvenir. Barger stated that many other Hells Angels members thought this was cool and began to put Nazi patches and medals on their colors. Barger (2001) says that he just needed a belt and it had no political meaning on his part (p. 38).

OMGs Practice Selective Membership

In order to protect themselves from infiltration by the police, outlaw motorcycle gangs (like many other gangs) practice selective membership. All new members must be vouched for by an existing member. Race is often a discriminator. Outlaw motorcycle gang members are generally white. However, the Mongols and the Vagos have always admitted Hispanics. The Wheels of Soul started as an African American group but is now multiracial. Another game changer is the expansion to countries overseas. This has relaxed the race requirement in some areas out of necessity. The requirement that the prospective member must be male and over 18 years of age seems to be universal.

Originally, most clubs had a requirement that prospective or active members must own an American-made motorcycle. However, the Pagans initially began by riding Triumphs. The Wheels of Soul simply requires the motorcycle to be larger than 750 cc engine size. All outlaw motorcycle gangs practice extensive screening of new members. Some clubs require a written application and polygraph test. Others even employ background investigators. Bureau of Alcohol, Tobacco, Firearms and Explosives (ATF) Agent William Queen (2005) infiltrated the Mongols and stated:

> Before you can become a full patch (wearer), they make copies of your picture and distribute it to every other charter in the club; every patch studies your face closely and considers whether they have a problem with you or may have known you at some point. Every patch stares hard at you and weighs the possibility that you might be a cop trying to infiltrate the club.
>
> (pp. 179–180)

Potential members start as "hang arounds." They are allowed to hang around the members and see if they fit in with the group. Then if they wish to progress with membership and the members of the outlaw motorcycle gang chapter agree, they are invited to "prospect" (begin the process of trying to become a member). Potential members must prospect (some clubs call the prospective members "probates" or "strikers") for as much as a year to join the club. Prospects are expected to perform service for club members and the club (Barger, 2001). Prospects have limited participation in club activities. Prospects may be allowed to wear the top and bottom rocker of the club on their colors. However, they may not wear the club's patch or get any club tattoo (Dobyns & Johnson-Shelton, 2009, p. 273).

Biker initiation rites are often violent; every tribe has a rite of passage that allows young people to transcend from childhood into full adult membership in the group with elaborate initiation rites to become members of the organization. These rites are often violent and involve the prospective member being physically or mentally abused (Falco & Droban, 2013, p. 27). Many groups require the prospective member to participate in or commit a witnessed crime. ATF agent Jay Dobyns faked the murder of a rival

Mongols gang member in order to get into Hells Angels (Dobyns & Johnson-Shelton, 2009, pp. 294–298).

Outlaw Motorcycle Gang Funerals

Just as a group member has a formal rite of passage into the group, when a member dies they are often given a formal rite of exit into the next world. Members of the group gather as a show of unity to mourn their deceased member. Biker funerals are in the tradition of the American Mafia. They are a large and showy event.

The deceased is usually buried in full colors or uniform of the group. Mourners from the group attend in full colors or uniform. Group affiliation is often listed on the funeral program and may be engraved on the tombstone. Bikers ride to and from the service in formation. If the OMG member was a member of the U.S. military, an honor guard is requested including a gun salute. In keeping with the pseudo-warrior tradition, if the deceased was not a veteran of the military, the bikers may provide a shotgun firearms salute at the gravesite. Generally, the club allows the funeral director to dig the grave, but not fill it. A tradition started by the Hells Angels states that nobody throws dirt into the face of an Angel but another Angel. Most other OMG groups follow that tradition as well. Thus, the gathered OMG members grab shovels and fill in the grave themselves.

Sometimes there is violence at the funeral of an OMG member. On October 16, 2011, 4,000 people attended the funeral for Hells Angels San Jose Chapter head Jeffery "Jethro" Pettigrew in San Jose, California. Pettigrew had been murdered by a member of the Vagos MC on September 25 in a casino shooting in Sparks, Nevada. Two other Vagos members were injured in that incident (Katrandjian, 2011). Pettigrew was employed by the city of San Jose as a heavy equipment operator. Steve Tausan (age 52, aka "Mr. 187"), who was the San Jose Hells Angels sergeant at arms, was shot and killed by fellow Hells Angel member Steve Ruiz. Ruiz had been tasked with protecting Pettigrew and was attacked by fellow Hells Angels members. In the ensuing fight, Ruiz shot and killed Tausan.

The Nature of Outlaw Motorcycle Gang Crime

The primary crimes of outlaw motorcycle gangs are economically motivated, such as drug trafficking, motorcycle theft, prostitution, and other illegal enterprises that provide funds for the club and individual members. Secondary crimes such as murder, assault, rape, kidnapping, or arson often either support the primary crimes or the biker culture. However, unlike members of other types of gangs, outlaw motorcycle gang members seldom use illicit income as their sole means of support. Most outlaw motorcycle gang members have "day" jobs as well.

Outlaw motorcycle gangs will often buy legitimate businesses that provide employment for group members (thus making their parole officers happy). Additionally, the business often acts as a front to commit other crimes. The business also provides the group a base from which to recruit. It also allows the group to launder illicitly acquired money. Thus, cash-heavy businesses are favored. Examples of such include bars, bail bonds, construction, motorcycle shops, roofing, security, strip clubs, T-shirt and leather goods shops, tattoo parlors, towing companies, trucking, used cars dealers, auto repair shops, and waste disposal.

Sometimes the violence is gang against rival gang for turf reasons. On April 27, 2002, 42 Hells Angel members stormed into the Harrah's Casino in Laughlin, Nevada, where the Mongols were staying during the Laughlin River Run and began shooting their rival bikers. In the ensuing fight, three bikers (two Hells Angels and one Mongol) were killed and 10 more were injured. Forty-two Hells Angels were indicted, six accepted

Figure 4.3

Hells Angels on Bikes. The Hells Angels MC have more than one hundred chapters spread over 29 countries.

iStock Photo/Jerry Grugin

plea bargains, and the rest of the charges against the Hells Angels members were dismissed (Snedeker, 2002).

Hells Angels Motorcycle Club (MC)

Many trace the history of the Hells Angels to the Pissed Off Bastards of Bloomington that was founded in 1946 in California. Other accounts place members of the POBOBs as charter members of the Angels. The Hells Angels deny evolving from a previous motorcycle club or group. According to Hells Angels history, on March 17, 1948, the first Hells Angels motorcycle club was founded in the Fontana/San Bernardino area in the United States (Hells-angels.com, 2014). The "mother" chapter of the Hells Angels is located in Oakland, California. Ralph "Sonny" Barger became the president of the Oakland Chapter in 1958 and later was the national president of the Hells Angels Club (Barker, 2007, p. 35). The Hells Angels is a hierarchical gang with an organized structure (Barker, 2007, p. 91), and by club tradition, the club admits white members. The Hells Angels have an estimated 3,000–3,600 members (Queen, 2005, p. 25) and has grown to be the largest outlaw motorcycle gang in the world.

The Hells Angels have intentionally left out the apostrophe in their name. The Hells Angels use the number 81 as a symbol for the letters H and A in the alphabet. The Hells Angels mottos are "Angels Forever, Forever Angels!" and "Three can keep a secret if two are dead!" The Hells Angels patch contains a winged death head. The patch and the emblem are copyrighted by the Hells Angels.

According to the U.S. Department of Justice (2014),

The Hells Angels are involved in the production, transportation and distribution of marijuana and methamphetamine. Additionally, the Hells Angels are involved in the transportation and distribution of cocaine, hashish, heroin, LSD (lysergic acid diethylamide), ecstasy, PCP (phencyclidine) and diverted pharmaceuticals. The Hells Angels are also involved in other criminal activity including assault, extortion, homicide, money laundering and motorcycle theft.

(USDOJ, 2014)

Where the Hells Angels Are

The Hells Angels claim an estimated 238 chapters in 27 U.S. states, as well as Canada, Europe, Africa, Australia, and South America.

Hells Angels Allies include the Aryan Brotherhood, Booze Fighters, Red Devils, Henchmen, Iron Horsemen, Sundowners, and Gypsy Jokers. Hells Angels Enemies include the Banditos, Mongols, Outlaws, Pagans, Sons of Silence, Hessians, and Pagans.

Figure 4.4

Hells Angels headquarters. Started in 1948, the Hells Angels Motorcycle Club is a worldwide motorcycle club whose members typically ride Harley-Davidson motorcycles.

iStock Photo

BOX 4.2 The Most Famous Hells Angel: Sonny Barger

Ralph "Sonny" Barger was born in California on October 8, 1938. His mother left at an early age and Barger was raised by his father who was often absent and off working. In 1955, Barger dropped out of high school at 16. Barger then lied about his age and joined the U.S. Army, serving with the 25th Infantry Division in Hawaii until his real age was discovered 14 months later. Barger was given an honorable discharge and sent home (Barger, 2001, pp. 21–22). Shortly after Barger returned home, he was arrested for the first time on April 14, 1957, in Alameda, California, for drunk driving. This was the first of many arrests that Barger was involved in over the next five decades. While not all of the arrests led to convictions, many did. Several of these arrests were for violent felonies and resulted in Barger serving multiple prison sentences. Barger does not deny this, and in his book he reveals his arrest and conviction record (Barger, 2001, pp. 257–259).

    In April 1957, Barger and some friends formed the Oakland Chapter of Hells Angels in Oakland, California. The Oakland Chapter is still considered to be the mother chapter of the organization. Barger was the president of the Oakland Chapter for many years.

According to Hunter S. Thompson (1967), on November 19, 1965, in response to demonstrations by Vietnam War protesters, Barger held a press conference in which he read a telegram that he had sent to the president of the United States, offering the services of the Hells Angels to the U.S. military in Vietnam. Thompson stated that the telegram read:

President Lyndon B. Johnson
1600 Penn. Ave.
Washington D.C.

Dear Mr. President:
On behalf of myself and my associates I volunteer a group of loyal Americans for behind the lines duty in Viet Nam. We feel that a crack group of trained gorillas (sic) would demoralize the Viet Cong and advance the cause of freedom. We are available for training and duty immediately.
Sincerely
Ralph Barger Jr.
Oakland, California
President of Hell's Angels (p. 323)

There is no record of any reply by President Johnson to Barger's offer. However, Barger said he did get a letter back from an Army officer who said if the Hells Angels wanted to fight in Vietnam, they had to join the army. Barger noted that this was not possible, as most of the group's members were convicted felons (Barger, 2001, p. 124).

In 1966, Sonny Barger incorporated Hells Angels and turned the club into a corporation. Among other things, this allowed the Hells Angels death's head insignia to be copyrighted (Lavigne, 1996, p. 1). Barger is the most famous member of the Hells Angels, and he is also probably the most flamboyant. Barger maintains his own website to promote his publications and his activities (http://sonnybarger.com/). He is an author and has written several books including his autobiography *Hell's Angel: The Life and Times of Sonny Barger and the Hell's Angels Motorcycle Club*. Barger's open embrace of a public leadership role in Hells Angels popularized "biker" culture. During his last incarceration after a felony conviction, "Free Sonny" T-shirts were sold on the internet and at biker gatherings. There is even a "Sonny" beer that has been marketed. Barger is the public face of Hells Angels.

Iron Horsemen MC

The Iron Horsemen MC was founded in the 1960s in Cincinnati, Ohio (Underwood, 2010), and is a hierarchical gang that admits mostly white members. It is estimated that the Iron Horsemen MC has from fewer than 100 to 425 members (Barker, 2007, p. 87).

Todd (2009) reported that several members of the Iron Horsemen MC were convicted in Maine on drug and conspiracy charges. Todd said: "Investigators were able to determine that the drugs were coming from Mexico, going to Atlanta, then to Haverhill, Mass., and from there to Maine for distribution" (para. 9). Confiscated in the raid according to Todd

> were nine motorcycles; three motor vehicles; two pieces of property in Old Orchard Beach; 10 kilos of cocaine; 600 pounds of marijuana; several weapons, including AK-47s, AR-15s, and handguns; and $37,000 cash. The sheriff's office displayed some of the items at a May 18 news conference in the Community Room of the York County Jail. Two large bales of marijuana, the size of a small suitcase, were stacked at one end of the table, along with three large bags of marijuana, a kilo of cocaine and a zip-lock bag of American currency. At the other side was an array of weapons, scales and cutting tools (para. 11).

Where the Iron Horsemen Are

The Iron Horsemen MC claims chapters in California, Colorado, Indiana, Kansas, Kentucky, Massachusetts, Maine, Maryland, New Jersey, New York, Ohio, Pennsylvania, Tennessee, and Washington, as well as Europe and Australia.

Iron Horsemen allies include Hells Angels, Sons of Silence, Phantoms. Iron Horsemen enemies include Outlaws, Hells Angels in Tennessee, and Banditos.

Kinfolk MC

Kinfolk MC are a one percenter motorcycle club founded in Texas in 2016. One of the Kinfolk key founding members is believed to have been Dan Schild, also known as "Chopper Dan," a former Bandidos national chapter officer (OnePercenterBikers, 2017). It has been stated that Dan Schild started the Kinfolk MC after being looked over for the role of Bandidos national president after former National President Jeff Pike was arrested in early 2016. The Bandidos national president role went to Bill Sartelle, known as "Big Deal." Many of the members of Kinfolk are former members of the Bandidos MC (OnePercenterBikers, 2017). The Kinfolk MC patch consists of a man, viewed from the rear, wearing a wide brim hat and long coat, holding a pistol behind his back, looking much like an Old West gunslinger. Kinfolk MC also wear the one-percenter diamond patch.

On July 30, 2017, three members of the Bandidos MC and a support club member were shot at Mulligan's Chopped Hog Bar in East El Paso, Texas. Those shot were Bandidos El Paso Chapter President Juan Martinez along with Ballardo Salcido, Juan Miguel Vega-Rivera, and David Villalobos. On August 2, Kinfolk

MC member Javier Gonzalez was arrested by police on aggravated assault charges relating to the shooting. On August 3, Bandidos Chapter President Juan Martinez died from his injuries. Gonzalez was later charged with engaging in criminal activity and murder, and was held on $1 million bond. Kinfolk member Manuel Gallegos was later charged with engaging in criminal activity and assault in connection with the event.

Where the Kinfolk Are

The Kinfolk MC claims chapters in Colorado, Louisiana, New Mexico, and Texas. Kinfolk enemies include Bandidos MC and Hangmen MC (OnePercenterBikers, 2017).

Mongols MC

The Mongols were founded in 1969 in Montebello, California. The first Mongols club national president was Louis Costello (Davis, D., 2011, p. 64; Cavazos, 2008, p. 74). The Mongols are one of the largest and most violent outlaw motorcycle gangs in the United States (Mongols MC NW, 2014). The Mongols are a hierarchical structured gang, and are estimated to have between 1,000 and 2,000 members worldwide. The Mongols admit both white and Hispanic members (Cavazos, 2008, p. 205; Queen, 2005, p. 29).

Mongols sayings include "When we do right nobody remembers, when we do wrong nobody forgets . . . Live Mongol, Die Mongol!" (Mongols MC NW, 2014). The Mongols' colors depict the head of a Mongol warrior on the patch. In the Mongols, a skull and crossbones patch worn on the biker's colors indicates that he has killed someone for the club (Queen, 2005, p. 4).

ATF agent William Queen was able to infiltrate the Mongols in 1998. Agent Queen conducted an investigation that resulted in the indictment of 54 Mongols members in 2000 for murder, firearms violations, narcotics cases, thefts, and violations of the Racketeer Influenced and Corrupt Organizations Act (RICO; Queen, 2005, pp. 263–265). In 2008, agents of the ATF again were able to infiltrate the Mongols and over 60 members were indicted for murder and drug sales in Operation Black Rain. The national Mongols president, Ruben Cavazos, was arrested and later turned state's witness. The Mongols then expelled him from the club. In an interesting move, the government tried to block the Mongols from using their logo by court order as an instrument of their criminality. The Mongols sued and after some lengthy court battles were able to keep their logo's copyright. However it did not help the Mongols with the criminal charges: almost all of those charged in Operation Black Rain by the ATF were convicted (AP, 2008a; Mongolsmc.com, 2014).

Although alliances come and go among outlaw motorcycle gangs, the Mongols have had a long-running war with the Hells Angels (Cavazos, 2008, p. 75; Queen, 2005, pp. 24–25). They are also at war with the Vagos MC and their former ally EME (the Mexican Mafia). Mongol allies include Nuestra Familia, Nazi Low Riders, Banditos MC, and the Arellano-Felix Mexican drug cartel. The Mongols' primary crimes are drug trafficking, theft, and interstate theft of stolen motorcycles.

According to the U.S. Department of Justice (2014)

The Mongols are engaged in the transportation and distribution of cocaine, marijuana and methamphetamine. The Mongols are also known to frequently commit violent crime including assault, intimidation and murder in defense of their territory, and to uphold the reputation of the club.

Where the Mongols Are

The Mongols claim active chapters in 19 U.S. states. The Mongols also have chapters in Australia, Belgium, Brazil, Canada, England, France, Germany, Israel, Italy, Malaysia, Mexico, Netherlands, Portugal, Singapore, Sweden, and Thailand (Mongolsmc.com, 2014; NGIC, 2013).

Figure 4.5

Mongols and Outlaws. Mongols are allied with the Outlaws against the Hells Angels, and have ties with Hispanic street gangs in Los Angeles.

iStock Photo. Department of Justice

Outlaws MC

The Outlaws MC were founded in 1935 in Matilda's Bar in McCook, Illinois (Thompson, 2011, p. 114). The group is sometimes known as the American Outlaws Association. The Outlaws are a hierarchical gang that admits mostly white members. The Outlaws have an estimated 1,100–1,700 members (Queen, 2005, p. 25).

The Outlaws MC patch has a skull with red eyes and displays crossed pistons beneath. The emblem is affectionately known as "Charlie." The Outlaws mottos include "God Forgives, Outlaws Don't," "Outlaws Forever, Forever Outlaws" and "Adios!" (Angels Die in Outlaw States) (Thompson, 2011, p. 321).

According to the U.S. Department of Justice (2014),

The Outlaws are involved in the production, transportation and distribution of methamphetamine, the transportation and distribution of cocaine, marijuana and, to a lesser extent, ecstasy. The Outlaws engage in various criminal activities including arson, assault, explosives, extortion, fraud, homicide, intimidation,

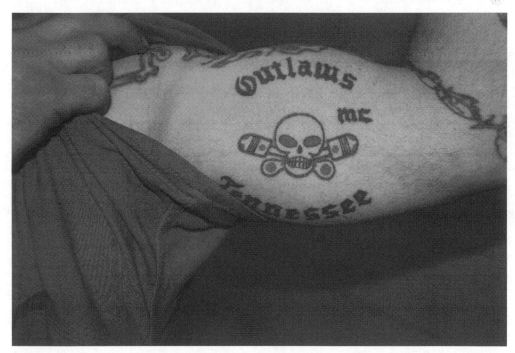

Figure 4.6

Outlaws MC patch. The patch consists of a skull with crossed pistons, also known as "Charlie."
Eric Qualls

kidnapping, money laundering, prostitution, robbery, theft and weapons violations. The Outlaws compete with the Hells Angels for both members and territory.

Outlaws allies include the Banditos, Black Pistons, Avengers, Pagans. Outlaws enemies include the Hells Angels, Red Devils, Iron Horsemen, and Devils Diciples [*sic*].

Where the Outlaws Are

The Outlaws claim chapters in 28 states as well as Canada, Europe, Australia, and Asia (NGIC, 2013).

Pagans MC

The Pagans MC was founded in 1959 in Prince George's County, Maryland, by Lou Dobkins. However, the club does not have a geographically fixed mother chapter. Pagan operations are guided by a mother club made up of 13 to 20 former chapter presidents that meets in various private homes in Long Island, New York in Suffolk and Nassau Counties. They wear a black number 13 on the back of their colors to indicate their special status. The Pagans are the largest outlaw motorcycle club on the East Coast. The Pagans admit mostly white members and have an estimated 900 members.

All About Bikes (2014) observed: "The official insignia of the Pagan's MC features the Norse fire-giant 'Surtr' sitting on the sun and wielding a sword. Above Surtr is the word 'Pagan's' and below it is 'MC,' both of which are written in red, white and blue."

According to California Department of Justice Criminal Intelligence Specialist Ann Richardson (1991),

> The Pagans are different from the other major gangs in that their bottom rocker doesn't delineate the state of which holds their membership; instead, it reads "East Coast." Pagans claim the entire East Coast as their dominion. Pagans no longer have clubhouses to carry on gang business; instead, meetings rotate from members' houses to members' houses. This came about after the 1983 RICO investigation into the Pagans. A case which was successful in prosecuting 20 plus members for assorted weapon, narcotic, and conspiracy charges.

Richardson (1991) observed that:

> Other organizational changes brought about from that RICO investigation was the change in the Pagans' national bylaws. Prior to the case, the bylaws said that

the Pagans' national president was paid the same salary as that of the President of the United States. It also stated the mother chapter oversaw the organizational activities. Each member of the mother chapter had certain chapters (a region) which reported to him and likewise. The bylaws (prior to the RICO investigation) determined which chapters would sell dope, where they would sell it, and to whom they would sell it to. It also stated the main responsibility of the members of the mother chapter was to collect the dope money. Their bylaws were the first piece of evidence presented in the RICO case.

According to the U.S. Department of Justice (2014), in addition to dealing drugs, "The Pagans have been tied to traditional organized crime groups in Philadelphia, Pittsburgh and New York and have engaged in criminal activities such as arson, assault, bombing, extortion and murder" (USDOJ, 2014). According to the Connecticut Gang Investigators Association (CTGIA) (2008), reprisal from a Pagan consists usually of a .38 caliber double automatic Colt, two shots in the back of the head, stomping on the victim just like a fish wrapped up in newspaper. That is the telltale sign of a Pagan hit.

Where the Pagans Are

The Pagans claim chapters in 14 states as well as England (NGIC, 2013; Thompson, 2011, p. 4).

Pagans allies include Thunderguards, Outlaws, Warlocks in Pennsylvania, and the Genovese and Gambino families (LCN). Pagans enemies include Hells Angels, and Warlocks in New Jersey.

Sons of Silence MC

The Sons of Silence were founded in 1966 in Colorado. The Sons of Silence are a hierarchical gang that admits mostly white members. It is estimated that the Sons of Silence have at least 250 members.

The Sons of Silence motto is "Sons Forever, Forever Sons!"

According to the U.S. Department of Justice (2014), "SOSMC members have been implicated in numerous criminal activities, including murder, assault, drug trafficking, intimidation, extortion, prostitution operations, money laundering, weapons trafficking, and motorcycle and motorcycle parts theft."

Where the Sons of Silence Are

The Sons of Silence claim chapters in 14 U.S. states. SOS allies include Banditos. SOS enemies include Hells Angels.

Vagos MC (aka the Green Nation)

The Vagos MC was founded in 1965 in San Bernardino, California. The Vagos were originally called the Psychos. According to George Rowe (2013), "As membership multiplied, the Psychos adopted a new name—Los Vagos, Spanish for 'The Vagabonds' or 'The Tramps'—and took green as their signature color" (p. 13). The Vagos are a hierarchical structured gang (Falco & Droban, 2013, p. 27; Rowe, 2013, p. 13), and admit white and Hispanic members. The Vagos are one of the most rapidly growing outlaw motorcycle gangs in the United States. Estimates of the membership range from greater than 600 Members to over 4,000 members in the United States and foreign locations.

Vagos sayings include "We give what we get." They call themselves the "Green Nation." The Vagos patch has a depiction of Loki, the Norse god of mischief, over a motorcycle wheel with wings (Rowe, 2013, p. 13).

According to the U.S. Department of Justice,

> The Vagos produce, transport and distribute methamphetamine and are also involved in the distribution of marijuana. The Vagos have also been implicated in other criminal activities including assault, extortion, insurance fraud, money laundering, murder, vehicle theft, witness intimidation and weapons violations.
>
> (USDOJ, 2014)

Where the Vagos Are

The Vagos claim chapters in 17 U.S. states as well as Brazil, Canada, Costa Rica, England, Germany, Mexico, Nicaragua, Scandinavia, and Switzerland (Vagosmcworld. com, 2014; NGIC, 2013).

Vagos allies include the Arellano-Félix Organization. Vagos enemies include the Mongols and Hells Angels.

Warlocks MC

The Warlocks were founded in 1967 in the Orlando, Florida, area by U.S. Navy veterans including Tom "Grub" Freeland from the aircraft carrier USS *Shangri-La* (Warlocks MC, 2014). The Warlocks are a hierarchical gang that admits mostly white members. It is estimated that the Warlocks have 500 members.

Warlocks mottos include "To find us, you must be good; to catch us, you must be fast; to beat us, you must be kidding" and "Warlocks Forever, Forever Warlocks!"

Members of the Warlocks have been involved in or convicted of drug trafficking, extortion, money laundering, and weapons trafficking.

Where the Warlocks Are

The Warlocks MC claims chapters in 10 U.S. states as well as Canada, England, and Germany (Warlocks MC, 2014).

Warlocks allies include the Pagans in Pennsylvania and the Hells Angels in Virginia. Warlocks enemies include the Pagans in New Jersey and South Carolina.

Wheels of Soul MC

The Wheels of Soul MC was founded in 1967 in Philadelphia, Pennsylvania (WOS, 2014; Thompson, 2011, p. 306). The mother chapter is still in Philadelphia (Salter, 2011). The Wheels of Soul is a hierarchical gang. They sometimes refer to themselves as the Wheels of Soul MC Nation. Originally a black motorcycle club, the Wheels of Souls MC now admits members of other races and is considered to be one of the few outlaw motorcycle gangs that is truly multiracial (Barker, 2007, pp. 52, 89). It is estimated that the Wheels of Soul has more than 100 members.

The Wheels of Soul (WOS) patch features a winged motorcycle wheel as its center logo. The WOS colors are also unique in the usage of three rockers. The top rocker says "Wheels." The middle rocker says, "of Soul." The bottom rocker gives the WOS member club's geographic location.

The NGIC (2013) observed:

> In December 2012, seven members of the Wheels of Soul MC were convicted in federal court of racketeering conspiracy and related charges, including murder, attempted murder, and conspiracy to commit murder, and tampering with evidence. Additionally, in April 2013, the final indicted members of the WOS were sentenced for their roles in a racketeering conspiracy, according to open source reporting.
>
> (p. 19)

Where the Wheels of Soul Are

The Wheels of Soul MC claims chapters in 15 U.S. states (WOS, 2014; NGIC, 2013). WOS allies include the Hells Angels and Red Devils.

Summary

Biker gangs or outlaw motorcycle clubs began in 1935 with the Outlaws MC, but they came into their own following World War II and expanded rapidly. They now exist in one form or another nationwide in the United States. Outlaw motorcycle clubs engage in crime for economic reasons, often at the wholesale level of drug trafficking or manufacture. They are expanding, but not as fast as some of the Chicago or L.A. based street gangs. However, some of the biker gangs have had significant expansion, especially overseas. The biker lifestyle appeals to a small minority of the motorcycle population.

DISCUSSION QUESTIONS

1. Explain the types of economic crimes committed by OMGs.
2. Compare and contrast the organizational structures of street gangs and OMGs.
3. Explain the basic biker philosophies expressed by OMG members.

CHAPTER 5 Prison Gangs

CHAPTER OBJECTIVES

After reading this chapter students should be able to do the following:

- Examine the history of prison gangs.
- Identify the effect of prison gang membership on inmate violence.
- Assess methods of prison gang communication.
- Consider the relationships between prison gangs and street gangs.
- Evaluate administrative issues with managing prison gangs.
- Identify the major prison gangs.

Introduction

The existence of a letter sent from one gang leader to another with rules for behavior by street gang members in Los Angeles should come as no surprise, but would it be different if the sender were an inmate in the Secure Housing Unit (SHU) at Pelican Bay State Prison in northern California? Arturo Castellanos, a convicted murderer and member of the Mexican Mafia (EME) prison gang, incarcerated at Pelican Bay since 1990, wrote the letter (Montgomery, 2013). Castellanos dispatched the letter to members of Florencia 13, a street gang in Los Angeles. The letter outlined rules (*reglas*) for EME associates on the streets. They included:

1. How street gangs and their subgroups were to be governed, including the election of a president and vice president by "majority votes."

2. How drug sales, prostitution and other illegal activities were to be organized and "taxed," with a percentage going to gang leaders behind bars.

3. How disputes were to be settled.

4. How assaults and murders were to be authorized.

5. How snitches and sex offenders were to be rooted out and punished.

Castellanos reminded the recipients, "We are Emeros (Mexican Mafia members) and we expect that these reglas are followed and respected by all true south-side Florencianos and Florencianas" (Montgomery, 2013).

Prison gangs exist in many prisons and jails throughout the U.S., and they influence criminal activity and behavior in the community. Prison gang members have ties to street gangs and influence much of the crime the street gangs commit and the profits they reap. This chapter will examine the definitions and history of prison gangs as well as the violence and other problems their existence brings to both the prisons and the streets. We will wrap up with an examination of prison gang management strategies and what we can expect from prison gangs in the future.

Gangs in Corrections

You might ask, "What is the difference between prison gangs and street gangs?" Previously, it was thought that many prison gangs existed only in prisons and were not expected to be a problem for local law enforcement, or for other criminal justice personnel (probation or parole officers, etc.). Those gangs and their street gang counterparts do exist outside of the context of correctional institutions. And prison gang membership will be in most cases equivalent to gang membership on the outside of the correctional environment as well. Obviously, however, there are situations where confined persons temporarily show an allegiance to a gang simply while in custody and somehow reduce—perhaps, to its absolute minimum—any such post-release gang affiliation. There are few if any "prison gangs" that do not represent a similar gang problem on the street.

Some researchers have concluded that "prison gangs" are totally independent of or totally different than their identical counterparts out on the streets or out in the "free world." Gangs get imported into prison when their members are effectively prosecuted for crimes. Other gangs form or reorient their structure in prison, some with drastic changes to the street gangs to which they are related. In summary, it is not where a gang operates, it is how it operates and functions that distinguishes it in terms of its sophistication and its objective crime threat. You will learn that we can distinguish between gangs in terms of their organizational capabilities, and this can be used to rate gangs in terms of the nature and extent of threat (quality and quantity) they pose to society.

Definitions

No analysis of such a phenomenon as prison gangs can be undertaken without ensuring a working definition has been identified. The most oft-cited and earliest identified definition of the term prison gang comes from Lyman, who defined a prison gang as "An organization which operates within the prison system as a self-perpetuating, criminally oriented entity, consisting of a select group of inmates who have established an organized chain of command and are governed by an established code of conduct" (1989, p. 48).

The Lyman (1989) definition centers on the commission of crime, not the location of the gang's origin. Knox (2012) identified a prison gang as any gang that operates in prison. The Federal Bureau of Investigation (FBI) distinguished prison gangs as criminal organizations that originated within the penal system and operated within correctional facilities throughout the U.S., although released members may be operating on the street (National Gang Intelligence Center [NGIC], 2011).

As we can see from the FBI definition, a tradition has developed where a prison gang was defined exclusively as "a gang that originated in the prison" (Knox, 2012). Thus, gangs like the Aryan Brotherhood and the Black Guerrilla Family would be "pure" prison gangs because they were gangs that originated within the prison system; they were not street gangs imported into the prison system. The NGIC (2013) has recently expanded the definition of prison gangs as "criminal organizations that originated within the penal system that have continued to operate within correctional facilities throughout the U.S., including self-perpetuating criminal entities that can continue their operations outside the confines of the penal system" (para. 13). Thus the potential for expansion and activity extends outside the prison while still requiring an origin within.

The term Security Threat Group (STG) has been used to describe groups that include prison gangs. A typical STG is a group of three or more persons with recurring threatening or disruptive behavior including but not limited to gang crime or gang violence (Knox, 2012). Recurring threatening or disruptive behavior may include violations of the disciplinary rules where said violations were openly known or conferred benefit upon the group. That might include gang crime or gang violence. More liberal definitions of STGs allow for any group of "two or more persons." That apparently became the ACA's (American Correctional Association) definition ("two or more inmates, acting together, who pose a threat to the security or safety of staff/inmates, and/or are disruptive to programs and/or to the orderly management of the facility/system"; see Allen, Simonsen & Latessa, 2004, p. 196).

In some jurisdictions, the STG is also called a "Disruptive Group." STGs or disruptive groups would include any group of three or more inmates who were members of the same street gang or prison gang, or the same extremist political or ideological group, where such extremist ideology is potentially a security problem in the correctional setting (e.g., could inflame attitudes, exacerbate racial tensions, spread hatred; Knox, 2012). While there may be a tendency to use the terms *prison gang* and *security threat group* interchangeably, this chapter intentionally focuses on the former.

Before the Gangs

Scholars of the mid-1900s noted that inmates in prisons used an *inmate social system*. Those systems provided a way to keep from internalizing the negative psychological effects of incarceration (McCorkle & Korn, 1954). The inmate social system allowed an inmate to be protected from the loss of his social group outside of prison while ensuring his acceptance into the group of inmates with whom he affiliated inside the prison. Members of those groups had similar values and adhered to similar codes. The system was rigidly hierarchical and included extreme authoritarianism (McCorkle & Korn, 1954).

Perhaps the main value of the inmate social system was possession and exercise of coercive power. That power was acquired by providing material aid to another inmate (McCorkle & Korn, 1954). The offering of cigarettes, as an example, was often used to demonstrate such a desire for power. The only way to refuse to accept such a submissive position to another was to insist that the gift be taken back by the giver (McCorkle & Korn, 1954).

Before prison gangs took over the governance of the prison system, there was an "inmate code." The inmate code (also known as the "convict code") identified the informal rules that have developed among inmate social systems. The inmate code helps define an inmate's image as a model prisoner. An inmate's ability to follow the code determined his "place in the social hierarchy" (Skarbek, 2014, p. 28). The code helped to emphasize unity of prisoners against correctional workers. If an inmate ignored the code, they would be relegated to a "low rung on the social ladder" (Skarbek, 2014, p. 19). The inmate code was an adaptation of the "thieves code," which was "thou shalt not snitch" (Irwin, 1980, p. 12).

Although each institution had a slightly different variation, the inmate code often included:

1. Don't interfere with inmate interests. Never rat on another inmate, don't be nosy, don't have loose lips, and never put an inmate on the spot.

2. Don't fight with other inmates. Don't lose your head and do your own time.

3. Don't exploit inmates. If you make a promise, keep it, don't steal from inmates, don't sell favors, and don't go back on bets.

4. Maintain yourself. Don't weaken, whine, or cop out. Be a man and be tough.

5. Don't trust guards or the things they stand for. Don't be a sucker, the officials are always wrong and the prisoners are always right (JailSergeant.com, 2015).

Older, respected convicts could break the code on occasion, but "the threat of violence and loss of respect kept most prisoners from doing so" (Irwin, 1980, p. 74). The code reduced conflict with others by "coordinating people's actions and expectations" (Skarbek, 2014, p. 27). Both the inmate social system and the inmate code lost their effectiveness over time, and became quite ineffective between 1950 and 1970 (Skarbek, 2012). The code began to break down once large demographic changes occurred within the prison system, and the code was no longer able to provide protection in the inmate social system (Skarbek, 2014).

Skarbek (2014) observed that order existed in contemporary prisons, despite the population's characteristics and the degradation of the inmate code. Order existed in prisons when there were relatively few violent acts like assault, rape, or murder. To some extent, the order in prisons could be attributed to the corrections officers, who punished inmates for unacceptable behavior. But Skarbek (2014) suggested that corrections officers provided only part of the governance of inmates, for a few reasons. The first was that corrections officers could not watch and protect everyone. With thousands of inmates often governed by dozens of corrections officers, it was not difficult to conceal criminality. Another reason that corrections officers did not constitute the entirety of governance was that they might shirk their responsibilities. That could happen for personal, professional, or monetary reasons. Finally, since prison rules prohibit inmates from lawfully possessing contraband or illegal items, corrections officers did not protect inmates from the theft of those items (Skarbek, 2014).

Prison Gang History

The first organization that could have been considered a prison gang according to today's standard definition appears to have been the Camorra, in Italy, in the 1800s. According to Lyman (1989), the Camorra formed in the Spanish prisons of Naples during the latter part of the nineteenth century (1860–1900). The Camorra was formed as a Mafia-like criminal organization and their influence and control quickly moved from within the prison to the nearby city of Naples. It was a highly structured and disciplined organization with a defined hierarchy (chain of command) and set of rules for the membership (code of conduct). Thus, the Camorra met Lyman's definition of a prison gang (Lyman's definition included the requirement of "an established code of conduct" [1989, p. 48], as well as the NGIC [2013] definition [except for being located in the U.S.]). The Camorra ultimately controlled much of the local government. It should be noted that other authors placed the existence of the Camorra in Sicilian jails in the early nineteenth century, as early as 1820 (Mooney, 1891).

Many scholars have made the claim that the first known prison gang in the U.S. was the Gypsy Jokers, formed in the 1950s in Washington state prisons. Camp and Camp

(1985) appear to be the earliest (and original) source of the information, and their work was cited as such by several authors. Camp and Camp conducted an exhaustive analysis of prison gangs in the U.S. At the time, they reported "the first gang was formed in 1950 at the Washington Penitentiary in Walla Walla" (Camp & Camp, 1985, p. 20), without identifying their source(s). In a table included in the report (replicated in Table 5.1), they listed the Gypsy Jokers (1950), Mexican Mafia (1957), (Gangster) Disciples and Vice Lords (1969) as the first prison gangs formed in the U.S. It was assumed that the source was one of their many interviewees or survey respondents, likely a correctional employee from the penitentiary, who obtained such information or allegation from an inmate.

The Camps authored two studies in the 1980s regarding prison gangs. The first, in 1985, titled *Prison Gangs: Their Extent, Nature, and Impact on Prisons*, was funded by the Office of Legal Policy's Federal Justice Research Program (personal communication, J. Brooks, May 4, 2015). That study was not focused on dates as much as a national inventory of gangs. The other was published in September 1988, titled *Management*

TABLE 5.1 When and Where Prison Gangs Began in the United States

Year	Jurisdiction	Gang
1950	Washington	Gypsy Jokers
1957	California	Mexican Mafia
1969	Illinois	Disciples
		Vice Lords
1970	Utah	Aryan Brotherhood
		Nuestra Familia
		Black Guerrilla Family
1971	Pennsylvania	Pennsylvania Street Gangs
1973	Iowa	Bikers
		Vice Lords
1974	North Carolina	Black Panthers
	Virginia	Pagans
	Arkansas	KKK
1975	Arizona	Mexican Mafia
	Texas	Texas Syndicate

Camp, G.M., and Camp, C.G. (1985). *Prison gangs: Their extent, nature, and impact on prisons.* South Salem, NY, page 20.

* This group was included in the original list. The authors of this textbook were unable to find support for that inclusion.

Strategies for Combatting Prison Gang Violence through the National Institute of Justice. That study focused on gangs at Walla Walla, California, and Nevada (personal communication, J. Brooks, May 4, 2015). The Camp and Camp report (1985) indicated "more detailed histories of individual gangs will be discussed in the case studies section of this report" (p. 20). The case studies section (pp. 65–189) made no mention of Washington State or the Gypsy Jokers.

Further research showed that the claim regarding the Gypsy Jokers was likely to be false. The Gypsy Jokers was founded as a motorcycle gang in California six years after their reported existence in the Washington State Penitentiary (WSP). According to one source, a Security Threat Group Coordinator for the Washington Department of Corrections, the WSP chapter of the Gypsy Jokers was one of the founding groups of the Washington State Penitentiary Motorcycle Association (WSPMA) along with the Hells Angels (personal communication, W. Riley, April 29, 2015). Outlaw motorcycle gang (OMG) members (those within the WSPMA) were allowed to wear a WSPMA patch, which easily identified them. The bikers were one of the two most powerful disruptive inmate organizations at the

Figure 5.1

Gypsy Jokers. Gypsy Joker Protest Run, Gawler, South Australia.

Roy Lister, Salisbury North, Australia [CC BY-SA 2.0 (https://creativecommons.org/licenses/by-sa/2.0)], via Wikimedia Commons

Figure 5.2

Inmates at Washington State Penitentiary. Grandfather Gabriel R. Morales is on the right at Big Red-WSP in 1948.

Gabe Morales

WSP during the gang period from 1973 to 1979 (Camp & Camp, 1988). The WSPMA was "an amalgam of about 200 inmates who were members of a variety of street motorcycle gangs" (Camp & Camp, 1988, p. 68). The WSPMA was a way for the locked-up bikers to associate with fellow members in and outside of the prison gates and wear colors while incarcerated (personal communication, R. Belshay, April 30, 2015).

The WSPMA was in existence for about 25 years. It has officially been defunct since 1988. Riley speculated that some early members may have been in prison in Washington when they created the concept of the Gypsy Jokers organization, but noted it was debatable the Gypsy Jokers were the first prison gang, as their own history clearly conflicted with the Camp report.

Further inquiry of prison gang expert Gabriel (Gabe) Morales confirmed the discounting of the claim. Morales reported that his grandfather did time at WSP, was there in 1950, and no such group as the Gypsy Jokers was active in the WSP at that time (personal communication, G. Morales, April 20, 2015). Morales specifically asked his grandfather about prison before he died in 1978. He said he was in what could be called a pre-Texas syndicate. They ran rackets like the prison gangs of the future, but there was no organization. His grandfather said there were no motorcycle gangs in the WSP during the times he was there (personal communication, G. Morales, April 20, 2015).

Mexican Mafia History

The Mexican Mafia formed in 1957 in the California prison system (Orlando-Morningstar, 1997). Hankins reported the early days of the Mexican Mafia, initially a loosely organized group of Mexican inmates with leadership experience as members of street gangs (2014). Hankins (2014) chronicled his experience as a prison gang investigator, from San Quentin starting in the 1950s, and later the California Department of

Corrections Special Services Unit. The early Mexican Mafia (known as EME) of 1959 included Louis Flores, known as "Huero"; Richard Ruiz, known as "Richie"; and 14 unidentified Mexican inmates. Members were handpicked from the "toughest and most-trusted Mexicans" who were equal members with "no leaders or shot callers" (Hankins, 2014, p. 7). The shared thought among members of the group was that because of their typically criminal behavior, they would spend much of their lives in prison. By joining together, their time in prison would be easier, and they would be able to make money in the process (Hankins, 2014). They agreed that they were EME for life, and if a member showed weakness or failed to carry out an order from the group, the person who recruited him would execute him. EME formed with the intent to control gambling, prostitution, cigarette sales, and other illegal activities (Hankins, 2014). Among the strategies that EME initially used to control the prisons was to attack the black inmates under the guise of a racial confrontation. Although they would keep quiet about the identity of their group in public, the word would spread throughout the prison population.

Nuestra Familia History

By 1968, many non-EME Mexican inmates decided to form their own organization for protection against EME. The group included Freddie Gonzales, Chalo Hernandez, and Black Jess Valenzuela, all from southern California, but most came from northern California (Hankins, 2014). They called themselves "Nuestra Familia" (Our Family; Hankins, 2014). Hankins (2014) was of the opinion that one of the reasons the Nuestra Familia (NF) formed was because the Mexican Mafia shunned many potential allies because they were not from the southern (Los Angeles area) part of California. EME attacked one of the NF members named Neri shortly after the group formed (Hankins, 2014, p. 86). That action predicated another in which Thomas "Sonny" Pena was murdered by the EME (Morales, 2011). Those murders led to the event known as the "Shoe War of 1968," which solidified the ongoing war between the two prison gangs for many years to come. In the Shoe War, an EME member, Carlos "Pieface" Ortega, stole a pair of shoes from Hector "Mad Dog" Padilla and gave them to a fellow EME gang member, Robert "Robot" Salas (Morales, 2011). Padilla confronted Salas and accused him of being a thief. The fight that broke out between the two polarized the prison yard and the rivalry of the two Hispanic gangs (Morales, 2011).

Black Guerrilla Family History

In the early 1970s, the Black Guerrilla Family (BGF) formed in response to the presence of a class struggle outside the corrections system. The founding leader of the BGF was George Lester Jackson, known as "The Dragon" (Hankins, 2014, p. 124). Jackson was an avowed Maoist who taught that the societal class struggle was along racial lines. The repressors in the government, including the corrections officers, were legitimate targets.

Contemporary Prison Gangs

Despite the disruptive effect that prison gangs have on prisons and society, very little has been learned about them (Buentello, Fong, & Vogel, 1991). Their secretive nature, along with a reluctance of prison administrators to acknowledge early indicators of a prison gang problem, has hindered both investigation and research of these groups (Buentello et al., 1991; Hankins, 2014). Prison gangs generally have fewer members than street gangs and OMGs and tend to be structured along racial or ethnic lines (NGIC, 2013). Typically, a prison gang consists of a select group of inmates who have an organized hierarchy and have chosen to be governed by an established code of conduct. Prison gangs vary in both organization and composition, from highly structured gangs to those with a less formalized structure (NGIC, 2013). Nationally, prison gangs pose a threat because of their role in the transportation and distribution of drugs. They are typically more powerful within state correctional facilities than they are within the federal penal system (NGIC, 2013).

As we have seen, many prison gangs originated to provide protection. Those same gangs, according to Skarbek (2014), essentially unify to provide much more than just individual protection. They provide governance, which is required in all societies. The institution cannot offer the governance provided by prison gangs. Prisoners engage in a marketplace where the transactions and items transacted are illicit. Prison gangs enforce the rules that allow prisoners to participate in that extralegal marketplace (Skarbek, 2014).

Prison Gang Development

Buentello, Fong, and Vogel (1991) identified a five-stage model for the development of prison gangs. The first stage occurs when a convicted offender is sent to prison, apart from his traditional support system. He realizes that he needs to learn how to engage with the officers and other inmates and abide by the inmate code of conduct. He moves into stage 2 and begins socializing with certain inmates—usually those with whom he shares a common interest. As these informal relationships develop and grow, some weaken and dissolve and others strengthen. The stronger groups may identify a need for self-protection from staff or other inmates. Leadership will begin informally, based on the charismatic influences and interactions of specific members (Buentello et al., 1991).

Stage 3, the transformation to a self-protection group, is possible when a group has a sizeable membership or when members perceive hostility by other groups.

Stage 4 in the development model begins when members agree to formal rules of conduct. They share many of the same viewpoints and exclude those who are weak or fail to contribute to group cohesion. Those members are part of a predator group, the precursor to a prison gang. Predator groups generate fear among other inmates, as they are willing to participate in a variety of criminal activities (Buentello et al., 1991). The power that members of predator groups demonstrate enables them to profit from criminal activities. Those that grow stronger (than other predator groups) became prison gangs. At stage 5, members of prison gangs see themselves as part of an organized crime group (Buentello et al., 1991). The extent of criminal activity may increase and they are likely to increase the awareness of their presence by taking credit for certain activities and advertising their gang's presence.

Prison gangs have attracted members for a variety of reasons. Jacobs (1977) observed that prison gangs served important functions for prisoners, both psychologically and economically. During the 1960s and 1970s, prisoners joined gangs to protect themselves or make money engaging in illegal prison activity like gambling and drug dealing (Orlando-Morningstar, 1997). The lure of money has served to bring a change to the dynamics of gang relationships, too. Jacobs (1974) explained how gang members who would have killed one another on the Chicago streets cooperated in prison. There was an absolute consensus among the leadership that "international war" must be avoided at all costs (Jacobs, 1974). It should be noted that "international" was meant to identify between-gang (inter-nation) conflict, as many of the gangs referred to themselves as nations. It was felt that the victors of a confrontation could only be the custodial staff. "Any fight between two or more members of rival gangs can have explosive repercussions" (Jacobs, 1974, p. 404).

The leaders developed international rules to which all of the gangs pledged to abide. The rules included:

I.   There will be no rip-offs between organization members.

II. Each organization must stay out of the other organizations' affairs. In a dispute between members of two organizations, members of a third are to stand clear and to attract no attention.

III. No organization will muscle in on a dealer already paying off to another organization.

IV. Organizations will discipline their own members in the offended party's presence.

V.   Organizations cannot extend their protection to non-members.

(Jacobs, 1974, p. 404)

While all the gangs did not equally support the rules, those rules provided a foundation for joint governance. While the framework could be seen as a truce, or ceasefire, and agreement to make peace with one's enemies, the guidelines were for less altruistic motives. Maintaining peace in a prison environment kept the prison staff from being too controlling and allowed the prison underground economy to flourish (Jacobs, 1977).

As the inmate social system filled some of the psychological need, prison gangs evolved to become even stronger unifiers. The economic function was a relatively new "benefit," though. Each of the gangs Jacobs studied had a poor box, storing cigarettes (often used as currency) for the needy. Prison gangs also functioned as a communications network, making sure members were advised of policy changes and events that were important to them (Jacobs, 1977). Prison gangs also served as a distribution network for contraband.

Roth and Skarbek (2014) suggested that "inmates join gangs to promote cooperation and trust" (p. 224). New inmates are advised by both corrections officers and fellow inmates to affiliate with a prison gang. Prison gangs resolve a variety of inmate-inmate conflicts (Roth & Skarbek, 2014).

How Many Prison Gang Members Are There?

Based on data provided by federal and state correctional agencies, the NGIC estimated that there were approximately 230,000 gang members incarcerated in federal and state prisons nationwide (NGIC, 2011). That number, at the time, represented approximately 16% of the 1.4 million gang members in the U.S. Their large numbers and dominant presence allows prison gangs to employ bribery, intimidation, and violence to exert influence and control over many correctional facilities. Gang density level refers specifically to the percentage of inmates who are gang members. It consists of those who came into the facility as gang members, the imported and larger portion of the gang density statistic, as well as those who joined while incarcerated (Knox, 2012).

Jacobs (1977) reported that by the summer of 1972, non-gang members, corrections officers, and administrators at the Stateville Correctional Center in Illinois estimated that "50 percent of the inmate population was affiliated with one of the four gangs" in the prison (Black P. Stones, Black Gangster Disciples, Conservative Vice Lords, and Latin Kings; p. 146). Camp and Camp (1985) estimated there were 114 prison gangs with 13,000 members in the 49 states reporting prison gangs. Carlie (2002) made an interesting observation in his estimation of the number of prison gang members in the U.S. He noted that Beck et al. (1991) surveyed inmates in state prisons in 1991, and gangs, as defined in that survey, were criminal organizations of inmates that shared five or six of the following characteristics:

- Formal membership with a required initiation or rules for members

- A recognized leader or certain members whom others follow

- Common clothing (such as jackets, caps, scarves or bandanas), group colors, symbols, tattoos, or special language

- A group name

- Members from the same neighborhood, street, or school

- Turf or territory where the group is known and where group activities usually take place (Beck et al., 1991).

Approximately 6% of inmates belonged to groups that could easily be classified as a prison gang, and another 6% engaged in illegal activities with groups exhibiting at least three gang characteristics (Beck et al., 1991). If a prison gang were defined as a criminal group of inmates sharing at least three of the six characteristics identified above, then approximately 12% of the prison inmates were involved in prison gangs in 1991 (Carlie, 2002).

Those (revised) numbers appeared similar to the findings in a more recent study. Adult and juvenile arrestees incarcerated in San Diego County, California, were questioned regarding drug use and other behaviors. Many of the juveniles (46% of groups of both males and females) reported they had some type of gang affiliation (Burke, 2009). The number of adults who reported gang affiliation was significantly lower (13% for males and 14% for females). Of those reporting gang affiliation, the first association with a gang occurred between the ages of 6 and 23 (mean age of 13.3). Most got involved because their friends (58%) or family (32%) were involved (Burke, 2009).

Jail populations had gang density rates that were similar to prisons (Ruddell, Decker, & Egley, 2006). The reasons include:

- The length of time gang members are held in jail relative to the normal (more short-term) jail population.

- The function of jails as entry points for prisons, causing jails to be filled by prison backlogs.

- While jails are known for housing misdemeanor offenders, jails, especially those in urban locations, are increasingly occupied by more serious offenders (Ruddell et al., 2006).

In 2004, Ruddell et al. (2006) surveyed jails throughout the U.S. regarding their special needs populations, including gang members. The researchers found that gang membership among jail inmates ranged from zero to 70 percent, with a mean of 13.2 percent.

Many (45%) of the responding jail administrators reported the problem had increased in the previous five years (Ruddell et al., 2006).

Based on results of their 2009 survey, Winterdyk and Ruddell (2010) estimated there were 307,621 gang members in U.S. prisons on January 1, 2009. Respondents to their survey reported a proportion of suspected gang members to the total prison population at 2–50 percent, with a mean of 19.1 percent. The total of validated gang members ranged from zero to 39 percent, with a mean of 11.7 percent. With 1.6 million federal and state prisoners in 2009, that meant there were 307,621 gang members in U.S. prisons, and 188,921 of them were validated (Winterdyk & Ruddell, 2010).

Respondents to Knox's (2012) recent nationwide survey reported a much higher percentage. The survey asked "overall, considering the percentage who were gang members before they came to your institution and considering the percentage who joined or quit after they came to your institution, what percentage of the inmates in your facility are gang members?" The results ranged from zero to 90 percent for males, with a mean score of 29.5 percent. The results for female gang density showed a range from zero to 30 percent, with a mean score of 3.61 percent (Knox, 2012). The 2004 survey responses showed a mean of 25.9 percent for males and 6.28 percent for females (Knox, 2004a). Surveys from prior years ranged from 9.4 to 24.7 percent for males and 3.5 to 7.5 percent for females, as depicted in Table 5.2.

Thus, over recent years, it appeared that the national gang density parameter has steadily increased for males and decreased for females inside American correctional institutions. The prison gang problem remains mostly a male problem, with female inmates having a significantly lower gang density rate.

While those numbers were higher than what has been reported in other studies, it appears that selected states have even higher prison gang problems. According to some inmates and correctional employees, prisons in Mississippi were run by STGs (prison gangs). The *Clarion-Ledger* (2014) reported that 13,154 inmates, more than half of Mississippi's 19,972-inmate prison population was classified as members of a STG. Many of

TABLE 5.2 Gang Density Rates

	1991	1993	1995	1999	2004	2012
Male	9.4	12.2	20.5	24.7	25.9	29.5
Female	3.5	2.3	3.1	7.5	6.28	3.61

George Knox (2012). The Problem of Gangs and Security Threat Groups (STG's) in American Prisons and Jails Today: Recent Findings from the 2012 NGCRC National Gang/STG Survey. *National Gang Crime Research Center*. www.ngcrc.com/corr2012.html

the gangs were able to compromise, and then control, correctional officers. A source said some of the officers even had gang tattoos, which they explained was part of their "past life" (*Clarion-Ledger*, 2014).

Prison Gangs and Violence

Membership in a prison gang has often been said to increase the level of violent misconduct that inmates display. In fact, the degree of violent misconduct was higher for core members studied than for peripheral affiliates (suspected members and associates; Gaes, Wallace, Gilman, Klein-Saffran, & Suppa, 2002). The peripheral associates, in turn, were more likely to engage in violent activities than inmates who were not gang-affiliated. In a more recent study, gang prevalence showed significant association with inmate-on-inmate violence (Worrall & Morris, 2012). That research, of inmates in a large southern state, did not show that the gang members were the source of the increased violence.

Scott (2014) found indications that increased time in a gang while incarcerated may lead to less of a propensity for violence. In a study of gang members in a youth correctional facility, he found a significant difference in the level of violence between gang members and non-gang members (Scott, 2014). Violent attitudes varied depending on whether youth had spent no time in a gang while institutionalized, whether they were currently in a gang, or whether they were formerly in a gang. The research showed a statistically significant and positive association between violent and aggressive attitudes and gang membership between one and two years. There was not such a relationship for former gang members or for youth who were in a gang more than two years (Scott, 2014). Additionally, there was a statistically significant negative association between length of institutionalized gang membership and violent and aggressive attitudes. Gang member demographics may also play a part.

In a study involving gang members in Canadian prisons, Ruddell and Gottschall (2011) examined whether all STG members posed the same types of threat of violence. They examined five categories of STGs: Aboriginal (indigenous people; terms such as "Indian" and "Eskimo" have largely fallen into disuse in Canada), Asian, OMG, street, and traditional organized crime (TOC). As with other studies, they found that non-gang members were involved in fewer acts of major or minor misconduct than gang members (2.5% compared to 3.8%). Street gang members had the highest rates of misconduct (5.33%; Ruddell & Gottschall, 2011). Aboriginal, Asian, and OMG groups were similarly lower (3.25–3.5). TOC members had the lowest rate of misconduct (less than 1%). Three of the five STG categories that had the highest percentage of members involved in major incidents, with just under three-quarters of the Asian, street, and Aboriginal gang members were involved in at least one major incident (Ruddell & Gottschall, 2011).

Gang members were more likely to be the victims of violence. According to research involving male inmates in a Texas prison, prison gang members were more likely to be victimized compared to non-gang members (Rufino, Fox, & Kercher, 2011). That was found to be true even when their involvement in criminal behavior was considered. The study also found that gang members who were victimized were likely to be under the influence of a substance. They were also more likely to be alone and attacked by a rival gang member (Rufino et al., 2011). The researchers also learned that victimized gang members were more likely than non-victimized gang members to have joined the gang before prison.

Decker and Pyrooz (2015) cautioned that symbolic violence (talking about it) and instrumental violence (doing it) should be studied separately. Groups who threatened violent activity without delivering it may accomplish their objectives, but when studying those groups the two activities should be examined separately. Including this reality in research is important because "official sources tend to exaggerate the extent of the problem and violence related to it" (Decker & Pyrooz, 2015, p. 108). Such activity is counterproductive and gives groups more recognition than they deserve.

Violent disputes over control of drug territory and enforcement of drug debts frequently occur among incarcerated gang members (NGIC, 2011). The recent NGCRC survey included the question, "in your estimate, what percentage of all violence among inmates in your facility is caused by gangs or gang members?" The results showed a range of values between a low of zero to a high of 100 percent. The mean score was 33.7 percent, meaning that on the average, gangs and gang members cause about a third of all the violence among inmates (Knox, 2012).

Prison Gang Communication

Prison gang members and other inmates can carry out a range of criminal activities, in large part because they are able to communicate with other people both inside and outside the prisons (State of New Jersey Commission of Investigation, 2009). They regularly exploit systemic weaknesses to obtain and use mobile devices such as cell phones and smartphones to send messages, post communications on social media and other internet sites, and communicate using traditional voice or video calls. They also use ever-changing encryption schemes to defeat detection of hidden physical messages by prison mail-room personnel, and they readily subvert the state's official inmate prison phone system (State of New Jersey Commission of Investigation, 2009).

Cell Phones

Although prohibited in prison, cell phones have been discovered in increasing numbers in prison, even in the most secure areas. The vast majority of confiscated cell phones were found to be "prepaid" cards or devices, available at many retail stores (State of New

Jersey Commission of Investigation, 2009). Although there is an activation process for such phones, the purchaser is not required to provide any type of personal identification, thus making him/her virtually untraceable by law enforcement (State of New Jersey Commission of Investigation, 2009).

The recent (Knox, 2012) survey included the question, "in your opinion, have gangs/STG's tended to result in more cell phones being smuggled in for use by inmates in your facility?," to which 47.2 percent of the respondents said "yes" and half of the respondents (52.8%) indicated "no" (Knox, 2012). There were no detection measures specific to cell phones at the points of entrance to most prisons or throughout the institutions (State of New Jersey Commission of Investigation, 2009).

Landline (Prison) Phones

State prison inmates have access to an official telephone system that enables them to place collect calls to persons outside. Inmates are each assigned an access number that must be used to activate the calls, and they must submit a call recipient list consisting of the names and residential telephone numbers. Calls to cell phones are prohibited. All calls placed by inmates on the prison phone system can be monitored and are recorded for security purposes and archived for up to one year (State of New Jersey Commission of Investigation, 2009).

Despite those safeguards, the commission found that the prison phone was easily subverted:

- Inmates make calls to persons not identified on call lists. This was usually accomplished by placing a call to an authorized recipient, who then connected the call to a third party.

- Inmates borrowed and/or accessed numbers to disguise the actual source of a call.

- Insufficient resources and staff have weakened the Department of Correction's (DOC) call-monitoring capability as a proactive investigative tool (State of New Jersey Commission of Investigation, 2009).

The recent NGCRC survey included the question, "in your opinion, is telephone monitoring an effective technique to prevent gang leaders from maintaining their ties to outside gang members?" Some 82.7 percent agreed that telephone monitoring was effective as a way to deal with incarcerated gang leaders. Only 17.3 percent of the respondents did not agree that telephone monitoring is effective in this regard (Knox, 2012).

Prison Mail

The use of correspondence by inmates to exchange information and messages with associates both inside and outside the correctional system is as old as the prison mail service itself (State of New Jersey Commission of Investigation, 2009). The volume of prison mail compounds security issues, as there is often no limitation on the number of letters inmates can receive or send, and DOC regulations require that they receive incoming mail within one day of receipt in the prison mail room. All of this presents special challenges for prison personnel. Incoming mail, with the exception of inmate legal documents, must be opened and examined for contraband (State of New Jersey Commission of Investigation, 2009). It must also be read in certain circumstances, such as when prison investigators have requested mail covers on an inmate's correspondence due to reasonable suspicion of criminal activity or a threat to institutional security. DOC personnel who staff prison mail rooms are also authorized to sight-scan the written text of all mail for unusual or suspicious markers (State of New Jersey Commission of Investigation, 2009).

The 2012 survey included the question, "in your opinion, is mail monitoring an effective technique to prevent gang leaders from maintaining their ties to outside gang members?" Some 87.2 percent agreed that mail monitoring was effective in this regard. Only 12.8 percent did not agree that mail monitoring was effective (Knox, 2012). Inmates develop special codes and ciphers to encode messages. Cryptanalysts often find hidden messages in their forensic analyses. For instance, the overt message of "AHG to Sammy" or "All Honorable Greetings to Sammy" might contain the alphanumeric childhood code of A = 1, H = 8, G = 7, thus what it really says in California illiterate-level gang cryptology is "187 to Sammy" or "kill Sammy" (Knox, 2012). Staff who work in the mail room and who monitor phones and visitation rooms need to know a lot more about the hidden codes and many words and phrases that have "double meanings" to most gangs (Knox, 2012).

Many prisons consider prisoner-to-prisoner mail a potential breach of security. In Pelican Bay, for instance, prison gang members were not allowed to write to other inmates. In spite of this, gang members developed their own communication technique. They used a bounce-back technique, in which they wrote a letter intended for another inmate; they mailed the letter to a cooperative third party who knew both persons; and the letter was "bounced" to the inmate for whom it was originally intended (Geniella, 2001a). Often, an inmate sent a letter using the *reverse bad* technique, in which he addressed the letter to a purposely bogus address so the letter was returned to the sender, the name and address of the person to whom he intended to send it (Morales, 2011).

The NGCRC survey also asked, "is prisoner to prisoner mail allowed in your facility?" Gang members routinely communicate this way, using various ploys and methods and intermediary contacts, as they often need to transmit messages to other institutions and to the outside world. Some 47.3 percent of the facilities did in fact allow prisoner-to-prisoner mail. In about half the cases (52.7%), prisoners were not allowed to send mail to other prisoners (Knox, 2012). The survey also asked the question, "in your opinion is prisoner to prisoner mail a major security problem in the field of corrections?"

Most of the correctional facilities (88.9%) said "yes," that allowing prisoner-to-prisoner mail was a major security problem. Only 11.1 percent of the respondents did not feel it was a major security problem to allow prisoner-to-prisoner mail (Knox, 2012).

Internet Access

Inmates were not typically given internet access, although many have access to email. "Current rules permit all federal inmates and most state prisoners to send and receive emails through special, monitored systems" (Lehrer, 2013, para. 2). All email messages are sent in plain text, with no attachments (Associated Press, 2008b). Potential contacts receive an initial email when a federal prisoner wants to add them as a contact. Prisoners can only send messages to contacts. The system pays for itself with proceeds from prison commissaries, and inmates also pay five cents per minute while reading or writing emails (Associated Press, 2008b). Email has added benefits, too. Lehrer noted that unlike physical mail, email cannot be used to smuggle contraband. Email can be monitored automatically and doesn't require the dedication of staff for its distribution. Additionally, there were dozens of cases of inmates running criminal operations by phone or mail, but thus far, there have been no documented cases involving email since the U.S. Bureau of Prisons began its pilot program eight years ago (Lehrer, 2013).

According to Branstetter (2015), Kansas, Louisiana, Hawaii, and Connecticut were experimenting with restricted online access. The email system to which federal prisoners were currently given access is a digital equivalent to prison mailing systems. Messages are text-only and subject to search by prison guards (Branstetter, 2015). While those might seem like understandable precautions, it's worth considering how prisoners use the illicit internet access they do get through the 3,000 cellphones that have been confiscated since 2012 (Branstetter, 2015).

Inmates already have access to the internet. Between the passing of messages for digital transmission and the use of internet-connected cell phones, many inmates have found a way to connect. For example, Mocospace, billed as the largest mobile gaming community in North America, was designed for mobile use. Shortly after its launch, photographs of what appeared to be inmates, posing in prison-type clothing in rooms with gray cinderblock walls with metal doors, permeated the site. It would not be difficult for prison gangs to communicate with associates on the street.

According to Branstetter (2015), as part of their Tech Behind Bars series, Fusion identified the social media account actively managed by an anonymous inmate. The AcieBandage account on Vine, a short-form video-sharing service acquired by Twitter in October 2012, had several videos shot in what appeared to be a prison cell. The account was suspended, but some of the Vines were saved on YouTube (Roose, 2015). Roose and Harshaw's investigation (2015) determined that some inmates accessed the internet through proxies—family members or friends who used the account to relay messages—while other inmates appeared to have accessed the sites directly. One inmate, who posted on Facebook for example, advised:

> Hello everyone, wanted to say hi and let u know I'm currently on an extended lock-down," said the post on an account with the name of a federal inmate serving time for armed robbery at a high-security facility in Texas. "Dont worry I'm nit [*sic*] in trouble the lock-down is due to a big incident that happened between two gangs at my location.
>
> (Roose & Harshaw, 2015, para. 9)

Figure 5.3

Prison guard lookout tower. While towers are used to physically secure the prison, they cannot ensure the marketplace of illicit goods.

iStock.com/OskariVara

Lehrer (2013) suggested that the time has come to allow internet access for inmates in jails and prisons. He observed that it would increase opportunities for them and improve their reintegration into society, at nearly no cost to taxpayers. Access to the internet might change the balance of power inside the prison. A problem inmate might only receive emails from prison administrators, while a well-behaved inmate pending release might be able to access education, employment, news, and perhaps even entertainment websites. At worst, this would simply prevent idleness—the main cause of violence behind bars Lehrer, 2013).

Control of the Marketplace

Skarbek (2012) observed that the increase of the number of people incarcerated meant potential expansion in the marketplace. The marketplace in prisons was very different than the typical marketplace, and it may be said to encourage the existence of prison gangs. When inmates want to engage in the marketplace and purchase drugs, sex, or contraband items, they often have to make a purchase from someone whose reputation they do not know. This type of transaction is called an impersonal exchange, meaning you don't know the reputation of the other person in the transaction; you don't have any reason to indicate that you would be doing future business with them, and if they engage unfairly in the transaction, you have no repercussion (Skarbek, 2014).

Skarbek (2014) noted that historically, people in need of security in such a transaction have established a Community Responsibility System (CRS). Such a system makes all members of the community "responsible for the actions and obligations of any other member" to establish order and promote trade (Skarbek, 2014). As a result, all a person in the marketplace needs to know is the reputation of the community, not the individual with whom he is contemplating a transaction. For a CRS to work, each community must establish a way for non-members to reliably verify someone's affiliation with their community and monitor their own members. Prison gangs perform this service, according to Skarbek (2014). Prison gang members are easily identifiable by their tattoos and other indicia, including their race or ethnicity. Prison gang leaders make a habit of monitoring the behavior of their membership and correcting behavior, when necessary.

The NGCRC survey asked, "what kind of economic rackets do gangs try to operate or control in your facility?" Here are the results in the order of their reported severity:

66.9% gambling
60.8% drugs
60.1% food
56.1% extortion
29.7% loan-sharking

28.4% clothing
16.9% sex (Knox, 2012).

The 2004 survey did not report the extent of prison gang drug trafficking involvement. The remainder of the percentages had the following responses:

73.2% gambling (higher than 2012)
56.7% food (lower than 2012)
70.1% extortion (higher)
60.4% loan-sharking (much higher)
40.2% clothing (higher)
45.1% sex (much higher; Knox, 2004a).

The 2004 survey asked, "what percentage of the illicit drug trade in your facility is brought in by prison gang members?" The results indicated a mean of 34.5—over one-third. The survey asked who was in control of the drug trade, and the response was higher in favor of prison gangs, with a mean of 41.7 percent. In the 1999 survey, the mean was 37.2 percent, up from 35 percent in 1995 and 31.4 in 1993.

Cigarettes were once the currency of the prisons. Generic brand cigarettes were sold in the prison commissary for about a dollar each, and packs were an effective unit of currency. But tobacco was outlawed in 2004, so prisoners started using postage stamps as currency (Ferranti, 2013a). A book of 20 stamps sold for $9 in the commissary, and represented a $6 value in the prison. Pouches of rolling tobacco wholesaled for 50 books of stamps, or $300 each (Ferranti, 2013a). Each pouch was then broken down into 80 to 100 cigarettes, which cost one book of stamps each, or $6. A cigarette was sold for $20, and a pack cost $200. The sale of tobacco has created a cash cow for prison gangs and the guards willing to work with them (Ferranti, 2013b). According to some inmates, guards don't care about contraband cigarettes since many of them also smoke (Ferranti, 2013a).

Prison gang members engage in many questionable and illicit financial transactions while incarcerated. On one level, they openly exploit fundamental weaknesses in an official system of inmate trust accounts, subverting such accounts for the unlawful purchase of narcotics and contraband and for gambling, money-laundering, extortion, and other criminal activities. Millions of dollars move through these accounts each year with no meaningful or effective oversight (State of New Jersey Commission of Investigation, 2009). Prison gangs' objectives are simply to generate as much money, and secure as much power and as much territory as possible. Territorial control extends to prison yards and street communities and to the gang members who occupy those areas.

The trust that prison gangs offer has facilitated illegal contraband markets. Prison gangs form to "provide extralegal governance in social and economic interactions"

(Roth & Skarbek, 2014, p. 224). Inmates clandestinely make illicit transactions by communicating with outside cohorts and associates who do their bidding directly on the streets (State of New Jersey Commission of Investigation, 2009).

In addition to exploiting weaknesses in the system, state prison inmates, including members of criminal street gangs, evaded that system altogether by communicating with fellow gang members, associates or relatives outside prison walls (State of New Jersey Commission of Investigation, 2009). Known as "street-to-street" transactions, those schemes presented a special challenge to law enforcement because they were not captured by the rudimentary procedures of most inmate account systems. Moreover, given the fact that private personal bank accounts were used to underwrite transactions of this nature, they tend to occur more frequently and often involve the movement of larger individual sums of money (State of New Jersey Commission of Investigation, 2009).

The survey included the question, "do you allow prisoners to exchange funds with each other?" The overwhelming majority (98.6%) of respondents indicated "no," that this was not allowed. Only 1.4 percent of the respondents indicated that prisoners were allowed to exchange funds with each other (Knox, 2012). Allowing inmates to exchange funds was bad policy. Where it was allowed, gangs and STGs were able to collect payments directly from the inmates they extort. The typical collection strategy is to have the inmate mail the money to a third party known or controlled by the gang on the streets (Knox, 2012). Typically, those transactions were triggered when an inmate arranged for someone on the outside to act as a go-between for the funneling of payments to others on the street, usually in the form of a money order. Current and former inmates reported that those payments were used for a variety of illicit purposes (State of New Jersey Commission of Investigation, 2009).

Gangs affect security even in well-run prisons. In prisons where security is less of a concern for administrators, prison gangs perform many of the functions, like controlling housing arrangements, permitting the use of cell phones and chargers, and the use of cash cards like Green Dot, which many prisoners use to extort money from others and pay for contraband (Southern Center for Human Rights, 2014). Those practices can be a gross breach of security.

Prison Gangs and Religious Services

One concern of administrators and other corrections professionals was that prison gang members may increase their level of dangerousness while incarcerated. Prison gang members, already an ideal target audience for radicalization, may do this by expanding their associations with foreign gang members or radical criminal organizations, both inside correctional institutions and in the community upon their release (NGIC, 2011).

Some street gangs were known to conduct their gang business during hosted prison religious services. Several gangs used this practice, but the Black P. Stones seemed to have perfected it. The Black P. Stone Nation (BPSN) was first known as the Blackstone Rangers gang. In the Blackstone Rangers, there were two gang leaders: Jeff Fort and Eugene "Bull" Hairston (aka "King Bull" and "King Ball," respectively). Only Jeff Fort survived. Jeff Fort learned early on that having some association with or appearance of a religious operation was very functional for an effective gang organization. That was another way in which gangs exploit a free society: they knew that religion was a "sacred" aspect of society that most do not want regulated, inspected, monitored, or investigated (Knox, 2003b). The BPSN adopted a decidedly Islamic belief system. So how and why would Jeff Fort have begun this tradition? Perhaps he was looking for a way to overcome the federal parole restrictions about "gang association" when he was released from his first federal prison sentence for embezzling federal monies. Jeff Fort adopted the cloak of a religious front: the Moorish American (Moorish Science Temple of America, or MSTA). Today that religious group has been adapted as a "front" for other prison inmates throughout the United States and is regarded in many correctional facilities as an STG.

Having worship services used as a front were not the only connections that radical Islamists have to prison gangs. Well-published attacks or attempts by ex-prisoners exposed to radical Islam include Richard Reid, who served time in a British prison before he became the "shoe bomber"; Jose Padilla, who served time in a Florida prison before becoming the "dirty bomber"; Muktar Said Ibrahim, who converted to Islam in a British prison before involvement in the London Underground bombing plot; and Kevin Lamar James, who founded Jam'yyat Al-Islam Al-Saheeh (JIS, Arabic for "Assembly of Authentic Islam") and orchestrated a plot to bomb several military bases, a number of synagogues, and an Israeli consulate in California from a California prison. James was the product of American gang culture (SpearIt, 2011).

Criminologists refer to this practice as "prison Islam" or "Prislam," in which gang leaders take on the practices of Islam to justify a violent and criminal lifestyle. While JIS is the only known "Prislam" group to come close to executing an attack, "Prislam" groups have wreaked havoc inside prisons for years (SpearIt, 2011). Prislam groups include the Michigan-based "Melanic Islamic Palace of the Rising Sun" and the British-based "Muslim Boys," who have waged war through assaults, batteries, and prison riots (SpearIt, 2011).

The 2012 survey included the question, "have inmates attempted to use religious services as a front for a Security Threat Group or gang?" Some 62.4 percent of the respondents indicated "yes," that inmates have tried to use religious services for their gang. Only 37.6 percent of the respondents reported not seeing this kind of abuse of religion behind bars (Knox, 2012). That was an increase from the 2004 survey responses, in which 61.4 percent indicated they had religious services that camouflaged gang meetings.

Street Gangs in Prisons

Once incarcerated, most street gang members join an established prison gang to ensure their protection (NGIC, 2011). Prison gang members, who exert control over many street gang members, often engage in crime and violence upon their return to the community. Gang members returning to the community from prison have an adverse and lasting impact on neighborhoods, which may experience notable increases in crime, violence, and drug trafficking (NGIC, 2011). Valdez (2009b) found that most street gang members respected prison gang members. Sadly, that amount of respect may be so strong that the street gang member aspires to become a prison gang member.

While *some* street gangs may have ties to established prison gangs and/or have incarcerated members who remained connected to the gang, it was important not to equate street and prison gangs, since substantial differences exist between them. Some notable examples include the organized, collective drug trade, strong ties, and covert behavior among prison gangs, compared with less structured, more individualistic drug trade, highly fluctuating ties, and overt behavior among street gangs (National Gang Center, n.d.).

In Jacobs's Stateville (IL) Correctional Center prison gang research (1977), no typical prison gangs were identified in the late 1960s, but established street gangs had a solid grip on the prison subculture. Four street gangs—three with primarily black members and one with primarily Hispanic members—competed for the inmates' membership. The black gangs included the Blackstone Rangers (later the Black P. Stone Nation), the Devil's Disciples (also known as the Black Gangster Disciple Nation), and the Conservative Vice Lords. The Latin Kings (a predominately Puerto Rican gang), although smaller in number, attempted to represent the interests of all Hispanic inmates—both Puerto Rican and Mexican (Jacobs, 1977).

The Bloods and Crips, traditional Los Angeles street gangs not typically considered prison gangs, were gaining strength in the prisons. The 415s, a group from the San Francisco area (415 was a San Francisco area code) was growing stronger in the prisons, according to Fleisher and Decker (2001). Morales (2011) explained that the group was first called "Bay Love," then 415, and then KUMI 415 (*kumi* is "10" in Swahili). In 1993, African American inmates at Rikers Island Correctional Facility in New York formed the United Blood Nation to protect themselves from other prison gangs (State of New Jersey Commission of Investigation, 2009).

Prison gangs and street gangs typically function in an interdependent capacity. As part of their arrangement, incarcerated gang members with lengthy sentences rely heavily on income provided by their street partners (NGIC, 2013). Street gangs benefit from their relationship with prison gangs primarily by securing protection in prison, as prison gangs protect their incarcerated street gang benefactors. Also, street gangs use their association with prison gangs to venture into different profitable endeavors. For example,

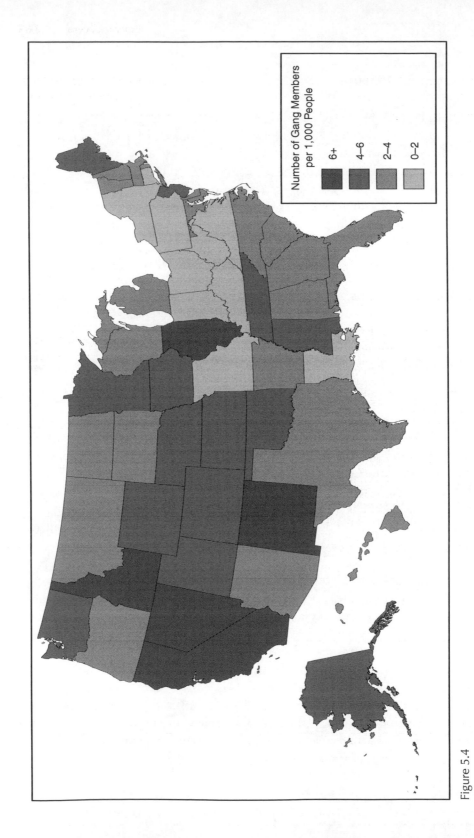

Figure 5.4

Nationwide Gang Presence per Capita per State.

NGIC and NDIC 2010 National Drug Survey Data and U.S. Census Population estimates 2010; NGIC (2011)

street gang members will often use the name and reputation of one of their incarcerated leaders to forge new relationships, extend their criminal networks, and expand their street and prison operations. In many ways, street gangs were largely the product of prison gang influence. Accordingly, prison gangs lie at the helm of the considerable threat street gangs pose to the nation (NGIC, 2013).

There was no state or national longitudinal data that tracked street gang expansion in the state or federal prison system. It was inferred, though, that the states with the highest per capita number of gang members had the highest number of gang members in their prisons (Pyrooz, Decker, & Fleisher, 2011). California, Colorado, Illinois, Nevada, and New Mexico had the highest per capita rate of gang members.

Wood, Alleyne, Mozova, and James (2014) found there was not a link between involvement in prison gang activity and street gang membership for prisoners in the UK. There was, however, a link between participation in group organized crime on the streets and involvement in prison gang activity. Some of the variables that predicted street gang membership were key predictors of prison gang membership (Wood et al., 2014).

Since they operated largely under the command of prison gangs, street gangs—both on the street and in prison—typically forwarded a percentage of their illicit proceeds to their incarcerated leaders. Thus it was ultimately through their street subordinates that prison gangs impact crime rates in communities and prison yards across the nation (NGIC, 2013).

Over 56 percent of NGIC survey respondents indicate that prison gangs control street gang activities outside of prison within their jurisdictions through means of visitation, notes and coded communication, defense attorneys, corrupt prison staff, court sessions, contraband, cell phones and institution phones, social media, and direction provided to released inmates (2013).

Although in the prison systems inmates typically self-segregated, incarceration in a jail facility did not have the same effect (Newhouse, 2009). In the local jails, most gangs "put their colors and conflicts aside" and made alliances (Newhouse, 2009). Reputation for violence played a big part in who received respect in the jails. The MS-13, for example, wielded much influence and respect in jails in the eastern United States (Newhouse, 2009). This influence allowed MS-13 members to get other inmates to assist them with making phone calls, running errands, passing contraband, and getting select housing concessions.

Who Controls the Prison?

Prison gangs partake in a host of criminal activities within correctional facilities and on the streets. Illicit activity varied from one prison gang to another, and not every prison gang committed every type of crime. However, a prison gang will typically engage in any crime to further its objectives (NGIC, 2013). Of those surveyed, 25 percent of respondents ranked prison gangs as their overall greatest criminal threat, while 17 percent cited prison gangs as the most violent and problematic type of gang in their jurisdictions. Prison gang crimes ranged from white-collar offenses to acts of extreme violence (NGIC, 2013). While traditional or lead prison gangs posed the greatest national threat, independent prison gangs (IPGs) were also a menace, most often at the regional level. While many IPGs operated exclusively in specific facilities, some have expanded and are represented in both state and federal facilities. Dead Man Incorporated (DMI), for example, originated in the Maryland Department of Public Safety and Correctional Services (MDPSCS) and advanced into the federal system (NGIC, 2013).

Gangs in other countries were less secretive about their control over the prisons. Jones, Narag, and Morales (2015) found that governance issues existed in Philippine prisons as well. With about 14,000 of the 23,000 inmates housed in maximum security (one of the largest maximum security populations in the world), about 95 percent of those inmates belonged to a gang. The 12 gangs represented in the prison occupied 13 of the 14 dormitory buildings (the fourteenth was unoccupied). The gangs all had their own disciplinary function, where "trials are conducted should a member attempt to challenge the leadership" or violate the rules (Jones et al., 2015, p. 13).

The gangs' rules varied slightly, but usually included:

- Give respect to all officers and member of the gang;

- Failure to pay debt to a gang mate will be given appropriate penalty;

- Stealing from a gang mate is strictly prohibited;

- Never fail to give a weekly due or contribution to the gang;

- Avoid any form of criticism to fellow inmates—any problem that may arise involving fellow members should be consulted to elders (bosyos) before taking action;

- Give due respect to visitors of gang mates—talking to them is allowed only with the consent of the fellow gang member;

- In cases of trouble among fellow gang members, the same should be deliberated fairly and justly;

- Voyeurism is strictly prohibited—violation shall receive the maximum penalty; and

- Having an affair with the wife or girlfriend of a gang mate is strictly prohibited—a maximum penalty shall be imposed for those who violate this rule.

(personal communication with Bosyo at NBP, November 28, 2012, as cited by Jones et al., 2015, pp. 13–14).

Connecting Prison Gang Membership to
Street Gang Membership

Since the study by Jacobs (1974) of Stateville prison gangs, the concept of importation has helped us understand that in places like Illinois, most of the gang members
were imported into the correctional system when street gang members were convicted
of felony crimes. So in the Stateville example of gang members behind bars, those were
not gang members who first joined inside a prison; they had been gang members prior
to entering the correctional stem. The vast majority of prison gang members in Illinois
appeared to be imported (Knox, 2012).

An inmate may enter the correctional system as a neutron, non-gang aligned, and
still join or be recruited into a gang. In other cases, an inmate may enter the correctional
system not as a full gang member, but as perhaps an associate of a gang or who may have
a brother or relative or close friend in the gang. And then, again while in custody, they
formally join the gang that they had a casual association with (Knox, 2012). The present
analysis provides one of, if not the very first, true quantitative estimate of the scope and
extent to which inmates join gangs after they enter the correctional system (Knox, 2012).
The 2012 NGCRC Corrections STG Survey asked, "please estimate what percentage of
inmates were not gang members on the streets, but who did in fact join a gang or an STG
after entering your institution." The statistical estimates for male inmates first joining a
gang while in correctional custody ranged from a low of zero to a high of 97 percent.
The mean was 19.8 percent of the inmates; literally one out of five inmates in America
may be joining a gang for the first time after they enter the correctional system (Knox,
2012). The statistical estimates for female inmates were somewhat lower, with the values showing a range between zero to a high of 98 percent, but with an overall mean of
13.1 percent.

The survey asked the question, "in general, which type of gang group poses more
danger to your facility: a street gang (has its origins outside of prison) or a prison gang
(has its origins inside of prison)?" Most (58.5%) picked "street gang," while 41.5 percent
felt that the prison gang posed the greater danger (Knox, 2012). The survey also asked,
"do the more dangerous security threat groups that exist in your facility also exist by the
same name in communities outside of the correctional environment?" Here the answer
was clear: yes, in most cases, as 89.5 percent of the respondents reported that the more
dangerous STGs existed by the same names on the street. Only 10.5 percent of the
respondents reported that their most dangerous STGs did not exist by the same name on
the streets (Knox, 2012).

A good example of prison gangs also existing outside of prison was the Nuestra
Familia (NF) prison gang, which was found to be responsible for a murder spree in Santa
Rosa, California (Geniella, 2001b). The NF had for a long time been in the business of

ordering "hits" on rival gang members and having younger members on the street carry out these contract murders. At one point, with seven dead bodies to their credit, the NF felt so emboldened that it wanted to assassinate an aggressive, no-nonsense prosecutor. The killings continued until someone noticed that a pattern seemed to account for a lot of homicides and many other crimes. It was only at that point that local officials "discovered" that the NF was not just a prison gang, but that it also operated on the streets of California communities (Knox, 2012).

Prison Gang Membership and the Propensity to Recidivate

Shelden (1991) found that prison gang members were more likely to have a drug problem. Perhaps related to that, they also typically had an unstable work history with no legitimate occupation. Prison gang members (obviously) had criminal records that could limit their chances of finding legitimate employment after prison (Shelden, 1991). More gang members in juvenile facilities had court referrals than non-gang members (30% with seven or more, compared to 8% of gang members). Two-thirds of the gang members had at least one prior commitment compared to half of the non-gang members (Shelden, 1991).

Some blame correctional institutions and prison gangs for increases in crime in the community outside. When Anchorage, Alaska, was named the fifth most dangerous city in the entire nation by Forbes (after Memphis, Tennessee, Springfield, Illinois, and Flint and Detroit, Michigan), many Alaska inmates found themselves forced to join prison gangs to survive (KTVA Alaska, 2014). When they were released after completing their sentences, they were likely to be worse than they went in, according to corrections professionals. The problem was relatively new, as for years, Alaska inmates were transferred down to prisons in the Lower 48 because prisons in Alaska were overcrowded (KTVA Alaska, 2014).

Dooley, Seals, and Skarbek (2014) observed that prison gang membership increased recidivism in three ways. First, prison gang membership potentially identified given and observable characteristics about an inmate. Only those dedicated to a criminal lifestyle would agree to join the gang. With such a propensity, recidivism was expected (Dooley et al., 2014).

Second, membership in a prison gang was likely to increase the potential for recidivism because it increased exposure to criminally minded individuals and they would be more likely to trust a fellow prison gang member. Such affiliations can more easily influence an individual's behavior. Third, membership in a prison gang was likely to draw the attention of law enforcement. While they cannot identify and contain all crime, if someone committing a crime was increasingly receiving attention from law enforcement, the likelihood of arrest was increased (Dooley et al., 2014).

The NGCRC survey included the question, "in your opinion, do gang members tend to have a higher recidivism rate?" Not surprisingly, 90.1 percent of the respondents to this survey answered in the affirmative, that gang members did tend to have a higher rate of recidivism (Knox, 2012). When gang members have a higher recidivism rate, they need more effective reentry services and more specialized supervision by a gang certified parole officer. The survey also asked, "do you believe that gang members generally have a stronger affiliation with their gang after serving time?" The results of the survey show that 88 percent felt "yes," that the incarceration experience enhanced the ties to the gang, that serving time increased their ties to the gang (Knox, 2012).

Prison Gangs and Racial Issues

Few problems were as entrenched as that of racial conflict behind bars in American corrections. It was initially characterized by the existence of white racial extremism among inmates, which was itself supported and nourished by white racist extremist groups in the free world. It was an entrenched problem and it was directly related to the prison gang problem (Knox, 2012). Those working in corrections were very pessimistic about the prospects for reducing the problem, and few if any program resources existed in American corrections to deal with this enduring problem (Knox, 2012).

In the late 1960s and early 1970s, Stateville (IL) prison inmates were overwhelmingly black (70%) (Jacobs, 1977). Twenty percent of the inmates were white, and 10% were Hispanic. Jacobs (1977) noted that members of the four minority (black and Hispanic) gangs he studied demonstrated a "rudimentary solidarity opposed to white society, white administration, and white inmates" (p. 153). At the Stateville prison in 1972, there was no organizational structure for white inmates, although there were several cliques, some of which provided security (Jacobs, 1977). Those deemed secure were seen that way because of "fighting ability, gangland ties, legal skills or alliance with staff members" (p. 159). Jacobs (1977) noted that the more vulnerable prisoners were exposed to physical assault, rape, extortion, and constant harassment. By 1974, two prison gangs devoted to white inmates began to develop elsewhere in the Illinois prison system: the Ku Klux Klan and the House of the Golden Dragon.

Prison gangs were often aligned primarily by race and ethnicity, although a 2005 U.S. Supreme Court decision (*Johnson v. California*, 2005) examined CDCR's unwritten policy of racially segregating prisoners in double cells for up to 60 days each time they entered a new correctional facility. The policy was based on the asserted rationale that it prevented violence caused by racial gangs. The Court decided that only the "necessities of prison security and discipline" could be used for rationale to segregate inmates in such a way. The decision appeared to be in response to the Court's observation that race functioned as a proxy for gang membership, and gang membership served as a proxy for violence (*Johnson v. California*, 2005).

The 2012 survey asked, "do white inmates have a separate gang?" A majority of the institutions responding to the survey, some 70.1 percent ($N = 96$), reported "yes," that white inmates had a separate gang. Typically, that would entail something like the Aryan Brotherhood, which was pretty much a "whites only" type of gang (Knox, 2012). The responses since 1999 have been consistently above 70 percent. Responses in the early to mid-1990s ranged from 27 to 57 percent.

Many prison systems have tried to remove, or at least limit, racial issues. The state corrections system in Texas developed a policy in which they separate and isolate gang leaders and members, and integrate all non-gang members. The process was dubbed "the most racially integrated prison system in the nation" (Trulson, Marquart, & Kawucha, 2006, pp. 29–30).

As we saw in our discussion of the Community Responsibility System (CRS), all inmates must integrate into existing groups (Skarbek, 2014). Inmates cannot opt out of the CRS. Even those who were not active members were considered associates, so group members could determine whom the other group members were in order to foster and encourage engagement in the marketplace. Gangs work together to encourage peace in the CRS (Skarbek, 2014).

Inmates have structures in the prison community to fulfill the two requirements of the CRS. First, they have an easy way to determine which group the inmate affiliates with (Skarbek, 2014). The simplest method of identification and distinguishing one person (inmate) from another is by their appearance, and their race or ethnicity is often the most visible distinguisher. Each group uses logos and symbols to further distinguish members, and actively disciplines any inmate who uses a representative logo without having group affiliation. Second, each gang has a process for determining and ensuring the reliability of their members (Skarbek, 2014). That helps the gang ensure their reputation remains intact with the CRS.

Prison gangs have historically been homogeneous with respect to race. Gangs like the Aryan Brotherhood want white members, while gangs like the Black Guerrilla Family want black members. It is also true that conflicts involving Hispanic/Latino/Mexican gangs found in conflict with African American gangs can manifest in racial conflict as well. Anything that has increased racial conflict behind bars has also increased the gang problem behind bars (Knox, 2012). It was not known if the reverse is true: would any program designed to reduce racial conflict behind bars automatically reduce the prison gang problem too? The biggest reason for a lack of such knowledge was of course the fact that no one is promoting programs for "racial harmony" behind bars. It was not a popular feature of adult American corrections to find "programs designed for the reduction of racial/ethnic conflict among the inmates" (Knox, 2012). Among gang experts, it was reasonable to assume that racial conflict was a surrogate measure of gang conflict, and this is true whether we were looking at gang/race conflicts in high schools, the community, or correctional settings (Knox, 2012).

The NGCRC survey asked the following question for the first time in prison gang empirical research. The survey asked, "do you believe housing all members of one gang together could reduce the racial conflict among inmates in your facility?" There was little support for the idea that this was true. The majority of respondents (72.2%) felt that "no," housing all members of one gang together would not reduce racial conflict. Only about a fourth (27.8%) believed that housing all members of one gang together could reduce racial conflict (Knox, 2012). Some systems depend on the process of gang renunciation to alter their racial tension levels. With racial tensions running high at high security facilities, validated gang members and other residents have spent their exercise time in 15" × 7" cages, called "dog runs" (Malm, 2015). Even though inmates were segregated and separated by the cages, they refused to exercise simultaneously. Instead, inmates alternated their workout routines, waiting until members of rival gangs had finished. In prisons where gang renunciation was made available to inmates, several inmates, who would previously have killed each other on sight due to their race or gang, played a friendly basketball game (Malm, 2015).

Figure 5.5

Rows of prison cells inside Alcatraz Prison. Prison management includes more than the structure of the prison.

iStock.com/Eric Broder Van Dyke

The survey included the question, "does your facility have any programs for inmates which seek to improve race relations among inmates?" Only 8.5 percent of the respondents indicated that "yes," their facility had a program for inmates which seeks to improve race relations. For the overwhelming majority of cases, though (91.5%), respondents indicated that their correctional facility does not have such a program feature (Knox, 2012).

The survey included the question, "do you think anything can be done to reduce racial conflicts among inmates?" The results show almost a 50/50 split, with 51.5 percent responding "yes," they do believe something could be done to reduce racial conflict. The other half (48.5%) was skeptical, and did not believe anything can be done to reduce racial conflicts among inmates (Knox, 2012). The survey also included the question, "do you believe a program that sought to improve race relations among inmates could reduce the gang violence problem in your facility?" Some 30.7 percent of the respondents agreed that a program to improve race relations could reduce the gang problem as well. Most (69.3%) did not agree with this premise, that a program that sought to improve race relations among inmates could reduce the gang problem as well (Knox, 2012).

Prison Management Strategies

Prison administrators have used many different strategies to manage prison gangs. Overt and covert strategies ranging from isolating prison gang leaders, segregating gang members, vigorous prosecution of criminal acts, and using inmate informants have been used (Pyrooz et al., 2011). Less traditional strategies include transferring prison gang leaders to another institution and formally identifying the inmate as a gang member (known as jacketing) to keep him in a high-risk status and maintained in a secure housing unit have been tried, as well. Pyrooz et al. observed that the process of transferring out the problem gang member simply exported gang activity to another location (2011). Others might argue that segregation without a predicating activity was unconstitutional behavior. The normal response to those claims by prison administrators was that gang members had an elevated propensity for violence, and keeping them out of the general population protected inmates who were not gang members (Pyrooz et al., 2011).

Alternative programming was an option for prison management strategies, although prison gang members rarely choose to participate (Pyrooz et al., 2011). Shelden (1991) found that almost half of the gang members studied were not enrolled in any programs, compared to one-third of the non-gang members. Non-gang members were about eight times more likely than gang members to be enrolled in two or more programs (Shelden, 1991).

The recent NGCRC survey included the question, "in your estimate, what percentage of all institutional management problems in your facility are caused by gangs or gang members?" The results showed a range between a low of zero to a high of 100 percent.

The mean score was 27.2 percent, meaning that on average, gangs and gang members cause about a fourth of all management problems in prisons and jails (Knox, 2012). As we know from elsewhere in that report, telephone and mail monitoring were very commonly used as strategies to control gangs. That was true because the monitoring of mail and phone information provided raw, actionable intelligence on gangs and gang members. But because there were so many dimensions to the prison gang problem behind bars, there were many different strategies that have been used over the years as well (Knox, 2012). Most (over 75%) reported using phone call and mail monitoring programs. Most (over 50%) reported their facility used informers, transfers of problem inmates, and segregation. At least one-third (33%) used interrupting communications, balancing the number of rival gang members in the same unit, displacing members to different facilities, isolating leaders, and using a task force to monitor and track prison gang members.

Ruddell et al. (2006) surveyed jails throughout the U.S. and found that jail administrators used similar strategies. The three strategies that were considered most effective were segregation or separation, intelligence gathering, and sharing information with other agencies (Ruddell et al., 2006). The strategies deemed least successful were the restriction of outside visitors, transfer of gang members to other facilities, and sanctions for criminal behavior (Ruddell et al., 2006).

Renouncing the Gang

One way to control the prison gang problem was to offer gang members the opportunity to leave the gang. This was a tremendously underutilized option, and previous research showed that many inmates have tried to leave the gang—they just did not have any safe place to go (Knox, 2012). They were, or at least they felt they were, trapped in the gang life until they were released from prison. This was true because few resources existed to help them quit the gang life while behind bars (Knox, 2012).

A successful example of this process was found in California. Since 1999, the California Department of Corrections and Rehabilitation (CDCR) has received an increased number of requests from inmates seeking special protection (Malm, 2015). Those inmates intended to drop out of their prison gangs, and California had several Sensitive Needs Housing Units (SNHU) that were designed to protect former members from the gangs. The SNHUs provide a safer environment, free from gang activity. Inmates of different races and gang affiliations mix during their daily exercise and in the cafeteria during lunch (Malm, 2015). Prisoners who would previously have killed each other on sight due to their race or gang now play a friendly basketball game on the SNHU court (Malm, 2015).

The 2012 survey asked, "does your facility have a special program that is able to get gang inmates to quit their gang?" A few (15.7%) indicated "yes," thus the vast majority did not have any special program to help their inmates quit gang life (Knox, 2012). One example of a program that encourages inmates to quit their gang is the GRAD program in the Texas state prison system. GRAD is the acronym for the federally funded "Gang Renouncement and Disassociation Process" (Riggs, 2004). In three stages during nine months of program services, they are taught "how to start new lives outside the gangs" (Riggs, 2004). Apparently more than 600 inmates are on the waiting list for the program.

Winterdyk, Fillipuzzi, Mescrier, and Hencks (2009) examined prison gang intervention strategies in Canada. Among the success stories, they found that "once the offender renounced their gang affiliation, they were less likely to be involved in violence than prior to their renunciation, and that they seldom returned to the gang" (p. 23). The survey showed that slightly more than one-third of respondents indicated that they had a formal gang renunciation program in place (Winterdyk et al., 2009). With the exception of "interventions based on a formal education or treatment program," none of the renunciation strategies was identified as being overly effective. Table 5.3 provides a breakdown of responses.

Morales (2011) suggested that there should be more gang renunciation programs to create distrust in the gangs and diminish their influence. If gang members know they

TABLE 5.3 Perceived Effectiveness at Increasing the Number of Members That Have Formally Renounced Involvement in STG Gang Renunciation Strategies

	Very Effective	Somewhat Effective	Not Effective	Not Applicable
Interventions using faith-based strategies	0	15.4%	7.7%	76.9%
Interventions using chaplains or other religious leaders	0	7.7%	0	92.3%
Interventions by counselors, casework staff, or unit managers	7.7%	38.5%	0	53.8%
Interventions based on racial, cultural, or ethnic values	0	23.1%	7.7%	69.2%
Interventions based on a formal educational, or treatment program	15.4%	30.8%	0	53.8%

Winterdyk, J., Fillipuzzi, N., Mescrier, J., and Hencks, C. (2009). *Prison Gangs: A review and survey of strategies*. Correctional Service of Canada.

can leave the gang, and will be protected, they might not "stay quiet about what their gangs are doing" (Morales, 2011, p. 196). Although it can be difficult to convince prison administration of the value of such a program, they can help improve the recidivism rate tremendously. It was important to start slow and make sure the program was very structured (Morales, 2011). Prison gang leaders may try to sabotage the program.

It was very common in gang reclamation and intervention (renunciation) programs, to have a member of a gang who wants to quit gang life, but who had a gang tattoo, often on a prominent area of the body. Gang tattoo removal services were seen as an effective tool, in combination with gang renunciation programs, to help people leave gang life behind (Knox, 2012). It was an especially effective tool inside correctional facilities, where having a gang tattoo removal service was essential in the effort to change the social identity of a gang member.

The 2012 survey asked the question, "does your facility have a gang tattoo removal program for inmates who want to quit gang life?" Only a small percentage, 2.1 percent ($N = 3$), reported having such a service (Knox, 2012). The overwhelming majority of adult correctional facilities responding to the survey reported that they did not have a gang tattoo removal service for their inmates. It would be very hard to assist inmates and prisoners to leave the gang life if they faced such an uphill battle to get rid of their gang tattoos.

The survey also asked, "what percentage of the inmates who come in as gang members actually quit their gang?" The results ranged from a low of zero to a high of 30 percent, with a mean score of 6.19 percent (Knox, 2012). The 2004 survey responses had a mean of 9.46 percent. There were many reasons why an inmate may quit the gang, and it may be unrelated to the existence or non-existence of a program or service designed to encourage inmates to detach from the gang life (Knox, 2012). It appeared that the inactive gang population was quite small in American prisons and jails. For self-protection perhaps, they may need to be active gang members (Knox, 2012).

Segregation and Classification of STGs

STG management by segregation and classification was a significant challenge, especially in the area of due process. The best practices approach, using lessons learned and evidence-based type strategies with reliable and valid criteria, provided for an objective classification system (Vigil, 2006). Classification reviews were typically determined by a number of factors: criminal and behavioral history, medical and mental health history and needs, length of sentence, and others. While classification alone cannot decrease violence, escape, or litigation, establishing a solid program and periodically evaluating and improving it can make managing dangerous and disruptive inmates less of a risk (Vigil, 2006).

Toch (2007) claimed that the classification process was flawed and was akin to "segregating gang members for life" (p. 275). He observed that hearings for gang members were often streamlined and did not provide the accused with information regarding the nature of the allegations against him. The CDCR promoted their comprehensive gang management strategy to include curtailing the ability of gangs to participate in crimes and enabling the offender to reintegrate into the general population (2012). Their policy noted that "offenders who do not engage in disruptive gang behavior" would be afforded the opportunity to do so (CDCR, 2012, p. 5).

Many corrections organizations advocate segregation as a management philosophy for gang members. Corrections Corporation of America (CCA) used the Inmate Management System, an inmate database of known gang membership and affiliations, photos of gang culture tattoos, and other identifying markings, to track confirmed inmate gang members and to monitor all suspicions of inmate gang affiliations and activities (Corrections Corporation of America, n.d.). In an effort to suppress facility gang activity, correctional administrators and staff members examined strategies from other correctional systems as well as company-wide best practices. Administrators from different regions worked to establish an aggressive strategy to address gangs and created what was CCA's gang management program. The admission phase was chosen as the prime time frame for inmates to undergo a rigorous, one-on-one interview session with a security threat group coordinator—a designated facility staff member responsible for managing gang intelligence, activities and investigations at the facility—to assess the likelihood of gang association (Corrections Corporation of America, n.d.). The security threat group coordinator also explains CCA's zero-tolerance policy for gang activity and strongly advises the inmate to divulge any gang affiliations the facility should know about when selecting a housing location—a key step in preventing violence in the facility.

Additionally, the security threat group coordinator examines the inmate for tattoos and other gang-culture markings that are photographed, catalogued in CCA's Inmate Management System 2 (IMS2) database and, if necessary, disseminated to fellow STG coordinators and facility staff for review and awareness. After identification, inmates who are suspected gang members are tracked and monitored daily by security threat group coordinators. Any suspicious or deviant behavior is relayed to staff at each shift change to ensure consistent monitoring and to maintain safety and security of the facility (Corrections Corporation of America, n.d.).

The survey included the question, "does your institutional system take gang membership into account?" Some 69.8 percent of the respondents indicated "yes" that their classification system takes gang membership into account. Still, some 30.2 percent said "no," that their classification system does not take gang membership into account (Knox, 2012). About 67% of the 2004 survey respondents indicated they took gang membership into account for classification.

Intensive Supervision Units (ISU)

When gang-affiliated inmates display behavioral problems or participate in violent activity, many corrections agencies place them in intensive supervision units

(ISU)—restrictive and structured housing away from the influence of other inmates in the general population (Corrections Corporation of America, n.d.). Inmates are isolated and remain there for a specified time, allowing the correctional facility to remove the high-risk inmate from the larger population and better manage staff resources.

In 2012, the CDCR adjusted their rules for the secure housing unit and began classifying prison gangs as STGs. The new rules included a step-down program for gang members to be released into the general population. The rules also include a validation system to identify STG affiliates using a point system. To be validated, a total of at least three sources must provide at least 10 of the optional points against an inmate (CDCR, 2012).

The points assigned to the categories are as follows:

- *Two points*: symbols (e.g., hand signs, graffiti, distinctive clothing), written materials identifying the prisoner that was not in the personal possession of the prisoner (e.g., membership or enemy lists);

- *Three points*: association with validated STG affiliates, informant information (however, validation cannot be based solely on hearsay informant information), debriefing reports;

- *Four points*: written materials that are in the personal possession of the prisoner, photos (no more than four years old), CDCR staff observations, information from other agencies, visits from people known to promote or assist STG activities, communications (e.g., phone conversations, mail, notes);

- *Five points*: self-admissions;

- *Six points*: crimes committed for benefit, at direction or in association with an STG, tattoos or body markings;

- *Seven points*: legal documents (15 CCR § 3378.2(b)(1)–(14); Prison Law Office, 2014).

The classification documentation must disclose all source items used in a validation and provide a copy of all non-confidential documents being relied upon (Prison Law Office, 2014).

If corrections administrators assign inmates affiliated with a prison gang to housing so that they were always held in a housing unit with their same or allied gang members, they give a unique power to the gang. Those that argue in favor of keeping the inmates locked in with their own gang preference will typically claim that this reduces conflicts between the gangs (Knox, 2012).

The NGCRC survey asked, "In your opinion, would it be best to incarcerate members of the same gang in the same prison housing area, or is it better to mix them up and disperse gang/STG members?" The responses showed that 28.1 percent felt it was good policy to segregate prison gang members by their specific gang identity (Knox, 2012). But over two-thirds of the respondents, some 71.9 percent felt the reverse was true. Additionally, the 2012 survey asked, "Do you believe that housing all members of one gang together could make that gang stronger and more powerful?" Most (83%) responded "yes." Only 17 percent did not believe that housing all members of one gang together would make them stronger.

Alternative Solutions

Skarbek (2014) identified the two approaches used by the CDCR. The primary strategy involved identifying gang-involved offenders, tracking and monitoring them, and applying sanctions when they engaged in gang activity. In the prisons, this strategy included housing gang members apart from the general population in highly restrictive areas. This strategy, according to Skarbek (2014), ignores the need of the population for governance, as it focuses mostly on removing one of many parts without fixing the problem. Another, quite different, approach was being used by the CDCR and about 150 facilities across the U.S. The California variation started by advising new inmates of the dangers of gang membership and then showing them alternatives to gang membership. Both practices have failed.

Governance theory suggests that to limit the effects of prison gangs, conditions that caused the environment in which they grow must be changed and substitutions for their inherited functions must be found. Skarbek (2014) identified three possible solutions:

1. Make prisons safer and more liberal

2. Incarcerate fewer people

3. Hire more police (p. 161).

Skarbek (2014) suggested making performance measurement system that tied the warden's pay to the inmates' post-release behavior. Prison administration should "interview released inmates about their experience and prison conditions" (Skarbek, 2014, p. 161). He also suggested that legalizing the use of tobacco by inmates and reducing the number of people incarcerated would reduce the need for extralegal governance and the prison gangs that administer it.

Respondents to the survey followed a different thought. The 2012 NGCRC survey asked, "do you believe it would be beneficial to have a new federal criminal law making it a felony to recruit new gang members while incarcerated?" Some 85.3 percent answered yes, while only 14.7 percent did not believe it would be beneficial to have such a new law.

The survey also asked whether the respondents thought "a zero-tolerance policy is the best approach for dealing with gangs and gang members." Some 61.5 percent answered "strongly agree," and another 26.6 percent answered "agree." Only 9.8 percent answered "neither agree or disagree" and 2.1 percent answered "disagree" (Knox, 2012).

Prison Gang Evolution

As gangs on the streets outside have evolved, so have prison gangs. A group of former prison gang associates or foot soldiers has started to challenge the established prison gang dynamic.

Many young Hispanic inmates in Texas prisons, especially those with prior street gang affiliations, have joined prison gang-like groups known as *Tangos* (Tapia, Sparks, & Miller, 2014). In the 1990s, affiliation with a Tango group amounted to serving as an *esquina*, or backup for fights between its parent gang and others. Tangos were foot soldiers, and the best had a chance of becoming a prospect of the prison gang (Tapia et al., 2014). By many accounts, too few of them were afforded the opportunity to be prospects (Tapia et al., 2014).

Contemporary Tangos have resisted the prison gang label. They have proposed to act as a support network for inmates who want to do their time peacefully and avoid coercion from traditional Latino prison gangs (Tapia et al., 2014). There were at least five distinct Tango factions throughout the state of Texas (Tapia et al., 2014).

The "H-town" or "Houstone" Tango was the originator and largest component of "Tango Blast," a statewide confederation of Tangos from different cities that have challenged the Texas Syndicate and the other traditional Latino prison gangs (Tapia et al., 2014). The Tango Blast model has grown in popularity and could change the landscape because it rejects old notions of prison gang exclusivity and lifelong commitments. Authorities say the trendy look and loose rules of the Tango Blast were proving irresistible to kids (Tapia et al., 2014). Tangos can maintain affiliations with gangs they joined outside prison, a hybrid approach to membership that allows them to plant tentacles in many established Hispanic neighborhood gangs (Tapia et al., 2014). Other groups are likely to follow the Tangos' lead, many for the same reasons.

Prison Gangs Today

There were many complex and intricate aspects of the prison gang problem behind bars.

This NGCRC has conducted studies like those cited in this chapter dating back to the early 1990s. We have not seen the prison gang problem level off yet, which means that gang density was on the rise. It may be possible for gangs to claim that they run the jails and prisons, because of the power they wield there (Knox, 2012). There was little optimism about the chances of reducing or curtailing the prison gang problem behind bars. Most of the respondents were pessimistic about the future: they expect the prison gang problem to increase in the next few years (Knox, 2012).

One of the challenges for corrections professionals going forward could be the transition to a younger generation for both their prison gang members and their corrections officers. With the increase in prison and street gang numbers, and the inclination of older prisoners to show some level of disrespect to the younger and less experienced prisoners (such as "boys trying to be men"; Hunt, Riegel, Morales, & Waldorf, 1993), problems as described previously were likely to continue. Additionally, with the corrections field being one of the fastest growing in the nation, supported by a growth in both public and private correctional agencies, the employment of younger staff will bring a combination of naiveté, inexperience, and innovative ideas that will likely confound the strategies of more experienced administrators (Marcell, 2006).

The top of the "wish list" for adult state prisons in terms of dealing with gangs would probably be improving their intelligence/information systems. The idea was to track and monitor the gang problem and make the information available to a wide variety of key personnel. Constant monitoring of gang inmates would mean watching who they talk to and when, monitoring their tattoos, and perhaps in strategic or tactical ways letting the inmates know that the corrections system knew what they were up to (Knox, 2012).

Directly tied to the issue of having an improved intelligence or management information system was "how" and "who" will collect the information, and this goes to the belief that one way to improve the capability of correctional institutions to respond to the prison gang problem was to organize local gang task force groups. The gang task force would be given the responsibility to conduct initial interviews of incoming inmates and track those who were gang members or who have had previous STG involvement of any kind. By establishing a gang or STG task force, this creates training opportunities for internal training and for greater involvement of line staff in a voluntary capacity: offer the training to all who want it, and recruit within this cadre of trained personnel for qualified persons to carry out the mission and mandates of the local gang task force. Getting outside involvement was key to a successful local task force (Knox, 2012).

Lastly, the category of what was said to be an innovative way to control gang activity in prison was linked to creating new programs or services for inmates. The biggest demand was for a program that would have inmates denounce or renounce their gang life; with this kind of program, then other rehabilitative efforts will be successful to ultimately reduce the "threat level" of the inmate and help him/her to be reintegrated back into society (Knox, 2012). Having a renunciation program basically means providing inmates a method of disassociating from gang life.

Similarly, some suggested that if a correctional agency was going to have a "renunciation program," then one level of measuring the effectiveness of the program would be indicated by the number of inmates willing to have their proudly worn gang tattoos removed. Offer them a tattoo removal service, help them start a new beginning somewhere, let them get good job training or education that will restore their pride—those were traditional aims of rehabilitation, but rehabilitation was not a major goal of adult correctional systems in most states (Knox, 2012).

These are key predictions made by those who work in correctional institutions.

- Most of the respondents (85.1%) expect the prison gang problem to increase. Less than one percent (0.7%) believe the problem will decrease, and 14.2 percent believe the problem will remain at about the same level (Knox, 2012).

- Most believe that assaults on corrections officers by prison gang members will increase. Some 62.5 percent of the respondents expressed the belief that the problem of prison gang members assaulting correctional officers and staff will increase in the next few years. Only 2.1 percent felt the problem will decrease, and over a third (35.4%) felt the problem would remain at the same level it was at now (Knox, 2012).

- Prison gangs will (continue to) infiltrate the correction officer ranks. Many correction officers, as well as senior DOC managers, openly expressed concern over the threat of gang infiltration into their ranks, and gang members told the commission that gangs actively try to achieve such infiltration. Until September 2008, the New Jersey Department of Corrections (NJ DOC) did not even ask whether such applicants were members or associates of a gang. The NJ DOC has also begun examining applicants' internet-based personal pages on social media websites. After one such set of reviews, the department rejected the applications of nine individuals whose pages openly displayed clear evidence of gang affiliation (State of New Jersey Commission of Investigation, 2009).

Some of the More Well-Known Prison Gangs

Aryan Brotherhood

White inmates established the Aryan Brotherhood (AB) in San Quentin State Prison in California to protect themselves from attack by black and Hispanic inmates in 1967 (Orlando-Morningstar, 1997). The AB was originally ruled by consensus but is now highly structured with two factions—one in the CDCR and the other in the Federal Bureau of Prisons system. The majority of members are Caucasian males, and the gang is primarily active in the Southwest and Pacific regions. Its main source of income is the distribution of cocaine, heroin, marijuana, and methamphetamine within the prison systems as well as on the streets. Some AB members have business relationships with Mexican DTOs that smuggle illegal drugs into California for AB distribution. AB was

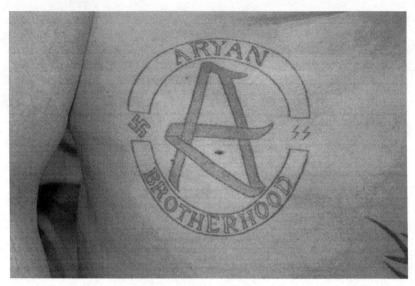

Figure 5.6
Aryan Brotherhood tattoo. Public domain.
U.S. Department of Justice

notoriously violent and is often involved in murder for hire. Although historically linked to the California-based Hispanic prison gang Mexican Mafia (La Eme), tension between AB and La Eme is becoming increasingly evident as seen in fights between Caucasians and Hispanics within the CDC (NDIC, 2008).

Barrio Azteca

Barrio Azteca is one of the most violent prison gangs in the U.S. The gang is highly structured and has an estimated membership of 2,000. Most members are Mexican national or Mexican American males. Barrio Azteca is most active in the Southwest region, primarily in federal, state, and local corrections facilities in Texas and outside prison in southwestern Texas and southeastern New Mexico (NDIC, 2008). The gang's main source of income is derived from smuggling heroin, powder cocaine, and marijuana from Mexico into the U.S. for distribution both inside and outside prisons. Gang members often transport illicit drugs across the U.S.-Mexico border for DTOs. Barrio Azteca members also are involved in alien smuggling, arson, assault, auto theft, burglary, extortion, intimidation, kidnapping, robbery, and weapons violations (NDIC, 2008).

Black Guerrilla Family

Black Guerrilla Family (BGF), originally called Black Family or Black Vanguard, is a prison gang that was founded in the San Quentin State Prison in 1966. The BGF was started by George Jackson, a member of the Black Panthers (Orlando-Morningstar, 1997). The gang is highly organized, along paramilitary lines, with a supreme leader and central committee. BGF has an established national charter, code of ethics, and oath of allegiance. BGF members operate primarily in California, Georgia, Maryland, and Missouri. The gang has 100 to 300 members, most of whom are African American males (NDIC, 2008). A primary source of income for gang members is the distribution of cocaine and marijuana. BGF members obtain these drugs primarily from Nuestra Familia/Norteños members or from local Mexican traffickers. BGF members are involved in other criminal activities including auto theft, burglary, drive-by shootings, and homicide (NDIC, 2008).

Four Horsemen, Tangos, and Tango Blast

Texas prison officials first noted the presence of a gang known as Four Horsemen in 1998. Some Hispanic gang members entering the Texas Department of Criminal Justice (TDCJ) from the cities of Austin, Dallas, Fort Worth, and Houston were not interested in joining an established prison gang and established Four Horsemen to protect one another and to engage in illegal activities, particularly drug trafficking, to make money. Four Horsemen became known as Tangos, because its members wore tattoos that reflected the town (or *tango*) in which they resided prior to incarceration (NDIC, 2008). As interest in Tangos grew among Hispanic gang members entering TDCJ from other areas of Texas, Tangos from West Texas, the Rio Grande Valley, San Antonio, and El Paso were accepted. Of the eight groups now recognized as Tangos, only six are part of Tango Blast, also known as Puro Tango Blast. Tango Blast includes Tangos from the four original cities as well as the West Texas and Rio Grande Valley areas. Tango Blast differs from Tangos in that separate Tango Blast gangs sometimes band together to help one another. The gang's rapid growth poses a significant new security threat, and elements of Tango Blast within TDCJ appear to be challenging Texas Syndicate for control of illegal prison activities. Tango members appear to return to their local street gangs when released from prison, rather than continue their prison-based affiliation (NDIC, 2008).

Hermanos de Pistoleros Latinos

Hermanos de Pistoleros Latinos (HPL) is a Hispanic prison gang formed in the TDCJ in the late 1980s. It operates in most prisons in Texas and on the streets in many communities in Texas, particularly Laredo. HPL is also active in several cities in Mexico, and its largest contingent in that country is located in Nuevo Laredo. The gang is structured and is estimated to have 1,000 members. Gang members maintain close ties to several Mexican DTOs and are involved in the trafficking of large quantities of cocaine and marijuana from Mexico into the U.S. for distribution (NDIC, 2008).

Melanics

The Melanics were formed in the prison in Jackson, Michigan, in 1981. The term *melanic* refers to members of the black or African American race. The gang appeared only in Michigan. They were listed as an STG known as the Melanic Islamic Palace of the Rising Sun (MIPRS; Knox, 2002). The MIPRS were fraught with violence and rebellion. They empowered members through military roles and titles, and encouraged them to fight as if they are in a revolution or rebellion (Knox, 2002). The group tended to follow leftist influences from the 1960s and 1070s (not unlike those promoted by the Black Panthers and Black Guerrilla Family). They maintained an alliance with the Gangster Disciples since December 12, 1998 (Knox, 2002). The group became defunct by name, but has hundreds of members operating in an underground capacity (Knox, 2004b).

Mexican Mafia

The Mexican Mafia prison gang, also known as La Eme (Spanish for the letter M), was formed in the late 1950s within the CDCR (NDIC, 2008). It is loosely structured and has strict rules that must be followed by the estimated 350 to 400 members. Most members are Mexican American males who previously belonged to a southern California street gang. Mexican Mafia is active in 13 states, but its power base is in California (NDIC, 2008). The gang's main source of income is extorting drug distributors outside prison and distributing methamphetamine, cocaine, heroin, and marijuana within the prison systems and on the streets. Some members have direct links to Mexican DTOs and broker deals for themselves and their associates. Mexican Mafia also is involved in other criminal activities including controlling gambling and homosexual prostitution in prison (NDIC, 2008).

Mexikanemi

The Mexikanemi prison gang (also known as Texas Mexican Mafia or Emi) was formed in the early 1984 within the TDCJ (Orlando-Morningstar, 1997). The gang is highly structured and is estimated to have 2,000 members, most of whom are Mexican national or Mexican American males who were living in Texas at the time of incarceration (NDIC, 2008). Mexikanemi poses a significant drug trafficking threat to communities in the Southwest region, particularly in Texas. Gang members reportedly traffic multikilogram quantities of powder cocaine, heroin, and methamphetamine, and multiton quantities of

Figure 5.7
Mexican Mafia tattoo. Public domain.
U.S. Department of Justice

marijuana, from Mexico into the U.S. for distribution inside and outside prison. Gang members obtain drugs from associates or members of the Osiel Cárdenas-Guillén and/ or Vicente Carrillo-Fuentes Mexican DTOs. In addition, Mexikanemi members possibly maintain a relationship with Los Zetas, which is associated with the Gulf Cartel (NDIC, 2008). The Mexikanemi is the largest prison gang in the Texas prison system and is becoming a significant threat in the federal prison system (Orlando-Morningstar, 1997).

Nazi Low Riders

Nazi Low Riders (NLR) is a violent California-based prison gang that subscribes to a white supremacist philosophy. The gang has 800 to 1,000 members, most of whom are Caucasian males with a history of street gang activity and drug abuse (NDIC, 2008). NLR operates in correctional facilities and communities, primarily in the Pacific and Southwest regions. The gang's primary sources of income are derived from the distribution of multiounce to multipound quantities of methamphetamine, retail-level distribution of heroin and marijuana, and extortion of independent Caucasian drug dealers and other white supremacist gangs. Members also engage in violent criminal activity such as armed robbery, assault, assault with deadly weapons, murder, and attempted murder; in addition, they commit identity fraud, money laundering, witness intimidation, and witness retaliation (NDIC, 2008).

Ñeta

Ñeta is a prison gang that began in Puerto Rico and spread to the U.S. Ñeta is one of the largest and most violent prison gangs, with about 7,000 members in Puerto Rico and 5,000 in the U.S. Ñeta chapters in Puerto Rico exist exclusively inside prisons; once members are released from prison they no longer are considered to be part of the gang. In the U.S., Ñeta chapters exist both inside and outside prisons within 36 cities in nine states, primarily in the Northeast region. The gang's main source of income is the retail-level distribution of powder and crack cocaine, heroin, marijuana and, to a lesser extent, LSD, MDMA, methamphetamine, and PCP. Ñeta members also commit such crimes as assault, auto theft, burglary, drive-by shootings, extortion, home invasion, money laundering, robbery, weapons and explosives trafficking, and witness intimidation (NDIC, 2008). Los Ñetas have spread from Puerto Rico to U.S. prison systems in Connecticut, Florida, Massachusetts, New Jersey, New York, Pennsylvania, and Rhode Island (Montalvo-Barbot, 1997). Other Puerto Rican gangs like El Grupo 25 de Enero del 1981, were started by Puerto Rican prisoners in response to a need for protection from Los Ñetas (Montalvo-Barbot, 1997).

Nuestra Familia (NF)

La Nuestra Familia ("Our Family") originated in Soledad State Prison in the mid-1960s. Most of the original members were Hispanic inmates from northern California who were seeking to protect themselves from the Mexican Mafia, a gang composed of Hispanic inmates from southern California cities. La Nuestra Familia has a formal structure and rules of conduct. It is governed by a group known as "La Mesa," which resembles a board of directors (Orlando-Morningstar, 1997). Several years ago a blood war developed between La Nuestra Familia and the Mexican Mafia over the control of drug trafficking inside prison. Recent evidence, however, indicates that the rivalry between the two gangs may be easing in California. CDCR officials report that the two gangs appear to have called a "partial truce"; some members have returned to prison without fulfilling obligations (Orlando-Morningstar, 1997).

Public Enemy Number One

Public Enemy Number One (PEN1) is the fastest-growing Caucasian prison gang, with an estimated 400 to 500 members operating in prisons and communities in California and, to a much lesser extent, in locations throughout the Northeast, Pacific, Southwest, Southeast, and West Central regions of the country (NDIC, 2008). PEN1 members espouse a white supremacist philosophy and pose a criminal threat inside and outside prison because of their alliance with AB and NLR. Gang members derive their income from distributing mid-level and retail-level quantities of methamphetamine. In addition, members engage in violent criminal activity such as assault, attempted murder, and homicide as well as auto theft, burglary, identity theft, and property crimes (NDIC, 2008).

Sureños

As individual Hispanic street gang members enter the prison systems, they put aside former rivalries with other Hispanic street gangs and unite under the name Sureños or Norteños. The original Mexican Mafia members, most of whom were from southern California, considered Mexicans from the rural, agricultural areas of northern California as weak and viewed them with contempt (NDIC, 2008). To distinguish themselves from the agricultural workers or farmers from northern California, members of Mexican Mafia began to refer to the Hispanic gang members that worked for them as Sureños (southerners). Sureños gang members' main sources of income are the retail-level distribution of cocaine, heroin, marijuana, and methamphetamine both within prison systems and in the community, as well as the extortion of drug distributors on the streets. Some members have direct links to Mexican DTOs and broker deals for Mexican Mafia as well as their own gang. Sureños gangs also are involved in other criminal activities such as assault, carjacking, home invasion, homicide, and robbery (NDIC, 2008).

Norteños

Inmates from northern California became known as Norteños (northerners) and are affiliated with NF. Norteños gang members' main sources of income are the retail-level distribution of cocaine, heroin, marijuana, methamphetamine, and PCP within prison systems and in the community, as well as the extortion of drug distributors on the streets. Norteños gangs also are involved in other criminal activities such as assault, carjacking, home invasion, homicide, and robbery (NDIC, 2008).

Texas Syndicate

Texas Syndicate (TS) is one of the largest and most violent prison gangs; it is active on both sides of the U.S.-Mexico border and poses a significant drug trafficking threat to communities in the Southwest region (NDIC, 2008). The TS is highly structured and is estimated to have 1,300 members, most of whom are Mexican American males between 20 and 40 years of age. Gang members smuggle multikilogram quantities of powder cocaine, heroin, and methamphetamine and multiton quantities of marijuana from Mexico into the U.S. for distribution inside and outside prison. Gang members have a direct working relationship with associates and/or members of the Osiel Cárdenas-Guillén DTO. In addition, TS members possibly maintain a relationship with Los Zetas (NDIC, 2008). Fong (1990) found that both the Texas Syndicate and the Mexican Mafia shared similar characteristics with respect to organizational structure, leadership style, and recruiting styles.

Trinitarios

The Trinitarios, the most rapidly expanding Caribbean gang and the largest Dominican gang, are a violent prison gang with members operating on the street. The Trinitarios are involved in homicide, violent assaults, robbery, theft, home invasions, and street-level drug distribution (NGIC, 2011). Although predominant in New York and New Jersey, the Trinitarios have expanded to communities throughout the eastern United States, including Georgia, Massachusetts, Pennsylvania, and Rhode Island. An increase in the Dominican population in several eastern U.S. jurisdictions has resulted in the expansion and migration of Dominican gangs such as the Trinitarios. This has led to an increase in drug trafficking, robberies, violent assaults in the tri-state area (NGIC, 2011).

DISCUSSION QUESTIONS

1. Describe how membership in a prison gang affects an inmate's inclination toward violence.
2. Identify the general forms of inmate crime.
3. Examine how prison gangs are alike and dissimilar to STGs.
4. Explain the premises with several of the more effective gang management strategies.
5. What evolutions in prison gangs can corrections professionals expect in the near future?

CHAPTER 6 Females in the Gang World

Introduction

Females have been part of gangs in the United States for many years. Asbury's (1927) early account of gangs identified both active female gang members and female auxiliary (support) gangs. While some criminal justice professionals and researchers may have doubts about the existence of legitimate female gang members, those suspicions don't make their existence any less real.

This chapter will review images of female gang members, female gangs, and the violence against females by gangs and gang members. We will examine rival theoretical ideas like the chivalry and convergence hypotheses. We will review the interesting results from a National Gang Crime Research Center (NGCRC) survey of female gang members in Chicago. From this we will learn about the social profile of a female gang member and the fact that sexual abuse is often found in the life span of female gang members. The chapter examines a number of scenarios in which violence occurs against females in the gang context, such as gang dating, gang rape, and prostitution.

Images of Female Gangs

There has been much academic research on female gangs. Joan Moore's (1991) description of female gang members from Los Angeles is that they fit the social profile of being from the economic underclass trapped in depressed competitive urban areas. That was consistent with Anne Campbell's findings in *The Girls in the Gang*, where Campbell interviewed three female gang members and described the underclass profile of unemployability, poverty, minority status, stigma, and educational failure. The study by Harris (1988) interviewed 21 Latino female gang members and showed we need school-based gang intervention and prevention programs for youth well before the age of 15.

Fishman (1988) studied black female gang members from a gang called the Vice Queens. Their social profile included urban poverty and economic deprivation. Cloward and Ohlin (1960), in advancing a theory of crime and delinquency specifically aimed at explaining the onset of gangs, noted that gangs tended to originate in those communities that lacked legitimate opportunities and which might have had conspicuous illegitimate opportunities.

Lauderback, Hansen, and Waldorf (1992) interviewed 65 female gang members in San Francisco, mostly Latinos (78.5%). They documented an all-female gang called the Potrero Hill Posse (PHP) that specialized in running rock houses (crack houses). According to their study:

> A very common occurrence at rock houses is the exchange of sex for crack. Called "hubba honeys" and "toss-ups," there are women of all ages who frequent these establishments merely to garner a small amount of crack by providing male patrons with sexual favors, generally oral copulation. Unlike female sex workers, who are usually very strict about what services they will perform for specific sums of money, there is no such standard with toss-ups who will provide virtually any type of sex for meager amounts of crack.

Felkene and Becker's (1994) study included 40 female gang members from Los Angeles and showed many prosocial characteristics: 91.9 percent believed in God, 59.5 percent were satisfied with their lives, 39.5 percent went to church several times a year, and so forth. The research by Rosenbaum (The Violent Few, 1996) focused on a sample of 214 juvenile females confined in the California Youth Authority. Of great interest was that Rosenbaum established that the gang density level in the sample of confined juveniles was 32 percent (70, or 32%, were considered female gang members).

A startling finding from Rosenbaum was that some 94 percent of the confined female gang members had been arrested for a violent crime. Some 58 percent reported being a sexual abuse victim and concludes "many were members of female-only gangs."

Chang (1996) studied female Chicago gang members at the Cook County Jail. In the sample of 307 female inmates, 97 were gang members. That showed a gang density of 30 percent for adult female gang member inmates, almost identical to the density of confined female juvenile gang members reported in the Los Angeles Rosenbaum sample (1996). Furthermore, some 40.2 percent of the female gang members in Chang's (1996) sample reported ever being sexually abused. Chang (1996) noted: "Our study supports Bowker and Klein's findings (1983) that female friendship was more important in determining gang membership than any other variables" (p. 12).

Referring to Chang, Knox (1995) observed: "This study confirmed previous studies that there are structural barriers to female gang involvement" (p. 21).

The 1997 NGCRC Female Gang Task Force Report (Knox, 1997a) compared 320 female gang members with 3,736 male gang members. The project involved 29 researchers who collected data in 17 states from 85 different correctional facilities (Project GANGFACT). A total of 57.2 percent of the females reporting having ever been forced to have sex that they did not want to have, compared to only 15 percent among male gang members. In one regard, females were more involved in nefarious gang activities than their male gang member counterparts. When asked "have you ever personally made false 911 calls to the police emergency number in connection with your gang activities?," 23.9 percent of the male members reported doing this, compared to 31.3 percent among female gang members. So female gang members were significantly more likely to make false 911 calls in gang activities than were the male gang members.

The report by Lurigio, Schwartz, and Chang (1998) made a secondary analysis of the Cook County Jail data (Chang, 1996). Among its findings:

> Female gang members in the present study were more likely than nongang members to report that their mothers had drinking problems, suggesting that they came from more troubled households (p. 28).

Another finding that is consistent with prior research related to the reasons why women leave gangs, such as the female gang members in Sikes's (1997) participatory research: "the women in our sample left the gang primarily because of the competing demands of childcare." Also in Sikes's research, the current data suggested that at a certain point in the women's lives, gangbanging is viewed as too costly or simply seems inappropriate because of their ages or household responsibilities. Sikes (1997) found that:

> Respondents' claims of gender equality in gangs, however, were contradicted by their reports that they engaged in rather stereotypic activities (e.g., serving as

"mules" by carrying drugs and weapons, and having sex with gang leaders). Also, none of our respondents stated that she was a leader in the gang (p. 105).

The analysis of literature by Anderson, Brooks, Langsam, and Dyson (2002) suggested the female gang member from 1990 to present was a "new" type of gang member different from previous generations and time periods. What is new is the modern female gang member is more violent, uses more weapons, has more gang influence over others, and is more motivated to achieve financial success through drug sales than previous cohorts of female gang members. They concluded that providing better employment and educational opportunities will be needed in any gang prevention strategy of the future.

The research by Turley (2003) examined detained female juvenile gang members in six Texas counties for the year 1998. Among other things, it showed gang density rates ranging from a low of 7.7 percent (Dallas County) to a high of 30 percent (San Antonio County). Noting that Texas was not witnessing many all-female gangs "that are autonomous and not connected to any male gang," Turley (2003) went on to explain that:

> This trend, while minor considering the arrest data that does not show females to be a major threat in gang violence or gang membership, does give credence to the work by some researchers that show a more self-determining agenda for female gangs (Lauderback et al., 1992; Knox et al., 1995; Felkenes & Becker, 1995).

Turley (2003) concluded that:

> The presence of male gang members does influence female gang membership, in that through coercion and peer pressure, male gang members proselytize potential female gang members in their neighborhoods to join. These male gangs will often have auxiliary female gang members that perform subordinate functions (sex roles and "muling" of drugs/guns) in the gang. Female gangs do not appear to be organized on their own in Texas' largest cities, but are created as a service unit of the main male gang (p. 7).

The research by Newbold and Dennehy (2003) involved oral interviews with 10 female gang associates, in this case women who associated with biker gangs in New Zealand. Child sexual abuse figured prominently as a causal factor, as "half (of the female gang associates) had experienced childhood sexual abuse." The study was built upon the research by Hopper and Moore (1990), which studied women involved in American biker gangs over a 17-year time period, which concluded that women are treated as inferior to male members who control them, dominate them, and abuse them.

The Newbold and Dennehy (2003) research therefore concludes that with regard to female associates of New Zealand biker gangs and stated:

Gangs are all-male organizations in which women are denied status or even membership. They are excluded from any say in gang politics or business and remain dependent on the men for acceptance and accreditation. Women are expected to display overt subservience to their partners and other gang members, especially on gang territory, with failure to do so likely to result in a beating.

The analysis by Sule (2005) used a sample of 114 eighth grade students who were identified as Hispanic female gang members. This was a secondary analysis of data from a GREAT Program evaluation (Esbensen, 2000). The main findings from Sule (2005) are that:

1. "There is a positive relationship between association with delinquent peers and Hispanic female gang membership." and

2. "Gang affiliation among Hispanic female juveniles seems to be attributable to family, peer influence, and individual characteristics such as attitude toward school."

Any gang prevention efforts aimed at Hispanic females would need to be implemented before the point at which the students begin to feel the effects of peer pressure, or it would be too late to be effective.

The analysis by Varriale (2008) involved a secondary analysis of the national longitudinal survey of youth collected by the Bureau of Labor Statistics. The study focused on examining gang desistance where pregnancy became an exit strategy for female Hispanic gang members. Fleisher and Krienert (2004) had argued that motherhood became a way for females to exit from gang life. Varriale's research found no support for the assertion by Fleisher and Krienert (2004).

The research by Brownfield (2012) was unique in that it was able to use data from a survey sample of 521 Canadian respondents. It provided a logistic regression analysis of gang membership on gender, and used variables from three theories (opportunity theory, differential association, and social control theory). Brownfield concluded that:

Most importantly, we find that gender has no significant effect on the likelihood of gang membership controlling for measures from all three theories. The gender difference in gang membership is accounted for fully by these independent variables.

The research by Kolb and Palys (2012) was based on interviews with 10 Latina gang members (18–36 years of age). They were interviewed at a well-known East Los Angeles gang intervention program site. The authors documented the important distinction in the two options of entering the gang. To join the gang they were either "jumped in" (e.g., beaten in) or "sexed in." There was a much higher status for gang members who were jumped in. They reported "every woman interviewed endured some form of abuse at the hands of their parents." Joining the gang simply exposed them to a more powerful and deadly form of abuse.

Kakar (2013) surveyed undergraduate college students and was able to develop a sample of 120 males and 81 females who had some form of affiliation with a gang or gang members (and had delinquent friends). Kakar described a kind of honeymoon effect in gang life regarding gender differences, where in the first six months of gang life males may be involved in more crime and violence than their female counterparts, but that after six months (e.g., after the honeymoon period) the inhibition among female gang members disappeared.

Kakar (2013) found that:

> The results also reveal that the perception that female role in gangs is minimal and limited to being "look outs" or providing sexual favors to the male members may not be as accurate as purported by earlier research. In the beginning, female members may assume these traditional expected roles, however, as members mature into gangs and become more experienced, the differences by gender begin to disappear and males and females engage in similar activities and equally serious crimes.
>
> (p. 36)

The research by Genty, Adedoyin, Jackson, and Jones (2014) was unique by studying the role of religion in a sample of adult incarcerated females in North Carolina. A total of 185 female inmates were interviewed, only 9 or 4.9 percent admitted to gang membership. Data showed all female inmates have a strong sense of religiosity. While there were too few female gang members in the sample to analyze, generally the gang members appeared in some regards to be somewhat more religious than the non-gang members.

The Chivalry Versus Convergence Hypotheses

The chivalry hypothesis is advanced as a way of explaining female crime generally. It assumes that there is a bias against locking up females. It may assume that at the gates to the criminal justice system, females are treated differently than males. An example would be if it could be shown that females are more likely to receive "discretion" and therefore screened out of the criminal justice system at the point of arrest.

Touted as the major rival explanatory hypothesis to the chivalry idea is the convergence hypothesis. The convergence hypothesis suggests that females may in some ways be "catching up" to their male counterparts in the criminal justice system as offenders. The convergence hypothesis rears its head every time anyone suggests there is a rise in any aspect of female crime, delinquency, or punishment.

If the chivalry hypothesis is that females receive special treatment in the criminal justice system, then actually, and more logically, the reverse of the chivalry hypothesis would not be convergence, but would rather be something akin to rudeness towards females (e.g., female harassment). Finally, and perhaps more likely, the possibility exists that males are simply more prone to crime than females cross-culturally.

How then do we explain the female gang situation today in criminological terms? First, enormous evidence suggests that in the overwhelming number of cases involving the larger and more formidable gangs that exist in America today, these are male-dominated activities: females play a role in these gangs, but not in the top leadership positions. Why would this be true? Criminal offenders are not generally known for being activists against sexism and for the women's rights movement. That criminals abuse women, plain and simple, would be the better bet.

By most actual empirical research conducted, the percentage of female gang members existing in America tends to roughly parallel the percentage of females in the American prison system. That would be about 5 to 6 percent of the overall gang members. Many gangs have female auxiliary units, which is a common phenomenon. Many gangs allow females to associate with them in a supportive capacity. Some gangs allow females to hold rank and even direct male members. But few major genuine criminal gangs exist that are in fact 100 percent female. If we wanted to use Thrasher's definition of gang (any group unsupervised by responsible adults that may engage in deviance), then obviously, such "gangs" would exist everywhere. But few all-girl gangs exist as autonomous gang organizations. How could they exist very long? What would they do? It would have to involve something other than claiming geographical turf, because they would attract every gang that ever heard of them. It would have to involve something other than drug sales, because eventually they would end up in competition with any of a number of male-dominated gangs.

There is only one place where we can easily find all-female gangs operating—behind bars: in juvenile detention centers, in juvenile correctional institutions, in adult jails, and in adult correctional institutions that, by definition, allow only females as inmates. Inside some of these facilities there are conflicts and rivalries between the members representing their various gang groups and organizations.

Findings on Female Gang Members

As reported previously (Knox, McCurrie, Laske, & Tromanhauser, 1992), gender is a factor that significantly differentiates self-reported gang membership among high school students. Females have a lower base rate for gang membership than do males. The research problem, then, was to oversample female students to such an extent that a sufficient group size could be obtained for female gang members. To accomplish this, two versions of the same survey were created: one for males and one for females.

Several public high schools on Chicago's South Side were used for data collection. The male version of the survey was not analyzed here and was not the primary research objective. It thus served a placebo function to keep the boys busy in the coed classrooms. Both versions of the survey instrument were five pages long and contained 99 different questions, some of which had multiple parts, and thus well over 99 different variables. Data collection began in early 1993 and continued until May 1993 when a sufficient number of self-reported female gang members had been reached.

All survey instruments were stored by the school and classroom in which they were collected. Manual checks were made to identify self-reported gang members, and then the gang member was matched by race, age, and grade level with a non-gang member respondent, often from the same classroom. The analysis reported here therefore reflects a matched-pair design of African American female high school students, half (100) of whom self-reported that they had previously joined a gang, and half (100) of whom reported that they had never joined a gang.

In the study, all of the female gang members (100) were members of the Folk Nation. More specifically, they self-identified as Sisters of the Struggle (S.O.S.), Intellectual Sisters, Intellectual Sisters of the Struggle (I.S.O.S.), or simply members of the Gangster Disciples gang. The "Intellectual Sisters" identity came from the written internal literature of the Brothers of the Struggle (B.O.S.), which was the conglomerate group of the Disciples Nation. While other Folks gangs that have female members existed, our data allowed the identification of specific gangs to which the respondents self-reported their membership. For all practical purposes, then, the female gang members analyzed here were "Intellectual Sisters" or S.O.S.—the female constituency of the clearly male-dominated B.O.S. organization.

According to the study, all of the African American females (100) who had never joined a gang are typically regarded as "Neutrons" in the context of the high school and community environment. A "Neutron" is a person who is not gang-affiliated, having never joined any gang and not being aligned with any gang nation (People or Folks, Brothers or Folks, Crips or Bloods, etc.).

Comparing Folks and Neutrons

Survey results can be summarized in terms of six profile patterns: family life, substance abuse, school discipline, dating, violence socialization, and aggressive personality characteristics.

- The Family Life Profile. Female gang members were significantly more likely to report that they had siblings (brothers or sisters) who were also gang members. Female gang members were significantly more likely to report prior pregnancies. Female gang members were significantly more likely to report that their family receives public aid. Female gang members were significantly less likely to report that they regularly attended church. Female gang members were significantly more likely to report having struck (hit) a parent one or more times. Female gang members were significantly more likely to report ever having run away from home. Female gang members were significantly less likely to report receiving an allowance from their family.

- The Substance Abuse Profile. Female gang members were significantly more likely to report that a lot of kids in their neighborhood use illicit drugs. Female gang members were significantly more likely to report using marijuana at least once a week. Female gang members were significantly more likely to report drinking alcohol at least once a week. Female gang members were significantly more likely to report having close friends who had shot up/injected drugs (e.g., IV drug use) and who used illicit drugs.

- The School Discipline Profile. The female gang member was significantly more likely to report knowing the police officers who worked at the school. The female gang member was significantly more likely to report having been (a) suspended from school, (b) having an "in-school" suspension, and (c) having an "in-school" detention. The female gang member had a lower educational aspiration by being significantly less likely to expect to graduate from a four-year college. The female gang member was significantly more likely to report also having been previously arrested.

- The Dating Profile. The female gang member was significantly more likely to report having a boyfriend who had an arrest record. The female gang member was significantly more likely to report having ever been beaten or assaulted by a boyfriend. The female gang member was significantly more likely to report that she could marry someone who was an active gang member—and, reminiscent of the classic movie *West Side Story*, apparently more willing to date a rival gang member if he showed respect. The female gang member was significantly less willing to marry someone of another race.

- The Violence Socialization Profile. The female gang member was significantly more likely to report having been previously threatened with gang violence. The female gang member was significantly more likely to report having ever carried a weapon to school for protection. The female gang member was significantly more likely to report having been in one or more fights during the last year. The female gang member was significantly more likely to report having ever had to pull a knife on someone. The female gang member was significantly more likely to report having had experience in shooting a handgun. The female gang member was significantly more likely to report having a permanent tattoo.

- The Aggressive Personality Profile. The female gang member was significantly more likely to believe she can take a beating just like a man. The female gang member was significantly more likely to report that she would never back out of a fight. The female gang member was significantly more likely to report that she sometimes felt like smashing things for no apparent reason. The female gang member was significantly more likely to think of herself as someone who fought first and asked questions later. The female gang member was significantly more likely to report that other persons considered her a very defiant individual and to distrust other people.

Has Equal Rights Affected Gang Life?

No, not really, is the short answer. Gang members being within the offender and subcultural population would not theoretically be expected to share such higher norms as that of feminist liberation. But let us proceed to the long answer. What do these female gang members report in terms of convergence and chivalry hypotheses? Are the females in this particular gang on equal status and enjoy equal opportunity for advancement as found in the male gang member counterparts (the convergence hypothesis)? Or are females given special duties because of their gender and are still basically relegated to a subservient position in a male-dominated organization (the chivalry hypothesis)? Here we can test these issues by taking a closer look at the viewpoints of our sample of female gang members. Research from the NGCRC found that:

1. About half of the female gang members (52.1%) report that their boyfriend was also a member of the same gang.

2. When asked "within the gang, were female members treated the same as males (i.e., do they have the same status and privileges as males)," some 60 percent said "yes." About a fourth (26.3%) said "no." The rest (13.7%) were not sure.

3. When asked if the females in the gang were used for specific jobs or tasks because they were females, about half (53.7%) said "no." About a fourth (28.4%) said "yes," and the rest (17.9%) were not sure.

4. When asked if females in the gang had special duties which males did not have, some 37.8 percent said "yes." About an equal proportion (40.8%) said "no." About a fifth (21.4%) were not sure.

5. When asked if female members were permitted to date males who were not members of the same gang, about two-thirds (65.6%) said "yes." Some 17.7 percent said "no," and the rest (16.7%) were not sure.

6. When asked if female members were allowed to be leaders within the gang, nearly three-fourths (74.2%) said "yes." Some 9.7 percent said "no," and the rest (16.1%) were not sure.

7. When asked if female members were allowed to lead or control male gang members, this story of equal opportunity tends to unravel. About half (51.6%) of the respondents said that they were not allowed to lead or control gang members in their gang. Still, some 29.5 percent said it would be possible for females to exert power over males, and some 18.9 percent were not sure.

8. One of the classical ways in which male gang members exploited female gang members and female gang associates was to use them to limit their risk of apprehension and arrest. Numerous examples existed in the literature, for example, showing that female gang members were often asked to carry guns for the male members, as Dawley described in his tenure with the Vice Lords that the females were used for "whatever was needed" including sex: "A Vice Lady was also used for carrying guns. The police couldn't search females so she could carry a shotgun up under her dress and the fellas could walk alongside" (Dawley, 1992, p. 31). When asked if female gang members were expected to carry guns for the male gang members, some 32.3 percent said "yes." About half (50.5%) said "no." The rest (17.2%) were not sure.

Theoretically, some gang organizations were expected to display more of the chivalry pattern than others. This was true, as documented elsewhere, because some gang organizations like the Black P. Stones and the Vice Lords had a tendency to mimic Islamic ideological influence in their internal beliefs and in their written gang internal literature and belief system. Historically, women have not gained the same power and status as men in Islamic groups or societies. The group studied here was not one that has a pronounced Islamic influence. Thus, theoretically it is possible to hypothesize that greater convergence would be found in this group (S.O.S.) than among gangs composed primarily of the same racial group representing a rival or opposition gang nation (Stones, Vice Lords, etc.).

No clear-cut answer, thus, was forthcoming on this issue. The data suggested a mixed set of findings in a gang that held the best possibility for convergence. To a large extent, however, it appeared that females had not exactly liberated that particular gang organization. What was very clear from this research was that female gang members differed in significant ways from their non-gang member counterparts matched by the same race, age, and school grade level. That still did not answer the more fundamental question of whether female gang members differed significantly from the social, psychological, and behavioral or background profile found among male gang members.

Females Represent About Six Percent of the Gang Problem

The study by George T. Felkenes and Harold K. Becker (1995) noted that "gang membership was predominantly male-oriented, 94 percent male and 6 percent female" (p. 5). Their study provided insight into Hispanic female gang members in the Los Angeles area. Among other findings, the research noted (1) females were more likely to want to be successful in life, (2) over half (61.1%) were from a two-parent family, (3) two-fifths (41.2%) had dropped out of school, and (4) while most believed in God (91%), only 18.4 percent attended church regularly.

Are There All-Female Gangs?

Yes, just as among males, gangs of varying levels of sophistication in terms of their organization and in terms of their level of crime threat included gangs composed almost entirely, if not exclusively, of female members. Most examples of that type of all-female gang were those at the lower level of the gang crime threat continuum. However, some research did show that the all-female criminal gang does exist. Perhaps the strongest evidence documenting the all-female criminal gang was the work titled "Sisters Are Doin' It for Themselves: A Black Female Gang in San Francisco" by Lauderback et al. (1992), published in what is now the *Journal of Gang Research*. In their work, they documented the group called the Potrero Hill Posse, or PHP. Their study showed this all-female gang to be primarily involved in drug sales operations. It seemed to attract less attention from the police; in fact their study showed that only half of the members had an arrest record. Was it possible that the chivalry hypothesis operated here; that is, citizens were more likely to call the police when a group of boys hang on the corner, and be less likely to call the police about a complaint of suspicious girls on the corner? That would make for a fascinating actual field experiment for those interested in future research on gangs.

What happened to male-dominated gangs also happened to female gangs was another finding of the Lauderback, Hansen, and Waldorf study. When one group forms, another will form to oppose it. That has been called the law of natural group opposition formation; where a blue gang starts, a red gang will shortly follow; where a Folks gang starts, a People gang will shortly organize to counteract it. The Potrero Hill Posse had their opposing local gang in a group called the Valencia Gardens Mob, also composed primarily of African American females.

The Rise and Fall of the GP Gang in Chicago in the Spring of 2004

In a *Chicago Sun-Times* article, Ihejirika (2004) reported that in the spring of 2004 a hue and cry arose on Chicago's south side as high school students and parents became alarmed at a new aggressive and violent gang that came out of nowhere, but suddenly commanded lots of news media attention. The girl gang was the "GPs."

The gang was a Level I gang and operated at the Dyett Academic Center, which was located in the Washington Park neighborhood on Chicago's South Side. News of a new vicious and violent female gang quickly attracted the attention of the Chicago Police Department, who issued the message "if you want to act like a gang we can treat you like a gang." The message being they could be locked up easily, charges could be pressed, arrests, and convictions in court—the message to the gang was they could get into a lot of trouble if they wanted to, and the police were ready.

Almost as quickly as the police arrived on the scene, Chicago State University President Elnora Daniel went to the school to talk to the students with some other successful role models. Then, just as quickly as the GP gang came on the scene, it just disappeared. It faded back into oblivion. The duration of the gang: about 3 weeks, during April and May 2004.

The Beat Down Girls: From Video Game to "Acting It Out"

In 1999, a group of teenage girls in Polk County, Florida, became the equivalent of what some experts regard as a female gang, even though the life history of the gang lasted only about two weeks. They had a name to their collective group identity: they called themselves the "Beat Down Girls." They liked to fight, particularly as a group, and were in the habit of starting confrontations that would lead to such fighting opportunities. They would beat other girls in their neighborhood. They had emulated what they learned on the video game Beat Down.

When the Beat Down computer game came out in 1999, it was criticized by groups like the Florida Gang Investigators Association (Atkins, 1999). Characters in the game include "The Don," who is an urban pimp and a gangster, so the game includes challenges like recruiting new gang members, collecting your money from the prostitutes, and so forth. The contagion effect, or the copycat phenomenon, occurs when impressionable youths emulate what they see in the media. Such was, it seems, the origin of the Beat Down Girls. So in this video game, gangbanging interacts with violence and pimping/prostitution.

As female gangs go, that one had a flash-in-the-pan start and a quick washout ending. As one of the gang investigators who handled the case explained, they quickly became notorious in their one neighborhood area for "beating the hell out of people." But those people who were beaten quickly had parents in court filing for "orders of protection" against members of the Beat Down Girls. Within days after filing this kind of domestic violence "civil remedy," the main cast of characters from The Beat Down Girls received subpoenas to appear in court. The judge told them, "ladies do you see the two gentlemen in the back of the courtroom in black coats, those are police officers, they are here today because of you."

The judge issued orders of protection, and ravaging violence from the Beat Down Girls quickly evaporated. In a 2003 follow-up inquiring about the current status of the Beat Down Girls, the "gang" had not resurfaced. Asked further if any of the members had gone on to other more mainstream street gangs, the investigator replied "no, but it wouldn't surprise me if you might see them mud wrestling when they become of age."

The Correctional Environment for Female Gang Members

Nationwide a lower gang density has always been reported for females than for males. That consistently appeared in research on the different types of correctional environments as well: juvenile short-term detention facilities, juvenile long-term correctional institutions, local jails, and adult state correctional institutions. However, the lower gang density was that reported as the official estimate only. There was reason to be somewhat skeptical about the official estimates from those who were the chief administrators of the same facilities.

The fact remained, however, that in the female component of the correctional system what we had were groups of females that interacted along gang lines. One thing appeared to be true and deserving of much more research: that females were in this context much less violent than their male counterparts. One can readily find numerous examples of male gang members behind bars who killed other inmates and who even assassinated correctional officers, and who routinely "rioted." In a gang riot at Cook County Jail, for example, the Vice Lords fought the Disciples over who would have first use of the shower. Seven male inmates were stabbed and two were killed in a frivolous fight over who showered first.

We have not heard as much such gang violence in the female correctional context. Is that a problem of statistical proportions that is masked and biased by the very nature of the use of the penal sanction in America? Possibly so. Historically in America, only about five percent of the prison inmates have been female, and that trend has been consistent over a very long period of the history of American criminal justice. One possibility we can rule out for those who would claim that female gang members are less violent in custody than their male counterparts is the idea that female inmates are treated better. The fact is most correctional programs are geared towards males, especially the rehabilitation and vocational training programs. Far fewer resources are allocated to the women's division of most state correctional systems. So one cannot effectively argue that women gang members are less violent because they are treated better than male inmates.

What we do know about inmate roles is that female inmates take on more of a quasi-family function and do appear to have social skills to be able to avoid and mediate conflicts. What we do know about male inmates is that many, particularly gang members, have a kind of combative personality syndrome that prefers conflict over all other options for problem solving. Still the issue deserves greater research. Our correctional institutions provide a natural arena in which to ascertain the nature of the differences in gang violence, and much more research needs to be done in this area.

The Study of Confined Juvenile Gang Girls by Rosenbaum (1996)

The study by Jill Leslie Rosenbaum (1996) pointed out that a lot of misconceptions about "female gang members" have been previously published in the criminological literature. Among the misconceptions was the generalization from Cohen (1955, p. 45) that female delinquency generally consists primarily of sexual delinquency. Rosenbaum studied 70 female gang members confined in the California state juvenile correctional system. The profile that emerged was this: 94% had been arrested for a violent crime; most joined the gang at age 12; about half "had other family members who had served time in jail or state prison" (p. 19); and about half of these female gang members reported being the early victims of sexual or physical abuse in their generally dysfunctional families.

Rosenbaum takes Chesney-Lind (1993) to task for the claim that violent girl gang behavior was a social construction of the mass media. Said Rosenbaum (1996): "she obviously has not looked closely at the female gang members who have found their way to the California Youth Authority" (p. 21).

Queens of Armed Robbery: Short-Lived All-Female Gang

In 2000, the *Chicago Tribune* reported that an example of a small all-female gang that specialized in armed robbery demonstrates that all-female gangs can exist and can be involved in violent crime. This particular example, though, is rare. Four girls made up the gang called the "Queens of Armed Robbery." They came from an affluent suburb of Houston, Texas. Their gang behavior: armed robbery, no graffiti, just armed robberies, typically convenience stores. The girls were linked to at least five different robberies during the summer of 1999. Two of the girls (both 17 years old), Lisa Warzeka and Katie Dunn, were sentenced to seven-year prison terms for their role in the armed robberies.

Burning Out: Disengaging From Gang Life as Some Approach Adulthood

A number of qualitative interviews with female gang members from NGCRC research have shown this type of scenario. The basic situation was that of where the female gang member of a larger male-dominated gang, usually a very structured criminal gang, slowly disengages from the gang's routine activities. The result was the ex-gang member or what could also be called the inactive gang member. Some simply "grew out of it"; their affiliation with the gang was contextually centered. That is typically in a high school situation, so when they reach their early twenties, their social network changes and they find themselves progressively avoiding the trouble that gang life provides. The following are examples of how female gang members disengaged from the gang, as observed by Dr. George Knox (2008) at the National Gang Crime Research Center:

Case #1: White Female Member of White Gang

A white female gang member of the Simon City Royals, a predominantly white gang in Chicago, found herself hanging out with the gang less and less over time as she had to find a job and pay her own bills. Quitting shortly after high school, relocating to a new neighborhood, and not renewing high school contacts, she established an entirely new social network of friends and associates. She still had the gang tattoo, but it was on an area of the body not normally exposed in public and so it was easy to simply act like she knows nothing about gangs and live a law-abiding existence. Gang life for her was a temporary adolescent fad: it had its value in high school, but it lost its value as she faced the need to seriously address how she was going to fit in to society and pay the bills and the rent. She became a highly responsible citizen who worked like anyone else for a living at ordinary jobs.

Case #2: African American Female Member of the Gangster Disciples

An African American female member of the Gangster Disciples provided another example of the disengagement theory about severing ties to the gang. The person began to sever the ties to the gang at the time she enrolled as a student in a university. By the time she had graduated, she still lived in the area where she grew up, but she no longer was active in gang life on the streets. In fact, she had thought that she was completely out of the gang until one night in 1993 some Gangster Disciples came to her house. While she still lived on the South Side of Chicago, she had moved and did not think her gang knew where she lived. But they appeared at her door one night and handed her a petition and basically ordered her to sign the petition. The petition that was being circulated in the Chicago area, which ultimately had over 5,000 names on it, demanded that the Illinois Prisoner Review Board (i.e., the parole board) grant Larry Hoover (their gang leader) parole because he was now rehabilitated.

Case #3: White Female Member of White Racist Extremist Gang

A white female member of a white racist extremist gang made a lot of bad decisions in her youth, and made a lot of good ones later as she matured. One of the good decisions she made later in life, after becoming a mother, was that she needed a college education.

She had joined the Aryan Nation thinking this was the coolest thing she could do. She was willing to show her level of support by getting a very large series of gang tattoos. Here is the problem: later in life, she would marry a black man and have children of mixed racial backgrounds, and she could never really join them at the "pool" or in any sunbathing type of situation. She had to cover up the tattoos. The tattoos included large Nazi symbols. She really wanted to know how to get them off. Her professor told her about a gang tattoo removal program. She got the tattoos removed, by laser, and was able to raise her children well. She graduated from college. She grew out of the gang. She matured. At some point, she realized the self-destructive nature of the gang life was not her primary goal in life. She did a 180-degree backflip on racial issues, and today is married to a man whose race she detested as a youth.

Case #4: Female Associate of Latin Gang

The case showed the classic situation of being dually integrated at a high level into conventional society and into the subculture, a kind of marginal adaptation. She prefers the barrio life even now as she is capable of moving out and starting a professional career. Why? Because that was where she grew up and has many friends there. She was able to basically leave the gang alone, and remained friendly with them, because they were part of the very fabric of the Hispanic Chicago community she lived in. She still knew the gang members and the gang leaders and had family members in the gang. She was not, however, likely to be active in any gang criminal operation or involved in its street life. She was cordial to the homies and was simply able to disengage over a period of years while working and attending college, a period of time that corresponded to her own maturation and entry into young adulthood. Not uncommonly, she had no arrest record and planned to work in the criminal justice system. She would like to work, in fact, for the FBI, and was considering going to law school.

Finally, when talking about females exiting gang life, sometimes the gang feels that they need to have an "exit beating" or "outing violation" for leaving the gang. That is a physical beating in a ritual ceremony; the same result happens to male members of gangs. If they do not take the punishment willingly, then they will be targeted for worse violence. That happened in the case of 15-year-old Connie Ayala in Elgin, Illinois, where the gang put out an S.O.S. (Shoot on Sight, or Slaughter On Sight) order on her for not taking her beating to get out of the gang. Then one day on the street with her aunt, Connie was again attacked by female members of the gang, who ended up stabbing her aunt.

The Tabula Rasa Treatment Program for Female Gang Members

The study by Ernest M. De Zolt, Linda M. Schmidt, and Donna C. Gilcher (1996) described a promising program for female gang members in Cleveland, Ohio, that grew out of a reported 22 percent increase in female delinquency. The project involved a "rites of passage" approach that included an educational component, a wellness component, and a job skills or vocational component. Thus tutoring and mentoring were part of this holistic approach. It included biweekly group counseling by a licensed psychologist as well.

Bind-Torture-Kill Case of a Female Gang Associate by Female Members

Not only are at-risk children susceptible to gang involvement, but middle class children can be drawn in as well. One particularly brutal case of violence was in the case of 20-year-old Kristin Ponquinette, a high school graduate and the daughter of the school superintendent in Aurora, Illinois. In this case, Ponquinette had simply been a wannabe, hanging out with lower level gang members. She witnessed the gang business operations, became sexually involved with some of the male gang members, and after a confrontation with jealous female members of the gang she was targeted for execution. The execution was described by Pelton (1994):

> On April 17, 1992, according to testimony in the trials, Mobley's gang tied and gagged Kristin Ponquinette in a basement garage, threatened her with a chain saw, chopped off her hair, beat her and locked her in a closet. Then they led her to a railroad bridge at 127th Street and Eggleston Avenue, where they smashed her over the head with a chunk of cement, wired a manhole cover to her feet and threw her into the Cal-Sag Channel. The body eventually broke loose from the manhole cover and was found floating miles downstream in Alsip nine days later by a Coast Guard boat.

Sexual Violence and Exploitation as a Function of Gang Organization

One scenario in which females were subjected to sexual violence and sexual exploitation occurred as a function of goal attainment for the gang organization itself. Some sexual violence and sexual exploitation of females occurred as a logical progression of the coercive type of criminal organization in some gangs. As criminal organizations, gangs should not be expected to exemplify higher levels of moral development. Gangs are mostly chauvinistic in culture, and if any ethos can be said to characterize their gender relationships it would be an extreme form of hypermasculinity. Thus it is violence and exploitation that is functional in some way for the gang, and it is openly approved of as such by the members of the gang. It is not carried out individually by one member or two members; it is true collective behavior. The sexual violence and exploitation of females is part and parcel of the gang culture, its values, norms, and beliefs.

The pattern of sexual exploitation and sexual violence includes the little-researched issue of being "sexed in," that is, for some females to become members of a male-dominated gang, they would have to have sex with the male gang members. It is interesting to note that in the gang research arena there are those who studied the gang as a problem of crime and violence, and there are others who study the gang to argue that society has overreacted to gangs by excessively labeling them with attributions such as "the super predator."

McCorkle and Miethe (2002) took print journalists to task for portraying gang members as "trigger-happy sociopaths." They extended the "moral panic" concept in sociology to say that American society has overreacted to the gang problem. They attacked with great vigor the kind of "bad rap" gangs get in America. Research by Miller (2001) demonstrates that animosity is sometimes so strong between rival gangs that in one rival female gang member's case this meant being first physically assaulted by a number of female gang members and then being viciously raped and left for dead by their male counterparts. So we know this kind of sexual violence occurs; it is simply so difficult to systematically study. Being "sexed in" to gang membership is not a status-enhancing admission, and it is further reasonable to believe that within the offender population, self-report methods may simply be biased downwards in gaining a true parameter of this factor. In other words, it may very well be the case that we are able to learn about some of these practices only through the courtroom testimony of victims or when the news media reports someone being killed in the process.

We will now systematically review a number of such different scenarios with the idea in mind that we need to identify these conditions and situations if we are going to be seriously committed to developing more effective ways to achieve gang prevention and intervention with regard to the female members and associates (Knox, 2008c).

Dating a Sureño, But Drinking With a Latin King: Drugged and Raped

There is no way to estimate how many times this happens in cities, large and small, across America and elsewhere. But it involves a typical scenario where a young woman is at a party, a bar, or nightclub, and makes the acquaintance of someone who is willing to buy her a drink. In this case, the young woman had admitted to her new "friend" that she was dating a member of the Sureños gang (SUR 13). She would only discover later, after being drugged and raped, that she was getting free drinks from a member of the Latin

Kings. It is common to gang subcultural argot to call such new friendly acquaintances "frenemies": they act like friends, but they are really enemies.

In this particular city where the drug-induced rape occurred, the SUR 13 gang was a hostile rival to the Latin Kings gang. We can cut right to the chase and tell you in advance the moral of the story: if you are a woman and you are dating or romantically involved with a criminal gang member, the last thing you want to do is informally disclose this information in a way that a rival gang might learn about it and view you as a target for sexual violence.

The victim takes the drink, and experiences the effects of alcohol and drugs, then she leaves with the Latin King. She passes out in his car, and he rapes her, and leaves her on the side of the road. She is discovered by a motorist. The police arrive and she is taken to the hospital. Interviewed the next day, she tells the investigating officer, "yes, I remember the last drink, there were like remnants of a pill or something at the bottom of the glass" (i.e., something that had not fully dissolved in the drink). Witnesses at the bar helped identify the drug-rapist. The suspect was a member of the Latin Kings. In his twisted view of the world, he had a "right," indeed a duty, to rape a rival gang members' girlfriend. In his "view of the world," raping her was just a logical extension of the "gang war" (Knox, 2008c).

Sexed in to the MS-13

The story surfaced in August 2002 when a 17-year-old female got more than she had bargained for by dabbling with gang membership. She wanted to join the notorious Mara Salvatrucha (MS-13) gang that was operating in her hometown of Manassas, Virginia. She was given the choice of a "beat-in" or to be sexed in. She chose the latter, not understanding how violent it would actually be.

While she had consented to be sexed in, what she did not know was that four MS-13 members would do this repeatedly and violently over an extended period of time. So when the gang members did finally finish with her, she was so injured, humiliated, and traumatized that she contacted police. The local police made two quick arrests of MS-13 members Reyes Avila-Villalta and Jose Hercules-Pineda, and issued warrants for two other members, Carlos Francisco Coreas-Melgar and Alfonso Oscar Rosales (Knox, 2008c).

Offering young females the choice of being "beat in" or "sexed in" can be found in a wide number of gangs throughout the U.S. A similar case to the MS-13 story was reported in the *Beloit Daily News* when a local man claimed to be the governor of the Elkhorn, Wisconsin, area for the Gangster Disciples. This GD's name was Markus W. Zielinski, from Dell Lake, Wisconsin, and he offered two teenage girls (13 and 14 years old) the same option: to be "beat in" or to be "sexed in," where the sex would involve having sex with him and two other GDs. They chose to be beaten in, but it got out of hand, and was reported to police. Zielinski was then promptly arrested (Knox, 2008c).

Gang Rape Tied to Gang Recruitment

Gang members present a collateral risk to anyone who associates with them. This includes everyone: police officers simply standing by gang members on the street, kids who just hang with gang members, and in some cases even those dating gang members or those who want to join can be a very serious "risk." Such was the case with Victor Garcia in Chicago, when he wanted to join a gang. The gang knew he had an attractive girlfriend, and the gang was willing to make a deal with him. Eager to join the gang, he would "set up" his girlfriend for a brutal gang rape from his new homies.

In June 1992 Victor Garcia, age 17, was convinced that he could join the gang if the gang could have sex with his girlfriend. Garcia agreed with this unique arrangement for his gang initiation ceremony in Chicago. The girl was subsequently lured to a party where the gang members lay in wait. She was then physically assaulted and repeatedly raped by four gang members until the following day when she was let go (Roeper, 1993).

Doris McLeod 1974–1991: Milwaukee BTK Gang Offender Case

Knox (2008b) observed that Doris McLeod indeed had a troubled past as a teenage girl. Her teen years were spent in various forms of foster care, until she ran away in 1991. She arrived by Greyhound bus in Milwaukee, Wisconsin. Doris barely made it off the bus before being intercepted by Joseph White. White was a self-appointed "welcoming committee" for any young female he could get his hands on. Joseph White was a gang-banger who wanted to be a Milwaukee pimp. Thus his efforts to befriend Doris were little more than a ruse for his larger plan, which quickly began to unfold. He did offer Doris food, a place to stay, and all the benefits of his "connections" to the underworld in Milwaukee. He was, after all, a member of the local Gangster Disciples street gang.

The tendency exists in the gang world today, where chapters of the Gangster Disciples formed outside of the original gang epicenter (Chicago), for such gangs to improvise and often modify their "gang literature." Gang literature here refers to their code, their constitution and bylaws. In Joseph White's faction of the Gangster Disciples (GD), there was a "rule" to the effect that any hooker who did not promptly pay up to a Gangster Disciple who was pimping her should receive a "V-50" for this "violation."

A "V-50" in this case meant 50 punches to the chest and head area. It was written down in the Milwaukee chapter "local rules" for the Gangster Disciples. It did not exist in Chicago where the Gangster Disciples were originally formed, before the Gangster Disciples rapidly spread to over 30 states in the 1990s. Thus the gang rules that Joseph White lived by basically empowered him to do what he did.

Another pimp had told Joseph White that in his opinion little Doris McLeod was not going to make a very good prostitute. Doris did not like the work that she was compelled and coerced to engage in by wannabe pimp Joseph White. So White decided to pummel Doris, as his GD constitution advised, with numerous blows to the chest and head area.

Joseph White decided that the girl needed an attitude adjustment, and he administered a "V-50" in the basement of an inner-city house in Milwaukee. Doris did not survive the beating. Joseph White then cut off her fingerprints and drove the body towards Madison, dumping it in an open field after also cutting off her hands. The hands were discovered, minus the finger prints, also in Dane County. Persistent investigators in Dane County eventually broke the case through posters and the media. White acted as his own lawyer at trial and was promptly convicted and is currently serving two sentences: first degree murder (life) and aggravated rape.

Gang Rape as a Hypermasculinity Function: The Mongolian Boys Society

The gang came to the attention of authorities in October of 1999 when 23 of its members were arrested for a number of different "gang rapes" that occurred in 1998. While the rapes actually took place in a motel room in Fresno, California, the gang involved was the "Mongolian Boys Society." Fresno, California, has a large number of Asian gangs. What the Mongolian Boys Society did was go to Fresno to vacation and party.

But in the party atmosphere, they lured three girls to their motel, and 23 of their gang members took turns raping the three girls. The "lures" used were common to the gang world: yes, we have lots of cocaine, we have whatever you want, good music, good food, and a great motel. Once the girls were in the spider web, they were given all the drugs they could consume; then they were isolated and systematically attacked for purposes of sexual violence.

In this kind of scenario, the "gang rape" is a hypermasculinity function. The idea is that you prove your manhood by violently assaulting a young girl. In the atmosphere of gang life, and its subcultural values, the gang members "take part" in this ritual because it shows they are "down with their gang nation." They are "dedicated" to the group identity.

The Wolf Pack Gang in Quebec, Canada

According to Knox (2008c), this story surfaced in late 2002 when 11 prominent Canadian older adult men, including a popular Quebec City radio host, were among those arrested for soliciting a juvenile prostitute. They had been involved in a juvenile prostitution ring that was operated by a street gang known as the "Wolf Pack." The age range of the juvenile prostitutes was 14–17. The Wolf Pack gang had a systematic way of recruiting young female gang members and lavishing them with praise and gifts. The

Wolf Pack gang also had a unique ability to penetrate and compromise some of the "higher society" in this Canadian province.

The Wolf Pack gang method of operation for recruiting underage prostitutes was to throw parties and "scout" for candidates. Once they found someone who fit their profile, they would disclose their gang status, promise protection, and actually give a number of "goodies" and "props" to the young girls. The Wolf Pack gang could give the girls drugs, status, excitement, and at least the promise of protection. These were not welfare girls; these were girls from middle class family backgrounds. But impressed with the money, drugs, attention, and the "lure" of gang excitement, a number of the juvenile females agreed to work for the gang as prostitutes. When they would be later interviewed by police while in custody, they would confess that they did it "for love of the gang" or because they had been threatened with violence from the gang if they did not continue what they had started. The gang was their pimp.

The Wolf Pack gang made a lot of money. It focused on clients with deep pockets who liked young girls. Among the social elite arrested were well-known restauranteurs and businessmen such as:

- Radio talk show host Robert Gilet

- Jacques Racine, president of a chain of drug stores

- Charles Nourcy, owner of a chain of food stores

- Yvan Cloutier, ex-president of the Quebec Winter Carnival.

In addition to the wealthy businessmen already arrested and others like them under investigation, a total of 17 juveniles and nine adult members of the Wolf Pack gang were also arrested once this juvenile prostitution ring was broken up in December of 2002.

Forced Prostitution to Pay Off Drug Debts to the Gang

Knox (2008c) observed that a case study in Chicago showed in some situations the gang's drug business becomes the basis for becoming involved in the prostitution business. The coerced or forced prostitution of females has one purpose: to allow the female drug addicts to pay off their drug debts to the gang. The particular case study was considered to have an extremely high level of validity, as will be explained.

The prostitute used for the case study reported she was in a phase of her career where she found it more profitable to rob her johns than to "turn tricks." Her forte was robbing Hispanic men after they had become extremely intoxicated. She worked the Mexican bars in an area on South 63rd Street between California and Kedzie in Chicago, Illinois. When some of the men were in this extremely intoxicated state, she equated the ease of robbing them as equivalent to "tipping over cows": "I was robbing 'em then, I was not trying to turn no dates, it was good money around there, when they get real drunk, all you had to do was trip them and they fall down, and take their money and run."

The reason she did not actively "prowl" for "dates" in the Mexican bars was because there was a more organized kind of prostitution activity that went on. As she described it:

> a lot of the young girls would get strung out on PCP from the Latin Souls, what they do is start them smoking PCP and when the girls get strung out on it, they get some on credit, and they have to pay off the drug debt. So, the gang would advocate for them, pimp them. The gang would go up into the Mexican bars and tell them they had a girl outside, see if anyone wanted to turn a date.

The area of Chicago did have several Hispanic gangs in the vicinity, including the Latin Souls just to the east. So, the story checked out regarding the identity of the specific gang involved. That would be a type of forced prostitution of a limited duration: once the young girl had enough money accumulated from tricks, she could pay off the gang, and perhaps get her credit line for drugs restored. That was a form of forced prostitution because failure to pay back the drug debt could mean facing summary execution from gangs involved in narcotics sales. So, when a young girl owed the gang money for unpaid drugs, there may have been a strong element of coercion involved if they told the girl, "well, let's go make some money then so you can pay us off."

Kidnapping, Slavery, and Forced Prostitution as a Gang Enterprise

Knox (2008c) stated that this scenario involving sexual violence and sexual exploitation reflects an intentional income-producing crime motivation by the gang or its members, but involving a higher level of threat by encompassing the issues of kidnapping, slavery, and forced prostitution. To the extent that money can be made by gangs in the areas of commercial vice, then this thesis reveals a fatal flaw of logic in the argument by Moore (1978) that if we only legalized heroin, this would eliminate gang violence in America. Heroin is not the only facet of the underground economy that gangs can compete for. Here we document some examples and patterns of the more organized forms of prostitution and gang involvement in patterns of sexual violence and the sexual exploitation of females.

In that kind of scenario, the gang will kill females who could potentially "put them away" through courtroom testimony. Those kinds of homicides may never be detected as homicides, because if the females are drug abusers (as many are), the gang need only give them a classic "hot shot" and they die of an overdose. All the police find is another dead junkie on the street or in a home somewhere. It is reasonable to believe that gangs are able to accomplish this with relative ease and that therefore it does occur.

Summary

Gang membership has attracted female gang members who have a history of abuse and abused them further. There are exceptions, but generally gang life for female members continues to pattern itself after an exploitive pattern of male chauvinism rather than providing genuine equal opportunity across gender lines. There were few female members in high command, but it remains a male-dominated business. The chapter examined the main research findings that have contributed to the literature on female gang members and female gangs. A troubled and at-risk family, social, and economic profile emerged for the background of female gang members. They were likely to be marginalized by the dual effects of urban poverty and being a racial minority and therefore subject to various forms of racism. They typically enter the gang abused, and become more abused inside gang life.

DISCUSSION QUESTIONS

1. Define the chivalry hypothesis in relation to female gangs.
2. Define the convergence hypothesis in relation to female gangs.
3. Describe why many female gang members choose to leave the gang.
4. Describe how female gang members use sex in their initiation rites, their crimes, and in their defenses against law enforcement.
5. Examine recent incidents of gang-related commercial sexual exploitation in the news.

CHAPTER 7 Gangs and Violence

Introduction

Residents were alarmed when they learned that gang members gunned down four men sitting in a parked car in a drive-by shooting in an upscale San Francisco neighborhood. The area had a more criminal past, but it had become a mecca for young professionals. About 10 p.m. one Friday night, residents started reporting more than a dozen gunshots in what was believed to be an incident of gang violence (Coleman, 2015). It was initially reported that the car in which the men were murdered was stolen. Many residents were shocked that something so terrifying could happen in their otherwise safe neighborhood of professionals with a mix of Victorian homes, boutiques and popular restaurants. One resident expressed his surprise on Twitter: "Moved from Brooklyn to SF for this?" (Coleman, 2015). This activity may have come as a surprise to many residents, but it was just another day for the gang members involved.

The area was one of many neighborhoods in the U.S. that have gone through a complete revitalization. Community leaders claimed success in halting the blight and welcomed new businesses and new residents. The new residents in those areas often had little knowledge of the history attached to their neighborhood. At most, they may know that it was transformed from an area of older homes known to have criminal activity to one known as a trendy up-and-coming part of the community. While the updated status is often the consensus among citizens, no one told the gangsters who claimed the territory as their own. Gang members need not live in a location to frequent it. They also do not require ownership to claim possession of a property or group of properties. That is best evidenced, perhaps, by the frequent use of spray paint that gang members use to mark their territory with graffiti. The gang mindset often discounts rules, especially those put in place without their involvement. Community leaders can change street names, raze government housing projects that attract criminals, and encourage development of new and exciting endeavors, but that will not prevent the gang members from coming around.

Many communities have seen an increase in gang membership in recent years. Gangs exist in all types and sizes of communities, from small town to large urban area and everything in between. Annual estimates of the number of gang members in the U.S. from the National Youth Gang Survey have averaged around 770,000. The most recent estimate of approximately 850,000 gang members represented an 8.6% increase over the previous year, as shown in Figure 7.1.

The numbers fluctuated somewhat from year to year in that survey and were not compared to any increase in population or other variables. Nonetheless, it appeared the

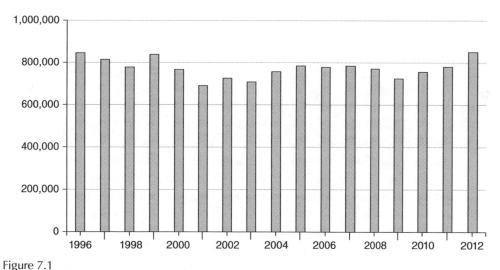

Figure 7.1

Estimated Number of Gang Members, 1996–2012.

National Gang Center (NGC). (2015). National Youth Gang Survey Analysis. NGC, U.S. Department of Justice. www.nationalgangcenter.gov/Survey-Analysis.

number of gang members in the U.S. was consistent. Nearly 1 in 5 of the larger cities reported they had more than 1,000 gang members, while only about 1 in 10 suburban counties did so. Suburban counties, rural cities, and rural counties were significantly more likely to report uncertainty of the number of gang members in their areas.

There were also some discrepancies between agencies that attempted to count the number of gang members in the country. According to a recent report by the U.S. Federal Bureau of Investigations (FBI), there were roughly 1.4 million gang members in the United States at the end of 2010 (National Gang Intelligence Center [NGIC], 2011). That figure represented an increase of 400,000 over the prior (2009) NGIC estimate, which was 200,000 more than their 2007 report. All in all, it appeared that there are roughly 1 million gang members in the U.S.

Gang-related crime and violence is increasing in our communities as gangs work to control their territory and criminal operations. Gangs may be responsible for up to 80% of the crimes occurring in communities across the nation (NGIC, 2009). NGIC analysis indicated that gang members were responsible for an average of 48 percent of violent crime in most jurisdictions and a much higher percentage in others. Gang-related violent crime is increasing in smaller urban areas (NGIC, 2009). Police in such diverse locations as Arizona, California, Colorado, Illinois, Massachusetts, Oklahoma, and Texas have reported that gangs are responsible for at least 90 percent of crime in their areas (NGIC, 2011).

In this chapter, we will examine gang violence and how it affects individuals, families, communities, and organizations. We will look first at how the presence of gangs affects the level of violence in the community. Then we will evaluate to what extent violence permeates the gang culture. Finally, we will examine ethnic and immigrant gangs and why violence is often a component of their presence in the community.

Gang Violence

Although gangs have always been in existence, contemporary gangs are more violent, more organized, and more widespread (Franco, 2008). Gang members often migrate from cities to suburbs and rural areas to grow their organization, recruit new members, expand drug distribution, and form new alliances (NGIC, 2011). A recent report by the NGIC showed that many gangs have advanced far beyond their traditional drug distribution roles and are more organized and influential in their communities. The negative impact of gangs throughout society is undeniable. They incite fear and violence within our communities. Gangs threaten our schools, our children, and our homes. Gangs today are more sophisticated and flagrant in their use of violence and intimidation tactics (NAGIA, 2005). In fact, it could be argued that mere membership in a gang means the member will be more likely to engage in violent activity than before they joined.

TABLE 7.1 **Violent Gang Safe Street Task Force Accomplishments**

Year	Complaints	Indictments & Information	Arrests	Convictions
2001	1,143	2,181	3,999	2,168
2002	1,024	1,951	3,512	1,964
2003	826	1,971	3,837	1,698
2004	980	2,183	4,162	1,773
2005	1,191	2,540	4,745	1,700
2006	1,421	2,695	5,537	2,199
2007	1,295	3,256	7,256	2,325
2008	633	4,017	7,792	2,839
2009	1,975	4,634	9,082	3,252
2010	1,681	3,845	7,184	3,176
Totals	12,169	29,273	57,106	23,094

Federal Bureau of Investigation (FBI). (2015). Fighting Gang Violence. Retrieved from www.fbi.gov/about-us/investigate/vc_majorthefts/gangs/recent-statistics

Gangs typically develop in areas that were already high-crime areas. Not surprisingly, those areas continue to experience higher crime rates than areas that are not populated by gang members (Tita & Ridgeway, 2007). Many areas are affected, although leaders may initially deny increases in gang violence (Huff, 1990). In the first decade of the twenty-first century, the FBI tracked the increase in gang violence, documenting a fluctuation in the numbers of complaints, indictments, arrests, and convictions from year to year, but overall there was an increase in all the categories. In particular, the number of arrests grew by almost 100% during the 10-year period, while the number of gang members was also increasing. Unfortunately, the number of indictments was roughly half of the number of arrests, and convictions occurred for only about one-third of arrests.

It should be noted that depending on the way arrests were counted, one individual may commit several crimes, each of which would be counted individually. For example, if one person was charged with five crimes, that could be reported as five arrests. The fluctuations in numbers from indictments to arrests to convictions might also represent a lack of prosecution or plea bargaining.

Gang members typically develop a code of conduct, which is often enforced using fear of violence or physical punishment (Thrasher, 1927). Codes of conduct for non-criminal groups typically set out the organization's values, ethics, objectives, and responsibilities. A well-written code gives guidance on how to deal with certain situations (Magloff,

2015). Codes of conduct for gangs include such things as not disclosing the details of their gang, so research about the inner-workings of the gang can be difficult.

Some gang members use gang violence to maintain or manage their reputation. The reputation or status of a gang or gang member allows them to manage present and future conflict (Papachristos, 2007). Taylor, Peterson, Esbensen, and Freng (2007) concluded that gang members were more likely (and more frequently) victims of violence than non-gang members. Given their propensity to carry weapons and settle disputes with violence, this was not surprising. Youth who join gangs were likely to be well acquainted with the likelihood of violence from their exposure to contemporary music, movies, and peers.

Gang members can be affected by a culture of violence in more ways than just an increased likelihood of arrest. Membership in a gang increased an individual's probability of arrest, as well as the probability of incarceration and violent victimization. The rates were not at all insignificant. Gang members have rates of violence about 100 times greater than the public (Decker & Pyrooz, 2010).

Factors Influencing Gang-Related Violence

Respondents to National Gang Center Surveys have identified the factors that significantly influenced gang-related violence in their jurisdictions. As shown in Figure 7.2, most agencies surveyed reported that intergang (between-gang) conflict and drug-related factors directly affected local levels of gang violence. More than one-third of the agencies in 2012 reported three main factors: the return of gang members from secure confinement, intragang (within-gang) conflict, and the emergence of new gangs. Two factors, gang members returning from confinement and intragang conflict, noticeably increased in importance from 2006 to 2012, while gang member migration and the emergence of new gangs noticeably decreased.

It may seem strange that gang members returning from a stint in jail or prison would increase the likelihood of violence. The effect of gang members returning from prison also results in increases in violent crime and drug trafficking in the community (Howell, 2006). While the existence of and involvement in prison gangs may account for the increase in violence and drug trafficking, they do not do much to explain the increase in violence. That may best be explained by the necessary replacement or change of leadership while the gang member was incarcerated and the unwillingness and refusal of those leaders to relinquish control of the gang or of the returning member to accept and submit to the authority of the new leadership.

Intragang conflict can increase the likelihood of gang-related violence for many of the same reasons. Violence between gang members often happens spontaneously over personal matters. Most gang members reported that gang leaders intervene to resolve intergang and intragang conflicts (Greene & Pranisand, 2007). Gang leaders try to control and contain violence themselves, often using violence or the threat of violence.

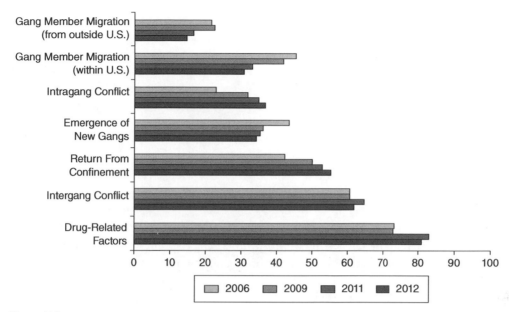

Figure 7.2

Factors Influencing Local Gang Violence.

National Gang Center (NGC). (2015). National Youth Gang Survey Analysis. NGC, U.S. Department of Justice. www.nationalgangcenter.gov/Survey-Analysis.

As was found in the surveys by the National Gang Center, intergang (between-gang) conflict increases the levels of local gang violence. Gang members may engage in violence against other gangs in disputes over territory, drug trafficking, or other issues. The status of a gang or gang member often depends on how responding actions or inactions are perceived by others. Many gangs will use violence to avoid losing status to other gangs (Papachristos, 2007). The use of violence can preclude being the victim of violence from another either in the present or in the future.

New gangs in the area may threaten established relationships between gangs and other members or organizations in the community, including other gangs. When gangs or other criminal elements have agreements regarding which of them is going to sell drugs and who is going to run the prostitution in the area, the addition of new players may cause confusion or competition. Given the natural tendency for gang members to use violence to encourage change, a violent response is often the result.

A study by Pyrooz, Wolfe, and Spohn (2011) examined whether gang members were more likely to be victims of crime than non-gang members. The research indicated that although many people (gang member and those who are not gang-affiliated alike) believe that gang membership offers protection, gang members were significantly more likely to be crime victims. Those findings suggest that gang membership increased the likelihood of victimization instead of decreasing it (Pyrooz et al., 2011). Gangs do not always provide protection against crime in their local community (Tita & Ridgeway, 2007).

Female gang members engaged in violence, although their status and involvement is likely to be different than their male counterparts. According to Miller and Decker (2001), male gang members did not perceive females as potential targets of gang retaliation, so the threat of violence that female gang members were exposed to was not as high as it was for male gang members.

Types of Violent Gang Activity

There are three well-known ways that gang members use violence. First, gang initiation and indoctrination, the testing of prospective gang members, often includes violent activity directed towards the prospect. Second, gang members who act contrary to the rules of the gang may face discipline, which is often meted out in a violent manner. Lastly, arguments and disagreements between gangs often become violent, especially when the disagreements regard which area of the city is controlled by which gang or who has the right to conduct business in a certain area.

Gang Indoctrination

As with many other groups or organizations, gangs often engage in the practice of indoctrination and initiation. This is often accomplished by providing the prospective gang member with a test of strength or will while enduring what is often called a beat-in or jump-in. A beat-in is an event in which one or more established gang members punch, kick, or otherwise strike the prospect for a predetermined time (Edmonton Police Service, 2015). That violence-infused introduction to the gang culture serves as a foundation for future acts of violence for the new gang member.

The beat-in may also consist of a series of beatings over a set period of time by a certain number of members (Edmonton Police Service, 2015). Each gang and gang set establishes the rules for these activities, depending on guidelines from the larger organization with which they affiliate. Other forms of initiation may include requiring the prospect to commit a robbery, shoplifting, rape, burglary, a drive-by shooting, stealing a gun, assaulting a rival, or self-mutilation (Edmonton Police Service, 2015).

Member Discipline

Discipline in gangs is critical to the success of the gang, as it is with any organization. With gangs, though, discipline of members is more likely to be violent. This may be due to the position of violence in the gang culture. A violation of the gang's rules usually results in a beating for the violator. By Sureño rules, for example, the violator is beaten for 13 seconds or more (The Tennessean, 2011). Other gangs have their own rules, often defining the number of assailants and length of time for the beating.

Quitting the gang can also be effected by agreeing to be "beaten down" or "jumped out," depending on the gang. Those beatings are often so severe that significant injury results. If a member chooses to leave the gang without being beaten down or jumped out, his former friends (gang members) may resort to extreme violence (Edmonton Police Service, 2015).

Drive-By Shootings

Another example of gang violence in the community is what is known as a drive-by shooting, when gang members shoot at other gang members, police, or regular citizens while driving on or in a motor vehicle. Using a vehicle allows the shooter to approach the intended target without being noticed and then to speed away before anyone reacts (Dedel, 2007). The vehicle may also offer some protection in the case of return fire or the ability to flee the area to avoid detection or capture. While firing a weapon is considered a potentially dangerous act, these acts become increasingly dangerous with the addition of a vehicle and often a moving target. Firing a weapon from a moving vehicle makes for an increased difficulty in hitting the intended target and an increased likelihood that an unintended target, such as a building, car, or person, will be hit.

No organizations collect nationwide data on drive-by shootings. National databases like the FBI's Uniform Crime Reports record the result (e.g., homicide, assault, aggravated assault) rather than the action (i.e., beat-in, street fight, drive-by shooting). The data that are available indicate that large metropolitan cities with mature and developed gang problems are more likely to be affected by drive-by shootings than smaller jurisdictions (Dedel, 2007).

Flash Gangs

Flash-mob violence periodically occurs in many cities across the U.S. Gang members and other criminals use the notification techniques that many non-criminal flash mobs have used to notify their members of a mass meeting. Coordination and communication is often made by email, text message, or use of one or more forms of social media, such as Twitter, YouTube, or Facebook. The coordinated and synchronized activity of the participants has caused onlookers to watch in awe without considering alternative responses like notifying law enforcement (Smith, Rush, Robinson, & Karmiller, 2012). These flash mob activities, if done well in the planning stages, appear to onlookers as a spontaneous activity. When violence is added to the activity, gang members operate in a shroud of perceived anonymity. These events often cause law enforcement challenges with investigating (Smith et al., 2012).

Gangs and Homicide

Globally the risk of being a homicide victim is highest for young men aged 15–29, with a rate of 21.2 per 100,000 (United Nations Office on Drugs and Crime [UNODC], 2011). The rate was the highest of all groups of males. For perspective, the rate was roughly double the rate of being a homicide victim for men in the 60–69 age group. That remarkable decrease in risk of such violence over a lifetime was easily attributed to the decreasing involvement in high-risk illicit activities such as street gang membership as men get older. Figure 7.3 depicts the global homicide rate.

In comparison, the global age-specific homicide rate for women is far lower, between 3 and 4 per 100,000 for all age groups after the age of 15.

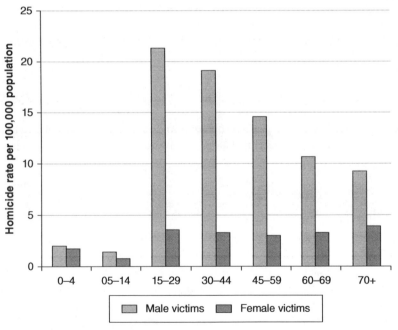

Figure 7.3

Global Homicide Rate by Sex and Age Group.

WHO, Causes of Death 2008 dataset (2011)

Studies have shown that 9% of homicide in the United States and as much as 25% of homicides in urban cities are gang related (Decker & Pyrooz, 2010; Pyrooz et al., 2011). This increased likelihood may come from the gang member experiencing a higher degree of violence during their upbringing. Gang members were found to be significantly more likely to have witnessed violence between their parents compared to non-gang members (Fox, Rufino, & Kercher, 2011).

The number of gang-related homicides reported from 2007 to 2012 grew in most areas of the U.S. The number of gang homicides averaged nearly 2,000 each year during that time. During roughly the same period, there were more than 15,500 homicides across the United States (FBI, 2012). Those estimates suggested that gang-related homicides accounted for around 13% of all homicides annually, as shown in Table 7.2.

Note that highly populated areas accounted for the clear majority of gang homicides, with nearly 67 percent of gang homicides occurring in cities with populations over 100,000, and 17percent occurring in suburban counties in 2012. In a typical year in cities with mature gang populations and problems like Chicago and Los Angeles, around half of all homicides were gang related. Overall, these figures show that gang violence is greatly concentrated in the largest cities across the United States.

TABLE 7.2 Number of Gang-Related Homicides

	2012		Percent Change, Previous 5-Year Average to 2012	
	% Total	N	% Total	
Agencies Reporting Gang Activity	—	999	—	—
Agencies Reporting Gang Homicide Statistics	—	829	—	—
Coverage Rate (%)	79.6%	—	83.0%	—
Total Gang Homicides	100.0%	2,363	100.0%	23.6
Cities With Populations Over 100,000	68.1%	1,587	67.2%	35.1
Suburban Counties	18.5%	408	17.3%	−7.6
Cities With Populations of 50,000–100,000	10.9%	255	10.8%	15.9
Smaller Areas	2.5%	113	4.8%	

National Gang Center (NGC). (2015). National Youth Gang Survey Analysis. NGC, U.S. Department of Justice. www.nationalgangcenter.gov/Survey-Analysis

Notes: "Not presented because of small base rate. "Smaller Areas" refers to cities and rural counties below 50,000 combined.

Pyrooz et al. (2011) determined that women were less likely to be homicide victims. They found that when a female gang member was the victim of a homicide, she was usually in the wrong place at the wrong time. They noted that the lower levels of involvement in gang homicide, as both victims and offenders, might be due to their lower rates of participation in gangs (Pyrooz et al., 2011).

Domestic Violence

In families that experience domestic violence, children often learn that violence is an appropriate response to settle disputes, manipulate and control, and express negative emotions (Brown, 2007). The process was like what the youth exposed to gangs learned. Abuse of females among gang members, including physical and sexual violence, becomes normal behavior (Brown, 2007). A physically abusive gang member was often an expert at intimidation (Brown, 2007). That intimidation was a powerful force when used against a partner in a relationship. Intimidation tactics used by gang members often included stalking or intimidating victims who left a relationship or chose to testify in court against a gang member.

Gang involvement further complicates the already difficult challenge of assisting victims of domestic violence. Due to the power of the typical gang network and the typical gang mentality, victims of domestic violence were likely to have multiple perpetrators within the gang, all of whom saw the victim as communal property (Darby & Annetts, 2014). The 2011 NGIC Threat Assessment indicated that gangs started to engage in more human trafficking and prostitution activities. The power and control in such a situation is intensified by the typical gang culture. Gang members who engaged in human trafficking and prostitution often used specific tactics to groom their victims (Darby & Annetts, 2014). They manipulated and coerced their victims to prostitute themselves with promises of drugs and alcohol, and they recruited other members to do the same.

Neighborhoods in Fear of Gang Violence

Melde and Rennison (2010) examined responses by community members to the possibility of gang violence. Fear of crime in general has been examined, and consistently showed that women were more afraid of crime and gang crime than men, and racial and ethnic minorities were typically more afraid than whites (Lane & Fox, 2012). Earlier research indicated that older people were more afraid of crime, but more recent studies show that younger people were more afraid of both crime generally and gang crime more specifically (Lane & Fox, 2012).

As we have seen, gangs have a propensity towards violence, and that propensity was well known in the community and may influence victim and bystander behavior in criminal incidents in hopes that they can lessen the possibility of retaliation by the gang (Melde & Rennison, 2010). The concern over the level of fear produced by street gangs has been recognized as a major problem in the arrest and later conviction of gang members, as it was believed that victims and witnesses were less likely to cooperate with authorities for fear of gang retaliation (Greene & Pranisand, 2007). Naturally, both prosecution and law enforcement officials were concerned with the effect that gangs have on their potential witnesses to crimes they commit.

The effect of fear of crime on community members appeared to be mixed and perhaps dependent upon the type of crime committed. For example, the odds of reporting decreased when a gang member committed a robbery (Melde & Rennison, 2010). It would stand to reason, and fit with the general public belief, that reporting of all violent crime was lower when a gang member is the suspect. To the contrary, the odds of reporting increased when a gang member committed violent crimes like rape or aggravated assault (Melde & Rennison, 2010). The effect of gang membership on victim and bystander behavior also appeared to be dependent upon the type or severity of a crime as well. For example, an increased likelihood of forceful victim resistance in acts of aggravated assault and a decreased likelihood of forceful resistance in simple assault were found when the offender was thought to be a gang member (Melde & Rennison, 2010). Those perhaps counterintuitive and unpredictable results may explain why the presence of gang members and the violence they bring can negatively impact the community.

The response of community members to crime, especially gang crime, was often fueled by the response to gang crime by media and community leaders. If the media inflated the number and severity of gang crimes, community leaders may then attribute higher importance to the activity (McCorkle & Miethe, 1998). The collective response influenced the perceptions of individual community members, and may lead to what has been termed moral panic. Such a determination may lead to an increase in attention toward gangs and gang crime, which may include more investigation and prosecution of gang members (McCorkle & Miethe, 1998).

Lane and Fox (2012) learned that current gang members felt significantly more at risk of personal victimization than former and non-gang members. Said another way, members of the group recognized that their current lifestyle made them a likely target. Lane and Fox (2012) observed that both current and former gang members reported committing more property and personal crime than non-gang members, and current gang members reported committing more personal crime than ex-gang members. Regarding gang crime specifically, current gang members felt significantly more at risk than ex-gang members who, in turn, felt significantly more at risk than non-gang offenders. So the further an individual got from gang membership, the less they felt threatened by gang crime (Lane & Fox, 2012).

Imported Gang Violence

The effect of war, corruption, and poverty in their home nations on refugees cannot be overstated. Those experiences naturally affect the people who flee from them, and experiences continue to influence them as citizens of a new country. Communities made up of immigrants from the same country often band together when they arrive in a new place. Some of those groups form based on a similar ethnicity, heritage, or former citizenship. Sometimes that leads to assimilation into the new community. Other times the new residents self-segregate, sticking together in all facets of their lives. For some, the attraction of criminal gangs is quite enticing. New immigrants may join to be part of the new culture, to increase their likelihood of success, or quite often, to defend themselves against gang members in the community that want to prey on the new citizens.

Contemporary youth in the U.S. and elsewhere have experienced few, if any, years when their country was not at war. The graphic images and stories available to all because of always-on connectivity via the internet provide insight into life in a wartime situation. But that does not effectively create the absence of hope and despair often found among the citizens in a country at war. It is possible that all that access has desensitized youth and young adults to the devastation caused by violence.

Let's examine five areas to see how that turmoil can affect the formation and activities of gangs. First, we will look at Mexico in North America, with a reputation as a tourist destination with a porous border used for drug trafficking for many years. Next, we will travel down to El Salvador and Central America, where war and insurgency has been a way of life. We will stop in the Caribbean, where communities outside of tourist spots conceal the far-reaching gang crime within. Then, we will examine Somalia, in eastern Africa, which in recent history has experienced a bloody civil war. Finally, we will look at Kurdistan, a region in the Middle East that traverses the borders of Turkey, Iraq, and Iran.

Mexico

Mexico has a rich history and is one of the world's largest economies. The country has been known for its hardworking people and for its corrupt politicians. Numerous instances of criminals partnering with police, military, and government officials have been reported over the years. But the danger associated with criminals and government officials having similar interests has not kept foreigners from spending time in that country. Many locations across Mexico have become prime tourist destinations because of the beauty and diversity of the country.

But Mexico has seen a fusion of its powerful drug cartels and gangs resulting in an ongoing drug war with numerous killings and decapitations. Cartels are large drug trafficking organizations that compete and fight with other cartels and some local drug trafficking rings for control of territory. The rivalries among Mexican cartels have resulted in bloody battles and have claimed many innocent lives (United Nations, 2009). The Zetas are a particularly violent group. They were initially the enforcement arm for the Gulf Cartel in the late 1990s. Made up of deserters from the Mexican special operations force, the Zetas brought military tactics like ambushes, defensive positions, and small-unit exercises to the organized criminal groups in Mexico (Sullivan & Logan, 2010a). The Zetas have created a brutal mystique, making their name synonymous with violence and fear across the Americas. In addition to drug trafficking, human trafficking, small arms trafficking, kidnapping, and murder, their skills included conducting raids and ambushes, using small unit infantry tactics to engage in close quarters battle with state security forces (Sullivan & Logan, 2010a).

Etter and Lehmuth (2013) observed that criminals and other gangs in Mexico had been trading drugs, humans, guns, and other goods for many years. There was a time when Mexican drug cartels transferred their shipments at the U.S.-Mexican border, and another organization smuggled the products further into the U.S. The cartels were more involved in the entire supply chain, and brought their products into the U.S. themselves. Many cartels had operations throughout North America, including all regions of the U.S. (Etter & Lehmuth, 2013).

The fact that the drug cartels have operated so freely within Mexico has astonished some observers. The history of corruption of the Mexican police and military forces, as well as members of the judiciary and other government officials, contributed significantly to the problem. Consequently, the Mexican government had a difficult time recruiting and retaining honest police personnel (Etter & Lehmuth, 2013). Many of the drug cartels have a reputation of violence, especially when their profit potential is attacked by either rival cartels or law enforcement.

The Mexican drug cartels also appeared to be able to operate freely along the border with the U.S. Rodriguez, Eve, Del Carmen, and Jeong (2014) observed that the enforcement problems were often magnified when they traverse international boundaries. They noted that many of these groups engaged in violent crimes such as assault, burglary, and robbery in addition to their drug distribution endeavors. The research also determined that violence was one of the top concerns for law enforcement in those areas. The main cartels operating out of Mexico at the time of this writing included:

- Cartel del Pacífico Sur

- Gulf Cartel

- Independent Cartel of Acapulco

- Jalisco New Generation Cartel

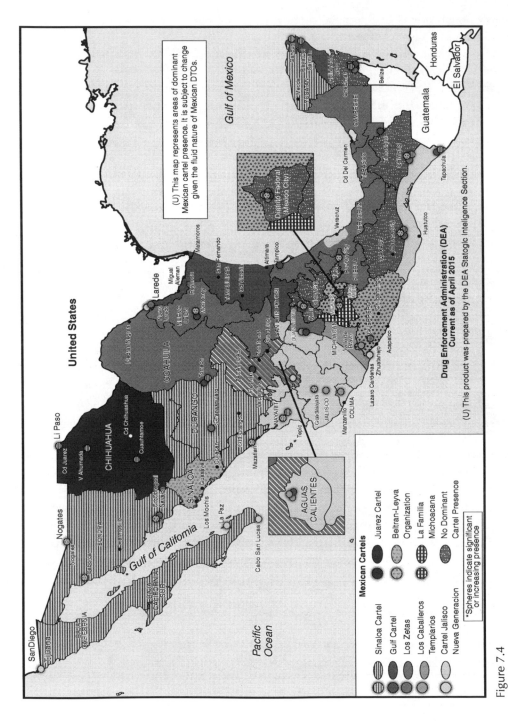

Figure 7.4

Map of DTO (Cartel) Areas of Dominant Influence.

U.S. Drug Enforcement Administration (DEA) (April 2016). The DEA identifies drug trafficking organizations (DTOs) as "cartels." The Knights Templar is identified in Spanish as Los Caballeros Templarios.

- Juárez Cartel

- Knights Templar

- Sinaloa Federation

- Tierra Caliente

- Tijuana Cartel

- Los Zetas.

Mexican drug gangs went through an adjustment in 2014. According to STRAT-FOR Global Intelligence (2015), the Sinaloa Federation had leadership issues in 2013 and 2014. Not only was one of their leaders arrested, but several of the subordinate groups grew more independent. Other Gulf Cartel factions had structural issues, too. The Knights Templar in Michoacan, as an example, were all but dismantled. Several other area crime groups filled the void.

Figure 7.4 identifies the areas of cartel influence in Mexico.

El Salvador and Central America

The growth of Mexican cartels has brought a new class of violence to Central America. Violent crime rates, especially in the region that included Honduras, El Salvador, and Guatemala, are among the highest in the world. To a certain extent, the location was part of the problem. Central America was situated between some of the world's largest drug producers in South America and the world's largest consumer of illegal drugs, the U.S. The region had high rates of poverty, relatively unlimited access to weapons and capable gunmen, and weak, underfunded, and sometimes corrupt governments (UNODC, 2011). Those factors make the area ripe for the active presence of organized crime syndicates.

Though the United States has aided Central American efforts to address criminal violence, it also has contributed to the problem because many of its citizens use illicit drugs (Shifter, 2012). Add to that the relatively relaxed gun control laws and deportation policies that have returned more than a million illegal migrants with violent criminal records, and you have the foundation of a supporting base for organized crime activities. In 2010, the U.S. instituted a regional strategy and listed all Central American countries as major drug transporters or producers. The resulting strategy, called the Central America Regional Security Initiative (CARSI), pledged to deliver over $301.5 million (Shifter, 2012). The focus was originally intended to be on three main activities: narcotics interdiction and law enforcement, institutional capacity building, and violence prevention. The transnational drug trade, which quickly became the most profitable organized criminal activity in the region, reaped significant benefits from the weakness of governments throughout Central America.

The Mara Salvatrucha (MS-13) is an example of a street gang that has transformed itself into a powerful transnational force. Formed on the streets of Los Angeles in the 1980s by immigrants fleeing civil war in El Salvador, MS-13 has transformed from a turf-oriented immigrant gang into a potent, brutal, transnational criminal organization (Sullivan & Logan, 2010b). MS-13 was initially formed to provide its members a way to avoid being victimized by other gangs. In doing so, it provided a gateway for its members into criminal activities. The early members of MS-13 included former guerrillas and soldiers with combat experience during the Salvadoran civil war (Franco, 2008). MS-13 developed a reputation of employing unusual methods of violence, including attacking their victims with machetes. Despite that reputation, Franco noted that little evidence existed to substantiate that the MS-13 gang was more violent than other street gangs (2008).

Transnational gangs operating throughout the Americas are widely known as *maras* (Sullivan & Logan, 2010b). Mara gangs are a significant security and stability concern throughout the Western Hemisphere. Honduras, El Salvador, Nicaragua, and Guatemala are all threatened by the Maras. Their existence may cause increases in a variety of crimes, notably homicides, as depicted in Figure 7.5.

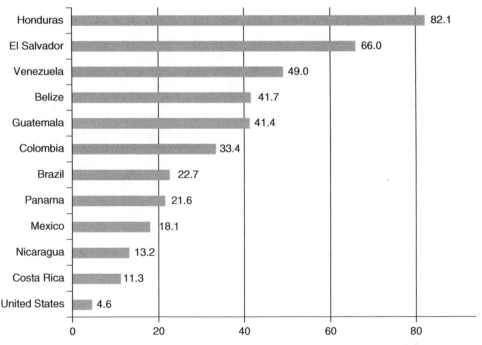

Figure 7.5

Homicide Rates per 100,000 Inhabitants.

United Nations Office on Drugs and Crime, Global Study on Homicide (2011)

Mara gangs and the local drug trafficking groups have historically been quite distinct, although the gangs would often be the local drug distributors and serve as contract killers for the drug trafficking groups. The maras are established throughout Central America, and although their activities are sometimes transnational in nature, they often lack a central command and have only minimal connections to large drug trafficking organizations (UNODC, 2011). Those gangs are extremely violent and responsible for a significant share of homicides in several of the region's countries, where they are increasingly involved in extortion, intimidation and protection rackets.

The Caribbean

Caribbean countries are also affected by violent crime driven by organized drug trafficking. Drug trafficking is among the illicit activities of gangs in Jamaica, where street gangs became progressively involved when the Caribbean became a trafficking route from Colombia in the 1980s (UNODC, 2011). Such shifts in the structure and focus of criminal groups and the reaction of law enforcement have profoundly influenced the nature and pattern of lethal violence in the Caribbean over the past decade. Figure 7.6 shows a comparison of various types of violent crime comparing Honduras and Jamaica.

According to Seepersad (2013), criminal gangs in Trinidad and Tobago have brought that country a notoriety that rivals Jamaica for levels of violence. Increases in the number

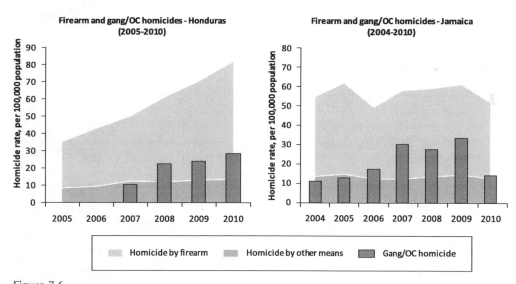

Figure 7.6

Firearm and Gang/Organized Crime Homicide: Honduras and Jamaica.

National Police, as cited in United Nations Office on Drugs and Crime, Global Study on Homicide (2011)

of murders and violent crimes have been attributed primarily to increases in gang activity. In fact, gang members are arrested in Trinidad and Tobago far more than non-gang criminals. While the average non-gang citizen has .68 arrests, the average gang member has over two. Almost one in three of the murders in the first decade of the twenty-first century was attributed to gangs there.

Somalia

Somali gang presence has increased in several cities throughout the United States according to the most recent FBI report on gangs (NGIC, 2011). Somali gangs are most prevalent in Minneapolis-St. Paul, Minnesota; San Diego, California; and Seattle, Washington. The gangs' presence in those areas was primarily due to the proximity to the Mexican and Canadian borders. Somali gang activity has also been reported in other

Figure 7.7

T-shirt of Somali Outlaws set in Minneapolis, Minnesota. Public domain.

Minneapolis Police Department/FBI

cities throughout the United States such as Nashville, Tennessee; Clarkston, Georgia; Columbus, Ohio; East Brunswick, New Jersey; and Tucson, Arizona.

Unlike most street gangs, Somali gang members usually align and adopt gang names based on clan or tribe, although a few have joined traditional street gangs like the Crips and Bloods (NGIC, 2011). Homicides involving Somali victims are often the result of clan feuds between gang members. Sex trafficking for the purpose of prostitution is also a growing trend among Somalian gangs.

Although some Somali gangs have adopted Bloods or Crips gang monikers, they typically do not associate with African American gangs (NGIC, 2011). Somali nationals have tended to migrate to low-income communities, which are often controlled by local Bloods and Crips street gangs. Somali youth may even emulate the local gangs, which frequently leads to friction between them.

Kurdistan

Kurdistan is a geographic region in the Middle East that spans the countries of Turkey, Iraq and Iran. Before World War I, traditional Kurdish life was nomadic, often consisting of sheep and goat herding throughout the Mesopotamian plains and highlands (Washington Post, 1999). With the Ottoman Empire's dismantling after the war came new nation states, but not a separate Kurdistan. The Kurds received harsh treatment from the Turkish government, which designated them "Mountain Turks," outlawed their language, and forbade them to wear traditional Kurdish costumes in the cities (Washington Post, 1999). In Iraq, Kurds have faced similar repression at the hand of former leader Saddam Hussein, who razed their villages and attacked them with chemical weapons in the mid-1990s.

That harsh treatment by the governments inspired many Kurds to move to the U.S. As children and youth in Kurdistan were raised in a culture in which war and turmoil was the norm, many of them had a propensity to dismiss government authority. They can also be desensitized to violence, which they experienced due to the long-term war in their country (Cavaliere, 2013). The Kurdish Pride Gang (KPG) formed around 2000 and grew out of the same need for a shared sense of identity that fueled the rise of other ethnic gangs, like the MS-13. The gang was formed in response to a need for protection from other street gangs in the area. The KPG soon dealt drugs, burglarized homes, and flashed gang signs, intimidating citizens and making area parks and playgrounds unsafe. They have been involved with illegal guns, assault, and attempted murder (Cavaliere, 2013).

The gang became quite a threat to the community, and the local police responded. In 2012, the KPG became the target of a street gang injunction by police in Nashville, Tennessee. A civil lawsuit in Davidson County Criminal Court alleged that KPG members engaged in violent crimes such as assaults, illegal possession and discharge of guns, burglaries, witness intimidation, street robberies, conspiracy to commit murder, and threatening police officers, among other crimes (Nashville.gov, 2012). Those acts took place on a regular basis and allowed the gang to maintain power over the community, recruit new members, and threaten and intimidate citizens to keep silent about KPG activities. That was the first gang injunction sought by Nashville government (Nashville.gov, 2012). The gang even infiltrated the Nashville Police.

Summary

To identify how increases in homicides can be attributed to gang activity, we should consider that the risk of being a homicide victim globally is highest for young men aged 15–29. The subsequent decrease in risk of violence over a lifetime is a direct reflection of the decreasing involvement, as men age, in high-risk illicit activities such as street gang membership. As much as 25% of homicides in urban cities are gang related, and the number of gang-related homicides is increasing.

Concern over the level of fear produced by street gangs has been recognized as a major problem in the arrest and later conviction of gang members. It is believed that victims and witnesses are less likely to cooperate with authorities for fear of gang retaliation. Gang members recognize that their current lifestyle makes them a likely target, and current gang members felt significantly more at risk than ex-gang members, who in turn felt significantly more at risk than non-gang offenders.

Communities made up of immigrants from the same country often band together when they arrive in a new place. New immigrants may join gangs to be part of the new culture, to increase their likelihood of success, or quite often, to defend themselves against gang members in the community that want to prey on the new citizens. While not all members of an immigrant community are likely to become gang members, those who do will add a new dimension to the criminal justice needs of the community.

DISCUSSION QUESTIONS

1. Describe how gang activity often results in violent acts.
2. How does the presence of gangs increase the level of violence in a community?
3. Describe the impact of fear of crime on communities.
4. How are increases in homicides attributed to gang activity?
5. To what extent might an increase of ethnic and immigrant gangs affect the community?

CHAPTER 8 Gangs and the Military

CHAPTER OBJECTIVES

After reading this chapter students should be able to do the following:

- Explain how military training adds to the dangerousness of gang members.
- Identify historical events regarding military-trained gang members.
- Analyze how the existence of military-trained gang members affects communities.
- Examine the necessary changes in police response policies when the community includes military-trained gang members.

Introduction

Military-trained gang members (MTGMs) have existed in the United States since the beginning. In each wartime era, they have been identified with varying degrees of responses by communities and governments. The presence of MTGMs in the community means an increase in the dangerousness of gang members there. The existence of those gang members often means a higher number of military tactics being used by gangs, such as home invasions and armed robberies, as well as the use of military-style weapons and explosives. In this chapter, we will examine the presence of military-trained gang members in our communities and how their presence significantly increases the potential for increased violence.

Military-Trained Gang Members in History

Clearly the first criminal groups led by men with military training were river pirates in the 1790s. One of the more notorious was river pirate Samuel Mason, a former militia captain in the American Revolution (Asbury, 2003). In 1777, Mason, a native of the area now known as Pennsylvania, left the military and searched for a new career. In the 1790s, he settled at Red Bank (now Henderson), Kentucky, and became a counterfeiter and later a river pirate. Mason and his gang moved their operation to Cave-in-Rock, Illinois, in the mid-1790s after the tax collectors from Pennsylvania hunted him down. They left Cave-in-Rock before the turn of the century and became land pirates (highwaymen) on the Natchez Trace (Asbury, 2003). Many a traveler traversing the 440 miles of wilderness between Nashville in Tennessee and Natchez in the Mississippi Territory reported attacks by the Mason gang before Sam Mason was captured in 1803.

In the 1840s, several street gang members joined the military in New York, seeking better opportunities and a fresh start at a new location. They were sent to Mexico City to fight in the Mexican-American War, and were later discharged from the military in what became San Francisco, California, shortly before the California Gold Rush. Many folks from around the world made their way to the California gold mines to find their treasure. Some traveled there by signing on with a ship as a commercial sailor, then neglected their responsibility to offload the ships in the bay once they arrived, dashing instead to the mines (Asbury, 2003).

The veteran New York gang members had formed a group they called the Hounds, and were hired by the ship's captains to retrieve the wayward sailors, for which they were paid about $25 a head (over $600 in today's dollars). The group began calling themselves the San Francisco Society of Regulators, the closest thing to a police or security force that the town had (Asbury, 2003). The Hounds/Regulators "served" the shopkeepers and barkeeps by drinking in their establishments and leaving without rendering payment, claiming the city owed *them*. In their spare time, they harassed or threatened the locals (many of whom were Mexicans, Chileans, and Peruvians).

Brothers Jesse and Frank James served as Confederate guerrillas, known as bush-whackers, ambushing the Union armies during the Civil War (Allender, 2001). In 1866, after the war, they began robbing banks, trains, and stagecoaches. For 16 years, the Jameses and their compatriots committed 11 bank robberies, 12 train robberies, and four stagecoach holdups, obtaining an estimated $350,000 (over $6 million in today's dollars; Clark & Palattella, 2015).

One of the more well-known and intriguing gang members with a military connection was the gangster known as Edward "Monk" Eastman. Eastman's self-named gang was active in New York at the same time as the Five Pointers. Gangs were not the only activity Eastman had in New York City, he owned a pet store, and served as a sheriff, a boxer, and a bouncer (Asbury, 1989). Eastman was a gangster's gangster and was very well connected politically. Eastman served in the Army during World War I, and when his service ended he was pardoned by the governor of New York. He did not change his ways, however, and sold bootleg alcohol and drugs until he was murdered in 1921.

Figure 8.1

Monk Eastman. Public domain. Eastman was a gangster's gangster in New York who joined the Army and fought in the trenches in France during World War I.

Gangs in the Military

Although military laws prohibit active membership, contemporary street gangs, prison gangs, and outlaw motorcycle gangs (OMG) all have service members who have enlisted. Some gang members specifically try to acquire military assault weapons, ammunition, body armor, and explosives. Gang members with military-type (assault) weapons may endanger citizens when they conduct drive-by shootings of rival gang members (NGIC, 2013). Military-trained gang members may also be more likely to initiate or engage in potentially deadly confrontations with police. As shown in Table 8.1, many gang members have been found in possession of weapons.

TABLE 8.1 **Number of Firearms Recovered by Gang (Top 10 Listed)**

Gang	2011	2012	Total
Bloods	577	543	1,120
Crips	456	415	871
Gangster Disciples	342	430	772
Vice Lords Nation	259	252	511
Sureños	218	205	423
Latin Kings	169	107	276
Norteños	93	115	208
Black P. Stone Nation	90	113	203
Black Disciples	37	42	79
No gang information/unidentified (NGI)	385	280	665
Total (minus NGIs)	2,241	2,241	4,463

Bureau of ATF, Violent Crimes Analysis Branch, as cited by National Gang Intelligence Center [NGIC]. (2013). *National Gang Report*. Washington, DC: National Gang Intelligence Center.

In 1992, Knox conducted an exploratory study of a convenience sample of Illinois National Guard soldiers. An incident involving the death of a child had occurred in a large public housing complex that was known for gang violence. The shooter, a gang member, had served in the military, and public officials had suggested the possibility that the National Guard could have been called to assist in suppressing the gang problem (Knox, 2006).

Survey respondents estimated that gang membership in the military ranged from a low of zero to a high of 75 percent with a mean of 21.5 percent (Knox, 2006). The responses indicated that the Army National Guard was thought to have the highest percentage of former or current gang members in its ranks (a mean of 21.5%). The Coast Guard was thought to have the lowest percentage, with a mean of 6.3 percent.

In 1996, in response to racially motivated homicide of a civilian couple by soldiers, members of a Department of the Army task force evaluated the effects of extremist groups and reported that "gang-related activities appear to be more pervasive than extremist activities as defined in Army Regulation (AR) 600–20" (U.S. Department of

Defense [DoD], 1996, para. 16). At the time, there was no prohibition against gang membership by U.S. service members. Both AR 600–20 and DoD Directive 1325.6 (later changed to DoD Instruction (DoDI)—Guidelines for Handling Dissident and Protest Activities Among Members of the Armed Forces) prohibited active membership in extremist groups, and many leaders and investigators considered street gangs to be extremist groups, although neither document specifically mentioned street gangs.

The authors of the 2006 U.S. Army Gang Activity Threat Assessment (GATA) reported an increase in both gang-related investigations and incidents in 2006 over previous years. The most common gang-related crime was drug trafficking, which encompassed (31%) of the gang-related offenses reported for the year (CID, 2006). Although drug-related criminal activity often existed where violent crime existed, that was not all that was learned from the survey. Three assaults, two homicides, and two robberies were also reported as gang-related crimes in 2006 (CID, 2006). More recent reports have yielded much the same results. The Department of Defense recently started distinguishing street gangs from groups and OMGs in their annual reports.

In a recent survey of law enforcement professionals working adjacent to a large military installation, 57 percent reported the use of military weapons and explosives by gang members in their jurisdiction (Smith, 2014a). That was in the higher range of responses from the previous five years. Typical responses in other surveys ranged between 18 and 66 percent.

Smith (2014a; 2014b; 2014c; 2014d) found that 6–11 percent of gang members in a sampling of communities had military training of some kind. Advanced combat tactics have become more available to gang members in civilian communities. MTGMs introduce military tactics and training to local gang members, creating an increase in the level of gang violence within the community (NGIC, 2007). In a recent survey, almost half (46%) of law enforcement professionals working adjacent to a large military installation reported that gang members in their jurisdiction used military-type tactics (Smith, 2014a). The percentage reporting military-trained gang members was higher than surveys from the previous five years, which ranged from 13 to 37 percent in agreement. Most (86%) respondents who reported a perception agreed that gang members in their jurisdiction were currently serving in the military. The percentage of those reporting agreement was also significantly higher than previous survey responses, which typically ranged from 16 to 33 percent in agreement.

Most of the respondents surveyed reported they had gang members that committed home invasions and armed robberies (Smith, 2014a). Those responses were consistent with survey responses in the previous five years. In a classic home invasion robbery, two or more gang members armed with weapons forcefully enter a private home or apartment to control the actions of the occupants with the goal of stealing property and committing other opportunistic crimes (McGoey, 2014). A gang home invasion may appear similar to the action of police executing a no-knock warrant or raiding a drug house. It also has similarities to the military tactic of breaching and clearing a dwelling as part of close-quarters combat tactics (U.S. Army, 1993).

There was a total of 1,598 gang-related Army Criminal Investigation Division (CID) reports, both Reports of Investigation/Law Enforcement Reports (ROI/LERs) and Criminal Intelligence (CRIMINTEL), identified from 2002 to 2015. Of those, 374 were felony criminal investigations by CID. An additional 1,224 cases did not rise to that standard, but were nonetheless investigated to some extent.

From 2012 to 2015, 94 total felony reports of investigation involved members of street gangs. Drugs were the focus of 48 of the investigations, while 14 were homicide related and 10 were sex crime related. The remaining cases comprised various offenses such as robbery, assault, extortion, larceny, and failure to obey. There were 90 subjects identified: 58 of them were soldiers, 48 of whom were active duty. Most of the street gang subjects were black males who were 20–24 years old, single, and junior enlisted (E1–E4).

In addition to the investigations, there were 147 CRIMINTEL reports associated with street gangs from 2012 to 2015. Within the CRIMINTEL reports, 209 individuals were identified as having suspected affiliation with street gangs. There were 114 soldiers, of whom 105 were active duty. The remaining individuals included 76 with no DoD affiliation and 16 otherwise DoD-affiliated persons.

Twenty-five of the felony investigations in 2012–2015 involved OMGs with 28 subjects, and all but one of them were active duty soldiers. The investigations involved the offenses of murder, wrongful distribution of drugs, assault, fraud, and failure to obey. Most subjects in the felony OMG investigations were white males who were 20–24 years old and senior enlisted (E5–E9).

There were an additional 356 CRIMINTEL reports associated with OMGs from 2012 to 2015. Within the CRIMINTEL reporting, 473 subjects were suspected of affiliation with OMGs. There were 297 soldiers, 264 of whom were on active duty. The remaining individuals included 92 with no DoD affiliation and 90 otherwise DoD-affiliated persons. The 2015 assessment reported the number of OMG investigations more than doubled. It was suggested that the increase was due to greater awareness and improved tracking and reporting by CID offices.

Military-Trained Street Gang Members and the Community

Some examples of street gang members with military training or equipment include the following.

In 1996, a suspected Sureños gang member shot and killed his executive officer and wounded the squadron commanding officer to protest the incarceration of his fellow gang members. Marine Sgt. Jessie Quintanilla entered his squadron's command suite and confronted his executive officer, Lieut. Col. (LTC) Daniel Kidd in his office, pointed a .45-caliber pistol at him and, as LTC Kidd attempted to run to an adjacent room, shot Kidd in the back (*Quintanilla v. United States*, 2010). As Quintanilla followed Kidd into the adjacent room, he encountered his commander, LTC Thomas A. Heffner, and shot him in the chest. Quintanilla then shot Kidd a second time in the back, killing him. Shortly thereafter, Quintanilla fired two shots at Gunnery Sgt. W. E. Tiller, missing with both. Quintanilla was then disarmed and apprehended.

In 1997, Jacqueline Billings, a soldier at Fort Hood, Texas, ordered three gang members to kill Basel Maaz, the manager of a nightclub in Killeen, Texas. Billings was the "governor" of a 40-member faction of the Gangster Disciples—many of whom were soldiers at Fort Hood. Billings had the distinction of being perhaps the first, and surely the most violent, female MTGM (*United States v. Billings*, 1999). Instead of killing Maaz, the gang members shot Dorian Ellsworth Castillo and Robert Jharel Davidson, who were driving Maaz's car from the nightclub to his home. Also in the summer of 1997, Billings's gang committed an armed robbery at the management office of the Monaghan Apartments, stealing approximately $2,500 in cash and a gold watch, valued at $18,500.95.

On January 8, 2005, Lance Cpl. Andres Raya shot and killed Ceres, California, police Sgt. Howard Stevenson and wounded Officer Sam Ryno with a semiautomatic SKS rifle outside a Ceres liquor store before police returned fire and killed him (DeFao, 2005). Raya, a U.S. Marine, was a Norteño gang member and was high on cocaine at the time. During the investigation, it was learned that he had just returned from Iraq, but had not faced combat. Raya had made odd statements when he entered the liquor store, left and fired off a couple of rounds from his rifle, and then returned to the store and told the clerk to call police because he had been shot. Officer Ryno and Sgt. Stevenson then arrived. The investigation also uncovered ties to the Norteño gang, including a book by a member of the related prison gang, Nuestra Familia, and numerous pictures of Raya wearing the gang's signature color red and making gang signs with his hands (DeFao, 2005).

On July 3, 2005, in Kaiserslautern, Germany, gang leader Rico Williams knocked out Juwan Johnson with one punch. Williams, a former airman, ran the Gangster Disciples in the area (Mraz, 2007). After two gang members helped Johnson to his feet, Williams punched him again. Johnson fell to the ground a second time. Johnson then stood up under his own power, at which time nine of the Gangster Disciples descended on him in a beating typical of those experienced for initiation and discipline. The punishment lasted six minutes. After six minutes and more than 200 blows, Johnson lost bowel control (Mraz, 2007). The other gang members helped him into his car, and drove him to their barracks and carried him to his room. Later, Johnson turned blue and was taken to the local hospital, where he died from his injuries. That afternoon, Williams concocted a cover story for all to tell: a bunch of Turks beat up Johnson in downtown Kaiserslautern the night before.

In the fall of 2006, four Marines in Columbia, South Carolina, were found to be recruiting local teenagers into the Crips street gang per the direction of a gang leader in Florida (WTOC, 2006). The Marines were contacted by the gang leader and asked to follow up on an online inquiry by the teenagers, who had used computers at schools and public libraries to make the connection. The teenagers met with the gang member Marines outside a high school, near a fun park, and at a home in the community. Many Crip gang members, including the Marines, were arrested for planning an attack at a high school football event in Columbia, South Carolina.

In 2008 a former soldier in Oklahoma City, Oklahoma, admitted to making multiple improvised explosive devices (IED) that he intended to sell to gang members (Johnson, 2008). The former soldier made weapons like those used against his fellow soldiers in Iraq and offered them for sale to gang members and other criminals in Oklahoma City for as little as $100.

In 2009, Private Michael Apodaca carried out a hit for the Juarez Cartel (Greig, 2013). Apodaca was paid $5,000 to shoot and kill Jose Daniel Gonzalez-Galeana. And military leaders, both non-commissioned and commissioned officers, are willing to use their military training to benefit criminal gangs. In 2011, Sgt. Samuel Walker and former Lieut. Kevin Corley agreed to kill members of a rival gang for $50,000 and cocaine. Corley negotiated with men purporting to be members of the Zetas cartel but were undercover

Figure 8.2

Improvised explosive device (IED). Buried IED blast in in Iraq. Public domain.

U.S. Army

agents to kill rival gang members (Greig, 2013). Corley said that he could train 40 cartel members in "room clearing, security and convoy security." He also said he could recruit other members from his unit to the gang and steal military weapons for the gang.

From August 2014 to March 2015, Jaime Casillas and Andrew Reyes worked at the National Guard Armory in El Cajon, California (Davis, 2015a). Reyes and Casillas agreed to sell military property including firearms, body armor plates, and ammunition to an undercover agent, who told them he wanted weapons for drug traffickers in Mexico. The two sold the agent six rifles, one pistol, body armor plates, ammunition, and magazines for a total of $15,450.

Cpt. Leon Brown IV was the leader of a violent street gang that ran a prostitution ring with underage girls, distributed marijuana and psilocybin, and gave alcohol to teenagers (Davis, 2015b). He was also convicted of sexual assault of a child younger than 16, the use of psilocybin, willful dereliction of duty, conduct unbecoming of an officer and a gentleman, pandering, unlawful entry, and communicating threats.

Outlaw Motorcycle Gang (OMG) Members in the Military

OMGs and their support clubs actively recruit active-duty military personnel for their knowledge, reliable income, tactical skills, and dedication to a cause. According to the Bureau of Alcohol, Tobacco, Firearms and Explosives (ATF), a large number of support clubs have recruited active-duty military personnel and DoD contractors and employees (2014). OMG members have represented their gang by flying (wearing) their colors while serving in Iraq, Afghanistan, and other locations where service members are deployed across the globe. The ATF has published reports in each of the last several years. Information in those reports include:

- OMG support clubs are recruiting a large number of active-duty military personnel.

- Outside Fort Bragg and Eglin Air Force Bases, explosives have turned up in residences of U.S. Army Special Forces operators—unsubstantiated connections to an OMG.

- Violence between OMGs increased from 2012 to 2013.

- OMG members, especially those affiliated with the Hells Angels, Bandidos, Warlocks, and Mongols continue to fly their colors while serving in Iraq, Afghanistan and other destinations across the globe.

Some examples of OMG members with military training include:

- Members of a Dutch motorcycle gang, armed with Kalashnikov rifles, recently offered their skills to Kurdish forces battling the Islamic State in Iraq and Syria (ISIS;

FoxNews.com, 2014). Three members of the gang No Surrender traveled to Mosul in northern Iraq to take up the fight against ISIS, according to a group leader of the gang, which has dozens of chapters in Europe. A Dutch public prosecutor said it was lawful for Dutch citizens to fight against the group, as long as they did not fight against the Netherlands.

- On March 3, 2012, gunfire erupted outside the Sin City Deciples [*sic*] clubhouse in Colorado Springs, Colorado. Virgil "Jason" Means was tossed out of the clubhouse after getting into a fight with a member. Means returned about an hour later to retrieve his wallet. Means was shot and killed. A U.S. Army soldier and Sin City Deciples sergeant-at-arms was convicted of manslaughter and sentenced to 21 years' imprisonment (ATF, 2014).

- On October 20, 2013, an officer with the Richmond, Virginia, Police Department conducted a traffic stop on Eric Roman for speeding. Roman was a member of the Down and Dirty MC, a support club for the Wheels of Soul OMG. Roman was wearing his colors and carrying an eight-inch knife and a handgun, both concealed under his colors (ATF, 2014). He explained to the police officer that he was employed as a federal police officer at Quantico Marine Corps Base. The officer determined that Roman was not authorized to possess a concealed firearm off-base, and arrested him.

Prohibiting Military Street Gangs and OMGs

Although policies and regulations differ in wording across the military branches of the Defense Department, most guidelines on participation in extremist organizations are the same. When there is no information, the other branches default to the Army. Service members must generally reject participation in organizations that:

- Espouse supremacist causes;

- Attempt to create illegal discrimination based on race, creed, color, gender, religion, or national origin;

- Advocate the use of force or violence or otherwise engage in efforts to deprive individuals of their civil rights.

Additionally, DoD policy instructions have prohibited service members from:

- Participating in supremacist or extremist rallies or demonstrations;

- Knowingly attending meetings or activities while on active duty, when in uniform, when in a foreign country, or in violation of off-limits restrictions or orders;

- Conducting fund-raising activities;

- Recruiting or training members (including encouraging others to join);

- Organizing or leading a supremacist or extremist group;

- Distributing extremist or supremacist literature on or off military installations.

There is no definition for "gang" in the Uniform Code of Military Justice (UCMJ). An MTGM is defined as a street gang, prison gang, or OMG group member per the applicable jurisdiction's definition, with military training or experience, as perceived by a reasonable, typical police officer. MTGMs display indicators that they received military training either directly or indirectly. Indicators of military training include the use of military tactics, weapons, explosives, or equipment to conduct gang activity, and the use of distinctive military skills, particularly if gang members are trained in weapons, tactics, and planning, and then passing the instruction on to other gang members. Military tactics include the techniques and strategies taught in a variety of military occupational specialties, ranging from tactical assault to organizational leadership strategies.

The Uniform Code of Military Justice (UCMJ)

Gang members who are in the military must abide by military law, known as the UCMJ. They must also follow the civilian law in the local jurisdiction when they are off-post. Gang members who are not in the military must follow the civilian law in the jurisdiction where they are. In addition to specific and focused legal prohibitions, the following sections of the UCMJ have been deemed relevant and useful when targeting the actions of MTGMs; they include, but were not limited to, the following.

Article 83, Fraudulent Enlistment, Appointment, or Separation

The crime punishes enlistment in the armed forces by falsely representing, or deliberately concealing, one's qualifications and receiving pay; or procuring one's own separation from the armed forces by false representation or concealing eligibility for that separation. It seems a bit ironic that the punishment for the crime is provided for by a court-martial, as the main "crime" is that the individual was not a legitimate member of the military, and yet the military has the authority to put him on trial. An example of the crime of fraudulent enlistment would be concealing from the recruiter a criminal record that would otherwise make a recruit ineligible, or providing false identification to enlist in the armed forces.

Article 92, Violation or Failure to Obey Lawful General Order or Regulation

The crime applies to service members who violate a lawful general order or regulation, having knowledge of the lawful order and his/her duty to obey, or being derelict in the performance of his/her duties. A general order is lawful, unless it is contrary to the Constitution, the laws of the U.S., or lawful superior orders. An example of the crime for street gang or OMG group members would be participation in demonstrations or distributions of gang-related literature without approval. Common violations were not commonly punished by court-martial but were generally handled through non-judicial punishment.

Article 116, Riot or Breach of Peace

Riot is a disturbance of the peace by three or more persons with a common purpose to act against anyone who might oppose them. Riots are committed in such a violent and turbulent manner as to cause, or be calculated to cause public terror. A breach of the peace is an unlawful disturbance of the peace by someone acting to disturb the public tranquility or impinge upon the peace and good order to which the community is entitled. Engaging in a fight and unlawful discharge of firearms in a public street are examples of conduct which may constitute a breach of the peace. Loud speech and unruly conduct may also constitute a breach of the peace. A speaker may also be guilty if he/she uses language which can reasonably be expected to produce a violent response.

Article 117, Provoking Speeches or Gestures

The charge of provoking speeches or gestures means there is an allegation that the accused made wrongful use of certain words and gestures toward another person, that the words the defendant used or the gestures made by him/her provoked or reproached the other person, and the person against whom the provoking or reproachful words/gestures were used was also covered under the UCMJ. The words or gestures used should have had a potential to cause a breach of peace in an average person and can elicit a retaliatory turbulent or violent act.

Article 134, General Article, Specifically, Conduct Which Is Prejudicial to Good Order and Discipline

The article criminalized three categories of offenses not covered elsewhere in the UCMJ: offenses to the "prejudice of good order and discipline"; offenses that "bring discredit upon the armed forces"; and offenses involving "noncapital crimes or offenses which violate Federal law." An example of the crime would be a service member violating policy by carrying and concealing a dangerous weapon, or wrongfully influencing, intimidating, impeding, or injuring a witness.

Figure 8.3

Counting gang members in the military. Soldiers on a ridge in silhouette demonstrating the difficulty with counting the number of gang members in the military.

iStock.com/Tomwang112

How Many MTGMs in the Civilian Community?

No one has found a way to determine how many active gang members are in the military. The best conservative estimate is between 20,000 (about 1% of the estimated number of gang members in the country) and 200,000 (about 10% of the estimated number of gang members in the country). If we use a conservative 7.5 percent estimation of the number of gang members in the United States to the last (2011) tally by the NGIC, and there were an estimated 2.1 million gang members identified by Pyrooz and Sweeten, with an adjusted NGIC adult to juvenile count (using a ratio of 53:47 as found by the New Jersey State Police), that would mean there were 147,500 MTGMs in the U.S. in 2017. If the higher adjustment were correct (approximately 85:15 by Katz and Webb), there would be 6.6 million gang members, which would mean there were 495,000 MTGMs in the U.S. in 2017.

Some will criticize the estimations and want to use a more conservative percentage, like the long-used estimate by the Army CID claiming that "less than one percent" of service members are gang members. That number may be intended to represent an insignificant amount, but the attempt at minimization of the issue misses the mark. At any given time, the number of military service members fluctuates, but the military had 1,333,240 active duty service members and 817,384 reservists at the start of 2017, for a total of 2.15 million. If less than 1/100th of them are gang members, then we only need to be concerned about 21,500 service members who could be simultaneously involved in criminal gangs.

One problem with such a low estimate is that those numbers were based on the number of gang members known by police. As criminologists and criminal justice students everywhere can tell you, the police are not aware of all the criminals in their jurisdictions— only those who have been caught! If what the International Outlaw Motorcycle Gang Investigators Association (IOMGIA) suggested about OMGs was also true for street gangs, there could be a much bigger problem than anyone has imagined.

Another problem with that number was that with approximately 22 million veterans among the 316 million people in the United States, that would still mean we had 220,000 MTGMs at any given time. And the number of MTGMs representing one percent of the military could be increasing in the civilian community as that number cycles out of the military.

If it were possible to determine how many gang members were active in the civilian community at the target age of military recruits, and compare that number to the same population in the military, it would likely show that a similar percentage of each population has gang ties. The possibility does not excuse the existence of gang members in the military; it simply explains it. To excuse the existence of gang members in the military would be to say that the military, like McDonald's or Walmart, with over a million youthful employees around the world, understandably draws a few gang members into its ranks from the gang lifestyle (Ackman, 2005; Business.gov, 2009). Neither McDonald's nor Walmart runs a background check that rivals the security clearance conducted as standard fare by the military, and neither trusts their global employees with an issued weapon and ammunition.

In the 2012 CID assessment, the authors suggested that commanders should continue to enforce DoD Instruction (DoDI) 1325.06, 22 Feb 12.

> The DoDI 1325.06 states military personnel must reject active participation in criminal gangs and other organizations that advocate supremacist, extremist, or criminal gang doctrine, ideology, or causes. Examples of active participation

include fundraising, recruiting, wearing colors or clothing, or having tattoos or body markings associated with gangs.

Thus the presence of gang members in the military should be aggressively examined, questioned, and reported. Instead of accepting the existence of gang members in the military community, the goal should be to limit opportunities to join and be retained and subsequently released to the civilian community (Smith, 2015). Although the MCIOs do well to identify the gang-related crimes committed in their ranks, the larger problem is not the presence, with or without criminal activity, of gang members in the military (Smith, 2015). More significant than gang members in the military is the increasing presence of MTGMs in the civilian communities and their ability to increase the dangerousness of the organized criminal element and avoid detection by law enforcement because of their skills.

Gangs are a problem for military communities, much as they are for civilian communities. Those engaging in the gang lifestyle are inherently a security threat to the community and cannot be depended on to support the community. There has been no empirical effort by either the military or gang scholars to examine why gang-involved individuals enlist in the military. Nor has there been much of an effort to examine their effect on the community once they are released from the military. What is known is that the presence of street gangs and OMGs in the military has served to undermine the values, equal opportunity, and legitimate authority of the community (Smith, 2017).

Constitutional Issues

It is not easy to rid a community of gangs—even in the military. Gangs are protected: they are a legal organization that anyone can join. According to some, that is because of the U.S. Constitution. The First Amendment says, in part, that Congress cannot:

1. Establish or prohibit religion

2. Restrict freedom of speech or freedom of the press

3. Restrict people from peaceably assembling.

Each of these provisions may apply to gangs. Some gangs have a religious component, and could be protected under the freedom of religion clause. Street gangs and OMGs may also enjoy the Constitution's protection of much of their freedom of speech. The third part is often found to permit groups to meet in public areas. But it is a strange twist on the freedom of speech clause, tied to the Fourteenth Amendment, that empowers those organizations to form. The "right of association" was identified in the 1958 decision of *NAACP v. Alabama ex rel. Patterson*. The state of Alabama had sought to compel the NAACP to produce membership lists to determine whether the organization was operating in violation of the law. Justice Harlan identified the "right of association" inherent in the Constitution, explaining:

Effective advocacy of both public and private points of view, particularly controversial ones, is undeniably enhanced by group association. It is beyond debate that freedom to engage in association for the advancement of beliefs and ideas is an inseparable aspect of the "liberty" assured by the Due Process Clause of the Fourteenth Amendment, which embraces freedom of speech.

Said another way, mere affiliation with or membership in a street gang or OMG does not automatically prevent service in the military. While there is a good argument that neither the Constitution nor the Bill of Rights "gave" us the freedom to do anything, both are often cited as the authority that allows gangs (and other legally behaving groups) to gather, or "assemble" without interference by government representatives (Smith, 2017).

Research on Military Service and Crime Commission

Recent attention has been paid to the relationship between service in the military and desistance from criminal activity. Galiani, Rossi, and Schargrodsky (2009) examined the process of drafting young men into military service in Argentina. They looked at a cohort of males born between 1958 and 1962. Galiani et al. (2009) determined that military service increased the likelihood of developing an adult criminal record, both during peacetime and wartime. They identified positive effects of military service:

- Military service teaches obedience and discipline, which can limit criminality.

- Military service might improve labor market prospects, preventing the inclination to commit property crime.

- Military service serves to incapacitate young men from the ability to commit crimes while in the service.

Galiani et al. (2009) also proposed alternative, negative effects of military service:

- Military service delays entrance into the labor market, limiting opportunities.

- Military service provides firearms training, reducing the entry costs to crime.

- Military service provides a social environment that is prone to violent responses.

Albaek, Leth-Petersen, le Maire, and Tranaes (2013) found that military service reduces the likelihood of criminality for those previously disposed to commit crime. In a study of Danish youth who were born in 1964 and drafted into the military while they were between ages 19 and 22, military service was found to reduce property crime for up to five years. Albaek et al. (2013) found no effect on the commission of violent crime from military service, and no effect for the majority of draftees.

Teachman and Tedrow (2015) suggested that voluntary military service did not affect the risk of committing or being convicted of violent crimes. In the first study to focus on the effect of military service on crime in the twenty-first century, Teachman and Tedrow (2015) found that voluntary military service reduced the likelihood of contact with the criminal justice system, especially for men with a history of delinquent or criminal behavior prior to enlisting. They studied a cohort of men born between 1980 and 1984. Teachman and Tedrow (2015) found that voluntary military service significantly reduced the risk of committing or being convicted of non-violent crimes.

Finally, Boucai (2007) made the argument that active recruitment of criminals would provide a recruitment pool for the military and provide a disciplinary foundation on which individual criminal reform could be attempted. Boucai (2007) noted that the U.S. Armed Forces regularly provides waivers for recruits with misdemeanor and felony crimes on their record. Additionally, the enlistment process often depends on the recruit to tell the truth about their criminal history, as juvenile records may be off-limits. As a result, some service members enlist with criminal histories and neither request nor receive a waiver. Most of those service members do well to avoid committing crime during the term of their enlistment, Boucai (2007) noted, as military service has been shown to help reduce an individual's criminal propensity (see, for example, Teachman & Tedrow, 2015). Why not, then, Boucai (2007) wondered, change the informal policy of allowing recruits with criminal history and actively solicit them?

Survey and Methodology

A recent study addressed the problem of the growing presence of MTGMs in civilian communities. The purpose of the study was to determine the perceived presence of MTGMs in jails and community corrections and to examine whether there was a relationship between the perceptions of sheriff's deputies regarding the presence and a number of variables.

On August 26, 2015, a survey was conducted of attendees at the Tennessee Corrections Institute (TCI) FTO training conference in Pigeon Forge, Tennessee. The survey instrument, the Modified Military Gang Perception Questionnaire (M-MGPQ; Smith, 2011), contained questions designed to identify the respondents' perceptions of the presence of MTGMs in their jurisdictions.

The survey asked for responses to questions using a Likert scale to assess the level of agreement with the statement/question (Strongly Disagree, Disagree, No Opinion, Agree, and Strongly Agree). The survey questions specifically referred to the respondents' perception of the use of military weapons, equipment, and tactics by gang members in the respondents' jurisdictions. Questions were asked to assess indicators of MTGMs, whether they directly obtained the training or training was passed on by someone else who received the training directly, and the knowledge and sources of knowledge regarding MTGMs in the respondents' jurisdictions. Limited demographic and employment-related questions were asked (Smith, 2017).

Data were sought from the population of 274 members of the TCI attending the 2015 conference. The final sample consisted of 242 participants who answered all or almost all of the questions on the survey. The response rate provided a 95% confidence level and a 2.16 margin of error. Most of the respondents (93.8%) reported working at the local level, with a few (3.6%) at the state level. The majority (96.3%) reported their primary assignment was in corrections. Most (81%) had not served in the military. The average conference attendee was described as a white male with some degree of rank (corporal or higher), 25–45 years old, with at least a high school diploma and no previous experience in the criminal justice system (Smith, 2017).

For the purpose of this survey, Tennessee was considered a mature gang state. That means that gangs and related groups have a significant presence in the state and that there has been acknowledgment of their presence and an official counterresponse by most law enforcement jurisdictions. It should be noted that the character of the sample limited its external validity. The findings cannot be generalized beyond Tennessee, as that was the population that was studied.

Survey Results

The primary questions were designed to determine the perception of the respondents regarding the presence of MTGMs in his or her community. The questions were as follows:

1. Gang members in my jurisdiction are increasingly using military-type weapons or explosives.
2. Gang members in my jurisdiction use military-type equipment (body armor, night-vision, etc.).
3. Gang members in my jurisdiction use military-type tactics.
4. Gang members in my jurisdiction commit home invasions.

TABLE 8.2 Responses to Primary Questions

	Weapons	Equipment	Tactics	Home invasions	Armed robberies	Current military	Past military	Advise
SD	2.1%	1.9%	2.1%	3.2%	2.1%	3.2%	1.6%	14.2%
D	23.1%	32.5%	29.6%	10.5%	6.7%	18.2%	8.4%	35.3%
NO	35.9%	43.5%	35.9%	20.5%	14.4%	56.1%	42.9%	45.3%
A	36.4%	21.4%	29.6%	53.2%	60.8%	19.8%	42.4%	4.7%
SA	2.6%	0.6%	2.8%	12.6%	16%	2.7%	4.7%	0.5%

Legend:

Weapon: Question 1	SD: strongly disagree
Equipment: Question 2	D: disagree
Tactics: Question 3	NO: no opinion
Home invasions: Question 4	A: agree
Armed robberies: Question 5	SA: strongly agree
Current military: Question 6	
Past military: Question 7	
Advise: Question 8	

5. Gang members in my jurisdiction commit armed robberies.

6. There are gang members in my jurisdiction that currently serve in the military.

7. There are gang members in my jurisdiction that have served in the military in the past.

8. Military representatives advise our department when gang members are discharged.

The results are summarized in Table 8.2.

Presence of Gangs in the Military

Street gangs and OMGs were represented by the MTGMs in the respondents' jurisdictions.

- Street gangs represented by the MTGMs in respondents' jurisdictions included (reported as the percentage of respondents reporting a presence):
  - Bloods 54.2%
  - Crips 52.5%

- Gangster Disciples 47.5%

- Vice Lords 52.5%

- Mara Salvatrucha 16.9%.

- OMGs represented by the MTGMs in respondents' jurisdictions included:

  - Outlaws 57.1%

  - Hells Angels 26.5%

  - Pagans 4.1%.

Gangs in the Military Today

In the 2016 U.S. Army Gang and Domestic Extremist Activity Threat Assessment (GDEATA), 14 different street gangs were identified. The most prominent gang involvement included the Bloods and Gangster Disciples. Of the street gang investigation subjects, most (69%) were African American, most (94%) were male, most (75%) were single, most (88%) were 20–24 years of age, and all (100%) were junior enlisted (E1–E4). Most of the street gang subjects identified (81%) graduated with an education no higher than a GED or high school diploma.

The Bandidos MC were the most prominent OMG in CID cases. Of the OMG suspects, most were white (60%) and most (80%) were non-commissioned officers. Table 8.3 includes the street gangs and OMGs identified by Army CID in FY16.

TABLE 8.3 Street Gangs and OMGs Identified by Army CID in FY16

Street Gangs

Bloods	Vice Lords	Gangster Disciples
Flossy Crooks	900 Gang	Savage Young Gunnas
MS-13	Folk Nation	Crips Get Money Click
Vatos Locos	Pacoima 13	Sureños
18th Street Gang	Walker Village Murder	Down South Georgia Boys
Flyboyz Set	Gang	Latin Kings
Norteños	Barrio Azteca	The Commission

Outlaw Motorcycle (MC) Gangs

Bandidos MC	Top Hatters MC	Reapers MC
Hells Angels MC	Commandos MC	Tuckahoe MC
No Surrender MC	Iron Order MC	Dirty Dawgs MC
Street Soldiers MC	Pagans MC	Kingsmen MC
Black Pistons MC	Toros MC	Red Devils
Infidels MC	Da Fam MC	MC Vagos MC
Organized Chaos MC	Joy Riders MC	Dirty South Stunners MC
Strikers MC	Queen City Hustlers MC	Krazy Aces MC
Block Burnaz MC	Tru Ikonz MC	Scallywags MC
Iron Coffins MC	Death Dealers MC	Veterans MC
Outcasts MC	Kandid Clutch MC	Dragon Riders MC
Thunderguards MC	Raiders MC	Los Caballeros MC
Bodean MC	Trump Tight Riders MC	Sin City Deciples MC
Iron Legacy MC	Desperados MC	Wheels of Soul MC
Outlaws MC	Killer Mans Sons MC	East Side MC
Los Solitarios MC		
Southern Iron MC		
Wingmen MC		
Family of Wheels MC		
Masonic Riders MC		
Southern Riders MC		
Freebird MC		
Mongols MC		
Steel Horseman MC		
Gypsy Joker MC		
Nam Knights MC		
Street Kuttaz MC		

U.S. Army. (2017). U.S. Army Criminal Investigation Command's Fiscal Year 2016 (FY16) Gang and Domestic Extremist Activity Threat Assessment (GDEATA).

Non-criminal Solutions

Treatment programs are often suggested to show offenders the error of their criminal ways. Most of them apply to street gangs, as they represent the highest number of gang members and are most often the ones to be considered "treatable." Meltzer

(2001) studied gang-involved adolescent males who were court-mandated to attend a gang reduction program. The program included weekly meetings where speakers from a variety of community and academic areas addressed the group regarding laws, behavior, treatment, and other topics designed to inform their judgment and actions. The primary goals identified for the program were to decrease gang involvement and illegal behavior.

Meltzer (2001) found an increase in knowledge regarding related laws and an increased concern about the risk and danger of gang association, which was presented by professionals and community representatives. Many of the participants were ready for change when they attended the program, and though many of the participants had been involved in gang-related activity, they did not appear to be very deeply involved.

Based on the premise that most gang-affiliated offenders will reenter society, treatment in prisons is often focused on reducing gang violence. Encouraging dissociation is often the strategy used, especially in prison settings. Treatment in corrections facilities has included programs for gang members who wanted to renounce their gang association. Those programs included interacting with members of other gangs, signing a renunciation form, and cultural awareness training.

The treatment programs that were most likely to reduce recidivism were those that followed the risk-need-responsivity principles. Treatment of gang members with the highest risk of reoffending was most effective. For treatment to be effective, needs that contributed to criminal activities must be assessed, identified, and targeted. The delivery of treatment should be adjusted to accommodate clients' characteristics to ensure treatment effectiveness. Gang members who wished to change had to perform a delicate balancing act to move away from criminal activities and association, especially in prison.

Gang-free zones and gang injunctions have enjoyed some success in limiting the negative effects of gangs in communities in recent years. In the 1980s, the Los Angeles County district attorney asked for a court order declaring gangs to be a form of quasi-corporate structure, so that each member could be held accountable for the actions of other members. The ruling was sought to enable the community to force gang members to remove their gang's graffiti.

Many states had enacted gang-related laws by that time, and 31 states had adopted laws like the federal Racketeer Influenced and Corrupt Organizations Act (RICO) laws. It was thought that the notification requirement of gang members that they were known members of a criminal street gang might contain the seeds for useful deterrence activity.

Innovative Responses to MTGMs

In contrast to the approaches taken by the military, some prison systems are using a system of treatment designed to deter recidivism. High-intensity cognitive-behavioral (HICB) treatments provide an opportunity to examine "what works" with those inside the prison system. While prison is clearly not the same as the military, there are a few notable similarities, including the increase in discipline and restriction of freedoms. The basics of the program includes using culturally sensitive teaching and therapeutic approaches to address the offenders' needs, providing the offenders with a supportive environment to practice and generalize the new skills, and requiring an exit strategy for the offenders (Di Placido, Simon, Witte, Gu, & Wong, 2006). Overall recidivism was significantly reduced, and for the few who reoffended, the activity was less serious. The process acknowledged the benefits of isolating gang members from the local community, encouraging them to renounce their gang association and engage in post-treatment analysis.

A military version of HICB might start with acknowledged gang members seeking to join the military. Instead of simply taking their word that they have stopped all gang activity and continue to do so, the military could assign counselors to debrief the admitted gang member as he enters the military. Working with the recruit, a plan of action could be designed to help him through the stressors and triggers likely to appear during the term of his enlistment. Periodic (quarterly, leading to annually, perhaps) follow-up could be scheduled to ensure the process is working.

Some scholars have suggested that gangs be considered a public health issue. Gang-involved youth are at increased risk for incarceration, as well as negative health and social outcomes. Community responses to gangs might improve if they were public health problems, as those programs are more defensive and focus on prevention (Sanders, 2017). A military version of the public health application might use medical specialists to categorize and track the progress of enlisted gang members, in coordination with many other administrative and investigative agencies, and report, as needed, to military leadership.

The approach known as pulling levers was designed to influence the behavior and environment of chronic offenders. The strategy attempts to prevent gang violence by making would-be offenders believe that severe consequences would follow. A variation of this strategy was used in programs like Operation Ceasefire, a problem-oriented deterrence program that used a zero-tolerance approach (Braga, 2003). It involved rounding up offenders and holding a community meeting to explain the consequences of their continued criminal actions (long and arduous prison sentences).

A military version of the pulling levers approach might include a contract with an individual sincerely seeking a way to exit the gang life. There should be a long-term commitment on both sides, with checks and balances. Perhaps an annual psychological evaluations and polygraph examinations could be agreed to in order to ensure against a reversion.

Summary

The Army CID (and other branch MCIOs) have been reporting on gang-related investigations since 2005. The CID has published an assessment annually, with varying degrees of detail and analysis, apparently dependent on the authors' focus. Examining the increased level of violence when the community includes military-trained gang members starts with understanding that the MCIOs have identified military personnel with gang membership or affiliation in every branch of the U.S. Armed Forces. Gang members and associates who join the military typically seek to acquire training and access to weapons and sensitive information. The presence of gang members in the military should be aggressively examined, questioned, and reported. The goal should be to limit opportunities to join and be retained and subsequently released to the civilian community. Although the MCIOs do well to identify the gang-related crimes committed in their ranks, the larger problem is not the presence, with or without criminal activity, of gang members in the military. More significant than gang members in the military is the increasing presence of MTGMs in the civilian communities, and their ability to increase the dangerousness of the organized criminal element and avoid detection by law enforcement because of their skills.

DISCUSSION QUESTIONS

1. How does military training add to the dangerousness of gang members?
2. What are some historical events that involved military-trained gang members?
3. Other than improving weapons proficiency, what skills can gang members learn in the military that would benefit the gang?
4. What policy changes could be used to mitigate the effects of MTGMs in the military? In the community?

CHAPTER 9 Asian, East Asian, and African Organized Crime

CHAPTER OBJECTIVES

After reading this chapter students should be able to do the following:

- Identify the major Chinese organized criminal groups.
- Explain the differences between the triads and tongs.
- Explain how Chinese organized crime became an international criminal justice problem.
- Explain the origins of the yakuza.
- Identify the major Japanese organized criminal groups.
- Explain how Japanese organized crime became an international criminal justice problem.
- Examine the beginnings of the Chaldean Mafia.
- Identify some activities of Nigerian organized crime.

Introduction

Chinese organized crime began with bandit groups in China. It became much more organized with the development of triads in the 1700s. Chinese immigration to other parts of the world spread it even further. In the United States, it developed into a unique type of organization known as tongs. In their examination of Asian organized crime groups, Lindberg, Petrenko, Gladden, and Johnson (1997) observed that:

A complex and fluid relationship exists between triads, tongs, street gangs and American-Chinese organized crime groups. Some of these groups evolved from street gangs into sophisticated organizations that rival the traditional mob in their violence, economic impact and expanse of illegal operations. Particularly in the drug trade, various groups cooperate at different levels to get the product to its final destination. Frequently, higher level Asian groups provide support to the lower level street gangs. In exchange, the street gangs act as enforcers for the higher level group, including performing contract murders and protecting illegal operations.

(p. 44)

Huston (2001) found that language was not only a shield against law enforcement in Asian gangs but it was a unifying element within the gang against all outsiders. Huston observed:

> Gangs tend to have similar origins and speak a particular dialect. For example, the Ghost Shadows and the White and Black Dragons are mostly from Hong Kong and speak Cantonese. The Fuk Ching are almost exclusively Chinese from Fukien province and speak the Fukienese dialect. The members of the United Bamboo are almost all from Taiwan and speak mostly Mandarin (or possibly Taiwanese). The members of the Tung On group are traditionally Hakka Chinese, primarily from Hong Kong and China, and Hakka is their dialect.
>
> (p. 115)

Ethnic Japanese gangs tend to draw their members at least initially from their own ethnic groups. They use language, religion, and culture to define their criminal identity. Those types of gangs initially tend to prey upon their own ethnic communities, especially among immigrants. They may or may not expand to the wider general population (Etter, 1998; Lindberg et al., 1997, p. 44).

The Chaldean Mafia has operated in the United States since 1985. Most of the Assyrian/Chaldean immigrant population speak Aramaic as their native tongue. The younger generation, like those of other immigrants, may be marginalized by other groups and respond by forming a gang based on their common community characteristics (ethnicity, religion, etc.). African organized crime groups like those in Nigeria originally centered on the drug trade. The Nigerian immigrant populations in other countries assisted in establishing a network for the transport and sale of drugs, as well as an extensive money laundering operation. Other primary crimes include weapons-trafficking, human trafficking, kidnapping, robbery, diamond smuggling, and extortion. This chapter examines the ethnic gangs that have transcended from common street gangs into larger criminal organizations that operate in one form or another in more than one locality.

Triads

The triads began in the days of the Imperial Chinese Empire, from 221 BC to AD 1911 (Huang & Wang, 2002). According to Huang and Wang (2002) secret societies have existed in Chinese society since the Han dynasty (AD 25–220). Many of those secret societies had religious or political beliefs that differed from the government of the time. Some of those groups developed into a cult-like status and became involved in rebellions against the government and into labor movements, especially among the boatmen that worked on the canals. Some of these groups became involved in smuggling, robberies, and other crimes (Huang & Wang, 2002, pp. 26–28).

Triads originated in China about 1760 as an anti-Manchu political movement. They advocated overthrow of the Qing emperor and restoration of the Ming Empire as represented by Hung Wu (Booth, 1990, pp. 19–33). Martin (1970) identified the beginning of the Heaven and Earth Societies during the reign of Yung Cheng (1723–1736). Martin found that "Members revealed their membership by pointing first up to heaven, then down to the ground and lastly to their hearts, thus suggesting a harmonious union of God, earth and man" (p. 38). Triad members still use gang hand signs to communicate. Hanes and Sanello (2002) observed that "By the nineteenth century, they had become associated with common piracy and banditry, though they maintained their hatred of the Qing" (p. 169). According to the Illuminated Lantern (2011), triads have a rather elaborate history which is partly based on reality and partly on myth. It involved not only a struggle against the Qing dynasty, but a retreat to the Shaolin monastery and the eventual burning of the monastery. Only five survived the fire, and these are said to be the "Five Ancestors" of modern triads. They went on a number of adventures which are still remembered by triad officials and sometimes represented in initiation rituals.

The defeat of the Chinese empire in the First Opium War (1839–1842) and again in the Second Opium War (1856–1860) forced China to allow the sale of opium. The

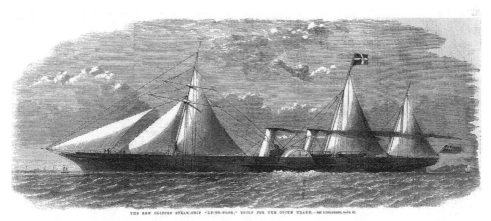

Figure 9.1

The clipper steamship Ly-ee-moon, built for the opium trade. Public domain.

London News c. 1859

terms of the peace treaty also gave the British possession of the island of Hong Kong and a part of Kowloon. The triads were originally called Heaven, Earth, and Man Societies and used a symbol that represented a triangle. The British called them triads. The triads were anxious to cooperate with the British against the Imperial Chinese government. However, the triads were just as anxious to engage in criminal activities to make money (Hanes & Sanello, 2002, p. 307). For their part, the British authorities in Hong Kong realized that some of the triads were criminal groups, and in 1845 they passed the first ordinance to prohibit the operation of such groups in the Royal Colony of Hong Kong (Morgan, 1960, p. 59).

Dr. Sun Yat-sen (1866–1925) began his association with the triads in 1885 while at medical school in Hong Kong. A fellow medical student named Cheng Shih-liang who was a triad member promised Sun Yat-sen that if he was ever to rebel against the Manchu-led Imperial Chinese government, he would have support from the triads (Schiffrin, 1980, p. 28; Martin, 1970, p. 38).

After China's defeat in the First Sino-Japanese War (August 1, 1894–April 17, 1895) and the resulting ceding of the island of Taiwan (Formosa) to the Japanese, Sun Yat-sen and Yeun Ku-wan along with others planned an uprising against the Qing government. On October 26, 1895, the First Guangzhou Uprising began, backed by Japan and the triads. It was a miserable failure. The Qing government discovered the plot, and the promised Japanese aid never arrived. The would-be revolutionaries were slaughtered and 72 of the rebels died. Sun Yat-sen was banned from Hong Kong for five years by the British Government. The Qing government sent assassins to Hong Kong and killed Yeun Ku-wan. Sun Yat-sen was forced to seek exile in Japan (Martin, 1970, p. 81; Schiffrin, 1980, pp. 45–46). Kaplan (1992) observed:

> From 1896 until the fall of the Quing Dynasty in 1911. China's founding father Sun Yat-Sen crisscrossed Southeast Asia and North America rousing local Chinese to support a revolution in the homeland.
>
> (p. 96)

Bergere (1998) found that in 1899, Sun Yat-sen traveled to Hawaii where his brother owned land and cattle. There he joined a triad to aid in his revolutionary quest. The triad's Hawaiian lodges provided him with letters of recommendation to the triads in San Francisco. He set sail for the United States in March 1904. Describing Sun Yat-sen's trip to the United States, Bergere observed:

> His first success was simply managing to set foot on American soil. The recent exclusion laws made it difficult for Chinese citizens to enter the country. Sun Yat-sen had taken the precaution of acquiring false papers that declared him to have been born in Hawaii and to be therefore eligible for American citizenship.

But upon arrival in San Francisco on April 6, 1904, he was recognized and denounced by employees of the Customs Service who happened to be Chinese members of the Society to Protect the Emperor. The intervention of a Chinese pastor and the head of the local triads helped to extricate Sun Yat-sen from this tricky situation. The cooperation between Chinese converts and secret societies upon which Sun Yat-sen had relied so heavily at the time of the first attempts in insurrection in Guangdong, now once again played in his favor.

(pp. 124–125)

During those travels, Sun Yat-sen visited and sought the support of the triads and tongs in San Francisco, Los Angeles, St. Louis, Atlanta, Philadelphia, New York, and Chicago (Schiffrin, 1980, pp. 99–100; Dillion, 1962, p. 180).

In 1911–1912 the Qing dynasty and the Imperial Chinese government were overthrown. The Republic of China was declared, and on December 29, 1911, Sun Yat-sen was elected as the first president of the new Republic of China (Schiffrin, 1980, p. 159). In 1912, the Kuomintang (KMT) or Nationalist Party was formed. Through the warlord period, the triads worked with the KMT and various factions alternately, doing whatever was to their advantage (Kaplan, 1992, p. 228; Lunde, 2004a, p. 111). In 1927, during the Autumn Harvest Uprising, the Communists (CPC) under Mao Tse-tung began a civil war against the forces of the KMT under President Chiang Kai-shek. For a time the KMT forces seemed to be winning, and in 1934–1935 they forced the CPC to undertake a retreat into the mountains that is often called "The Long March." When Japan invaded China in 1935, the KMT and the CPC called a truce and made an uneasy alliance to fight the Japanese. In 1945 after the defeat of Japan in World War II, the island of Taiwan was returned to the control of the Republic of China (ROC). After Japan was defeated in 1945, the truce was off and the civil war resumed. During this conflict KMT forces often elicited the aid of the triads against the CPC forces (Kaplan, 1992, p. 228).

In 1949, the Communist forces of Mao Tse-tung were victorious over the ROC forces of the KMT and the People's Republic of China was declared. Chiang Kai-shek, the government of the ROC and the KMT were forced to flee to the island of Taiwan. Many triad members either fled with the KNT forces to Taiwan or went to Hong Kong to join other lodges of their triad, although the KMT used triad members as intelligence sources on the mainland after 1949 to spy on the Communists (Kaplan, 1992).

There are an estimated 57 triad groups operating out of Hong Kong. Some are very large (70,000+), while others are very small. Triad criminal activities do not involve the whole triad but are carried out by a faction or a splinter segment. The area boss directs criminal activities with independence and autonomy (McKenna, 1996). Triad extortion, protection, and blackmail rackets operate in the realm of illegal gambling, public transportation, taxis, and many other areas of everyday life. Prostitution, pornography, fraud, and drug dealing are controlled by the area bosses (McKenna, 1996). McKenna (1996) noted that in the movie industry, "the claim has been made that triads control 80 to 90 percent of it" (pp. 322–323).

The return of Hong Kong to the Chinese government in 1997 caused some of the triads to move assets and operations to the United States, Canada, the United Kingdom, and other parts of Europe (Dombrink & Song, 1996, p. 329). Although Chu (2005) found that after Hong Kong returned to the administration of the Chinese government, many triads used this opportunity to expand their operations into mainland China (p. 8).

Zhang and Chin (2003) observed:

> Triads and other traditional crime groups rely heavily on such factors as group identity, loyalty and familial relationships to create a sense of belonging and extract personal commitment to sustain their profit-orientated activities. Consequently, triad societies have developed different levels of organizational imperatives such as rules, rituals, oath, code of conduct and chains of command which are often sophisticated and elaborate. Violence is frequently used to strengthen group identity or cohesion, to reduce competition and to maintain monopoly over certain industries or neighborhoods.
>
> (p. 483)

BOX 9.1 The 36 Triad Oaths Taken During Initiation

1. After having entered the Han gates I must treat the parents and relatives of my sworn brothers as my own kin. I shall suffer death by five thunderbolts if I do not keep this oath.
2. I shall assist my sworn brothers to bury their parents and brothers by offering financial or physical assistance. I shall be killed by five thunderbolts if I pretend to have no knowledge of their troubles.
3. When Han brothers visit my house, I shall provide them with board and lodging. I shall be killed by myriads of knives if I treat them as strangers.
4. I will always acknowledge my Han brothers when they identify themselves. If I ignore them I will be killed by myriads of swords.
5. I shall not disclose the secrets of the Han family, not even to my parents, brothers, or wife. I shall never disclose the secrets for money. I will be killed by myriads of swords if I do so.
6. I shall never betray my sworn brothers. If, through a misunderstanding, I have caused the arrest of one of my brothers I must release him immediately. If I break this oath I will be killed by five thunderbolts.
7. I will offer financial assistance to sworn brothers who are in trouble in order that they may pay their passage fee, etc. If I break this oath I will be killed by five thunderbolts.
8. I must never cause harm or bring trouble to my sworn brothers or Incense Master. If I do so I will be killed by myriads of swords.

9. I must never commit any indecent assaults on the wives, sisters, or daughters, of my sworn brothers. I shall be killed by five thunderbolts if I break this oath.

10. I shall never embezzle cash or property from my sworn brothers. If I break this oath I will be killed by myriads of swords.

11. I will take good care of the wives or children of sworn brothers entrusted to my keeping. If I do not I will be killed by five thunderbolts.

12. If I have supplied false particulars about myself for the purpose of joining the Han family I shall be killed by five thunderbolts.

13. If I should change my mind and deny my membership of the Han family I will be killed by myriads of swords.

14. If I rob a sworn brother or assist an outsider to do so I will be killed by five thunderbolts.

15. If I should take advantage of a sworn brother or force unfair business deals upon him I will be killed by myriads of swords.

16. If I knowingly convert my sworn brother's cash or property to my own use I shall be killed by five thunderbolts.

17. If I have wrongly taken a sworn brother's cash or property during a robbery I must return them to him. If I do not I will be killed by five thunderbolts.

18. If I am arrested after committing an offence I must accept my punishment and not try to place blame on my sworn brothers. If I do so I will be killed by five thunderbolts.

19. If any of my sworn brothers are killed, or arrested, or have departed to some other place, I will assist their wives and children who may be in need. If I pretend to have no knowledge of their difficulties I will be killed by five thunderbolts.

20. When any of my sworn brothers have been assaulted or blamed by others, I must come forward and help him if he is in the right or advise him to desist if he is wrong. If he has been repeatedly insulted by others I shall inform our other brothers and arrange to help him physically or financially. If I do not keep this oath I will be killed by five thunderbolts.

21. If it comes to my knowledge that the Government is seeking any of my sworn brothers who has come from other provinces or from overseas, I shall immediately inform him in order that he may make his escape. If I break this oath I will be killed by five thunderbolts.

22. I must not conspire with outsiders to cheat my sworn brothers at gambling. If I do so I will be killed by myriads of swords.

23. I shall not cause discord amongst my sworn brothers by spreading false reports about any of them. If I do so I will be killed by myriads of swords.

24. I shall not appoint myself as Incense Master without authority. After entering the Han gates for three years the loyal and faithful ones may be promoted by the Incense Master with the support of his sworn brothers. I shall be killed by five thunderbolts if I make any unauthorized promotions myself.

25. If my natural brothers are involved in a dispute or law suit with my sworn brothers I must not help either party against the other but must attempt to have the matter settled amicably. If I break this oath I will be killed by five thunderbolts.

26. After entering the Han gates I must forget any previous grudges I may have borne against my sworn brothers. If I do not do so I will be killed by five thunderbolts.

27. I must not trespass upon the territory occupied by my sworn brothers. I shall be killed by five thunderbolts if I pretend to have no knowledge of my brothers' rights in such matters.

28. I must not covet or seek to share any property or cash obtained by my sworn brothers. If I have such ideas I will be killed.

29. I must not disclose any address where my sworn brothers keep their wealth nor must I conspire to make wrong use of such knowledge. If I do so I will be killed by myriads of swords.

30. I must not give support to outsiders if so doing is against the interests of any of my sworn brothers. If I do not keep this oath I will be killed by myriads of swords.

31. I must not take advantage of the Hung brotherhood in order to oppress or take violent or unreasonable advantage of others. I must be content and honest. If I break this oath I will be killed by five thunderbolts.

32. I shall be killed by five thunderbolts if I behave indecently towards small children of my sworn brothers' families.

33. If any of my sworn brothers has committed a big offense I must not inform upon them to the Government for the purposes of obtaining a reward. I shall be killed by five thunderbolts if I break this oath.

34. I must not take to myself the wives and concubines of my sworn brothers nor commit adultery with them. If I do so I will be killed by myriads of swords.

35. I must never reveal Han secrets or signs when speaking to outsiders. If I do so I will be killed by myriads of swords.

36. After entering the Han gates I shall be loyal and faithful and shall endeavor to overthrow Ch'ing and restore Ming by coordinating my efforts with those of my sworn brethren even though my brethren and I may not be in the same professions. Our common aim is to avenge our Five Ancestors.

(Morgan, 1960, pp. 157–160)

Triad Organizational Structure

Triads are a hierarchical organizational structured group with specific offices that are dictated by tradition (Booth, 1990, pp. 33–39). The U.S. Department of Justice (DOJ, 1988) found:

Under the traditional leadership structure, Triad ranks are based on Chinese numerology and occultism. The number "4" is of special importance representing the four elements, the four seas and four cardinal points of a compass. Each Triad member is assigned a rank that begins with that number. The leader of a Triad is a 489 or San Chu (sometime know as: General, Dragon head or Mountain Lord); his deputy or second in command is a 438. The Incense Master (Heung Chu) and Vanguard (Sing Fung) are both 438s and of equal rank. Vanguards handle recruiting, Incense Masters officiate at ceremonial rituals. Below the 438s are 426s or Red Poles. These men are usually trained in weapons and martial arts. Red Poles are enforcers and hit men who directly control some Triad groups. A 415 or White Paper Fan (Pak Tsz Sin) handles general administrative matters and a 432 or Straw Sandal (Cho Hai) handles liaison within Triad branches and among other organizations. Ordinary members of soldiers are called 49s.

(pp. 23–24)

Big Circle Boys (大圈仔) aka Big Circle Gang (大圈幫)

The Big Circle Gang originated in China and is organized in cells and practices triad-like secret membership rites, although it is not considered to be a traditional triad. Huston (2001) observed: "Members must go through an ignition ceremony and swear oaths that are considered to be stricter and more binding than those of a traditional triad society" (p. 110).

According to Berry et al. (2003), the Big Circle

originated in the late 1960's from a group of purged or imprisoned Red Guard soldiers who initially engaged in armed robberies (the name refers to the designation of prisons on Chinese maps of that period). After expanding operations successfully into Hong Kong from its mainland bases, diversified its criminal activities and became prosperous. Key members emigrated to Canada, South America, and the United States, establishing operations in those countries and ultimately diversifying into credit card fraud, counterfeiting, and trafficking humans and narcotics.

(p. 63)

The primary crimes of the Big Circle Boys include armed robbery, credit card fraud, counterfeiting, drug trafficking, and human trafficking (Huston, 2001, p. 109). The Big Circle has an estimated membership of 5,000+.

Where the Big Circle Boys Are

The Big Circle Boys are found in Canada, China, South America, United States (Huston, 2001, p. 65).

Sun Yee On Triad (新義安), aka Yee On Commercial and Industrial Guild

The Sun Yee On Triad was founded in 1919 in Hong Kong. Many of the Sun Yee On Triad leaders were arrested and deported back to mainland China in 1953 by the Royal Hong Kong Police (RHKP) (Booth, 1990, p. 54). Lindberg et al. (1997) found that:

> Members of this group are natives of Chiu Chau and possess a strong group identity. The group is extremely cautious about admitting new members; however, it interacts with numerous U.S-based Asian gangs and some criminally-influenced Tongs. The Sun Yee On follow traditional Triad rituals, adhere to a strict command and control structure, and are extremely disciplined.
>
> (p. 48)

Sometimes Sun Yee On members use legitimate businesses to shield their criminal operations. Chu (2005) found:

> Although indicators have shown that individual Sun Yee On members may have been involved in some specific legitimate businesses such as the catering business, the film industry, or even the stock market, their roles in the legitimate economy are uncertain. For instance, it is difficult to confirm whether they are simply legal entrepreneurs, using their triad reputation to monopolize the business, or laundering their money through investing in legitimate businesses. Compared with other triad groups, it is quite clear the Sun Yee On members tend to participate in more non-violent crime such as black market crime and economic crime. In addition, they have more connections with legitimate business entrepreneurs and professionals such as lawyers and accountants.
>
> (p. 10)

The primary crimes of the Sun Yee On include drug trafficking, human trafficking, prostitution, and counterfeiting (Berry et al., 2003). The Sun Yee On also exercises a great deal of control and influence on the movie industry in Hong Kong (Lindberg et al., 1997, p. 48). The Sun Yee On has an estimated membership of 56,000+.

Where the Sun Yee On Are

The Sun Yee On are based in Hong Kong and Guangdong Province on the mainland. They operate in the United States, Australia, Canada, the United Kingdom, Belgium, France, Germany, Japan, Netherlands, Russia, Spain, and Thailand (Berry, Curtis, Elan, Hudson, & Kollars, 2003).

14 K Triad (十四K)

The 14 K Triad was formed in 1945 by Nationalist Chinese military general Lieut. Gen. Kot Siu-Wong as an anti-Communist group called the Hung Fat Shan Chung Lee Tong (Booth, 1990, pp. 57–59; Morgan, 1960, p. 305). The group fled to Hong Kong after the Communist victory in 1949. The 14 K have maintained their ties with the KMT over the years (Booth, 1990, pp. 57–59; Chu, 2005, p. 11). The various factions of the Hung Fat Shan were headquartered at 14 Po Wah Road, Canton, and eventually changed their name to the 14 K. The 14 K is based in Hong Kong and has 30 subgroups. The subgroups operate independently and autonomously (Lindberg et al., 1997, p. 48). The 14K has an estimated 24,000 members (Kaplan & Dubro, 1986, p. 214).

Chu (2005) found:

> Individual 14 K members may get involved in drugs, street level selling of pirated VCDs/DVDs, London Gold scams, money laundering, vehicle theft and smuggling, prostitution, extortion, loan sharking, illegal gambling, and so on. . . . These are their private businesses and all profits will remain in their hands.
>
> (p. 11)

Lindberg et al. (1997) found that the 14K has an estimated 24,000 members and

> the 14 K's are involved in illegal gambling, extortion, prostitution, drug trafficking, murder, money laundering, illegal alien smuggling and firearms smuggling. Law enforcement sources also report the 14 K drug trafficking proceeds are laundered through East Coast casinos and counterfeit U.S. currency is smuggled from Hong Kong through San Francisco.
>
> (p. 48)

Where the 14 K Are

Members of the 14 K have been reported as being active worldwide including in the United States, United Kingdom, Netherlands, Australia, New Zealand, and Hong Kong, and they have extensive Canadian operations in Vancouver and Toronto.

Luen Triad (聯字頭)

The Luen Triad was operating in Hong Kong as early as 1931 (Booth, 1990, p. 43). The Luen Triad is headquartered in Hong Kong and has 17 subgroups (DOJ, 1988, p. 23; Morgan, 1960, pp. 295–296). According to Booth (1999):

The Luen founded several ironworkers' associations in Hong Kong's commercial shipyards and held sway over shipworkers in HMS Tamar, Hong Kong's Royal Naval Base and one of the biggest establishments east of Suez.

The Luen Triad is noted for being involved in extortion, prostitution, and gambling (Morgan, 1960, pp. 295–296) and has an estimated 8,000 members (Berry et al., 2003).

Where the Luen Are

The Luen Triad has been reported in California, Massachusetts, and New York, as well as Australia, Canada, the Czech Republic, Europe, Hong Kong, Russia, Slovakia, and Southeast Asia (Berry et al., 2003).

United Bamboo Gang (竹聯幫)

The United Bamboo Gang (UBG) was formed in 1956 from a youth gang in Taiwan. It was one of the largest of the three main triads on Taiwan (United Bamboo, Four Seas, Celestial Way). The United Bamboo Gang has been tied with corrupt Kuomintang officials and became involved in Taiwanese politics in the 1980s (Bishop, 2005; Chang, 2005; Kaplan, 1992, pp. 368–371). Lindberg et al. (1997) stated:

> UBG members and associates in the United States are involved in drug trafficking, money laundering, contract murder, extortion, bank fraud, illegal gambling, prostitution, alien smuggling and weapons trafficking. Each chapter of the UBG contributes to a common fund in the U.S. to support its leaders, members and activities. These funds are often used to pay legal fees of indicted members, and to support families of incarcerated members. The UBG also has an established network capable of providing members with guns, narcotics and fraudulent passports and identification. Its ability to produce counterfeit identification and its sophisticated network allow members sought by law enforcement to be easily transported out of the country.
>
> (p. 47)

Chin (1996) noted in 1986, nine members of United Bamboo had been indicted and convicted under the RICO Act in an investigation by the FBI and the New York Police Department (NYPD) of their drug dealing operations. Chin stated:

> In 1986, a RICO case was brought against the Taiwan-based United Bamboo gang. Nine United Bamboo members in California, Texas, and New York were charged with leading a racketeering enterprise that was involved in many serious crimes. The FBI was able to infiltrate the gang getting two undercover agents

formally inducted into the gang. At the trial, all the defendants were found guilty of racketeering activities.

(pp. 173–174)

The United Bamboo Gang is allied with the Japanese yakuza clan Yamaguchi-gumi (Bishop, 2005; Kaplan, 1992, pp. 373–374). The United Bamboo Gang has also been involved with the KMT intelligence services (Kaplan, 1992, p. 371). The United Bamboo Gang has an estimated 20,000+ members (Berry et al., 2003).

Where the United Bamboo Are

The United Bamboo Gang has been reported in Taiwan, Asia, Australia, Canada, France, South America, the United Kingdom, and the United States (Bishop, 2005).

Wo Hop To (和合桃)

The Wo Hop To was established in Hong Kong in 1908 as a part of the Wo group of triads (Lindberg et al., 1997, p. 48; Booth, 1990, p. 53). According to Booth (1990), during the Japanese occupation of Hong Kong (1941–1945) the Wo group collaborated with the Japanese. Booth (1990) stated: "When the Japanese occupied Hong Kong the Wo group consolidated their power under the aegis of the Japanese administration" (p. 53).

After being the focus of a U.S. Senate hearing on Asian organized crime in 1991, 10 members of the Wo Hop To were arrested by the FBI on charges of murder for hire, conspiracy to distribute heroin, and illegal weapons possession (Lindberg et al., 1997, p. 48; Chin, 1996, pp. 173–174). The Wo Hop To leader Peter Chong fled to Hong Kong but was captured and extradited back to the United States in 2000 (Isaacs, 2000). Another Wo Hop To leader, Raymond "Shrimp Boy" Chow, was arrested in this investigation and convicted of narcotics offenses in 1996 (Booth, 1999, p. 310). Chow later testified for the government against Chong. Chow was also the leader of the Chee Kung Tong in San Francisco at the time of his arrest (FBI, 2014c).

In March 2014, the FBI arrested Chow and California State Senator Leland Yee on weapons trafficking and political corruption charges (Burke, 2014). The Wo Hop To are sometimes allied with the Sun Yee On Triad. Davidson (1996) observed: "There is also evidence that some Chinese triads, in particular the Wo Hop To of Hong Kong have acquired direct influence over some San Francisco Asian street gangs" (p. 298). Huston (2001) noted the alliance between the Vietnamese street gang Hung Pho (Red Fire) and the Wo Hop To in the San Francisco area (p. 226). The Wo Hop To are involved in drug trafficking, weapons trafficking, gambling, extortion, protection rackets, and loan-sharking (Lindberg et al., 1997, p. 48).

Where the Wo Hop To Are

The Wo Hop To has been reported in Hong Kong, and Canada, as well as the U.S. states of California and Illinois.

Wo Shing Wo (和勝和)

The Wo Shing Wo triad was established in 1930 after breaking away from the Wo Hop To triad (Chu, 2005, p. 10). Their leader is called Dragon Head and is elected every two years. The Wo Shing Wo is composed of nine subgroups. During World War II, the Wo Shing Wo supported the Japanese against Great Britain (Booth, 1999, pp. 153–154). Wo Shing Wo members have been involved in some legitimate businesses such as catering and the entertainment business (Chu, 2005, p. 11). Chu (2005) found:

> Individual Wo Shing Wo members may get involved in drugs, street level selling of pirated VCDs/DVDs, London Gold scams, money laundering, vehicle theft, and smuggling, prostitution, extortion, loan sharking, illegal gambling, and so on . . . They will not transfer part of their profits to the Society.
>
> (p. 10)

The Wo Shing Wo triad deals in dock workers, loan-sharking, protection rackets, pirated DVDs, drug trafficking, and so forth (Booth, 1999, p. 179). The Wo Shing Wo has an estimated 70,000+ members.

Where the Wo Shing Wo Are

The Wo Shing Wo have been reported in Australia, Hong Kong, China, Canada, Japan, the Netherlands, the United Kingdom, and the United States.

The Effects of U.S. Immigration Law on Chinese Crime in the United States

It was the government of the United States that forced the Chinese into the human trafficking business. Prior to 1882, Chinese immigrants were welcomed into this country. Although there was a great deal of anti-Chinese sentiment that began to develop, it was not altogether much different than that anti-immigrant sentiment expressed against the Irish immigrants of a previous generation during the 1820s–1840s. Huston (2001) found in 1868 that the Burlingame Treaty was reversed when the Chinese Exclusion Act of May 8, 1882, suspended the immigration of Chinese laborers, skilled and unskilled, for 10 years. Previously teachers, students, and merchants were guaranteed free and equal immigration and travel for both Chinese and Americans in the others' country. The law was extended for another 10 years on May 5, 1892, and renamed the Geary Act, and on April 27, 1904, it was made permanent. Huston (2001) observed how with the passage of some new federal laws the attitudes regarding the Chinese appeared to have changed. There was an anti-Chinese riot in 1877 in San Francisco, California. Huston (2001) found:

> The Scott Act of October 1, 1888, prohibited the return of all Chinese laborers who had temporarily left the United States with plans to return. The reentry certificates of 20,000 men in this category were summarily declared void. The Immigration Act of 1924 prohibited all Chinese wives from immigrating to the United States. Ironically, the whites had gone from complaining that the Chinese did not bring their wives to America in sufficient numbers to prohibiting them from bringing them at all. These laws are the only pieces of legislation in U.S. history that excluded members of a specific nationality by name.
>
> (p. 79)

The Chinese were now forced to sneak into the United States. Soon the triads and their American cousins the tongs were smuggling would-be Chinese immigrants into the United States on a wholesale basis (Dillion, 1962, p. 193).

Tongs

Tongs were started in the United States during the mid-1800s by Chinese immigrants as a type of self-help association (Asbury, 1933, p. 184). The word *tong* means hall or gathering place (Zhang & Chin, 2003, p. 471). The tongs exist openly and are based chiefly on business affiliations (MafiaNJ, 2015). Some of the tongs quickly became involved in organized Chinese criminal activities. In his study of tongs, Asbury (1933) observed:

> Occasionally they engaged in legitimate business, but in particular they were the lords of the underworld—they operated gambling resorts, opium dens and houses of prostitution, and exercised practical control over the slave trade, for although the actual buying and selling of girls was done by individuals, the tongs usually collected a head-tax for every slave imported for immoral purposes.
>
> (p. 185)

Daye (1997) found that in the United States, tongs often

functioned as surrogate families to help Chinese people when there was no one else to help them. However, while this holds true for the most part today and almost all Tong engage in many legal and admirable activities, some Tongs have been found to be engaged in some illegal activities as well, most often gambling. It would appear that the intentions of the Tong chairman seem to determine the Tong's activities. And while the Tongs may use Asian youth gangs as muscle to protect their local gambling activities, they do not always have direct paramilitary control over the Chinese youth gangs.

(p. 188)

According to Jackson and McBride (1990):

The early tongs at the turn of the century started out being involved in protection, gambling, and vice rackets. However, wars began to break out among tongs over rights to exploit territories. Then as blood was shed and passions calmed and age advanced on the tong members, they began to settle their disputes, for the most part, in non-violent ways. However, occasions still arise in which the tongs resort to violence to settle their differences.

(p. 48)

Asbury (1933) found that the first tong war started in the 1860s in Marysville, California. The war began when a Chinese woman claimed by a Hop Sing member was stolen by a member of the Sing Suey Tong. The Hop Sings declared war to avenge their honor. Several people on both sides were killed before the Suey Sings admitted defeat and gave the woman back (p. 182).

The conflicts that developed between the tongs led them to maintain groups of armed men to protect their criminal and other interests. Each of the organizations had hit men and fighters. Asbury observed:

In later years the tong warriors fought with revolvers, bombs, and even machine guns, but in earlier times the favorite weapons were hatchets, daggers, knives, and bludgeons, which he carried in a long silken belt wrapped around his body beneath a loose blouse. When abroad on his murderous business, his queue was wound around his head, and he wore a broad-brimmed, low-crowned black slouch hat, pulled well down over his eyes. If he succeeded in dispatching an enemy, he left beside the body the weapon with which he had struck the fatal blow. The boo how day, popularly known as hatchetmen or highbinders, received regular salaries, with extra pay for exceptional bravery in battle, and bonuses based on the number of men they killed. They were subjected to strict discipline and were required to obey at all times, without question, the orders of the man who had chosen by their tong to command them in action.

(pp. 185–186)

Because of their competing interests, a series of tong wars broke out in San Francisco between 1880–1913. Huston (2001) found:

In the 19th and early 20th centuries the various tongs frequently came into conflict, and this led to a series of bloody wars between them, notably in San Francisco in the 1890's and in New York in the 1920's.

(pp. 62–63)

In examining the tong wars in San Francisco (1880–1913), Chin (1996) found:

Tong conflicts continued unabated until the establishment of the Wo Ping Peace Treaty (Peace Committee) in San Francisco in 1913. It brought temporary peace to the warring groups.

(p. 6)

In his study of the tong wars in New York City (1899–1907) between the Hip Sing Tong and the On Leong Tong, McIllwain (1997) observed:

The turn-of-the-century tongs were involved with police and political corruption, labor racketeering, price fixing, prostitution, gambling, immigrant smuggling, slavery, drug trafficking, and violent crimes. They are still associated with those activities.

(p. 25)

The tong wars in the 1920s did not only occur in New York City. There were also tong wars in Cleveland, Ohio (Trickey, 2008), Butte, Montana (Mai Wah Society, 2015), and Seattle, Washington (Paciotti, 2005). Sometime the conflict would start in one city and expand into violence in another city. Lee (1960) observed:

To offset unfavorable reactions as well as hide the persistence of their activities, tongs became known as "Merchants' Associations" or clubs. These organizations, especially those affiliated with Chinese Masonry, have formed an "underground" network in the United States.

(p. 162)

Figure 9.2

Mock Duck and Tom Lee factions in Chinatown. Photograph shows Chinese American men arrested for being involved in a war between On Leong Tong and Hip Sing Tong organizations for control of Chinatown. Public domain.

New York World-Telegram and the Sun Newspaper Photograph Collection (Library of Congress)

That the tongs still function in the United States is a historical fact. FBI Special Agent Linda Keene (1989) observed:

Many of the tongs in the United States are national organizations with chapters in cities that have large Chinese communities. While the tongs serve primarily as "merchant associations," several of the tongs are used as fronts for vicious Chinese organized crime groups that prey mainly on Chinese immigrants and Chinese Americans. And, while the economic mainstay of the criminally involved tongs is illegal gambling, some members have been known to direct gang enterprises that include extortion, drug trafficking, robbery and "protection" schemes for prostitution and pornography.

(p. 14)

A Chinese organization that is often confused with and sometimes intertwined with the tongs is the Chinese Consolidated Benevolent Association (CCBA). It is also known as the Chinese Six Companies because the original organization that formed in San Francisco had six associations as members, including the Hop Wo Company, Kong Chow Company, Ning Yung Company, Sam Yup Company, Yan Wo Company, and Yeong Wo Company (Asbury, 1933, p. 141; Lee, 1960, p. 147; Dillion, 1962, p. 71; Huston, 2001, p. 150). These Chinese associations began around 1882 and attempted to benefit the Chinese immigrants. Asbury (1933) observed:

> For many years, until soon after the beginning of the present century, practically every business enterprise in Chinatown was dominated by an organization of merchants call the Six Companies, which also exercised supervisory control over most of the Chinese in California, particularly those of the coolie or laboring class. Through their agents in China the Six Companies advanced money to emigrants who desired to come to the United States, and as early as 1852 had set aside a fund of two hundred thousand dollars which was used solely for this purpose. When the immigrant arrived in this country, the Six Companies obtained a job for him or outfitted him for the mines and saw to it that he repaid the loan, with interest. According to various investigating committees, the organization also required him to pay into it coffers a certain portion of his earnings as long as he remained in America.
>
> (pp. 140–141)

These CCBAs quickly formed in areas with large Chinese populations such as New York, Chicago, Los Angeles, Seattle, Washington, DC, and cities in Canada. Chin (1990) found:

> Three permanent associations of the CCBA are tongs in nature. They are the On Leong Merchant Association, comprise of mostly Cantonese-speaking businessmen; The Hip Sing Association, formed by predominately Toisanese-speaking working-class immigrants; and the Chih Kung tong, the overseas branch of the Hung societies.
>
> (p. 49)

Huston (2001) found that the Fukien American Association is a member of the CCBA in New York City (p. 183). After 1912 they had a very strong association with the KMT, which many have kept to this day (Huston, 2001, p. 94; Chin, 1996, p. 12; Chin, 1990, pp. 49, 60; Kaplan, 1992, p. 111). Chin (1996) advocated that there are two types of social order in Chinatown: the legitimate and illegitimate. Chin (1996) stated:

> The legitimate social order regulates political, economic, and social behavior, while the illegitimate social order dictates territorial rights for the operation of

gambling places, and the level and intensity of involvement in other illegal activities such as heroin trafficking, loansharking, and human smuggling. Most community associations play a role only in the maintenance of the legitimate social order, but a few are influential in both the legitimate and illegitimate worlds. It is the latter groups that are closely associated with Chinese gangs.

(p. 12)

Bing Kong Association (秉公堂) aka Bing Kung

The Bing Kong Tong was established in the late 1800s and early 1900s in Los Angeles and later moved to San Francisco, California (Dillion, 1962, p. 186). The Bing Kong Tong fought in the tong wars of 1880–1913. During this period, the Bing Kong dealt extensively in prostitution (Dillion, 1962, p. 200). The Bing Kong was the largest tong in Seattle during the 1920s (Paciotti, 2005). The Bing Kong Tong was a strong supporter of the government of the ROC (and by implication the KMT as well). As an example of this, Huston (2001) noted:

On October 9, 1949, 18 days after Mao established the People's Republic of China, several hundred inhabitants of San Francisco's Chinatown gathered to celebrate the event. A few minutes into the speeches, members of either the Hop Sing or Bing Kung Tongs invaded the auditorium, tore down the flag, sprayed much of the audience with blue dye, and may have assaulted some of the speech makers (report vary). The next day, a tong-war-style "hit list" with the names of 15 of the prominent speakers was posted, offering a $5,000.00 award for the death of each one.

(p. 94)

Toy (1997) discovered that in the 1970s the Bing Kong Tong reacted when their interests were threatened by newly formed Chinese immigrant gangs such as the Yow Yee (latter the Suey Sing):

The Bing Kong Tong issued a public notice that stated that if the gang interfered with any of its member's stores or restaurants, they would be dealt with severely.

(p. 234)

Where the Bing Kong Are

The Bing Kong have been reported in California, Oregon, Utah, and Washington.

Chee Kung Tong aka Chinese Freemasons, Hung League, Sam Hop To, Ko Lo Woi, Chi Hung Tong, Chih Kung Tong

Chin (1990) observed that the Chih Kung Tong was the overseas branch of the Hung societies (p. 49). Huston (2001) found as early as the 1850s that the Chee Kung Tong was involved in violence and extortion attempt against fellow Chinese immigrants in California (p. 73). Dillion (1962) observed that the Hung Society was operational in California in 1854 (p. 54). According to Lee (1960):

> This secret society and its variations originated in China during the Ming Dynasty and acquired different names, or created various sub-branches, as its members sought divergent objectives under its auspices. It is the only society of international scope, with branches throughout the world. It has always been debatable whether Chee Kung Tong or Triad is an underground revolutionary party (its initial objective), an organization bent on righting alleged or real in justices suffered by its members at the hands of non-members, or an alliance of persons dealing in illegal traffic in gambling, narcotics, prostitution, kidnapping, and so on. It has been known to engage in all of these activities in China and abroad. The first North American branch of the Chee Kung Tong was established around 1858 in British Columbia, Canada; by 1863 one was organized in San Francisco. During the height of its power in America, a branch existed wherever sojourners and their kinsmen gathered.
>
> (pp. 168–169)

The Chee Kung Tong claimed to have hosted Dr. Sun Yat-sen in their San Francisco lodge during his trips to the United States. The tong claimed that Dr. Yat-sen maintained an office in their lodge and has preserved the office as a sacred place used by the president of the ROC. The tong even made a YouTube video about this (www.youtube.com/watch?v=5sM33tnWakU).

The Chee Kung Tong fought in the tong wars of 1880–1913. Lee (1960) further observed:

> The Chee Kung Ton declined in importance in America after the 1920's when a majority of its members either died, returned to China, or were incarcerated and latter deported for partaking in liquor, narcotic, and other illegal traffic.
>
> (p. 169)

However, after World War II, there was a resurgence of activity within the Chee Kung Tong in the United States. According to Huston (2001), unlike many tongs, the Chi Hung Tong had no affiliated gang with the group (p. 117).

Where the Chee Kung Tong Are

The Chee Kung Tong has been reported in California, Hawaii, Massachusetts, and New York.

Fukien American Association

The Fukien American Association attempts to serve the needs of immigrants from Fujian Province in China. The Fukien American Association is allied with the Fuk Ching gang (Huston, 2001, p. 117; Keefe, 2009, p. 76; English, 1995, p. 87). In the early 1990s the Fukien American Association's leader was Alan Man Sin Lau (Keefe, 2009, p. 76). Keefe (2009) found:

> A Senate subcommittee found in 1991 that the tong is instrumental in assisting other ethnic Fukienese to immigrate to the United States. And seemed to be involved in the heroin trade as well. It outlined the relationship between Alan Man Sin Lau and the Fuk Ching gang and determined that the leader of the Fuk Ching gang is. . . 'Ah kay.
>
> (p. 77)

Chin (1996) observed that although the Fukien American Association vigorously denied any involvement in human smuggling: "The tongs, especially the Fukien American Association have often been implicated in this lucrative business" (p. 159). In 1993, a ship called the *China Venture* carrying illegal Chinese immigrants grounded in New York with disastrous results (Chin, 1996, p. 157; NYT, 1993). Fried (1998) reported that:

> The nightmarish, four-month journey of the Golden Venture began off the coast of Thailand and wound through the Indian and Atlantic Oceans. It ended on June 6, 1993, when the freighter was ordered to run aground on the Rockaway peninsula in Queens and the nearly 300 immigrants aboard were told to swim ashore in the early morning darkness. Ten of the passengers drowned or died of hypothermia from the effort, which required a long swim through rough waters because the ship ended up on a sandbar 200 yards offshore. The immigrants, who had made various down payments to get aboard, were to pay the rest of the $30,000 fee after their illegal arrivals in the United States. Nearly all of those who made it to shore were quickly rounded up and many spent up to three and a half years in American jails after their voyage, which cast a sharp spotlight on the widespread and lucrative smuggling of Chinese people to America.

Where the Fukien American Association Is

The Fukien American Association has been reported in New Jersey and New York.

Hip Sing Association (協勝公會)

The Hip Sing Tong was established around 1875 and was formed by predominately Toisanese-speaking working class immigrants from China (Chin, 1990, p. 49). The Hip Sing Tong fought in the tong wars of 1880–1913 in both California and New York (Asbury, 1989, pp. 301–315; Booth, 1999, pp. 299–300). Dillion (1962) noted that during this period, the Hip Sing was noted for running illegal gambling dens (p. 201). Members of the Hip Sing Tong dealt drugs with the Kuomintang in the 1930s and 1940s (Kaplan, 1992). On February 6, 1996, Dick Chin, the West Coast president of the Hip Sing Tong, was arrested by the FBI on seven counts of conspiracy and money laundering in Operation Highbind (Rosenfeld, 1996). On July 12, 2012, the Portland, Oregon Police Department and the Metro Gang Task Force arrested several Hip Sing Tong members on drug and weapons charges (Simpson, 2012). Much of the modern Hip Sing illegal gambling activities are confined to the tong building or lodge (MafiaNJ, 2015). The Hip Sing Tong uses Chinese street gangs to protect their illegal activities (MafiaNJ, 2015), and are allied with the Flying Dragons and Wah Ching Asian street gangs (Huston, 2001, p. 117; English, 1995, p. 52; Booth, 1999, p. 303; Chin, 1990, p. 80). Primary criminal activities of the Hip Sing include drug trafficking, prostitution, gambling, and money laundering.

Where the Hip Sing Are

The Hip Sing have been reported in California, Colorado, Georgia, Idaho, Illinois, Maryland, Massachusetts, Minnesota, Missouri, New York, Ohio, Oregon, Pennsylvania, Texas, Washington State, and Washington, DC (Chin, 1990, p. 57).

Hop Sing Tong (合勝堂)

The Hop Sing Tong was established as early as the 1860s in California (Asbury, 1933, p. 184) and fought in the tong wars of 1880–1913. The Hop Sing Tong is allied with the Hop Sing Boys gang (Huston, 2001, p. 117).

Where the Hop Sing Are

The Hop Sing have been reported in California, Colorado, Idaho, Oregon, and Washington.

On Leong Merchant's Association (安良工商會)

The On Leong Merchant's Association was founded in 1893. According to Chin (1990), the On Leong was originally formed of mostly Cantonese-speaking businessmen (p. 49). In his study of the tong wars in New York City (1899–1907), McIllwain (1997) found:

> The On Leong was a merchant-based tong whose members controlled large portions of legitimate businesses such as Chinese restaurants, mercantile enterprises, and import-export firms. Members included some of the most prestigious, most powerful businessmen in Chinatown. This power and influence allowed them to control and regulate Chinatown's vice industries: gambling, opium, and prostitution.
>
> (p. 37)

The On Leong Tong fought in the tong wars of 1899–1913 in New York. During this time, the On Leong was receiving protection from the NYPD and the corrupt city government of Tammany Hall due to the political efforts of the On Leong leader of the time, Tom Lee (Asbury, 1989, pp. 303–305; Booth, 1999, p. 299; McIllwain, 1997, p. 37). Dillion (1962) noted that during this period the On Leong was extensively involved in the importation and selling of "slave girls" (p. 201). According to Russick (2010), the On Leong fought in the tong wars of the 1920s in Chicago and

> some of the association's revenue came from illegal activities, including traditional Chinese gambling games such as Fan Tan and Pai Gow, a game played with dominos. In 1988, after years of investigation, the FBI, along with the Chicago Police, raided and seized the building and charged the On Leong leadership with gambling violations. In 1991, sixteen of those arrested pled guilty to tax evasion and racketeering charges.

In examining that 1991 Chicago case and the guilty plea of On Leong leader Wilson M. Moy in 1994, O'Connor (1994) also found:

> The On Leong also acknowledged taking steps to fix a 1981 murder trial by having a Cook County judge bribed, but Moy denied he knew of or was involved in that bribery. . . . Circuit Court Judge Thomas Maloney was convicted last year in federal court of fixing the murder trial of three New York gang members who were brought to Chicago by On Leong to kill an alleged troublemaker. Moy admitted he was involved personally in passing bribes to an undisclosed number of Chicago police officers from the mid-1960s through the early 1980s to protect the casino from raids. Several of the officers were in "supervisory law

enforcement positions," according to Moy's plea agreement. The Chicago On Leong also admitted that from the early 1970s through April 1988 it regularly made "street tax" payments of as much as $8,000 a month to various Chicago mob members in order to operate the gambling business.

The On Leong uses Chinese street gangs to protect their illegal activities (MafiaNJ, 2015) and are allied with the Ghost Shadows (Huston, 2001, p. 117; English, 1995, p. 52; Booth, 1999, p. 303). MafiaNJ (2015) found that the On Leong members involved in illegal gambling activities operations usually confine those activities to the tong building or lodge. The On Leong's primary crimes include bribery, fraud, illegal gambling, racketeering, and prostitution (Anastasia, 1990). The On Leong has over 30,000 members.

Where the On Leong Are

The On Leong have been reported in California, Florida, Illinois, Louisiana, Maryland, Massachusetts, Michigan, Minnesota, Missouri, New York, New Jersey, Ohio, Pennsylvania, Rhode Island, Texas, Virginia, and Washington, DC.

Suey Sing Association (萃勝工商會) aka Suey Sing Tong (萃勝堂)

The Suey Sing Tong was established in 1867 in California (Asbury, 1933, p. 184) and fought in the tong wars of 1880–1913. The Suey Sing are allied with the Wo Hop To Triad (Toy, 1997). The Suey Sing Association also maintains ties with the Suey Sing Boys gang (Mark, 1997, pp. 41–42). Their primary crimes include gambling and prostitution (Toy, 1997, pp. 240–241), and it is estimated that they have more than 1,000 members.

Where the Suey Sing Are

The Suey Sing Tong has been reported in California, Oregon, and Utah.

Tung On Association (東安公所)

The Tung On Association was established in New York in the early twentieth century. Faison (1994) observed:

In most of its functions, the Tung On is a legitimate association of businessmen and immigrants from the same part of China, with an executive board, monthly meetings and a banquet at Chinese New Year. When it was established early this century, named for two counties abutting Hong Kong whence its members came, the tong was like an unofficial social service center, helping new immigrants locate relatives and find a place to stay.

However, in 1994, Faison reported:

Members of the Tung On like to say that their association is as innocent as their afternoon gatherings. But Federal prosecutors say they can prove otherwise, and they have charged Clifford Wong, the Tung On's longtime president, with leading a criminal enterprise that killed 10 people and participated in many other crimes, like armed robbery and heroin trafficking.

Chin (1996) found that 15 Tung On members were indicted for murder by the NYPD, Drug Enforcement Agency (DEA) and Bureau of Alcohol, Tobacco, and Firearms (ATF) and that they were convicted (p. 173). Chin (1996) also observed that the Tung On engaged in the protection racket and extortion (p. 53). The Tung On is involved in illegal gambling activities that are confined to the tong building or lodge (MafiaNJ, 2015), and uses Chinese gangs to protect their illegal activities (MafiaNJ, 2015). The Tung On Tong is allied with the Tung On Boys gang (Huston, 2001, p. 117) and the Sun Yee On Triad (Booth, 1990, p. 127).

Where the Tung On Are

The Tung On have been reported in New York and Pennsylvania.

Yakuza

The yakuza is a Japanese organized crime group. A *yakuza* is also a losing hand in a Japanese card game called *oicho-kabu*. The object of the game is to get as close to 19 without going over. Ya-ku-za is 8–9–3 or a losing combination. Thus, the yakuza consider themselves to be "born to lose," misfits and outcasts from society. Many yakuza see themselves as *bakuto* or gamblers that were once influential in Japanese village life (Siniawer, 2012, p. 625; Maruko, 2002, p. 14; Kaplan & Dubro, 1986, p. 24).

According to Kaplan and Dubro (1986), some people trace the origins of the yakuza to the *kabuki-mono* (the crazy ones). They were unemployed *ronin* (samurai), documented as early as 1612, and preyed on villagers (p. 14). The yakuza claim that they came from the *okondate* (chivalrous ones), formed about the same time to protect the villages. Either way, the yakuza see themselves as the last section of society to maintain the samurai traditions of the past. Siniawer (2012) observed:

During the early modern Tokugawa period (1600–1868), yakuza and their violence were viewed critically by local societies in which they operated. Yakuza built their organizations and expanded their territories in part through physical violence—armed fights, bloody brawls, and murders. They engaged in predatory activities such as extortion, blackmail, and burglary.

(p. 625)

The role of the yakuza as a gambler and sometimes criminal began to change with the times at the end of the Tokugawa period in 1868 (Maruko, 2002). The new Japanese government in the Meiji Restoration was a time of change in Japan. Change often offers opportunities. Maruko (2002) observed:

It was the beginning of the Meiji period (1868–1912) that yakuza had new opportunities to participate in politics, and that the nature of their involvement was violent. During the Freedom and People's Rights Movement (Jiyu minken undo) of the 1870s and 1880s, gamblers are known to have been part of the rioting crowd in at least the Gumma Incident, the Chichibu Incident, and the Nagoya Incident. In the case of the Chichibu Incident (1884), members of the regional Poor People's Party (Komminto) and others armed themselves with rifles, bamboo spears, and swords, and attacked the offices of officials and the homes of usurers, stole money and weapons, and burned documents. The crowd not only included a number of gamblers, but was also led by a gambling boss (bakuto no oyabun) named Tashiro Eisuke. By the late 1880s, yakuza were hired as strongmen for political parties to disrupt speeches, intimidate opposition candidates, and scare electors. The elections in 1890 and 1892 were notoriously violent, in part because of the activities of political ruffians.

(pp. 14–15)

In the early twentieth century, the yakuza began to be involved in Japanese nationalist politics (Kaplan & Dubro, 1986, pp. 32–37). In 1915, a yakuza boss was even elected to the lower house of the Japanese Diet (Maruko, 2002, p. 15). After World War I, yakuza officials met with Japanese government leaders in the capital at the Home Ministry. Siniawer (2012) stated:

The cooperation between yakuza and the state challenges conventional assumptions about the illegitimacy of the mafia, on one hand, and the legitimacy of the state, on the other. In the 1920s and 1930s, yakuza were not unequivocally condemned as criminals or parasitic mafiosi by the societies in which they operated or the political universe in which they thrived, and they were considered just legitimate enough by those who decided to do business with them. And the state, intentionally or not, capitalized on this blurring of boundaries between legitimate and illegitimate because in supporting the yakuza violence instead of flagrantly wielding that of the police or military, it could forward its ideological,

financial, and political interests while taking cover in a gray area where state violence was not patently identifiable and therefore more difficult to criticize. Or to
put it another way, this modern and arguably democratic state cooperated with
nonstate violence specialists in order to violently suppress dissent while evading
questions about the legitimacy of such use of force.

(p. 624)

In the 1930s and 1940s the yakuza expanded its operations along with those of the
Japanese military operations during the years before and during World War II. Being
patriotic nationalists, many of the yakuza served in the Japanese military or naval forces,
especially in China, Korea, and Manchuria (Saga, 1991, p. 108; Kaplan & Dubro, 1986,
p. 39). During the Japanese occupation of Hong Kong (1941–1945), many ties were
made between some of the Chinese triads and the yakuza members who were serving in
the Japanese military occupation forces there (Booth, 1999, pp. 153–154).

After World War II and during the American Occupation Government in Japan
(1946–1952) the yakuza was busy dealing in black market goods, drugs, gambling, and
prostitutes (Saga, 1991, p. 241; Kaplan & Dubro, 1986, pp. 43–44). Siniawer (2012)
discovered:

The yakuza rebounded from the dry years of the early 1940s by running the
black market that sprung up across the country after the war's end. Having
staked out their turf, yakuza bosses managed vendors who sold various necessities like food and clothing, as well as amphetamines, to impoverished customers.
As the economy recovered, the yakuza transitioned out of the black markets and
returned to traditional industries such as gambling, bars, restaurants, prostitution, and labor racketeering. Fueled by the proceeds from their successful business
ventures, the postwar yakuza developed into expansive and sophisticated mafia
syndicates.

(p. 632)

After the Allied Occupation of Japan ended in 1952, a unique relationship developed
between the yakuza and the Japanese government. The government was aware of their existence and had tried to regulate them rather than eliminate them. Keene (1989), in noting
that relationship, observed: "Today, due to their openly recognized existence the Yakuza
constitutes a separate class with its wealth, members, culture and political ties" (p. 15).

Adelstein (2012) agreed with Keene that the unique relationship existed between the
Japanese government and the yakuza, and stated:

Today the yakuza are embedded into Japanese society. The major gang bosses
are almost well-known celebrities. Bosses for the second and third largest crime

group, the Sumiyoshi-kai and the Inagawa-kai grant interviews to publications and television. Politicians are seen having dinner with them.

(p. 158)

Yakuza Organizational Structure

The yakuza engage in a uniquely Japanese style of organized crime. Yakuza gangs are rigidly hierarchical and follow strict codes of behavior. According to Lunde (2004b), the typical yakuza organization includes the Oyabun (Supreme Boss), Saiko Komon (Senior Advisor), Waka Gashira (Number 2 Man), Shatei Gashira (Number 3 Man), Komon (Advisors), Kaikei (Accountants), Kumicho Hisho (Secretaries), Sharei (Senior Bosses) and Wakashu (Junior Bosses) (p. 95). Yakuza conduct themselves as a business in a land of businessmen. Lunde (2004b) noted that the yakuza members have business cards denoting their clan, organization, and rank, and that one of the clans actually publishes an internal telephone directory (p. 95). There are over 21 yakuza groups, but the three largest are the Yamaguchi-gumi, Inagawa Kai, and Sumiyoshi Rengo Kai.

The Yamaguchi-gumi began around 1915 in Kobe and was involved in dockworkers' unions (Kaplan & Dubro, 1986, p. 38). The Yamaguchi-gumi still maintains its head-quarters in Kobe. The group has an internal newsletter for its members. In an effort to keep up with the times, the Yamaguchi-gumi clan of the yakuza now maintains a website, and its own theme song (Arrouas, 2014). Adelstein (2010) observed that the politicians in Japan often still seek support from the yakuza and that the Yamaguchi-gumi ordered its members to vote for a specific political party in the 2007 Japanese elections (p. 63). The Yamaguchi-gumi have an estimated 40,000 members.

The Inagawa Kai was founded in 1945 among groups of gamblers in Yokohama. Their headquarters is in Tokyo. The Inagawa Kai has an estimated 10,000 members (Hoover, 2011).

The Sumiyoshi Rengo Kai was founded in 1958. It is considered to be a union of several smaller yakuza groups and has undergone several name changes. Their headquarters is in Tokyo. The Sumiyoshi Rengo Kai has an estimated 12,000 members.

Strict Rules and Discipline

The leader of the yakuza group maintains control over his subordinates. If he cannot, he will not remain as the leader. If a yakuza member fails in a specific task or offends the yakuza leader, they are often required to participate in a unique Japanese gang ceremony called *yubizume*. Yubizume is a traditional yakuza ritual in which the member who has offended or failed in some way chops off part of a finger and presents it to the Oyabun (leader) as an act of contrition (Kaplan & Dubro, 1986, p. 25; Lunde, 2004b, p. 96). If the offering is accepted, the member is forgiven. If not, the member is often killed. It is not uncommon to find members of the yakuza to have missing digits on their hands denoting some real or perceived transgression against the gang boss.

Yakuza and the Wider Japanese Community

The yakuza are a part of Japanese culture. The yakuza engage in legitimate businesses, such as travel agencies (especially those offering "sex tours" of the Philippines or Thailand), hotels, restaurants, construction, pachinko parlors, dockworkers, labor unions, real estate, and entertainment (especially professional sumo wrestling). The Japanese have an obsession with the game of pachinko, an upright form of pinball game that is played for money. The yakuza controls much of the pachinko parlor trade in Japan. The various yakuza organizations overtly display signs at their headquarters and are often listed in the local phone directory.

Figure 9.3

Yakuza-Marukin at Sanja Matsuri. Yakuza take the opportunity to show their tattoos during Sanja Matsuri, one of the biggest festivals in Tokyo, Japan.

Uploaded by Jorge, Tokyo, Japan/20 May 2007 [CC BY-SA 2.0 (https://creativecommons.org/licenses/by-sa/2.0)], via Wikimedia Commons

However, not everybody in Japan likes the yakuza. Some businesses post signs that state that yakuza are not welcome. Other business have posted signs that prohibit people with rainbow tattoos (yakuza). Other businesses exploit the yakuza images in fashion, comics, and cartoons. The presence of the yakuza is kind of an accepted open secret.

For example, while it is illegal for the yakuza to show their tattoos in public, an exception is made for the Sanja Matsuri Festival at the Asakusa Shrine in Tokyo. Held the third weekend in May, the festival draws over 2 million participants and is one of the biggest festivals in Tokyo (Japan National Tourism Organization, 2017). Asakusa is one of the oldest parts of Tokyo and is also home to quite a few yakuza members, who come out to show their colors. Yakuza members often carry the Mikoshi portable shrine as a part of the parade during the festivities (Japan National Tourism Organization, 2017). The yakuza are considered to be *ujiko*, or part of the community, and are thus allowed to participate in the celebrations.

Yakuza as a Robin Hood Organization

The yakuza view themselves as the *okondate* or chivalrous ones, with a duty to protect the Japanese traditions and people (Lunde, 2004b). Thus, sometimes they rise from the role of criminal and become willing saviors providing relief efforts to the people in times of disaster. After the 1995 earthquake in Kobe, Jones (2011) stated the members of the yakuza were often the first persons to respond to the disaster even before the government forces had arrived. After a devastating earthquake and tsunami hit Japan in 2011, Jones (2011) observed:

> Tons of relief goods have been delivered to victims of Japan's catastrophic earthquake and tsunami from a dark corner of society: the "yakuza" organized crime networks. Yakuza groups have been sending trucks from the Tokyo and Kobe regions to deliver food, water, blankets and toiletries to evacuation centers in northeast Japan, the area devastated by the March 11 earthquake and tsunami which have left at least 27,000 dead and missing.

Commenting on the yakuza relief efforts for the 2011 earthquake, yakuza expert Jake Adelstein (2011) said:

> The day after the earthquake the *Inagawa-kai* (the third largest organized crime group in Japan which was founded in 1948) sent twenty-five four-ton trucks filled with paper diapers, instant ramen, batteries, flashlights, drinks, and the essentials of daily life to the Tohoku region. An executive in *Sumiyoshi-kai*, the second-largest crime group, even offered refuge to members of the foreign

community—something unheard of in a still slightly xenophobic nation, especially amongst the right-wing yakuza. The *Yamaguchi-gumi*, Japan's largest crime group, under the leadership of Tadashi Irie, has also opened its offices across the country to the public and been sending truckloads of supplies, but very quietly and without any fanfare.

In 2014, yet another earthquake hit Japan, and Reuters (2014) reported:

Tons of relief goods have been delivered to victims of Japan's catastrophic earthquake and tsunami from a dark corner of society: the "yakuza" organized crime networks. Yakuza groups have been sending trucks from the Tokyo and Kobe regions to deliver food, water, blankets and toiletries to evacuation centers in northeast Japan, the area devastated by the March 11 earthquake and tsunami which have left at least 27,000 dead and missing. Yakuza are better known for making money from extortion, gambling, pornography and prostitution, as well as for the often-elaborate tattoos covering much of their bodies. But disasters bring out another side of yakuza, who move swiftly and quietly to provide aid to those most in need.

Yakuza and the Police

The Japanese police are very efficient. Lunde (2004b) reported that in the 1980s and 1990s the yakuza attempted to bribe Japanese police in Kobe, Osaka, and Tokyo, causing a scandal (p. 105). The Japanese police call the yakuza the *boryokudan*, or violent ones, which the yakuza consider a great insult. The word refers to degenerate, violent gangsters with no sense of tradition or honor (Keene, 1989, p. 14).

Yakuza and Crime

The yakuza practice a uniquely Japanese style of organized crime. For example, when attempting to extort money from a Japanese corporation, the yakuza has a tactic that they disrupt stockholders' meetings of Japanese corporations called "greenmail." The corporations often pay greenmail to the yakuza to avoid the fistfights and shouting that these demonstrations bring, or the threatened leak of bad information that could affect stock prices of the company (Szymkowiak, 2002, pp. 167–168).

The primary crimes of the yakuza include drug trafficking, extortion, gambling, racketeering, prostitution, money laundering, human trafficking, and weapons trafficking (Kaplan & Dubro, 1986, pp. 76–77). According to Keene (1989), the yakuza has over 2,500 groups with an estimated membership of over 110,000 (p. 14).

Common Yakuza Markings

Unlike many gangs or organized crime groups who strive for secrecy, according to Keene (1989):

> Yakuza members are known to boast outwardly about their affiliation and each group has its own distinctive lapel pin that the members proudly wear. Gang insignias and flags are also openly displayed on their meeting places and buildings.
>
> (p. 15)

The yakuza member takes great pride in his tattoos. Tattoos worn by the yakuza are often considered to be a rebellion against society's norms in a society that values conformity. They are badges of clan, honor, and endurance (it can take 100 hours to tattoo a member's entire back). The custom of yakuza tattoos is thought to be originated with the *bakuto* (medieval unions of gamblers) who tattooed a black ring around their arm for each crime that they committed (Kaplan & Dubro, 1986, p. 25; Fellman, 1986, p. 15; Etter, 1995, pp. 53–54). Keene (1989) observed:

> Yakuza members undergo almost continuous tattoo operations, displaying snakes, dragons, waves and mythical figures which symbolize their ancestral or adopted organization and demonstrate their permanent commitment. Tattoos worn by 75 percent of the Yakuza members are used to intimidate people outside the organization, even though they are usually concealed by the individual's apparel.
>
> (p. 15)

Where the Yakuza Are

The yakuza have been reported in Brazil, Japan, Korea, the Philippines, Singapore, Thailand, and the United States (Lunde, 2004b, p. 104; Adelstein, 2012, p. 158).

Asian Street Gangs

Asian street gangs often tend to be from second or third generation immigrant youth who are disaffected from the family values of their elders (Song, Dombrink, & Gels, 1992, pp. 1–12). These gangs may or may not be affiliated with other Asian organized crime groups such as triads and tongs (Toy, 1992, p. 16). Valdez (2009a) observed that Asian street gangs tend to develop around members of their own ethnic immigrant groups, thus in California you will find Chinese, Japanese, Korean, Filipino, Samoan, and Vietnamese gangs (pp. 155–163). Most of these Asian street gangs affect only their local communities. However, some have an extended influence beyond their local cities or states.

Born to Kill aka BTK

BTK is a Vietnamese gang that was started in 1989 in New York City (English, 1995, p. 17). BTK is allied with the Flying Dragons and are rivals with the Ghost Shadows. The BTK's primary crimes include protection and extortion (Chin, 1996, p. 53). The BTK has an estimated membership of 6,000.

Where the BTK Are

Members of Born to Kill have been reported in California, Georgia, Mississippi, New York, and Texas.

Four Seas Gang (四海幫)

The Four Seas Gang formed as a Taiwanese triad in the 1955 (Chin, 1990, p. 71). Their organizational structure strongly resembles that of a triad, although many consider them to be just another gang (Huston, 2001, pp. 65–66). The Four Seas Gang are rivals of the United Bamboo Gang (Kaplan, 1992, p. 470) and is allied with the yakuza (Booth, 1990, p. 142).

Chin (1990) observed:

> After Four Seas members arrived in the United States (sometimes illegally), they became active in collecting debts, operating gambling houses and nightclubs, and investing in legal businesses such as restaurants and trading companies.
>
> (p. 71)

The Four Seas Gang's primary crimes are gambling, extortion, kidnapping, and human trafficking (Butterfield, 1985; Chin, 1990, p. 71). While many Four Seas members on Taiwan took advantage of the 1997 offer of amnesty (Operation Self-Renewal) by the Chinese government, many others did not and the gang remains active (Booth, 1999, p. 332). The Four Seas Gang has an estimated 5,000 members.

Where the Four Seas Are

The Four Seas Gang has been reported in California and Taiwan.

Flying Dragons

The Flying Dragons was formed around 1968 in New York under the auspices of the Hip Sing Tong (Chin, 1990, p. 80). The Flying Dragons, while mostly made up of Chinese youth, also admit Korean or Fujianese teenagers (Chin, 1996, p. 104). The Flying Dragons are a hierarchical gang with formal initiation rites and oaths similar to those taken by tong members (Chin, 1996, p. 110). The Flying Dragons are allied with the Hip Sing Tong and the BTK (Huston, 2001, p. 117; English, 1995, p. 52). The Flying Dragons primary crimes include illegal gambling, protection, extortion, and drug trafficking (Chin, 1996, pp. 51, 153).

Where the Flying Dragons Are

The Flying Dragons have been reported in New Jersey and New York.

Fuk Ching

The Fuk Ching gang is allied with the Fukien American Association (Huston, 2001, p. 117). The Fuk Ching specialize in heroin trafficking (DOJ, 1988, p. 38). Primary crimes of the Fuk Ching also include human trafficking, robbery, protection, and extortion (Zhang, 1997, p. 327; Berry et al., 2003, p. 28; English, 1995, pp. 62–63; Chin, 1996, pp. 51, 53). Keefe (2009) states that the Fuk Ching was suspected of being involved in the *Golden Venture* human trafficking case along with the Fukinese American Association and extortion in the Chinatown neighborhood. Chin (1996) found:

> Approximately three months after the golden Venture incident, the FBI and the NYPD's Major Case Squad arrested twenty leaders and members of the Fuk Ching gang. The gang was charged with being a racketeering enterprise that was heavily involved in extortion, kidnapping, human smuggling, and murder. The leader of the gang was arrested in Hong Kong and extradited to the United States to stand trial.
>
> (pp. 173–174)

Where the Fuk Ching Are

The Fuk Ching have been reported in New Jersey and New York.

Ghost Shadows

The Ghost Shadows were formed in 1971 by Yin Poy aka "Nicky" Louie in New York City from Chinese immigrants (Levitt, 1994). The Ghost Shadows are allied with the On Leong Tong (Huston, 2001, p. 117; English, 1995, p. 52). Chin (1996), discussing the Ghost Shadows, noted:

> The gang was indicted in 1985, after the NYPD, the Jade Squad of the Manhattan District Attorney's Office, and the FBI had worked together for two years collecting evidence on the gang's criminal activities. The 85-count indictment included 13 murders and numerous incidents of attempted murder, robbery, extortion, kidnapping, bribery, and illegal gambling. In May 1986, most of the defendants pleaded guilty and received the maximum sentence of 15 years.
>
> (pp. 173–174)

Twenty-five Ghost Shadows were indicted and among those convicted in that indictment was Yin Poy aka "Nicky" Louie, the Ghost Shadows' leader (AP, 1985). Levitt (1994) observed:

> Louie was the Ghost Shadows' co-founder and head until 1978, when he was deposed after surviving numerous assassination attempts. In 1986, he was convicted of racketeering along with 24 other Ghost Shadows. He was released from prison in 1994.

The Ghost Shadows primary crimes include: extortion, protection, robbery, kidnapping, illegal gambling and bribery (Chin, 1996, pp. 51, 173–174).

Where the Ghost Shadows Are

The Ghost Shadows have been reported in Illinois, Louisiana, Massachusetts, New Jersey, and New York, as well as Hong Kong and Taiwan (Huston, 2001, pp. 64–65; AP, 1985).

Wah Ching (華青)

The Wah Ching was founded 1966 in San Francisco (Huston, 2001, p. 103). The Wah Ching began as street toughs that served as lookouts for the Hop Sing Tong's gambling houses (DOJ, 1988, p. 32; Chin, 1990, p. 68). The DOJ (1988) observed:

> Wah Ching leaders now control a vast array of legal and illegal business enterprises in North America including nightclubs, entertainment holdings, jewelry stores, travel agencies, medical services, gambling clubs and gas stations. Several years ago the California Bureau of Organized Crime and Criminal Intelligence (BOCCI) upgraded the Wah Ching from a street gang to an organized criminal group.
>
> (p. 32)

At one time the Wah Ching attempted to control all Asian street gangs in California but were unsuccessful in their quest. This led to conflict with other Chinatown street gangs in San Francisco. On Sunday, September 4, 1977, members of the Joe Boys Chinese street gang went to the Golden Dragon restaurant in San Francisco's Chinatown looking to kill members of the Wah Ching. The Joe Boys opened fire in the crowded restaurant and killed five people and injured 11 more. Most of the Wah Ching members in the restaurant ducked behind tables and escaped injury. This incident became known as the Golden Dragon Massacre. Five members of the Joe Boys gang were convicted in the attack (Valdez, 2009a, p. 193; Chin, 1990, p. 69; UPI, 1977).

According to the California Department of Justice (CDOJ), Division of Law Enforcement, Criminal Intelligence Bureau (2003), on January 23, 2002,

> [Eleven] Wah Ching members were arrested in Los Angeles on charges including conspiracy to commit assault with a dangerous weapon, murder in aid of racketeering, carrying and possessing a firearm during and in furtherance of a crime of violence, conspiracy to distribute marijuana, and distribution of methylendioxymethamphetamine (ecstasy). The charges relate to the Wah Ching's efforts to further its criminal enterprises in the Southern California region.
>
> (CDOJ, 2003, p. 11)

The Wah Ching originally were allied with the Hop Sing Tong (Huston, 2001, p. 117), but switched their alliance to the Hip Sing Tong in 1977 (Toy, 1997, p. 238). The Wah Ching are also allied with the Sun Yee On and 14 K Triads (DOJ, 1988, p. 32). The enemies of the Wah Ching include the Asian Boyz (Crips) and the Wo Hop To Triad. The Wah Ching has an estimated membership of over 3,000.

Where the Wah Ching Are

The Wah Ching have been reported in California, Colorado, Massachusetts, New York, Oklahoma, Oregon, South Dakota, Texas, and Virginia (Huston, 2001, pp. 103–104).

Chaldean Mafia

The Chaldean Mafia began in the United States around 1985 among the Assyrian/Chaldean immigrant population that had moved to Wayne County, Michigan, in the Detroit area. Most of the Assyrian/Chaldean immigrant population practices the Chaldean Catholic religion and are Christians. They speak Aramaic as their native tongue (Knox, 2003a, pp. 65–76). The Chaldean Mafia was involved in a gang war in the late

1980s in Detroit. One Chaldean Mafia leader, Bahaa Kalsko, was convicted of murder and armed robbery in 1985 and is currently serving a life sentence in the Michigan Department of Corrections (Knox, 2003a, p. 71). According to Burnstein (2014),

> Around the summer of 1988, according to court filings and federal documents, Kalasho and Akrawi and some of their syndicate's lieutenants had a falling out, resulting in the starting of a deadly shooting and firebombing war that lasted well into the next decade and in which their rivals had backing from the Italian mafia.

In this conflict, reputed Chaldean godfather Lou "The Hammerhead" Akrawi was opposed by splinter factions lead by Sam "The Candy Man" Goggo and Mark "The Terminator" Salem. As a result, Akrawi's nephew, Harry Kalasho aka "Harry the Blonde," was murdered. This touched off a series of killings in the Detroit area. Burnstein (2012) observed that Akrawi "was convicted in Wayne County Recorder's Court in 1996 of second-degree murder and sentenced to 15 to 25 years behind bars." Akrawi remains in custody.

According to the FBI (2015a),

> The Chaldean Mafia, composed predominantly of Iraqi nationals, operated a narcotics distribution network moving drugs from Phoenix and San Diego to Detroit. Involved in violent crimes such as homicide, assault, kidnaping, armed robbery, and arson, the gang used intimidation and brutal force to move the narcotics and collect drug proceeds. The work of the Detroit Metropolitan Violent Crime Task Force resulted in the conviction of 111 subjects and the seizure of $5.3 million, 6.5 tons of marijuana, 25 kilograms of cocaine, five pounds of crystal methamphetamine, and 78 firearms.

According to Davis (2011), in 2011, DEA working with "Immigration and Customs Enforcement, Border Patrol, Internal Revenue Service, sheriff's and FBI bomb squads, and the Bureau of Alcohol, Tobacco, Firearms and Explosives" participated in "Operation Shadowbox." This operation resulted in the arrest of 60 individuals that were smuggling drugs from Mexico into California and then to Detroit. Davis (2011) stated that:

> The investigation has culminated in the seizure of more than 13 pounds of methamphetamine; more than 5 pounds of ecstasy, pharmaceuticals, crack cocaine, heroin and cocaine; and more than 3,500 pounds of marijuana, most of which was likely smuggled through maritime routes controlled by the Sinaloa Federation.

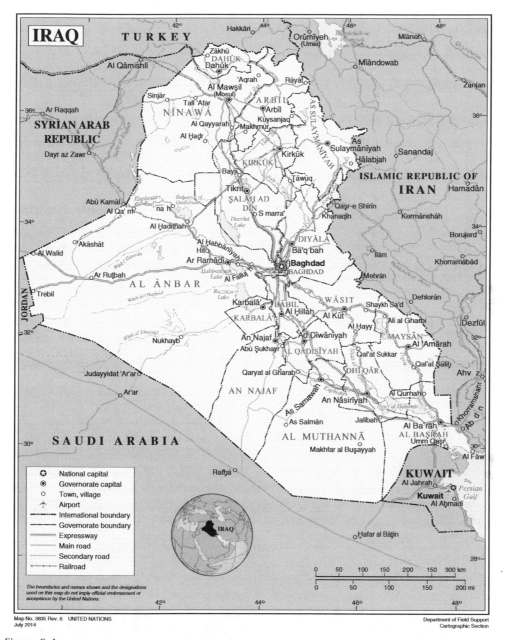

Figure 9.4

Map of Iraq. The Chaldean Mafia is a gang composed almost exclusively of individuals tracing their roots to the country of Iraq. Public domain.

United Nations

The Chaldean Mafia is allied with Colombian drug cartels, the Sicilian Mafia, the Tijuana cartel and the Sinaloa cartel in their drug dealing operations. The Chaldean Mafia is estimated to have fewer than 100 members (DOJ, 2007, p. 4; Knox, 2003a, p. 75).

Common Chaldean Mafia Markings

Although the Chaldean Mafia does not use any specific colors, they have been known to use the number 313. This represents the third and the thirteenth letters of the alphabet, or CM (Chaldean Mafia; Knox, 2003a, p. 72).

Where the Chaldean Mafia Are

Members of the Chaldean Mafia have been reported in Arizona, California, Illinois, and Michigan (Carpenter & Cooper, 2015, p. 6; Davis, K., 2011).

Nigerian Organized Crime

While many African countries have organized crime that may cross a border or two, it is Nigerian organized crime that is truly transnational in nature due to the number of countries that it operates in. Nigerian organized crime originally centered on the drug trade. Ethnic Nigerian immigrant populations in various countries assisted in the transport and sale of drugs, especially heroin. Political unrest has caused some rebel groups to engage in the drug trade to finance their revolutionary activities. The profits from these drug sales have also caused Nigerian organized crime to be involved in extensive money laundering operations (FBI, 2015g). Other primary crimes include weapons trafficking, human trafficking, kidnapping, robbery, diamond smuggling, and extortion (Babatunde, 2012). Nigerian organized crime is often involved in various frauds. According to the FBI (2015g):

> Nigerian groups are famous globally for their financial frauds, which cost the U.S. alone an estimated $1 billion to $2 billion each year. Schemes are diverse, targeting individuals, businesses, and government offices. Here's just a partial list of their fraudulent activities: insurance fraud involving auto accidents; healthcare billing scams; life insurance schemes; bank, check, and credit card fraud; advance-fee schemes known as 4–1–9 letters; and document fraud to develop false identities. The advent of the Internet and e-mail have made their crimes more profitable and prevalent.

In oil-rich Nigeria, organized crime is also involved in massive theft of natural resources. Sieff (2008) observed:

In Nigeria, organized crime cartels control vast swaths of land in the oil-producing Niger Delta. Theft is rampant. Gangs in the delta illegally install valves on pipelines and load the oil onto barges. The barges then move out to sea where they rendezvous with tankers. The tankers blend the stolen oil in with legitimate oil and carry it away for sale to world markets. Nigeria's oil theft is a lucrative business: hundreds of millions of barrels are stolen each day, earning syndicates an estimated $60 million a day. Over the past few years, gang warfare over turf and smuggling routes has killed or displaced thousands of people living in the main Niger Delta city of Port Harcourt and the villages scattered across the delta.

Where the Nigerian Organized Crime Groups Operate

According to the FBI (2015g):

African criminal enterprises have been identified in several major metropolitan areas in the U.S., but are most prevalent in Atlanta, Baltimore, Chicago, Dallas, Houston, Milwaukee, Newark, New York, and Washington, D.C. Nigerian criminal enterprises are the most significant of these groups and operate in more than 80 other countries of the world.

Summary

Beginning as bandit groups in China, triads spread with Chinese immigration across the world. They restrict membership to members of their own ethnic groups and provide a variety of illicit goods and services to their clients. Chinese gangs use language, culture, race, religion, and ethnicity to shield them from law enforcement. Many of the crimes of Chinese gangs are initially committed against members of their own ethnic groups. Tongs developed in the United States as a result of Chinese immigration and are often allied with triads. Both the Chinese triads and the Chinese tongs have an almost rigid hierarchical organizational structure and have set offices for their leaders. The lack of understanding by law enforcement of the language, culture, religion, and ethnicity hinders the investigation of these groups by law enforcement.

Japanese groups like the yakuza have a long and concealed history. Although they have a worldwide presence, they are primarily located in areas with a significant Japanese population. Yakuza have elaborate tattoos that they conceal from public view. They are typically embedded in the culture like Chinese organized crime groups and are well established in the community. Asian gangs that aren't quite determined to be at the level of organized crime take on many of the characteristics of the organized crime groups.

The Chaldean Mafia has operated in the United States since 1985. Most of the Assyrian/Chaldean immigrant population practice the Chaldean Catholic religion and are Christians. They speak Aramaic as their native tongue. The younger generation, like those of other immigrants, may be marginalized by other groups and respond by forming a gang based on their common community characteristics (ethnicity, religion, etc.).

African organized crime groups like those in Nigeria originally centered on the drug trade. The Nigerian immigrant populations in other countries assisted in establishing a network for the transport and sale of drugs, as well as an extensive money laundering operation. Other primary crimes include weapons trafficking, human trafficking, kidnapping, robbery, diamond smuggling, and extortion.

DISCUSSION QUESTIONS

1. Explain the differences between a Chinese triad and a tong.
2. Explain why a tong may or may not be a criminal organization in any given instance.
3. Describe the differences in a hierarchical and non-hierarchical Chinese gang structure.
4. Explain the role language has in the operation of ethnic gangs.
5. Explain what makes the Chaldean Mafia unique among gangs that originated from Middle Eastern immigrants.
6. What sorts of crimes could Nigerian organized crime groups commit?

CHAPTER 10 Italian Organized Crime

CHAPTER OBJECTIVES

After reading this chapter students should be able to do the following:

- Describe Italian organized crime.
- Explain the difference between organized crime and street gangs.
- Describe how Italian organized crime is structured and the various criminal groups involved.
- Describe what criminal enterprises that Italian organized crime engages in.
- Explain how Italian organized crime has become a transnational threat.

Introduction

While organized crime has always dealt in illegal goods and services, Naim (2003) noted that they have expanded their dealing to include trafficking in human organs, endangered species, stolen art, and toxic waste. Organized crime differs from other types of crime mainly due to the scale of their criminality and the scope of their operations. Organized crime is usually an international criminal enterprise.

The leaders of organized crime groups often view themselves in the context of a "man of honor" or a "social bandit" rather than as an evil entity. In his work on social bandits, Hobsbawm (1969) described the social bandit as a type of noble robber who steals from the rich and gives some to the poor. It is a style of political and social resistance often referred to in folklore and legend (Etter and Lehmuth, 2013; Robinson, 2009; Seal, 2009; Edberg, 2004; Hobsbawm, 1969). Many bandits and smugglers are viewed as "Robin Hood" type characters.

The criminals often try and live up to that image, donating money, food, jobs, medical care, education, and other benefits to the people in the areas in which they operate.

That does not preclude them from exploiting, terrorizing, or killing anybody they choose, but the myth survives. The image buys the criminals support against government forces, and citizens will often not inform on them to the police (Etter & Lehmuth, 2013). Chicago Mafia leader Al Capone, Colombian cartel leader Pablo Escobar, and Mexican cartel leader Joaquín Archivaldo Guzmán Loera aka "El Chapo" are examples of organized crime figures that either viewed themselves as, or were viewed by the public, as "social bandits."

Due to the common view of themselves as "men of honor" and as "social bandits," it became the custom that when one of those leaders died, a lavish and public funeral would often be held that not only demonstrated the importance of the deceased but also of the organized crime group that they represented. It became a public show of the power of the group. In the United States, the practice with La Cosa Nostra began as early as the 1920s during Prohibition (Zion, 1994, p. 28; Dorigo, 1992, pp. 36–37). The practice has also been observed with the Mexican drug cartels, the Colombian drug cartels, the Russian Mafia, and recently (copying their American cousins) by the Sicilian Mafia.

In a recent example of the 2015 funeral of a Italian organized crime leader in Rome, life imitated art when Sims (2015) reported:

> The lavish funeral held for the boss of a notorious Rome crime gang in which a brass band played the theme tune from the *Godfather* movie and a helicopter dropped red rose petals on mourners has been condemned. Hundreds of mourners turned out to pay their respects to Vittorio Casamonica, 65, at the San Giovanni Bosco church on the outskirts of Rome yesterday. Six ornamental horses pulling a black and gold embossed carriage carried Casamonica's coffin to front of the church while a band played tunes from the *Godfather* and bouquets of flowers were tossed at the casket as it was carried in to the church.

International gangs present a unique series of challenges to law enforcement. Since they operate across international borders, they present law enforcement with issues of jurisdiction, language, culture, and a scale of operations that makes efforts to eradicate or contain them much more difficult.

Italian Organized Crime

Italian organized crime is not one monolithic organization as it is often portrayed in the media and entertainment industries. Italian organized crime is divided into several parts that are unique in their scope and criminal activities. In their investigations of Italian organized crime, the FBI (2015b) found:

There are several groups currently active in the U.S.: the Sicilian Mafia; the Camorra or Neapolitan Mafia; the 'Ndrangheta or Calabrian Mafia; and the Sacra Corona Unita or United Sacred Crown. We estimate the four groups have approximately 25,000 members total, with 250,000 affiliates worldwide. There are more than 3,000 members and affiliates in the U.S., scattered mostly throughout the major cities in the Northeast, the Midwest, California, and the South. Their largest presence centers around New York, southern New Jersey, and Philadelphia. Their criminal activities are international with members and affiliates in Canada, South America, Australia, and parts of Europe. They are also known to collaborate with other international organized crime groups from all over the world, especially in drug trafficking.

Figure 10.1

Sicilian Mafia. Sketch of the 1901 maxi trial of suspected mafiosi in Palermo. Public domain.

From the newspaper *L'Ora*, May 1901

Lavorgna, Lombardo and Sergi (2013) agreed with the FBI's observations about Italian organized crime when they found that:

> In spite of its historical ties to Sicily, the word mafia has become an umbrella term used to describe "mafia-like" organizations such as the Calabrian 'Ndrangheta, the Apulian Sacra Corona Unita, and the Campanian Camorra or at least the Casalesi clan, the most powerful Camorra group. These mafia groups are regarded as the ideal-type of organized crime. They are large-scale, stable, and structured organizations.
>
> (p. 267)

Although most experts consider the Sicilian Mafia and the American Mafia (La Cosa Nostra) to be two separate entities, the two are unquestionably related. Italian organized crime as a whole has a patriarchal organizational structure, and within the United States it is organized into families with defined territories of operations. Full members or "made men" are usually of Italian ancestry. Others may be involved with or employed by the Mafia as associates.

Sicilian Mafia (Based in Sicily, Italy)

Some have claimed that the history of the Sicilian Mafia can be traced back as far as the Sicilian Vespers Rebellion of March 30–April 28, 1282, when the people of Sicily rebelled against Charles I who was the French-imposed king of the Kingdom of Sicily (Dorigo, 1992, p. 12). Other historians have denied this and have traced the origins of the Mafia to the early 1700s in Sicilian feudal society (Spadafora, 2010). Spadafora further observed:

> It was fiefdoms, and more specifically feudalism, that spawned the Mafia, albeit gradually and indirectly. By 1700, most of the more important noble families who controlled "urban" fiefs (including towns as well as land) were spending ever more time in the larger cities (Palermo, Catania, Messina, Siracusa, Agrigento, Marsala) where political power was centered—particularly Palermo, which was the capital. In doing so, they left the day-to-day administration of their estates to others . . . Not only did feudatories enjoy specific feudal rights (abolished with feudalism in 1812), some also had the authority to mete out justice for certain petty crimes (such as theft of sheep, poaching of game or encroachment of property) . . . Banditry was endemic, but in the gabelloti the bandits found willing accomplices. Lax law enforcement, along with Sicilians' natural distrust of authority, facilitated development of this parallel power structure.

As the criminals enjoyed the cooperation of the corrupt gabelloti, who legally represented the landholders, there was little to be done. Most people accepted the status quo, being poor, illiterate and disenfranchised (they could not vote).

In that atmosphere, strong men or "dons" would often decide local problems and make rules that only applied to their small territorial holdings or village. But most authors agree that by the Bourbon period of Neapolitan kings in the early to mid-1800s, the Mafia was a growing concern in Sicily (Lupo, 2009, pp. 3–5; Dickie, 2004, p. 35; Paoli, 2003, pp. 179–180; Allen, 1962, p. 12).

In his examination of the Sicilian Mafia, Lunde (2004a) observed that power in that time and area was arbitrary. He reported it appeared the larger and more extended the family, the more protected the individual, as safety lay in the family. This was true especially in a social system that included vendettas where no offense was allowed to pass unavenged for the sake of honor. During the military conflicts that accompanied the Risorgimento (1815–1871) or Italian reunification, the Sicilian Mafia took sides in the conflict. Lupo (2009) found:

> there was already a well-defined Mafia in the period of the Risorgimento. That Mafia allied itself with the forces supporting Victor Emmanuel II, and opposed Garibaldi, who wished to give land to the peasants.
>
> (p. 204)

Dickie (2004) observed that the Mafia in Sicily came with the unification of Italy during the Risorgimento. By having backed Victor Emanuel II, the Mafia in Sicily was often able to exert an undue, corrupting influence on local police and government officials. This became the subject of several governmental investigations, such as the one conducted by Leopoldo Franchi and Sidney Sonnino in 1876 (Dickie, 2004, pp. 50–54). Although the government was unsuccessful in suppressing the Mafia in Sicily, many Sicilians and other Italians fled to the United States either as a result of the Risorgimento or the attempts by the unified Italian government to suppress the Mafia (Dickie, 2004, p. 69; Delzell, 1965).

Even with the attempted suppression by the Italian government, the Mafia flourished in Sicily during the period 1876–1924. With few exceptions, the "men of honor" had a unique position in Sicilian society due to the massive difference between the rich who were supported by the government and the poor who were supported by nobody. Sterling (1990) observed:

> The poor turned to the Mafia because they had nobody else. There was no state apart from tax collectors, where they were concerned. The Church, omnipotent in a solidly Catholic country, was in league with the barons and the establishment in

Rome. The Mafia, though in league with all three, took pride in administering a degree of even handed justice. This was a necessary ingredient of power, and power was once thought to be more intoxicating than money for a Mafia don. A simple citizen with none but honorary titles, he could command respect bordering on reverence, dispute wisdom and patronage, mediate disputes, choose public servants (including police chiefs and judges), elect lawmakers, and shape governments.

(p. 48)

Thus, there developed a group of clans in Sicily that were ruled by dons who viewed themselves as "Robin Hood" type figures and "social bandits," providing a service to their people in exchange for "respect." This was more a patriarchal type of organization rather than a hierarchical one. If a don got into more trouble than he could handle, he often fled by emigrating to the United States. Dorigo (1992) found:

By the middle of the nineteenth century, therefore, there existed in Sicily a "parallel" government that lacked only one thing: the opportunity to make a lot of money. There were plenty of opportunities for petty crime, it was true, such as protection money from small businesses, "number games" (illegal lotteries), minor league confidence tricks, and cattle theft. It was possible to do a little better out of prostitution, provided you controlled enough girls, but for a Mafioso this would probably offend against *omerta*. The occasional kidnapping could make a lot more money, but there was just not a large enough reservoir of potential victims, and few people could afford really significant ransoms. With a relatively small, poor island, the Mafia was limited in what it could do.

(p. 15)

During the period of the 1880s to 1924, the Sicilian Mafia embedded itself as a functioning part of the island's society. However, that was about to change. Sterling (1990) observed that with the rise of Mussolini in Italy, the Fascists had their own ideas about order and observed that:

Mussolini had decided, on his first tour of Sicily in 1924, that the Mafia would have to go. The mayor and *Capo-Mafia* of Piana dei Greci, Don Cicco Coccia, was showing him around, and remarked of his large police escort: "Excellency, you're with me, and you have nothing to worry about. Why do you need so many cops?" Il Duce instantly understood the Mafia in Sicily. This was its kingdom, and he its guest—not at all his style. He was unlikely in any case to put up for long with this alternative power to his own. Within a month, Don Cicecio was in jail and Mussolini's war on the Mafia had begun. His Iron Prefect, Cesare Mori, set out to uproot the Mafia "as a surgeon penetrates the flesh with fire and steel, until he cauterizes the pus sacks of the bubonic plague." Thousands were flung into prisons and tortured, guilty or innocent, their property seized and their families ruined. Where evidence was lacking, they were framed.

(p. 51)

In describing the conflicts between Mussolini and the Sicilian Mafia, Lunde (2004a) reported that Mussolini was determined to destroy the Mafia when he gained control of Italy in 1924. He appointed a prefect of Palermo in 1924 and granted the first person to hold that position, Cesare Mori, extraordinary powers. Mass trials were held, with the defendants held in huge iron cages, earning Mori the title "Prefect of Iron." Most, overwhelmingly from the lowest levels of the Mafia, were found guilty and sent to penal colonies.

This had two basic results for the Sicilian Mafia: first, many Mafia fled to the United States to avoid arrest (many joined their cousins in the American La Cosa Nostra), and second, those members of the Mafia that remained in Sicily developed a healthy dislike for Mussolini and the Fascist government of Italy prior to and during World War II. In

Figure 10.2

Benito Mussolini and Adolf Hitler stand together on a reviewing stand during Mussolini's official visit in Munich. Public domain.

Muzej Revolucije Narodnosti Jugoslavije, via the U.S. Holocaust Memorial Museum

1943, when the Allies invaded Sicily, some members of the Mafia assisted U.S. military forces in scouting and acquiring intelligence against the Germans and their Italian Fascist allies. Some authors suggest that this assistance was provided at the request of American Mafia don Lucky Luciano, but other authors deny his involvement (Fijnaut, 2012, pp. 133–134; Lupo, 2009, pp. 187–188; Newark, 2007a, pp. 32–38; Dickie, 2004, pp. 191–203; Lunde, 2004a, p. 59; Kross, 2003; Bonanno, 1999, pp. 45–46; Lacey, 1991, pp. 124–125; Sterling, 1990, pp. 55–57).

After the Allied victory in Sicily in 1943, the Allied occupation forces attempted to restore order in Sicily and removed all of the previous Fascists that had served in local government. Many of their replacements were either Sicilian Mafia members (who were certainly anti-fascist) or others who were associated with the Sicilian Mafia. That led to corruption problems and a thriving black market in which the Sicilian Mafia dominated (Lupo, 2009, p. 189; Dickie, 2004, pp. 191–203; Sterling, 1990, pp. 55–57). Sterling (1990) found:

> Men of Honor were everywhere after the Allies invaded Sicily in July 1943. The entire fascist establishment having collapsed, they took its place. Local Mafia bosses were doubling as mayors in scores of Sicilian towns. The incoming *capo di tutti cappi*, Don Calogero Vizzini, ran a thriving black market from the City Hall of Villalba, his hometown. Vizzini, whose onetime criminal dossier had included thirty-nine murders, six attempted murders, thirty-six robberies, thirty-seven thefts, and sixty-three extortions, now owned a gun permit "for protection against fascist attacks." The U.S. Army had made him an honorary colonel.
> (p. 55)

After World War II, Italy began to rebuild, and the Allied occupiers began to prepare to face new enemies such as the communists. With Yugoslavia and Albania having become communist states and a civil war going on in Greece between the Greek government and communist-backed insurgents (1946–1949), there was a pressing need for the fledgling new Italian government and the Allied occupiers to prevent Italy from falling into the hands of the communists. Thus, Lunde (2004a) found, the relationship between the Mafia and the Allied occupiers of Sicily in 1943 ensured that Sicily voted for the Christian Democratic Party (CDP) for almost 50 years. That kept the communists and the socialists out of the government and gave the CDP a free hand in Sicily. Over the next decade, dozens of left-wing leaders were murdered and the Mafia began a systematic elimination of left-wing politicians. That lasted until the mid-1960s.

In the 1950s the Sicilian Mafia began to look beyond Sicily to conduct their criminal enterprises. In the period 1950–1963, Sicilian Mafia leaders like Tommaso Buscetta (1928–2000) helped to expand the Mafia's enterprises into cigarette smuggling and into rigged construction bids involving concrete (Lupo, 2009, p. 224; Dickie, 2004, pp. 217–239; Arlacchi, 1987, pp. 66–67). Most Mafia historians agree that the heavy multinational involvement in the drug trade by the Sicilian Mafia began in the 1950s in an alliance with their American Mafia cousins. On October 10–14, 1957, a four-day meeting was held at the Grand Hotel des Palmes in Palermo for the purpose of facilitating the Sicilian Mafia's participation in heroin smuggling to the American Mafia, using the cigarette smuggling routes already established by the Sicilian Mafia from France to Italy. American Mafia leaders such as Joe ("Joey Bananas") Bonanno and Charles "Lucky" Luciano met with Sicilian Mafia leaders to cement their illicit narcotics trade agreement (Lupo, 2009, pp. 224–225; Raab, 2006, pp. 111–113; Dickie, 2004, pp. 234–235; Lunde, 2004b, p. 61; Sterling, 1990, pp. 82–86).

The Sicilian Mafia had smuggled drugs to the United States on a small scale prior to 1957. Dickie (2004) observed:

> The Sicilian mafia's involvement in the US drug trade was not a novelty in 1957. Morphine was already being smuggled through Palermo, in cases of oranges and lemons, back in the 1920's. Nick Gentile mentions how drugs would be hidden in shipments of cheese, oil, anchovies, and other Sicilian products. New York boss Joe Profaci's Mamma Mia Importing Company was one of many commercial fronts for narcotics trafficking. But the pattern of arrests and drug seizures in the years after Joe Bananas' holiday in Sicily show a marked increase in Sicilian involvement, and much closer cooperation between the two shores of the criminal Atlantic; the effects of the decisions taken among the red carpets and gilt-framed mirrors of the Hotel des Palmes are measurable. As a US attorney would latter remark, everyone at the meeting was a "narcotics track star." Heroin was to be the new transatlantic sport for men of honor.
>
> (p. 235)

Part of the reason for this meeting was political and part was geographical. The American Mafia had been smuggling drugs into the United States from Cuba for years (Lacey, 1991, pp. 172–175). However, in the 1950s, Batista's Cuba was rife with revolutionary activity and the American Mafia was afraid that the government (which was pro-Mafia) would fall to Castro's communists (which it did in 1959). Looking for a different narcotics trade route, the American Mafia turned to their Italian cousins. Referring to the European narcotics trade, Lunde (2004a) observed:

> In the 1950's, the main narcotics suppliers were Corsicans in the south of France, where they refined morphine base brought from Turkey and the Lebanon. With their U.S. connection, the Sicilian Mafia became the Corsicans' best customers. Heroin was sent to Sicily then to the United States, usually packed in shipments of Italian specialties, such as oranges, cheese, and olive oil.
>
> (p. 62)

There were of course fights between the various Sicilian Mafia families for territory and trade routes. According to Dickie (2004), the "First Mafia War" was fought between 1962 and 1963 and began among Palermo's Mafia families (p. 241). While there had been a considerable amount of killing between the Mafia members on all sides of the conflict, matters came to a head on June 30, 1963. Lunde (2004a) reported:

> Another car bomb exploded on Ciaculli on June 30, 1963, killing seven police-men. This time the Italian government reacted. Police cordoned off Palermo street by street, confiscating weapons and arresting 1,900 men. Some 250 Mafia leaders were brought to trial and many sent to jail. Some were sent into exile in the north of Italy, allowing the Mafia to gain a foothold there.
>
> (pp. 62–63)

Lunde observed most of the exiled Mafiosi escaped. Some went into hiding, while others set up a global network by moving to the Americas. In response to the Ciaculli bombing, the Italian government passed new laws and reestablished the Anti-Mafia Commission.

The "Second Mafia War" (1977–1980s) was an internal conflict between clans of the Sicilian Mafia and the Corleonesi led by Luciano Leggio (1925–1993) and his deputy Salvatore Riina. Leggio had been imprisoned in 1974 by Italian authorities and was running the Corleonesi and the Sicilian Mafia Commission from prison through Riina, who was on the outside (Cimino, 2014a, p. 24; Dickie, 2004, p. 262). The conflict began in 1977 when Leggio arranged for the leader of the Sicilian Mafia Commission, Gaetano Badalamenti (1923–2004), who was also the leader of the Mafia in Cinisi, to be deposed from his post on accusations of hiding drug revenues from other members. Badalamenti fled to Brazil where he attempted to enlist the aid of Buscetta in his fight with the Corleonesi (Lupo, 2009). The roots of the conflict were social as well as economic, as the Palermo clans, who considered themselves the true Mafia, regarded the Corleonesi with both fear and contempt, considering them peasant upstarts attempting to move into Palermo territory.

Thus the conflict developed with the forces of Leggio and Riina on one side and those of Stefano Bontade (1939–1981) and Salvador Inzerillo (1944–1981) on the other. Leggio and Riina had been planning to take control of the organization for years (Lunde, 2004a). They did deals and formed partnerships with "men of honor" from other families. Those moves had to be completed without their bosses' permission because narcotics trafficking was not considered traditional Mafia activity. In assessing the causes of the Second Mafia War, Sterling (1990) agreed with Lunde (2004a), observing:

> According to the losers, Buscetta in particular, the war had nothing to do with drugs; it was purely a struggle for power. In reality, the two were indivisible. Even if Leggio cared nothing for money—a ridiculous idea—he could certainly have wielded no power over the Mafia by 1981 without controlling the source

of its sudden, unimaginable wealth. For that if nothing else, he had to eliminate Inzerillo and Bontade.

(p. 206)

Many Mafia members were killed along with their families during this conflict. On April 23, 1981, Bontade was killed on the orders of Riina as Bontade was driving his car in Palermo. Inzerillo was murdered about three weeks later. Italian police discovered that the same weapon had been used in both killings. The violence had reached such levels that some Mafia members began to turn state's evidence for the Italian police. In 1983, after losing two sons in this conflict, Tommaso Buscetta turned state's evidence against his former comrades in the Mafia. Cimino (2014a) reported that Buscetta became a *pentito* (an informant) and was the first senior Mafia figure to do so in 1983. He revealed that the Mafia was not many separate groups but a single organization run by a commission, or *cupola*, led by Riina. Riina organized a terrorist-style attack known as the Christmas Massacre. A bomb was detonated in a tunnel between Florence and Bologna, killing 17 and injuring 267, to divert resources from the investigation. Nevertheless, Buscetta's cooperation led to the convictions of 338 Mafiosi.

Giovanni Falcone (1939–1992) was a prosecuting judge and magistrate in Palermo, Sicily. He was noted for his vigorous investigations and prosecutions of the Mafia in Sicily (Ehrenfeld, 1992, p. 14; Sterling, 1990, p. 141). Ehrenfeld (1992) interviewed Falcone, who told her of connections between the Sicilian Mafia and arms trafficking deals with Syria, Libya, and Iraq, as well as ties with Colombian drug cartels. She stated:

He declared immediately that the biggest problem he faced was not from the Mafia; but from the corrupt politicians who were paid by it. He described political harassment during the "Maxi Trial" and attempts to assassinate him. We spoke about the Syrian government's involvement in drug and arms trafficking with the Sicilian Mafia, and he pulled out files to illustrate the ties.

(p. 15)

Falcone later worked in the Ministry of Justice in Rome. Jamieson (1993) reported that Falcone's investigations of the Sicilian Mafia and his involvement in such high-profile Mafia prosecutions as Palermo's "Maxi Trial" in 1986 and 1987, in which 475 Mafia members were defendants, made Falcone a primary target for assassination by the Sicilian Mafia. Jamieson stated:

Falcone was murdered together with his wife and three bodyguard on May 23, 1992. The attack was followed less than two months later (July 19) by the assassination of Judge Paolo Borsellino with his five bodyguards.

(p. 304)

Falcone was murdered on the orders of Sicilian Mafia leader Salvatore Riina aka "the Beast," who contracted with Giovanni Brusca aka "the pig" aka "the butcher" aka "the people slayer," to do the deed. According to Cimino (2014a):

> Twelve drums containing 770 pounds of explosive in all were placed under the freeway, transported beneath the road on a skateboard. Then for weeks Brusca and his men kept watch, looking for Falcone. Twice they missed him. Once he was with his friend and fellow prosecutor Paolo Borsellino. "If we had known, we'd have killed two birds with one stone," said Brusca.
>
> (pp. 86–87)

Falcone and his wife were spotted on the afternoon of May 23, 1992. Their armor-plated car was one of a convoy of three. Brusca flicked the switch to the remote control, detonating the explosives in the drums, causing an explosion so powerful that it registered on an earthquake monitor on the other side of the island (Cimino, 2014a). The lead car in the convoy was blown into an olive grove 60 yards away, and the three bodyguards inside were killed. Meanwhile, the judge, his wife and his driver were badly injured. Falcone and his wife died shortly after they arrived in hospital. Only the driver survived (Cimino, 2014a). Brusca was paid handsomely and celebrated with champagne.

The murders of Falcone and Borsellino in 1992 caused immediate repercussions of the Sicilian Mafia. There was a huge public outcry for the Italian government to do something about the Mafia. Cimino (2014a) found:

> The murder of Falcone and, soon after Borsellino provoked an unprecedented crackdown on the Mafia. In January 1993, Riina was arrested after 24 years as a fugitive. Brusca, Bagarella and Provenzano decided to continue the war against the state that Riina had begun. They discussed poisoning children's snacks, planting HIV-infected syringes on the beaches of Rimini and toppling the Leaning Tower of Pisa. Instead they opted for a series of bomb attacks.
>
> (p. 90)

The Sicilian Mafia began a series of bomb attacks across Italy, notably including Rome and Florence (Lunde, 2004a, p. 73; Dickie, 2004, pp. 316–317). The Italian government began a massive crackdown on the Sicilian Mafia. Leoluca Bagarella was captured in 1995 and sentenced to life imprisonment. Brusca was captured in 1996, became a pentito and turned state's evidence against his fellow Mafia members. Provenzano remained on the run until his arrest in 2006. He was also sentenced to life imprisonment.

A disciple of Riina, Matteo Messina Denaro became a Mafia celebrity after *L'Espresso* put his picture on the cover of their April 2001 issue announcing "*Ecco il nuovo capo della mafia*" (here is the new boss of the Mafia). Like his American counterparts Al Capone

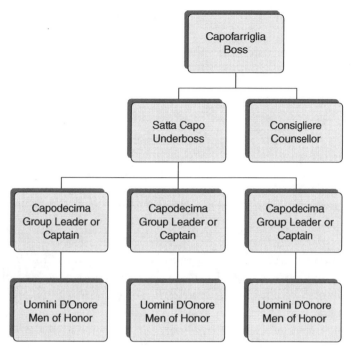

Figure 10.3

Typical Sicilian Mafia Organizational Structure.

Lunde (2004a, p. 55)

and John Gotti, Denaro was not shy of publicity and seemed to enjoy the press. He had been on the run from Italian authorities for over 20 years. He was the image of the social bandit and was considered a folk hero according to Cimino (2014a, pp. 124–15). The local people considered him a benefactor because he provided jobs in his supermarkets that some say are used for money laundering by the Mafia.

The modern Sicilian Mafia is a multinational criminal organization whose primary crimes include extortion, money laundering, political corruption, drug trafficking, bid rigging, loan-sharking, and smuggling. They are allied with other Italian organized criminal groups such as the Camorra, 'Ndrangheta, and the Sacra Corona Unita. They are allied with the American Mafia, Albanian organized crime, Colombian cartels, and Russian organized crime.

Where the Sicilian Mafia Operates

In addition to Sicily and Italy, Labrousse (2003) noted that the Sicilian Mafia had expanded its operations and expanded its international presence to Brazil, Canada,

Eastern Europe, and South Africa. The Sicilian Mafia conducts drug trafficking and money laundering operations. They also often used these countries as an escape route to hide fleeing Mafiosi on the run from Italian authorities (p. 27).

Initiation and Omerta

While not all Mafia families used the same initiation, the ceremony usually involved a dagger, a revolver, and a blood oath. That signified that the prospect lived by the knife and the gun and would thus die if he violated his oath of Omerta. However, Lupo (2009) observed that in the Sicilian Mafia, Omerta was often proclaimed in theory, but not always in practice (p. 116). Lunde (2004a) described the Sicilian Mafia initiation rites as told by Mafia informer, Tommaso Buscetta:

> Buscetta described Mafia initiation rites, remarkably similar to 19th century descriptions and those described by Joe Valachi. Initiation consisted of a blood oath and an oath of obedience. The aspiring member had to be presented for initiation by at least three "men of honor" from the family. Blood was drawn from the initiate's finger and sprinkled on the picture of a saint, which was set on fire and passed from hand to hand while the initiate swore to keep the code of Cosa Nostra, which he was bound to for life. His cosa was his new family, and he could not switch allegiances.
>
> (p. 68)

Lunde (2004a) observed that the Sicilian Mafia restricted its membership to Sicilian men. Other rules outlined the expected sexual morality of the prospective member and prohibited adultery with another Mafia member's wife. Violation of these rules was punishable by death. Lunde (2004a) further noted that very strict rules applied to Mafia killings, only for certain specified reasons, and the *capofamiglia* had to approve the action, which must be carried out in the cosa's territory. Although the Mafia code prohibited killing non-Mafia members, the rule was never taken very seriously.

American Mafia (La Cosa Nostra)

New Orleans: The Beginnings of the American Mafia

The Mafia first came to the United States when Italian Mafia members began to arrive in New Orleans in the 1870s after Garibaldi took over Italy, although some sources point to some Italian Mafia members arriving in New Orleans as early as 1865. They quickly began to engage in the traditional crimes of extortion and controlling the docks. Conflicts developed in the late 1880s over control of the docks in New Orleans between two Mafia families: the Provenzano family (said to be Camorras) led by brothers George, Joe, and Peter versus the Matranga family (said to be Sicilians) led by brothers Carlo aka "Charles" (1857–1943) and Antonio aka "Tony," as well as the family led by Joseph P. Macheca (1842–1891) (Hunt & Sheldon, 2010, pp. 217–263; Asbury, 2003, pp. 409–410).

New Orleans Police Chief David Hennessey (1858–1890) chose the wrong side in the Matranga-Provenzano feud. By backing the Provenzanos he became a target for the

Figure 10.4

New Orleans Police Chief David Hennessy. "Scene of the Assassination." Shows location of the murder of police chief David Hennessy and artist's conception of the event. At top left is a portrait of Hennessy. Public domain.

The Mascot newspaper, October 18, 1890 issue, via (overly dark) microfilm in New Orleans Public Library, photographed by Infrogmation

other family. Hennessey threatened to reveal some damaging information on his opponents that he had obtained from the Italian government when he was ambushed and killed on October 16, 1890. Over 250 Italian immigrants were arrested in the following investigation. However, only 19 were indicted, including Charles Matranga.

On March 13, 1891, all of the defendants were acquitted. According to Asbury (2003), there was much speculation in the press about jury tampering. Anti-Italian riots and lynchings followed the acquittal (pp. 415–421). Joseph P. Macheca was among those Italians and Sicilians that were killed by the mob (Hunt & Sheldon, 2010, p. 359). At the time, the incident created a diplomatic crisis, as the Italian government demanded an explanation of why its citizens were not being protected. They even threatened war against the United States. The American government under President Harrison eventually paid an indemnity payment to the Italian government of 125,000 francs (about $24,000) (Hunt & Sheldon, 2010, pp. 263–264). As a result, the Matranga family came to control the Mafia crime in what became known as the "Dixie Mafia" (Hunt & Sheldon, 2010, p. 269).

"Millionaire Charlie" Matranga ruled the New Orleans underworld until 1922 when he decided to retire. He died in retirement in 1943. Upon Matranga's retirement in 1922, control of the Mafia in New Orleans passed to Sylvestro "Silver Dollar Sam" Carolla (1896–1970). Carolla was in and out of both state and federal prison (in 1933 his Louisiana state prison term was cut short by a pardon from Louisiana Governor John B. Fournet). Carolla was deported back to Sicily in 1947, after which Carlos Marcello (1910–1993) took over the "Dixie Mafia." Marcello worked closely with other Mafia leaders like Meyer Lansky and Frank Costello in various gambling rackets (Davis, 1989, pp. 33–43; Davidson, 1964, pp. 15–21). Marcello was bitter enemies with President John F. Kennedy and Attorney General Robert Kennedy. Marcello was rumored to have been involved in the assassination of President Kennedy in 1963, but it was never proven (Carter, 2009, p. 6; Davis, 1993b, pp. 210–211; Davis, 1989, pp. 81–179). However, Marcello was convicted in 1981 of violations of the Racketeer Influenced and Corrupt Organizations (RICO) Act and spent 1983–1989 in federal prison. Upon his release as a result of his conviction being overturned, Marcello was in ill health and retired. He died in 1993. Anthony Carollo had assumed control in 1990 and remained as don until his death in 2007.

New York: The Beginnings

Initially, the arrival of large numbers of Italian immigrants into the New York City area through Ellis Island was just another wave of immigration into the United States. Most of the immigrants were honest and hardworking people. Some were not, and those included immigrants that had been involved in the Mafia back home in Italy. They found themselves in a new land with many established gangs in the city (Irish, Jewish, and others). The members of the Mafia began to establish themselves among the Italian immigrant community and to adapt to the new conditions they found themselves in. The effects that the new wave of Italian Mafiosi had on the "white slave" trade and other street crime in New York City and the lack of cooperation by immigration authorities or Italian government officials was explained by New York City Police Commissioner Theodore A. Bingham (1908) in a controversial article that he wrote for *The North American Review*. Bingham also noted that the Italian criminals conducted their own surveillance on the police and stated:

> The best-known men in all New York to the Italian criminals are Lieutenant Petrosino and the other members of the Italian squad. Indeed, the first thing an Italian criminal does on arriving here is to make himself acquainted with the appearance of the Italian detectives. Similarly, every pickpocket, every thief, every "white slave" master, every professional criminal in whatever line, familiarizes himself as far as possible with the appearance of the members of the police force, as they freely say themselves.
>
> (pp. 393–394)

The Black Hand or La Mano Nera

Contrary to popular folklore, the Black Hand was not a specific criminal group. It was an extortion racket that was practiced by Italian and Sicilian criminal groups such as the Mafia and the Camorra. The practice is alleged to have originated in the Kingdom of Naples around 1750. The scam worked this way. A letter was sent to the intended victim threatening kidnap, violence, or death if the victim did not pay the extortionists money. The letter (sometimes called a knife letter) was adorned with symbols of a black hand and other threatening symbols such as daggers, smoking guns, skulls, and so forth. The letters were usually only sent to those in the Italian immigrant community (Lombardo, 2010, pp. 119–160; Short, 2009, pp. 29–32; Landesco, 1968, p. 108). Among the victims threatened by the scheme was famed Italian American tenor Enrico Caruso (1873–1921), who initially paid and was then swarmed by more extortion threats (Pitkin & Cordasco, 1977, p. 138). The scam was practiced in several Italian American communities across the United States from the 1880s until about World War I (Petacco, 1974, pp. 29–47).

Police lieutenant Joe Petrosino made a career with the New York City Police Department (NYPD) investigating crimes involving the Italian immigrant community including the Mafia and Black Hand plots after a victim was found inside a barrel in a New York City alley in 1903 (Pitkin & Cordasco, 1977, p. 38; Petacco, 1974, pp. 1–14). Petrosino formed a squad of Italian-speaking NYPD officers and made a point of identifying Mafia

Figure 10.5

Black Hand. Army officers established a group called Unification or Death (aka the Black Hand), against the king and queen of Serbia in 1901. They killed the royal couple in May 1903. Uploaded by Gabriel Van Helsing via Wikimedia Commons. Public domain.

Bain News Service, Library of Congress

members for further investigation. Petrosino was murdered on March 12, 1909, while he was in Palermo, Sicily, investigating the past records of some New York Mafia members (Lupo, 2009, pp. 145–146). His funeral in New York City was attended by over 200,000 mourners. It was one of the largest funerals of its time (Lombardo, 2010, p. 183).

Beginning in 1911, the Chicago Police Department formed its own "Black Hand Squad" to investigate those crimes (Lombardo, 2010, pp. 69–106). Many other major urban police departments followed suit and formed specialized units that concentrated on ethnic gang crimes. That activity, as well as the existence of organized crime groups who included the name Black Hand in their names, kept the legend alive.

The Era of the Mustache Petes

The Mustache Petes were the local Mafia leaders of the Mafia in the United States in New York and the East Coast from about the late 1800s until the Castellammarese War of

1929–1931. They were very traditional and formed hierarchical and patriarchal family-type criminal organizations that operated primarily within the Italian immigrant community. They tried to adhere to Sicilian Mafia traditions and engaged in traditional Sicilian crimes such as smuggling and attempting to fix problems within the immigrant community. Power was obtained by trading favors for jobs and patronage. Of course, gambling, loan-sharking, extortion, prostitution, and other traditional crimes were not neglected.

The Mafia's expansion into the United States was greatly aided by the passage of Prohibition in 1919. Smuggling booze became the Mafia's ticket to power and wealth beyond the immigrant community. Labor unions and drug running were added into the mix later. The dons in the Mustache Pete era were hampered by tradition and a narrow world view of criminality. They were accustomed to operating in their own neighborhoods and not much farther. The rapid expansion of the American Mafia during 1919–1928 changed everything. The era of the Mustache Petes is said by many to have ended in the Castellammarese War (1928–1931).

Alphonse "Al" Gabriel Capone aka "Scarface" (1899–1947)

Alphonse Capone was born in Brooklyn, New York, on January 17, 1899. His parents had immigrated to the United States from Naples, Italy, and he had become a naturalized U.S. citizen in 1906 (Schoenberg, 1992, p. 20). Al began his criminal career working for Frankie Yale, leader of the Five Points Gang in New York City (Balsamo & Balsamo, 2012, pp. 41–46).

In 1917, Al Capone was given the scars on his face by another gangster named Frank Galluccio after Capone made a pass at Galluccio's sister in a dance hall. To prevent a vendetta killing, Galluccio appealed to his boss Joe "The Boss" Masseria. A meeting was set up between Masseria, Lucky Luciano (who had witnessed the cutting), Galluccio on one side and Frankie Yale and Capone on the other side. Money changed hands and apologies were issued (Balsamo & Balsamo, 2012, pp. 109–124). Schoenberg (1992) observed:

> Capone also recognized the justice of the settlement and the dishonor of his scars. He later put out the story that they had come to him in service with the Lost Battalion of World War I. In fact, he had never been called up in the draft. He once told Galluccio he realized it had been wrong to insult his sister, especially so publicly. In his days of greatness, on visits to New York, Capone would hire Galluccio as a supernumerary bodyguard for $100 a week.
>
> (p. 34)

Al Capone was sent to Chicago in 1919 by Frankie Yale after Capone was involved in a fight with a member of "Wild" Bill Lovett's White Hand Gang. Capone was sent to work for Johnny Torrio, who had been Yale's mentor before he left for Chicago in 1909 (Balsamo & Balsamo, 2012, pp. 153–156). Torrio had risen to become one of the leading mob bosses in Chicago and operated out of the suburb of Cicero (Landesco, 1968, p. 85). Capone's brother Frank was killed in Cicero during a 1924 police raid. Capone served Torrio loyally. Torrio's arch rival in Chicago, Charles Dean O'Banion,

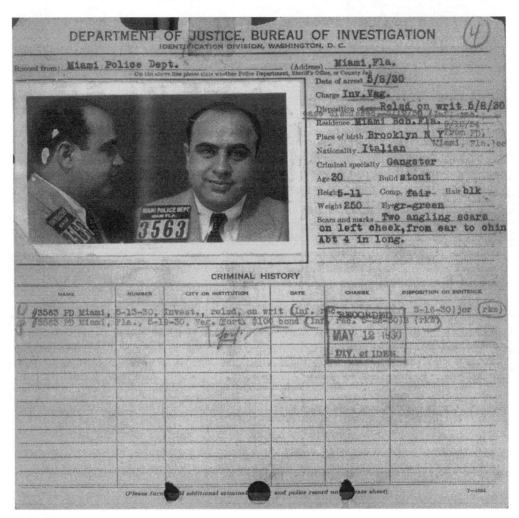

Figure 10.6

Al Capone's arrest record. Alphonse Gabriel "Al" Capone started his life of crime as a Five Points New York City gangster. He became infamous as a gangster in Chicago during the late 1920s and 1930s. Public domain.

FBI

was murdered in a mob hit by Frankie Yale and two others at Torrio's orders in 1924. When Torrio decided to retire after an assassination attempt on his life by rival O'Banion gangsters Earl "Hymie" Weiss and George "Bugs" Moran left him nearly dead in 1925, he left control of "the Outfit" to Capone (Lindberg, 2016, pp. 245–246; Lunde, 2004b, p. 132; Schoenberg, 1992, p. 136; Landesco, 1968, pp. 94–95).

Capone's Outfit was engaged in bootlegging, prostitution, extortion, and labor union racketeering. They ruthlessly eliminated their competition among Irish and other Italian gangs (Lunde, 2004b, p. 129). The FBI (2016) stated:

> Capone had built a fearsome reputation in the ruthless gang rivalries of the period, struggling to acquire and retain "racketeering rights" to several areas of Chicago. That reputation grew as rival gangs were eliminated or nullified, and the suburb of Cicero became, in effect, a fiefdom of the Capone mob.

After his men attempted to kill Capone, Earl "Hymie" Weiss (aka Henry Earl J. Wojciechowski) was killed in a gang shootout in 1926 at Capone's orders (Lindberg, 2016, pp. 246–247). Capone then negotiated a truce with his successor, Bugs Moran (Lunde, 2004b, p. 134). However, Capone was suspected of masterminding the St. Valentine's Day Massacre that occurred in Chicago on February 14, 1929. The massacre killed seven of Bugs Moran's gang, but did not get Moran as he was not present at the attack (Lindberg, 2016, p. 248; Lunde, 2004b, p. 141; Schoenberg, 1992, pp. 207–216).

Capone had trusted Frankie Yale to assist with his shipments of illegal liquor from New York. After Capone found out that Yale was behind the hijacking on several of those shipments. Capone acted. Frankie Yale was killed in an ambush in Brooklyn, New York, in 1928 (Lunde, 2004b, p. 139; Schoenberg, 1992, pp. 201–203).

At the behest of Masseria in New York, Capone began to oppose the interests of rival Chicago gangster Giuseppe "Joe" Aiello (1891–October 23, 1930), who was on the Castellammarese side of the conflict. After Aiello had made several attempts to kill Capone, Capone arranged for the murder of Aiello in Chicago during the Castellammarese War in 1930 (Lindberg, 2016, p. 230). Masseria was credited with allowing Capone (a Neapolitan and not a Sicilian by ancestry) to join La Cosa Nostra during the Castellammarese War (Newark, 2007b, p. 61).

While most criminals attempted to avoid pubic attention in any form, Capone was flamboyant and enjoyed it. Beshears (2010) found:

> Al Capone who became one of the most notorious crime lords of the 1920's and 1930's, epitomized the Prohibition-era gangster figure. Typically dressed in pinstripe suits, fedoras, and fancy neckties, he served as a model of under- world fashion. Like Capone, many well-known criminals of the time wore sharp suits, hats, and accessories. Other signature items of gangster fashion included

overcoats, spectator shoes, watch fobs, and jewelry. The multitude of photographs and historical documents that depict gangsters sporting these styles supports the notion that fashionable, yet flashy, business-like apparel served as typical gangster garb. While these sartorial elements portrayed gangster as formally, though sometimes ostentatiously, dressed, gangsters' style carries greater significance when examined in its historical context.

(pp. 197–198)

Capone's flashy style and cars spoke of wealth and power to the people of Chicago. That was especially true after the Great Depression began in 1929. During the Depression, Capone set up soup kitchens in Chicago and tried to help some of the poor (Schoenberg, 1992, p. 292). That made him a folk hero with many of the poor who lamented the lack of action by the government to help them. He loved to be photographed and gave interviews to the press. On March 24, 1930, Capone even appeared on the cover of *Time* magazine (Beshears, 2010, p. 201). He was a social bandit who set the model for generations of would-be gangsters to come.

However, trouble was brewing for Capone. In 1927, the U.S. Supreme Court had ruled in *United States v. Sullivan* (1927) that income from illicit traffic in liquor was subject to the income tax, and that the Fifth Amendment did not protect the recipient of such income from prosecution for willful refusal to make any return under the income tax law. Woodiwiss (1987) observed:

Capone became the world's most famous criminal because he was the first of the racket bosses to attract saturation treatment in the press, and not because of his criminal success. In fact, in relative terms Capone was not a success, his power and freedom in Chicago were short-lived. His downfall was a direct result of receiving too much publicity. The federal administration of President Herbert Hoover was committed to a show of effective liquor law enforcement and someone had to pay the price. Capone's national notoriety ensured that only he could fit the bill properly. In 1931 he was convicted of tax evasion, sentenced to eleven years in a federal penitentiary and thus finished as a criminal power.

(p. 8)

Capone served seven years in federal custody and became very ill during his confinement. The FBI (2016) observed:

On November 16, 1939, Al Capone was released after having served seven years, six months and fifteen days, and having paid all fines and back taxes. Suffering from paresis derived from syphilis, he had deteriorated greatly during his confinement. Immediately on release he entered a Baltimore hospital for brain treatment and then went on to his Florida home, an estate on Palm Island in Biscayne Bay near Miami, which he had purchased in 1928.

After Capone was released from prison, he was in such ill health that he retired to his home in Florida, where he died in 1947. Capone's other brother, Ralph "Bottles" Capone Sr. (January 12, 1894–November 22, 1974) remained with the Outfit and became a sort of advisor and spokesman until his death.

Chicago

The Chicago Outfit has remained a force in organized crime since the early 1900s. While gangs and organized crime have always existed in Chicago (Asbury, 1940), the organization that became the Outfit began about 1910 under the leadership of Giacomo "Big Jim" Colosimo (1878–1920), who ruled the group until his murder in 1920. Giovanni "Johnny" Torrio (1882–1957) took over and ruled the Outfit until his retirement in 1925 (Lindberg, 2016, p. 244). Torrio left control of the Outfit to Al Capone, who expanded its reach and scope until 1931 when he was imprisoned. Lunde (2004b) found:

> When Al Capone arrived in Chicago . . . the city was a patchwork of ethnic gangs, battling for territory. Ten years later, when Capone was jailed, the situation had completely changed. After Prohibition was repealed in 1933 the old ethnic gangs vanished, their members absorbed into the Capone organization, the legitimate world, the prison system—or the cemetery. It might be expected that with Capone in Alcatraz, his organization would break up. The press created the false impression that Capone was a criminal mastermind, solely responsible for political corruption and the violence and mayhem on Chicago's streets.
>
> (p. 146)

His prosecutors also thought organized crime in the city would quickly disappear once Capone was incarcerated. In reality, Capone had inherited a very efficient organization from Torrio, and had subsequently transformed it into a diverse and sustainable cooperative. Prohibition had helped create a network linking the Outfit to crime groups in New York, New Jersey, Buffalo, Cleveland, Kansas City, and in Canada and the Caribbean (Lunde, 2004b). Those places were all part of the network of illicit liquor production, smuggling, shipping and trucking, and technology like the automobile, the interstate highway system, the telephone, and the telegraph, had facilitated those contacts and strengthened the web of organized crime.

The Outfit survived the demise of Capone and remained a major criminal presence in Chicago for many years (Lindberg et al., 1997, pp. 8–22). Lavorgna et al. (2013) found:

> In Chicago, the term organized crime has historically referred to the Outfit, the city's traditional organized crime group. Tracing it roots to Prohibition and the Capone Syndicate, the Outfit has played a significant role in Chicago's underworld since the 1920's. The outfit sold narcotics, muscled labor unions, and forced saloon keepers and restaurant owners to install their jukeboxes and pinball machines. They also ran handbooks, dice games, gambling casinos, and brothels. During much of their reign, the Outfit operated with impunity because of its association with the Democratic political machine that controlled Chicago.
>
> (p. 285)

The Chicago Outfit was hit with a significant RICO prosecution by the U.S. Department of Justice in 2005. In 2007, Frank Calabrese Jr., son of Outfit boss Frank Calabrese Sr., turned state's evidence and aided the FBI in what became known as the Family Secrets trial and resulted in the convictions of several Outfit leaders (Calabrese, 2011, pp. 267–283).

The Castellammarese War 1928–1931

The Castellammarese War was over power and money, like most Mafia conflicts. According to Dickie (2004), the Castellammarese War got its name "because one side was dominated by Mafiosi who originated from Castellammare del Golfo" (p. 183). Salvatore Maranzano was from Castellemmare del Golfo in Sicily. This area is west of Palermo, where most of the American Mafioso had ties. Maranzano arrived in the United States in 1927. He was a refugee from Mori's anti-Mafia campaign and the Fascists (Hortis, 2014, p. 79; Dickie, 2004, p. 184). Newark (2007b) observed:

> Maranzano quickly took to the bootlegging business, made money, and came to dominate the Castellammarese clan in Brooklyn and Manhattan. By 1928, Maranzano and his mob were attracting the attention of Giuseppe Masseria, known as Joe the Boss. Masseria was a squat, fat Sicilian who had made his reputation in street shoot-outs in the early 1920's. He too made a fortune out of bootlegging and attracted many of the toughest gangsters of New York. One of them was Charlie "Lucky" Luciano. They concluded a gang alliance over a table groaning with Italian food.
>
> (p. 60)

TABLE 10.1 The Combatants

Pro-Masseria Coalition	Anti-Masseria Coalition
Joseph Masseria family (Manhattan)	**Castellammarese Clan (Central Brooklyn)**
Joe Masseria, boss of bosses 1928–1931	Salvatore Maranzano, boss of bosses 1931
Giuseppe Morello, Masseria consigliere	Joseph Bonanno, Maranzano lieutenant
Joseph Catania	Nichola Schrio, ex-boss of Castellammarese
	Vito Bonventre
1931 cabal in Masseria family	**Castellammarese clan's hit team**
Charles "Lucky" Luciano	Nick Capuzzi
Vito Genovese	Sebastiano "Buster" Domingo
Frank Livorsi	Joe Valachi
Joseph Stracci	
Al Capone "The Outfit" (Chicago)	**Joseph Aielio family (Chicago)**
Chester LaMare faction (Detroit)	**Gaspare Milazzo family (Detroit)**
Joseph Pinzoto family (Bronx/Harlem)	**Reina family faction (Bronx/Harlem)**
Would be successor boss to Reina family	Tom Gaglino
	Tommy Lucchese
Alfred Mineo family (South Brooklyn)	**Joseph Profaci family (Central Brooklyn)**
Steve Ferrigno, lieutenant	
	Stephan Magaddino family (Buffalo)

(Hortis, 2014, p. 76).

There was a good deal of killing on both sides during the Castellammarese War and it was beginning to affect business. In the spring of 1931, Lucky Luciano, from the pro-Masseria coalition, attended a party with Salvatore Maranzano, the leader of the Castellammarese clan. They came to an agreement that in order to end the war, Masseria had to go (Hortis, 2014, p. 85). On April 15, 1931, Luciano invited Masseria to the Nuova Villa Tammaro restaurant for lunch and to play cards. Luciano excused himself to go to the bathroom. Several gunmen including Albert Anastasia, Vito Genovese, Joe Adonis, Bugsy Seigel, and John "Silk Stockings" Giustra entered the restaurant and shot Masseria (Hortis, 2014, pp. 86–87).

The Aftermath of the Castellammarese War

One of the most tangible results of the Castellammarese War was that organized crime in New York became really organized. In May 1931, a Mafia conference meeting was held at the Congress Plaza Hotel in Chicago, Illinois. At that meeting, a Mafia commission of six was proposed. The commission was to be led by an elected boss of bosses. Hortis (2014) cited the research of Gentile (1963) and observed:

> The ambitious Salvatore Maranzano outmaneuvered them. Maranzano cynically cut a deal with the Neapolitan Al Capone, the man whom Maranzano only recently had said was "staining the organization" of the Mafia. In exchange for Capone agreeing to "affirm Maranzano's supremacy in the national scene," he would recognize Capone in Chicago after all. Next, Maranzano cajoled or intimidated the smaller clans. It worked. "Maranzano was thus elected boss of the bosses of the United States Mafia." Explained Gentile.
>
> (pp. 87–88)

There were other implications for both the American and Sicilian Mafia. Varese (2011) discovered:

> The U.S. groups were also becoming autonomous, rescinding any dependency on the Sicilian homeland. By the end of the war that pitted Masseria against Maranzano and led to the death of both leaders in 1931, dual Sicilian and U.S. Mafia membership was forbidden. Furthermore, membership of a Sicilian cosa was no longer a sufficient qualification to join a U.S. family. Buscetta dates the full separation between the two entities at around 1950. Because of the Castellammare War, the families had turned to new sources for recruitment. In order to increase their ranks to fight the war, families started to look beyond Sicilians and, anathema to a Sicilian Mafioso, admitted Neapolitans, the most famous being Joe Valachi, who testified against the Mafia in 1963. Over time, typical new recruits came to be youths of Italian descent who had grown up in the inner-city neighborhoods of New York City. The candidates would be observed for a while and then, if deemed worthy, schooled for full membership. This is a sure sign that the U.S. Mafia had become an autonomous organization.
>
> (p. 123)

Luciano had formed partnerships with Jewish gangsters such as Meyer Lansky and Ben "Bugsy" Siegel. On September 10, 1931, four gangsters (working for Luciano) posing as IRS agents "raided" the New York office of Maranzano and shot him to death (Hortis, 2014, pp. 91–93; Roemer, 1990, pp. 34–35). After the murder of Maranzano, the commission was convened. Hortis (2014) found:

> The Commission, as it became to be called, had seven charter members. Given Gotham's importance, each of the five bosses of the New York families received

Figure 10.7

Meyer Lansky was a major organized crime figure who, along with his associate Charles "Lucky" Luciano, was instrumental in the development of the National Crime Syndicate in the United States.

Library of Congress. New York World-Telegram & Sun Collection (Al Ravenna)

a seat. These included the incumbent bosses Charles Lucino, Tom Gaglino, and Joseph Profaci, and two new bosses from Brooklyn: Vincent Mangano (who replaced a Maranzano loyalist) and Joseph Bonanno (who replaced Maranzano himself). Steve Magaddino of Buffalo got the sixth seat as an influential Castella-mmarese with surprising strength in upstate New York. Al Capone held the seventh seat for Chicago, which also represented by proxy the smaller western clans.

(pp. 96–97)

When Capone was arrested in 1931, his seat on the commission was taken by Paul "The Waiter" Ricca (1897–1972), who was also from Chicago. Ricca assumed control of the Outfit and led it for the next 40 years.

Charles "Lucky" Luciano aka Salvadore Luciana (1897–1962)

Salvadore Luciana was born in the village of Lercara Friddi on the island of Sicily in the Kingdom of Italy on November 24, 1897. His father had been a sulfur miner in Sicily, but in 1906 he moved his family to Manhattan in New York City when Salvadore was nine (Newark, 2010, pp. 11–13; Gosch & Hammer, 1975, p. 3). Young Salvadore attended New York City public schools until he dropped out at the age of 14 after being sent to the Brooklyn Truant School for four months in 1911 (Gosch & Hammer, 1975, pp. 7–8). Luciana became childhood friends with Meyer Lansky. He also began to run with local street gangs. In 1916, Luciana was arrested and convicted of a narcotics violation when he was caught delivering a vial of heroin. Luciana was sentenced to eight months at the New Hampton Farms Reformatory at 18 (Newark, 2010, p. 18; Gosch & Hammer, 1975, p. 16). Luciana became a member of New York's Five Points Gang along with Vito Genovese and Frank Costello (Newark, 2010, p. 19).

In 1920, Luciana went to work for Joe "The Boss" Masseria. By this time Luciana was going by the name of Charles rather than Salvadore. He also began to deal in bootleg liquor with gangster Arnold Rothstein. Luciana became a valued lieutenant for Masseria. In spite of this, Luciana was once again arrested for narcotics in 1923. He avoided a conviction by telling law enforcement where some more drugs and cash were located, but he did not give up any other mobsters (Newark, 2010, pp. 34–35).

In 1929, Luciana was kidnapped on Staten Island and severely beaten by rival mobsters. When questioned by the police, he refused to give any information even though his face had been cut badly. Later, when arrested by the police on suspicion of auto theft, Luciana was forced to appear before a grand jury. He gave his name as Charles Luciano. He used the name Charles "Lucky" Luciano until his death (Newark, 2010, pp. 45–51).

After fighting for the pro-Masseria coalition as one of Masseria's chief lieutenants, Luciano accepted an offer from Maranzano. Newark (2010) observed:

> The Castellammarese War was bad for business and Maranzano let it be known that the best way to end the fighting was for someone to knockoff Masseria. Once that had been completed, he vowed, he would not take vengeance on any of Masseria's gang. It was a temping solution and Luciano visited him in March 1931 to discuss it further. Joseph Bonanno was at the meeting and said it was his first opportunity to see the man he had heard so much about.
>
> (p. 57)

Luciano arranged the ambush that ended the Castellammarese War by killing Joe "The Boss" Masseria in 1931 (along with Albert Anastasia, Vito Genovese, Joe Adonis, and Bugsy Siegel). Later that year, Luciano arranged the murder of Maranzano, thus

Figure 10.8

Lucky Luciano. Charlie "Lucky" Luciano, an Italian mobster born in Sicily. Luciano is considered the father of modern organized crime in the United States. Public domain.

Remo Nassi

clearing the field for Luciano to assume the leadership of the commission with the five Mafia families in New York.

Luciano's reign did not last long. In 1936, Luciano went to prison for promoting prostitution (pandering) in New York City. He was sentenced to 30–50 years after being prosecuted by New York City Prosecutor Thomas Dewey along with several other Mafia defendants (Newark, 2010, pp. 117–129). Luciano continued to run his gang from prison until his appeal was denied in 1938 (Newark, 2010, pp. 136–137). Luciano then turned over the day-to-day operations of his gang to Frank Costello.

During World War II, after instances of alleged sabotage against Allied shipping on the docks of New York, Luciano was approached by officers of U.S. Naval Intelligence in 1942. Luciano aided the Navy in keeping the docks safe and allegedly arranged for aid for the American Army forces that invaded Sicily in 1943. Luciano did not do this out of the goodness of his heart; he provided assistance in exchange for a reduced sentence. In 1946, after World War II had ended, Thomas Dewey, then governor of New York, commuted Luciano's sentence (Newark, 2010, pp. 153–172; Short, 2009, pp. 154–158; Lunde, 2004b, p. 157; Dorgio, 1992, pp. 66–69; Gosch & Hammer, 1975, pp. 276–278). Luciano was released from prison but was immediately deported to Italy.

Although he was not allowed to return to the United States for the remainder of his life, Luciano was still influential with the American Mafia until his death. He died in 1962 in Italy from a heart attack. Luciano's body was allowed to be returned to New York and was interred in the Luciana family mausoleum (Gosch & Hammer, 1975, p. 450).

The American Mafia and Political Corruption

The American Mafia did not invent political corruption. However, political corruption was a key element in the successful expansion of the American Mafia in many American cities. The relationship between various political machines and the mob was often one of mutual benefit. Short (2009) observed that "In America's big cities politics in the nineteenth century was bound up with organized crime: it was organized crime" (p. 132).

The politicians provided protection and the mob got out the vote from the neighborhoods that they considered to be in their territories. They also suppressed any real opposition. Those mutually beneficial arrangements continued well into the twentieth century and involved the Democratic political machines in at least three major American cities (New York, Chicago, and Kansas City). Tammany Hall began in New York as early as 1786, but it was a major force in New York City Democratic politics from about 1850 to 1933. Tammany Hall was infamous for its corruption and involvement with various criminal groups. However, the election of Fiorello La Guardia in 1933 and reform district attorneys like Thomas Dewey spelled the end of Tammany Hall in New York (Lingberg, 2016, p. 41; Short, 2009, pp. 132–148).

In Chicago, it was William Hale Thompson (mayor, 1915–1923 and 1927–1931) who allowed the mobs and gangs to expand in Chicago. He was often condemned as one of the most unethical mayors in the United States. Thompson was voted out in 1931 by Anton Cermak in an election defeat that has been described as a landslide. In contrast to Tammany Hall and the Pendergast Machine, Thompson was a Republican. He also had the distinction of being the last Republican Mayor of Chicago as of 2016 (Lindberg, 2016, pp. 92–96).

In Kansas City, Thomas Joseph Pendergast ran the Democratic political machine in Kansas City and Jackson County, Missouri, from 1925 to 1939. He maintained open alliances with known criminals and wielded his political power like a monarch. He envisioned Kansas City as a "wide open" town with every vice imaginable available. The effects of the political corruption of Pendergast on the Kansas City crime family was described by Ouseley (2011):

From 1928, when John Lazia seized by force the political machinery of the North End, the city was doomed to suffer under an alliance forged between him and political boss Thomas J. Pendergast. In that era, the mob was above the law, brazenly displaying its political clout, dealing directly with politicians and public officials and openly running its rackets. Enforcers were put to work shaking down gamblers, pimps, bootleggers, drug dealers, fences and the like, generating millions of dollars in revenue that financed the corrupt Pendergast machine and filled the coffers of organized crime. The Outfit manufactured thousands of ghost voters and generated large blocks of votes through violence and intimidation at the polls, using every tactic imaginable to rig-elections. In return it was protected, free to operate openly, with free access to public officials and the Police Department.

(pp. 35–36)

In 1939, Pendergast was convicted of failing to pay income tax on bribes he received to pay gambling debts. Pendergast also was involved in other insurance frauds and criminal activities (*United States v. Pendergast*, 1941).

Las Vegas and the Mob

Nevada legalized casino-style gambling in 1931. Several casinos that had no affiliation with organized crime or the mob had begun to locate in Las Vegas (such as the El Rancho and the Last Frontier) on an area of Highway 91 that became known as "The Strip" (Dorigo, 1992, p. 84). Capeci (2004) noted that there were other factors that combined to make Las Vegas an attractive location and observed:

Besides the legalization of gambling, Las Vegas received three other huge boosts starting in 1931—an abundance of jobs, water and electricity—courtesy of the gigantic Hoover Dam. Nevada also simplified its divorce laws that same year. Unhappy spouses from California and elsewhere would set up shop in Las Vegas and Reno for the required six-week waiting period. Not surprisingly, they filled some of their spare time by doing a little gambling.

(p. 164)

The mob got a foothold in Las Vegas when Benjamin "Bugsy" Siegel (1906–1947) decided to build a casino there in 1944–1945. Siegel was a long time Jewish mobster and associate of Meyer Lansky. Siegel had been involved in the Bugs and Meyer mob, Murder, Inc., and now was associated with the Genovese family. Siegel had been a bootlegger and occasional drug dealer, but he was mainly known as a mob hit man. At the direction of Lucky Luciano, Siegel had been involved in the killing of both Joe "The Boss" Masseria and Salvadore Maranzano that ended the Castellammarese War (Dorigo, 1992, pp. 34–35; Jennings, 1967, pp. 29–34).

Figure 10.9

Las Vegas. "Welcome to Las Vegas" sign with sunset sky.

iStock.com/trekandshoot

Siegel moved to the Los Angeles area in the late 1930s, financed by Luciano, and began to work in the local and prostitution markets there (Jennings, 1967, pp. 35–36). He began to circulate socially in the Hollywood movie industry crowd. In 1945, Siegel bought into a Las Vegas casino called the El Cortez and sold his interest for a profit of $160,000 in 1946 (Dorigo, 1992, p. 84).

In 1944, Siegel bought a failed motel in Las Vegas on Highway 91 called Folsom's Guest Cottages. He arranged for the closed motel to be torn down, and in 1945 the Flamingo Club arose in its place. This project was financed with mob money from New York. Fischer (2007) found that among the original 13 investors listed on the paperwork for the Nevada Projects Corporation that was building the Flamingo Club, at least four had major mob connections (Siegel, Louis Pokross who was acting for 15 New York mobsters, Morris Rosen acting as a front for Frank Costello, and Meyer Lansky). The construction of the Flamingo Club was essentially financed by the Genovese family of New York (Fischer, 2007, pp. 9–10).

Siegel might have been a good gangster, but he was not a talented businessman. The construction of the Flamingo Club took longer than expected and went way over budget. When the casino finally did open, it began to lose money and even closed for 60 days between January and March 1947. On June 20, 1947, Benjamin "Bugsy" Siegel was murdered in his girlfriend's Beverly Hills home (Short, 2009, pp. 106–107; Roemer, 1990, pp. 44–51). Mo Sedway (an associate of Lansky) was one of the three men who took over the Flamingo. According to several sources, the decision to kill Siegel came after a Mafia summit that was held in Havana, Cuba, on December 25, 1946. Attending this meeting were representatives from the Five Families in New York including Anastasia, Bonanno, Costello, Lansky, Lucchese, and Luciano, among others (Fischer, 2007, pp. 25–38; Roemer, 1990, pp. 48–49).

The murder of Siegel was never solved. There were of course political repercussions (albeit somewhat temporary ones). Jennings (1967) observed that

> in Nevada the political leaders suddenly saw the Siegel murder as a threat to their growing gold mine—the gambling business that supplied the cash they couldn't get in taxes or any other way from the state's meager population, then about 140,000. It was not just the killing that made them uneasy. It was the sudden realization that the big money was coming from the underworld, that they knew very little about the hoodlums in their midst, and any homicidal thug like Siegel could get a gambling license by applying to city authorities.
>
> (p. 224)

Noting that in the early 1950s the Mafia had begun to formulate rules about mob conduct in Las Vegas, Short (2009) stated:

> The Mafia's National Commission bans killings in Las Vegas because they scare off gamblers and could upset the cozy relationship which exists between organized crime and the local authorities.
>
> (p. 46)

The New York Mafia and the Chicago Outfit began to invest in other casinos in Las Vegas. The mob became involved in the Thunderbird, the Sahara Hotel, the Stardust Hotel, the Tropicana, and the Riviera. Many casinos and hotels were financed by money provided by loans from labor unions that were controlled by the mob (Fischer, 2007, pp. 135–142; Roemer, 1990, pp. 60–61). In the casinos that the mob had invested in or controlled, money was skimmed from gambling winnings and never reported to the State of Nevada or the Internal Revenue Service. The mob also used the casinos to launder money from some of their other illegal enterprises (Fischer, 2007, pp. 175–184). In spite of a short resurgence from the mid-1960s to the 1970s, the mob's involvement in

Las Vegas diminished significantly as a result of government investigations and competition by legitimate businessmen such as Howard Hughes (Short, 2009, pp. 303–304; Dorigo, 1992, pp. 98–99; Roemer, 1990, p. 262).

Fulgencio Batista, Cuba, and the Mob

Fulgencio Batista Zaldívar (1901–1973) was a sergeant in the Cuban army when he led the Revolt of the Sergeants in 1933 that overthrew the government of President Geraldo Machado and caused Machado to flee to Miami. As a reward, Batista became a colonel in the Cuban Army and was appointed as head of the Cuban Armed Forces. In 1937, the Cuban government turned over Cuba's gambling establishments to military control. Bastista wanted gambling to be a stable income source for the government, and he hired an American, Lou Smith, to run things for him. Smith had been a successful dog and horse track operator, but he was not a very good casino manager. Smith recommended his friend Meyer Lansky. According to Lacey (1991):

> In 1938, Meyer Lansky took his gambling services to Cuba. Fulgencio Batista, the handsome young sergeant who had made himself the strongman of Cuban politics five years earlier, wanted to boost the country's gaming revenues. Before the Depression, Havana's two casinos that were associated with Oriental Park, the city's racetrack, had been meccas for rich American winter visitors. But now both the track and the casinos were doing badly, and it was Meyer Lansky's job to help put them straight.
>
> (p. 108)

Lansky was very good at what he had been assigned to do, and thus a profitable mutual relationship was formed between the Mafia and Batista that was fueled with generous bribes and only grew stronger as Batista's personal power rose. Batista was the elected president of Cuba from 1940 to 1944. He then led a military coup that returned him to the presidency from 1952 to 1959 (Lacey, 1991, p. 223; Dorigo, 1992, pp. 88–89). The Mafia controlled the gambling, drug trade, and prostitution in Cuba during this period. Short (2009) observed:

> By the 1950's every major American syndicate boss had a piece of Cuban gambling, courtesy of Meyer Lansky. His brother Jake worked as a pit boss at the Nacional, minding Meyer's interests. Improved air travel opened up the island to far more gamblers and organized crime's offshore profits soared.
>
> (p. 193)

The Mafia felt secure enough in the safety and political protection of Cuba that they sometimes held their national commission meetings in Havana (Fischer, 2007, pp. 25–38; Roemer, 1990, pp. 48–49). In February 1947, Luciano had attempted to move to Havana from Italy, where he had been deported, but this was short-lived. Luciano was arrested by Cuban authorities at the request of the U.S. Federal Bureau of Narcotics in March 1947 and deported (Lacey, 1991, p. 172). All of this came crashing down in 1959 when Fidel Castro overthrew the Batista government and the Communists took over Cuba. Lansky and the other Mafia members were expelled from Cuba and it cost them millions in investments and lost revenues (Lacey, 1991, pp. 252–254). That has often been cited as the reason that Mafia members were willing to work with the CIA in various unsuccessful plots to assassinate Castro (Short, 2009, p. 117; Raab, 2006, pp. 144–145; Dorigo, 1992, pp. 90–91).

Rats, Snitches, and the End of Omerta

Law enforcement officers and prosecutors for years had a very difficult time obtaining convictions against Mafia members. Witnesses became blind or forgetful, or simply disappeared. The Mafia members themselves largely adhered to a Mafia code of conduct known as Omerta that demanded silence about the family's affairs. Violators were severely sanctioned, usually by death. Looking at the example of Edward J. O'Hare, Lindberg (2016) found that:

> Federal informant O'Hare, who managed Capone's dog-racing track and Sportsman's Park in Cicero, paid with his life. On November 8, 1939, at the end of a normal business day, O'Hare motored south down Ogden Avenue from Sportsman's Park when his vehicle was overtaken by Capone gunmen. O'Hare was killed in the ambush. It was later revealed that he had agreed to inform on the Capone mob, knowing full well of the dangers because he needed a governmental recommendation that would allow his son to attend the Naval Academy at Annapolis, Maryland. That was the price of his heroism.
>
> (p. 253)

In 1950–1951, Senator Estes Kefauver (D-Tenn.) led the U.S. Senate Special Committee to Investigate Crime in Interstate Commerce. The hearings by this committee were held in 14 cities and had hundreds of witnesses. The Kefauver hearings were televised and became very popular television viewing for the American public. Even threatened by jail sentences for contempt of Congress, mob leader after mob leader steadfastly refused to answer questions, citing their Fifth Amendment rights (Short, 2009, pp. 182–183; Lunde, 2004b, p. 162; Lacey, 1991, pp. 190–201).

The solid wall of Mafia member silence was broken in 1963 by Joseph Valachi (1904–1971). Short (2009) described Valachi's defection, saying:

> The first Mafioso to turn public informer and betray the true structure of the Mafia in America was Joseph Valachi, a thirty-year veteran of organized crime. Serving twenty years for narcotics in Atlanta Penitentiary, he became convinced that his Mafia boss, Vito Genovese, had given him the kiss of death. Genovese, who by this time was also in Atlanta for a narcotics offense, ordered another inmate to kill him. Valachi mistook another prisoner for his would-be assassin and clubbed him to death. When he realized he had killed the wrong man he became so consumed with fear and remorse that he turned government witness and informed on the Mafia. Ironically it was only because Genovese wrongly believed Valachi to be an informer that he decided to have him killed. That at least was Valachi's story.
>
> (pp. 36–37)

Valachi became the first in a long line of Mafia members who would turn state's witness to save their own lives or reduce their criminal charges. In 1980, Lucchese family member Henry Hill turned state's evidence (Pileggi, 1985, pp. 247–251). In 1990, Chicago Outfit gangster James LaValley began cooperating with FBI agents (Lindberg et al., 1997, p. 17). It wasn't just Mafia soldiers that began to talk: Lucchese crime family underboss Alfonso "Little Al" D'Arco turned FBI informant in 1991 (Capeci & Robins, 2015, p. 419), and in 1992 Gambino family underboss Salvatore "Sammy the Bull" Gravano turned state's evidence (Capeci, 2004, pp. 267–270; Davis, 1993a, p. 2). Using mob informants quickly became one of the FBI's most effective tactics.

The Pizza Connection

The Pizza Connection was a plot that occurred between 1975 and 1984 to smuggle heroin and cocaine into the United States. Participants included members of the Bonanno crime family and the Sicilian Mafia including deposed Sicilian Mafia leader Gaetano Badalamenti. Drugs were smuggled into the United States and dealt thru a number of pizza restaurants controlled by the Bonanno crime family. The pizza restaurants were not only used to deal drugs but also to launder money for the Mafia. The arrests of the Mafia suspects involved an extensive investigation by the FBI, DEA, U.S. Customs, and European law enforcement authorities including famed Italian lawman Giovanni Falcone. Sicilian Mafia informer Tommaso Buscetta testified as a government witness at trials in the United States and Italy. The trials began in September 1985 and did not end until March 1987. Twenty-one Mafia defendants were convicted (Lunde, 2004b, p. 170; Blumenthal, 1988).

John J. Gotti Jr., the "Teflon Don" (1940–2002)

John Gotti was born on October 27, 1940, in the South Bronx. He dropped out of school at 16. Gotti began his criminal career in a local street gang and worked his way into a position inside the Gambino family after several years (Dorigo, 1992, p. 102). Gotti took over the Gambino family after the death of Castellano in 1985. Allegedly, Gotti and Gravano were in another car watching when Castellano was murdered (Cimino, 2014a, p. 14).

In his examination of Gotti, Zion (1994) stated:

> Soon after the assassination of Paul Castellano, John Gotti, who is said to have ordered the hit, was installed as the new boss of New York's Gambino family. Federal prosecutors considered him a tempting target. Gotti was a twice-jailed felon (for hijacking in his younger days and for participating in a 1973 murder to avenge the death of old man Carlo's nephew); a third conviction would result in serious time. But the wise guy from Howard Beach, Queens, had a long history of making people whom he didn't like to disappear. In addition to rival gangsters, these included a neighbor who in 1990 had been unable to brake in time when Gotti's 12-year-old son, Frank, darted out into the street on his bike; according to mob informers, that hapless soul was chainsawed to death. But making even a single charge to stick was another matter, thanks to the lawyerly skills of Bruce Cutler. Indeed, by indicting Gotti twice in four years—and losing both times—the government inadvertently turned him into a perverse folk hero.
> (p. 140)

Gotti was called the "Dapper Don" because of his fancy dress and sense of style. Gotti did not shy away from the press and was often photographed. He was later called the "Teflon Don" because although he was charged with several criminal offenses, no charges would stick. Davis (1993a) observed:

> While he was active in the middle to late 1980's, John Gotti epitomized the traditional Italian Mafia more than any of his contemporaries in organized crime. Here was a boss with swagger and style and panache who actually did wield considerable power. With his partner in crime, Sammy the Bull Gravano, he controlled the concrete industry in New York; and through his capos in private garbage carting, the garment district, and the Brooklyn waterfront, he exerted

Figure 10.10

John Gotti Jr. and company. An FBI surveillance photo of suspected mobsters Thomas (Tommy Sneakers) Cacciopoli, John (Junior) Gotti and John Cavallo. Public domain.

Uploaded by TUBS, CC BY-SA 3.0 (https://creativecommons.org/licenses/by-sa/3.0)], via Wikimedia Commons

considerable influence on those industries as well. But, above all, he was the disciple of Anastasia's gunman Dellacroce, was perhaps the last of the dons to believe passionately in the codes and goals and rituals of the 120-year-old criminal brotherhood that sprung up in nineteenth century southern Italy and was so successfully transplanted in most of the major cities of the United States.

(pp. 485–486)

After his underboss, Salvatore "Sammy the Bull" Gravano, turned state's evidence and testified against him, Gotti was convicted in 1992 of RICO and several other offenses including involvement in several murders. He died in federal custody in 2002 (Cimino, 2014a, pp. 12–17; Lunde, 2004b, p. 170; Blum, 1993, pp. 325–333).

American Mafia Organization and Criminality

The American Mafia or La Cosa Nostra developed a patriarchal and hierarchical organizational structure that was similar to their Sicilian cousins. The basic unit was the crime family and those families were primarily located in cities within the United States. Typically, the family consisted of about 25 to 100 "made men" and a much larger number of "associates" who perform work for the family in various criminal enterprises.

While not monolithic, the American Mafia is a multibillion-dollar criminal enterprise. Common crimes of the American Mafia include drug trafficking, human trafficking, weapons trafficking, gambling, money laundering, political corruption, labor union racketeering, cargo theft and hijacking, stock manipulation, fraud (including healthcare and insurance fraud), bid rigging (especially construction, concrete, trash services, etc.), extortion, fencing, and auto theft (Lindberg et al., 1997, pp. 10–13; Smith, 2009). American Mafia allies include Albanian organized crime, Russian organized crime, the yakuza, Colombian cartels, Mexican cartels, triads, and tongs.

Where La Cosa Nostra Operates

American Mafia families have been reported in Buffalo, New York (Magaddino family); Chicago, Illinois (the Outfit); Cleveland, Ohio (Cleveland crime family aka Licavoli family aka Mayfield Road Mob); Dallas, Texas (Dallas crime family 1921–1990); Denver, Colorado (Colorado crime family aka Smaldone family 1910s–2006); Detroit, Michigan (Detroit crime family aka Detroit Partnership aka Zerilli family); Kansas City, Missouri (Kansas City crime family aka Civella family); Los Angeles, California (Los Angeles crime family); Milwaukee, Wisconsin (Milwaukee crime family aka Balistireri family); New England (Boston, Massachusetts; Providence, Rhode Island; Connecticut; New Hampshire; and Maine) (Patriarca family aka New England crime family aka Boston crime family aka Providence crime family aka the Office); New Jersey (DeCavalcante crime family); New York City, New York (the Five Families: Bonanno family, Colombo family, Gambino family, Genovese family, and Lucchese family); New Orleans, Louisiana (New Orleans crime family aka Dixie Mafia, formerly Matranga family and Marcello family); Northeastern Pennsylvania (Bufalino family aka Pittston family aka Scranton Wilkes-Barre family 1900–2008); Philadelphia, Pennsylvania (Philadelphia crime family aka Philadelphia Mafia); Pittsburgh, Pennsylvania (Pittsburgh crime family aka LaRocca family); Rochester, New York (Rochester crime family 1950s–1993); San Francisco, California (San Francisco crime family aka Lanza family 1928–2006); San Jose, California (San Jose crime family aka Cerrito family 1900s–2009); St. Louis, Missouri (St. Louis crime family aka Giordano family); and Tampa, Florida (Trafficante family aka Tampa Mafia) (FBI, 2015a).

Camorra or Neapolitan Mafia (based in Naples, Italy)

The word *camorra* means "gang." The Camorra first appeared in the mid-1800s in Naples, Italy, as a prison gang. Once released from prison, members formed clans in the cities and continued to grow in power. Lunde (2004a) found:

> The Camorra is a crime group based in Naples. Evidence that it is highly structured dates back to 1820, when police found documents on its policies and initiation rites. The Camorra originally controlled the city's prisons, collecting a tax from prisoners as well as a fee from the authorities for keeping order. They also organized gambling and theft in Naples and took a 10 percent cut on all cargo arriving on the docks.

The Camorra was a big part of controlling Naples during the campaign for Italian unification in 1860. One member of the Camorra was even made chief of police (Lunde, 2004a). However, after the government arrested many Camorra members near the end of the nineteenth century, the Camorra's involvement in politics was limited to guaranteeing votes for the Liberal Party. Some *camorristi* emigrated during that time, and several founded a Camorra branch in Brooklyn, New York (Lunde, 2004a).

The Camorra has more than 100 clans and approximately 7,000 members, making it the largest of the Italian organized crime groups (Lavorgna et al., 2013, p. 269). Matthews (2014) found that the Camorra was the most successful among the traditional Italian organized criminal groups and stated that the

> Camorra is the most successful of these groups, raking in an estimated $4.9 billion per year on everything from "sexual exploitation, firearms trafficking, drugs, counterfeiting, gambling . . . usury and extortion . . ." And Camorra has been at it a long time. Based in Naples, the groups history dates back to the 19th century, when it was formed initially as a prison gang. As members were released, the group flourished during the bloody political struggles in Italy during the 1800's by offering protection services and as a force for political organization among Italy's poor.

One of the primary ways that the Camorra makes money is cigarette smuggling. The Camorra receives payoffs from other criminal groups for any cigarette traffic through Italy. In the 1970s, the Sicilian Mafia convinced the Camorra to convert their cigarette smuggling routes into drug smuggling routes with the Sicilian Mafia's assistance. Not all Camorra leaders agreed, leading to the Camorra Wars that cost

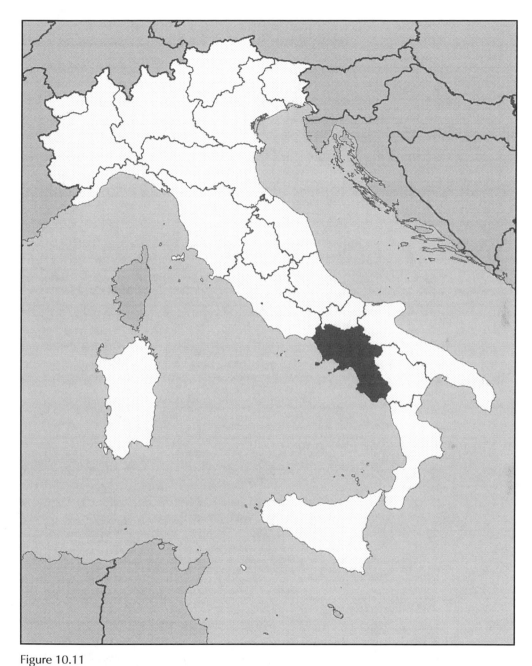

Figure 10.11

The Camorra has its roots in the Italian region of Campania. The Camorra is one of the oldest and largest criminal organizations in Italy, dating back to the seventeenth century.

400 lives. Opponents of drug trafficking lost the war (FBI, 2015a). Sterling (1994) found:

> The Camorra's contraband tobacco moves through an elaborate circuit from Switzerland, Belgium, and Holland (manufacturing states) to Hungary, Romania, Bulgaria and Turkey (storage depots) to Yugoslavia and Albania (staging areas for the final run across the Adriatic into Italy). This circuit in reverse constitutes the famous Balkan route. The biggest two-way trade in arms and drugs ever uncovered has depended on it since the 1960's. Three-quarters of the heroin reaching Western Europe and a substantial portion of America's travels along it.
> (p. 83)

In 2004 and 2005 a conflict broke out between rival Camorra clans over control of the drug and prostitution trade in the Naples area. Sometimes called the Secondigliano War and sometimes called the Scampia Feud, the conflict resulted in several deaths among various Camorra members. However, after the death of an innocent civilian, the Italian government cracked down hard and several Camorra leaders were either arrested or fled the country (Saviano, 2006, pp. 60–135).

Along with cigarette smuggling and drug trafficking, other primary Camorra crimes include money laundering, extortion, human trafficking, robbery, blackmail, kidnapping, political corruption, and counterfeiting. The Camorra are allied with other Italian organized criminal groups, Albanian organized crime, and Russian organized crime.

Where the Camorra Operates

The Camorra has been reported in Italy, France, the United Kingdom, and the United States. According to the FBI (2015a), it is believed that nearly 200 Camorra affiliates reside in this country, many of whom arrived during the Camorra Wars.

'Ndrangheta or Calabrian Mafia (Based in Calabria, Italy)

Varese (2011) found the word 'Ndrangheta was first recorded in 1909 (p. 31). In their study of Italian organized crime, the FBI (2015a) reported:

> The word "'Ndrangheta" comes from the Greek meaning courage or loyalty. The 'Ndrangheta formed in the 1860s when a group of Sicilians was banished from the island by the Italian government. They settled in Calabria and formed small criminal groups.

However, Lunde (2004a) found:

The 'Ndrangheta originated in the late 19th century. Its precursor was Calabrian banditry. When the railroad between Reggio di Calabria and Eboli was built in the 1880's, the government waged a major offensive against the bandits in the Aspromonte Mountains. The criminals were displaced to the towns and cities. By 1900, family-based criminal gangs were active in many Calabrian towns. They were the nuclei of the 'Ndrangheta, now the largest and most violent of Italian criminal associations.

(p. 76)

In the 'Ndrangheta that extended family or clan forms a basic unit called a *'ndrina*. 'Ndrina comes a Greek word meaning a man who does not bend (Lunde, 2004a, p. 76; Varese, 2011, p. 31; Lavorgna et al., 2013, p. 269). In his examination of the organization of the 'Ndrangheta, Varese (2011) found:

Each 'ndrina is autonomous on its territory and no authority stands above the 'ndrina boss. The 'ndrina is usually in control of a small town or neighborhood. If more than one 'ndrina operate in the same town, they form a locale. In some cases, sotto 'ndrine have been established. A rather elaborate internal structure is shared by most 'ndrine, and includes the boss and six lower ranks. Each rank could be further differentiated into further internal ranks.

(pp. 31–32)

The FBI (2015a) stated: "There are about 160 'Ndrangheta cells with roughly 6,000 members. Cells are loosely connected family groups based on blood relationships and marriages."

The FBI (2015a) claims that in the United States, there are an estimated 100–200 'Ndrangheta members and associates, primarily in New York and Florida. The 'Ndrangheta specialize in kidnapping and political corruption, but also engage in drug trafficking (cocaine), murder, bombings, counterfeiting, gambling, frauds, thefts, labor racketeering, loan-sharking, and alien smuggling (FBI, 2015a). Noting the 'Ndrangheta's extensive involvement in Italian cocaine trafficking, arm trafficking, prostitution and extortion, Squires (2010) reported:

For decades, the 'Ndrangheta has been based in the southern region of Calabria, in the toe of the Italian boot, but has in recent years thrived on cocaine trafficking and spread its tentacles to northern Europe, the United States, South America and Australia. It has also established a formidable presence in northern Italy, laundering its dirty money and investing in ostensibly legitimate enterprises such as hotels, restaurants, supermarkets, and even the healthcare sector.

In describing the extent of the involvement of the 'Ndrangheta in the overall Italian economy, Blundell (2013) reported that the 'Ndrangheta was adept in investing in legitimate Italian businesses to shield or facilitate its criminal enterprises. He noted that the 'Ndrangheta was invested in Italian banks, malls, building firms, supermarkets, and clubs across Italy. Blundell (2013) stated that:

> If you are Italian, you can avoid the organization only if you give up food, booze, cigarettes, clothes, travel, drugs, porn, betting, share-trading and renting a flat because it has interests in every aspect of daily life.

Matthews (2014) noted the success of the 'Ndrangheta and estimated their annual income at over $4.5 billion, stating:

> Based in the Calabria region of Italy, the 'Ndrangheta is the country's second largest mafia group by revenue. While it is involved in many of the same illicit activities as Camorra, 'Ndranga has made its name for itself by building international ties with South American cocaine dealers, and it controls much of the transatlantic drug market that feeds Europe. It has also been expanding its operations in the U.S. and has helped prop up the Gambino and Bonanno crime families in New York. In February (2014), Italian and American police forces arrested dozens of 'Ndranga and Gambino family members and charged them with crimes related to the transatlantic drug trade.

The *National Post* (2015) found that the 'Ndrangheta were attracted to Canada by the secrecy of Canadian banking laws and the opportunity to smuggle drugs into the United States and Canada, observing:

> The 'Ndrangheta's presence in Canada is long and storied. It has been here since at least the 1950s, with its Canadian branch labelled the "Siderno Group" because its members primarily came from the Ionian coastal town of Siderno in Calabria. Siderno is also home to one of the 'Ndrangheta's biggest and most important clans, heavily involved in the global cocaine business and money laundering.

Allies of the 'Ndrangheta include Albanian organized crime, Colombian drug cartels, Camorra, Mexican drug cartels, and the Sicilian Mafia.

Where the 'Ndrangheta Operates

The 'Ndrangheta has been reported in Argentina, Australia, Belgium, Canada, Colombia, Italy, Germany, Mexico, the Netherlands, the United Kingdom, and the United States.

Sacra Corona Unita or United Sacred Crown (Based in the Puglia Region, Italy)

The Sacra Corona Unita (SCU) was formed on Christmas Day 1981 in Bari prison (Italy) by Giuseppe Rogoli to block the Camorra gang (DeDonto, Santoro, Rossi, Grattagliano, & Introna, 2009, p. 895; Lunde, 2004a, p. 77). The group has adopted a parochial and hierarchical organizational structure consisting of 15 unique ranks. Unlike other Italian organized crime groups, the members of Sacra Corona Unita often bear tattoos indicating their rank and position within the criminal organization (DeDonto et al., 2009, p. 896).

The Sacra Corona Unita members use ritualism to initiate new members. DeDonto et al. (2009) found:

> A solemn oath binds each members to the others: during the swearing-in ceremony a fellow member binds the new member's index finger with a thread and pricks it, splattering a few drops of blood on a holy picture (generally St. Michael the Archangel), that is indissoluble bond between the new member and his fellows, the blood bears witness that he is ready to give his life for the others, the holy image is society itself, and the scattered ashes shows that in the same way as the picture cannot be pieced together, so the member cannot recede or fail in the obligations that he has taken on.
>
> (p. 895)

DeDonto et al. (2009) observed that the oath taken by new SCU members consisted of four promises of loyalty and fidelity to the SCU. The oath states:

> I swear by the point of this bloody dagger to be faithful to this body of society made up of active, free, frank, and forthright men, and to all the rules and social prescriptions.
>
> I swear to abjure father, mother, brothers, and sisters, up to the seventh generation.
>
> I swear to share cent by cent, thousandth by thousandth as our elder founders shared: the Count of Ugolino, Herald of Russia, and Knight of Spain who bore a dagger in the right hand that cut and slashed skin, flesh and bone up to the last drop of blood.
>
> I swear to put one foot in the grave and the other in chains to embrace jail.
>
> (p. 896)

The rituals are made as elaborate as possible to impress upon the initiate the seriousness of what they are swearing allegiance to. DeDonto et al. (2009) observed:

Sometime the ritual is enriched by other symbols: the pin used to prick the finger, named the armour; the picture of St. Michael the Archangel; white silk handker-chiefs symbolizing the purity of the soul of the new adept; the booty consisting of a few cigarettes representing the gains of the society to be shared out fairly; a pill for committing suicide if the member betrays faith with his companions; a gun symbolizing an exemplary punishment of unfaithful members; a lemon to "heal the wounds of the wise companions"; and a puff of cotton wool that, according to the most accredited tradition represents the Monte Blanco, considered as a holy place.

(p. 895)

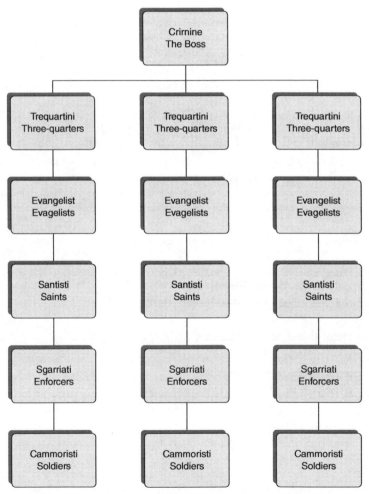

Figure 10.12

Organization of the Sacra Carona Unita.

Lunde (2004a, p. 75)

According to the FBI (2015a), the Sacra Corona Unita is headquartered in Brindisi, located in the southeastern region of Puglia in Italy. The FBI states that the Sacra Corona Unita consists of about 50 clans with approximately 2,000 members. Although very few Sacra Corona Unita members have been identified in the United States, some individuals in Illinois, Florida, and New York have links to the organization.

In examining the criminal activities of the SCU, the FBI (2015a) reported:

> The Sacra Corona Unita specializes in smuggling cigarettes, drugs, arms, and people. it is also involved in money laundering, extortion, and political corruption. The organization collects payoffs from other criminal groups for landing rights on the southeast coast of Italy, a natural gateway for smuggling to and from post-Communist countries like Croatia, Yugoslavia, and Albania.

Where the Sacra Corona Unita Operates

The Sacra Corona Unita primarily operates in Italy and the Balkans. However, some members have been reported in the United States. The Sacra Carona Unita is allied with Albanian organized crime, Chinese triads, Colombian drug cartels, the Russian Mafia, Sicilian Mafia, and the yakuza.

Summary

As can be seen, Italian organized crime is made up of numerous, often competing criminal organizations. It is not the monolithic "Mafia" as portrayed in the media. However, these independent Italian organized criminal groups have managed to survive for often hundreds of years. They are a distinct phenomenon in the study of organized criminal organizations.

DISCUSSION QUESTIONS

1. Explain why and how the Mafia in Italian organized crime is not just one organization.
2. Explain the crimes that Italian organized crime is involved in.
3. Explain how and why the American Mafia separated from the Sicilian Mafia.
4. Describe the effect the effects of transnational crime on Italian organized crime.

CHAPTER 11 Russian and Other European Organized Crime

Introduction

There have always been organized crime groups in Russia. Chalidze (1977) found that "In previous centuries the Russian word *vor*, which now means 'thief' was a generic term for a criminal or foreign enemy. *Tat* was the word for thief" (p. 4).

The Russian usage of *vor*, meaning "thief" and being a public criminal outcast, was documented by Baldaev, Vasiliev, and Sidorov (2014). They found that the Russian practice of branding criminals was a prototype of the modern criminal tattoo. Until about 1846, criminals were branded *VOR* (thief) if they were sentenced to hard labor. The marking was typically done as a tattoo, and allowed any citizen to recognize a convicted criminal, even after they had served their time.

Brands were often applied to either the cheeks and forehead or to shoulder blades and the right forearm. There were three types of brands: the letters SK (SsylnoKatorzhny: hard labor convict); SP (SsylnoPoselenets: hard labor deportee); and B (Begly: escapee).

If they were repeat offenders, a new brand was applied below the previous one. In 1846, when the Decree on Punishments came into effect, the brand *VOR* was replaced with *KAT*, the first three letters of the word for hard labor convict: *katorzhnik*.

Specifically, Baldaev et al. (2014) found:

> The letter *K* was applied to the right cheek, *A* to the forehead, and *T* to the left cheek. Since that date, the word *kat* has come to mean a scoundrel for whom nothing is sacred. The decree remained in effect up until 1863. These lifelong marks on the body and face of hard labour convicts can be considered the earliest symbols of membership in the world of outcasts: the first criminal tattoos. Though forcibly applied, they never the less began to function as caste markings.
>
> (p. 21)

The pervasiveness of theft in Russia was demonstrated when Chalidze (1977) observed that Tsar Nicholas I was reported by a Russian newspaper to have told his son during the Crimean War (1853–1856): "I believe you and I are the only people in

Figure 11.1

The Russian police are responsible for investigating organized crime in Russia.

iStock.com/olegkozyrev

Russia who don't steal" (p. 28). Although there have always been criminals in Russia, the Russian Mafia developed as a prison gang during Soviet times and thus adopted a unique criminal culture. Developing in the Soviet gulag system, Russian organized crime adopted a patriarchal and hierarchical organizational structure. Unlike prison gangs in the United States, which developed along ethnic and racial lines, prison gangs in the former Soviet Union developed their own unique cultural view of their "thieves' world" in spite of the wide diversity of indigenous populations in the former USSR. According to Finckenauer and Voronin (2001):

> Ethnicity did not play the significant role in Soviet organized crime that it played in the United States. Instead, the Soviet prison system, in many ways, fulfilled the functions that were satisfied by shared ethnicity in the United States. In the Soviet Union, a professional criminal class developed in Soviet prisons during the Stalinist period that began in 1924—the era of the gulag. These criminals adopted behaviors, rules, values and sanctions that bound them together in what was called the thieves world, led by the elite "vory v zakone," criminals who lived according to the "thieves' law." This thieves' world, and particularly the vory, created and maintained the bonds and climate of trust necessary for carrying out organized crime.

Starting as a prison gang, the Russian Mafia became very fond of tattoos. Like the Japanese yakuza, many if not most members of the Russian Mafia have tattoos. The tattoos are an expression of the member's acceptance and adherence to the code of the thieves' world (Baldaev, Vasiliev, & Plutser-Sarno, 2006, p. 35). The tattoos can show the offense committed, number of times incarcerated, or the length of incarceration. Nicknames and affiliations with their clan or group may also be present. The Canadian Customs Service developed an excellent guide to Russian Mafia tattoos (Radanko, 2011, p. 271; Baldaev et al., 2009; Lambert, 2003, p. 4; Finckenauer & Waring, 1998, pp. 102–103; Chalidze, 1977, pp. 66–67). In addition to the numerous tattoos, the vor often spoke a language of their own called *fenya* (Varese, 2001, p. 146).

According to Finckenauer and Waring (1998) the vor society that developed in the Soviet prisons adopted a Thieves Code that forbade cooperation in any way with the state and included:

- The vor is expected to turn his back on his birth family and to have no family of his own except for the criminal community that is his family.

- The vor is forbidden to work and must live only by criminal activity.

- The vor must give moral and material assistance to other thieves.

- The vor must recruit and teach his craft to the young.

- The vor must limit his drinking and gambling. Becoming drunk or being unable to pay gambling debts is prohibited.

- The vor must not become involved with the authorities, participate in social activities, or join social organizations.

- The vor must not take up weapons on behalf of the authorities or serve in the military.

- The vor must abide by and carry out punishments determined by the thieves' meeting (a combination dispute resolution and court forum)

- The vor must fulfill all promises made to other thieves (p. 105).

The prohibition of the Thieves Code against aiding the authorities and taking up weapons for them was absolute (Chalidze, 1977, p. 49). Freidman (2000) observed that even during World War II when the motherland was threatened by Nazi invaders, the vor were expected to honor the Thieves Code. Freidman found:

> During the Second World War, Stalin devised a plot to annihilate the thriving *vor* subculture by recruiting them to defend the motherland. Those who fought with the Red Army, defying the age-old prohibition of helping the State, were rewarded by being arrested after the war and thrown into the same prison camps with the *vors* who had refused to join the epic conflict. The "collaborators" were branded *suki*, or bitches. At night, when the Artic concentration camps grew miserably cold, knives were unsheathed, and the two sides hacked each other to pieces, barracks were bombed and set on fire. The "*Vor Wars*" lasted from 1945 to 1953. When they were over, only the *vors* who refused to battle the Nazis had survived. By then, they wielded ultimate authority in prison, even over wardens, importing liquor, narcotics, and women.
>
> (p. 10)

Another type of thief that occupied the Thieves World were the "Thieves in Authority" or *avtoritety*. Those were employees and associates of the government that stole from the state or misappropriate state property, services or funds to their own benefit. Those *avtoritety* were not exactly *nomenklatura* (senior government officials) or even *apparatchiks* (party functionaries). They served the government and the Communist Party of the Soviet Union as directors, managers, and supervisors in the vast Soviet empire while looting the government for their own benefit (Finckenauer & Waring, 1998, pp. 92–93).

The *avtoritety* often acted in concert with or in full cooperation with the Vory v Zakone in conduct of their criminal enterprises. A Vory v Zakone, literally "thieves in law," describes an elite organized crime group member. The group has roots in the prison camps and can be compared to the Mexican Mafia in the United States. In noting the illegal diversion of consumer goods from the official state economy in the Soviet Union, Serio (2008) found that by the late 1960s:

> The traditional criminal world generally began to interact more frequently with the upperworld, as the so-called shadow economy operators (*teniviki*) and the workshop managers (*tsekhoviki*) were pulling in massive amounts of money by providing the black market with products that should have been going into the state distribution network. They needed protection from the government, from their competition, and from criminals. They sought it through bribing state officials but also by entering into agreements with protectors in the criminal world.
>
> (p. 145)

Most of the crime committed by Russian Mafia clans during Soviet times involved economic crimes within the state system. These crimes often included misappropriation of government goods and services, black market activities to obtain Western goods, drug trafficking, bootleg liquor, untaxed cigarettes and illegal (for profit) carpentry, plumbing, and electrical work (Finckenauer & Waring, 2001; Albini et al., 1995).

The fall of communism (1989–1991) was a time of rapid change in the former Soviet Union. The strictly regulated economy and governmental structure of the USSR was replaced by unregulated type of capitalism that has been described by many as "Wild West" in nature. The breakaway of many of the former Soviet republics into separate nation states only accelerated this. Russian organized crime seized on these opportunities as a chance to expand and evolve (Frickenauer & Voronin, 2001; Waller & Yasman, 1995). Shelley (1998) observed:

> In 1994 Russia's then interior minister, Mikhail Yegorov, said the number of organized crime groups in the former Soviet Union had grown from 785 during Gorbachev's reign to 5,691. By 1996 this estimate had grown to 8,000 groups, each with memberships of between 50 and 1,000. The government in Moscow estimates the Russian mafia controls 40% of private business and 60% of state-owned companies. Unofficial sources said 80% of Russian banks are controlled either directly or indirectly by criminals.

According to Serio (2008), the collapse of the Soviet Union and the subsequent reorganization of the Russian government provided an atmosphere that Russian organized crime was able to expand and flourish. This in turn led to conflict within the Russian organized crime groups for control and resulted in the Great Mob War of 1992–1994. This was in turn followed by the collapse of the ruble in 1998, which sent many Russian organized crime groups looking for other opportunities in their foreign holdings. All of these factors contributed to the rapid rise of the Russian Mafia and their transnational approach to criminality (Serio, 2008, pp. 206–207).

The Great Mob War of 1992–1994 and the Continued Violence of the Russian Mafia

Competition among the various Russian Mafia clans led to violence and the rise of flamboyant mob bosses. As they became more organized, the Russian Mafia groups claimed territory and sought dominance in their illegal trades. Varese (2001) observed:

The ability to mobilize a number of well-armed individuals is a crucial requirement for survival in the underworld. Since the early 1990's, the post-Soviet criminal landscape started to be populated by territorially based groups with this ability.

The Great Mob War of 1992–1994 was an attempt by various Russian organized crime groups and the organized crime groups of some of the former Soviet Republics to dominate the criminal community in the former Soviet Union. Klebnikov (2000) found:

The "Great Mob War" was fought mostly in Moscow, but its echo was heard as far as Vladivostok, Krasnoyarsk, Sverdlovsk (Yekaterinburg), Samara, St. Petersburg, Tbilisi, Grozny, London, and New York. The root of the conflict was economic. Dozens of top gangster bosses had come out of prison after Communism fell, and they found the nation's prime economic assets up for grabs. Huge industrial companies, mines, and oil fields were being privatized. Anyone ruthless enough could attain unimaginable wealth almost overnight. One popular analogy of what was happening in Russia at this time was that of a car wreck—a vehicle stuffed with dollar bills crashes, the money is scattered on the ground, and the bystanders push one another away, trying to grab the biggest bundle. Both the older mob bosses (the thieves-professing-the-code) and the younger "gangster businessmen" engaged in a savage struggle with one another to stake their claim.

(p. 21)

Klebnikov (2000) observed that although the mob war was chaotic, the factions soon divided into two primary alliances. The Chechen and the thieves-professing-the-code formed one faction. The other faction included the Solntsevo Brotherhood or Solnt-sevskaya Brigade (Varese, 2001, p. 170) and their allies, Ivankov operating from New York, Otarik, and Sergei Timofeyev (aka "Sylvester" because of his alleged resemblance to the American movie star Sylvester Stallone). This group was often called the Slavic Alliance and was considered to be very anti-Chechen (pp. 21–25).

Otari Kvantrishvili aka "Otarik" (1948–1994) had been a wrestler and was involved with the Dynamo Sports Club. He had been charged with rape in 1966 and sent to a psychiatric hospital (Serio, 2008, p. 186; Klebnikov, 2000, p. 18). Otarik used his involvement with the sports club as a front for his racketeering activities (Varese, 2001, p. 68). He was known as someone who could act as a mediator between warring Russian Mafia factions. Otarik was a good friend and associate of Ivankov (Serio, 2008, p. 145). Otarik was murdered by a sniper in 1994 while leaving a bathhouse (Varese, 2001, p. 228).

Sergei Timofeyev aka "Sylvester" was the leader of the Orekhovskaya gang (Serio, 2008, p. 198; Varese, 2001, p. 170). Timofeyev was involved in several gang murders and had operations in Cyprus. He was murdered in 1994 when a car bomb exploded (Varese, 2001, p. 170; Freidman, 2000, pp. 125–126). His gang, the Orekhovskaya, began to fight among themselves and later merged with the Solntsevskaya Bratva. Schreck (2005) reported:

> Orekhovskaya, which rose to prominence for racketeering in the early 1990s, is thought to have organized the slayings of at least 35 people, including an investigator, a senior police official and many rival gangsters. The group's influence all but vanished after a series of arrests in the late 1990s.

Boris Berezovsky (1946–2013) was a Russian businessman and made his fortune during the turbulent transition between the Soviet Union and modern Russia. Klebnikov (2000) reported:

> In 1992, according to Moscow police sources, Berezovsky approached Mikhas to buy the Orbita, a Solntsevo-controlled super-market on Smolensk Square, next to the Foreign Ministry building; he wanted this prestigious site for one of his car dealerships. The price Mikhas demanded was supposedly $1 million; Berezovsky apparently found the price too high. Whether on the advice of his partner, Badri, or on his own initiative, Berezovsky ultimately teamed up with the enemies of the Solntsevo Brotherhood: the Chechens. Meanwhile, Berezovsky's rivals in the auto market, beholden to other organized-crime groups, were jealous of his success. They resented his inside deal with Russia's largest auto company, Autovaz, and his successful lobbying of the Ministry of Foreign Trade to impose high customs duties on imported automobiles. Thus,

Berezovsky found himself in the middle of a war between Moscow's predominant gangster families.

(pp. 20–21)

In 1993, Berezovsky traveled to Israel and obtained Israeli citizenship, but retained his Russian citizenship (Klebnikov, 2000, p. 23). In 1994, Berezovsky survived a car bombing attack on his life in Moscow (Klebnikov, 2000, p. 38). While back in Russia, due to his political connections and ownership of a Russian television station (ORT), he became involved with Russian President Boris Yeltsin serving in the Duma (Russian Parliament) (Varese, 2001, p. 33). Berezovsky's wealth rose to an estimated $3 billion. His business tactics fell under suspicion because of his ties with organized crime. Analysts at GlobalSecurity.Org (2015) reported:

> Berezovsky's business policies and actions were continuously scrutinized, however, and have often been considered corrupt. Those within the business community questioned how the oligarch's enterprises continuously floundered while Berezovsky's wealth increased considerably. Numerous investigations were launched against Berezovsky and his companies and corporations. The authorities uncovered numerous instances of embezzlement, fraud, and tax-evasion, but were incapable of prosecuting Berezovsky because of his political power and influence.

Berezovsky's fortunes began to fade as Yeltsin left office and was replaced by Vladimir Putin. The Putin government began an anti-oligarch campaign, publicly denouncing oligarchs and describing their negative impacts on domestic and economic affairs in July 2000. Later that year, the state prosecutor's office launched several inquiries against Berezovsky and his many business operations. Berezovsky no longer enjoyed the level of political protection he had in the past, and he fled Russia in November 2000 and was granted asylum in Britain. In 2001, he was officially charged with fraud and political corruption, but Britain refused to extradite him.

Berezovsky was convicted of fraud and embezzlement in absentia. He became a very vocal critic of Putin, filing lawsuits in British courts over some of his Russian business holdings and issues of libel. In 2013, Berezovsky was found hanging in his London home (GlobalSecurity. Org, 2015). The coroner's 2014 verdict made no decision on whether his death was suicide or murder. A renowned German expert on asphyxiation said that the tycoon was strangled, and then hung on a bathroom rail in an imitation of suicide (GlobalSecurity.Org, 2015).

Since the Great Mob War of 1992–1994, the violence among Russian organized crime groups continued, but on a smaller scale. Shelley (1998) found:

> Russia sees around 10,000 fatal shootings a year, 600 of which are contract killings. In the last five years 95 bankers have been murdered. Assassins, who often

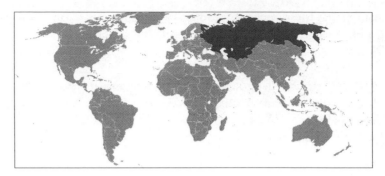

Figure 11.2

The Soviet Union. The Solntsevskaya Bratva is the biggest and most powerful part of the Russian Mafia. The organization was founded in the late 1980s in the area of Moscow, Russia, when it was part to the former Soviet Union.

C records [Public domain or CC BY-SA 4.0 (https://creativecommons.org/licenses/by-sa/4.0)], via Wikimedia Commons

kill for as little as £600 ($1,000), have targeted hotel bosses, restaurateurs, sports figures, businessmen, politicians, journalists and Afghan war veterans. In Soviet times the KGB kept the lid on the Russian mafia but its successor, the FSB, is under-funded and demoralized.

The Russian law enforcement authorities are still engaged in their attempt to stem the violence and frequent conduct raids on Russian Mafia leaders and gatherings (Livesey, 2015).

Solntsevskaya Bratva aka Solntsevo Brigade

The Solntsevskaya Bratva is the largest of the Russian organized crime groups. Matthews (2014) reported:

The group is composed of 10 quasi-autonomous "brigades" that operate more or less independently of each other. The group does pool its resources, however, and the money is overseen by a 12-person council that "meets regularly in different parts of the world, often disguising their meetings as festive occasions."

It's estimated that the group claims upwards of 9,000 members, and that it's bread and butter is the drug trade and human trafficking. Russian organized crime in general is heavily involved in the heroin trade that originates in Afghanistan: It is estimated that Russia consumes about 12% of the world's heroin, while it contains just 0.5% of the world's population.

Matthews also estimated the group's income at over $8.5 billion annually (Matthews, 2014). Varese (2001) described the Solntsevo as an umbrella organization that was made up of different crews that were active in several different countries (p. 171). Porter (2015) claims that the Solntsevskaya Bravtva has ties with the Russian FSB and that

> The group's tentacles are now believed to extend as far as Indonesia and Latin America, where they have established cocaine trafficking networks in collusion with Mexican cartels.

Russian Organized Crime

A free market economy in the new Russia also led to the expansion of the types of crime the Russian Mafia was engaged in. Russian organized crime quickly adapted to the fluid economic conditions and the newfound access to foreign trade and travel. Finckenauer and Waring (1998) observed that the primary crimes of the Russian Mafia now were drug trafficking, weapons trafficking, human trafficking, sex trafficking, pornography, black market goods, antiquities trafficking, stolen cars, precious metals, and money laundering (p. 118). The Russian Mafia is also extensively involved in the trafficking of untaxed cigarettes and counterfeit tax stamps throughout Europe (Billingslea, 2004).

Drug trafficking is an area that the Russian Mafia excels in. The Russian Mafia is not only engaged in the sale and transport of drugs, but also in their production. A specialty is Krokodil or desomorphine, a very powerful synthetic opioid. Albini et al. (1995) observed:

> It is in the realm of drug-trafficking, where much of the high profit is made . . . the Russian former republics produce 25 times more hashish than the rest of the world and opium poppies flourish in abundance in Afghanistan, Uzbekistan, and other territories of the former U.S.S.R. (p. 213).

The changes in the Russian economy brought on by the fall of communism benefited Russian organized crime greatly. Lindberg et al. (1997), in observing the extent and the effect the Russian organized crime had on the overall Russian economy, noted:

> It is estimated that between 80% and 90% of all businesses pay some sort of street tax to organized crime groups, many up to one-third of their profits.

Organized crime groups, in turn, pay one-third of their income to bribe public officials. Incredibly, much of the money generated through the sale of formerly state-owned capital and resources is funneled abroad into the private bank accounts of government officials and organized crime members at the rate of $1 billion per month, draining the Russian economy of much needed cash. Money that stays home is laundered through investment in legitimate enterprises, blurring the line between legitimate business and criminal enterprises. Consequently, a significant portion, over 50%, of the legitimate economy is controlled by organized crime, including 35,000 Russian businesses and 60% of banks, according to the Interior Ministry. It is also reported that the majority of privatized real estate in Moscow is now under the influence of criminal groups.

(pp. 92–93)

As the criminal operations of the vor infiltrated the Russian banking system, bank fraud and illegal money laundering quickly became staples of the criminal activities of Russian organized crime. Emanuel E. Zeltser, director and general counsel of the American Russian Law Institute, testified before the House Committee on Banking and Financial Services on September 29, 1999. His testimony dealt with the hearing on the Bank of New York, Russian organized crime, and money laundering. Zeltser testified that the collapsed Russian Inkombank had been controlled by members of the Russian Mafia. Zeltser (1999) testified that:

According to Inkombank's own promotional material this mob-controlled bank had correspondent relationships with top banks in the United States, Canada, Switzerland and many other Western countries. Its representative offices and branches were licensed in Switzerland, UK, Germany and Cyprus. Illicit proceeds could flow to any point in the world at the touch of a button in Moscow. In May of 1996, the US Security and Exchange Commission approved a $10 M Inkombank/Bank of New York joint securities issue, known as ADR. The American public was given the opportunity to buy an equity stake in the world's most profitable enterprise, Russian Organized Crime.

Many of these Russian mob bosses modeled themselves after the flamboyant lifestyles that they saw in American movies about American gangsters from La Cosa Nostra in the 1920s and 1930s. They surrounded themselves with very visible signs of wealth, such as expensive cars and clothing, and adopted a very visible public "tough guy" persona. As noted by Shelley (1998), this led to violence, so, like their American Mafia counterparts of the 1920s and 1930s, Russian mob bosses began to favor elaborate public funerals.

Members of other mobs often attended or sent notes or elaborate floral arrangements. Elaborate, large, laser engraved tombstones have been favored by the narcissistic tastes of the Russian mob bosses.

Krysha "The Roof"

In describing the organization and tactics of Russian organized crime, the Center for Strategic and International Studies [CSIS] (1997) used the Russian term *krysha*, and observed:

> One of the most prominent terms of the new Russian criminal jargon is krysha, which literally means "roof." Throughout the Cold War, Soviet intelligence services used this term to refer to a cover set up for intelligence of officers in a foreign country. In the context of ROC, however, krysha is now used to refer to an umbrella of protection, or "bandit roof." This protection can come in the form of a criminal overlord protecting members of his organization. It also can come in the form of a criminal group's declaring that a specific business is paying it extortion money and is therefore under its protection. Finally, a krysha also can include certain forms of corrupt government protection, including the militsiya, tax police, the military, customs, and border guards.

The Great Russian Immigrations

The migrations of Russians into other countries came in several waves. Many Russians emigrated during Tsarist times (1890–1920) for better opportunities or to escape perceived religious oppression. After the 1917 revolution and the civil war that followed, there was a wave of immigration to escape the takeover of Communism as the Union of Soviet Socialist Republics (USSR) replaced the previous Tsarist Russian Empire, although restrictions in the United States immigration laws, such as the Johnson Act of 1921 and the Reed-Johnson Act of 1924, greatly restricted immigration from Eastern Europe to the United States (Finckenauer & Waring, 1998, p. 40).

As the Soviet Union began to have political troubles and eventually dissolved, there were two more main waves of Russian immigration. Finckenauer and Waring (1998) found:

> By the late 1970's, for example, the cause of the "refuseniks"—Jews who applied for permission to emigrate from the Soviet Union but were not permitted to do so—had become a major cause and a political issue in the United States. Russian Jews eventually were allowed almost unlimited immigration because of the

discriminatory treatment they received in the Soviet Union, and other Russians were likewise permitted to emigrate from the USSR to the United States as political refugees.

(p. 40)

This new wave of immigration from the Soviet Union beginning in 1968 turned into an exodus as hundreds of thousands fled the USSR and Communism. Rosner (1986) found that this wave of Russian immigrants was educated and often had technological job skills, unlike the immigrants of earlier waves of immigration (p. 125). Siegel and Bovenkerk (2000) observed:

Emigration from the former Soviet Union and the creation of an expatriate Red Mafia provide a magnificent opportunity to study the process of ethnic organized crime. The immigration itself constitutes a recent and ongoing movement of people, many of whom have not decided to settle.

(p. 428)

Sporadically from 1968 to 1983 and again since 1988, waves of immigrants have left the former Soviet Union. Major Russian-speaking communities were established in many Western countries including the United States, Israel, Germany, Canada, and South Africa. While most of the immigrants were Jews, there were also Germans, Ukrainians, and Armenians (Siegel & Bovenkerk, 2000).

Russian Organized Crime in the United States

After and during the first wave of Russian immigration into the United States (1890–1920), Russian immigrants who chose to participate in organized crime often did so in partnership or association with members of established La Cosa Nostra (LCN) Mafia families in their areas. That collaboration between Jewish Russian immigrants and local Italian criminals was first noted in a controversial *North American Review* article by NYPD Police Commissioner Theodore A. Bingham as early as 1908. Bingham (1908) observed that:

The crimes committed by the Russian Hebrews are generally those against property. They are burglars, firebugs, pickpockets and highway robbers—when they have the courage; but, though all crime is their province, pocket-picking is the one to which they seem to take most naturally. Indeed, pickpockets of other nationalities are beginning to recognize the superiority of the Russian Hebrew in that gentle art, and there have been several instances lately where a Hebrew and an Italian had formed a combination for theft in the streets, the former being always selected for the "tool," as the professionals term that one who does the actual reaching into the victim's pocket, while the others create a diversion to distract attention, or start a fight in case of the detection and pursuit of the thief.

(p. 384)

Bingham was police commissioner of New York City from 1906 to 1909, and may have obtained some of his views on immigrants and crime from his predecessor, William McAdoo, who was police commissioner from 1904–1905. McAdoo had a very negative, almost anti-Semitic, view of Russian Jewish immigrants and their perceived criminality (Finckenauer & Waring, 1998, p. 48).

Radanko (2011) found that many Russian immigrants who came during the first wave of Russian immigration were Russian Jews from provinces in Russia, Ukraine, and what is now Poland. They were fleeing religious persecution. Those Russian immigrants who participated in some type of organized crime began to do so during Prohibition and in league with various LCN families. Mobsters like David Berman aka "Davie the Jew" (1903–1957) worked with the Genovese family in Minneapolis and later Las Vegas in booze and gambling rackets (Radanko, 2011, pp. 289–290; Fischer, 2007, p. 13). Others like Isadore Blumenfeld aka "Kid Cann" aka "Issy" (1900–1981) operated in Minnesota and partnered with Chicago's Al Capone to run illegal liquor. He also engaged in narcotics trafficking and prostitution. Cann was also the associate of another Russian Jewish immigrant, Meyer Lansky (Radanko, 2011, p. 293). Yet another Russian-Jewish gangster of the period was Charles "King" Solomon (1884–1933), who was one of the largest bootleggers in Boston. It was rumored, but never proven, that he ran illegal liquor with Joseph Kennedy during this period. Solomon also ran narcotics, prostitution, and gambling. Solomon cooperated with the LCN families and the Irish Mob. He was a powerful enough gangster that he attended the 1927 Atlantic City crime conference arranged by Meyer Lansky. Solomon was murdered in a Boston nightclub called the Cotton Club in 1933. Although dying, Solomon refused to name the four gangsters who shot him, taking that knowledge to the grave (Radanko, 2011, pp. 301–305).

Evsei "Little Don" Agron came to the United States in 1975 as a part of the wave of Soviet Jews that were allowed to leave the USSR during the 1970s. A Vory v Zakone who had served time in the Soviet gulags for murder, he set up his criminal operations in the Brighton Beach area of Brooklyn, New York (Freidman, 2000, pp. 23–42). Agron was allied with the Genovese family of LCN. He was murdered in New York City in 1985.

Marat Balagula came to the United States in 1977 as a refugee and settled in Brighton Beach, New York. He began to operate a nightclub there, which he used as a front for his criminal activities. Balagula worked for Agron and served as his consigliere. He is suspected of ordering Argon's death, but it was never proven (Freidman, 2000, pp. 41–42). Balagula was heavily involved in gasoline tax fraud and credit card fraud. He was also involved in a diamond smuggling operation from Sierra Leone in Africa and a heroin smuggling operation from Thailand. In 1986, he was arrested and convicted in federal court in a U.S. Secret Service case on credit fraud and gasoline tax fraud charges. Although he fled to Belgium and later Germany, in 1989 he was captured, extradited back to the United States and sent to federal prison (Freidman, 2000, pp. 42–67). Balagula was released from federal prison in 2004.

Boris Nayfeld came to the United States from Gomel, Russia, in the 1970s as a religious refugee and settled in Brighton Beach, New York (Freidman, 2000, pp. 25–26; Radanko, 2011, p. 232). Nayfeld became the chauffeur of the local Russian mob leader Evsei Agron (Freidman, 2000, p. 38). After Agron was murdered in 1985, Nayfeld became Balagula's chauffer. Nayfeld later took over the Bratva gang after Balagula's arrest and was involved in extensive heroin trafficking into the New York area from Thailand. Nayfeld was also involved in a violent struggle for control of criminal enterprises in New York with other Russian organized crime figures such as Monya Elston (Radanko, 2011, pp. 233–236; Freidman, 2000, pp. 3–21). In January 1994, he was arrested by federal agents for drug trafficking. Later, he and his co-defendants, the Dozortsev brothers, pleaded guilty to laundering the drug money that belonged to themselves and Ricardo Fanchini (Finckenauer & Waring, 1998, p. 157, pp. 246–247). Siegel (2003a) stated:

> Boris Nayfeld ("Beeba," or "Daddy"), the former boxer settled in Edegem, a suburb of Antwerp, after he escaped an attempt on his life. He had contacts in Berlin in connection with the Chechen Mafia. In Belgium, he has built a strong network, including drugs smuggling on a large scale.
>
> (p. 55)

An increase of Russian organized crime (ROC) came to the United States with the fall of the Soviet Union and the mass migration of Russian immigrants into the United States after 1991. Noting the rise of the Russian Mafia in the United States, Finckenauer (2015) observed that approximately 15 of those criminal groups operated in the United States, and eight or nine of them (comprising 5,000–6,000 members) maintained links to Russia. Supportive reports indicate about 200 large ROC groups operating in 58 countries worldwide, including the United States.

The New York State Organized Crime Task Force (NYSOCTF et al., 1996) report on Russian émigré crime noted American law enforcement was hampered in the investigation of Russian organized crime by the distrust of the governmental authorities by Russian immigrants. The report stated that

> opportunities to obtain information from Russian emigres are further hampered by the lack of Russian speaking police officers. Most law enforcement agents investigating Russian—émigré crime do not speak Russian and are unfamiliar

with the peculiarities of the language, such as the use of the Cyrillic alphabet, the feminization of surnames, and the inversion of birthdates.

(p. 180)

That often resulted in inaccurate recording of biographic data, a problem that was exacerbated by the limited cooperation of translators. To add to the challenges of law enforcement, Finckenauer (2015) noted Russian émigrés tended to be highly educated and thus are very resourceful and sophisticated in their methods of operation. They may carry false identification documents or use variations of the spelling of their names to thwart background investigations, so identification and apprehension of Russian émigré criminals is quite difficult.

The Russian Mafia is very flexible in the crimes that it promotes to make money. The Russian Mafia's primary crimes in the United States include auto theft (Albini et al., 1995), auto chop shops, drug trafficking, extortion, fraud, fuel tax evasion, gambling, insurance fraud, staged automobile accidents, confidence schemes, credit card fraud, check frauds, identity theft, document forgery (passports, etc.), pornography, sex trafficking, human trafficking, and weapons trafficking (Finckenauer & Waring, 1998).

Vyacheslav Kirillovich Ivankov aka "Yaponchick"

For a time, Ivankov was one of the most notorious Russian Mafia criminals and operated in the United States and Russia. Vyacheslav Kirillovich Ivankov was born in Tbilisi, Georgia, on January 2, 1940. Ivankov was commonly known as Yaponchick which means "little Japanese." Some say it was because of his slightly oriental facial features (Radanko, 2011, p. 60). Others have implied that that he took the name after Moisey Volfovich Vinnitskiy aka Mishka Yaponchik (1891–1919), a famous Russian outlaw who fought on the Soviet side during the Russian Revolution and Civil War.

Ivankov first went to prison in the USSR for a bar fight. Upon his release, he continued his criminal career selling goods on the black market and burglarizing houses (Radanko, 2011, p. 61). Imprisoned once more, he was known as a Vory v Zakone in 1974 while in Butyrka Prison in the USSR (Klebnikov, 2000, p. 17). Ivankov was arrested again in 1982 for weapons violations, forgery, and drug trafficking. He was released in 1991 (Lunde, 2004a; Durden-Smith, 1995).

In his 1996 testimony before the Permanent Subcommittee on Investigations of the Committee on Governmental Affairs before the U.S. Senate, Russia's Deputy Minister of Interior Igor Nikolayevich Kozhevnikov testified that he believed that Ivankov fled to the United States to avoid further arrest in Russia (Radanko, 2011, p. 62). Ivankov immigrated to the United States in 1992 on a business visa. He claimed that he was planning to work in the movie industry (Finckenauer & Waring, 1998, p. 110).

Examining Ivankov's travels, Durden-Smith (1995) reported that in 1992, Ivankov appeared in Los Angeles to become the Russian mob's link to the Colombian cartels. He then moved his base of operations to New York and traveled frequently from there to Vienna and Dusseldorf, and had a number of meetings with Russian organized crime figures. In 1991, just outside of Moscow, there was a meeting of 100 of the top Russian Mafia members to discuss how to operate in the new circumstances prevailing after the recent overthrow of leadership. The previous August, the godfather of Brighton Beach, Evsei Agron, was killed outside his Brooklyn apartment. His successor, Marat Balagula, known as "The Georgian" or "The Giant," was arrested in Frankfurt in 1989, two years later. Balagula was the man who had brought the American-based Organizatsiya to maturity through a series of jewelry heists, insurance frauds, and an enormous gasoline bootlegging and tax scam. It was clear that new leadership was necessary.

Ivankov was a member of the Solntsevskaya Bratva and was their representative in the United States (Radanko, 2011, p. 61; Varese, 2001, p. 170; Serio, 2008, pp. 69–70). He supported the group in the Great Mob War of 1992–1994 from his position in New York (Klebnikov, 2000, pp. 11–43). Ivankov was rumored to have ties with the KGB (Klebnikov, 2000, p. 75). Sinelnikov (2011) reported for *Pravda* that:

> Russian criminals are highly sophisticated and uncatchable for the West. As soon as the Soviet Union collapsed, Russian criminals started to look for new homes far away from the motherland. Vyacheslav Ivankov, for example, bought a ticket to the United States as soon as he came out of prison in Russia. That was a perfect opportunity for him to change his image. In Russia, he was known as a jailbird. In the States, he earned the reputation of Robin Hood; US newspapers referred to him as the new Solzhenitsyn. Afterwards, Mr. Ivankov showed the States how to love freedom. The deeds of Mr. Ivankov in particular and the Russian mafia in general are dramatized and demonized in the West. The Russian mafia definitely exists, but it does not stand out from others of the ilk, such as Cosa Nostra, Yakuza, Ndrangheta, etc. The myth that has been created is much more profitable.

In the United States, Ivankov ruled a Russian criminal group with over 100 members that operated out of the Brighton Beach neighborhood of Brooklyn (CBS, 2000). Ivankov was allied with at least three of LCN's Five Families in the NYC area (Williams, 2000, pp. 199–200). Ivankov was arrested on June 8, 1995, by the FBI (working with the Royal Canadian Mounted Police) for extortion and conspiracy (FBI, 2015d; Serio, 2008, p. 172; Raab, 1995). Ivankov was convicted along with several others and sentenced to prison (*United States v. V. K. Ivankov*, 1998). After he served his time in federal prison in the United States, Ivankov was deported back to Russia on July 13, 2004, to face charges that he was involved in the 1992 double murder of two Turkish nationals.

Ivankov was acquitted by a Russian court in 2005 of the murder charges. Radanko (2011) observed that the trial only lasted one day and "The witnesses, a police officer among them, claimed to have never seen him in their lives" (p. 61). Ivankov was shot by a sniper on July 28, 2009, while leaving a Moscow restaurant. He died of his injuries on October 9, 2009. Ivankov's funeral was a grand mob affair and was attended by hundreds of Russian mobsters (Schwirtz, 2009; Radanko, 2011, p. 62).

Semion Mogilevich

According to Varese (2001), during the mid-1990s Semion Mogilevich acted as the Solntsevo's representative in Hungary (p. 170). During that time, Mogilevich was also very active in the United States and Canada. Radanko (2011) observed that many European and U.S. federal law enforcement authorities believed that Mogilevich was the "Boss of Bosses" of the Russian Mafia worldwide. He had nicknames of "Don Semyon" and "The Brainy Don" (p. 10). According to the FBI (2015e):

> Simon Mogilevich is wanted for his alleged participation in a multi-million-dollar scheme to defraud thousands of investors in the stock of a public company incorporated in Canada, but headquartered in Newtown, Bucks County, Pennsylvania, between 1993 and 1998. The scheme to defraud collapsed in 1998, after thousands of investors lost in excess of 150 million U.S. Dollars, and Mogilevich, thought to have allegedly funded and authorized the scheme, was indicted in April of 2003.

Mogilevich was indicted in U.S. federal court on charges by the U.S. Department of Justice for fraud by wire, RICO conspiracy, money laundering conspiracy, money laundering, aiding and abetting, securities fraud, filing false registration with the SEC, false filings with the SEC, and falsification of books and records. He fled the country and was last reported hiding in Russia. In October of 2009 he was placed on the FBI's Ten Most Wanted fugitive list, where he remained until 2015 (FBI, 2015e).

In 1999, Semion Mogilevich also attempted to run for a seat in the Russian Duma (parliament) on the LDPR (Russian Liberal Democratic Party) ticket (Varese, 2001, p. 183). Mogilevich was involved in drug trafficking. According to Freidman (2000), Mogilevich "also fortified his organization by coordinating activities with non-Russian crime groups such as the Japanese Yakuza and the Italian Camorra" (p. 242). Mogilevich shielded his illegal activities by running a number of legitimate enterprises that supported his illegal businesses. For example, he purchased the controlling share in an arms manufacturing company in Hungary, thus he obtained a Hungarian license to sell weapons as a legitimate armaments manufacturer. However, Mogilevich has been accused of also selling illegally acquired Warsaw Pact weapons (Freidman, 2000, pp. 244–245).

Russian Organized Crime (ROC) as a Transnational Criminal Organization (TCO)

ROC as a TCO: Belgium

Russian organized crime has expanded into a transnational criminal organization. Belgium is especially attractive to Russian organized crime because of its extensive diamond markets. Dunn (2000) remarked that

> Antwerp's port has a reputation for being a major smuggling base. The city's diamond dealers, many of them Russian Jews, have links to many Russian Gangs and are allegedly among the world's most experienced in the art of laundering money and dodging taxes.
>
> (p. 81)

Noting the transnational nature of Russian organized crime, Siegel (2003a) observed:

> The transnational character of Russian organized crime can also be illustrated by the position of Belgium, and especially Antwerp, on the criminal map of the Russian Mafia. Russian Crime Bosses take refuge in Belgium when they are in danger somewhere else. Belgium has the reputation of an ideal location for Russian criminal networks. Drugs and women trafficking, money laundering and trade in stolen and counterfeit gold and diamonds are the main activities of Russian speaking criminals in Belgium.
>
> (p. 55)

ROC as a TCO: Colombia

Colombia is a major source of drugs. The Russian Mafia has formed alliances with Colombian drug cartels to facilitate drug trafficking operations. Those alliances included the Russian mobsters providing technical assistance to the Colombian drug cartels in the development of new ways to transport drugs. As an example of this, *Los Angeles Times* reporter Darling (2000) stated:

> The three foreigners first raised suspicions in the Andean mountain village of Facatativa because they never smiled or waved. Then people noticed that they always had food delivered and seldom emerged from the warehouse where they worked.
>
> Finally, someone called the police. Officers, shocked by what they discovered when they entered the warehouse during a predawn raid Sept. 7, made two phone calls: one to the U.S. Drug Enforcement Administration office here

and another to the Russian ambassador. Thanks to the offended villagers, law enforcement officers had found a 100-foot submarine under construction, the first tangible evidence of a long-suspected alliance between the latest generation of Colombian drug traffickers and the Russian mafia.

In describing the partnership between the Colombian cartels and ROC, CSIS (1997) found:

> Cooperative efforts between ROC groups and the Colombian drug cartels are centered in Miami, where the local FBI office characterized the Russian gangsters as "very brutal . . . they are very sophisticated. They are computer literate. They hit the ground running." Miami represents a gateway to both the United States and Latin America. The Drug Enforcement Agency (DEA) and FBI disrupted one scheme that involved a plan to use a Russian-built submarine to smuggle cocaine from Colombia to the United States.

ROC as a TCO: Cyprus

Cyprus was attractive to Russian organized crime because of its banks and the favorable banking laws of the country. When you engage in illegal businesses, you find yourself in need of somewhere to stash the cash that you have acquired. You want somewhere that the local government will not seize it and that the banking regulations are favorable to your needs. The Russian Mafia has found that the banking system in Cyprus fills the bill (Siegel, 2003a, pp. 60–61; Dunn, 2000, p. 82; Fisk, 1994). This gives them somewhere to stash the cash and to launder the money. According to Webster (2015), Cyprus has become one of the major places for the Russian Mafia to launder money.

ROC as a TCO: Israel

As masses of Soviet Jews fled Russia, in the period from 1968 to 1983 and from 1988 onward, many immigrated to Israel (Siegel & Bovenkerk, 2000). The vast majority of those immigrants were not criminals, but some were. Siegel (2003a) noted that Israel was a favorite spot for many Russian Mafia to immigrate to because of Israel's favorable immigration and banking laws. The members of Russian organized crime found that it is much easier to travel with an Israeli passport than a Russian one (pp. 52–55). According to Connolly (1998), "Former police chief Asaf Hefetz says £2.5bn ($4bn) of organized crime money from the former Soviet Union has been invested in Israeli real estate, businesses and banks in the past seven years."

One of these immigrants who was also a member of ROC was Grigory Lerner aka Gregory Lerner aka Zvi Ben-Ari. According to Connolly (1998), "Gregory Lerner, who was arrested in 1997 for defrauding four Russian banks of £70m ($106m), was reputedly sent to Israel to head up one of the money laundering operations." Lerner, 47, served six years in jail after reaching a plea bargain with Israeli prosecutors.

However, after being released from prison, Lerner resumed his criminal life. Grayeff (2006) reported:

> Gregory Lerner, who had already served six years in prison for fraud, has been arrested in Paraguay after fleeing from Israel two weeks ago following a second conviction for embezzlement, forgery and money-laundering, the police said on Monday. Investigators at the Serious and International Crimes Unit traced Lerner (Zvi Ben-Ari) to South America after receiving intelligence information. In cooperation with the Israel Police's representative in the region, the local authorities tracked Lerner to a hotel in the Paraguayan capital, Asuncion. He is believed to have escaped from Israel under an assumed identity. According to Asuncion reports, Lerner was drunk when apprehended and had to be hauled off to hospital before being formally arrested. Cash and a forged passport were found in his hotel room.

ROC as a TCO: Eastern Europe, the Balkans, and Italy

Russian organized crime is one of the dominant criminal groups in central Europe, Eastern Europe, and the Balkans (Plywaczewski, 2003, pp. 63–72; Dunn, 2000, pp. 82–84). Russian organized crime is also allied with some segments of Italian organized crime (Freidman, 2000, p. 242). The primary crimes of the Russian Mafia organizations in these areas include auto theft, drug trafficking, human trafficking, weapons trafficking, and art or antiquities smuggling or theft.

ROC as a TCO: Germany

There is a large Russian-speaking population in Germany and many Russian Mafia dons like to do business there. The German newspaper *Die Welt* (2009) reported that the Russian Mafia was active in Berlin and that many of the cars that were stolen in Germany ended up in Russia. Siegel (2003a) found that the Russian Mafia in Germany was engaged in weapons trafficking (including nuclear materials), human trafficking, smuggling art and antiquities, auto theft, prostitution, and money laundering (pp. 57–60).

ROC as a TCO: The Netherlands

Siegel and Bovenkerk (2000) estimated that approximately 10,000 Russian-speaking immigrants moved into the Netherlands. They observed that many of the immigrants were Soviet Jews and had first immigrated to Israel. They also observed that many of the immigrants arrived in the Netherlands with forged documents (p. 424). Siegel and Bovenkerk (2000) found that the immigrants suffered from a public perception that they were somehow involved with the Russian Mafia. While indeed some were, the vast majority were not (p. 431).

However, the Netherlands is attractive to the members of Russian organized crime because of their relaxed views on some drugs and prostitution. The Russian Mafia in the Netherlands is involved in human trafficking, drug trafficking, weapons trafficking, auto theft, art and antiquities theft or smuggling, and money laundering (Siegal & Bovenkerk, 2000, p. 433; Dunn, 2000, p. 84).

Russian Organized Crime as a Prison Gang

The Russian Mafia began in the Soviet gulag prison system before coming out of prison and into the streets. But because they are still operating as a criminal organization, it is logical to assume that if you commit crimes, sometimes you are going to get caught. The numbers of Russian Mafia members in prison in the United States is relatively small. However, in Europe (especially in Eastern Europe) the number is much higher. Plywaczewski (2003) found that when there were significant numbers of Russian Mafia inmates in a prison, they tended to become one of the most dominant prison gangs in the prison and intimidated other prisoners into compliance or cooperation.

The Russian Mafia is a transnational criminal organization that spans over 50 countries. Beginning in the Soviet gulags, they rapidly adapted to changing times. It is this flexibility and willingness to change that makes them a dangerous threat to law enforcement.

The Irish Mob

The Irish Mob were the dominant organized crime group in the United States from about 1820 to 1920. Irish American gangs like the Dead Rabbits, Forty Thieves, Gopher Gang, Roach Guards, Whyos, and the White Hand Gang fought for control of the city streets of New York, especially in the Five Points District (Asbury, 2008). Irish American gangs developed a strong presence in areas with a large Irish American population such as Boston, Chicago, Cleveland, Providence, Philadelphia, New York, and Minneapolis. The advent of Prohibition triggered a series of gang wars with the Sicilian gangs that became the American Mafia. As a result of those conflicts from 1920 to 1932, the influence of Irish American criminal organizations was severely diminished. At one time, the Irish Mob was a major trafficker of weapons to the Irish Republican Army in Ireland. However, although smaller, the Irish Mob survived and continued operating in those cities. Some gangs, like the Westies in New York City and the Winter Hill Gang in Boston, are still considered to be major players (Carr, 2012; English, 2014; English, 2006; Lehr & O'Neill, 2012).

Current crimes include political corruption, hijacking, labor racketeering, weapons trafficking, horse race fixing, gambling, prostitution, drug trafficking, extortion, and loan-sharking.

Where the Irish Mob Operates

In addition to Boston, Chicago, Cleveland, Providence, Philadelphia, New Jersey, and Minneapolis in the United States, the Irish Mob has been reported in Australia, Canada, the United Kingdom, Ireland, and New Zealand.

Albanian Organized Crime (Albanian Mafia aka Mafia Shqiptare)

In 1991, with the fall of communism across Europe, Albania found that its international isolation had ended. Lunde (2004a) observed that

> Albania emerged from more than 40 years isolation under a repressive communist regime in 1991, only to descend into social and political chaos soon afterward. Many Albanians, including criminals left the country and settled abroad. Having gained experience of organized crime by working with other groups, an independent Albanian criminal network emerged a few years later.
>
> (pp. 92–93)

Albanian communities have a long tradition of suspicion of the state. In northern Albania in 1991, a collapse of law and order led to the renewal of the Kanun, traditional medieval laws that stressed close family ties, honor, revenge, and blood feuds. The Kanun is strongly patriarchal and allows a man to beat, imprison, or even kill his son or daughter, or kidnap a woman he wishes to marry. The Kanun generally considers woman and children to be property.

Arsovska (2015) disagreed with Lunde (2004a) on the effects of Kanun law on Albanian organized crime. While acknowledging that the Kanun of Lek Dukagjini might have some cultural influence on some Albanian criminal's behavior, Arsovska (2015) observed that

> The Kanun code is not a "mafia" code; criminals may use their own their own interpretations of some cultural themes to justify their behavior, but in general, Albanian criminals do not respect or follow the Kanun laws.
>
> (p. 227)

The idea of the Italian Mafia's code of Omerta or silence does not always apply to Albanian organized crime. Arsovska (2015) observed that

> The clan-based structure of Albanian society, Albanians' general distrust of state institutions, and the fear of reprisal make some of these groups hard to infiltrate, but this doesn't mean that specific codes of secrecy are strictly followed; in return for lesser sentences, many Albanian criminals have become defectors and testified against their associates in court. They also tend to talk over the phone and be careless in discussing their crimes.
>
> (p. 227)

The Albanian Mafia is organized around a familial clan structure with a strong internal discipline among members that centers around the concept of *besa* (trust) and *ndera* (honor). Arsovska (2015) found that Albanian organized criminals divided into "core

Figure 11.3

Map of Albania. Albania, a small European country on the Balkan Peninsula, is situated very close to Italy, hence the connections between the Italian Mafia and Albanian organized crime. Public domain.

CIA

groups" to accomplish their criminal acts. Although there are no Albanian "godfathers" as such, these "core groups" were organized around leaders. When the leaders were arrested or killed, the group often lost continuity and sometimes dissolved (pp. 226–227).

Ghosh (2012) found that "Ethnic Albanian gangs have taken an ever-increasing role in the trafficking of hard drugs, including heroin, across Europe." Ghosh (2012) also found that it is estimated that approximately 80% of the heroin distributed in Europe is managed or trafficked by the Albanian Mafia. In 2009, the FBI (2009) in Operation Black Eagle arrested several members of the Albanian Mafia on charges of conspiring to smuggle heroin into the United States in the New York and New Jersey area.

In another drug trafficking case in the United States in 2011, 49 members of the Albanian Mafia were indicted in federal court for smuggling large amounts of marijuana from Canada and Mexico into the United States using semitrailers. The U.S. Immigration and Customs Enforcement Agency (ICE, 2012) announced the arrest of the group's leader, stating:

> Arif Kurti, 42, also known as "the Bear," "Arty," and "Nino," was arrested in Albania on a provisional warrant issued from the Eastern District of New York. According to the indictment and other court filings submitted by the government, the syndicate comprises several inter-related ethnic Albanian family clans (also known as "fis"), with hundreds of associated members, workers and customers. In operation for more than a decade, the syndicate is allegedly responsible for organizing the importation and distribution of tens of thousands of kilograms of hydroponic marijuana from Canada and Mexico, substantial quantities of MDMA from the Netherlands and Canada, hundreds of kilograms of cocaine from Mexico, Colombia, Venezuela and Peru, and large quantities of diverted prescription pills, such as oxycodone. The drugs were distributed in various locations in the United States, including New York, California, Georgia, Colorado and Florida, as well as in Canada and Europe.

In addition to drug trafficking, Albanian organized crime has engaged in weapons trafficking, human trafficking, sex trafficking, bribery, extortion, fencing, gambling, loan-sharking, money laundering, robbery, and theft (FBI, 2015c). The Albanian Mafia is heavily involved in the sex trade in Europe and other places. Arsovska (2006) discovered that

> In the last decade, the ethnic Albanians have been massively involved in the trafficking of human beings, particularly women and children for sexual purposes. They have been actively involved in exploitation of prostitution, very often linked to slavery. Interviewed women and children have reported that all

of them have experienced some kind of abuse, such as being regularly raped or beaten. Victims of trafficking are usually left as prey for their Albanian pimps, who strictly control all aspects of their lives. Those who do not comply are seriously harmed by their pimps. The Italian Ministry of Interior reported that 168 foreign prostitutes were killed in 2000, mainly Albanian and Nigerian women murdered by their pimps.

It is important to understand why, according to a recent internal British governmental briefing, ethnic Albanians now control more than 75% of the prostitution in London and other European cities. Concerted police raids on Soho brothels revealed that around 80% of women working as prostitutes were from overseas, mostly from the Balkans and the Baltic states. It is estimated that approximately 70% of women working in these U.K. brothels are Albanians or Kosovar Albanians. According to the British National Criminal Intelligence Service, Albanian women are also being moved by Albanian criminals to red-light areas in the north of England and the Midlands (p. 172).

Allies of Albanian organized crime include Camorra, La Cosa Nostra, 'Ndrangheta, Russian Mafia, Sacra Corona, Sicilian Mafia, and Turkish organized crime.

Where Albanian Organized Crime Operates

The Albanian Mafia has been reported in Albania, Australia, Belgium, Canada, the Czech Republic, China, Croatia, France, Germany, Greece, Honduras, Israel, Italy, Kosovo, Macedonia, Scandinavia, Slovakia, Slovenia, Spain, Switzerland, Turkey, the United Kingdom, and the United States (especially in Illinois, New Jersey, and New York).

Summary

Russian organized crime including the Russian Mafia began as a prison gang in the gulags of the Stalinist Soviet prison system. The vor has developed into a unique Russian criminal class with its own code of conduct. The Russian Mafia in now a transnational criminal operation and poses a significant threat to international law enforcement. The Irish Mob has clear ties to the United States but still maintains a presence in many other countries. The length of time they have been in existence should not be overlooked, nor should their potential worldwide network. Albanian organized crime is closely related to, and its origins closely located to, those of Italian organized crime. Differences exist and should not be discounted, as each group has their own specialties and subtleties.

DISCUSSION QUESTIONS

1. Explain how and why the Russian Mafia started.
2. Describe the vor's code and explain its effects on the thieves who adhere to it.
3. Describe the "War of the Bitches."
4. Explain how immigration affected the operations of the Russian Mafia.
5. Explain how the Russian Mafia became a transnational criminal group.
6. Identify events in the history of the Irish Mob.
7. Examine the connections Albanian organized crime has with nearby countries of origin.

CHAPTER 12 Drug and Other Trafficking Organizations in the Americas

CHAPTER OBJECTIVES

After reading this chapter students should be able to do the following:

- Explain the difference between organized crime and a common street gang.
- Explain how drug trafficking affected the criminality of Mexican and Colombian cartels.
- Explain how human trafficking affects the world economy and human rights.
- Examine how organized crime groups engage in property trafficking.

Introduction

Drug trafficking organizations (DTOs) operate at will whenever the government, especially police, are unable to exert their control. In addition to trafficking in large amounts of drugs, these organizations engage in, or are connected to organizations that engage in, human trafficking, sex trafficking, and counterfeiting. Human trafficking includes the transport of humans across geographic areas without proper documentation. Sex trafficking often involves the kidnapping of young adults to be sold as sex slaves or prostitutes. Counterfeiting is the making of what appears to be a legitimate instrument or branded product outside of the authority of the organization responsible for the quality of the instrument or product. These crime areas are interconnected.

Mexican Drug Cartels

The organization of Mexican criminal groups can be traced to several specific periods in history and politics. Etter and Lehmuth (2013) found that

> There has always been smuggling along the U.S.-Mexican border. It follows that there have always been smugglers and banditos in Mexico and in the United States that work with each other. The trade in drugs, humans, guns and other goods is an old one. During the Mexican Revolution (1910–1923) guns went south into Mexico by the train load. During Prohibition (1919–1932), the traffic was northbound into the United States with illegal liquor.
>
> (p. 3)

Prior to 2000, along the U.S. border, Mexican smuggling rings were prolific and were organized around familial ties (Nagle, 2011). The smuggling rings grew or manufactured or drugs (largely marijuana and some heroin), then transported them to the border where they would be picked up by the U.S. buyers. Penetration into the interior of the United States was largely limited to border areas. The smuggling rings relied on political corruption within the Mexican government and police to protect their operations. They avoided attracting too much attention to themselves and avoided contact with the Mexican Army at all costs. They were aware that the Mexican government would not extradite them to the United States no matter what they did.

Political Corruption in Mexico Prior to 2000

The almost open criminality in Mexico prior to 2000 could have never existed without the knowledge and complicity of people in the government. The Institutional Revolutionary Party (PRI) ruled Mexico with an iron fist from 1929 to 2000. Grillo (2011) observed that

> The PRI system relied on corruption to keep taking over smoothly. Businessmen could pay off small town caciques, who could pay off governors, who could pay off the president. Money rose up like gas and power flowed down like water. Everybody was happy and stayed in line because everybody got paid. Historians have noted this paradox in Mexican politics—corruption was not a rot but rather the oil and glue of the machine. In this system, heroin money was just one more kickback flowing up. The drug market was a fraction of the size of today,

and officials didn't see it as a huge deal. It was a misdemeanor—the way many people today view pirated music.

(p. 35)

In describing the role of the PRI in the corruption that plagued Mexico prior to 2000, Williams (2009) found:

In Mexico under the PRI, there was a degree of acceptance by the elite of organized crime. Some analysts go even farther, arguing that this was an example of the elite exploitation model of organized crime in which politicians used organized crime to consolidate their positions while maintaining plausible deniability.

In spite of treaty agreements, under the rule of the PRI, the Mexican government would not ordinarily extradite wanted Mexican nationals to the United States to face trial for crimes they had committed there. From 1996 to 2002, Mexico extradited an average of 14 fugitives per year to the United States, in spite of hundreds of outstanding requests for extradition (U.S. Senate Concurrent Resolution 79, 108th Congress: 31 UST 5059).

Describing the arrangement that the PRI seemed to have with the drug cartels prior to 2000, Terrance Poppa (1998) observed that the Mexican government under the PRI was only paying lip service to anti-drug efforts, stating:

Mexico goes through the motions of dealing with drug trafficking as a part of an elaborate deception. It will burn a field of marijuana in the presence of the media, but only after the tops have been harvested. It will stage public burnings of seized cocaine, but it more likely to be corn starch inside the packages, the cocaine having been removed and sold to the favored groups. It will allow DEA agents in the field, but block and frustrate every investigative effort. Its facilitation of drug trafficking pump-primed drug addiction throughout North America, yet it routinely blames the victims and rages and fumes whenever it is accused of involvement. It will offer up a sacrificial lamb, some trafficker whose time has come, as a way of placating the victims. It will even offer up an occasional official. But then business will continue as usual.

(pp. 333–334)

The rules for the drug traffickers were basically stay low (out of the public eye), stay quiet (don't kill anyone important) and pay up. If you violated any of those rules, the government would suddenly discover your criminal activities and take action. Grillo

(2011) stated that the most brazen era of PRI corruption was during the 1988–1994 presidential term of Carlos Salinas (p. 84). The three biggest cartels prior to 2000 were the Guadalajara Cartel, the Juarez Cartel and the Gulf Cartel.

The Guadalajara Cartel Prior to 2000

Examining the Guadalajara Cartel, Cimino (2014b) found that

The Guadalajara Cartel was formed in Central Mexico in the 1970's by Rafael Caro Quintero, Miguel Angel "El Padrino" Felix Gallardo and Ernesto "Don Neto" Fonseca Carrillio.

(p. 11)

Gallardo was a former policeman with the Policia Judicial Federal (PJF). Gallardo expanded the marijuana and heroin selling operations of the cartel by allying with the Medellin cartel of Colombia to sell Colombian cocaine. Mahadevan (2011) reported that

During the early 1980s, the biggest trafficking organization in Mexico was the Guadalajara cartel. . . . it initially desisted from overt displays of force, preferring to deflect law enforcement efforts through bribery. However, it ruinously broke with this restraint in February 1985, when it ordered the abduction and murder of a U.S. Drug Enforcement Administration operative. Intense pressure from the United States forced Mexican authorities to gradually begin dismantling the cartel.

(p. 8)

The Juarez Cartel Prior to 2000

Pablo Acosta Villarreal aka "El Zorro de Ojinaga" (d. 1987) and his partner Amado Carrillo Fuentes aka "El Señor de Los Cielos" (Lord of the Skies; 1956–1997) ran the Juarez Cartel from around 1984 to 1997 (Poppa, 1998, p. 320). About 1986, they forged alliances with Colombian Cartels to smuggle cocaine into the United States in addition to the marijuana and heroin that they were already smuggling (Poppa, 1998, pp. 255–256). Observing that Acosta was a social bandit, Cimino (2014b) stated:

Known as "*El Pablote*," "The Czar," "The Ojinaga Fox," "The Ojinaga God-father" and "The Ojinaga Robin Hood," Acosta Villarreal helped the poor in Ojinaga, buying school books for working class students and sometimes even paying for their university or private school tuition. He was also said to be one of a new breed of narco-trafficker-flamboyant, openly defiant of authority, impulsive and unpredictably violent. Often boasting of payoffs and murders, he would do anything to consolidate his power. He had a penchant for fine Texas Stetsons, AR-15 machine guns, brand new Ford Broncos, drinking tequila, snorting cocaine and smoking Marlboro cigarettes laced with crack cocaine. In April 1987, Acosta Villarreal was killed in an ambush orchestrated by the FBI.

(p. 66)

After Acosta was killed in 1987 by Mexican PJF authorities who were working with the FBI, Carrillo Fuentes assumed command (Poppa, 1998, pp. 301–321). Carrillo introduced more modern smuggling methods, flying the drugs into the United States using Boeing 727s and French Caravelles. Carrillo died in 1997 after a botched attempt to change his appearance through plastic surgery. He too was considered to be a social bandit, having given cattle and cars to local residents and contributing "narco-alms" to the Catholic Church (Cimino, 2014b, p. 67).

The Gulf Cartel Prior to 2000

Juan Nepomuceno Guerra Cárdenas and Juan Garcia Abrego turned a local smuggling operation that had roots in Prohibition-era liquor smuggling in the 1930s into a full-blown drug smuggling operation. In the period of the 1930s to 1970s, the cartel continued smuggling contraband but diversified their criminal activities to include car theft, extortion, gambling, gunrunning, and prostitution. The Gulf Cartel began smuggling marijuana into the United States in the 1970s. The cartel formed an alliance with the Cali Cartel to smuggle cocaine into the United States. Guerra Cardenas retired in 1991. Abrego was captured in 1996 and in a rare move was extradited to the United States shortly thereafter. A power struggle resulted within the cartel and they went through a series of leaders but continued to exist (Cimino, 2014b, pp. 24–35).

The Election of 2000 and the End of an Era

In Mexico, politics as usual ended with the defeat of the Institutional Revolutionary Party (PRI) by the National Action Party (PAN) in 2000. The new president, Vicente Fox, began to extradite wanted criminals to the United States and attempted to deal with corruption in the Mexican government. His successor, Felix Calderon, campaigned on the promise to restore the "rule of law" to Mexico. He was elected and in 2006 began to attempt to end the traditional corruption and live up to his election promise by inserting

Figure 12.1

Vicente Fox (right) and Gerhard Schröder, German chancellor (left). Public domain.

Noticias e Información de la Presidencia

the army into drug enforcement and reforming the federal police. The result was a drug war between the government and the cartels (Etter & Lehmuth, 2013, p. 4; Mahoney, 2010).

After 2000, the Cartels Adapt and Expand

The cartels became much more organized in their criminal activities. They expanded both horizontally and vertically in organizational structure. Every aspect of drug trafficking was now embraced by the cartels including growth/manufacture, transport, wholesale distribution, and marketing. The range of drugs produced and sold expanded from the traditional marijuana and heroin to include methamphetamine, ecstasy, and other designer drugs. Alliances were made with Colombian cartels to transport and distribute cocaine into the United States. The range of operations of the individual cartels expanded rapidly following the immigration smuggling routes across the borders into Central America and across the United States, especially in the cities. In order to protect

Figure 12.2

The Mexican drug cartels often transport and store illicit drugs in tunnels. This one was controlled by the Sinaloa cartel, a cement-lined passage thought to link warehouses on either side of the border. Public domain.

U.S. Drug Enforcement Administration

their newly expanded operations, the cartels developed paramilitary capabilities with sophisticated communications systems that were capable of not only fighting other cartels, but the Mexican military as well.

The Narco-wars in Mexico 2000–Present

The drug war that resulted in Mexico after President Calderon committed the Mexican military into the fight against the Mexican drug cartels has claimed over 100,000 lives. Hundreds of thousands more have been wounded and hundreds of thousands more forced out of their homes as refugees. The war has been compared to a square dance to narco-*corrido* music, in which the participants attempt to stab fellow dancers in the back as they change partners.

It what has become a type of asymmetric warfare that covers many but not all of the Mexican states. The Mexican military is using counterinsurgency tactics combined with a "Kingpin Strategy" to combat the drug cartels. The cartels have created paramilitary forces to protect their drug trafficking operations. These paramilitary forces have adopted guerrilla-style tactics to combat the government forces, although the various cartel forces have adopted more conventional infantry tactics when it suited their goals, even using homemade World War I style armored vehicles not only against the government forces but against each other.

The result has been a type of three-way split in the conflict. The government forces include the Mexican military and law enforcement or police that remain loyal to the government. The cartels have divided into two basic sides: the Sinaloa Cartel and their allies and the Los Zetas Cartel and their allies. Because of corruption issues, these allies have often included local police forces who have actually fired on government forces.

The goals of the government forces include the complete elimination or suppression of the cartel forces of both alliances. They wish to restore the rule of law to Mexico and end the open criminality and corruption that plagues Mexico. The government has prosecuted corrupt politicians and relieved entire police forces in attempts to achieve their goals.

The goals of the cartels include survival, protection of their sources of income, maintaining some support from the people, and the ability to conduct their criminal business operations without interference from government. In order to do this, the cartels must import weapons and ammunition. The cartels have on occasion taxed iron mine operators for raw iron ore and avocado farmers for a portion of their crops, using the proceeds to trade for or buy weapons.

Although in some isolated areas the cartels have levied taxes in areas they control, they have no intention of becoming the permanent government. There has been no attempt thus far by any cartel to march on the capital of Mexico City and displace the government. This is very different from the Mexican Civil War of 1910–1923. In order to solicit support from the people, the cartels portray themselves as protectors of the people against the other cartels or corrupt officials. An example of this are the narco-*placas* (or explanation signs) that are often left at the scenes of cartel violence. An example is being made or a political statement is being made and this requires, in the cartel leader's mind, an explanation to the people. This practice was copied from a Colombian group that worked for the Cali Cartel called Los Pepes.

Mexican cartels have developed a leader-centered patriarchal organizational structure that is often family-oriented in the line of succession. While this can aid in unity of command of the cartel and help to prevent infiltration by outside forces, it can prove to be a great weakness if the leaders are killed or captured. Several Mexican cartels have disbanded because the government forces targeted the leaders using the "Kingpin Strategy," having killed or captured all of the leaders, leaving no family members to replace them. Table 12.1 shows the alliances of the Sinaloa Cartel, along with their location of operation and the status of their leadership.

In his description of the size and scope of the Sinaloa Cartel, Matthews (2014) observed that

---

TABLE 12.1 Sinaloa Cartel Alliances (as of 2016)

Cartel	Location	Leaders
Sinaloa Cartel Allied with FARC, Norte del Valle Cartel, Shining Path, Russian Mafia, Sicilian Mafia, Sung Ye On Triad, 14K Triad, MS-13, Mexican Mafia	Sinaloa and 18 other Mexican states, United States, Asia, Australia, Argentina, Brazil, Chile, Colombia, Costa Rica, Europe, Guatemala, Honduras, Nicaragua, Panama, and West Africa	Joaquín Archivaldo "El Chapo" Guzmán Loera: captured 1993, escaped 2001, captured 2014, escaped 2015, captured 2016. Ismael Zambada García
Gulf Cartel (Cartel del Golfos or CDG) Allied with 'Ndrangheta, MS-13	Tamaulipas and Northeastern Mexico, United States	Juan Nepomuceno Guerra Cárdenas: died 2001 Osiel Cárdenas Guillén: captured 2003, extradited to United States 2007 Antonio Ezequiel Cárdenas Guillén: killed 2010 Jorge Eduardo Costilla Sánchez: captured 2012, extradited to United States 2015
Knights Templar Cartel (Los Caballeros Templarios)	Michoacán and four other Mexican states	Nazario Moreno González "El Mas Loco": killed 2014 Enrique Plancarte Solís "Las Chiva": killed 2014 Servando Gómez Martínez "La Tuta": captured 2015 Dionisio Loya Plancarte "El Tio": captured 2014

Cartel	Location	Leaders
Jalisco New Generation Cartel (Cartel de Jalisco Nueva Generacion or CJNG)	Jalisco and four other Mexican States	Nemesio Oseguera Cervantes "El Mencho"
		Martín Arzola Ortega "El 53": captured 2011
		Emilio Alejandro Pulido Saldaña "El Tiburon"
		Erick Valencia Salazar "El 85": captured 2012
		Alex Vega "El Compa Pekas"
Los Antrax Paramilitary Group (Sinaloa)	Sinaloa	Rodrigo Arechiga Gamboa "El Chino Antrax": captured 2013
		Jesus Pena "El 20": captured 2014
		Melesio Beltrán Medina "El Mele": killed 2014
Artist Assassins (Doble A or AA) Street Gang (Sinaloa)	Chihuahua	
La Barredora	Acapulco	Christian Hernández Tarín "El Chris": captured 2011
		Víctor Manuel Rivera Galeana "El Gordo": captured 2011
		Eder Jair Sosa Carvajal "El Cremas"
Gente Nueva Paramilitary Group (Sinaloa)	Sonora and three other Mexican states	Noel Salgueiro "El Falco": captured 2011
		José Antonio Torres Marrufo "El Jaguar": captured 2012
		Mario Nuñez Meza "El Mayito": captured 2013
		Jesús Gregorio Villanueva Rodríguez "El R5": killed 2013
Los Mexicles Street Gang (Sinaloa, Gulf)	Northern Mexico and Texas	Jose Marquez
La Familia Michoacan (LFM) Disbanded after internal conflicts in 2011. Many members regrouped as Knights Templar Cartel.	Michoacan and nine other Mexican states, United States	Carlos Alberto Rosales Mendoza: killed 2015
		Nazario Moreno González "El Mas Loco": killed 2014

Sinaloa is Mexico's largest drug cartel, one of several gangs that have been terrorizing the Mexican population as it serves as the middleman between South American producers of illegal drugs and an unquenchable American market. The White House Office of Drug Control Policy estimates that Americans spend $100 billion on illegal drugs each year, and the RAND Corporation says that about $6.5 billion of that reaches Mexican cartels. With an estimated 60% market share, the Sinaloa cartel is raking in approximately $3 billion per year.

Table 12.2 shows the alliances of Los Zetas, along with their location of operation and the status of their leadership.

TABLE 12.2 **Los Zetas Cartel Alliances (as of 2016)**

Cartel	Location	Leaders
Los Zetas Formed in 1997 from 30 deserters from the Mexican Military Special Forces. Originally allied with the Gulf Cartel until 2002. Allied with 'Ndrangheta, MS-13, Texas Syndicate, Gangster Disciples.	Tamaulipas and 23 other Mexican states, United States, Guatemala	Arturo Guzmán Decena "Z-1": killed 2002 Rogelio González Pizaña "Z-2": captured 2004 Heriberto Lazcano Lazcano "Z-3": killed 2012 Miguel Treviño Morales "Z-40": captured 2013 Omar Treviño Morales "Z-42": captured 2015
Juarez Cartel (Cartel de Juarez or Vicente Carrillo Fuentes Organization)	Chihuahua and 21 other Mexican states, United States	Pablo Acosta Villarreal: killed 1987 Rafael Aguilar Guajardo: killed 1993 Amado Carrillo Fuentes: died 1997 Vincente Carrillo Leyva: captured 2009 Alberto Carrillo Fuentes: captured 2013 Vicente Carrillo Fuentes: captured 2014 Juan Pablo Ledezma

Cartel	Location	Leaders
Tijuana Cartel (Cartel de Tijuana or Arellano-Félix Organization or Cartel Arellano Felix-CAF) Allied with Cali Cartel, Norte del Valle Cartel, FARC.	Tijuana and 15 Mexican states, United States	Francisco Rafael Arellano Félix: captured 1993, extradited 2006, released 2008, killed 2013 Benjamín Arellano Félix: captured 2002, extradited 2011 Eduardo Arellano Félix: captured 2008, extradited 2012 Ramon Arellano Félix: killed 2002 Francisco Javier Arellano Félix: captured 2006 Alberto Arellano "El Piloto"
Oaxaca Cartel	Oaxaca	Pedro Díaz Parada: captured 2007 Eugenio Jesús Díaz Parada Domingo Aniceto Díaz Parada
La Lina Paramilitary Group (Juarez)	Chihuahua	Juan Pablo Ledezma "El JL or José Luis Fratello" Juan Pablo Guijarro "El Monico": captured 2010 Luis Carlos Vázquez Barragán "El 20": captured 2010 Marco Antonio Guzmán "Brad Pitt": captured 2011 José Guadalupe Rivas González "El Zucaritas": captured 2011 José Antonio Acosta Hernández "El Diego": captured 2011 Jesús Antonio Rincón Chavero "El Tarzan": captured 2011 Luis Guillermo Castillo Rubio "El Pariente": captured 2012
Barrio Azteca Street Gang that began in El Paso, Texas	United States and Chihuahua	
Beltran-Leyva Cartel (Beltran-Leyva or BLO or Cartel de los Beltran-Leyva-CBL) Disbanded in 2014 after all of their leaders were killed or captured	Sinaloa and five other Mexican states, United States	Marcos Arturo Beltrán Leyva: killed 2009 Carlos Beltrán Leyva: captured 2009 Alfredo Beltrán Leyva: captured 2008 Héctor Beltrán Leyva: captured 2014

Cartel	Location	Leaders
Milenio Cartel Disbanded in 2012 after most of their leaders were arrested. Allied with Medellin Cartel.	Michoacan and six other Mexican states, United States	Armando Valencia Cornelio: captured 2003 Óscar Nava Valencia: captured 2009, extradited to United States 2011 Juan Nava Valencia: captured 2010

Colombian Drug Cartels

Colombia did not start supplying marijuana on a large scale until the late 1960s. The origin of the marijuana boom can be traced to a search by U.S. drug dealers for a new supply source of marijuana. Soon money hungry Colombians seized the opportunity to make a lot of money in a stagnant economy by becoming marijuana exporters. The new Colombian drug lords soon took over the producing and distributing of the marijuana that was produced in Colombia. This was the beginning of the Colombian participation in the trafficking of illegal drugs to the United States and the rest of the world (Streatfeild, 2001, p. 207).

The Colombian cartels developed new patriarchal hierarchical organizational structures that expanded horizontally and vertically to encompass all aspects of the cocaine trade. Filippone (1994) found that

> These cartel bosses did more than direct the processing and distribution of cocaine. They built the organization into a multinational entity that influenced events well beyond the scope of the international drug business. As their wealth and power grew, they expanded into politics, the media, private armies, real estate, and international banking. They espoused an ideology to legitimate and support their operations. It should be noted that they are motivated not by ideology but by greed and the phenomenal wealth of the drug trade. Their ideology is centered on the fact that they are businessmen and their power is a function of their wealth, which is derived in a way that is considered illegal. Therefore, their ideology seeks to protect them from prosecution, give legitimacy to their organization, and ensure the continued operation of their business. The ideology has three pillars: It is pro-Colombian, pro-status quo, and anti-United States.
>
> (p. 326)

The Colombian cartels began to also grow poppies and process them into heroin. The heroin was sold by the cartels along with the cocaine. All of this required logistical support. The cartels set up landing fields, drop-off points, and banking services in the Bahamas, Cuba, Panama, and Nicaragua (Moore, 1990, pp. 131–140; Gugliotta & Leen, 1989, pp. 263–264).

The Colombian cartels began to set up operations to distribute cocaine inside the United States, especially in Miami and New York City. This caused conflict with those groups that thought that they were in charge of local drug distribution and resulted in the "cocaine wars" of the late 1970s and 1980s (Rempel, 2011, p. 22; Gugliotta & Leen, 1989, pp. 355–358). The conflicts carried over into Colombia, and the Medellin Cartel often found itself fighting forces of the Cali Cartel. Both cartels developed paramilitary forces to guard their interests.

In order to respond to this type of organized crime, the DEA adopted a "Kingpin Strategy." Drug operations were set up working with the Colombian government to capture cartel leaders and extradite them to the United States for trial. This strategy has resulted in the arrest of many of the cartels' main people (DEA, 2016).

Sieff (2008, p. 190) found that "South American drug cartels, which have operated for years in South Africa, have started using West African nations to transit cocaine to lucrative European markets. West African body couriers transport the drugs via land, air, and sea routes."

Medellin Cartel 1972–1993

The Medellin Cartel was a Colombian drug cartel that operated from Medellin, Colombia, from 1972 to 1993. Filippone (1994) observed that:

> The structure of the Medellin Cartel is somewhat complex. The cartel is actually a conglomerate made up of the pooled resources of the individual groups. In addition to the large cocaine production, transportation, and distribution organizations, there are equally extensive and sophisticated organizations for political action, security and protection, and financial management. Each of these subordinate activities operates in slightly different ways, recruits from different segments of society, and performs unique, yet critical, functions in the overall scheme. Within each organization the division of labor is highly complex and organized. At the low and middle levels of these organizations, the managers are easily transferred but the positions remain constant.
>
> (p. 327)

Describing the extent and depth of the Medellin Cartel, Filippone (1994) observed that

> The international nature of the Medellin cartel's operations was demonstrated by the Drug Enforcement Agency's (DEA's) special enforcement operation Bolivar, which targeted the cartel. Bolivar involved 15 countries, 51 separate DEA offices, and 201 separate investigations. The Medellin cartel has remained at the center of attention because of its tactics, which are violent and conspicuous, and the fact that it has traditionally controlled at least 60% of the Colombian cocaine traffic. The organization that it has developed employs up to 120,000 people, including 2,000 to 3,000 in the United States. This vast organization is controlled by a select few individuals, mostly the infamous Pablo Escobar, who continued to manage the cartel's operations even while incarcerated in his specially built prison in Envigado.
>
> (p. 324)

Pablo Emilo Escobar Gaviria (1949–1993)

Although he was the undisputed leader of the pack, Pablo Escobar worked with several other drug dealers, including the Ochoa brothers in Medellin, to form a cartel to sell drugs (Gugliotta & Leen, 1989, pp. 17–18). Expanding his organization vertically and horizontally, at one point Escobar controlled the means of production, transportation, and wholesale distribution of over 80% of the cocaine that went into the United States. Bowden (2001) observed that Pablo was a creature of his time and place, stating that

> He was a complex, contradictory, and ultimately very dangerous man, in large part because of his genius for manipulating public opinion. But this same crowd-pleasing quality was also his weakness, the thing that eventually brought him down. A man of lesser ambition might still be alive, rich, powerful, and living well in Medellin. But Pablo wasn't content to be just rich and powerful. He wanted to be admired. He wanted to be respected. He wanted to be loved.
>
> (p. 15)

Thus Pablo became the public face of the Medellin cartel. He also attempted to exercise political power and ran for the Colombian House of Representatives in 1982, becoming an alternate from Antioquia. This also had the advantage of making Escobar exempt from arrest under Colombian law and allowed him a diplomatic passport (Bowden, 2001, pp. 30–31; Filippone, 1994, p. 336). In 1989, he was named one of the

Figure 12.3

Pablo Escobar. A mug shot taken by the regional Colombia control agency in Medellin in 1977.

Colombian National Police [Public domain], via Wikimedia Commons

10 richest people on earth by both *Forbes* and *Fortune* (Bowden, 2001, p. 15). His cartel was ruthless in maintaining the power of their drug trafficking organization. There were allegations that his cartel funded some guerrilla operations in Colombia such as FARC, ELN, and M-19 (Bowden, 2001, p. 27).

Pablo Escapes Prison and Is Hunted Down (1992–1993)

Being the public face of the cartel had its advantages, but it had its hazards too. This included voiding the chance of being extradited to the United States. In 1991, Escobar surrendered to Colombian authorities in a brokered deal that mandated he serve five years and would not be extradited to the United States. Escobar was incarcerated in La Cathedral prison in Medellin. The prison had a bar, swimming pool, and Jacuzzi. Escobar continued to run the cartel from the prison and had his own phone. When it looked like Escobar might be transferred to another prison in Bogota, Escobar walked away in July 1992, triggering a massive manhunt that led to his death (Escobar, 2010, pp. 88–101; Bowden, 2001, pp. 109–130; Streatfeild, 2001, p. 445). Escobar was killed on December 2, 1993, in a gunfight with members of Colombian National Police Col. Martinez's Search Bloc at a safe house where he was hiding. That effectively ended the Medellin Cartel (DEA, 2016; Lunde, 2004b, p. 185).

Pablo the Folk Hero

Escobar admired Al Capone and copied many of his actions, including seeing to the needs of the poor (Bowden, 2001, p. 237). He was the model of a social bandit. Escobar funded houses, clinics, a zoo, sports teams, and other social work projects, ensuring the loyalty of the poor population of Medellin. Thousands attended his funeral, and many still see him as a folk hero championing the interests of the poor versus the rich in Colombia (Bowden, 2001, p. 266). As a memorial, the Latin musical group Los Tigres del Norte wrote a song about Pablo Escobar and his donations to the poor. T-shirts bearing his image and commemorative plates are still sold on the streets of Colombia.

Carlos Lehder Rivas

Known as Carlos Lehder, he was the brains behind the setting up of cocaine transportation routes for the Medellin Cartel to the United States via aircraft, boats, and overland (Gugliotta & Leen, 1989, pp. 263–264). In 1977, Lehder set up a base of operations on the island of Norman's Cay in the Bahamas (Moore, 1990, p. 74; Gugliotta & Leen, 1989, pp. 57–74). Lehder also set up a distribution system for the cocaine all over the United States. Noting the change in cocaine smuggling tactics developed by Lehder, Filippone (1994) stated that

> The origins of the cocaine trade in Colombia go back to the 1950's, when the Colombians produced a small amount of cocaine and shipped it to the Cuban Mafia. When the Cubans went to the United States in the 1960's, so did the cocaine. The primary method of smuggling cocaine into the United States was by using "mules," people who hide a relatively small amount of cocaine on their body or in their personal luggage and enter the United States through normal entry points. This all changed in 1976, when Carlos Lehder Rivas, a small-time car thief and marijuana smuggler serving time in a U.S. prison, conceptualized an important change in the cocaine-trafficking industry. Instead of using "mules," he would use small private aircraft to smuggle cocaine into the United States. This took advantage of the existing trafficking routes and distribution networks the Colombians had established for marijuana smuggling. The main differences were that the cocaine was easier to transport, required fewer people, and was far more profitable.
>
> (p. 324)

Feeling the heat from U.S. law enforcement, in early 1985 Lehder boldly and publicly announced that he would pay $350,000 to anyone who could kill or capture the U.S. DEA chief. In 1987, Lehder was captured in Colombia and extradited to the United States (Lunde, 2004b, p. 184; Eddy, Sabogal, & Walden, 1988, p. 325). He made a plea agreement and testified against Panama's former President Manual Noriega in U.S. federal court in exchange for a reduction in sentence to 55 years.

George Jung

George Jung was a marijuana smuggler who met Lehder in prison at Federal Corrections Institution (FCI) Danbury, where Lehder was his cellmate. They began to fly cocaine into the United States for Escobar as partners. Jung and Lehder later split up and worked for Escobar separately (Streatfeild, 2001, pp. 215–219; Gugliotta & Leen, 1989, pp. 57–59; Eddy et al., 1988, pp. 147–148). In 1994, Jung was arrested in Topeka, Kansas, with a large amount of cocaine (796 kg). He pleaded guilty to several counts of conspiracy and was in federal custody until 2014.

José Rodriguez-Gacha aka "The Mexican" (1947–1989)

José Rodriguez-Gacha aka "The Mexican" was one of the founders of the Medellin Cartel (Gugliotta & Leen, 1989, p. 17; Eddy et al., 1988, pp. 289–290). He was often considered the most violent of the Medellin Cartel leaders. Rodriguez-Gacha spent his cocaine wealth in the purchase of horses, soccer teams, and massive amounts of land in the jungle. Although Rodriguez-Gacha was involved with Muerte a Secuestradores (Death to Kidnappers; MAS) death squads in Colombia, he also intimidated through bribery and violence. For example, an army major was flabbergasted at an offer, delivered by an emissary of Rodriguez-Gacha: in return for destroying confiscated documents and computer disks that provided a detailed blueprint of Gacha's cocaine empire, the officer, whose monthly salary was $300, would receive $1.2 million cash. If he refused, the drug Mafia would hunt him down and kill him.

After being blamed by the Colombian government for a series of terrorist attacks that killed over 200 people and several bombings including the bombing of a Colombian airliner, Rodriguez-Gacha was hunted down and killed by Colombian authorities in 1989 (Bowden, 2001, pp. 82–83; Gugliotta & Leen, 1989, p. 591). Rodriguez-Gacha was seen as a social bandit who gave money to rehabilitate buildings by some people in the town of Pocho. Thousands of mourners from the town attended his funeral (Bowden, 2001, p. 83).

Jorge Ochoa Vasquez "El Gordo"

Jorge Ochoa Vasquez was one of the original founders of the Medellin Cartel (Gugliotta & Leen, 1989, pp. 17–18). Jorge became responsible for coordinating Medellin cartel operations in Western Europe and in the United States (Moore, 1990, pp. 84–86; Eddy et al., 1988, pp. 55–56). In 1983, feeling pressure from the Colombian government, the Ochoa brothers, Rodriguez-Gacha, Lehder, and Escobar hid in Panama for some time (Bowden, 2001, p. 45). In 1986, Spanish police arrested Ochoa on a U.S. warrant and both the United States and Colombia applied for his extradition. As a result, the Medellin Cartel publicly threatened to murder five Americans for every Colombian extradition. The Spanish courts ultimately ruled in favor of Colombia's request and Ochoa was deported. He served a month in jail on charges of bull smuggling before he was paroled (Gugliotta & Leen, 1989, pp. 430–431). Jorge surrendered to the Colombian National Police in January 1991 and was sentenced to prison for drug trafficking. Jorge served five years and was released. Ochoa now lives quietly in Medellin.

Fabio Ochoa Vasquez

Fabio Ochoa Vasquez was the bother of Jorge. He acted as a pilot for the cartel and sometimes dealt with Milenio Cartel of Mexico. He allegedly ordered the killing of Barry Seal inside the United States in 1986. Fabio moved to the United States and lived in Miami, where he supervised shipments of Medellin Cartel cocaine to the United States (Gugliotta & Leen, 1989, pp. 349–350). Fabio was arrested in Colombia in 1999 and extradited to the United States in 2001 (Lunde, 2004b, p. 185). Upon conviction in federal court in 2003, he was given a 30-year prison sentence (O'Neil, 2003).

Tranquilandia Lab Raid 1984

By tracking the illegal sale of massive amounts of ether to Colombia, the DEA and Colombian police discovered Tranquilandia, a laboratory operation deep in the Colombian jungle. In the subsequent raid on March 10, 1984, law enforcement officials destroyed 14 laboratory complexes containing 13.8 metric tons of cocaine, seven airplanes, and 11,800 drums of chemicals, conservatively estimated at $1.2 billion. The operation confirmed the consolidation of the Medellin Cartel's manufacturing operation (Gugliotta & Leen, 1989, pp. 217–218).

The Body Count

In an effort to maintain power and influence in Colombia and avoid extradition to the United States, the Medellin Cartel resorted to violence. It cost the lives of three Colombian presidential candidates, the Colombian Minister of Justice (Rodrigo Lara-Bonilla), Attorney General Carlos Mauro Hoyos-Jiminez, more than 200 judges, dozens of journalists, and over 1,000 police officers. In the 1980s the Medellin Cartel began a series of bombings of cars, public buildings and police stations. The bombings were to exert political power and to prevent the extradition of drug lords to the United States. The bombings continued through the 1990s. The drug dealers known as "the Extraditables" said: "Better a tomb in Colombia than a jail cell in Miami!" (Bowden, 2001, pp. 51–72).

In order to further their point to the Colombian government, the Medellin Cartel engaged in political assassination, often using forces from various guerrilla movements to assist in the bombing or hits. Louis Carlos Galan was assassinated in August 1989. He was the front-runner in the race for the presidency of Colombia and had campaigned against drug trafficking and corruption (Gugliotta & Leen, 1989, pp. 556–560). His death caused the U.S. government to commit U.S. Delta forces to become involved in the hunt for Pablo Escobar. On October 11, 2007, Alberto Santofimio was sentenced to 24 years in prison for ordering a hit squad belonging to late drug baron Escobar to kill Galan. Santofimio was also running for election and was an associate of Escobar, who was facing U.S. extradition.

Cali Cartel 1977–1998

The Cali Cartel was a drug cartel that operated around the city of Cali, Colombia, from 1977 to 1998. Robinson and Cooper (1991) reported that

> Authorities say the Cali group isn't a cartel, really, but rather a consortium of loosely affiliated and cooperating trafficking groups. The Drug Enforcement Administration estimates that the Cali group is now responsible for up to 70 percent of the cocaine reaching U.S. shores, including as much as 85 percent of the lucrative New York market. Cali traffickers are also strong in Houston, Miami and Southern California, and they are establishing beachheads in Europe as well. Cali cocaine, packaged in rectangular blocks marked with distinctive red and yellow dots, recently appeared as far away as Czechoslovakia. The Cali traffickers, says DEA Administrator Robert Bonner, represent "the most powerful criminal organization the world has known."

Describing the tactics used by the Cali Cartel to protect itself, Robinson and Cooper (1991) went on to report that

> Even more than Medellin, the Cali cartel uses bribes, threats and its political clout to escape punishment. Few publicly criticize the most notorious Cali boss, Gilberto Rodriguez Orejuela, who has allegedly laundered his money into legitimate, lucrative investments including a top-flight soccer team, a chain of

pharmacies, banks and other businesses. Last September, Colombia's Supreme Court annulled his 1988 acquittal on trafficking charges, as well as that of his colleague Jose Santacruz Londono. But no arrest warrants are being served.

However, as Chepesiuk (2010) observed, the Cali Cartel also used modern technology and intelligence tactics to protect themselves. Chepesiuk found that

> The technological and counter-intelligence sophistication of the Cali rivaled the resources available to a first-world state. Following a raid in 1995, the Colombian authorities discovered that the cartel had been able to monitor all telephone traffic in and out of Cali and Bogota, including the Ministry of Defense and the U.S. embassy. Whether through bribery or threat, they cultivated contacts in official ministries, seemed to know when their phones were bugged, even by remote, and had complete copies of Colombia's up-to-date car-registration records. The possessed encryption software that outfoxed the knowledge of Colombian and DEA IT experts. In short, much as a modern nation-state's intelligence service would, they understood that blanket coverage was less hit-and-miss than the old ways of intrigue and espionage. On their payroll were a rumored 5,000 Cali taxi-drivers, who yielded precise details of the comings and goings of the officials they were contracted to drive, together with news of who was entering and leaving the city as a whole. Time magazine ran a story in 1991 about how DEA and U.S. Customs agents were monitoring a cocaine shipment being offloaded in Miami, while themselves being under surveillance by the Cali cartel.
>
> (pp. 132–133)

Unlike the Medellin Cartel, which preferred to transport cocaine by airplane, the Cali Cartel preferred to transport its wares by merchant marine. But they had a high degree of situational awareness of the nature and successes of their law enforcement opponents. Above all, the Cali Cartel was adaptable. When the DEA began to make things too hot in Miami and New York, the Cali Cartel simply moved their operations. Noting their adaptability, Chepesiuk (2010) found that

> the greatest change they brought about in distribution patterns, and through it geopolitics, was to recruit Mexican gangs to move the drug on to its market in the U.S. Traditionally, the Cali cartel had dominated the cocaine route into Florida from their tame state of Panama, while Escobar and Lehder had operated out of the Bahamas. But when the Colombian government bowed to US pressure over extradition, the Cali came up with the solution of cutting in the Mexicans because, by no longer exporting directly to the US, they hoped to

avoid eligibility for extradition under the terms of the relevant legislation. In so doing, the Cali have been partly responsible for the growth of Mexican gang warfare (having raised the stakes over and above those provided by the traditional crops of cannabis and heroin) and the social disorder that parts of the country are undergoing.

(p. 133)

The Cali Cartel also forged alliances with Italian organized crime to distribute cocaine in Europe (Chepesiuk, 2010, pp. 135–155). The cartel dealt with guerrilla and paramilitary groups to protect their interests. They even formed a group called Los Pepes (People Persecuted by Pablo Escobar) to attack Medellin Cartel members and to hunt for Escobar (Streatfeild, 2001, p. 445).

Gilberto Rodriguez-Orejuela aka "The Chess Player"

Gilberto Rodriguez-Orejuela was the leader of the Cali Cartel. Gilberto openly bragged that he was responsible for the 1994 election of the Liberal Party candidate, Ernesto Samper after contributing over $6,000,000 to his campaign (Rempel, 2011, p. 157). However, that did not save Gilberto from being arrested by the Colombian National Police in 1995 after his donations to the election campaign had been publicly revealed (Rempel, 2011, pp. 185–186; Streatfeild, 2001, p. 459). Gilbeto was sentenced to 13 years but he was extradited to the United States in 2004 (Chepesiuk, 2010, p. 184). Gilberto pleaded guilty in 2006 and was sentenced to 30 years and fined $2.1 billion (Rempel, 2011, pp. 315–316).

Miguel Rodriguez-Orejuela

Miguel Rodriguez-Orejuela founded the Cali Cartel along with his brother Gilberto and Jose Santacruz-Londono. Miguel took over day-to-day management of the cartel around 1990 (Rempel, 2011, pp. 111–112; Chepesiuk, 2010, p. 187). Miguel was arrested by the Colombian National Police in 1995 (Rempel, 2011, pp. 265–276) and was sentenced to 21 years. Miguel was extradited to the United States and pleaded guilty in 2006. He was sentenced to 30 years and fined $2.1 billion (Rempel, 2011, pp. 315–316).

Jose Santacruz-Londono aka "Chepe" (1943–1996)

Jose Santacruz-Londono was the number three man in the Cali Cartel and was one of the founding members of the cartel. Jose was involved in production of cocaine, transportation, distribution, and money laundering. He was arrested by the Colombian National Police in 1995 but escaped custody. Jose Santacruz-Londono was killed in a shootout with the Colombian National Police in 1996 (Rempel, 2011, p. 316; Lunde, 2004b, pp. 186–187).

Francisco Hélmer Herrera Buitrago aka "Pacho" aka "H7" (1951–1998)

Herrera was number four in command of the Cali Cartel. He established Cali ties with the New York City drug market and with Mexican drug traffickers. Herrera ran money laundering operations for the cartel. He was also suspected of negotiating with various Colombian rebel groups. Herrera also imported cocaine base into Colombia from Peru and Bolivia for the cartel. He surrendered to the Colombian National Police in 1996 (DEA, 1996). Herrera was murdered in a Colombian prison in 1998 by a man who entered the maximum security Palmira Prison east of Cali, posing as a lawyer (Rempel, 2011, p. 317; Chepesiuk, 2010, p. 145).

Victor Patino-Fomeque

Victor Patino-Fomeque was a former Colombian policeman. He was recruited to be the bodyguard for the Rodriguez brothers. Patino-Fomeque ran the Cali's maritime drug smuggling operations. He surrendered to the Colombian National Police in 1995 and was sentenced to 12 years. Victor was extradited to the United States in 2005. He later testified as a witness for the U.S. government in several trials of cartel members. As a result, over 30 friends and family have been killed because he testified for the government.

Henry Loaiza-Ceballos aka "El Alacran" (The Scorpion)

Henry Loaiza-Ceballos oversaw the Cali Cartel's military structure. He was considered to be the most violent of the group. Loaiza-Ceballos oversaw three different massacres in Colombia's drug wars (including the Massacre of Trujillo that killed between 245 and 342 people during 1988–1994). He surrendered to the Colombian National Police in 1995.

Norte del Valle Cartel 1990s–2012

The Norte del Valle Cartel was a Colombian drug cartel that operated in the Valle del Cauca department of Colombia from the 1990s to 2012. Although it was never as large as the Medellin or Cali Cartels, between 1990 and 2004 the Norte del Valle Cartel was responsible for exporting more than 1.2 million pounds of cocaine to the United States, worth roughly $10 billion. The cartel was considered the largest and most feared drug organization in Colombia, responsible for roughly 30% to 50% of the cocaine smuggled to the United States (DEA, 2004). After internal conflicts over leadership and the arrest of most of its leadership cadre, the cartel disbanded in 2012.

Diego Leon Montoya-Sanchez

Diego Leon Montoya-Sanchez was one of the leaders of the Norte del Valle Cartel. He sought help from some of Colombia's guerrilla and paramilitary groups to protect the operations of his cartel (Economist, 2004). Diego Leon Montoya-Sanchez was arrested in 2007 in Colombia, and on December 12, 2008, he was extradited to the United States.

Luis Hernando Gomez-Bustamante

Luis Hernando Gomez-Bustamante was a leader of the Norte del Valle Cartel. He was arrested in Cuba in 2004 for attempted entry using a false passport. He had been indicted in both the United States and Colombia for drug trafficking and was extradited from Cuba to Colombia in 2007. He was then extradited to the United States later that same year (BBC, 2008).

Arcangel de Jesus Heno-Montoya

Arcangel de Jesus Heno-Montoya was the number two man in the Norte del Valle cartel. He was captured in Panama in 2004 and extradited to the United States that same year.

Jhonny Cano-Correa, aka "Flechas" aka "Santiago"

Jhonny Cano-Correa was the number three man in the Norte del Valle Cartel. He was an enforcer for the cartel and oversaw the security of the cartel's cocaine laboratories. He oversaw financing for cartel operations and also found new smuggling routes. Cano-Correa was arrested by the Colombian National Police and Immigration and Customs Enforcement in Colombia in 2005 (U.S. Department of State, 2005a).

Jose Aldemar Rendon-Ramirez

Jose Aldemar Rendon-Ramirez was the Norte del Valle Cartel finance officer. He was a key lieutenant in the Colombian Norte del Valle Cartel (NVC), and was responsible for importing significant amounts of cocaine into the United States and Spain. He was also responsible for arranging for the laundering of tens of millions of dollars from drug trafficking for several major NVC traffickers. He was arrested in 2005 by the Colombian National Police outside Medellin (U.S. Department of State, 2005b).

Juan Alberto Monsalve, aka "El Loco"

Juan Alberto Monsalve was the owner of the Tele-Austin business in Queens, New York, that laundered money for the Norte del Valle Cartel. He was involved in the murders of people over drug debts in the United States (DEA, 2004). He was arrested in 2000 in the United States. Monsalve was convicted of homicide and drug trafficking. He was sentenced to two life sentences.

Fuerzas Armadas Revolucionarias de Colombia (FARC) 1964–Present

The FARC is a Marxist-Leninist guerrilla movement that has opposed the government forces of Colombia since 1964. Although at its height the FARC had an estimated 18,000 fighters, the strength of the FARC was recently estimated at between 9,000 and 12,000 fighters (Walsh, 2016, p. 8). The FARC has conducted bombings, assassinations, kidnappings, mortar attacks, hijackings, and guerrilla military actions against Colombian targets. They have also kidnapped foreigners for ransom. As a Communist revolutionary movement, prior to 1991 the FARC received assistance from Cuba and the former Soviet Union. Assistance from North Korea ended in about 2011. The FARC uses the drug trade to finance operations (Walsh, 2016, p. 8). They are currently allied with the Sinaloa cartel. The FARC has been known to trade drugs for military-grade weapons (Parker, 2010, pp. 190–239; Guglietta & Leen, 1990, p. 544). The FARC sometimes runs its smuggling operations through the Amazonas state of Venezuela (Wyss, 2015). Wyss (2015) found that

> The estimates about FARC manpower in Venezuela may be inflated. (Colombia says there are fewer than 7,000 active guerrillas.) But Colombian authorities do acknowledge that the group, which is considered a terrorist organization, often hides along the porous border. And there's evidence that the guerrillas are becoming more reliant on illegal mining as they've seen their drug routes squeezed. Organizations that study the conflict estimate that gold mining in Colombia alone might represent 20 percent of FARC income.

However, the times are changing, and on August 29, 2016, the Colombian government and the FARC signed a ceasefire that effectively ended the war that has raged in Colombia since 1964 (Walsh, 2016, pp. 7–9). It is unknown what effect, if any, this will

Figure 12.4

FARC—Revolutionary Armed Forces of Colombia.

FARC-EP [CC BY-SA 4.0 (https://creativecommons.org/licenses/by-sa/4.0)], via Wikimedia Commons.

have on FARC's drug selling operations. Several mini-cartels have already sprung up and are engaging in a mom-and-pop cocaine trade in Colombia.

Where Colombian Drug Cartels Operate

After the Medellin Cartel, the Cali Cartel, and the Norte del Valle Cartel disbanded, the FARC was left as the largest operating cartel in Colombia. However, many smaller independent cartels developed as a result. These cartels operate all through Central and South America. They have alliances with Mexican cartels, Italian organized crime, Russian organized crime, and many other criminal organizations. They even have limited operations and dealings in West Africa.

Transnational Gangs

Like traditional organized crime, transnational gangs deal in illegal goods and services. Naim (2003) observed that

The illegal trade in drugs, arms, intellectual property, people, and money is booming. Like the war on terrorism, the fight to control these illicit markets pits governments against agile, stateless, and resourceful networks empowered by globalization. Governments will continue to lose these wars until they adopt new strategies to deal with a larger, unprecedented struggle that now shapes the world as much as confrontations between nation-states once did.

While transnational crime has existed throughout the centuries, the global political changes and economic problems of the twenty-first century have brought new players into transnational crime (Bratton, 2007). Naim (2012) found that

The global economic crisis has been a boon for transnational criminals. Thanks to the weak economy, cash-rich criminal organizations can acquire financially distressed but potentially valuable companies at bargain prices. Fiscal austerity is forcing governments everywhere to cut the budgets of law enforcement agencies and court systems. Millions of people have been laid off and are thus more easily tempted to break the law. Large numbers of unemployed experts in finance, accounting, information technology, law, and logistics have boosted the supply of world-class talent available to criminal cartels. Meanwhile, philanthropists all over the world have curtailed their giving, creating funding shortfalls in the arts, education, health care, and other areas, which criminals are all too happy to fill in exchange for political access, social legitimacy, and popular support. International criminals could hardly ask for a more favorable business environment. Their activities are typically high margin and cash-based, which means they often enjoy a high degree of liquidity—not a bad position to be in during a global credit crunch.

Sex and Human Trafficking

The trafficking of humans for slaves or sexual exploitation is nothing new. It has been going on for centuries. In modern times this trafficking is often associated with other types of organized crime such as drug trafficking, weapons trafficking, or counterfeit goods trafficking (DOS, 2005, p. 13). Some people are trafficked for sexual exploitation or for exploitation of their labor. Some people are just being smuggled into another country to avoid the immigration laws (Police Chief, 2014).

The United Nations (2000) defined human trafficking as

> the recruitment, transportation, transfer, harboring or receipt of persons, by means of the threat or use of force or other forms of coercion, of abduction, of fraud, of deception, of the abuse of power or of a position of vulnerability or of the giving or receiving of payments or benefits to achieve the consent of a person having control over another person, for the purpose of exploitation.
>
> (p. 42)

Naim (2003) observed that:

> The man or woman who sells a bogus Hermes scarf or a Rolex watch in the streets of Milan is likely to be an illegal alien. Just as likely, he or she was transported across several continents by a trafficking network allied with another network that specializes in the illegal copying, manufacturing, and distributing of high-end, brand-name products. Alien smuggling is a $7 billion a year enterprise and according to the United Nations is the fastest growing business of organized crime. Roughly 500,000 people enter the United States illegally each year, about the same number as illegally enter the European Union, and part of the approximately 150 million who live outside their countries of origin. Many of these backdoor travelers are voluntary migrants who pay smugglers up to $35,000, the top-dollar fee for passage from China to New York. Others, instead, are trafficked; that is, bought and sold internationally—as commodities. The U.S. Congressional Research Service reckons that each year between 1 million and 2 million people are trafficked across borders, the majority of whom are women and children. A woman can be "bought" in Timisoara, Romania, for between $50 and $200 and "resold" in Western Europe for 10 times that price. The United Nations Children's Fund estimates that cross-border smugglers in Central and Western Africa enslave 200,000 children a year. Traffickers initially tempt victims with job offers or, in the case of children, with offers of adoption in wealthier countries, and then keep the victims in subservience through physical violence, debt bondage, passport confiscation, and threats of arrest, deportation, or violence against their families back home.

Many people are desperate to escape poverty, oppression, or war and voluntarily enlist the aid of human traffickers in order to seek a better life by being smuggled into a different country (DOS, 2005, p. 20). Valdez (2009a) found that

Human trafficking generates billions of dollars a years and is becoming one of the fastest growing criminal activities. Some experts assess human trafficking operates at the same level of arms and drug smuggling. There is a difference between human trafficking and human smuggling. A key distinction between trafficking and smuggling is the individual's freedom of choice. A person may choose and arrange to be smuggled into a country. When that person is then forced into a situation of exploitation where their freedom is taken away, they become a victim of human trafficking.

(p. 430)

While acknowledging that many (if not most) women who are trafficked for the purposes of prostitution are involuntary participants in sex work, Siegel (2003b) also found that some women were prostitutes in their native countries and utilized organized crime to transport them to another country to ply their trade as sex workers (pp. 73–84). Petersen (2015) also noted that not all women who were involved in sex work were forced into the job. Other factors often came into play. She noted that there was often legal confusion between sex work and human trafficking, stating:

Women's accounts of sex work are affected by a multitude of factors, including economic inequality; the presence or absence of legal rights; and gender, ethnic, and class discrimination. The state plays an important role as it largely determines whether sex workers (both migrant and domestic) are viewed as victims, criminals, or working persons.

(pp. 115–116)

With the constant flow of refugees due to war, poverty and political oppression, there exist opportunities for organized crime to engage in human trafficking on a worldwide scale. This often results in exploitation of a vulnerable population that often is forced into bonded labor, slavery, and sexual exploitation. The human trafficker preys on society's weakest and poorest members to exploit them for financial gain (Lunde, 2004b, pp. 20–27).

Although many countries prohibit human trafficking, sanctions of traffickers are rarely enforced (Haynes, 2004). Clients are often reluctant to cooperate with law enforcement, so prosecution can be difficult (Chuang, 2010). Convictions for trafficking is rare, and those who are convicted do not receive sentences that deter them or others. The International Labour Organization (ILO; 2014) claimed sex trafficking brings in $99 billion worldwide. The ILO estimates annual profit potential per victim at an average of $21,800 (Haynes, 2004).

In the United States, the criminal groups that engage in a significant amount of human and sex trafficking may surprise you. According to Bouché (2017), they included:

- Mom-and-pop groups (small or medium groups of 30 people or fewer, made up of family and/or friends without a proper name), 71% of which engage only in sex trafficking (either minor only, adult only, or both minor and adult). The sex trafficking venues include brothels or massage parlors (33%) and internet prostitution (25%).

- Crime rings (small or medium groups made up of other than family or friend without a proper name), for which about half (47%) of all the sex trafficking cases are internet prostitution cases.

- Gangs, operating either locally or nationally, but not transnationally, are involved in commercial sex trafficking. Gang trafficking cases involve only street prostitution and internet prostitution, and the vast majority of victims in these cases are minors.

- Illegal enterprises, such as officially operating and named brothels, massage parlors, or strip clubs, have the most adult sex trafficking cases of any other type. About 50% of illegal enterprise sex trafficking cases are in brothels/massage parlors, with another 19% in strip clubs.

Counterfeit Products

The piracy of intellectual property and the counterfeiting of goods cost the United States billions of dollars every year (Valdez, 2009a, p. 431). Ene and Mihaescu (2014) observed:

> While in the past the most common counterfeit products were luxury goods, at present, the phenomenon of counterfeiting has grown alarmingly, covering almost all categories of goods and affecting economies throughout the entire world.

Looking at the phenomena of the theft of intellectual property and counterfeiting, Naim (2003) found that

> Global marketing and branding are also playing a part, as more people are attracted to products bearing a well-known brand like Prada or Cartier. And thanks to the rapid growth and integration into the global economy of countries, such as China, with weak central governments and ineffective laws, producing and exporting near perfect knockoffs are both less expensive and less risky. In the words of the CEO of one of the best known Swiss watchmakers:

We now compete with a product manufactured by Chinese prisoners. The business is run by the Chinese military, their families and friends, using roughly the same machines we have, which they purchased at the same industrial fairs we go to. The way we have rationalized this problem is by assuming that their customers and ours are different. The person that buys a pirated copy of one of our $5,000 watches for less than $100 is not a client we are losing. Perhaps it is a future client that someday will want to own the real thing instead of a fake. We may be wrong and we do spend money to fight the piracy of our products. But given that our efforts do not seem to protect us much, we close our eyes and hope for the better.

This posture stands in contrast to that of companies that sell cheaper products such as garments, music, or videos, whose revenues are directly affected by piracy.

Melton (2014) noted that:

Typically, pirated and counterfeit recordings represent "dubbing" which is the process involved in the technically advanced mechanical, electrical, or acoustical transfer of sounds from a copy of an authorized recording onto unauthorized blanks.

Melton (2014) went on to observe that the packaging of the pirated product was often different than the original. The counterfeiting of products and theft of intellectual property costs industry billions of dollars in lost revenues each year.

Summary

Organized crime implies that the criminality will extend beyond individual criminality and generally considered to be a group act. Another factor is the ability to survive the death or arrest of a gang leader. Many of these organized criminal groups conduct transnational criminal operations. They maintain alliances with other organized criminal groups to conduct their criminal activities or to protect them from other criminal groups. These groups engage in peripheral activities. Many of them are illegal, such as human trafficking, often for purposes of prostitution and slavery. The groups often have counterfeiters connected to them as well.

DISCUSSION QUESTIONS

1. Explain the operations of a typical Mexican drug cartel.
2. Describe the effect the Colombian drug cartels' operations had on the Mexican drug wars.
3. Describe Albanian organized crime.
4. Explain the criminal activities of Nigerian organized crime.
5. Define the differences between human smuggling and human trafficking.
6. How could you determine if a prostitute was being trafficked for sex?
7. Imagine the merchandise in a local high-end department store. Which items would be profitable to counterfeiters?

CHAPTER 13 Investigation and Prosecution of Gangs and Organized Crime Groups

---

CHAPTER OBJECTIVES

After reading this chapter students should be able to do the following:

- Understand the requirements for retention of gang intelligence files.
- Align specific gang activities with the generations of gangs they represent.
- Evaluate the process of gang member identification using the point system.
- Remember the reasons for confidential informant development.
- Differentiate the methods used for gang prevention, treatment, and suppression.

Introduction

Six members of the Devils Diciples [*sic*], an outlaw motorcycle gang (OMG) that intentionally misspells its name, were convicted in a racketeering trial which was prosecuted under the Racketeer Influenced and Corrupt Organizations (RICO) Act (Baldas, 2015). The statute is described in Section 1961(4) of Title 18 of the U.S. Code. The investigation and prosecution was the result of coordinated effort by several agencies including the FBI, the Michigan State Police, and the Macomb and St. Clair County Sheriff's Offices. The Devils Diciples is a violent organization with chapters across the United States, in Canada, and the United Kingdom that has engaged in methamphetamine manufacturing and stolen motorcycles and requires its members to intimidate others and lie to the police (Baldas, 2015). The group has also made money by drug trafficking, gambling, and robbery.

The Devils Diciples members were convicted because they kidnapped and attempted to murder other members of the group for violating the gang's rules (Baldas, 2015). The victims were bound, beaten, and left to die in the desert. More than 60 firearms and 6,000 rounds of ammunition were seized, and eight methamphetamine labs were dismantled (Baldas, 2015). These types of investigations and prosecutions often involve multiple actions by many participants over a long time. Coordinating the efforts requires a series of complex activities that are coordinated with the actions of others in the criminal justice system.

Gang and organized crime investigators are tasked with conducting street patrols; supporting probation, parole, and search warrant requests; and making arrests of gang and organized crime group members. Gang and organized crime prosecutors conduct in-depth analysis of gang and organized crime problems and the effects of the crime on the victim and the community. Prosecutors must be adept at educating the judge and jury about group culture and habits (Jackson, 2004). Gang and organized crime evidence gives the jury insight into the conduct of both defendants and witnesses living the gang lifestyle. A prosecutor can use evidence for a variety of purposes, including proving intent, motive, and identity of gang members to prosecute gang-related cases. Successful gang prosecutions result from a coordinated effort of the prosecutor's office and local gang or other investigators. The strength of a case rests on the strength of the evidence and the credibility of the expert (Anderson, Nye, Freitas, & Wolf, 2009). As detailed as each investigation and prosecution must be in order to have a successful prosecution, there is much investigative work to be done.

In this chapter, we will begin with an overview of investigations, examine proper handling of intelligence, and look at the various types of crime and gang and organized crime group types. We will then look at ways investigators use to identify gang and organized crime group members and develop confidential informants. Some basic strategies used to prevent, treat, and suppress the groups in the community will be identified, and then continuing criminal enterprise and the RICO laws, as well as the importance of witness protection in gang and organized crime cases. We will wrap up with expert testimony and an overview of the more educated gang and organized crime group members.

Investigating Gangs

It is important to record and maintain all contacts with gang and organized crime group members in a database. This is necessary to facilitate investigation and subsequent prosecution (Anderson et al., 2009). Gang and organized crime investigators should also maintain good rapport with other members of the department and criminal justice system. Patrol officers may spend time interacting with gang and organized crime group members, and their knowledge can help with cases if they are trained in the proper methods for collecting and disseminating information and intelligence, and if the investigators have a way of accessing the information. Corrections officers or deputies working in the local jail interact with group members who have been incarcerated or locked up for a period. Additionally, members of the court interact with gang members, both for criminal trials and for other criminal justice system–related contacts. The more sources of information the investigator has, the more information the gang and organized crime unit will have (Anderson et al., 2009).

Gang and organized crime investigators must be familiar with the many dynamics at work in their jurisdictions. They need to know the history of the various gangs and organized crime groups, as well as information on the membership size, territory, local hangouts, rivalries, and types of crimes the members commit (Anderson et al., 2009). This information is critical to know the group members well enough to identify their criminal activity and to prosecute a case against them in court. Additionally, investigators need to identify the leaders, whether formal or informal. Formal leaders are often those who are readily identified and prominent in public settings. They lead, guide, and direct the gang activities. Informal leaders are those who help keep the gang intact. Like any other organization, disputes happen between members and the formal leaders may not be aware of them. Informal leaders may know of potential issues long before they are visible or become a problem. Informal leaders have a considerable amount of power and authority—sometimes rivaling that of the formal leadership.

Investigating Basics

Investigating is the process used to examine, study, or inquire about the detailed particulars of a specific subject. Investigators attempt to learn the facts about something hidden, unique, or complex, often trying to find a motive, a cause, or a culprit (Investigate, 2018). To effectively conduct an investigation, investigators must develop the *investigative mindset*. The mindset centers on a way of disciplined thinking supported by the principle that *from information comes evidence* (Association of Chief Police Officers [ACPO], 2005). The application of an investigative mindset brings order to the way investigators make decisions, involving five principles:

- Understanding the source of material

- Planning and preparation

- Examination

- Recording and collation

- Evaluation (ACPO, 2005).

The United Nations (UN) Uniform Guidelines for Investigations provide fundamental standards for investigations and investigators. The basic investigative principles include:

- Investigation is a profession that requires the highest personal integrity.

- Persons who conduct investigations should demonstrate competence.

- Investigators should remain objective, impartial, and fair throughout the investigation and disclose any conflicts of interest to supervisors in a reasonable time.

- Investigators should strive to maintain both the confidentiality of and, to the extent possible, the protection of witnesses.

- The conduct of an investigation should demonstrate the investigator's commitment to determining the facts of the case.

- Investigative findings should be based on substantiated facts and related analysis, not on suppositions or assumptions.

- Recommendations should be supported by the investigative findings (UN, 2009).

Figure 13.1

The justice system. Gang and organized crime investigators should also maintain good rapport with other members of the department and criminal justice system.

iStock.com/Mik_photo

A good investigation has five qualities: objectivity, thoroughness, relevance, accuracy, and timeliness (ASIS International, 2013). Objectivity requires investigators to avoid prejudging someone or something while maintaining a working hypothesis regarding what occurred, based on the information we have gathered. The requirement for relevance means that the information gathered should both relate to the subjects and have sufficient detail (ASIS International, 2013). The need for accuracy cannot be overstated. Many law enforcement and professionals believe that eyewitnesses give the best information. In fact, eyewitness accounts are the least accurate of all (ASIS International, 2013).

Gang Investigation Associations

It is often helpful for investigators to associate with others, even those who do not work in adjacent jurisdictions. Gangs and organized crime groups across the globe operate in similar ways, and the strategies used to catch them are numerous as well. Gang investigator associations exist in many areas of the United States and Canada. These associations are often formed based on the extent of the perceived gang threat, based on state, regional, or topical area. Gang investigators associations often include local, state, and federal law enforcement, corrections, and court system professionals whose interest or primary investigative responsibilities include the identification and prosecution of crimes related to gang activity (Tennessee Gang Investigator's Association [TNGIA], 2015). Some of the state and regional associations include:

- Alabama Gang Investigator's Association
- Arizona Gang Investigators' Association
- California Gang Investigators' Association
- Central Coast Gang Investigators' Association
- East Coast Gang Investigators' Association
- Florida Gang Investigators' Association
- International Outlaw Motorcycle Gang Investigators' Association
- Midwest Gang Investigators' Association
- Mississippi Gang Investigator's Association
- New Jersey Gang Investigators' Association
- North Carolina Gang Investigators' Association
- Northern California Gang Investigators' Association

- Northwest Gang Investigators' Association

- Ontario Gang Investigators' Association

- Southern Nevada Gang Investigators' Association

- Tennessee Gang Investigator's Association

- Texas Gang Investigators' Association

- Virginia Gang Investigators' Association.

Additionally, the National Alliance of Gang Investigator Associations (NAGIA) (2015) is a cooperative organization representing most (23) of the state and regional gang investigators associations in the United States. NAGIA has over 20,000 members and provides leadership and strategies to prevent and control gang crime. The association reduces the threat of gang violence by increasing public awareness, providing training, monitoring legislative efforts, disseminating intelligence, and partnering in efforts to prevent, intervene, and suppress gang activity.

Gang Research Centers

In addition to gang investigators, members of other organizations investigate and research gangs in one form or another. Among those groups are:

- National Gang Center (NGC), which works to further the mission of the Department of Justice (DOJ) by providing national leadership, information, training, and technical assistance that target gangs and street gang members of all ages. Serving researchers, policymakers, and practitioners nationally, NGC activities contribute to reductions in gang-related crime and violence and gang activity by juveniles and adults (NGC, 2015).

- National Gang Crime Research Center (NGCRC), a non-profit independent agency with the mission statement to promote research on gangs, gang members, and gang problems in cooperation with federal, state, and local government agencies; disseminate up-to-date valid and reliable information about gangs and gang problems; and provide training and consulting services about gangs to federal, state, and local government agencies (NGCRC, 2018).

- The National Gang Intelligence Center (NGIC), established by the FBI in 2005 to help curb the growth of gangs and related criminal activity, integrates gang intelligence from across federal, state, and local law enforcement on the growth, migration, criminal activity, and association of gangs that pose a significant threat to the United

States (FBI, 2015a). Analysts from multiple federal agencies man the NGIC, permitting centralized access to gang information from each of the agency databases. In addition, the NGIC provides operational and analytical support for investigations.

Intelligence Files

It is important that investigators abide by local, state, and federal guidelines or restrictions when maintaining intelligence files. Gang and organized crime units should include the entire department in their intelligence collection efforts (Anderson et al., 2009). Gang and organized crime investigators need to conduct regular briefings and training sessions so officers and detectives with primary investigative responsibility for other types of crimes can be aware of gang indicators. New officer orientation is also important (Anderson et al., 2009).

Intelligence files should be used to maintain an organization's records. The files should be kept digitally (in a computer database), both as part of a regional intelligence collection effort and locally for times when regional databases are unavailable. Regional databases are helpful because they offer access to records of gangs and gang members from many jurisdictions (Anderson et al., 2009). They should not be relied on exclusively, however, as a technical issue or security of the investigation might dictate that more limited or secure access is needed.

The First Amendment of the U.S. Constitution prohibits criminalizing mere membership in a gang (or other organization, even those with a criminal nature); however, associating with members of a criminal organization and committing crimes can be criminalized (*Scales v. United States*, 1961). To make things more complicated, law enforcement has a legitimate interest in monitoring individuals and groups that engage in criminal group behavior (Anderson et al., 2009). To address these competing interests, Congress passed the Omnibus Crime Control and Safe Streets Act in 1968, which attempted to recognize the need for intelligence databases and the right to privacy. The act resulted in the passage of the Code of Federal Regulations, Title 28, Part 23 (28 CFR Part 23), which outlines the requirements for entering information about an individual or a group into an intelligence system and purging the data from such a system (Anderson et al., 2009). Under the guidelines in 28 CFR Part 23, Section (b)(6), information intelligence database must be evaluated for its relevance and importance at least every five years.

Intelligence files are often used to ensure gang and organized crime investigators and other officers can maintain and update their awareness of current gang trends. The files should be arranged so they are gang specific and include evidence and information showing the existence, territory, and dynamics of the gangs in the jurisdiction (Anderson et al., 2009). Intelligence files should include photos of gang graffiti and the location

Figure 13.2

Hispanic gang graffiti on a resident's van. Intelligence files should include photos of gang graffiti and the location where it was displayed.

Anderson, J., Nye, M., Freitas, R., & Wolf, J. (2009, July). *Gang Prosecution Manual*. Institute for Intergovernmental Research.

where it was displayed; examples of the names and symbols used to identify the gang; photos of the various tattoos of individual gang members; and group photos and/or photos of gang members throwing hand signs, holding weapons, dressed in gang attire, or having other indications of gang affiliation (Anderson et al., 2009).

Gang intelligence files serve as a way to collect and maintain gang records and photographs of individual members. They should include photographs of all known gang members from a gang identified by self-admission or through other reliable sources. The files are used for possible suspect identification when the circumstances of an offense indicate a member or members of a gang committed. Gang intelligence files should be continually updated so they can assist with investigative, enforcement, and prosecution efforts (Anderson et al., 2009).

Regional Information Sharing Systems (RISS)

The Regional Information Sharing Systems (RISS) provides services and resources to successfully resolve criminal investigations and prosecute criminal offenders. RISS is congressionally funded and administered by the U.S. Department of Justice (USDOJ) and supports efforts against organized and violent crime, gang activity, drug activity, terrorism, human trafficking, identity theft, and other regional priorities while promoting officer safety (RISS, 2015).

RISSGang is a comprehensive gang resource hosted by RISS that offers gang investigators a criminal intelligence database, a website, and informational resources, providing access to gang information, including suspects, organizations, weapons, photographs, and graffiti. RISSGang is available to all authorized law enforcement, and provides access tools and resources, including gang-specific news, documents, and publications in categories such as:

- Motorcycle gangs
- Drug gangs
- Hate groups
- Hand signs
- Terminology

- Prison gangs
- Ethnic gangs
- Graffiti
- Colors

- Street gangs
- Youth gangs
- Tattoos
- Crypto/codes

RISS serves thousands of local, state, federal, and tribal criminal justice agencies through its subordinate organizations that partner with local, state, federal, and tribal agencies (RISS, 2015). Those organizations include:

- Middle Atlantic-Great Lakes Organized Crime Law Enforcement Network (MAGLOCLEN), serving Delaware, Indiana, Maryland, Michigan, New Jersey, New York, Ohio, Pennsylvania, and the District of Columbia, as well as Australia, Canada, and England.

- Mid-States Organized Crime Information Center (MOCIC), serving Illinois, Iowa, Kansas, Minnesota, Missouri, Nebraska, North Dakota, South Dakota, and Wisconsin, as well as parts of Canada.

- New England State Police Information Network (NESPIN) serving Connecticut, Maine, Massachusetts, New Hampshire, Rhode Island, and Vermont, as well as parts of Canada.

- Rocky Mountain Information Network (RMIN), serving Arizona, Colorado, Idaho, Montana, Nevada, New Mexico, Utah, and Wyoming, as well as parts of Canada.

- Regional Organized Crime Information Center (ROCIC), serving Alabama, Arkansas, Florida, Georgia, Kentucky, Louisiana, Mississippi, North Carolina, Oklahoma, South Carolina, Tennessee, Texas, Virginia, and West Virginia, as well as Puerto Rico and the U.S. Virgin Islands.

- Western States Information Network (WSIN), serving Alaska, California, Hawaii, Oregon, and Washington, as well as Canada, Guam, and New Zealand.

Figure 13.3

Regional Information Sharing Systems (RISS) logo. The RISS supports local, state, and federal police efforts against organized crime and gang activity, and other regional priorities. Public domain.

Institute for Intergovernmental Research

Fusion Centers

Many states and some large cities have established fusion centers to facilitate the sharing of information and intelligence. Fusion centers are designed to provide a comprehensive understanding of the criminal and terrorist threat in their area of operation (AOR). Fusion centers assist with both information sharing and broad-based data collection. Fusion centers have been said to capitalize on the wisdom of crowds (Guidetti, 2010). In other words, when multiple agencies pool their resources under one roof, the results multiply exponentially for all.

Primary fusion centers are the highest priority for the allocation of available federal resources, including the deployment of personnel and connectivity with federal data systems. Primary centers are often state specific. State fusion centers are owned and operated by the state and are designated by the governor. In accordance with the federal Resource Allocation Criteria (RAC) policy, the federal government recognizes these designations and supports the national network of fusion centers (Department of Homeland Security [DHS], 2015). The following is a current list of primary fusion centers. The centers serve as the focal points within the state for the receipt, analysis, gathering, and sharing of threat-related information (DHS, 2015).

Box 13.1 Primary Fusion Centers

- Alabama Fusion Center
- Alaska Information and Analysis Center
- Arizona Counter Terrorism Information Center
- Arkansas State Fusion Center

- California State Threat Assessment Center
- Colorado Information Analysis Center
- Connecticut Intelligence Center
- Delaware Information and Analysis Center
- Florida Fusion Center
- Georgia Information Sharing and Analysis Center
- Hawaii Fusion Center
- Idaho Criminal Intelligence Center
- Illinois Statewide Terrorism and Intelligence Center
- Indiana Intelligence Fusion Center
- Iowa Intelligence Fusion Center
- Kansas Intelligence Fusion Center
- Kentucky Intelligence Fusion Center
- Louisiana State Analytical and Fusion Exchange
- Maine Information and Analysis Center
- Mariana Regional Fusion Center (Guam)
- Maryland Coordination and Analysis Center
- Massachusetts Commonwealth Fusion Center
- Michigan Intelligence Operations Center
- Minnesota Fusion Center
- Mississippi Analysis and Information Center
- Missouri Information Analysis Center
- Montana Analysis and Technical Information Center
- Nebraska Information Analysis Center
- New Hampshire Information and Analysis Center
- New Jersey Regional Operations Intelligence Center
- New Mexico All Source Intelligence Center
- New York State Intelligence Center
- North Carolina Information Sharing and Analysis Center
- North Dakota State and Local Information Center
- Ohio Strategic Analysis and Information Center
- Oklahoma Information Fusion Center
- Oregon Terrorism Information Threat Assessment Network
- Pennsylvania Criminal Intelligence Center
- Puerto Rico National Security State Information Center
- Rhode Island State Fusion Center
- South Carolina Information and Intelligence Center
- South Dakota Fusion Center
- Southern Nevada Counter-Terrorism Center (Las Vegas, Nevada)
- Tennessee Fusion Center
- Texas Joint Crime Information Center
- U.S. Virgin Islands Fusion Center

- Utah Statewide Information and Analysis Center
- Vermont Intelligence Center
- Virginia Fusion Center
- Washington Regional Threat and Analysis Center (Washington, DC)
- Washington State Fusion Center
- West Virginia Intelligence Fusion Center
- Wisconsin Statewide Information Center

Types of Gang Crime

The National Crime Information Center (NCIC; 2013) reported that gang members committed a variety of crimes, most notably drug trafficking, robbery, burglary, prostitution, and assault. Many of the identified crimes are typical street crimes, such as assault, larceny, and robbery. Those are the crimes for which many gangs are often well-known. Law enforcement often focuses on those types of crimes because they are more visible to the citizens in the community.

Less violent crimes, like extortion, mortgage fraud, and counterfeiting, generally have fewer numbers of reported incidents. This may be because gangs are not committing those crimes with the same frequency as the more violent street crimes. It might also be that the less violent crimes are being committed but not detected or not being reported. These less violent crimes are not as visible to the general public. Gangs and other organized crime groups often advance to these crimes as part of a natural evolution or maturing process, as they realize that they can be more profitable and result in less time off the streets due to arrests. The degree to which gangs are involved in other crimes may fluctuate, but was estimated by respondents to the NGIC survey, as depicted in Figure 13.4.

Advanced Gangs

It is important that investigators focus not only on the most visible and easy to catch gangs, but also focus on those gangs that are more difficult to investigate and prosecute. In addition to making money by committing crime, the more advanced groups may have a desire to control the government, with political agendas bordering on insurgency. Gang activity can contribute to instability in any affected level of government, reducing the ability to control territory, and eroding the legitimacy of the government.

One method of distinguishing between the traditional gangs and more advanced organizations suggests that three elements should be considered: sophistication, politicization, and internationalization. There are three generations (or types) of gangs: turf

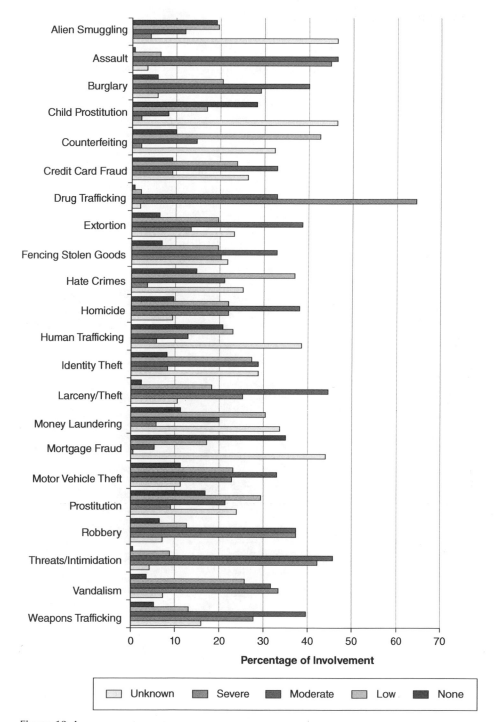

Figure 13.4

Criminal gang involvement. Survey respondents' rating level of gang involvement in various crimes.

NGIC. (2013). *National Gang Report*. Washington, DC: National Gang Intelligence Center.

gangs, drug or entrepreneurial gangs, and gangs with a mix of political and mercenary elements that are more globally oriented (Sullivan & Bunker, 2007). Figure 13.5 shows the characteristics that distinguish the generations along a continuum.

First generation gangs have been characterized as traditional street gangs. Members of first generation gangs are often what are being discussed when gangs are the topic of conversation (Knox, 2006; NGIC, 2007). Most anti-gang legislation (e.g., injunctions and restrictive ordinances) and anti-gang activity has been used to target those gangs. The 2009 NGIC report identified first generation gangs as local-level street gangs, constituting the highest number of gangs in the U.S.

Second generation gangs typically have a more organized structure and the leaders operate the gang like a business, with a market orientation (Sullivan & Bunker, 2007).

Figure 13.5

Publicizing prosecution strategies. U.S. Attorney Beth Phillips and Jackson County Prosecutor Jim Kanatzar announced new strategies to combat gang activity. U.S. Department of Justice (2015).

U.S. Attorneys—Western District of Missouri Narcotics and Violent Crimes Unit. Retrieved from www.justice.gov/usao-wdmo/narcotics-violent-crimes-unit.

Those gangs usually have a more centralized and developed leadership and operate in a broader geographic area (Sullivan & Bunker, 2007). Anti-gang activities rarely give gang investigators the ability to make the investment of time and intensity necessary to investigate these gangs. Authors of the NGIC report (2009) identified these gangs as regional-level gangs, which may have some ties to drug trafficking and other criminal organizations in the United States. In this analysis, the second generation gangs can be compared to the more advanced organized crime groups.

Third generation gangs are highly sophisticated, often having goals of political power or financial acquisition (Sullivan & Bunker, 2007). The organizational structure of most third generation gangs resembles a military organization, where promotions and rank are based on performance, time, and grade (Valdez, 2007). Third generation gangs tend to operate in a global environment and are highly organized and sophisticated criminal organizations (Sullivan & Bunker, 2007). Local anti-gang legislation (e.g., civil injunctions or abatement laws) has little impact on the operations of these gangs. Authors of the NGIC report (2009) identified these gangs as national-level street gangs. These gangs often have established cells in foreign countries that assist the gangs operating in the United States in developed associations with global drug trafficking and other criminal organizations. Although some claimed that gangs and terrorist groups were always separate entities and should be treated that way, third generation gangs have shared many of the characteristics of terrorists and insurgents (Wilson & Sullivan, 2007).

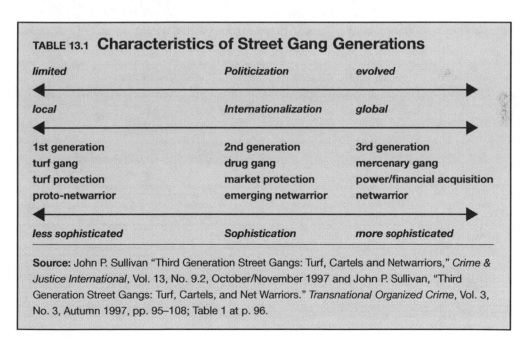

TABLE 13.1 Characteristics of Street Gang Generations

limited	*Politicization*	*evolved*
◄──────────────────────────────────────►		
local	*Internationalization*	*global*
◄──────────────────────────────────────►		
1st generation	2nd generation	3rd generation
turf gang	drug gang	mercenary gang
turf protection	market protection	power/financial acquisition
proto-netwarrior	emerging netwarrior	netwarrior
◄──────────────────────────────────────►		
less sophisticated	*Sophistication*	*more sophisticated*

Source: John P. Sullivan "Third Generation Street Gangs: Turf, Cartels and Netwarriors," *Crime & Justice International*, Vol. 13, No. 9.2, October/November 1997 and John P. Sullivan, "Third Generation Street Gangs: Turf, Cartels, and Net Warriors." *Transnational Organized Crime*, Vol. 3, No. 3, Autumn 1997, pp. 95–108; Table 1 at p. 96.

Street gangs are positioned "in one corner of the intersection (or gray area) between crime and war" (Sullivan & Bunker, 2007, p. 7). Third generation gangs have threatened the national security of many Latin American countries (Sullivan & Bunker, 2007). Although some have claimed that gangs and terrorist groups were always separate entities and should be treated that way, third generation gangs have shared many of the characteristics of terrorists and insurgents (Wilson & Sullivan, 2007).

Investigators must be able to discern between gangs in the different generations in order to effectively investigate and ultimately prosecute them. It is important the judges and the juries also know the difference, as the punishment for gang crimes is often designed to correct behavior. The more advanced the gangs and gang members get, the more advanced the correction of behavior that is necessary.

One way the potential advancement of gangs can be identified is by the ways they bring in money. Put another way, the funding methods used by gangs may show the level of advancement of the gang (Langton, 2010). Over 90% of gang units dealt with gangs that were financed though street-level drug sales. The average number of gang funding methods used ranges from three methods reported by gang units with fewer than 50,000 residents to six among units serving 500,000 residents or more (Langton, 2010). Table 13.2 shows the different types of funding used.

TABLE 13.2 Gang Financing Methods Reported by Specialized Gang Units, by Method of Financing and Population Served, 2007

Method of financing	Total gang units		Percent of gang units by population served				
	Number	Percent	Under 50,000	50,000–99,999	100,000–249,999	250,000–499,999	500,000 or more
Number of gang units	365	100%	16	96	119	56	78
Street-level drug sales[a]	340	93%	81%	94%	95%	89%	95%
Drug trafficking[a]	320	88	69	89	86	89	92
Weapons trafficking	258	71	50	64	70	73	85
Dues paid by members with legitimate employment	177	48	31	38	53	52	56
Economic crimes[b]	173	47	25	38	45	54	64
Prostitution	150	41	25	32	33	45	65
Sales of forged identity documents	142	39	13	29	34	50	56
Gambling	114	31	38	30	21	32	45

Method of financing	Total gang units		Percent of gang units by population served				
	Number	Percent	Under 50,000	50,000– 99,999	100,000– 249,999	250,000– 499,999	500,000 or more
Human trafficking	57	16	6	15	7	13	35
Other[c]	47	13	0	9	18	13	13
Pornography	32	9	0	5	5	7	22

[a] Street-level drug sales typically involve individual sellers who deal in small amounts for personal use rather than for resale. Street-level drug sales are distinguished from drug trafficking, which involves the production and distribution of large amounts of controlled substances for the purpose of buyer resale.

[b] Includes such offenses as credit card theft, forged checks, money laundering, embezzlement, and mortgage fraud.

[c] Includes such offenses as burglary, robbery, auto theft, theft of auto parts, and extortion.

Gang Member Identification

Civilian police in many locations have a process for identifying gang members called the *points system*. It was designed to make the process of determining whether someone has gang membership as objective as possible. Presumably, even someone with little in the way of training or familiarity regarding gangs could consider the available information and determine whether someone was gang affiliated. That is the best sort of process to use when it comes to the legal system.

Points systems are in place in jurisdictions across the country—both communities and corrections facilities. Local, state and federal corrections and local, state and federal law enforcement use point systems to identify individuals as gang members. An example of the rational for the point system was found in the Minnesota Violent Crime Coordinating Council (MVCCC), created in 1997 (2012). The goal was to determine an objective and consistent set of gang membership identifiers that could be used throughout the state. The criteria chosen were based on criteria used in other states around the country. The criteria were based on the premise that members of criminal gangs identify themselves with a specific organizational name, symbols, hand signs, colors, and language (MVCCC, 2012). These factors, in addition to the gang member's criminal activity, help officers identify and track gang organizations using objective criteria.

The gang affiliation of an individual is assessed based on their involvement in criminal activity and evidence of any of the established indicators (MVCCC, 2012).

- Admits gang membership

- Arrested with a gang member

- Displays a gang tattoo or brand

- Wears clothing or symbols intended to identify with a gang

- Appears in a photograph or image with a gang member engaging in gang-related activity

- Name appears on a gang roster

- Identified as a gang member by a reliable source

- Is regularly observed or communicates with a gang member in furtherance or support of gang-related activity

- Produces gang-specific writing or graffiti in furtherance or support of gang-related activity.

In addition to police at the local, state, and federal level, officers in the U.S. Bureau of Prisons and all state departments of corrections can identify gang members using a similar point system. The Appendices provide a sample point system for combining gangs and security threat groups.

Confidential Informant (CI) Development

Confidential informants (also called cooperating individuals or CIs) are a necessary investigative "tool" in law enforcement. According to Anderson et al. (2009), a CI is

any person who knowingly provides information to law enforcement related to another's criminal activity, whose motivation for doing so is other than that of an uninvolved witness who is a victim or private citizen primarily acting through a sense of civic responsibility, and who, as a general rule but not necessarily, expects some sort of personal benefit or advantage or the same for another individual.

(p. 20)

The use of informants can pose a significant risk to gang investigators if they are not properly managed and controlled (Gang Intelligence Strategy Committee [GISC], 2008). Learning how to develop and manage CIs is critical to the success of all investigators, and especially gang investigators. CIs in gang cases typically include those considered mercenaries (informing in return for payment), gang members who cooperate with law enforcement and prosecution to receive leniency in another case, codefendants in a trial, or friends not involved in the present crime (Anderson et al., 2009).

CIs should only be used when the circumstances preclude other types of investigation, such as surveillance or undercover work. CIs should only be used after both parties agree to and sign a written agreement between the CI, the police, and the prosecution (Anderson et al., 2009). Police should also maintain a record of all investigative direction and supervision of a CI and should document all known activities of the CI, whether good or bad, while the agreement was in effect.

Methods Used to Restrict Non-criminal Gang Activity

Responses to the traditional gang problem have typically included either prevention, treatment, or suppression (Klein, 1995). In the late 1980s, federal funding provided an incentive to initiate several prototypes for anti-gang program development. Solutions as varied as Gang Resistance Educational Assistance and Training (GREAT), which focused on prevention by informing youth of the dangers of gang involvement, and Community Oriented Policing Services (COPS), which focused on gang suppression using data-driven, community-wide gang responses, were implemented nationwide (Curry & Decker, 2003). Although these programs provided the foundation for contemporary solutions, a more diverse approach is used to address a variety of problems.

Gang Prevention

Gang prevention programs have often failed to follow through with promised measures of evaluation, and those that have been evaluated showed little if any effect on youth regarding gang joining and gang-related behavior (Klein, 2007). Meltzer (2001), for example, studied gang-involved adolescent males who were court mandated to attend a gang reduction program. The program included weekly meetings where speakers from a variety of community and academic areas addressed the group regarding laws, behavior, treatment, and other topics. The primary goals identified for the program were to decrease gang involvement and illegal behavior. Meltzer found an increase in knowledge regarding related laws, and an increased concern about the risk and danger of gang association, which was presented by professionals and community representatives. Many of the participants were ready for change when they attended the program, and though many of the participants had been involved in gang-related activity, they did not appear to be very deeply involved (Meltzer, 2001).

Gang Treatment

Based on the premise that the majority of gang-affiliated offenders will reenter society, treatment in prisons was often focused on reducing gang violence, including interacting with members of other gangs, signing a renunciation form, and cultural awareness training (Di Placido, Simon, Witte, Gu, & Wong, 2006). The treatment programs that were most likely to reduce recidivism were those that follow the risk-need-responsivity principles and treating gang members with the highest risk of reoffending. For treatment to be effective, needs that contributed to criminal activities must be assessed, identified, and targeted. Treatment works best when it is adjusted to accommodate a client's characteristics (Di Placido et al., 2006).

Gang Suppression

Law enforcement officers often oversee gang suppression programs to target the perpetrators of gang felony crimes and the leaders of their gangs. Police leaders traditionally preferred the military approach to that of the social worker (Jankowski, 1991). The usual focus was based on the notion that with increased enforcement and sanctions, gang members and leaders would be logically discouraged from committing future crimes. Many residents in inner-city communities reported that gang members were more able to deter crime in their community than police (Jankowski, 1991). The main types of police gang control activities were intelligence and information processing, prevention, enforcement, and follow-up investigations (Huff & McBride, 1993). The success of these operations depended on the ability of the gang unit to work closely with members of the units assigned to work narcotics, juveniles, patrol, homicide, and organized crime.

Gang Injunctions

In the 1980s, the Los Angeles County district attorney asked for a court order declaring gangs to be a form of quasi-corporate structure, so that each member could be held accountable for the actions of other members (Klein, 1995). The ruling was sought to enable the community to force gang members to remove their gang's graffiti. The 1995 Los Angeles City Attorney Gang Prosecution Section Report identified the focus on gang suppression and deterrence, noting that civil gang abatement strategies were often limited to a legal proceeding against a criminal element (often a gang) to prohibit them from engaging in conduct that promoted criminal activity. The strategy could then include obtaining an injunction with input from police, prosecutors, merchants, property owners, and other community members (Klein, 1995).

Maxson, Hennigan, and Sloane (2005) examined the effect and implications of injunctions as policy in California. The report was the first scientific examination regarding the impact of gang injunctions on the community, including the effect on gang presence, gang intimidation, and fear of confrontation with gang members in primary and secondary injunction areas. The researchers focused on changes in the quality of life in the neighborhood as a result of injunctions rather than the effect on gang members. They found that the gang injunction impacted the level of gang member intimidation and the level of fear of gang members by residents almost immediately (Maxson et al., 2005).

Project T.O.U.G.H. was a property abatement program that significantly curtailed gang activity in Los Angeles neighborhoods. Prosecutors using this strategy targeted the properties where gang members regularly committed crimes (Cristall & Forman-Echols, 2009). Although the attorneys were criminal prosecutors, they used civil lawsuits to abate gang activity at private properties, seeking injunctive relief for the community from the gangs. Both the owner and the gang members were sued with this strategy because they had either directly or indirectly caused or permitted a public nuisance to exist on the property (Cristall & Forman-Echols, 2009). Resolution of the injunction against the property owner required that he or she make comprehensive physical improvements to the property (such as installing surveillance systems, gates, or lighting) and alter their management practices (such as using better tenant screening, hiring new managers, or implementing the eviction process for certain occupants). The injunction against the gang member was designed to prevent them from (legally) returning to the property (Cristall & Forman-Echols, 2009).

Gang Prosecution

Gang cases present unique challenges. In the absence of specific gang legislation, it is the prosecutor's responsibility to educate the courts regarding gang issues within their jurisdictions. This may include conducting an in-depth background analysis of gang problems with each prosecution. The foundation of a gang's existence in the community, along with the history of the gang, can paint the picture for the court regarding the level of involvement the gang has in the community (Wennar, 2005). The gang-related crime, in context, should be expounded upon to not only include the law violations, but also the effect the crime committed by the gang's members had on the victim(s) and the community.

The gang culture is complex and often functions in ways that most citizens have difficulty understanding. As a result, in order to prosecute gang cases, the prosecutor must also be adept at educating the jury about gang culture and habits (Jackson, 2004). Gang evidence gives the jury insight into the conduct of both defendants and witnesses living the gang lifestyle, and it should not be assumed that the jury is familiar with the activities of the gang. A prosecutor can use gang evidence for a variety of purposes, including proving intent, motive, and identity (Jackson, 2004).

Prosecutor's Comprehensive Gang Response Model

The National District Attorneys Association's American Prosecutors Research Institute initiated the Prosecutor's Comprehensive Gang Response (PCGR) Model effort to help prosecutors formulate a comprehensive response to gang problems in their communities. Combining the expertise of professionals from prosecution, policing, juvenile justice, state and local government, schools, community-based organizations, faith-based groups, and researchers, the PCGR identified successful approaches in gang prevention, intervention, suppression, and reentry (Troutman, Nugent-Borakove, & Jansen, 2007).

Drawing on the experiences of the experts from those various disciplines and research on gang prevention, intervention, and suppression, the model suggested:

- Conducting an assessment to accurately identify the scope of the gang problem in each jurisdiction;

- Aligning the forces in the community and the prosecutor's office to provide an open line of communication and available resources and prevent duplicated efforts;

- Implementing a gang task force, making legislative changes, and providing education to the community to strengthen the response to gang activity;

- Evaluating the comprehensive gang response model to ensure success at each of the stages (Troutman et al., 2007).

An evaluation should be considered as an ongoing feedback loop of information to improve the elements within the gang model (Troutman et al., 2007).

Continuing Criminal Enterprise

One of the obvious and visible behaviors of gang members is criminal activity. Many gang members are repeat offenders who have specific modus operandi (Lyddane, 2006). The existence of a group (gang) of people who repeatedly commit criminal activity is likely to lead to a continuing criminal enterprise (CCE).

The FBI (2015a) defined a criminal enterprise as a group of individuals with an identified hierarchy or comparable structure that are engaged in significant criminal activity. The Continuing Criminal Enterprise statute, Title 21 of the U.S. Code, Section 848I(2), specifically defined a criminal enterprise as any group of six or more people, where one of them serves as an organizer, a supervisor, or any other management position with respect to the others, and which generates substantial income or resources, and is engaged in a continuing series of violations of specific portions of Title 21.

Those organizations often engage in multiple criminal activities and have extensive supporting networks. The terms organized crime and criminal enterprise are similar and often used synonymously. However, various federal criminal statutes specifically define the elements of an enterprise that need to be proven in order to convict individuals or groups of individuals under these statutes. An investigator can anticipate that high-level gang members will repeat certain criminal activities (Lyddane, 2006). Knowledgeable investigators can anticipate that suspects may change geographical locations or proceed in a more clandestine manner, but they will likely remain criminally active (Lyddane, 2006). By remaining alert and prepared for such behavior, gang investigators can increase the likelihood of identifying criminal gang activity.

Racketeer Influenced and Corrupt Organizations (RICO) Act

RICO was created as Title IX of the Organized Crime Control Act of 1970, which had as its stated goal "the eradication of organized crime." Congress determined that organized crime was draining billions of dollars from the U.S. economy annually, and created legislation to slow that loss. The criminal charges under RICO focus on prohibiting racketeering activity, defined as acts of murder, kidnapping, arson, robbery, bribery, extortion, obstruction of justice, and other crimes.

The FBI (2015a) defined significant racketeering activities as those predicate criminal acts that were chargeable under the RICO statute. These were listed in Title 18, Section 1961(1) of the U.S. Code, and include the following federal crimes:

- Bribery
- Sports bribery
- Counterfeiting
- Embezzlement of union funds
- Mail fraud
- Wire fraud
- Money laundering
- Obstruction of justice
- Murder for hire
- Drug trafficking
- Prostitution

- Sexual exploitation of children

- Alien smuggling

- Trafficking in counterfeit goods

- Theft from interstate shipment

- Interstate transportation of stolen property.

The following state crimes are also included:

- Murder

- Kidnapping

- Gambling

- Arson

- Robbery

- Bribery

- Extortion

- Drugs.

Gangs are increasingly being charged with RICO violations. There are two significant differences between a gang member tried for state violations and one taken to federal court. The first is the significance of the charges: a violation of federal law, not just one state or jurisdiction. The second effect is that prison time in the federal system is typically much longer that what is received in the state system. That means that, by default, some level of crime prevention occurs for the local jurisdiction.

Penalty Enhancements

Lawmakers often create penalty enhancements to show their constituents they are serious about decreasing crime in the community. According to the Nevada State Legislature (2011), a penalty enhancement does not create a separate offense but provides an additional penalty for the primary offense. The additional penalty must not exceed the sentence imposed for the underlying crime, and it runs consecutively with the sentence for the crime, as ordered by the court (Jackson, 2004). Nothing requires that prosecutors allege a penalty enhancement or charge a gang crime in order to use gang evidence. In reality, most cases in which gang evidence is applicable include no specific gang allegation (Jackson, 2004). In those cases, the prosecutor must simply explain why the gang evidence should be admitted.

Federal law gives us an example of a penalty enhancement. Currently, U.S. federal law *defines* the term *criminal street gang* as

an ongoing group, club, organization, or association of 5 or more persons—

(A) that has as 1 of its primary purposes the commission of 1 or more of the criminal offenses described in subsection (c);

(B) the members of which engage, or have engaged within the past 5 years, in a continuing series of offenses described in subsection (c); and

(C) the activities of which affect interstate or foreign commerce.

(18 USC § 521(a))

The offenses described in this section are:

(1) A federal felony involving a controlled substance (as defined in Section 102 of the Controlled Substances Act (21 USC § 802)) for which the maximum penalty is not less than 5 years;

(2) A federal felony crime of violence that has as an element the use or attempted use of physical force against the person of another; and

(3) A conspiracy to commit an offense described in paragraph (1) or (2).

(18 USC § 521(c))

The circumstances described in this section are that the offense described in subsection (c) was committed by a person who:

(1) Participates in a criminal street gang with knowledge that its members engage in or have engaged in a continuing series of offenses described in subsection (c);

(2) Intends to promote or further the felonious activities of the criminal street gang or maintain or increase his or her position in the gang; and

(3) Has been convicted within the past five years for:

(A) An offense described in subsection (c);

(B) A State offense—

(i) Involving a controlled substance (as defined in Section 102 of the Controlled Substances Act (21 USC § 802)) for which the maximum penalty is not less than five years' imprisonment; or

(ii) That is a felony crime of violence that has as an element the use or attempted use of physical force against the person of another;

(C) Any federal or State felony offense that by its nature involves a substantial risk that physical force against the person of another may be used in the course of committing the offense; or

(D) A conspiracy to commit an offense described in subparagraph (A), (B), or (C).

(18 USC § 521(d))

An examination of State Anti-Gang Statutes by the National Gang Center in their Highlights of Gang-Related Legislation (updated August 2014), showed:

• All 50 states and the District of Columbia had enacted some form of legislation relating to gangs or gang-related activity.

• 43 states and DC had legislation that defines "gang."

• 14 states had legislation that defines "gang member."

• 31 states defined "gang crime/activity."

• 28 states had passed gang-prevention laws.

• 31 states had laws that provided enhanced penalties for gang-related criminal acts.

• 14 states and DC had enacted anti-carjacking statutes.

• More than half of the states had laws against graffiti.

• 27 states and DC had legislation on gangs and schools.

• 12 states had enacted laws that dealt with gang-related databases.

(National Gang Center, 2014)

In Florida, Section 874.03 "Criminal gang-related activity" means activity committed with the intent to benefit, promote, or further the interests of a criminal gang, or for the purposes of increasing a person's own standing or position within a criminal gang; in which the participants are identified as criminal gang members or associates acting individually or collectively to further any criminal purpose of a criminal gang; activity that is identified as criminal gang activity by a documented reliable informant; or activity that is identified as criminal gang activity by an informant of previously untested reliability and such identification is corroborated by independent information.

Florida's law is individual oriented, meaning the law focuses on an individual activity to benefit, promote, or further the interests of the gang or increasing a person's standing or position in a gang, acting individually or collectively. Kansas (§ 21–4226), South Carolina (§ 16–8–230), and Texas (Fam. Code § 54.0491) are among the states that use a similar application as Florida.

The law in Illinois is more gang-related. Illinois law (740 ILCS 147/10) says that gang activity is any criminal activity, enterprise, pursuit, or undertaking directed by, ordered by, authorized by, consented to, agreed to, requested by, acquiesced in, or ratified by any gang leader, officer, or governing or policy-making person or authority, or by any agent, representative, or deputy of any such officer, person, or authority:

- Intent to increase gang's size, membership, prestige, dominance, or control in any geographical area; or

- Intent to provide the gang with any advantage in, or any control or dominance over any criminal market sector, or

- Intent to exact revenge or retribution for the gang or any member of the gang; or

- Intent to obstruct justice, or intimidate or eliminate any witness against the gang or any member of the gang; or

- Intent to otherwise directly or indirectly cause benefit, aggrandizement, gain, profit or other advantage whatsoever to or for the gang, its reputation, influence, or membership.

Illinois' law is more group or leader oriented. It proscribes (activity) directed by, ordered by, authorized by, consented to, agreed to, requested by, acquiesced in, or ratified by any gang leader, officer, or governing or policy-making person or authority, or by any agent, representative, or deputy of any such officer, person, or authority intent to increase gang's size, membership, prestige, dominance, or control in any geographical area. The laws in states like Mississippi (§ 97–44–3) and Washington (§ 9.94A.030) tend to follow Illinois.

Witness Problems in Gang Cases

Most victims and witnesses end up involved in the criminal justice system through no fault of their own (Wilkinson, Mallios, & Martinson, 2013). Witnesses can often make or break a case, and witnesses in gang cases are no exception. Several types of witnesses can be involved in a gang case. The *normal citizen* is a witness who is unaffiliated with any gang, and just happened to be in the wrong place at the wrong time and is being asked to testify (Jackson, 2004). These "clean" witnesses often have very limited information. If they can identify tattoos, weapons, or the number of perpetrators, their testimony may be able to support another, less credible, witness (Cartwright & Walutes, 2006). The normal citizens are generally extremely fearful of retaliation because he or she often lives in an area claimed by members of the gang as their turf. This witness's fear is legitimate, and prosecutors have a difficult time pacifying that fear (Jackson, 2004).

Another type of problem witness is a victim who belongs to a rival gang (to the defendant). These witnesses will likely be uncooperative simply because of the gang culture and mindset (Jackson, 2004). They are often a challenge because they do not want to use law enforcement to fix the problems they are having with a rival gang (Cartwright & Walutes, 2006). Even if they identify the defendant directly after the crime occurs, their cooperation may cease before the trial.

A third problem witness is a member of the defendant's own gang. These witnesses will try to protect the defendant at every step along the way and can be expected to try to actively sabotage the case against the defendant (Jackson, 2004). These witnesses are hard to recruit if the prosecutor doesn't have leverage (potential charges) against them.

Sometimes the prosecutor can use a codefendant as a witness (Jackson, 2004). The codefendant may be the best witness. These are often members of the same gang who have pleaded guilty and agreed to cooperate with the prosecutor (Cartwright & Walutes, 2006). They can explain the rules and structure of the gang and the terminology used by members of the gang. Getting a codefendant to agree to testify will probably require a deal of some kind, whether allowing them to plead to a lesser charge or granting them immunity or something in between.

Cartwright and Walutes (2006) identified another type of witness: gang members' girlfriends. Girlfriends of male gang members can be good source of information about gang activities. These witnesses may have only limited information, but they can most often be used to corroborate the testimony of other witnesses.

Witness Intimidation and the Anti-snitching Culture

Witnesses to gang violence are frequently subjected to intimidation tactics because they have provided information to or cooperated with law enforcement (Garvey, 2013). Gang members are likely to maintain an atmosphere of fear and intimidation in the neighborhoods where they operate. This kind of community-wide intimidation contributes to a "no snitching" culture in the community. That culture often frustrates the ability of law enforcement to investigate and prosecute gang crimes (Garvey, 2013). Gang case defendants or their fellow gang members may intimidate others by committing violence against witnesses, other gang members, or the entire community (Garvey, 2013).

Witness intimidation negatively affects the community and the criminal justice system. Any organized attempt or policy to control or limit gang crime requires the inclusion of actions to minimize the incidents and effects of witness intimidation (Anderson, 2007). Witness intimidation includes conduct that discourages witnesses from meaningful participation in the criminal justice process. Meaningful participation means activities such as involvement in the investigation, prosecution, and decision making of a case, and testifying in the trial, if needed (Wilkinson, Mallios, & Martinson, 2013).

Perhaps the most common form of witness intimidation is the use of direct threats of physical violence (Anderson, 2007). Intimidation of that form often prevents victims and witnesses from coming forward and reporting crimes. It is accomplished with behavior such as isolation, control, threats, and actual violence or offering incentives not to participate (Wilkinson et al., 2013). Sometimes, gang members intimidate witnesses without physical violence by simply staring at the witness or driving slowly past the witness's house (Anderson, 2007). Gang members who are associates of the defendant may also appear in court just to frighten witnesses into not testifying. Four approaches have been used to prevent or minimize the effects of witness intimidation.

- Requesting high bail
- Vigorous witness intimidation prosecution
- Conscientious witness management
- Creating and utilizing victim/witness assistance programs

(Anderson, 2007)

Requesting high bail keeps gang members locked up and reduces their ability to intimidate witnesses or victims. Seeking high bail is especially appropriate when judges are able to consider a defendant's danger to the community (Anderson, 2007). Vigorous, immediate prosecutions of those who intimidate witnesses is critical, as they send a message that such action will not be tolerated (Anderson, 2007). Unfortunately, some states have weak intimidation laws or very minimal penalties. A comprehensive program is required to successfully prosecute gang-related crime. Providing services such as crisis intervention, emergency assistance (food, clothing, shelter, and medical care), and orientation to the criminal justice system (explaining the court process and accompanying victims and witnesses to court) can show witnesses they are an important part of the process (Anderson, 2007). Victims and witnesses may also be able to receive financial reimbursement for medical expenses, loss of wages or support, funeral expenses, professional counseling, or job retraining or rehabilitation (Anderson, 2007). These accommodations might help provide them with a visible incentive to participation.

During the trial, prosecutors should work closely with bailiffs, the court, and the marshals to prevent and address intimidation. One strategy to hamper courtroom intimidation is to have the court personnel check the identification of anyone entering the courtroom (Seabrook & Stewart, 2014). Each person in the courtroom can be checked for outstanding warrants, and see who is on probation or under supervised release. Prosecutors can also request that the court reserve the first row of seats in the courtroom for attorneys or police officers so that witnesses may not have a clear view of anyone in the courtroom trying to intimidate them during testimony (Seabrook & Stewart, 2014).

Protecting Witnesses

If a witness has been threatened or harmed as a result of participation in the prosecution of a case, the prosecutor can help ensure their safety and well-being by placing them in protective custody of some sort. The Emergency Witness Assistance Program (EWAP) was designed to provide relocation and other services to victims and witnesses who have been threatened or have fears about testifying (Seabrook & Stewart, 2014). EWAP was first used in the 1990s when witness retaliation was at an all-time high. Witnesses who agreed to participate in prosecutions were being threatened, assaulted, and even murdered (Seabrook & Stewart, 2014). EWAP provides resources for the immediate relocation of victims and witnesses who are concerned about their safety or the safety of their family members when they are involved in a pending prosecution or investigation. EWAP assistance can include transportation to a safe location, emergency lodging, temporary placement with a friend or relative, or placement in a hotel. Permanent relocation assistance can include assistance with moving expenses or making homes more secure. EWAP can be a useful in providing immediate services to victims and witnesses (Seabrook & Stewart, 2014).

The Federal Witness Security Program (WITSEC) provides government witnesses and their authorized family members, whose lives are in danger as a result of their cooperation with the U.S. government, with a secure and safe alternative (U.S. Department of Justice [DOJ], 2015b). WITSEC is run by the U.S. Marshals Service and typically is used in the most serious cases, including federal organized crime and racketeering offenses, federal drug trafficking offenses, and other serious violent crimes (DOJ, 2015b).

Figure 13.6

Witness protection. A protected witness guarded by U.S. Marshals armed with a machine pistol and a shotgun.

U.S. Marshals Service [Public domain], via Wikimedia Commons

WITSEC provides 24-hour protection to all witnesses while they are in dangerous environments (Seabrook & Stewart, 2014).

Operation Hardcore

Operation Hardcore is a specialized unit that was designed to prosecute serious and complex violent gang cases in Los Angeles, California. The Hardcore Gang Investigations Unit was created by the district attorney's office (CrimeSolutions.gov, 2015). The unit began prosecuting gang-related felony cases in 1979. The unit targets gang offenders who have a history of committing violent offenses and prosecutes them in either juvenile or criminal court. Prosecutors in the unit develop an expertise in gang relations and gain a better understanding of the lifestyle, allegiance, and family relationships that contribute to offender motives for committing serious offenses (CrimeSolutions.gov, 2015). This aids prosecutors in creating cases against gang-affiliated offenders and helps them to convince juries of the credibility of their argument at trial.

Prosecutors in Operation Hardcore work closely with witnesses to develop a rapport to gain their support and testimony for trial (CrimeSolutions.gov, 2015). Prosecutors in the unit select their cases based on criteria designed to identify established patterns of criminal behavior that are likely to lead to more serious violent offenses. Prosecutors in the unit are able to work a reduced caseload and receive additional investigative support from the police and other agencies. They are also able to work an assigned case continuously, from beginning to end. This allows them to work more closely with witnesses and restrict any settlements to long before the actual trial (CrimeSolutions. gov, 2015). Prosecutors can take the time needed to meet with witnesses and reassure them of the importance of their cooperation. Prosecutors also have the funds available to relocate witnesses or provide them with additional police protection if they are threatened.

Expert Testimony

Among the most important decisions a prosecutor can make while preparing for a gang trial is deciding whom to call as an expert (Jackson, 2004). The expert he or she chooses must have an intimate and working knowledge of the defendant's gang. Simply having a passing knowledge will not impress the judge or the jury. The expert must be able to show that his or her opinions are based on personal history with and knowledge of the gang (Jackson, 2004). Experienced gang investigators base their opinion and expertise on their knowledge of gangs in the area, as well as their methodology, information provided by any number of street contacts, and other gang records (Anderson et al., 2009). The expertise of local gang investigators can be used to establish the defendant's identity, often by identifying tattoos or nicknames used in conversation (Wennar, 2005).

Rule 703 of the Federal Rules of Evidence addresses the bases of opinion testimony by experts. The Rule suggests that the facts or data upon which an expert bases an opinion or inference may be those perceived by or made known to the expert at or before the hearing. Of particular interest is that the facts the expert considers in order to form an opinion need not be admissible as evidence. Facts that are otherwise inadmissible are not typically disclosed to the jury.

The expert witness must exude confidence and professionalism. As soon as the expert takes the witness stand, the jury begins making personal judgments. The jury will ultimately be asked to believe the opinion of the expert, a person of whom they had previously never heard and had never met (Jackson, 2004). If the expert acts unsure, the jury will notice. If the expert is obnoxious or pompous, the jury will notice that as well. The expert should find a way to strike a balance between confidence and modesty to enhance his or her credibility and persuasion with the jury (Jackson, 2004). Most of the jury's impression will be based on the expert's qualifications, as drawn out by the prosecutor. Appendix A provides a Sample Direct Examination for Gang Expert for suggestions on the questions used to establish expertise.

The important piece of the gang expert's testimony will come as answers to hypothetical questions asked by the prosecutor. The hypothetical (based on the prosecutor's theory of the case) as seen through the eyes of the expert will be the culmination of the prosecutor's gang evidence. If the prosecutor has introduced gang evidence to prove intent, motive, or identity, the hypothetical should be tailored to that point, and the expert can then direct the jury to the facts that prove it (Jackson, 2004).

Educated Gang Members

As gangs evolve, they can progress through the three generations identified previously. Meanwhile, many gang investigators and prosecutors may not notice, and may find that they have increased challenges with identifying gang activity. This may be because gang members no longer fit the stereotypes they once did—poor, undisciplined, socially unaware juveniles with few leadership skills. As gangs evolve, their leaders are increasingly suggesting they attend colleges and universities to educate themselves. These gang members have no significant police record and are capable of serving the gang with one of many traditional occupations. Many gangs have become quite sophisticated criminal networks, and their crimes are not limited to acts of violence. These gangs distribute wholesale quantities of drugs, and develop and maintain close working relationships with transnational criminal and drug trafficking organizations (NGIC, 2011). The lack of a focus on violence is often the reason they do not attract the attention of law enforcement. Members of the more advanced gangs engage in crimes like counterfeiting, identity theft, and mortgage fraud, primarily due to the high profitability and much lower visibility and risk of detection and punishment of those white collar crimes than drug and weapons trafficking (NGIC, 2011). These crimes often require a more technical set of skills. Gangs have become increasingly adaptable and sophisticated in their crimes, and have employed new and advanced technology to facilitate criminal activity, enhancing their criminal operations (NGIC, 2011).

Gang members may not limit their activity to off-campus venues, though they may not hide their gang affiliation. Alpert, Rojek, Hansen, Shannon, and Decker (2011) found that many (19.5%) campus police chiefs reported they knew of a student-athlete who retained his or her gang membership while at their university. And very little research has been conducted to determine to what extent gang members have penetrated the higher education community. In research by Smith (2012) at a large, four-year public university in the southern United States, most of the students (62%) and law enforcement (69%) reported up to 10% of the students were active gang members. Most (88%) police thought gang members were responsible for up to 10% of crime on campus, while half (50%) of the student respondents thought gang members were responsible for over 10% of crime on campus. The Bloods, Crips, and Gangster Disciples were the top three gangs seen in the campus community for both groups. Drugs crimes, assaults, assorted weapons crimes, robberies, and sexual assaults were reported as gang-related crimes.

The presence of gangs on campuses across the country should be considered troubling, both for law enforcement and for members of the greater community. What gang members are doing on campus should be troubling in the long term. If gangs get more adept at avoiding detection because they have learned in criminal justice courses how the system operates, or in business courses how an audit works, or in computer science courses how to communicate without being detected, they will be more able to commit crime without concern for arrest.

Summary

It is important to know that the U.S. Constitution prohibits criminalizing mere membership in a gang. Aligning specific gang activities with the generations of gangs they represent requires a determination of the level of sophistication, politicization, and internationalization of the gang. Three generations (or types) of gangs have been identified. To evaluate the process of gang member identification using the point system, you should choose an objective and consistent set of gang membership identifiers. Confidential informant (CI) development begins with acknowledging that the use of CIs can pose a significant risk to investigators if they are not properly managed and controlled. Differentiating the methods used for gang prevention, treatment, and suppression allows one to identify the appropriate treatment. The primary goals for the program are often to decrease gang involvement and illegal behavior.

DISCUSSION QUESTIONS

1. Describe the process that local gang investigators would use to process intelligence on a gang operating in the region.
2. Examine the points system in the reading. Imagine what other types of groups (both those advocating lawful and unlawful activity) could be identified by a similar system.
3. Why should prosecutors use RICO laws or enhancements when prosecuting gangs? Should there be circumstances when those laws are not appropriate?
4. Examine the balance between maintaining a witness's safety in a gang case and the constitutional right of the accused to confront witnesses.
5. You are scheduled to be called as an expert witness in an upcoming gang trial. What material will the prosecutor need to get from you?
6. Identify the group behaviors and dynamics that would distinguish a first generation gang member from one in the second or third generation. How would you explain the differences to someone who knew very little about gangs or the criminal justice system?

APPENDIX A
Sample Direct Examination for Gang Expert

Qualifications

What do you do for a living?

How long have you done that?

What other positions have you held that qualify you to testify in this case?

How long were you involved directly in gang investigations?

What were your duties as a gang investigator?

What education, training, and background qualify you to perform those duties?

Have you ever lectured or taught classes regarding gangs? To whom?

Are you a member of any recognized professional organizations related to studying and sharing information on gangs and gang members?

Is it part of your job to stay current on gang trends, including rivalries, alliances, customs, habits?

How do you do this?

Have you ever qualified as a gang expert in the past?

Gang Culture

Are there typical qualities and characteristics that most gangs display?

What motivates the typical gang member to join a gang?

Once in, do gang members typically just quit?

Do gang members typically place a high degree of value on loyalty?

How is providing information to law enforcement viewed by gang members?

Does revenge have special significance in the gang culture?

Is there a time limit on revenge in the gang culture?

How should "imminence" be seen with respect to revenge by a gang?

Case at Hand

Are you familiar with [gang name]?

How do you know about that gang?

Is the gang typical compared to other gangs in Nashville or Middle Tennessee?

What, in your expert opinion, is unique about the [gang name]?

Do you know [defendant]?

Have you had personal contact with the defendant?

Is the defendant a member of [gang name]?

How do you know?

Has the defendant admitted his membership to you?

Is [defendant] a typical gang member?

Is the defendant personally aware of the inner workings of [gang name]?

Was the defendant aware of the circumstances surrounding the government case with which he was assisting?

Did he cooperate with law enforcement during the investigation?

Did the defendant have an agreement with law enforcement to assist with the investigation?

Did the agreement appear to be a typical informant–law enforcement agreement?

Did either side act in such a way that could be considered contrary to the agreement?

Why do you think [defendant] stopped cooperating with law enforcement?

Do you think [defendant] stopped cooperating because he was motivated by a desire to thwart further prosecution?

Do you think [defendant] was more in fear of retaliation by the gang against himself or his family?

In your expert opinion, did the defendant have reason to be in fear for his own and his family's safety?

In your expert opinion, did the defendant have reason to stop cooperating?

On what do you base your opinion?

How important is the ability to manage informants to gang investigations?

Are informants typically easy to convince that the law enforcement officer is a better ally than their fellow gang members?

How fragile is the law enforcement–informant relationship?

Did [defendant] have a potential predisposition against cooperating with law enforcement based on his upbringing and culture?

In your expert opinion, who is responsible for managing the law enforcement–informant relationship?

Were you able to form an opinion about the law enforcement–informant relationship in this case?

How well was the law enforcement–informant relationship handled in this case?

To what lengths will typical gang members go to discourage testimony against gang members?

Is the [gang name] a typical gang in this regard?

In your expert opinion, was there reason to believe that there was a direct causal relationship between [defendant's] potential testimony and the safety of his family?

Adapted from Jackson, Alan (2004) *Prosecuting Gang Cases: What Local Prosecutors Need to Know*. Washington, DC: Bureau of Justice Assistance.

APPENDIX B
Proposed State Policy: Gangs and Security Threat Groups

This is a comparison/proposed compilation of the policy for State Departments of Corrections and local Police. For each topic below, paragraph a indicates primary policy and paragraph b indicates policy while incarcerated. Paragraph c proposes those opportunities where a combination of the two can be made without negative effect on the application of either.

Confirmation

a. Confirmed Gang Member: an individual will be considered a confirmed gang member when he/she achieves 10 or more points from the below criteria.

b. Confirmation as an STG suspect/confirmed member will be based on the ten-point scale of identifiers contained in the Criminal Intelligence Submission Report CR-3536. STG files will be initiated once an inmate has one or more of the identifiers listed below:

1. Self Admission

a. Self Admission: (describe in narrative). (9 points)

b. Inmate admits to being an STG member and signs a statement of admission or admits in the presence of two staff members who will sign attesting to the admission. (9 points)

c. *Individual admits to being a Gang/STG member and signs a statement of admission or admits in the presence of two witnesses who will sign attesting to the admission. (describe in narrative) (9 points)*

- Admission must be documented with date of admission and name of officer or investigator who heard the admission in a police report, corrections report, field contact memo, or recorded statement.

- A vague admission about membership, for example, "I hang with the ** (gang name) **," should be clarified, and the precise admission documented (MVCCC, 2012).

2. Tattoos

a. Gang Tattoos/Brands (attach photo or describe). (8 points)

b. STG tattoos: Has tattoo(s) that are recognized as being associated with a particular group or set. (pictures of tattoo(s) to be placed in the STG intelligence file) (8 points)

c. *Gang/STG tattoos/brands: Has tattoo(s), brands, or other permanent or semi-permanent marking on skin/facial hair recognized as associated with a particular gang, crime group, or set. (pictures of tattoo(s), brand, marking placed in intelligence file and described in narrative) (8 points)*

- Tattoos and brands must be photographed or described in detail, using factual, non-subjective language. For example: "6-Pointed Star obtained 6 months ago" is a good description; "** (gang name) ** Star" is not.

- To be considered a "gang tattoo" or "gang brand," the gang-related nature of the tattoo or brand must be confirmed by an officer or investigator with adequate training and experience (MVCCC, 2012).

3. Hand Signs/Symbols/Logos

a. Use of hand signs, possession/use of symbols, logos, graffiti that clearly indicate gang affiliation. (list specific symbols/signs used) (3 points)

b. Use/possession of symbols or logos, hand signs, colors, etc. (copies of supporting evidence are to be placed in the STG file) (3 points)

c. *Use of hand signs, possession/use of symbols, logos, graffiti, colors, etc. that indicate Gang/ STG affiliation. (list specific symbols/signs used in file and described in narrative) (3 points)*

- Graffiti should be described in detail using factual, non-subjective language. Example: "132 SGC painted on wall" is a good description; "** (gang name) ** graffiti painted on wall" is not.

- Graffiti and gang-specific writings found on walls, notebooks or other items should be photographed or described in detail in a police report, corrections report or other documentation and, if possible, property inventoried.

- The gang-related nature of the writings or graffiti must be confirmed by an officer or investigator with adequate training and experience.

(MVCCC, 2012)

4. Wearing of Gang/STG Colors, Gang Clothing, Gang Paraphernalia

a. Wearing of gang colors, gang clothing, gang paraphernalia in such a way that indicates gang affiliation. (list specific items and colors in narrative) (1 point)

b. Wearing of STG colors. (photos or other supporting documentation is to be placed in the STG file) (1 point)

c. *Wearing of Gang/STG colors, clothing, paraphernalia in such a way that indicates affiliation. (include photos, other documentation and list specific items and colors in narrative) (1 point)*

- Suspected gang symbols and clothing worn or possessed must be evaluated in the context of how they are worn or the location they are recovered.

- Clothing, jewelry or items with suspected gang symbols or gang-related monikers should be photographed and, if possible, property inventoried.

- When items cannot be photographed or inventoried, the gang-related items should be described in detail using factual, non-subjective language. For example: "Blue jersey with # 13 on back" is a good description; "** (gang name) ** jersey" is not.

- Many symbols have multiple meanings and may not be a gang symbol to everyone. The gang-related nature of the clothing or symbols must be confirmed by an officer or investigator with adequate training and experience (MVCCC, 2012).

5. Possession of Gang/STG Documents

a. Possession of Gang Documents—roster, procedure, by-laws, etc. (describe in narrative). (3 points)

b. Possession of STG documents: rosters, bylaws, and codes, etc. (copies of documents to be placed in the STG file) (3 points)

c. *Possession of Gang/STG documents: rosters, procedures, bylaws, codes, etc. (copies of documents and description in narrative) (3 points)*

6. Possession of Commercial Gang/STG Publications

a. Possession of commercial Gang-related publications (describe in narrative). (1 point)

b. Possession of STG commercial publications. (copies of publication are to be placed in the STG file) (1 point)

c. *Possession of Gang/STG commercial publications. (copies of publication are to be placed in the STG file, describe in narrative) (1 point)*

7. Participation in Commercial Gang/STG Publications*

a. Participation in gang publications—submitting articles, illustrations, etc. (describe in narrative) (8 points) *

b. Participation in commercial STG publications: submitting articles, artwork, etc. (copies of publication are to be placed in the STG file). (9 points) *

c. *Participation in commercial Gang/STG publications: submitting articles, illustrations, artwork, etc. (copies of publication to be placed in file (describe in narrative). (9 points)*

8. Consistently in Contact With Gang/STG Members

a. Consistent observed contact with confirmed gang members (document observations—describe in narrative). (2 points)

b. Consistently observed contact with STG members. (documented contact by use of written statement, LCDG contact note, or e-mail from staff observing contact to be placed in STG file) (2 points)

c. *Consistently observed contact with Gang/STG members. (document by written statement, internal memo/note, or e-mail from department/organization employee observing contact to be placed in file) (2 points)*

- Family interactions are not considered to be gang-related unless there is criminal activity involved.

- Interactions must be voluntary and related to gang activity. For example, a person associating with a gang member because both work at the same location, absent gang-related activity between the two, does not meet this criterion.

- Observations must be documented in a police report, corrections report or field contact memo and include the date, time, and location of the interactions.

- A minimum of three documented observations of gang-related interaction in the previous 12-month period is needed to meet the "regularly observed with" portion of this criterion (MVCCC, 2012).

9. Contact With Gang/STG Members

a. Known contact with confirmed gang members. (document contact and list confirmed gang member) (1 point)

b. Known contact with STG members. For example, inmate is involved in an STG related incident along with confirmed STG members. (1 point)

c. *Contact with STG members. (interacting in person, verbally, digitally, or otherwise communicating with other gang members, directly or indirectly, or involved in Gang/STG-related incident with confirmed STG members) (1 point)*

- Individual is arrested with a gang member for an offense consistent with gang-related criminal activity.

- Arrests must be documented in a police report, corrections report or field contact memo and include the date, time, and location of the arrest (MVCCC, 2012).

10. Participating in a Photo With Gang/STG Members

a. Participating in a photo with confirmed gang members (attach photo or describe in narrative). (2 points).

b. Participating in a photo with known STG members. (copy of photo(s) are to be placed in the STG file). (2 points)

c. *Participating in photo with known Gang/STG members. (copy of photo(s) to be placed in file, describe in narrative). (2 points)*

- Photographs or images should depict evidence of gang-related criminal activity, such as a person holding a gun or wearing or displaying gang-related signs, symbols, clothing or graffiti.

- A single photograph or image with a gang member, absent any depiction of criminal gang-related activity or displaying gang-related signs, symbols, clothing or graffiti, may count only as one of three documented occasions of association in the previous 12-month period under criterion #8.

- Photographs or images recovered from or depicting gang members obtained by consent or during a lawful search should be inventoried or otherwise preserved and the chain of custody maintained.

- Images from social networking sites or other online sources should be downloaded and identified with the name of the person who posted it (if known), the date of posting (if known) and the URL of the site.

- The gang-related nature of the clothing or symbols must be confirmed by an officer or investigator with adequate training and experience (MVCCC, 2012).

11. Outside Jurisdiction Documents

a. Outside jurisdiction information/documents (document correspondence). (5 points)

b. Outside jurisdiction intelligence/documents. (identify source and place copies in the STG file). (5 points)

c. *Outside jurisdiction intelligence or information/documents (identify source, place copies in and document correspondence in file). (5 points)*

12. Correspondence With Gang/STG Members

a. Sending/receiving correspondence to/from confirmed gang members (document correspondence). (3 points)

b. Sending and receiving correspondence to/from STG members. Correspondence must contain Gang/STG content and must be to/from a confirmed member. (copy of correspondence is to be placed in the STG file). (3 points)

c. *Sending and receiving correspondence to/from Gang/STG members. Correspondence must contain Gang/STG content and must be to/from a confirmed gang/STG member (copy of correspondence to be placed in file). (3 points)*

- Correspondence or other communication between gang members, especially to and from incarcerated individuals, frequently contains references to other gang members and criminal and gang-related activity. They should be documented and, if possible, property inventoried.

- Messages and/or online conversations about criminal or gang-related activity on social networking sites should be downloaded or otherwise electronically preserved (MVCCC, 2012).

13. Named a Gang/STG Member in Correspondence[#]

a. (1) Named a gang member in correspondence[#] (document correspondence). (8 points)

(2) Subject's name appears on a gang roster, hit list, or gang-related graffiti[#] (describe in narrative). (8 points)

b. Named a STG member in correspondence[#] Suspect is named in correspondence involving a confirmed member or is listed as a member on a confiscated STG roster. (copy of material is to be placed in STG file). (8 points)

- Gang rosters on any media, including on clothing or in graffiti, should be photographed, and, if possible, property inventoried.

- There must be sufficient documented information matching the name with a specific individual before this may be counted as a criterion.

- Graffiti containing threats against an individual should be photographed or described in detail.

- A list of suspected gang members generated by a law enforcement agency is NOT a gang roster (MVCCC, 2012).

14. Confirmation Through Outside Agency Gang Unit or Database*

a. Confirmation through outside agency gang unit (document information source). (10 points)*

b. Confirmation through outside agency gang unit or gang database. (copy of documentation to be placed in STG file). (9 points) *

c. *Confirmation through outside agency Gang/STG unit or gang database (copy of documentation to be placed in file. (9 points)*

- Is identified as a gang member by a person with sufficient knowledge of gang activity to qualify him/her as a reliable source.

- Reliable sources must have a demonstrable basis for their knowledge; rumor and speculation are insufficient. Reliable sources may include persons of authority or those with a personal connection to the individual.

- Reliable source information must be documented in a police report, corrections report or field contact memo. A reliable source may be called upon to testify about his/her knowledge of an individual's gang involvement (MVCCC, 2012).

15. Engaged in Gang/STG Crime or Activity*

a. (1) Subject involved in criminal gang incidents (describe in narrative). (8 points)*

(2) Subject's victims or targets of crime are members of a rival gang. (document the victim and list confirmed gang name). (5 points) *

b. STG related disciplinary. Inmate is convicted of possession of STG materials, participating in STG activity, or as a perpetrator with confirmed STG members in a disciplinary involving STG activity i.e. homicide, assault, strong arm activity, etc. (5 points) *

Subject identified as a gang member by another gang member (document the contact and list confirmed gang name). (8 points)

Subject identified as a gang member by a reliable informant. (9 points)

---

 * indicates a discrepancy or difference between a & b versions of more than terminology (Gang to STG).

 # need to determine application based on case law (Crawford v. Washington, 541 U.S. 36 (2004). P59: Testimonial statements of witnesses absent from trial have been admitted only where the declarant is unavailable, and only where the defendant has had a prior opportunity to cross-examine. P 68: Where nontestimonial hearsay is at issue, it is wholly consistent with the Framers' design to afford the States flexibility in their development of hearsay law—as does Roberts, and as would an approach that exempted such statements from Confrontation Clause scrutiny altogether. Where testimonial evidence is at issue, however, the Sixth Amendment demands what the common law required: unavailability and a prior opportunity for cross-examination. P69: Where testimonial statements are at issue, the only indicium of reliability sufficient to satisfy constitutional demands is the one the Constitution actually prescribes: confrontation.

APPENDIX C
Gang Member Renunciation Form
The Gang Denunciation and Gang Renunciation Form (GDGRF)

George W. Knox, Ph.D. NGCRC
Copyright 2018, National Gang Crime Research Center.

Background

The Gang Denunciation and Gang Renunciation Form (GDGRF) was designed for use with persons exposed to the risk of gang membership who sincerely want and desire to abandon gang life and all it represents.

Types of Uses

The GDGRF is designed for a host of categories such as the following:

(1) adults or juveniles on probation or parole need to complete the GDGRF to reduce the probability of recidivism if they have ever been gang affiliated,

(2) juveniles in special educational programs designed to target "at-risk youth" or children who are starting to develop gang ties can benefit from completing the GDGRF particularly in conjunction with family counseling,

(3) juveniles in K-12 schools who may experience gang contamination when a parent, sibling, other relative or significant other is a gang influence will benefit from the GDGRF if used in conjunction with school counseling,

(4) whereas gang fights and gang conflicts and gang threats (sometimes involving the issue of workplace violence or threat of violence) can erupt in the work place setting, employers have found the GDGRF useful in dealing with employees who have been accused, whether true or false, of being gang members or displaying gang behavior that is inappropriate to the work place or place of business, using this form as an alternative to firing decisions may help restore the employee to a positive role in the workplace,

(5) the GDGRF is ideal for parents who are trying to reclaim their children from the grip of gang membership in conjunction with psychological counseling or similar professional social service help and intervention,

(6) the GDGRF is highly recommended for every publicly funded program providing services to the offender and ex-offender populations, juvenile and adult, as the factor of gang membership mitigates against rehabilitation efforts that may be implied in said services (e.g., re-entry services, job placement, training, etc.),

(7) any person working in a drug treatment program, gang prevention program, gang intervention program, gang outreach program, at any level of prevention (primary, secondary, or tertiary prevention levels) should probably complete the GDGRF as a part of their personnel package to ensure the integrity of the program staff are not allowed, by default, to maintain their gang affiliations, as it is generally recognized that "ex-gang member" needs a form like the GDGRF to ensure by testimony and self-proclamation that they are genuinely "former gang members."

(8) The GDGRF can be used on persons in short or long term correctional custody and is ideal for jail or prison inmates or confined juveniles as a way to achieve a cessation of gang activity through contract programming.

(9) The GDGRF is also ideal for persons who are in private or public in-patient treatment programs who are undergoing treatment or intervention counseling for multiple diagnostic issues (e.g., gangs, drugs, etc.); it is also highly recommended for use in conjunction with clients receiving gang tattoo removal services.

(10) The GDGRF should be used in any context where you have a person, male or female, juvenile or adult, in custody or at-large, who is at risk of knowingly associating with street gangs, outlaw motorcycle gangs, prison gangs, hate and extremist groups, etc.

Clergy members, social workers, psychologists, and all others in the helping profession may find situations where it is useful to use the GDGRF. Research has shown that when persons sign a "contract" like the GDGRF there is a kind of symbolic declaration, a publication of will and purpose, that impacts on human identity in a positive way.

Usage Instructions

In most applications, the GDGRF simply has two copies of the form signed, one goes to the person signing the form, and the other to the supervising authority (agency, program, hospital, psychologist, officer, employer, etc.). Sometimes it is useful to provide one to the client's parent(s) or other designated significant others (family members, guardian, caregiver, etc.).

Past Conduct Not Admitted, Future Conduct Promised

The GDGRF is not an admission of prior criminality, wrongdoing, or subcultural deviance (e.g., it is possible to join a gang and never get arrested for anything at a juvenile or adult level). Rather, the GDGRF form focuses on promises of future behavior to steadfastly avoid gang life and all the "risks" that stem from routine contact with gangs and gang members.

In short, the GDGRF is like a "promissory note" to avoid gang members and the negative things that can happen from hanging out with gangs.

The GDGRF obviously can be used very effectively in cooperation with debriefing initiatives. It works well with witness and testimony agreements for persons who are assisting in the prosecution of gang crime. Debriefing and helping the government suppress gangs is good for a complete identity transition from gang-associate or gang-member to becoming "gang-free" or a "recovering gang-impacted person." Sometimes the dosage of intervention requires only the GDGRF itself, it is an agreement, a contract with a significant other or official, and it is the equivalent of contractual programming for a "gang-free future." It focuses on future conduct, not past conduct.

The Gang Denunciation and Gang Renunciation Form (GDGRF)

Whereas, gangs are criminal and violent forces in society, I do hereby solemnly promise by affixing my signature in front of a witness to henceforth and for the entire duration of my life to have no intentional association with gangs or gang members; and I recognize that "gangs" means any street gang, drug gang, prison gang, or group of three or more persons who are recurrently involved in crime; and I recognize that hate/extremist groups are also included in what is meant in this declaration as a "gang" (e.g., the KKK is a gang, outlaw 1% biker clubs are a gang, party crews that violate drug laws are a gang, etc.).

I will carefully avoid gang life, by which I mean I will not intentionally want to hang out with or associate with gang members or persons involved in the gang lifestyle.

I will not conduct any personal business of any kind with gangs or gang members.

I hereby declare my intent to completely avoid the influence of gangs and gang members for the rest of my natural life.

I will accept no new close personal friends and associates who are members of gangs or extremist groups. I will begin immediately to distance myself from any existing close personal friends and associates who might be members of gangs or extremist groups. If I discover someone I am friendly with is a member of a gang or extremist group, then I will cease and desist from further efforts to have ongoing contact with such a person.

I will not knowingly associate with persons who are gang members, indeed even if I am accidentally put in contact in a random way with persons involved in the gang life I will find some way to quickly extract myself from the social situation to minimize my risk of being drawn into the negative influences of gang life.

In my mind I will endeavor to develop 1,001 ways of saying "NO" to gang members and gang life, I will always be ready to say "NO, I am not interested in becoming involved directly or indirectly with gangs or gang members," I will find creative and non-risky ways of saying "NO" when asked to get involved in gang activities, gang events, gang parties, gang meetings/reunions, and any gang relationships whatsoever.

From this day onward and for the rest of my natural life, I will not use gang slang; I will not wear gang clothing; I will not "represent gang affiliation," I will not display gang colors or gang symbols, I will not utter gang threats or put-downs against rival gangs, I will not visit gang websites on the Internet, I will not leave "gang messages" on Internet blogs where gang members may communicate on the internet, I will neither attack nor approve of gang members in writing on the Internet where it is easy to leave messages about other gangs and gang members.

I will not watch gang movies or listen to gang-related music.

I will not visit a gang-dominated or gang-owned business, club house, home, apartment, or location where gangs and gang members can be expected to be found.

I will change my preferences for goods and services if I encounter gangs or gang members in my daily, regular routine activities; if I see a former gang associate at the park, I will find a new park to visit; if I see a gang member I knew from the gang life at a local health club, I will find a new health club to attend; if I see former gang friends at a restaurant, I will find a different place to eat. I will avoid any possible contact with gangs or gang members.

I will not provide loyalty, support, help or assistance of any kind to my former gang or gang friends/associates, or to gangs or gang members generally. I will provide no material support and no emotional support to anyone caught up in the gang life, including former or current gang friends/associates, or to gangs or gang members generally, or members of hate/extremist groups generally.

If I am ever asked to do something illegal or illicit by a gang or gang member or extremist group, while I am at my place of employment, I will immediately report it to___(example, "My Supervisor," "My Probation Officer," etc.) _____ or to the local police having jurisdiction over the potential crime if it happens outside of the work environment.

I have no loyalty to any "gang nation" or extremist organization, I have loyalty only to my true nation, the United States of America. I may also have legitimate loyalty to God, my country, my family, and my employer.

Standing and placing my right hand over my heart, in witness whereof, I now read out aloud, as respectfully as I can, all of the words of the Pledge of Allegiance as I face the Flag:

I pledge allegiance to the flag, of the United States of America, And to the Republic for which it stands, One nation, under God, indivisible, With Liberty and Justice for all.

CLIENT:

Print your name: _____

Sign your name: _____

Today's Date: _____

WITNESS:

Witnessed by: _____

Today's Date: _____

A copy of this goes to the client, who should be congratulated for being, by self-proclamation, "gang-free."

APPENDIX D
Gang Laws in the United States

Brief Review of Federal and State Definitions of the Terms

"GANG," "GANG CRIME," and "GANG MEMBER" (as of December 2016)
Federal Law

Currently, federal law *defines* the term "criminal street gang" as "an ongoing group, club, organization, or association of 5 or more persons—

(A) that has as 1 of its primary purposes the commission of 1 or more of the criminal offenses described in subsection (c);

(B) the members of which engage, or have engaged within the past 5 years, in a continuing series of offenses described in subsection (c); and

(C) the activities of which affect interstate or foreign commerce." 18 U.S.C. § 521(a).

"The offenses described in this section are—

(1) a Federal felony involving a controlled substance (as defined in section 102 of the Controlled Substances Act (21 USC § 802)) for which the maximum penalty is not less than 5 years;

(2) a Federal felony crime of violence that has as an element the use or attempted use of physical force against the person of another; and

(3) a conspiracy to commit an offense described in paragraph (1) or (2)." 18 U.S.C.§521(c).

"The circumstances described in this section are that the offense described in subsection (c) was committed by a person who—

(1) participates in a criminal street gang with knowledge that its members engage in or have engaged in a continuing series of offenses described in subsection (c);

(2) intends to promote or further the felonious activities of the criminal street gang or maintain or increase his or her position in the gang; and

(3) has been convicted within the past 5years for

(A) an offense described in subsection (c);

(B) a State offense—

(i) involving a controlled substance (as defined in section 102 of the Controlled Substances Act (21 USC § 802)) for which the maximum penalty is not less than 5 years' imprisonment; or

(ii) that is a felony crime of violence that has as an element the use or attempted use of physical force against the person of another;

(C) any Federal or State felony offense that by its nature involves a substantial risk that physical force against the person of another may be used in the course of committing the offense; or

(D) a conspiracy to commit an offense described in subparagraph (A), (B), or (C)." 18 U.S.C. § 521(d).

State Law

A review of current state laws for various states' definitions of the words "gang," "gang member," and "gang crime" reveals the following information:

"Gang" Definitions

- 44 states and Washington, DC, have legislation that defines "gang."

- 36 states define a gang as consisting of three or more persons.

- 30 states include a common name, identifying sign, or symbol as identifiers of gangs in their definitions.

- 43 states refer to a gang as an "organization, association, or group."

- 28 states and Washington, DC, use the term "criminal street gang" to describe a gang.

- Every definition includes criminal/illegal activity or behavior.

"Gang Member" Definitions

- 11 have legislation that defines a "gang member."

- 5 states have a list of criteria, some of which a person must meet to be considered a gang member.

- Of those, 6 states require that a person must meet at least two criteria to be considered a gang member.

"Gang Crime" Definitions

- 31 states define "gang crime/activity."

- 20 states refer to it as a "pattern of criminal gang activity."

- 25 states enumerate the exact crimes that are to be considered criminal gang activity.

From National Gang Center December 2016—www.nationalgangcenter.gov/Content/Documents/Definitions.pdf

REFERENCES

Ackman, D. (2005). McAmerica. *Forbes* [online edition]. April 15. Retrieved from www.forbes.com/2005/04/15/cx_da_0415topnews.html

Acoli, S. (n.d.). An updated history of the new Afrikan prison struggle. In *Imprisoned Intellectuals: America's Political Prisoners Write on Life, Liberation, and Rebellion*, James, J. (2003, Ed.). New York, NY: Rowman and Littlefield.

Adelstein, J. (2012). Global Vice and the Expanding Territory of the Yakuza. *Journal of International Affairs*, Fall/Winter, 66(1), pp. 155–161.

Adelstein, J. (2011). Even Japan's infamous mafia groups are helping with the relief effort. *Daily Beast*. May 18. Retrieved from www.businessinsider.com/japan-yakuza-mafia-aid-earthquake-tsunami-rescue-efforts-2011-3

Adelstein, J. (2010). The Last Yakuza. *World Policy Journal*, Summer, pp. 63–71.

Ahmed-Ullah, N., and Ruzich, J. (2009). Police crackdown on burglaries: Western suburbs seen targeted by gangs. *Chicago Tribune*. November 12. Retrieved from http://articles.chicagotribune.com/2009-11-12/news/0911110837_1_burglaries-riverside-police-crack

Albaek, K., Leth-Petersen, S., le Maire, D., and Tranaes, T. (2013). *Does Peacetime Military Service Affect Crime?* IZA Discussion Paper No. 7528. Retrieved from SSRN: http://ssrn.com/abstract=2314823

Albini, J., Roger, R., Shabalin, V., Kutushev, V., Molseev, V., and Anderson, J. (1995). Russian Organized Crime: Its History, Structure and Function. *Journal of Contemporary Criminal Justice*, December, 11(4), pp. 213–243.

All About Bikes. (2014). *A History of the Pagan's Motorcycle Club*. Retrieved from www.allaboutbikes.com/feature-articles/motorcycle-stories/6941-a-history-of-the-pagans-motorcycle-club

Allen, E. (1962). *Merchants of Menace-The Mafia: A Study of Organized Crime*. Springfield, IL: Charles C. Thomas.

Allen, H. E., Simonsen, C. E., and Latessa, E. J. (2004). *Corrections in America: An Introduction* (20th ed.). Upper Saddle River, NJ: Pearson/Prentice Hall.

Allender, D. (2001). Gangs in Middle America. *FBI Law Enforcement Bulletin*, 70(12).

Alonso, A. A. (2004). Racialized identities and the formation of black gangs in Los Angeles. *Urban Geography*, 25, 658–674.

Alonso, A. A. (1999). *Territoriality among African-American street gangs in Los Angeles*. Unpublished master's thesis, University of Southern California.

Alpert, G., Rojek, J., Hansen, A., Shannon, R. L., and Decker, S. H. (2011). *Examining the Prevalence and Impact of Gangs in College Athletic Programs Using Multiple Sources*. Final Report to the Bureau of Justice Assistance, Washington, DC.

Anastasia, G. (1990). Affidavit: Chinatown leader involved in mob. *Philly.com*. March 6. Retrieved from http://articles.philly.com/1990-03-06/news/25905464_1_massage-parlor-prostitution-operation-affidavit

Anbinder, T. (2001). *Five Points: The 19th Century New York City Neighborhood That Invented Tap Dance, Stole Elections, and Became the World's Most Notorious Slum*. New York, NY: Free Press.

Anderson, J. (2007). Gang-Related Witness Intimidation. *National Gang Center Bulletin No. 1*, February, pp. 1–9.

Anderson, J., Brooks, W., Langsam, A., and Dyson, L. (2002). The 'New' Female Gang Member: Anomaly or Evolution? *Journal of Gang Research*, Fall, 10(1), pp. 47–65.

Anderson, J., Nye, M., Freitas, R., and Wolf, J. (2009). Gang Prosecution Manual. *Institute for Intergovernmental Research*, July, pp. 1–116.

Anonymous. (2006). US Street Gangs-Mara Salvatrucha. *Crimes, Criminals, Scams and Frauds*. Retrieved from http://crimeandcriminalsblog.blogspot/2006_09_11_archive.html

Arlacchi, P. (1987). *Mafia Business: The Mafia Ethnic and the Spirit of Capitalism*. London: Verso.

Armstrong, T., Bluehouse, P., Dennison, A., Mason, H., Mendenhall, B., Wall, D., and Aion, J. (1999). *Finding and Knowing the Gang Nayee-Field-Initiated Gang Research Project, the Judicial Branch of the Navajo Nation*. Washington, DC: Office of Juvenile Justice and Delinquency Prevention.

Arrouas, M. (2014). Japan's Biggest Crime Syndicate Has Its Own Website. *Time*. April 2. Retrieved from http://time.com/46477/japan-yakuza-website/

Arsovska, J. (2015). *Decoding Albanian Organized Crime: Culture, Politics, and Globalization*. Oakland: University of California Press.

Arsovska, J. (2006). Understanding a 'Culture of Violence and Crime': The 'Kanun of Lek Dukagjini' and the Rise of the Albanian Sexual-Slavery Rackets. *European Journal of Crime, Criminal Law and Criminal Justice*, 14(2), pp. 161–184.

Asbury, H. (2008). *Gangs of New York: An Informal History of the Underworld*. New York, NY: Vintage Books (reprint of the 1927 edition).

Asbury, H. (2003). *The French Quarter: An Informal History of the New Orleans Underworld*. New York, NY: Thunder's Mouth Press (reprint of the 1936 edition).

Asbury, H. (1989). *The Gangs of New York: An Informal History of the New York Underworld*. New York, NY: Dorset Press (reprint of the 1927 edition).

Asbury, H. (1986). *The Gangs of Chicago: An Informal History of the Chicago Underworld*. New York, NY: Thundermouth Press (reprint of the 1940 edition).

Asbury, H. (1940). *The Gangs of Chicago*. New York, NY: Perseus Books.

Asbury, H. (1933). *The Gangs of San Francisco: An Informal History of the San Francisco Underworld*. London, England: Arrow Books.

Asbury, H. (1927). *The Gangs of New York: An Informal History of the Underworld*. New York, NY: Alfred A. Knopf.

ASIS International. (2013). *Protection of Assets (POA)*. Kindle Version. [Investigation]. ASIS International.

Association of Chief Police Officers [ACPO]. (2005). Practice Advice on Core Investigative Doctrine. *National Centre for Policing Excellence*. Retrieved from www.caerphilly.gov.uk/pdf/Health_SocialCare/POVA/Core_Investigation_Doctrine_Interactive.pdf

Associated Press (AP). (2008a). Dozens of outlaw bikers arrested in ATF sting. October 21. Retrieved from www.nbcnews.com/id/27296867/ns/us_news-crime_and_courts/t/dozens-outlaw-bikers-arrested-atf-sting/#.VF06dJ3nbyM

Associated Press (AP). (2008b). Letters from federal prisoners going electronic: Inmates now have inboxes at more than 20 federal facilities across U.S. August 17. Retrieved from www.nbcnews.com/id/26253031/ns/us_news-crime_and_courts/t/letters-federal-prisoners-going-electronic/#.VVOZVGC26AA

Associated Press (AP). (1985). 25 Chinatown gang members indicted on racketeering charges. *Associated Press*. February 18. Retrieved from www.apnewsarchive.com/1985/25-Chinatown-Gang-Members-Indicted-on-Racketeering-Charges/id-41022e6a6daa474399bde0f948710d47

Atkins, A. (1999). Computer Gang Makes Gang Warfare Kid's Play. *Tampa Tribune*. June 22.

AVM.gangs.tripod.com. (2007). Gangster two-six. Retrieved from http://avm.gangs.tripod.com/id29.html

Babatunde, R. (2012). Nigeria: Organized crime—Rosanwo Babatunde. *Nigerians Talk*. Retrieved from http://nigerianstalk.org/2012/05/15/nigeria-organized-crime-rosanwo-babatunde/

Baldaev, D., Vasiliev, S., and Plutser-Sarno, A. (2009). *Russian Criminal Tattoo Encyclopaedia Vol. 1*. London: Fuel.

Baldaev, D., Vasiliev, S., and Plutser-Sarno, A. (2006). *Russian Criminal Tattoo Encyclopaedia Vol. 2*. London: Fuel.

Baldaev, D., Vasiliev, S., and Sidorov, A. (2014). *Russian Criminal Tattoo Encyclopaedia Vol.3*. London: Fuel.

Baldas, T. (2015). Ringleaders of Devils Diciples biker gang guilty of RICO. *Detroit Free Press* [online]. February 20. Retrieved from www.freep.com/story/news/local/michigan/macomb/2015/02/20/disciples-gang-verdict/23742675/

Ball, K. R. (2011). *Terry the Tramp: The Life and Times of a One Percenter*. Minneapolis, MN: Motorbooks.

Ball, R. A., and Curry, G. D. (1997). The logic of definition in criminology: Purposes and methods for defining 'gangs'. In *Gangs and Gang Behavior*, Mays, G. L. (Ed.), (pp. 3–21). Chicago, IL: Nelson-Hall. (Reprinted from *Criminology*, 33(2), pp. 225–245, 1995).

Balsamo, W., and Balsamo, J. (2012). *Young Al Capone: The Untold Story of Scarface in New York 1899–1925*. New York, NY: Skyhorse.

Barger, R. (2001). *Hells Angel: The Life and Times of Sonny Barger and the Hells Angel Motorcycle Club*. New York, NY: Perennial.

Barker, T. (2007). *Biker Gangs and Organized Crime*. Newark, NJ: LexisNexis/Anderson.

BBC. (2008). Colombian drug baron admits guilt. October 18. Retrieved from http://news.bbc.co.uk/2/hi/americas/7677592.stm

Beck, A. J., Gilliard, D., Greenfeld, L., Harlow, C., Hester, T., Jankowski, L., Snell, T., Stephan, J., and Morton, D. (1991). *Survey of State Prison Inmates, 1991*. Washington, DC: Bureau of Justice Statistics, U.S. Department of Justice.

Bergere, M. (1998). *Sun Yat-Sen*. Stanford, CA: Stanford University Press.

Berry, L., Curtis, G., Elan, S., Hudson, R., and Kollars, N. (2003). *Transnational Activities of Chinese Crime Organizations*. Washington, DC: Library of Congress, Federal Research Division.

Beshears, L. (2010). Honorable Style in Dishonorable Times: American Gangsters of the 1920s and 1930s. *Journal of American Culture*, 33(3), pp. 197–206.

Billingslea, W. (2004). Illicit Cigarette Trafficking and the Funding of Terrorism. *Police Chief*, February, 71(2).

Bing, L. (1991). *Do or Die!* New York, NY: HarperCollins.

Bingham, T. (1908). Foreign Criminals in New York. *North American Review*, September, pp. 383–394.

Bishop, M. W. (2005). Taiwan's gangs go global. *Asia Times*. June 4. Retrieved from www.atimes.com/atimes/China/GF04Ad06.html

Blau, R., and O'Brien, J. (1991). Rise and fall of El Rukn—Jeff Fort's evil empire. *Chicago Tribune*. September 8. Retrieved from http://articles.chicagotribune.com/1991-09-08/news/9103070697_1_el-rukns-rukn-organization-jeff-fort

Bloch, H., and Niederhoffer, A. (1958). *The Gang: A Study in Adolescent Behavior*. New York, NY: Philosophical Press.

Block, C., and Block, R. (1993). *Street Gang Crime in Chicago: National Institute of Justice: Research in Brief*. NCJ 144782. Washington, DC: OJJP.

Blum, H. (1993). *Gangland: How the FBI Broke the Mob*. New York, NY: Simon and Schuster.

Blumenthal, R. (1988). *Last Days of the Sicilians: The FBI's War Against the Mafia*. New York, NY: Pocket Books.

Blundell, N. (2013). New godfathers: Deadlier and more secretive than the Sicilian mafia. *Mirror*. December 8. Retrieved from www.mirror.co.uk/news/world-news/ndrangheta-mafia-deadlier-more-secretive-2902919

Bonanno, B. (1999). *Bound By Honor: A Mafioso's Story*. New York, NY: St. Martin's Press.

Bonn, R. L. (1984). *Criminology*. New York, NY: McGraw-Hill.

Booth, M. (1999). *The Dragon Syndicates*. New York, NY: Carrol and Graf.

Booth, M. (1990). *The Triads: The Growing Global Threat from the Chinese Criminal Societies*. New York, NY: St. Martin's Press.

Botsch, R. J. (2008). Jesus Malverde's significance to Mexican drug traffickers. *FBI Bulletin*, 77(8), pp. 19–22.

Boucai, M. (2007). Balancing Your Strengths Against Your Felonies: Considerations for Military Recruitment of Ex-Offenders. 61 *University of Miami Law Review* 997.

Bouché, V. (2017). *An Empirical Analysis of the Intersection of Organized Crime and Human Trafficking In the United States*. National Criminal Justice Reference Service (NCJRS). Retrieved from www.ncjrs.gov/pdffiles1/nij/grants/250955.pdf

Bourgois, P. (1989). In Search of Horatio Alger: Culture and Ideology in the Crack Economy. *Contemporary Drug Problems*, 16, pp. 619–650.

Bovsun, M. (2013). Motorcycle riot in Hollister, Calif., captures the attention of writers and Hollywood and gives birth to great American anti-hero. *New York Daily News*. October 19. Retrieved from www.nydailynews.com/news/justice-story/hell-wheels-bikers-spark-calif-riot-article-1.1489888

Bowden, M. (2001). *Killing Pablo: The Hunt for the World's Greatest Outlaw*. New York, NY: Atlantic Monthly Press.

Bowker, L., and Klein, M. (1983). The Etiology of Female Juvenile Delinquency and Gang Membership: A test of Psychological and Social Structural Explanations. *Adolescence*, 18, pp. 739–751.

Braga, A. A. (2003). *Responses to the Problem of Gun Violence Among Serious Young Offenders, Guide No. 23*. Retrieved from www.popcenter.org/problems/gun_violence

Branstetter, B. (2015). The case for internet access in prisons. *The Daily Dot, via The Washington Post*. February 9. Retrieved from www.washingtonpost.com/news/the-intersect/wp/2015/02/09/the-case-for-internet-access-in-prisons/

Bratton, W. (2007). The Mutation of the Illicit Trade Market. *Police Chief*, May, 74(5), pp. 22–24.

Breve, F. (2007). The Maras—A Menace to the Americas. *Military Review*, July/August, pp. 88–95.

Brightwell, E. (2012). *A Brief (and By No Means Complete) History of Black Los Angeles*. Retrieved from www.amoeba.com/blog/2012/01/eric-s-blog/a-brief-and-by-no-means-complete-history-of-black-los-angeles-happy-black-history-month-.html

Brown, G. C., Vigil, J. D., and Taylor, E. R. (2012). The Ghettoization of Blacks in Los Angeles: The Emergence of Street Gangs. *Journal of African-American Studies*, 16, pp. 209–225.

Brown, M. (2009). Funeral for last Don draws the whole gang. *Chicago Sun-Times*. September 15. Retrieved from www.highbeam.com/doc/1N1-12ABEE0EE586A8B0.html

Brown, V. A. (2007). Gang Member Perpetrated Domestic Violence: A New Conversation. *University of Maryland Law Journal of Race, Religion, Gender and Class*, 7(2), pp. 395–413.

Brownfield, D. (2012). Gender and Gang Membership: Testing Theories to Account for Different Rates of Participation. *Journal of Gang Research*, Fall, 19(1), pp. 25–32.

Buccellato, J. (2013). Gangs of Detroit: Examining Youth Violence. *CBS WWJ TV 62*. Retrieved from http://detroit.cbslocal.com/2013/10/31/gangs-of-detroit-examining-youth-violence/

Buentello, S., Fong, R. S., and Vogel, R. E. (1991). Prison Gang Development: A Theoretical Model. *Prison Journal*, 71, pp. 3–9.

Burch, J. H., and Chemers, B. M. (1997). *A Comprehensive Response to America's Youth Gang Problem*. OJJDP Series Fact Sheet #40, March. Washington, DC: Office of Juvenile Justice and Delinquency Prevention. Retrieved from www.ncjrs.org/txtfiles/fs-9640.txt

Bureau of Alcohol, Tobacco, Forearms, and Explosives (ATF). (2014). *OMGs and the Military 2014*. Washington, DC: U.S. Department of Justice.

Burke, C. (2009). *Gang Involvement Among San Diego County Arrestees in 2008*. San Diego, CA: SANDAG.

Burke, G. (2014). FBI sting shows San Francisco Chinatown underworld. *Associated Press*. March 28. Retrieved from www.reviewjournal.com/news/fbi-sting-shows-san-francisco-chinatown-underworld/

Burnstein, S. (2014). Chaldean mob war escalated 25 years ago. *Oakland Press*. March 7. Retrieved from www.theoaklandpress.com/apps/pbcs.dll/article?avis=OP&date=20140307&category=NEWS&lopenr=140309544&Ref=AR&profile=1030112&template=printart

Burnstein, S. (2012). Chaldean 'Godfather' and former Oakland County restaurateur's parole rescinded. *Oakland Press*. May 15. Retrieved from www.theoaklandpress.com/general-news/20120515/chaldean-godfather-and-former-oakland-county-restaurateurs-parole-rescinded-with-video

Business.gov. (2009). *Pre-Employment Background Checks*. Retrieved from www.business.gov/business-law/employment/hiring/pre-employment.html

Butterfield, F. (1985). Chinese Organized Crime Said to Rise in US. *New York Times*. January 13. Retrieved from www.nytimes.com/1985/01/13/us/chinese-organized-crime-said-to-rise-in-us.html

Calabrese, F. (2011). *Operation Family Secrets: How a Mobster's Son and the FBI Brought Down Chicago's Murderous Crime Family*. New York, NY: Broadway Books.

California Department of Corrections and Rehabilitation (CDCR). (2012). *Security Threat Group Prevention, Identification and Management Strategy*. Sacramento, CA: CDCR.

California Department of Justice (CDOJ). (2003). *Organized Crime in California*. Report to the legislature. California Department of Justice, Division of Law Enforcement, Criminal Intelligence Bureau. Retrieved from http://ag.ca.gov/publications/org_crime.pdf

Camp, C. G., and Camp, G. M. (1988). *Management Strategies for Combatting Prison Gang Violence*. South Salem, NY: Criminal Justice Institute.

Camp, G. M., and Camp, C. G. (1985). *Prison Gangs: Their Extent, Nature, and Impact on Prisons*. South Salem, NY: Criminal Justice Institute.

Capeci, J. (2004). *The Complete Idiot's Guide to the Mafia*. New York, NY: Alpha Books.

Capeci, J., and Robins, T. (2015). *Mob Boss: The First Boss to Turn Government Witness*. New York, NY: St. Martin's Paperbacks.

Carlie, M. (2002). *Into the Abyss: A Personal Journey into the World of Street Gangs*. Retrieved from http://people.missouristate.edu/michaelcarlie/what_i_learned_about/prisons.htm

Carpenter, A., and Cooper, S. (2015). Understanding Transnational Gangs and Criminal Networks: A Contribution to Community Resilience—A Social Network Analysis of the San Diego/Tijuana Border Region. *Journal of Gang Research*, Spring, 22(3), pp. 1–24.

Carr, H. (2012). *Hitman: The Untold Story of Johnny Martorano, Whitey Bulger's Enforcer and the Most Feared Gangster in the Underworld*. New York, NY: Forge.

Carter, R. (2009). Was Lee Harvey Oswald real killer of President Kennedy? *New York Amsterdam News*. November 19–25, p. 6.

Carter, S. (2007). MS-13 gang seeks to unite nationwide. *Washington Times*. July 25.

Cartwright, C., and Walutes, R. L., Jr. (2006). Victim and Witness Challenges in Gang Prosecutions. In Gangs, United States Department of Justice Executive Office for United States Attorneys. *United States Attorneys' Bulletin*, May, 54(3).

Cavaliere, V. (2013). The rise and fall of Kurdish gangs in Nashville. *Vocativ*. November 20. Retrieved from www.vocativ.com/underworld/crime/rise-fall-kurdish-gangs-nashville/

Cavazos, R. (2008). *Honor Few, Fear None: The Life and Times of a Mongol*. New York, NY: HarperCollins.

CBS. (2000). Russian mafia's worldwide grip. *CBS News*. July 21. Retrieved from www.cbsnews.com/news/russian-mafias-worldwide-grip/

CDOJ. (2003). *Organized Crime in California, 2002.* Sacramento, CA: California Department of Justice, Division of Law Enforcement, Criminal Intelligence Bureau.

Chalidze, V. (1977). *Criminal Russia: Essays on Crime in the Soviet Union.* New York, NY: Random House.

Chang, J. (1996). A Comparative Study of Female Gang and Non-gang Members in Chicago. *Journal of Gang Research*, Fall, 4(1), pp. 9–18.

Chang, R. (2005). Police begin probe into Bamboo Union after airport clash. *Taipei Times.* May 8. Retrieved from www.taipeitimes.com/News/taiwan/archives/2005/05/08/2003253653

Chepesiuk, R. (2010). Drug lords: The rise and fall of the Cali cartel. In *The Mammoth Book of Drug Barons*, Copperwaite, P. (Ed.). London: Constable and Robinson.

Chicago Gang History. (2017). *Notorious Street Gangs.* Retrieved from https://chicagoganghistory.com/notorious-street-gangs/

Chicagogangs.org. (2014). *Almighty Ambrose.* Retrieved from http://chicagogangs.org/index.php?pr=ambrose

Chicagogangs.org. (2014). *Almighty Bishops.* Retrieved from http://chicagogangs.org/index.php?pr=BISHOPS

Chicagogangs.org. (2014). *Almighty Gaylords.* Retrieved from http://chicagogangs.org/index.php?pr=gaylords

Chicagogangs.org. (2014). *Almighty Saints.* Retrieved from http://chicagogangs.org/index.php?pr=SAINTS

Chicagogangs.org. (2014). *Almighty Simon City Royals.* Retrieved from http://chicagogangs.org/index/php?pr=ALMIGHTY_SCR

Chicagogangs.org. (2014). *Ashland Vikings.* Retrieved from http://chicagogangs.org/index.php?pr=ASH LAND_VIKINGS

Chicagogangs.org. (2014). *BGD: Black Gangster Disciples.* Retrieved from http://chicagogangs.org/index. php?pr=BGD

Chicagogangs.org. (2014). *Black Disciples.* Retrieved from http://chicagogangs.org/index.php?pr=BDN

Chicagogangs.org. (2014). *Black Souls.* Retrieved from http://chicagogangs.org/index.php?pr=BLACK_ SOULS

Chicagogangs.org. (2014). *BPSN Black P-Stones.* Retrieved from http://chicagogangs.org/index.php? pr=BPSN

Chicagogangs.org. (2014). *Conservative Vice Lords.* Retrieved from http://chicagogangs.org/index.php?pr=CVL

Chicagogangs.org. (2014). *Cullerton Duces.* Retrieved from http://chicagogangs.org/index.php?pr=CULLER TON_DUCES

Chicagogangs.org. (2014). *Familia Stones.* Retrieved from http://chicagogangs.org/index.php?pr=FAMILIA_ STONES

Chicagogangs.org. (2014). *Four Corner Hustlers.* Retrieved from http://chicagogangs.org/index.php?pr=4CH

Chicagogangs.org. (2014). *Fourth Generation Messiahs.* Retrieved from http://chicagogangs.org/index. php?pr=4GM

Chicagogangs.org. (2014). *Gangster Disciples.* Retrieved from http://chicagogangs.org/index.php?pr=GDN

Chicagogangs.org. (2014). *Harrison Gents.* Retrieved from http://chicagogangs.org/index.php?pr=HARRI SON_GENTS

Chicagogangs.org. (2014). *Imperial Gangsters.* Retrieved from http://chicagogangs.org/index.php?pr=IMP_GA NGSTERS

Chicagogangs.org. (2014). *Insane C-Notes.* Retrieved from http://chicagogangs.org/index.php?pr=INSANE_ CNOTES

Chicagogangs.org. (2014). *Insane Deuces.* Retrieved from http://chicagogangs.org/index.php?pr=INSANE_ DEUCES

Chicagogangs.org. (2014). *Insane Dragons.* Retrieved from http://chicagogangs.org/index.php?pr=INSANE_ DRAGONS

Chicagogangs.org. (2014). *Insane Unknowns.* Retrieved from http://chicagogangs.org/index.php?pr=INSANE_UNKNOWNS

Chicagogangs.org. (2014). *Insane Popes Northside.* Retrieved from http://chicagogangs.org/index.php?pr=INSANE_POPES_NORTH

Chicagogangs.org. (2014). *Insane Popes Southside.* Retrieved from http://chicagogangs.org/index.php?pr=SSPOPES

Chicagogangs.org. (2014). *KGB: Krazy GetDown Boys.* Retrieved from http://chicagogangs.org/index.php?pr=KGB

Chicagogangs.org. (2014). *La Raza.* Retrieved from http://chicagogangs.org/index.php?pr=LA_RAZA

Chicagogangs.org. (2014). *Latin Angels.* Retrieved from http://chicagogangs.org/index.php?pr=LATIN_ANGELS

Chicagogangs.org. (2014). *Latin Brothers.* Retrieved from http://chicagogangs.org/index.php?pr=LATIN_BROTHERS

Chicagogangs.org. (2014). *Latin Counts.* Retrieved from http://chicagogangs.org/index.php?pr=LATIN_COUNTS

Chicagogangs.org. (2014). *Latin Dragons.* Retrieved from http://chicagogangs.org/index.php?pr=LATIN_DRAGONS

Chicagogangs.org. (2014). *Latin Eagles.* Retrieved from http://chicagogangs.org/index.php?pr=LATIN_EAGLES

Chicagogangs.org. (2014). *Latin Jivers.* Retrieved from http://chicagogangs.org/index.php?pr=LATIN_JIVERS

Chicagogangs.org. (2014). *Latin Kings.* Retrieved from http://chicagogangs.org/index.php?pr=LATIN_KINGS

Chicagogangs.org. (2014). *Latin Lovers.* Retrieved from http://chicagogangs.org/index.php?pr=LATIN_LOVERS

Chicagogangs.org. (2014). *Latin Pachucos.* Retrieved from http://chicagogangs.org/index.php?pr=LATIN_PACHUCOS

Chicagogangs.org. (2014). *Latin Souls.* Retrieved from http://chicagogangs.org/index.php?pr=LATIN_SOULS

Chicagogangs.org. (2014). *Latin Stylers.* Retrieved from http://chicagogangs.org/index.php?pr=LATIN_STYLERS

Chicagogangs.org. (2014). *MLD: Maniac Latin Disciples.* Retrieved from http://chicagogangs.org/index.php?pr=MLD.

Chicagogangs.org. (2014). *Mickey Cobras.* Retrieved from http://chicagogangs.org/index.php?pr=MICKEY_COBRAS

Chicagogangs.org. (2014). *Milwaukee Kings.* Retrieved from http://chicagogangs.org/index.php?pr=MKN

Chicagogangs.org. (2014). *Morgan Boys.* Retrieved from http://chicagogangs.org/index.php?pr=MORGAN_BOYS

Chicagogangs.org. (2014). *New Breed.* Retrieved from http://chicagogangs.org/index.php?pr=NEW_BREED

Chicagogangs.org. (2014). *Orchestra Albany.* Retrieved from http://chicagogangs.org/index.php?pr=ORCHESTRA_ALBANY

Chicagogangs.org. (2014). *Racine Boys.* Retrieved from http://chicagogangs.org/index.php?pr=RACINE_BOYS

Chicagogangs.org. (2014). *Party People.* Retrieved from http://chicagogangs.org/index.php?pr=PARTY_PEOPLE

Chicagogangs.org. (2014). *Party Players.* Retrieved from http://chicagogangs.org/index.php?pr Retrieved from =PARTY_PLAYERS

Chicagogangs.org. (2014). *Satan Disciples.* Retrieved from www.chicagogangs.org/index.php?pr=SATAN_DISCIPLES&nosessionkill=1

Chicagogangs.org. (2014). *Sin City Boys.* Retrieved from http://chicagogangs.org/index.php?pr=SIN_CITY_BOYS

Chicagogangs.org. (2014). *Spanish Cobras.* Retrieved from http://chicagogangs.org/index.php?pr=SPANISH_COBRAS

Chicagogangs.org. (2014). *Spanish Gangster Disciples.* Retrieved from http://chicagogangs.org/index.php?pr=SGD

Chicagogangs.org. (2014). *Spanish Lords.* Retrieved from http://chicagogangs.org/index.php?pr=SPANISH_LORDS

Chicagogangs.org. (2014). *Two Six.* Retrieved from http://chicagogangs.org/index.php?pr=TWO_SIX

Chicagogangs.org. (2014). *Two Two Boys.* Retrieved from http://chicagogangs.org/index.php?pr=_22_BOYS

Chicagogangs.org. (2014). *12th Street Players.* Retrieved from http://chicagogangs.org/index.php?pr=12th_STREET_PLAYERS

Chicagonations.webs. (2014). *Insane Gangster Satan Disciples.* Retrieved from http://chicagonations.webs.com/Insane%20Gangster%20Satan%20Disciples.htm

Chicagonations.webs. (2014). *Insane Latin Brothers.* Retrieved from http://chicagonations.webs.com/Insane%20Latin%20Brothers.htm

Chicagonations.webs. (2014). *Latin Souls.* Retrieved from http://chicagonations.webs.com/Latin%20Souls.htm

Chicago Police Department (CPD). (2005). *Street Gangs, the New Organized Crime: A Chicago Police Department Report.* Retrieved from http://chicagocop.com/resources/documents_archive/publications/Street%20Gangs%20The%20New%20Organized%20Crime.pdf

Chin, K. (1996). *Chinatown Gangs: Extortion, Enterprise, and Ethnicity.* New York, NY: Oxford University Press.

Chin, K. (1990). *Chinese Subculture and Criminality: Non-traditional Crime Groups in America.* New York, NY: Greenwood Press.

Chu, Y. (2005). Hong Kong Triads After 1997. *Trends in Organized Crime,* Spring, 8(3), pp. 5–12.

Chuang, J. (2010). Rescuing Trafficking from Ideological Capture: Prostitution Reform and Anti-Trafficking Law and Policy. *University of Pennsylvania Law Review,* 158(6), pp. 1655–1728.

Cimino, A. (2014a). *The Mafia Files: Case Studies of the World's Most Evil Mobsters.* London: Arcturus.

Cimino, A. (2014b). *Drug Wars: The Bloody Reign of the Mexican Cartels.* London: Arcturus.

Clarion-Ledger. (2014). Inmates, experts: Gangs rule Miss.'s prisons. October 6. Retrieved from www.correctionsone.com/corrections/articles/7639259-Inmates-experts-Gangs-rule-Miss-s-prisons/

Clark, J., and Palattella, E. (2015). *A History of Heists: Bank Robbery in America.* Lanham, MD: Rowman and Littlefield.

Clemons, G., Rossi, R., and Van De Kamp, J. (1990). *Crips & Bloods Street Gangs.* Sacramento, CA: Division of Law Enforcement, Investigation and Enforcement Branch, Bureau of Organized Crime and Criminal Intelligence, California Department of Justice. NCJ Number: 146790.

Cloward, R., and Ohlin, L. (1960). *Delinquency and Opportunity: A Theory of Delinquent Gangs.* Glencoe, IL: Free Press.

Cohen, A. (1955). *Delinquent Boys: The Culture of the Gang.* Glencoe, IL: Free Press.

Coleman, A. (2015). Residents express their shock at shooting that left four dead in trendy Bay Area neighborhood—as cops say it was a gang attack. *Daily Mail.* January 11. Retrieved from www.dailymail.co.uk/news/article-2905365/I-moved-Brooklyn-San-Francisco-Residents-express-shock-shooting-left-four-dead-trendy-Bay-Area-neighborhood-cops-say-gang-attack.html

Connecticut Gang Investigators Association (CTGIA). (2008). Combating the rise in violent youth and gang activities. Retrieved from http://www.segag.org

Connolly, K. (1998). How Russia's mafia is taking over Israel's underworld. *BBC News*. November 21. Retrieved from http://news.bbc.co.uk/2/hi/special_report/1998/03/98/russian_mafia/69521.stm, accessed August 5, 2015.

Corbiscello, G. (2008). Border Crossings: A look at the Very Real Threat of Cross Border Gangs to the U.S. *Journal of Gang Research*, Winter, 15(2).

Corrections Corporation of America. (n.d.). *Gang Management: Identifying and Monitoring Security Threat Groups*. Nashville, TN: CCA.

Cressey, D. R. (1969). *Theft of the Nation: The Structure and Operations of Organized Crime in America*. New York, NY: Harper and Row.

CrimeSolutions.gov. (2015). *Program Profile—Operation Hardcore (Los Angeles, CA) CrimeSolutions.gov*. National Institute of Justice. Retrieved from www.crimesolutions.gov/ProgramDetails.aspx?ID=316

Cristall, J., and Forman-Echols, L. (2009). Property Abatements—The Other Gang Injunction Project TOUGH. *National Gang Center Bulletin, No. 2*, September, pp. 1–17.

Cross, W. (1973). The Negro-to-Black conversion experience. In *The Death of White Sociology*, Ladner, J. (Ed.). New York, NY: Vintage Books.

CSIS. (1997). Russian Organized Crime. *Frontline*. Center for Strategic & International Studies. Retrieved from www.pbs.org/wgbh/pages/frontline/shows/hockey/mafia/csis.html

Cureton, S. R. (2009). Something Wicked This Way Comes: A Historical Account of Black Gangsterism Offers Wisdom and Warning for African-American Leadership. *Journal of Black Studies*, 40, pp. 347–361.

Cureton, S. R. (2008). *Hoover Crips: When Cripin' Becomes a Way of Life*. Lanham, MD: University Press of America.

Curry, G. D., and Decker, S. H. (2003). *Confronting Gangs: Crime and Community* (2d ed.). Los Angeles, CA: Roxbury Publishing.

Darby, D., and Annetts, P. (2014). Q and A About the Intersection of Gang Culture and Domestic Violence. *Bulletins—Fall 2013 OPDV Bulletin*. Retrieved from www.opdv.ny.gov/public_awareness/bulletins/fall2013/gangsdv.html

Darling, J. (2000). Submarine Links Colombian Drug Traffickers with Russian Mafia. *L.A. Times*. November 10. Retrieved from http://articles.latimes.com/2000/nov/10/news/mn-49908

Davidson, B. (1964). New Orleans: Cosa Nostra's Wall Street. *Saturday Evening Post*, February 29, 237(6), pp. 15–21.

Davidson, R. (1996). Asian Gangs and Asian Organized Crime in Chicago. *Journal of Contemporary Criminal Justice*, December, 12(4), pp. 295–306.

Davis, D. (2011). *Out Bad: A True Story About Motorcycle Outlaws*. San Bernardino, CA: Donald Charles Davis.

Davis, J. (1993a). *Mafia Dynasty: The Rise and Fall of the Gambino Crime Family*. New York, NY: Harpertorch.

Davis, J. (1993b). *The Kennedy Contract: The Mafia Plot to Assassinate the President*. New York, NY: HarperCollins.

Davis, J. (1989). *Mafia Kingfish: Carlos Marcello and the Assassination of John F. Kennedy*. New York, NY: McGraw-Hill.

Davis, K. (2015a). Feds: Guardsmen tried to sell guns to cartel. *San Diego Union Tribune*. April 15. Retrieved from www.sandiegouniontribune.com/news/2015/apr/15/army-reservists-arrested-in-gun-sale-scheme/

Davis, K. (2015b). AF: Missileer who ran 'violent street gang' gets 25 years. *Air Force Times* [online edition]. February 3. Retrieved from www.airforcetimes.com/story/military/crime/2015/02/02/minot-air-force-base-missileer-leon-brown-sentenced-25-years/22753751/

Davis, K. (2011). 60 arrested in El Cajon Chaldean organized crime case. *San Diego Union Tribune.* August 18. Retrieved from www.utsandiego.com/news/2011/aug/18/60-arrested-el-cajon-chaldean-organized-crime-case/

Davis, T. (2006). *MS-13 and Counting: Gang Activity in Northern Virginia.* Hearing before the Committee on Government Reform. House of Representatives. 109th Congress, Second Secession. July 14, 2006. Serial No. 109–174. Washington, DC: Government Printing Office.

Dawley, D. (1992). *A Nation of Lords: The Autobiography of the Vice Lords* (2nd ed.). Prospect Heights, IL: Waveland Press.

Daye, D. (1997). *A Law Enforcement Sourcebook of Asian Crime and Cultures: Tactics and Mindsets.* Boca Raton, FL: CRC Press.

DEA. (2004). *Indictments Charging Leaders of the Norte Valle Colombian Drug Cartel Unsealed.* Retrieved from www.dea.gov/pubs/states/newsrel/nyc050604.html

DEA. (1996). *Surrender of Last Cali Mafia Leader.* Retrieved from www.dea.gov/pubs/pressrel/pr960904.htm

DeCesare, D. (1998). The Children of War. *NACLA Report on the Americas,* July/August, 1071439, 32(1). Retrieved from http://web.ebscohost.com/ehost/detail?vid=5&sid=0c376997-1c4b-48b9-9669-3db6

Decker, S. H., and Pyrooz, D. C. (2015). 'I'm Down for Jihad': How 100 Years of Gang Research Can Inform the Study of Terrorism, Radicalization and Extremism. *Perspectives on Terrorism,* 9(1), pp. 104–112.

Decker, S. H., and Pyrooz, D. C. (2011). Gangs, Terrorism, and Radicalization. *Journal of Strategic Security,* 4(4), pp. 151–166. https://doi.org/10.5038/1944-0472.4.4.7

Decker, S. H., and Pyrooz, D. C. (2010). Gang violence: Context, culture, and country. In G. McDonald (Ed.), *Small Arms Survey.* Cambridge: Cambridge University Press.

Dedel, K. (2007). *The Problem of Drive-By Shootings, Guide No. 47.* Washington, DC: Center for Problem-Oriented Policing.

DeDonto, A., Santoro, V., Rossi, A., Grattagliano, I., and Introna, F. (2009). Manners of Killing and Rituals in Apulian Mafia Murders. *Journal of Forensic Sciences,* 84(4), pp. 895–899.

DeFao, J. (2005). Marine who killed cop linked to gang activity: Family members dispute account by investigators. *SFGATE.* January 16. Retrieved from http://www.sfgate.com/bayarea/article/CERES-STANISLAUS-COUNTY-Marine-who-killed-cop-2738399.php

Delzell, C. (1965). *The Unification of Italy, 1859–1861: Cavour, Mazzini, or Garibaldi?* New York, NY: Holt, Rinehart and Winston.

Department of Homeland Security. (n.d.). IED Attack Fact Sheet. *The Academies.* Retrieved from www.dhs.gov/xlibrary/assets/prep_ied_fact_sheet.pdf

Department of State. (2005). *Trafficking in Person Report.* June. U.S. Department of State. Publication 11252. Washington, DC: Office of the Undersecretary for Global Affairs.

DeZolt, E., Schmidt, L., and Gilcher, D. (1996). The 'Tabula Rasa' Intervention Project for Delinquent Gang-Involved Females. *Journal of Gang Research,* Spring, 3(3), pp. 37–43.

Dickie, J. (2004). *Cosa Nostra: A History of the Sicilian Mafia.* New York, NY: Palgrave Macmillan.

Die Welt. (2009). Russian mafia taking hold in Berlin. January 7. Retrieved from www.thelocal.de/20090107/16591

Dillion, R. (1962). *The Hatchet Men.* New York, NY: Coward-McCann.

Di Placido, C., Simon, T. L., Witte, T. D., Gu, D., and Wong, S.C.P. (2006). Treatment of Gang Members Can Reduce Recidivism and Institutional Misconduct. *Law and Human Behavior,* 30(1), pp. 93–114.

Dobyns, J., and Johnson-Shelton, N. (2009). *No Angel: My Harrowing Undercover Journey to The Inner Circle of the Hells Angels*. New York, NY: Crown/Random House.

Domash, S. (2005). America's Most Dangerous Gang. *Police*, February, pp. 30–34.

Dombrink, J., and Song, J. (1996). Hong Kong After 1997: Transnational Organized Crime in a Shrinking World. *Journal of Contemporary Criminal Justice*, December, 12(4), pp. 329–339.

Donnermeyer, J. F., Edwards, R., Chavez, E., and Beauvais, F. (2000). Involvement of American Indian Youth in Gangs. *Free Inquiry in Creative Sociology*, 24(2), pp. 167-174.

Dooley, B. D., Seals, A., and Skarbek, D. (2014). The Effect of Prison Gang Membership on Recidivism. *Journal of Criminal Justice*, 42(3), pp. 267–275.

Dorigo, J. (1992). *Mafia*. Secaucus, NJ: Chartwell Books.

Drug Enforcement Administration (DEA). (2016). *History, 190–194*. Retrieved from www.dea.gov/about/history/1990-1994.pdf

Dunn, G. (2000). Major mafia gangs in Russia. In *Russian Organized Crime: The New Threat?* Williams, P. (Ed.). London: Frank Cass.

Durden-Smith, J. (1995). True story of the 'Japanese'. *Moscow Times*. June 20. Retrieved from www.themoscowtimes.com/news/article/true-story-of-the-japanese/338114.html

Durkheim, E. (1965). *The Elementary Forms of the Religious Life* (J. W. Swain, Trans.). New York, NY: Free Press (Original work published 1912).

Dwyer, B. (2012). Who are the Four Corner Hustlers? *Chicago Sun-Times*. January 30. Retrieved from www.suntimes.com/photos/galleries/10331808-417/who-are-the-four-corner-hustlers.html

Economist. (2004). Lording It over Colombia. *Economist*, 373(6398), pp. 35–36.

Edberg, M. (2004). *El Narcotraficante: Narcocorridos & the Construction of a Cultural Persona on the U.S. Mexican Border*. Austin: University of Texas Press.

Eddy, P., Sabogal, H., and Walden, S. (1988). *The Cocaine Wars*. New York, NY: W. W. Norton.

Edmonton Police Service. (2015). Traits of Gang Members. Retrieved from www.edmontonpolice.ca/CommunityPolicing/OrganizedCrime/Gangs/TraitsofGangMembers.aspx

Egley, A., Jr., Howell, J. C., and Harris, M. (2014). *Highlights of the 2012 National Youth Gang Survey* (OJJDP Juvenile Fact Sheet, December. NCJ 248025). Washington, DC: Office of Juvenile Justice and Delinquency Prevention.

Ehrenfeld, R. (1992). The Sicilian: The Mafia's nemesis goes down. *New Republic*. June 29. pp. 14–16.

Ene, C., and Mihaescu, G. (2014). The Fight Against Consumer Goods Counterfeiting-Dimensions, Challenges, Solutions. *Petrileum—Gas University of Plolesti Bulletin*, Technical Series, 66(4), pp. 53–67.

English, T. (2014). *Paddy Whacked: The Untold Story of the Irish-American Gangster*. New York, NY: HarperCollins.

English, T. (2006). *The Westies: Inside New York's Irish Mob*. New York, NY: St. Martin's Press.

English, T. (1995). *Born to Kill: America's Most Notorious Vietnamese Gang, and the Changing Face of Organized Crime*. New York, NY: William Morrow.

Esbensen, F. (2000). *Evaluation of the GREAT Program in the United States, 1995–1999*. Omaha: University of Nebraska.

Escobar, R. (2010). Escobar: The inside story of Pablo Escobar, the world's most powerful criminal. In *The Mammoth Book of Drug Barons*, Copperwaite, P. (Ed.). London: Constable and Robinson.

Etter, G. W. (2010). Mara Salvatrucha 13: A Transnational Threat. *Journal of Gang Research*, Winter, 17(2), pp. 1–17.

Etter, G. W. (1998). Common Characteristics of Gangs: Examining the Cultures of the New Urban Tribes. *Journal of Gang Research*, Winter, 5(2), pp. 19–33.

Etter, G. W. (1995). Tattoos and the New Urban Tribes. *Journal of Gang Research*, Fall, 3(1), pp. 51–54.

Etter, G. W., and Lehmuth, E. (2013). The Mexican Drug Wars: Organized Crime, Narco-Terrorism, Insurgency or Asymmetric Warfare? *Journal of Gang Research*, Summer, 20(4), pp. 1–34.

Etter, G. W., and Swymeler, W. G. (2008). Examining the Demographics of Street Gangs in Wichita, Kansas. *Journal of Gang Research*, 16(1), pp. 1–12.

Faison, S. (1994). Charges against Tong President threaten a Chinatown Institution. *New York Times*. June 1. Retrieved from www.nytimes.com/1994/06/01/nyregion/charges-against-tong-president-threaten-a-chinatown-institution.html

Falco, C., and Droban, K. (2013). *Vagos, Mongols and Outlaws: My Infiltration of America's Deadliest Biker Gangs*. New York, NY: St. Martin's Press.

Federal Bureau of Investigation (FBI). (2016). *Famous Cases and Criminals: Al Capone*. Retrieved from www.fbi.gov/about-us/history/famous-cases/al-capone

Federal Bureau of Investigation (FBI). (2015a). *FBI: What We Investigate/Organized Crime/Glossary*. Retrieved from www.fbi.gov/about-us/investigate/organizedcrime/glossary

Federal Bureau of Investigation (FBI). (2015b). *Italian Organized Crime*. Retrieved from www.fbi.gov/about-us/investigate/organizedcrime/italian_mafia

Federal Bureau of Investigation (FBI). (2015c). *Gang Success Stories: Detroit: The Chaldean Mafia*. Retrieved from www.fbi.gov/about-us/investigate/vc_majorthefts/gangs/success

Federal Bureau of Investigation (FBI). (2015d). *The MS-13 Threat: A National Assessment*. Retrieved from www.fbi.gov/news/stories/2008/january/ms13_011408/

Federal Bureau of Investigation (FBI). (2015e). *Investigative Programs: Organized Crime, Vyacheslav Kirillovich Ivankov*. Retrieved from www.fbi.gov/about-us/investigate/organizedcrime/cases/vyacheslav-kirillovich-ivankov

Federal Bureau of Investigation (FBI). (2015f). *FBI Ten Most Wanted*. Retrieved from www.fbi.gov/wanted/topten

Federal Bureau of Investigation (FBI). (2015g). *African Criminal Enterprises*. Retrieved from www.fbi.gov/about-us/investigate/organizedcrime/african

Federal Bureau of Investigation (FBI). (2015h). *Balkan Criminal Enterprises*. Retrieved from www.fbi.gov/about-us/investigate/organizedcrime/balkan

Federal Bureau of Investigation (FBI). (2014a). *Bloods and Crips Gang*. Retrieved from http://vault.fbi.gov/Bloods%20and%20Crips%20Gang%20/Bloods%20and%20Crips%20Gangs%20Part%201%20of%201/view

Federal Bureau of Investigation (FBI). (2014b). *Imperial Gangsters*. Retrieved from http://vault.fbi.gov/imperial-gangsters

Federal Bureau of Investigation (FBI). (2014c). *California State Senator and Chee Kung Tong Leader Among 26 Defendants Charged in Federal Criminal Complaint*. Retrieved from www.fbi.gov/sanfrancisco/press-releases/2014/california-state-senator-and-chee-kung-tong-leader-among-26-defendants-charged-in-federal-criminal-complaint

Federal Bureau of Investigation (FBI). (2012). *Crime in the United States—2011. Uniform Crime Reports*. Retrieved from www.fbi.gov/about-us/cjis/ucr/crime-in-the-u.s/2011/crime-in-the-u.s.-2011/tables/table-1

Federal Bureau of Investigation (FBI). (2009). *Albanian Organized Crime*. Retrieved from www.fbi.gov/news/podcasts/inside/albanian-organized-crime.mp3/view

Felkenes, G., and Becker, H. (1995). Female Gang Members: A Growing Issue for Policy Makers. *Journal of Gang Research*, Summer 1995, 2(4), pp. 1–10.

Fellman, S. (1986). *The Japanese Tattoo*. New York, NY: Abbeville Press.

Ferranti, S. (2013a). With cigarettes banned in most prisons, gangs shift from drugs to smokes: Smoking bans have transformed the prison economy. *Daily Beast*. June 2. Retrieved from www.thedailybeast.com/articles/2013/06/02/with-cigarettes-banned-in-most-prisons-gangs-shift-from-drugs-to-smokes.html

Ferranti, S. (2013b). *Inside the Simon City Royals*. Retrieved from www.gorillaconvict.com/2013/03/inside-the-simon-city-royals/

Ferrell, J. (1993). *Crimes of Style: Urban Graffiti and the Politics of Criminality.* New York, NY: Garland.

Fijnaut, C. (2012). Twenty Years Ago: The Assassination of Giovanni Falcone and Paolo Borsellino. *European Journal of Crime, Criminal Law and Criminal Justice,* 20, pp. 131–136.

Filippone, R. (1994). The Medellin Cartel: Why We Can't Win the Drug War. *Studies in Conflict and Terrorism,* 17, pp. 323–344.

Finckenauer, J. (2015). Russian Organized Crime in the United States. *American Russian Law Institute.* Retrieved from http://russianlaw.org/roc_us.htm

Finckenauer, J., and Voronin, Y. (2001). *The Threat of Russian Organized Crime.* NCJ 187085. Washington, DC: U.S. Department of Justice Office of Justice Programs.

Finckenauer, J., and Waring, E. (2001). Challenging the Russian Mafia Mystique. *NIJ Journal,* April, pp. 2–7.

Finckenauer, J., and Waring, E. (1998). *Russian Mafia in America.* Boston, MA: Northeastern University Press.

Fischer, S. (2007). *When the Mob Ran Vegas.* New York, NY: MJF Books.

Fishman, L. (1988). "The Vice Queens: An Ethnographic Study of black female gang behavior." Paper presented at the Annual Meeting of the American Society of Criminology, Chicago, IL.

Fisk, R. (1994). Moscow's mafia finds an island in the sun: Cyprus is awash with dubious dollars from Russia. *Independent.* August 3. Retrieved from www.independent.co.uk/news/world/europe/moscows-mafia-finds-an-island-in-the-sun-cyprus-is-awash-with-dubious-dollars-from-russia-robert-fisk-reports-from-limassol-on-the-visitors-with-private-jets-bulging-suitcases-and-a-reluctance-to-answer-questions-1381056.html

Fleisher, M. S., and Decker, S. H. (2001). An Overview of the Challenge of Prison Gangs. *Corrections Management Quarterly,* 5(1), pp. 1–9.

Fleisher, M. S., and Krienert, J. L. (2004). Life-course events, social networks, and the emergence of violence among female gang members. *Journal of Community Psychology* 32(5), pp. 607–622. doi: https://doi.org/10.1002/jcop.20022

Florida Department of Corrections (DC FL). (2014). *Street Gangs—Chicago Based or Influenced. Florida Department of Corrections.* Retrieved from www.dc.state.fl.us/pub/gangs/sets4.html

Florida Department of Law Enforcement. (2007). *2007 Statewide Gang Survey Results.* Retrieved from http://myfloridalegal.com/webfiles.nsf/WF/JFAO-789KGG/$file/2007GangSurvey.pdf

Fong, R. S. (1990). The organizational structure of prison gangs: A Texas case study. *Federal Probation,* (1).

Fox, K. A., Rufino, K. A., and Kercher, G. A. (2011). *Crime Victimization and Gang Membership.* Crime Victims' Institute, Criminal Justice Center. Huntsville, TX: Sam Houston State University.

FoxNews.com. (2014). Dutch biker gang grabs rifles, joins Kurds in fight against ISIS. *Fox News/Associated Press.* October 15. Retrieved from www.foxnews.com/world/2014/10/15/dutch-biker-gang-grabs-rifles-joins-kurds-in-fight-against-isis/

Franco, C. (2008). *The MS-13 and 18th Street Gangs—Emerging Transnational Gang Threats.* Congressional Research Service (CRS) Report to Congress.

Fried, J. (1998). Mastermind of Golden Venture smuggling ship gets 20 years. *New York Times.* December 2. Retrieved from www.nytimes.com/1998/12/02/nyregion/mastermind-of-golden-venture-smuggling-ship-gets-20-years.html

Freidman, R. (2000). *Red Mafiya: How the Russian Mob Has Invaded America.* Boston, MA: Little Brown.

Freng, A., Davis, T., McCord, K., and Roussell, A. (2012). The New American Gang? Gangs in Indian Country. *Journal of Contemporary Criminal Justice,* 28(4), pp. 446–464.

Friedan, T. (2005). Two convicted, two acquitted in suburban Virginia street gang trial. *CNN News.* May 17. Retrieved from www.cnn.com/2005/LAW/05/17/ms13.trial.verdicts/

Gaes, G. G., Wallace, S., Gilman, E., Klein-Saffran, J., and Suppa, S. (2002). The Influence of Prison Gang Affiliation on Violence and Other Prison Misconduct. *Prison Journal*, September, 82, pp. 359–385.

Galiani, S., Rossi, M. A., and Schargrodsky, E. (2016). The effects of peacetime and wartime conscription on criminal activity, *Scandinavian Journal of Economics* 119(3). April 2016 DOI: 10.1111/sjoe.1218.

Gang Intelligence Strategy Committee (GISC). (2008). *Guidelines for Establishing and Operating Gang Intelligence Units and Task Forces*. GISC, Global Intelligence Working Group, Criminal Intelligence Coordinating Council, Global Justice Information Sharing Initiative. *U.S. Department of Justice*, October.

Gangworld. (2009). *Gangland-Hustle or Die (4CH Gang in Chicago)*. Retrieved from http://ghettogangs. blogspot.com/2009/09/gangland-hustle-or-die-4ch-gang-in.html

Garvey, T. M. (2013). Witness Intimidation: Meeting the Challenge. Washington, D.C.: *AEquitas*, pp. 14–18.

Geniella, M. (2001a). Pelican Bay inmates communicated via underground mail. *Press Democrat*. April 22. Santa Rosa, CA.

Geniella, M. (2001b). Links Found to Seven Santa Rosa Slayings. *Press Democrat*. April 21. Santa Rosa, CA.

Gentile, N. (1963). *Vita di Capomafia*. Rome, Italy: Editori Riuniti.

Genty, N., Adedoyin, A. C., Jackson, M., and Jones, M. (2014). Does Religion Matter? A Study of the Impact of Religion on Female Incarcerated Gang Members in a Bible Belt State, *Journal of Gang Research*, Winter, 22(2), pp. 1–16.

Ghosh, P. (2012). Tip of the iceberg: French Police arrest Albanian heroin traffickers, but Balkan criminal gangs tighten grip across Europe. *International Business Times*. October 16. Retrieved from www.ibtimes. com/tip-iceberg-french-police-arrest-albanian-heroin-traffickers-balkan-criminal-gangs-tighten-grip

GlobalSecurity.Org. (2015). *Boris Abramovich Berezovsky*. Retrieved from www.globalsecurity.org/military/world/russia/berezovsky.htm

Gore, B. (2014). *Origins of the CVL*. Retrieved from http://gangresearch.net/cvl/cvlhistoryfinal/stchstart.html

Gorn, E. (1987). Good-bye Boys, I Die a True American: Homicide, Nativism, and Working-Class Culture in Antebellum New York City. *Journal of American History*, 74(2), pp. 388–410.

Gosch, M., and Hammer, R. (1975). *The Last Testament of Lucky Luciano*. Boston, MA: Little, Brown.

Grant, C. (2013). *Native American Involvement in the Gang Subculture: Current Trends & Dynamics*. Community Corrections Institute. Washington, DC: BJA.

Grant, C., and Feimer, S. (2007). Street Gangs in Indian Country: A Clash of Cultures. *Journal of Gang Research*, 14(4), pp. 27–66.

Grascia, A. (2004). Gang Violence: Mara Salvatrucha—Forever Salvador. *Journal of Gang Research*, Winter, 11(2), pp. 29–26.

Grayeff, Y. (2006). Gregory Lerner arrested in Paraguay. *Jerusalem Post*. March 27. Retrieved from www. jpost.com/Israel/Gregory-Lerner-arrested-in-Paraguay

Greene, J., and Pranisand, K. (2007). *Gang Wars: The Failure of Enforcement Tactics*. A Justice Policy Institute Report.

Greig, A. (2013). Mexican drug cartels are using U.S. military personnel as guns-for-hire. *Daily Mail*. August 4. Retrieved from www.dailymail.co.uk/news/article-2384325/Mexican-drug-cartels-use-U-S-military-guns-hire.html

Griffith, K. (2017, August 5). Barrio 18: Meet the terrifying gang with 50,000 foot-soldiers across the US and so unashamedly violent it rivals MS-13. *Daily Mail*. August 5. Retrieved from www.dailymail. co.uk/news/article-4764744/Barrio-18-Meet-terrifying-gang-rivals-MS-13.html#ixzz51GGw3P5F

Grillo, I. (2011). *El Narco: Inside Mexico's Criminal Insurgency*. New York, NY: Bloomsbury Press.

Gugliotta, G., and Leen, J. (1989). *Kings of Cocaine: An Astonishing True Story of Murder, Money, and Corruption*. New York, NY: Harper Paperbacks.

Guidetti, R. (2010). Rethinking the purpose of Fusion Centers. *Police Chief Magazine* [online]. February. Retrieved from www.policechiefmagazine.org/magazine/index.cfm?fuseaction=display_arch&article_id=2017&issue_id=22010

Gusfield, J. R. (1980). "Taking the Starch Out of Social Problems." Paper presented at the SSSP Symposium on Social Theory of Social Problems, August.

Hagedorn, J. (1998). *People and Folks: Gangs, Crime and the Underclass in a Rustbelt City* (2nd ed.). Chicago, IL: Lakeview Press.

Hagedorn, J., and Macon, P. (1988). *People and Folks: Gangs, Crime and the Underclass in a Rustbelt City*. Chicago, IL: Lakeview Press.

Hanes, W. T., and Sanello, F. (2002). *The Opium Wars: The Addiction of One Empire and the Corruption of Another*. New York, NY: Barnes and Noble.

Hankins, W. (2014). *Alpha Guard*. Santa Ana, CA: Police and Fire Publishing.

Harding, S. (2014). *The Street Casino: Survival in Violent Street Gangs*. Chicago, IL: Policy Press.

Harris, M. (1988). *Cholas: Latino Girls and Gangs*. New York, NY: AMS Press.

Haskins, J. (1974). *Street Gangs: Yesterday and Today*. Wayne, PA: Hastings Books.

Hayes, B., and Quattlebaum, J. (2009). *The Original Wild Ones: Tales of the Boozefighters Motorcycle Club, Est. 1946*. Minneapolis, MN: MBI.

Haynes, D. (2004). Used, Abused, Arrested, and Deported: Extending Immigration Benefits to Protect the Victims of Trafficking and to Secure the Prosecution of Traffickers. *Human Rights Quarterly*, 26(2), pp. 221–272.

Hells-angels.com. (2014). *History*. Retrieved from http://affa.hells-angels.com/hamc-history/

Hill, J. (1997). Slayer of 2 sentenced to life in prison. *Chicago Tribune*. April 15. Retrieved from http://articles.chicagotribune.com/1997-04-15/news/9704150131_1_murders-penalty-gang

Hobsbawm, E. (1969). *Social Bandits*. Harmondsworth: Penguin.

Holmes, R. (2008). *Part II of the Biker Gangs Trilogy—The Evolution of Biker Gangs: The Way We Are: The Criminal Emerges*. Presented at the National Gang Crime Research Center 11th International Gang Specialist Training Conference. Chicago, IL, August 6–8, 2008.

Hoover, W. D. (2011). *Historical Dictionary of Postwar Japan*. Lanham, MD: Scarecrow Press.

Hopper, C., and Moore, J. (1990). Women in Outlaw Motorcycle Gangs. *Journal of Contemporary Ethnography*, 18, pp. 363–387.

Hortis, C. A. (2014). *The Mob and the City: The Hidden History of How the Mafia Captured New York*. Amherst, NY: Prometheus Books.

Howell, J., and Decker, S. (1999). *The Youth Gangs, Drug, and Violence Connection*. Washington, DC: OJJDP.

Howell, J., and Moore, J. (2010). History of Street Gangs in the United States. *National Gang Center Bulletin*, May, (4). Washington, DC: BJA/OJJDP.

Howell, J. C. (2015). *The History of Street Gangs in the United States: Their Origins and Transformations*. Lanham, MD: Lexington Books.

Howell, J. C. (2012). *Gangs in American Communities*. Thousand Oaks, CA: Sage, p. 24.

Howell, J. C. (2006). The Impact of Gangs on Communities. *National Youth Gang Center Bulletin*, 8(6), p. 2.

Huang, H., and Wang, J. (2002). From Religious Cult to Criminal Gang: The Evolution of Chinese Triads (Part I). *Journal of Gang Research*, Summer, 9(4), pp. 25–32.

Hubbard, J., Wyman, K., and Domma, F. (2012). *The Chicago Crime Commission Gang Book: A Detailed Overview of Street Gangs in the Chicago Metropolitan Area*. Chicago, IL: Chicago Crime Commission.

Huff, C. R. (1990). Denial, overreaction and misidentification: A postscript on public policy. In *Gangs in America*, Huff, R. (Ed.). Beverly Hills, CA: Sage.

Huff, C. R., and McBride, W. D. (1993). Gangs and the police. In *The Gang Intervention Handbook*, Goldstein, A. P., and Huff, C. R. (Eds.). Champaign, IL: Research Press.

Hunt, G., Riegel, S., Morales, T., and Waldorf, D. (1993). Changes in Prison Culture: Prison Gangs and the Case of the 'Pepsi Generation'. *Social Problems*, 40(3), pp. 398–409.

Hunt, T., and Sheldon, M. (2010). *Deep Water: Joseph P. Macheca and the Birth of the American Mafia* (2nd ed.). Lexington, KY: Hunt and Sheldon.

Huston, P. (2001). *Tongs, Gangs and Triads*. Lincoln, NE: Author's Choice Press.

ICE. (2012). *Alleged Leader of Ethnic Albanian Organized Crime Syndicate Extradited to the US to Face Drug and Money Laundering Charges*. Retrieved from www.ice.gov/news/releases/alleged-leader-ethnic-albanian-organized-crime-syndicate-extradited-us-face-drug-and

Ihejirika, M. (2004). Girl Gang stalks S. side schools halls. *Chicago Sun-Times*. April 30. p. 11.

Illinois State Police. (1997). *Street Gang Awareness*. Springfield, IL: Intelligence Bureau, Illinois State Police. Retrieved from www.state.il.us/ISP/gng00006.htm

The Illuminated Lantern. (2011). *An Introduction to Triads*. Retrieved from http://web.archive.org/web/20020818045315/www.illuminatedlantern.com/triads/page1.html

International Labor Organization. (2014). *Profits and Poverty: The Economics of Forced Labour-Executive Summary*. Geneva, Switzerland: International Labor Organization.

Investigate. (2018). *Dictionary.com*. Unabridged. Based on the Random House Dictionary. Retrieved from http://dictionary.reference.com/browse/investigate

Irwin, J. (1980). *Prisons in Turmoil*. Boston, MA: Little, Brown.

Isaacs, M. (2000). Twice burned. *SF Weekly News*. January 14. Retrieved from www.sfweekly.com/2000-06-14/news/twice-burned/

Jackson, A. (2004). *Prosecuting Gang Cases: What Local Prosecutors Need to Know*. Washington, D.C.: American Prosecutors Research Institute—Bureau of Justice Assistance.

Jackson, R., and McBride, W. (1986). *Understanding Street Gangs*. Placerville, CA: Custom.

Jackson, T. (2005). Man's fingers severed in Va. machete attack. *Washington Post*. January 5, p. B2.

Jacobs, J. B. (1977). *Stateville: The Penitentiary in Mass Society*. Chicago, IL: University of Chicago Press.

Jacobs, J. B. (1974). Street Gangs Behind Bars. *Social Problems*, 21(3), pp. 395–408.

JailSergeant.com. (2015). Inmate Code. *Sergeant Sandvig's JailSergeant.com*. Retrieved from www.jailsergeant.com/Jail_Prison_Inmate_Stories_.html

Jamieson, A. (1993). Giovanni Falcone-In Memoriam. *Studies in Conflict and Terrorism*, 18, pp. 303–313.

Jankowski, M. S. (1991). *Islands in the Street: Gangs and American urban society*. Los Angeles, CA: University of California Press.

Japan National Tourism Organization. (2017). *Asakusa Sanja Matsuri*. Retrieved from www.jnto.go.jp/eng/spot/festival/asakusasanja.html

Jennings, D. (1967). *We Only Kill Each Other: The True Story of Mobster Bugsy Siegel the Man Who Invented Las Vegas*. New York, NY: Pocket Books.

Johnson v. California, 543 U.S. 499 (2005).

Johnson, C., Webster, B., and Connors, E. (1995). *Prosecuting Gangs: A National Assessment*. (NIJ Research in Brief Series, February. NCJ 151785). Alexandria, VA: Institute for Law and Justice. Retrieved from www.ncjrs.org/txtfiles/pgang.txt

Johnson, J. (2008). Oklahoma City war veteran accused of selling bombs to gang members. *Oklahoman* [online edition]. December 25. Retrieved from http://newsok.com/oklahoma-city-war-veteran-accused-of-selling-bombs-to-gang-members/article/3332977

Johnson, K. (2006). MS-13 gang growing extremely dangerous, FBI says. *USA Today*. January 5.

Jones, C. R., Narag, R. E., and Morales, R. S. (2015). "Philippine prison gangs: Control of chaos?" RegNet Research Papers—Working Paper No. 71, 2015. Regulatory Institutions Network.

Jones, T. (2011). Yakuza among first with relief supplies in Japan. *Reuters*. March 25. Retrieved from www.reuters.com/article/2011/03/25/us-yakuza-idUSTRE72O6TF20110325

Kakar, S. (2013). Gang Membership and Gender: Does Being a Female Gang Member Affect the Type, Frequency and Intensity of Crimes Committed? *Journal of Gang Research*, Winter, 20(2), pp. 27–40.

Kaplan, D. (1992). *Fires of the Dragon*. New York, NY: Atheneum.

Kaplan, D., and Dubro, A. (1986). *Yakuza: The Explosive Account of Japan's Criminal Underworld*. Reading, MA: Addison-Wesley.

Kass, J., and Blau, R. (1992). Gang link probed in Cabrini death: Boy's great-uncle heads disciples. *Chicago Tribune*. October 18. Retrieved from http://articles.chicagotribune.com/1992-10-18/news/9204040327_1_rival-gang-confession-chicago-police-department

Katrandjian, O. (2011). Hells Angels leader dead and two injured in shooting in Nevada casino. *ABC News*. September 25. Retrieved from http://abcnews.go.com/US/hells-angels-leader-jeffrey-jethro-pettigrew-dead-injured/story?id=14601542

Katz, C. M., and Webb, V. J. (2006). *Policing Gangs in America*. New York, NY: Cambridge University Press.

Keefe, P. (2009). *The Snakehead: An Epic Tale of the Chinatown Underworld and the American Dream*. New York, NY: Anchor Books.

Keene, L. (1989). Asian Organized Crime. *FBI Law Enforcement Bulletin*, October, pp. 12–17.

Keiser, R. L. (1969). *The Vice Lords: Warriors of the Streets*. New York, NY: Holt, Rinehart and Winston.

Kirk-Duggan, C. A. (1997). Kindred Spirits: Sister Mimetic Societies and Social Responsibility. *Journal of Gang Research*, Winter, 4(2), pp. 23–36.

Klebnikov, P. (2000). *Godfather of the Kremlin: The Decline of Russia in the Age of Gangster Capitalism*. Orlando, FL: Harcourt.

Klein, M. W. (2007). *Chasing After Street Gangs: A Forty-Year Journey*. Upper Saddle River, NJ: Pearson Prentice Hall.

Klein, M. W. (1995). *The American Street Gang: Its Nature, Prevalence, and Control*. New York, NY: Oxford University Press.

Klein, M. W. (1990). *Having an Investment in Violence: Some Thoughts About the American Street Gang*. The Edwin H. Sutherland Award Address to the American Society of Criminology, 42nd Annual Meeting, November 9, Baltimore, MD.

Klein, M. W. (1971). *Street Gangs and Street Workers*. Englewood Cliffs, NJ: Prentice-Hall.

Klein, M. W., and Maxson, C. L. (2006). *Street Gang Patterns and Policies*. New York, NY: Oxford University Press.

Knox, G. W. (2012). *The Problem of Gangs and Security Threat Groups (STG's) in American Prisons and Jails Today: Recent Findings from the 2012 NGCRC National Gang/STG Survey*. National Gang Crime Research Center. Retrieved from www.ngcrc.com/corr2012.html

Knox, G. W. (2010). *Gang Profile: The Latin Kings*. Retrieved from www.ngrc.com/ngrc/page15.htm

Knox, G. W. (2008a). *The Satan Disciples: A Gang Profile*. Retrieved from www.ngcrc.com/ngcrc/sataprof.htm

Knox, G. W. (2008b). Gang Profile: The Gangster Disciples. *Journal of Gang Research*, 3(1), pp. 58–76.

Knox, G. W. (2008c). *Females and Gangs: Sexual Violence, Prostitution and Exploitation*. Retrieved from www.ngcrc.com/ngcrc/proffem2.htm

Knox, G. W. (2006). *An Introduction to Gangs* (6th ed.). Peotone, IL: New Chicago School Press.

Knox, G. W. (2004a). The Problem of Gangs and Security Threat Groups (STG's) in American Prisons Today: A Special NGCRC Report. *Journal of Gang Research*, 12(1), pp. 1–76.

Knox, G. W. (2004b). *Gang Threat Analysis: The Black Disciples*. Retrieved from www.ngcrc.com/bdprofile.html

Knox, G. W. (2003a). The Chaldean Mafia: A Preliminary Gang Threat Analysis. *Journal of Gang Research*, Spring, 10(3), pp. 65–76.

Knox, G. W. (2003b). *Gang Profile Update: The Black P. Stone Nation (BPSN)*. Retrieved from www.ngcrc.com/bpsn2003.html

Knox, G. W. (2002). Melanics: A gang profile analysis. *Journal of Gang Research*, 9(3), pp. 1–76.

Knox, G. W. (1997a). Research Note: The Facts About Female Gang Members, a Special Report of the NGCRC Task Force. *Journal of Gang Research*, Spring, 4(3), pp. 41–59.

Knox, G. W. (1997b). Crips: A Gang Profile Analysis. *Journal of Gang Research*, 4(3), pp. 61–75.

Knox, G. W. (1996). Gang Profile: The Black Gangsters, aka 'New Breed'. *Journal of Gang Research*, 3(2), pp. 64–76.

Knox, G. W. (1994). *An Introduction to Gangs* (Rev. ed.). Bristol, IN: Wyndham Hall.

Knox, G. W. (1981). Differential Integration and Job Retention Among Ex-offenders. *Criminology*, 18(4), pp. 481–501. https://doi.org/10.1111/j.1745–9125.1981.tb01379.x

Knox, G. W. et al. (1995). *The Economics of Gang Life: A Task Force Report*. Peotone, IL: National Gang Crime Research Center.

Knox, G. W., and Fuller, L. (1995). Gang Profile: The Gangster Disciples. *Journal of Gang Research*, 3(1), pp. 58–76.

Knox, G. W., McCurrie, T. F., Laskey, J. A., and Tromanhauser, E. D. (1996). *The 1996 National Law Enforcement Gang Analysis Survey: A Preliminary Report*. NGCRC—National Gang Crime Research Center. Retrieved from http://www.ngcrc.com/ngcrc/page8.htm.

Kolb, A., and Palys, T. (2012). Are You Down? Power Relations and Gender Reconstruction Among Latina Gang Members in Los Angeles. *Journal of Gang Research*, Fall, 20(1), pp. 19–32.

Konkol, M. (2012). Black Disciples leader who ran drug, gun trade, dead at 60. *Chicago Sun-Times*. January 8. Retrieved from www.suntimes.com/news/metro/9897741-418/black-disciples-leader-ran-drug-gun-trade.html

Kross, P. (2003). 'Lucky' Strikes a Deal. *World War II*, March, 17(7).

KTVA Alaska. (2014). Prison gangs recruiting on Anchorage streets. *KTVA Alaska*. June 11. Retrieved from www.ktva.com/prison-gangs-recruiting-on-anchorage-streets-411/

Labrousse, A. (2003). The war on drugs and the interests of governments. In *Global Organized Crime: Trends and Developments*, Siegal, D., van de Bunt, H., and Zaitch, D. (Eds.). Dordrecht, Netherlands: Kluwer Academic.

Lacey, R. (1991). *Little Man: Meyer Lansky and the Gangster Life*. Boston, MA: Little, Brown.

Lambert, A. (2003). *Russian Prison Tattoos*. Atglen, PA: Schiffer.

Landesco, J. (1968). *Organized Crime in Chicago*. Chicago, IL: University of Chicago Press.

Lane, J., and Fox, K. A. (2012). Fear of Crime Among Gang and Non-Gang Offenders: Comparing the Effects of Perpetration, Victimization, and Neighborhood Factors. *Justice Quarterly*, 29(4), pp. 491–523. Retrieved from https://doi.org/10.1080/07418825.2011.574642

Langton, L. (2010). Gang Units in Large Local Law Enforcement Agencies. *Bureau of Justice Statistics*. October. Special Report-Census of Law Enforcement Gang Units, 2007.

Laskey, J. (1996). Gang Migration: The Familial Gang Transplant Phenomenon. *Journal of Gang Research*, 3(2), pp. 1–15.

Latino Prison Gangs: Gang Identification Task Force. (2009a). *18th Street Gang*. Retrieved from http://latinoprisongangs.blogspot.com/2009/09/18th-street-gang.html

Latino Prison Gangs: Gang Identification Task Force. (2009b). *Surenos*. Retrieved from http://latinoprisongangs.blogspot.com/2009/09/surenos.html

Latino Prison Gangs: Gang Identification Task Force. (2009c). *Nortenos*. Retrieved from http://latinoprisongangs.blogspot.com/2009/09/nortenos.html

Latinoprisongangs.blogspot. (2009a). *Latin Kings*. Retrieved from http://latinoprisongangs.blogspot.com/2009/09/latin-kings.html

Latinoprisongangs.blogspot. (2009b). *Maniac Latin Disciples*. Retrieved from http://latinoprisongnags. blogspot.com/2009/09/maniac-latin-disciples.html

Lauderback, D., Hansen, J., and Waldorf, D. (1992). Sisters Are Doin' It for Themselves: A Black Female Gang in San Francisco. *Journal of Gang Research*, Fall, 1(1), pp. 57–72.

Lavigne, Y. (1996). *Hell's Angels: Into the Abyss*. New York, NY: Harper Collins.

Lavorgna, A., Lombardo, R., and Sergi, A. (2013). Organized Crime in Three Regions: Comparing the Veneto, Liverpool, and Chicago. *Trends in Organized Crime*, 16, pp. 265–285.

Lee, R. (1960). *The Chinese in the United States of America*. Hong Kong: Hong University Press.

Lehr, D., and O'Neill, G. (2012). *Black Mass: Whitey Bulger, the FBI, and a Devil's Deal*. New York, NY: Public Affairs.

Lehrer, E. (2013). Internet Access for Prisoners? Don't scoff; it would be a good idea. *Weekly Standard*. July 22. Retrieved from www.weeklystandard.com/articles/internet-access-prisoners_739266.html

Levitt, L. (1994). Ex-Gang Boss Sees Dollar Signs. *NYPD Confidential*. Retrieved from www.nypdconfiden tial.com/columns/1994/940912.html

Levitt, S., and Venkatesh, S. (2000). An Economic Analysis of a Drug-Selling Gangs Finances. *Quarterly Journal of Economics*, August, pp. 755–789.

Lindberg, K., Petrenko, J., Gladden, J., and Johnson, W.A. (1997). *The New Faces of Organized Crime*. Chicago, IL: Chicago Crime Commission.

Lindberg, R. (2016). *Gangland Chicago: Criminality and Lawlessness in the Windy City*. Lanham, MD: Rowman and Littlefield.

Livesey, J. (2015). Russian mafia 'godfather and henchmen' rounded up as footage shows armed police storm restaurant. *Mirror*. October 14. Retrieved from www.cbsnews.com/news/russian-mafias-worldwide-grip/

Lombardo, R. (2010). *The Black Hand: Terror by Letter in Chicago*. Champaign: University of Illinois Press.

Lunde, P. (2004a). *Organized Crime*. London: Dorling Kindersley.

Lunde, P. (2004b). *Organized Crime: An Inside Guide to the World's Most Successful Industry*. New York, NY: Barnes and Noble.

Lupo, S. (2009). *The History of the Mafia*. New York, NY: Columbia University Press.

Lurigio, A. J., Schwartz, J. A., and Chang, J. (1998). Descriptive and comparative analysis of female gang members. *Journal of Gang Research*, 5(4), pp. 23–33.

Lyddane, D. (2006). Understanding Gangs and Gang Mentality: Acquiring Evidence of the Gang Conspiracy. In Gangs, U.S. Department of Justice Executive Office for U.S. Attorneys. *United States Attorneys' Bulletin*, May, 54(3).

Lyman, M. D. (1989). *Gangland: Drug Trafficking by Organized Criminals*. Springfield, IL: Charles C. Thomas.

MafiaNJ. (2015). Chinese-Asian Organized Crime Groups: Tong and Street Gangs. *The Mafia in New Jersey*. Retrieved from www.mafianj.com/asian/tongs.shtml

Magloff, L. (2015). Examples of a Code of Ethics for Business. *Houston Chronicle*. Retrieved from http:// smallbusiness.chron.com/examples-code-ethics-business-4885.html

Mahadevan, P. (2011). *A War Without 'Principals': Narco-Violence in Mexico*. Athens, Greece: Research Institute for European and American Studies.

Mahoney, C. (2010). Mercenaries in Mexico. *Revolve*. June 17. Retrieved from http://www.revolve-magazine. com/2010/06/17/mercenaries-in-mexico/

Mai Wah Society. (2015). *Tong Wars*. Retrieved from www.maiwah.org/tong.shtml

Main, F. (2013). Funeral held for founder of the Conservative Vice Lords. *Chicago Tribune*. March 21. Retrieved from https://m.nationalreview.com/nrd/articles/340053/gangsterville/page/0/1

Main, F. (2012). Violence at gang funerals 'has gotten out of control': McCarthy. *Chicago Tribune*. December 2. Retrieved from www.suntimes.com/news/metro/16702202-418/brazen-violence-at-gang-funerals-has-gotten-way-out-of-control-mccarthy.html#.U9aBPp0o7yM

Major, A., Egley, A., Howell, J., Mendenhall, B., and Armstrong, T. (2004). *Youth Gangs in Indian Country*. Washington, DC: Office of Juvenile Justice and Delinquency Prevention.

Malm, S. (2015). Anywhere else, these pictures would get them killed: Inside the US prison unit for gang drop-outs where former Aryan Brotherhood members dine with ex-Black Guerilla Family and rival Mexican mafias play basketball. *Daily Mail*. May 9. Retrieved from www.dailymail.co.uk/news/article-3030092/Building-bridges-Inside-California-prison-unit-gang-drop-outs-former-Aryan-Brotherhood-members-dine-ex-Black-Guerilla-Family-rival-Mexican-mafias-play-basketball.html

Marcell, F. (2006). Security Threat Groups: Effect on Corrections During the Past Decade. *Corrections Today*, April, pp. 56–59.

Mark, G. (1997). Oakland China Town's First Youth Gang: The Suey Sing Boys. *Free Inquiry*, May, 25(1), pp. 41–50.

Martin, A., and Thomas, J. (1996). Book it: A new venture for the disciples. *Chicago Tribune*. September 18. Retrieved from http://articles.chicagotribune.com/1996-09-18/news/9609190250_1_gangster-disciples-larry-hoover-drug-conspiracy

Martin, B. (1970) *Strange Vigor: A Biography of Sun Yat-Sen*. Port Washington, NY: Kennikat Press.

Maruko, E. (2002). The 'Underworld' Goes Underground: Yakuza in Japanese Politics. *Harvard Asia Quarterly*, Summer, pp. 14–18.

Marx, G. (1999). Alleged gang kingpin faces drug charge. *Chicago Tribune*. September 9. Retrieved from http://articles.chicagotribune.com/1999-09-09/news/9909090291_1_latin-kings-federal-investigators-gang

Matthews, C. (2014). Fortune 5: The biggest organized crime groups in the world. *Fortune*. September 14. Retrieved from http://fortune.com/2014/09/14/biggest-organized-crime-groups-in-the-world/

Maxson, C. (1998). *Gang Members on the Move*. Washington, DC: Office of Juvenile Justice and Delinquency Prevention.

Maxson, C. L., Hennigan, K. M., and Sloane, D. C. (2005). It's getting crazy out there: Can a civil gang injunction change a community? *Criminology & Public Policy*, 4(3), 577–605.

McCorkle, L. W., and Korn, R. (1954). In Annals of the American Academy of Political and Social Science. *American Academy of Political and Social Science*, 293, pp. 88–98.

McCorkle, R. C., and Miethe, T. D. (2002). *Panic: The Social Construction of the Street Gang Problem*. Upper Saddle River, NJ: Prentice-Hall.

McCorkle, R. C., and Miethe, T. D. (1998). The Political and Organizational Response to Gangs: An Examination of a 'Moral Panic' in Nevada. *Justice Quarterly*, 15(1), pp. 41–64.

McGoey, C. E. (2014). *Home Invasion Robbery: Protect Your Family with a Security Plan*. Retrieved from www.crimedoctor.com/homeinvasion.htm

McIllwain, J. (1997). From Tong Wars to Organized Crime: Revisiting the Historical Perception of Violence in Chinatown. *Justice Quarterly*, March, 14(1), pp. 25–52.

McKenna, J. (1996). Organized Crime in the Royal Colony of Hong Kong. *Journal of Contemporary Criminal Justice*, December, 12(4), pp. 316–328.

Melde, C., and Rennison, C. M. (2010). Intimidation and Street Gangs: Understanding the Response of Victims and Bystanders to Perceived Gang Violence. *Justice Quarterly*, 27(5), pp. 619–666. https://doi.org/10.1080/07418820903228858

Melton, G. (2014). An Examination of the Bootleg Record Industry and Its Impact upon Popular Music Consumption. *Journal of Popular Music Studies*, 26(2–3), pp. 399–408.

Meltzer, G. R. (2001). *Evaluation of a probation department gang reduction and suppression program*. Unpublished doctoral dissertation, Pepperdine University.

Merton, R. (1938). Social Structure and Anomie. *American Sociological Review*, October, 3, pp. 672–682.

Miller, J. (2001). *One of the Guys: Girls, Gangs, and Gender*. New York, NY: Oxford University Press.

Miller, J., and Decker, S. H. (2001). Young Women and Gang Violence: Gender, Street Offending, and Violent Victimization in Gangs. *Justice Quarterly*, 18(1), pp. 115–140. https://doi.org/10.1080/07418820100094841

Miller, W. B. (1975). *Violence by Youth Gangs and Youth Groups as a Crime Problem in Major American Cities*. Washington, DC: U.S. Department of Justice.

Miller, W. B. (1958). Lower Class Culture as a Generating Milieu of Gang Delinquency. *Journal of Social Issues*, May, 14(3), pp. 5–19.

Mills, C. W. (1959). *The Sociological Imagination*. New York, NY: Oxford University Press.

Mills, S., and Brunuel, D. (1998). Small gang's big grip troubles neighborhood: The saints have grown more violent and more diverse since forming in the 1960s. *Chicago Tribune*. February 11. Retrieved from http://articles.chicagotribune.com/1998-02-11/news/9802110270_1_gangster-disciples-gang-combat-neighborhood

Minnesota Violent Crime Coordinating Council (MVCCC). (2012). *Gang Criteria Recommendation to the Commissioner of Public Safety [MN Statutes §299A.642, subd. 3(8)]*. Adopted June 13, 2012.

Mongols MC Northwest. (2014). *History*. Retrieved from http://mongolsmcnorthwest.com/history/

Mongolsmc.com. (2014). *Chapters*. Retrieved from http://mongolsmc.com/chapters

Montalvo-Barbot, A. (1997). Crime in Puerto Rico: Drug Trafficking, Money Laundering, and the Poor. *Crime and Delinquency*, 43(4), pp. 533–548.

Montgomery, M. (2013). How imprisoned Mexican mafia leader exerts secret control over L.A. street gangs. *KQED News*. September 19. Retrieved from http://ww2.kqed.org/news/2013/09/17/111570/secret-letter-from-mexican-mafia-gang-leader-to-la-street-gangs

Mooney, J. A. (1891). The Two Sicilies and the Camorra. *American Catholic Quarterly Review*, 16, pp. 723–748.

Moore, J. (1991). *Going Down to the Barrio: Homeboys and Homegirls in Change*. Philadelphia, PA: Temple University Press.

Moore, J. (1978). *Homeboys: Gangs, Drugs, and Prison in the Barrios of Los Angeles*. Philadelphia, PA: Temple University Press.

Moore, J. P. (1997). *Highlights of the 1995 National Youth Gang Survey* (OJJDP Series Fact Sheet, April #63). Tallahassee, FL: Institute for Intergovernmental Research. Retrieved from www.ncjrs.org/txtfiles/fs9763.txt

Moore, J. W. (1998). Understanding youth street gangs: Economic restructuring and the urban underclass. In *Cross-cultural Perspectives on Youth and Violence*, Watts, M. W. (Ed.). Stamford, CT: JAI Press.

Moore, N., and Williams, L. (2011). *The Almighty Black P. Stone Nation: The Rise, Fall and Resurrection of an American Gang*. Chicago, IL: Chicago Review Press.

Moore, R. (1990). *The Man Who Made It Snow: By the American Mastermind Inside the Colombian Cartel Max Mermelstein*. New York, NY: Simon and Schuster.

Morales, G. C. (2011). *La Familia—The Family: Prison Gangs in America* (2nd ed.). San Antonio, TX: Mungia Printers.

Morales, G. C. (2007a). Nortenos. *Gang Prevention Services*. Retrieved from https://web.archive.org/web/20140420194249/http://gangpreventionservices.org/norteno.asp

Morales, G. C. (2007b). Native Gangs. *Gang Prevention Services*. Retrieved from https://web.archive.org/web/20140420194122/http://gangpreventionservices.org:80/nativegangs.asp

Morgan, W. P. (1960). *Triad Societies in Hong Kong*. Hong Kong: Government Press.

Morris, D. (2008). *The War of the Bloods in My Veins: A Street Soldier's March Toward Redemption*. New York, NY: Scribner.

Mraz, S. (2007). Sgt. Juwan Johnson: His death and what it's meant for a gang. *Stars and Stripes*. May 13. Retrieved from www.stripes.com/news/sgt-juwan-johnson-his-death-and-what-it-s-meant-for-a-gang-1.63944

Nagle, L. (2011). Corruption of politicians, law enforcement, and the judiciary in Mexico and complicity across the border. In *Narcos over the Border: Gangs, Cartels and Mercenaries*, Bunker, R. J. (Ed.). New York, NY: Routledge.

Naim, M. (2012). Mafia States. *Foreign Affairs*, May/June, 91(3), pp. 100–111.

Naim, M. (2003). Five Wars of Globalization. *Foreign Policy*, January/February, (134), pp. 28–38.

Nashville.gov. (2012). *Nashville Government Seeks to Have Kurdish Pride Gang and 24 Members Collectively Declared a Public Nuisance.* Retrieved from www.nashville.gov/News-Media/News-Article/ID/143/Nashville-Government-Seeks-to-Have-Kurdish-Pride-Gang-and-24-Members-Collectively-Declared-a-Public-Nuisance.aspx

National Alliance of Gang Investigator Associations (NAGIA). (2015). About. *NAGIA*. Retrieved from www.nagia.org/

National Alliance of Gang Investigator Associations. (2005). *National Gang Threat Assessment.* Retrieved from www.nationalgangcenter.gov/threatassessments.cfm

National Drug Intelligence Center (NDIC). (2008). *Attorney General's Report to Congress on the Growth of Violent Street Gangs in Suburban Areas: Appendix B: National-Level Street, Prison, and Outlaw Motorcycle Gang Profiles.* Retrieved from www.justice.gov/archive/ndic/pubs27/27612/appendb.htm

National Drug Intelligence Center (NDIC). (2004). *Intelligence Bulletin: Mara Salvatrucha Update.* Johnston, PA: U.S. Department of Justice.

National Drug Intelligence Center (NDIC). (2003). *Drugs and Crime, Gang Profile: Gangster Disciples.* Johnstown, PA: National Drug Intelligence Center.

National Drug Intelligence Center (NDIC). (1998). *Street Gangs '98: National Street Gang Survey Report-1998.* Johnstown, PA: National Drug Intelligence Center.

National Gang Center (NGC). (2015). National Youth Gang Survey Analysis. *NGC, U.S. Department of Justice.* Retrieved from www.nationalgangcenter.gov/Survey-Analysis

National Gang Center (NGC). (2014). Highlights of Gang-Related Legislation. *NGC, U.S. Department of Justice.* Retrieved from www.nationalgangcenter.gov/Legislation/Highlights

National Gang Center (NGC). (2013). *National Youth Gang Survey Analysis.* June. Retrieved from www.nationalgangcenter.gov/Survey-Analysis

National Gang Center (NGC). (n.d.). Frequently Asked Questions About Gangs: What Kinds of Gangs Are There? *National Gang Center.* Retrieved from www.nationalgangcenter.gov/About/FAQ

National Gang Crime Research Center (NGCRC) (2018). *About NGCRC.* NGCRC. Retrieved from https://ngcrc.com/about/about.html

National Gang Intelligence Center (NGIC). (2015). *National gang report—2013.* Washington, DC: National Gang Intelligence Center.

National Gang Intelligence Center (NGIC). (2013). *2013 National Gang Report (NGR).* National Gang Intelligence Center. Retrieved from www.fbi.gov/stats-services/publications/national-gang-report-2013/

National Gang Intelligence Center (NGIC). (2011). *2011 National Gang Threat Assessment—Emerging Trends.* National Gang Intelligence Center. Retrieved from www.fbi.gov/stats-services/publications/2011-national-gang-threat-assessment

National Gang Intelligence Center (NGIC). (2009). *National Gang Threat Assessment—2009.* Washington, DC: National Gang Intelligence Center.

National Gang Intelligence Center (NGIC). (2007). *Intelligence Assessment: Gang-Related Activity in the US Armed Forces Increasing.* Crystal City, VA: National Gang Intelligence Center.

National Post. (2015). Why Italy's scariest mob loves Canada. *National Post.* Retrieved from www.nationalpost.com/news/story.html?id=78bf4dea-ad71-4ecb-ba1d-d6c18fb311cf

National Youth Gang Center. (2009). *National Youth Gang Survey Analysis.* Retrieved from www.national gangcenter.gov/Survey-Analysis

National Young Lords. (2014). *Jose (Cha-Cha) Jimenez.* Retrieved from http://nationalyounglords.com/?page_id=15

Neely, D. E. (1997). The Social Reality of African American Street Gangs. *Journal of Gang Research*, Winter, 4(2), pp. 37–46.

Nevada State Legislature. (2011). Fact Sheet. *Facts About Mandatory Penalty Enhancements for Felonies Under Nevada Revised Statutes.* Retrieved from www.leg.state.nv.us/Division/Research/Publications/Fact-Sheets/CrimeCharts/Enhancements.pdf

New Jersey State Police. (2007). *Gangs in New Jersey: Municipal Law Enforcement Response to the 2007 NJSP Gang Survey.* New Jersey Department of Law and Public Safety Division of the New Jersey State Police Intelligence Section. Retrieved from www.state.nj.us/njsp/info/pdf/njgangsurvey-2007.pdf

New York State Organized Crime Task Force (NYSOCTF), New York State Commission of Investigation, and New Jersey State Commission of Investigation. (1996). *An Analysis of Russian Émigré Crime in the Tri-State Region.* NCJ 174068. Washington, DC: NCJRS.

New York Times: NYT. (1993). Immigrants' ship runs aground in N.Y. 7 perish 300 Chinese spent 3 months at sea. *New York Times.* June 7. Retrieved from http://articles.baltimoresun.com/1993-06-07/news/1993158001_1_golden-venture-aground-ship-ran

Newark, T. (2010). *Lucky Luciano: The Real and the Fake Gangster.* New York, NY: St. Martin's Press.

Newark, T. (2007a). Pact with the Devil. *History Today*, April, 57(4), pp. 32–38.

Newark, T. (2007b). *Mafia Allies: The True Story of America's Secret Alliance with the Mob in World War II.* St. Paul, MN: Zenith Press.

Newbold, G., and Dennehy, G. (2003). Girls in Gangs: Biographies and Culture of Female Gang Associates in New Zealand. *Journal of Gang Research*, Fall, 11(1), pp. 33–53.

News 5. (2012). MS-13 Gang Member deported again. February 23. Retrieved from http://edition.channel-5belize.com/archives/67367

O'Conner, M. (1996a). U.S. says Hoover controlled gang, prison. *Chicago Tribune.* January 30. Retrieved from http://articles.chicagotribune.com/1996-01-30/news/9601300069_1_gangster-disciples-gang-members-larry-hoover

O'Conner, M. (1996b). Hoover prison life boast on tape. *Chicago Tribune.* February 16. Retrieved from http://articles.chicagotribune.com/1996-02-16/news/9602160038_1_gang-member-gangster-disciples-larry-hoover

O'Connor, M. (1994). On Leong, Moy plead guilty to running longtime casino. *Chicago Tribune.* February 13. Retrieved from http://articles.chicagotribune.com/1994-02-13/news/9402130225_1_gambling-conspiracy-gambling-operation-chicago-police-officers

Olivo, A. (2011). Federal sting targets Belizean Bloods gang: Suspects arrested as they allegedly plotted to rob drug cartel members in Berwyn. *Chicago Tribune.* November 4. Retrieved from http://articles.chicagotribune.com/2011-11-04/news/ct-met-belizean-bloods-charges-2-20111104_1_drug-cartel-cartel-members-gang-members

O'Neil, A. (2003). Drug kingpin gets 30 years. *Sun Sentinel.* August 27. Retrieved from http://articles.sun-sentinel.com/2003-08-27/news/0308270065_1_prison-term-alejandro-bernal-madrigal-sentence

OnePercenterBikers. (2017). *Kinfolk.* Retrieved from www.onepercenterbikers.com/kinfolk-mc-motorcycle-club/

Operation Safe Streets (OSS). (1992). *'Los Angeles Style': A Street Gang Manual of the Los Angeles County Sheriff's Department.* January. Los Angeles, CA: Los Angeles County Sheriff's Department.

Orlando-Morningstar, D. (1997). Prison Gangs. *Special Needs Offender Bulletin*, October, 2, pp. 1–13.

Ouseley, W. (2011). *Mobsters in Our Midst: The Kansas City Crime Family*. Kansas City, MO: Kansas City Star Books.

Paciotti, B. (2005). Homicide in Seattle's Chinatown, 1900–1940: Evaluating the Influence of Social Organizations. *Homicide Studies*, August, 9(3), pp. 229–255.

Padilla, F. (1993). *The Gang as an American Enterprise*. New Brunswick, NJ: Rutgers University Press.

Paoli, L. (2003). *Mafia Brotherhoods: Organized Crime, Italian Style*. New York, NY: Oxford University Press.

Papachristos, A. V. (2007). *Murder by structure: A network theory of gang homicide*. Unpublished dissertation, University of Chicago.

Papajohn, G. (1994). 'King' Wheat's killing mirrors change in gangs. *Chicago Tribune*. August 19. Retrieved from http://articles.chicagotribune.com/1994-08-19/news/9408190365_1_four-corners-vice-lords-gang

Papajohn, G., and Kass, J. (1994). 21st century vote giving gangs taste of real power. *Chicago Tribune*. September 28. Retrieved from http://articles.chicagotribune.com/1994-09-28/news/9409280241_1_larry-hoover-total-empowerment-drug-trafficking

Parker, N. (2010). Dangerous people, dangerous places. In *The Mammoth Book of Drug Barons*, Copperwaite, P. (Ed.). London: Constable and Robinson.

Pearson, G. (1983). *Hooligan: A History of Reportable Fears*. London: Macmillan Press.

Pelton, T. (1994). Gang leader guilty in woman's murder. *Chicago Tribune*. June 17. Section 2.

Petacco, A. (1974). *Joe Petrosino: The True Story of a Tough, Turn-of-the-Century New York Cop*. New York, NY: Macmillan.

Perkins, U. E. (1987). *Explosion of Chicago's Black Street Gangs: 1900 to Present*. Chicago, IL: Third World Press.

Petersen, C. (2015). Sex Work, Migration, and the United States Trafficking in Persons Report: Promoting Rights or Missing Opportunities for Advocacy? *Indiana International & Comparative Law Review*, 25(1), pp. 115–157.

Petrone, F. (1997). *People-Folks: The Street Gang Identification Manual* (Rev. ed.). Chicago, IL: Gang Prevention.

Pileggi, N. (1985). *Wise Guy: Life in a Mafia Family*. New York, NY: Pocketbooks.

Pitkin, T., and Cordasco, F. (1977). *The Black Hand: A Chapter in Ethnic Crime*. Totowa, NJ: Littlefield, Adams.

Plywaczewski, E. (2003). The Russian and Polish mafia in Central Europe. In *Global Organized Crime: Trends and Developments*, Siegal, D., van de Bunt, H., and Zaitch, D. (Eds.). Dordrecht, Netherlands: Kluwer Academic.

Police Chief. (2014). Human Trafficking 101 for Law Enforcement. *Police Chief*, July, 81(7).

Poppa, T. (1998). *Drug Lord: The Life & Death of a Mexican Kingpin*. Seattle, WA: Demand.

Porter, T. (2015). Gangs of Russia: Ruthless mafia networks extending their influence. *International Business Times*. April 9. Retrieved from www.ibtimes.co.uk/gangs-russia-ruthless-mafia-networks-extending-their-influence-1495644

Poston, R. (1971). *The Gang and the Establishment*. New York, NY: Harper and Row.

Pranger, B., and Etter, G. (2011). Psychological and Cultural Aspects of Outlaw Motorcycle Gangs. *Journal of Gang Research*, 19(1), pp. 21–36.

Prison Law Office. (2014). *Gang Validation and Debriefing Information*. November. Retrieved from www.prisonlaw.com/pdfs/GangLetter,Nov2014.pdf

Prison Offenders.Com. (2014). *Crips*. www.prisonoffenders.com/crips.html

Prisonoffenders.com. (2017). *Northern Structure*. Retrieved from www.prisonoffenders.com/northern_structure.html

Pyrooz, D. C., Decker, S. H., and Fleisher, M. S. (2011). From the Street to the Prison, from the Prison to the Street: Understanding and Responding to Prison Gangs. *Journal of Aggression, Conflict, and Peace Research*, 3(1), pp. 12–24. https://doi.org/10.5042/jacpr.2011.0018

Pyrooz, D. C., and Sweeten, G. (2015). Gang Membership Between Ages 5 and 17 Years in the United States. *Journal of Adolescent Health*, 1, p. 3.

Pyrooz, D. C., Wolfe, S. E., and Spohn, C. (2011). Gang-Related Homicide Charging Decisions: The Implementation of a Specialized Prosecution Unit in Los Angeles. *Criminal Justice Policy Review*, 22, p. 3. https://doi.org/10.1177/0887403410361626

Queen, W. (2005). *Under and Alone*. New York, NY: Random House.

Quicker, J., and Batani-Khalfani, A. (1998). From Boozies to Bloods: Early Gangs in Los Angeles. *Journal of Gang Research*, 5(4), pp. 15–22.

Quintanilla v. United States. (2010). *Petition for Extraordinary Relief*. March 30. Retrieved from www.jag. nay.mil/courts/documents/archive/2010/QUNITANILLA,%20J.A.pdf

Raab, S. (2006). *Five Families: The Rise, Decline, and Resurgence of America's Most Powerful Mafia Empires*. New York, NY: St. Martin's Press.

Raab, S. (1995). Reputed Russian crime chief arrested. *New York Times*. June 9, p. B3.

Radanko, L. (2011). *The Russian Mafia in America*. Lexington, KY: Create Space.

Rather, D. (2005). The Fight Against MS-13. *CBS NEWS 60 Minutes*. Retrieved from www.cbsnews.com/news/the-fight-against-ms-13/2/

RCMP Gazette. (2007). Biker gang structure. In *The Mammoth Book of Bikers*, Veno, A. (Ed.). Philadelphia, PN: Running Press Book.

Recktenwald, W. (1997). Study probes drop in state violence. *Chicago Tribune*. May 26. MetroLake Section, pp. 1–2.

Regional Information Sharing Systems (RISS). (2015). *Regional Information Sharing Systems (RISS) Program*. Retrieved from www.riss.net/default/Overview

Rempel, W. (2011). *At the Devil's Table: The Untold Story of the Insider Who Brought Down the Cali Cartel*. New York, NY: Random House.

Reuters. (2014). Yakuza among first with relief supplies in Japan. November 30. Retrieved from www.freemalaysiatoday.com/category/world/2014/11/30/yakuza-among-first-with-relief-supplies-in-japan/

Richardson, A. (1991). *Outlaw Motorcycle Gangs: USA Overview*. Sacramento, CA: California Department of Justice. Retrieved from www.ncjrs.gov/pdffiles1/Digitization/147691NCJRS.pdf

Riggs, R. (2004). State offers way out for violent prison gang members. *CBS-11 News*. July 26. Retrieved from http://cbs11tv.com/investigations/local_story_208180734.html

Robinson, A. (2009). Mexican Banditry and Discourse of Class: The Case of Chucho Roto. *Latin American Research Review*, 44(1), pp. 5–31.

Robinson, L., and Cooper, M. (1991). New Target: The Cali Cartel. *U.S. News & World Report*, December 23, 111(26).

Rodriguez, J. J., Eve, R. A., Del Carmen, A., and Jeong, S. (2014). Transnationalism: Law enforcement perceptions of gang activity on the Texas/Mexico border. *Journal of Gang Research*, 21(3), pp. 1–15.

Roemer, W. (1990). *War of the Godfathers: The Bloody Confrontation Between the Chicago and New York Families for Control of Las Vegas*. New York, NY: Donald I. Fine.

Roeper, R. (1993). Here's your chance, gang peacemakers. *Chicago Sun-Times*. November 10. p. 11.

Roose, K. (2015). Watch these fascinating vines taken by a prisoner in his cell. *Fusion*. February 3. Retrieved from http://fusion.net/story/42137/watch-these-fascinating-vines-taken-by-a-prisoner-in-his-cell/

Roose, K., and Harshaw, P. (2015). Inside the prison system's illicit digital world. *Fusion*. February 3. Retrieved from http://fusion.net/story/41931/inside-the-prison-systems-illicit-digital-world/

Rosenbaum, J. (1996). A Violent Few: Gang Girls in the California Youth Authority. *Journal of Gang Research*, Spring, 3(3), pp. 17–23.

Rosenfeld, S. (1996). Daly city man arrested in sting. *SF Gate*. February 6. Retrieved from www.sfgate.com/news/article/Daly-City-man-arrested-in-sting-3151959.php

Rosner, L. (1986). *The Soviet Way of Crime: Beating the System in the Soviet Union and the U.S.A.* South Handley, MA: Bergin and Garvey.

Roth, M. G., and Skarbek, D. (2014). Prison Gangs and the Community Responsibility System. *Review of Behavioral Economics*, 1, pp. 223–243.

Rowe, G. (2013). *Gods of Mischief.* New York, NY: Simon and Schuster.

Ruane, D. (2011). Gang linked to suspect in cop shooting came from Chicago. *News Press.* April 18. Retrieved from http://archive.news-press.com/article/20110419/CRIME/104190344/Gang-linked-suspect-cop-shooting-came-from-Chicago

Ruddell, R., Decker, S. H., and Egley, A., Jr. (2006). Gang Intervention in Jails. *Criminal Justice Review*, 31(1), pp. 33–46.

Ruddell, R., and Gottschall, S. (2011). Are All Gangs Equal Security Risks? An Investigation of Gang Types and Prison Misconduct. *American Journal of Criminal Justice*, 36(3), pp. 265–279. https://doi.org/10.1007/s12103-011-9108-4

Rufino, K. A., Fox, K. A., and Kercher, G. A. (2011). Gang Membership and Crime Victimization Among Prison Inmates. *American Journal of Criminal Justice*, 37, pp. 321–337.

Russick, J. (2010). The On Leong Merchant's Association. *Chicago History Museum.* Retrieved from http://blog.chicagohistory.org/index.php/2010/02/on-leong-merchant-association/

Saga, J. (1991). *Confessions of a Yakuza: A Life in Japan's Underworld.* Tokyo: Kodansha International.

Sale, R. (1971). *Blackstone Rangers: A Reporter's Account of Time Spent with the Street Gang on Chicago's South Side.* New York, NY: Random House.

Salter, J. (2011). Wheels of soul motorcycle gang members face, murder, drug charges. *Huffington Post.* January 9. Retrieved from www.huffingtonpost.com/2011/07/12/wheels-of-soul-motorcycle-gang-murder-drug_n_895728.html

San Diego County Deputy Sheriffs' Association. (1990). Gangs, groups, cults. In *Gangbangs and Drivebys: Grounded Culture and Juvenile Gang Violence*, Sanders, W. B. (1994, Ed.) (pp. 6–7). Hawthorne, NY: Aldine de Gruyter.

Sanchez-Jankowski, M. (1991). *Islands in the Street: Gangs and the American Urban Society.* Berkeley: University of California Press.

Sanders, B. (2017). *Gangs: An Introduction.* New York, NY: Oxford University Press.

Sanders, W. B. (1994). *Gangbangs and Drivebys: Grounded Culture and Juvenile Gang Violence.* Hawthorne, NY: Aldine de Gruyter.

Sante, L. (1991). *Low life: Lures and Snares of Old New York.* New York, NY: Vintage Books.

Sarconi, P. (2017). Now's probably the time to consider one of these burner phones. *Wired.* February 3. Retrieved from www.wired.com/2017/02/7-great-burner-phones/

Saviano, R. (2006). *Gomorrah: A Personal Journey into the Violent International Empire of Naples' Organized Crime System.* New York, NY: Picador.

Scales v. United States, 367 U.S. 203, 223 (1961).

Schiffrin, H. (1980). *Sun Yat-Sen.* Boston, MA: Little, Brown.

Schoenberg, R. (1992). *Mr. Capone: The Real-and Complete-Story of Al Capone.* New York, NY: William Morrow.

Schreck, C. (2005). 11 sent to prison for 18 brutal slayings. *Moscow Times.* August 18. Retrieved from www.themoscowtimes.com/news/article/11-sent-to-prison-for-18-brutal-slayings/210511.html

Schwirtz, M. (2009). For a departed mobster, wreaths and roses but no tears. *New York Times.* October 13. Retrieved from www.nytimes.com/2009/10/14/world/europe/14mobster.html

Scott, D. W. (2014). Attitude Is Everything: Youth Attitudes, Gang Involvement, and Length of Institutional Gang Membership. *Group Processes and Intergroup Relations*, 17(6), pp. 780–798. https://doi.org/10.1177/1368430214548285

Scott, M. (2009). *Lords of Lawndale.* Shelbyville, KY: Wasteland Press.

Seabrook, L. A., and Stewart, J. (2014). Snitches get stitches: Combating witness intimidation in gang-related prosecutions. In *Gang Prosecutions: U.S. Department of Justice Executive Office for United States Attorneys*, May, 62(3).

Seal, G. (2009). The Robin Hood Principle: Folklore, History and the Social Bandit. *Journal of Folklore Research*, 46(1), pp. 67–89.

Seepersad, R. (2013). Street Gangs and Violence in Trinidad and Tobago. *Journal of Gang Research*, 21(1), pp. 17–24.

Serio, J. (2008). *Investigating the Russian Mafia*. Durham, NC: Carolina Academic Press.

Shalur, S. (1993). *Monster: The Autobiography of an LA Gang Member*. New York, NY: Grove Press.

Shapira, I. (2005). Gangs sharpen intimidation: Machetes used increasingly in attacks. *Washington Post*. January 16. p. C3.

Shelden, R. G. (1991). A Comparison of Gang Members and Non-Gang Members in a Prison Setting. *Prison Journal*, 71(2), pp. 50–60. https://doi.org/10.1177/003288559107100206

Sheldon, R. G., Tracy, S. K., and Brown, W. B. (2001). *Youth Gangs in American Society* (2nd ed.). Stamford, CT: Wadsworth/Thomson Learning.

Shelley, L. (1998). The rise and rise of the Russian mafia. *BBC News*. November 21. Retrieved from http://news.bbc.co.uk/2/hi/special_report/1998/03/98/russian_mafia/70095.stm

Shifter, M. (2012). *Countering Criminal Violence in Central America*. Council on Foreign Relations (CFR). Center for Preventative Action, Council Special Report No. 64, April 2012.

Short, M. (2009). *The Rise of the Mafia: The Definitive Story of Organized Crime*. London: John Blake.

Short, J., and Strodtbeck, F. (1974). Youth, Gangs and Society: Micro and Macrosociological Processes. *Sociological Quarterly*, 15, pp. 3–19.

Short, J., and Strodtbeck, F. (1965). *Group Process and Gang Delinquency*. Chicago, IL: University of Chicago Press.

Sieff, M. (2008). Africa: Many Hills to Climb. *World Policy Journal*, Fall, 25(3), pp. 185–195.

Siegel, D. (2003a). The transnational Russian mafia. In *Global Organized Crime: Trends and Developments*, Siegal, D., van de Bunt, H., and Zaitch, D. (Eds.). Dordrecht, Netherlands: Kluwer Academic.

Siegel, D. (2003b). Natashas and Turkish men: New trends in women trafficking and prostitution. In *Global Organized Crime: Trends and Developments*, Siegal, D., van de Bunt, H., and Zaitch, D. (Eds.). Dordrecht, Netherlands: Kluwer Academic.

Siegel, D., and Bovenkerk, F. (2000). Crime and Manipulation of Identity Among Russian-Speaking Immigrants in the Netherlands. *Journal of Contemporary Criminal Justice*, November, 16(4), pp. 424–444.

Sikes, G. (1997). *8-Ball Chicks*. New York, NY: Anchor Books.

Simpson, C., and Pearlman, A. (2006). *Inside the Crips*. New York, NY: St. Martin's Press.

Simpson, P. (2012). Update on old town search warrant at hip sing association building. *Portland Police Bureau*. July 12. Retrieved from www.portlandoregon.gov/police/news/read.cfm?id=3164

Sims, A. (2015). Godfather-style funeral music played at funeral of purported mafia boss. *Independent*. August 21. Retrieved from www.independent.co.uk/news/world/europe/godfather-style-funeral-music-played-at-funeral-of-purported-mafia-boss-10465561.html

Sinelnikov, M. (2011). Russian mafia most powerful in the world? *Pravda*. July 11. Retrieved from http://english.pravda.ru/russia/politics/07-11-2011/119544-russian_mafia-0/

Siniawer, E. (2012). Befitting Bedfellows: Yakuza and the State in Modern Japan. *Journal of Social History*, 45(3), pp. 623–641.

Sirpal, S. K. (1997). Causes of Gang Participation and Strategies for Prevention in Gang Members' Own Words. *Journal of Gang Research*, Winter, 4(2), pp. 13–22.

Skarbek, D. (2014). *The Social Order of the Underworld: How Prison Gangs Govern the American Penal System*. New York, NY: Oxford University Press.

Skarbek, D. (2012). Prison Gangs, Norms, and Organizations. *Journal of Economic Behavior and Organization*, 82(1), pp. 702–716.

Smith, C. F. (2017). *Gangs and the Military: Gangsters, Bikers, and Terrorists with Military Training*. Lanham, MD: Rowman and Littlefield.

Smith, C. F. (2015). Military-Trained Gang Members-Two Different Perspectives. *Journal of Gang Research*.

Smith, C. F. (2014a). *Military-Trained Gang Member (MTGM) Security Threat Group Assessment: Tennessee [Montgomery County]*. A review of Security Threat Group (Gang and Extremist) Activity.

Smith, C. F. (2014b). *Military-Trained Gang Member (MTGM) Security Threat Group Assessment: Tennessee*. A review of Security Threat Group (Gang and Extremist) Activity.

Smith, C. F. (2014c). *Military-Trained Gang Member (MTGM) Security Threat Group Assessment: Northwest U.S*. A review of Security Threat Group (Gang and Extremist) Activity.

Smith, C. F. (2014d). *Military-Trained Gang Member (MTGM) Security Threat Group Assessment: Arizona*. A review of Security Threat Group (Gang and Extremist) Activity.

Smith, C. F. (2012). "Gang investigators' perceptions of military-trained gang members in the Southern U.S." Submitted to American Society of Criminology conference proceedings.

Smith, C. F. (2011). A comprehensive literature review of military-trained gang members. *Journal of Gang Research*, Fall, 19(1), pp. 9–20.

Smith, C. F., Rush, J. P., Robinson, D., and Karmiller, M. (2012). Flashgangs and Flashgangbanging: How Can Local Police Prepare? *Journal of Gang Research*, Fall, 20(1), pp. 33–50.

Smith, G. (2009). *Nothing but Money: How the Mob Infiltrated Wall Street*. New York, NY: Berkley Publishing Group.

Snedeker, L. (2002). Biker-gang violence a shock to gambling town that caters to older vacationers. Associated Press. April 27. Retrieved from www.freerepublic.com/focus/f-news/674043/posts

Song, J., Dombrink, J., and Gels, G. (1992). Lost in the Melting Pot: Asian Youth Gangs in the United States. *Journal of Gang Research*, 1(1), pp. 1–12.

Southern Center for Human Rights. (2014). *THE Crisis of Violence in Georgia's Prisons*. Author.

Spadafora, F. (2010). Origins of the Sicilian mafia. *Best of Sicily Magazine*. Retrieved from www.bestofsicily.com/mag/art345.htm

SpearIt. (2011). Radical Islam in prison: Made in the USA. *Huffington Post*. June 21. Retrieved from www.huffingtonpost.com/spearit/radical-islam-prison_b_880733.html

Spergel, I. A. (1993). *Youth Gangs: Problem and Response: NYGIC Document D0027*. Arlington, VA: National Youth Gang Information Center.

Spergel, I. A. (1991). *Youth Gangs: Problem and Response*. Washington, DC: Office of Juvenile Justice and Delinquency Prevention.

Squires, N. (2010). 'Ndrangheta Mafia' undone: Italy arrests 300 in huge crackdown. *Christian Science Monitor*. July 13.

Stallworth, R. (1994). *Gangster Rap: Music, Culture & Politics* (5th ed.). Salt Lake City: Utah DPS.

State of New Jersey Commission of Investigation. (2009). *Gangland Behind Bars: How and Why Organized Criminal Street Gangs Thrive in New Jersey's Prisons . . . and What Can Be Done About It*. State of New Jersey Commission of Investigation.

Sterling, C. (1994). *Thieves' World: The Threat of the New Global Network of Organized Crime*. New York, NY: Simon and Schuster.

Sterling, C. (1990). *Octopus: How the Long Reach of the Sicilian Mafia Controls the Global Narcotics Traffic*. New York, NY: Touchstone.

Stockwell, J. (2005). In MS-13, a culture of brutality and begging. *Washington Post*. May 2. Retrieved from www.washingtonpost.com/wp-dyn/content/article/2005/05/01/AR2005050100814.html

Stonegreasers.com. (2014a). *12th Street Players*. Retrieved from www.stonegreasers.com/greaser/12th_street_players.html

Stonegreasers.com. (2014b). *Northside Popes and Larry Larkin*. Retrieved from www.stonegreasers.com/greaser/larkin_popes.html

Stonegreasers.com. (2014c). *Simon City Royals and Simon City Gang*. Retrieved from www.stonegreasers.com/greaser/scr.html

STRATFOR Global Intelligence. (2015). In Mexico, the delineation of cartel power becomes more complex. *STRATFOR Global Intelligence*. January 22.

Streatfeild, D. (2001). *Cocaine: An Unauthorized Biography*. New York, NY: St. Martin's Press.

Sule, D. (2005). Correlates of Hispanic Female Gang Membership. *Journal of Gang Research*, Summer, 12(4), pp. 1–23.

Sullivan, J. P., and Bunker, R. J. (2007). Third Generation Gang Studies: An Introduction. *Journal of Gang Research*, 14(4), pp. 1–10. Chicago, IL: National Gang Crime Research Center.

Sullivan, J. P., and Logan, S. (2010a). Los Zetas: Massacres, Assassinations and Infantry Tactics. *Homeland1 News: The Counter Terrorist*, October/November.

Sullivan, J. P., and Logan, S. (2010b). MS-13 Leadership: Networks of Influence. *Counter Terrorist*, August/September.

Sutherland, E. H. (1947). *Principles of Criminology* (4th ed.). Philadelphia, PA: Lippincott.

Sutherland, E. H. (1940). White-Collar Criminality. *American Sociological Review*, 5(1), p. 1. https://doi.org/10.2307/2083937

Szymkowiak, K. (2002). *Sokaiya: Extortion, Protection, and the Japanese Corporation*. Armonk, NY: M. E. Sharpe.

Tapia, M., Sparks, C. S., and Miller, J. M. (2014). Texas Latino Prison Gangs: An Exploration of Generational Shift and Rebellion. *Prison Journal*, 94(2), p. 1–21. https://doi.org/10.1177/0032885514524694

Taylor, T., Peterson, D., Esbensen, F., and Freng, A. (2007). Gang Membership as a Risk Factor for Adolescent Violent Victimization. *Journal of Research in Crime and Delinquency*, 44, pp. 351–380.

Teachman, J., and Tedrow, L. (2015). *Military service and desistance from contact with the criminal justice system*. Unpublished paper. Research in support of National Institute of Child Health and Human Development grant R15 HD069968, accompanying Poster submission Poster Session on Demography of Crime. Population Association of America, 2015 Annual Meeting.

The Tennessean. (2011). The Gangs of Middle Tennessee. Retrieved from www.tennessean.com/includes/publicus/projects/projects04/paper/photos.html

Tennessee Gang Investigator's Association (TNGIA). (2015). About us. Retrieved from www.tn-gia.org

Thompson, H. S. (1967). *Hell's Angels: The Strange and Terrible Saga of the Outlaw Motorcycle Gangs*. New York, NY: Ballantine Books.

Thompson, T. (2011). *Outlaws: One Man's Rise Through the Savage World of Renegade Bikers, Hell's Angels and Global Crime*. New York, NY: Penguin Books.

Thorton, J., and Blau, R. (1988). Police say shooting may have been ordered by Rukns. *Chicago Tribune*. September 23. Retrieved from http://articles.chicagotribune.com/1988-09-23/news/8802010544_1_el-rukn-jeff-fort-black-p-stone-nation

Thrasher, F. M. (2000). *The Gang: A Study of 1,313 Gangs in Chicago*. Peotone, IL: New Chicago School Press. (Original work published 1927)

Tita, G., and Ridgeway, G. (2007). The Impact of Gang Formation on Local Patterns of Crime. *Journal of Research in Crime and Delinquency*, May, 44(2), pp. 208–237.

Toch, H. (2007). Sequestering Gang Members, Burning Witches, and Subverting Due Process. *Criminal Justice and Behavior*, 32(2), pp. 274–288.

Todd, E. (2009). *Members of Iron Horsemen Motorcycle Club Convicted on Drug Charges in Maine*. Fosters/Seacoast online. Retrieved from http://www.fosters.com/article/20090519/gjnews_01/705199918

Toy, C. (1997). A short history of Asian gangs in San Francisco. In *Gangs and Gang Behavior*, Mays, G. L. (Ed.). Chicago, IL: Nelson-Hall.

Toy, C. (1992). Coming out to Play: Reasons to Join and Participate in Asian Gangs. *Journal of Gang Research*, 1(1), pp. 13–29.

Trejo v. Hulick, 380 F.3d 1031 (7th Cir. 2004).

Trickey, E. (2008). The Tong Wars. *Cleveland Magazine*. August. Retrieved from www.clevelandmagazine.com/ME2/dirmod.asp?sid=E73ABD6180B44874871A91F6BA5C249C&nm=Arts+%26+Entertainemnt&type=Publishing&mod=Publications%3A%3AArticle&mid=1578600D80804596A222593669321019&tier=4&id=86A43D308FA0457293FF350EC6995F5A

Troutman, D. R., Nugent-Borakove, M. E., and Jansen, S. (2007). *Prosecutor's Comprehensive Gang Response Model*. September. American Prosecutors Research Institute, National District Attorneys Association.

Trulson, C. R., Marquart, J. W., and Kawucha, S. K. (2006). Gang Suppression and Institutional Control. *Corrections Today*, April, pp. 26–31.

Tuerina, E. (1993). Warden Says Attack by Inmate Grew out of Grudge over Funeral. *Milwaukee Journal*, September 12, p. B5.

Turley, A. (2003). Female Gangs and Patterns of Female Delinquency in Texas. *Journal of Gang Research*, Summer, 10(4), pp. 1–12.

Underwood, B. (2010). Iron Horsemen Call Cincinnati Home. *Fox 19 TV*. September 20. Retrieved from www.fox19.com/story/13186471/iron-horsemen-call-cincinnati-home

United Gangs. (2014). *Grape Street Watts Crips*. Retrieved from http://unitedgangs.com/2010/04/08/grape-street-watts-crips/

United Nations (UN). (2009). *Investigations Manual*. Investigations Division, UN Office of Internal Oversight Services. Retrieved from www.un.org/Depts/oios/pages/id_manual_mar2009.pdf

United Nations. (2000). *United Nations: Optional Protocol to Prevent, Suppress and Punish Trafficking in Persons, Especially Women and Children, Supplementing the United Nations Convention Against Transnational Organized Crime, G.A. Res.* New York, NY: United Nations General Assembly.

United Nations Office on Drugs and Crime (UNODC). (2011). *Global Study on Homicide: 2011*. UNODC. Retrieved from www.unodc.org/documents/data-and-analysis/statistics/Homicide/Globa_study_on_homicide_2011_web.pdf

United Nations Office on Drugs and Crime. (2004). *United Nations Convention Against Transnational Organized Crime and the Protocols Thereto*. Retrieved from www.unodc.org/documents/treaties/UNTOC/Publications/TOC%20Convention/TOCebook-e.pdf

United States v. Billings, ARMY 9900122. 1999. Retrieved from www.jagcnet.army.mil/Portals%5CFiles%5CACCAOther.nsf/OD/FA47861329FA617D85256D44004B 9A04/$FILE/oc-billings,j%20.pdf

United States v. Pendergast et al., 39 F. Supp. 189 (W.D. Mo. 1941).

United States v. Sullivan, 274 U.S. 259 (1927).

United States v. V. K. Ivankov, 146 F.3d 73 (2nd Cir. 1998).

UPI. (1977). S.F. Chinatown Massacre Victims Were Just All Innocent Bystanders. *Lodi Sentential News*. September 6. Retrieved from https://news.google.com/newspapers?nid=2245&dat=19770903&id=7WUzAAAAIBAJ&sjid=NTIHAAAAIBAJ&pg=5372,402519&hl=en

U.S. Army. (2017). *US Army Criminal Investigation Command's Fiscal Year 2016 (FY16)*. Gang and Domestic Extremist Activity Threat Assessment (GDEATA).

U.S. Army. (2013). *US Army Criminal Investigation Command's Fiscal Year 2012 (FY12)*. Gang and Domestic Extremist Activity Threat Assessment (GDEATA).

U.S. Army. (1993). Close Quarters Combat Techniques. *Appendix K, Field Manual (FM) 19–10*. (Change 1, 1995). Retrieved from www.globalsecurity.org/military/library/policy/army/fm/90–10/90–10apg.htm

U.S. Army Criminal Investigations Command (CID). (2006). *Summary Report Gang Activity Threat Assessment: A Review of Gang Activity Affecting the Army*. Retrieved from http://militarytimes.com/static/projects/pages/2006_CID_Report.pdf

U.S. Census Bureau, Population Division. (2013). Annual Estimates of the Resident Population for Selected Age Groups by Sex for the United States, States, Counties, and Puerto Rico Commonwealth and Municipios: April 1, 2010 to July 1, 2012. *2012 Population Estimates*. June. Washington, DC: U.S. Census Bureau. Retrieved from http://factfinder.census.gov/faces/tableservices/jsf/pages/productview.xhtml?src=bkmk

U.S. Department of Defense. (2007). *Enlistment/Reenlistment Document*. Armed Forces of the United States: DD Form 4/1. Retrieved from www.dtic.mil/whs/directives/infomgt/forms/eforms/dd0004.pdf

U.S. Department of Defense. (1996). *Army Task Force Report on Extremist Activity*. Retrieved from www.defenselink.mil/releases/release.aspx?releaseid=793

U.S. Department of Homeland Security (DHS). (2015). *Fusion Center Locations and Contact Information*. Retrieved from www.dhs.gov/fusion-center-locations-and-contact-information

U.S. Department of Justice. (2016). *Outlaw Motorcycle Gangs*. Retrieved from www.justice.gov/criminal-ocgs/gallery/outlaw-motorcycle-gangs-omgs

U.S. Department of Justice (DOJ). (2015a). *Street Gangs*. Retrieved from www.justice.gov/criminal/ocgs/gangs/street.html

U.S. Department of Justice (DOJ). (2015b). Office of Public Affairs, DOJ, U.S. Marshals Service. *Fact Sheet: Witness Security*. Retrieved from www.usmarshals.gov/duties/factsheets/overview.pdf

U.S. Department of Justice (USDOJ). (2014). *Motorcycle Gangs*. Retrieved from www.justice.gov/criminal/ocgs/gangs/motorcycle.html

U.S. Department of Justice. (1988). *Report on Asian Organized Crime*. Washington, DC: U.S. Department of Justice, Criminal Division.

U.S. Department of Justice, Bureau of Alcohol, Tobacco, Firearms and Explosives (ATF). (2014). *OMGs and the Military 2014*. Office of Strategic Intelligence and Information, ATF.

U.S. Department of State. (2005a). *Narcotics Reward Program: Jhonny Cano Correa*. Retrieved from http://m.state.gov/md115383.htm

U.S. Department of State. (2005b). *Narcotics Rewards Program: Jose Aldemar Rendon Ramirez*. Retrieved from www.state.gov/j/inl/narc/rewards/115382.htm

U.S. Senate Concurrent Resolution 79, 108th Congress: 31 UST 5059. Retrieved from www.escapingjustice.com/scongres79.htm

Vagosmcworld.com. (2014). *Charters*. Retrieved from www.vagosmcworld.com/#!charters/c1ooh

Valdemar, R. (2010). Sureño Tattoos and Symbols. *Police: The Law Enforcement Magazine*. Retrieved from www.policemag.com/blog/gangs/story/2010/03/sur-tattoos-and-symbols.aspx

Valdez, A. (2007). *Gangs Across America: History and Sociology*. San Clemente, CA: LawTech Custom.

Valdez, A. (2001). A History of the Crips and Bloods: An Inauspicious Rivalry Between Small-Time Neighborhood Gangs Gives Birth to a Bloody Legacy. *Police*, April, pp. 72–74.

Valdez, A. J. (2009a). *Gangs: A Guide to Understanding Street Gangs* (5th ed.). San Clemente, CA: Law Tech.

Valdez, A. J. (2009b). Prison Gangs 101. *Corrections Today*, February, pp. 40–43.

Varese, F. (2011). *Mafias on the Move: How Organized Crime Conquers New Territories*. Princeton, NJ: Princeton University Press.

Varese, F. (2001). *The Russian Mafia: Private Protection in a New Market Economy*. Oxford: Oxford University Press.

Varriale, J. (2008). Female Gang Members and Desistance: Pregnancy as a Possible Exit Strategy. *Journal of Gang Research*, Summer, 15(4), pp. 35–64.

Vigil, D.A. (2006). Classification and Security Threat Group Management. *Corrections Today*, April, pp. 32–34.

Virginia Commission on Youth. (1996). *Study of Youth Gangs* (House Joint Resolution 92, Virginia survey results). October 21. Retrieved from http://www.mcquigg.com/gang.html

Waldorf, D. (1993). When the Crips Invaded San Francisco—Gang Migration. *Journal of Gang Research*, 1(3), pp. 11–16.

Walker, R. (2014). *Crips and Bloods History: A First-hand Account of Their Real History and the Myths Surrounding the Origin and Founders of the Gangs*. Retrieved from www.gangsorus.com/crips_bloods_history.htm

Waller, J.M., and Yasman, V. (1995). Russia's Great Criminal Revolution: The Role of the Security Services. *Journal of Contemporary Criminal Justice*, December, 11(4), pp. 276–297.

Walsh, B. (2016). How Peace-Finally-Came to Reign Throughout the Western Hemisphere. *Time*, September 12–19, pp. 7–9.

Warlocks, M.C. (2014). *Chapters*. Retrieved from http://warlocksmc.net/chapters.html

Washington Post. (1999). Who Are the Kurds? Retrieved form www.washingtonpost.com/wp-srv/inatl/daily/feb99/kurdprofile.htm

Webster, W. (2015). *Russian Organized Crime*. Center for Strategic and International Studies. Retrieved from http://csis.org/programs/transnational-threats-project/past-task-forces/russian-organized-crime

Weinstein, H. (1992). FBI Smashes L.A. Drug Ring Linked to Medellin Cartel: Crime: Six People Are Charged and Three Arrested. The Case Shows Growing Ties Between Local Street Gangs and Major Colombian Dealers. *L.A. Times*. January 9. Retrieved from http://articles.latimes.com/1992-01-09/local/me-2290_1_los-angeles-drug, accessed June 16, 2014.

Weisberg, R. (2003). Norms and Criminal Law, and the Norms of Criminal Law Scholarship. *Journal of Criminal Law & Criminology*, 93(2–3), p. 467.

Wennar, J.T. (2005). View from the Field: Memorandum in Support of Gang Expert Testimony. *Journal of Gang Research*, 12(4), pp. 73–76.

Wheels of Soul (WOS). (2014). Retrieved from http://wheelsofsoul.wordpress.com/

White Prison Gangs. (2014a). *Chicago Gaylords*. Retrieved from http://whiteprisongangs.blogspot.com/2009/08/chicago-gaylords.html

White Prison Gangs. (2014b). *Simon City Royals*. Retrieved from http://whiteprisongangs.blogspot.com/2009/05/simon-city-royals.html

Whyte, W. (1943). *Street Corner Society: The Social Structure of an Italian Slum*. Chicago, IL: University of Chicago Press.

Wilkinson, J., Mallios, C., and Martinson, R. (2013). Evading Justice: The Pervasive Nature of Witness Intimidation. *Strategies in Brief*. March. p. 16.

Williams, P. (2009). Illicit Markets, Weak States and Violence: Iraq and Mexico. *Crime, Law, Social Change*, 52, pp. 323–336.

Williams, P. (2000). *Russian Organized Crime: The New Threat?* London: Frank Cass.

Williams, S. (2007). *Blue Rage, Black Redemption*. New York, NY: Touchstone Book, Simon and Schuster.

Williams, S., and Becnel, B. (2003). *Gangs and Violence (Tookie Speaks out Against Violence)*. San Francisco, CA: Sea Star Books.

Williamson, K. (2013). Gangsterville: How Chicago Reclaimed the Projects but Lost the City. *National Review Online*. Retrieved from https://m.nationalreview.com/nrd/articles/340053/gangsterville/page/0/1

Wilson, G.I., and Sullivan, J.P. (2007). On Gangs, Crime and Terrorism. *Special to Defense and the National Interest*. Retrieved from http://d-n-i.net/fcs/pdf/wilson_sullivan_gangs_terrorism.pdf

Winterdyk, J., Fillipuzzi, N., Mescrier, J., and Hencks, C. (2009). *Prison Gangs: A Review and Survey of Strategies*. Correctional Service of Canada.

Winterdyk, J., and Ruddell, R. (2010). Managing Prison Gangs: Results from a Survey of U.S. Prisons. *Journal of Criminal Justice*, 38(4), pp. 730–736.

Wojceichowski, C. (2013). Cops Nab First Chicago Gang Members Under RICO Law. *NBC Chicago*. June 13. Retrieved from www.nbcchicago.com/news/local/black-souls-rico-law-arrests-211481821.html

Wolf, S. (2012). Mara Salvatrucha: The Most Dangerous Street Gang in the Americas? *Latin American Politics & Society*, Spring, 64(1), pp. 65–99.

Wood, J. L., Alleyne, E., Mozova, K., and James, M. (2014). Predicting Involvement in Prison Gang Activity: Street Gang Membership, Social and Psychological Factors. *Law and Human Behavior*, 38(3), pp. 203–211. https://doi.org/10.1037/lhb0000053

Woodiwiss, M. (1987). Capone to Kefauver: Organized Crime in America. *History Today*, June, pp. 8–15.

Worrall, J. L., and Morris, R. G. (2012). Prison Gang Integration and Inmate Violence. *Journal of Criminal Justice*, 40(5), pp. 425–432. https://doi.org/10.1016/j.jcrimjus.2012.06.002

WTOC. (2006). *Beaufort Marines Charged in Gang Activity*. October 5. Retrieved from www.wtoctv.com/Global/story.asp?S=5501411

Wyss, J. (2013, January 18). Colombia's FARC says peace deal might fail after member accused of cocaine deal. *Miami Herald*. Retrieved from http://www.miamiherald.com/news/nation-world/world/americas/colombia/article208438554.html

Yablonsky, L. (1970). The Delinquent Gang as a Near-group. In *The Sociology of Subcultures*, Arnold, D. O. (Ed.). Berkeley, CA: Glendessary Press.

Yablonsky, L. (1962). *The Violent Gang*. New York, NY: Macmillan.

Zeltser, E. (1999). *Testimony of E. Zeltser on the Hearing on the Bank of New York, Russian Organized Crime and Money Laundering to the House Committee on Banking and Financial Services on September 29, 1999*. American Russian Law Institute. Retrieved from http://russianlaw.org/022.htm

Zhang, S. (1997). Task Force Orientation and Dyadic Relations in Organized Chinese Alien Smuggling. *Journal of Contemporary Criminal Justice*, November, 13(4), pp. 320–330.

Zhang, S., and Chin, K. (2003). The Declining Significance of Triad Societies in Transnational Illegal Activities. *British Journal of Criminology*, 43(3), pp. 469–488.

Zion, S. (1994). *Loyalty and Betrayal: The Story of the American Mob*. San Francisco, CA: Collins.

INDEX

Note: Page numbers in italic indicate a figure and page numbers in bold indicate a table.